Biographical Memo
Fellows of the British Academy
XVIII

HOWARD ERSKINE-HILL

Howard Henry Erskine-Hill

19 June 1936 – 26 February 2014

elected Fellow of the British Academy 1985

by

RICHARD McCABE
Fellow of the Academy

BRIAN WATCHORN

Howard Erskine-Hill, Professor of Literary History at Cambridge University and Fellow of Pembroke College, Cambridge; he specialised in eighteenth-century English literature with particular interest in Alexander Pope. His major publications include *The Social Milieu of Alexander Pope* (1975); *The Augustan Idea in English Literature* (1983); *Poetry and the Realm of Politics* (1996); and *Poetry of Opposition and Revolution* (1996). Editions include Pope's *Horatian Satires and Epistles* (1964) and *Selected Letters* (2000).

Biographical Memoirs of Fellows of the British Academy, XVIII, 1–13
Posted 8 April 2019. © British Academy 2019.

HOWARD ERSKINE-HILL

Writing the memoir of a friend can be surprisingly disconcerting. As you work through the personal archive you encounter, if not exactly a stranger, a more complex and complicated individual than you had imagined. We knew Howard in very different capacities but, as the personal 'Commonplace Books' now deposited in the library of Pembroke College, Cambridge, attest, neither knew him fully. He had many other students, colleagues, and friends, and a difficult family history of which he seldom spoke. This, then, is very much a collaborative effort attempting to convey something of the rich diversity of Howard's life, drawing upon both personal reminiscence and the written remains.

Held in the chapel of Pembroke College, Cambridge, Howard's memorial service was remarkable for the sheer number of former pupils, many from years long past, who turned up to pay their respects. But Howard was an exceptional and devoted teacher who evoked affection and admiration in equal measure. In a 'Commonplace Book' entry for 14 June 2005 he records how,

> Last week, after the regular lunch for third-year Pembroke English students, one of them said to me: 'You're not like a lot of the other university dons who are always looking at their watches to go back to their computers or the UL. You like to teach us!' This was said very casually but intentionally. I was *so* pleased! How unexpected! What a grace! It is of course what I hope to be.

In the aftermath of Howard's passing pupil after pupil confirmed that sense of dedication, writing of his kind but firm oversight, his dry, if often mischievous, sense of humour, and his unfailing humanity. It is important to begin with that. While the world at large will remember the scholar, those who knew Howard well will recall how the scholarship reflected the man.

Howard was born on 19 June 1936 in Wakefield, Yorkshire, the only child of Henry Erskine-Hill (1902–1989), a Scottish architect, and his first wife, Hannah Lilian Poppleton (1910–1991). His mother stemmed from a well-known family of worsted spinners and knitters in the nearby mill town of Horbury where Howard grew up with his cousin, John. The town is perhaps best known as the place where Sabine Baring-Gould, curate in the 1860s, wrote for the Sunday School procession the hymn 'Onward Christian Soldiers'—not quite Howard's taste in hymnody, militant though he could be. Howard's father came close to designing a new Episcopal cathedral for Aberdeen but was pipped at the post by Ninian Comper. There was a strong Anglican tradition in the Erskine-Hill family; Howard's grandfather became first Provost of what was to become Aberdeen Cathedral and his great uncle was Vicar of Horbury and Canon of Wakefield.

Despite such strong Anglican leanings, however, Howard was educated at Ashfield College in Harrogate, a Methodist boarding school, where he formed some lifelong friendships, notably with the future author Arnold Pacey. He credited the English teacher, Bill Radley, with cultivating his love of literature and inspiring his future career. So it was that, exempt from National Service on account of his asthma, Howard read English and Philosophy at Nottingham University, graduating BA in 1957, then PhD in 1961 with a dissertation entitled 'Tradition and Affinity in the Poetry of Pope'.

During the Second World War Howard's father served as an army officer but moved to Ireland shortly after when the marriage fell apart. He was to remarry and have two children, Stephen and Diana, whom Howard eventually discovered and got to know. After Stephen's death Howard developed a particularly strong bond with his half-sister, though she was profoundly deaf, and they went walking together in the north, following up family traces and places. In a poem entitled 'Family Affairs' (dated October 2013), Howard recorded how it felt 'Strange to meet half-brother and half-sister, / And through them see again my errant Dad.' The allusion was doubtless to Tasso's 'padre errante', and conjures up a complex mixture of affection and critique. Howard was on sabbatical at the Research Triangle in North Carolina when he received news of his father's death in 1989. His mother had accompanied him, and he felt unable to leave her to attend the funeral because, as the same poem records, she 'at least never walked out on me'. Although their relationship was often difficult, Howard was immensely protective of Hannah, who had been left in such difficult circumstances after the divorce that he sent her ten shillings each week from his student grant, a notable sum at the time. Eventually she joined him in Cambridge and they lived together in the comfortable surroundings of 194 Chesterton Road until her death in 1991. It is evident that Howard saw in their relationship a strong reflection of that eulogised by Pope in the concluding section of his 'Epistle to Dr Arbuthnot':

> Me, let the tender office long engage
> To rock the cradle of reposing age,
> With lenient arts extend a mother's breath,
> Make langour smile, and smooth the bed of death.
> Explore the thought, explain the asking eye,
> And keep awhile one parent from the sky!
> ('Epistle to Dr Arbuthnot', ll, 408–12)

Commenting on this passage, Howard writes that 'a personal, even confessional poem, comes to rest with allusion to an unusual circumstance of Pope's life: his own unmarried position and his mother's great age. It is a situation as peculiar to him as Horace's having a freedman father was to the Roman poet.'[1] But it was a 'peculiarity' Howard shared with Pope. Not for the only time the critic found personal empathy

[1] H. Erskine-Hill, *The Augustan Idea in English Literature* (London, 1983), p. 314.

with his poet. In Howard's case, the loss of his mother was partly filled by Diana, herself a published poet, who to his grief in turn developed cancer and died in Dun Laoghaire just as Howard himself was losing his bearings.

Following the award of the PhD, Howard taught in the English Department at the University of Wales, Swansea, from 1960 to 1965, reaching the grade of Senior Lecturer. Appointed to a lectureship at the University of Cambridge in 1965, he was promoted to Reader in 1984 and Professor of Literary History in 1994, a post he held until his retirement in 2003. He was conferred with a LittD in 1988. A Fellow of Jesus College from 1969 to 1980, Howard moved in that year to Pembroke College where he remained for the rest of his career. Following his election to the British Academy in 1985 he proved to be an active member of the Fellowship, regularly attending section meetings and serving on the Publications Committee for seven years from 1987 to 1994. He also organised a major symposium in May 1994 to mark the 250th anniversary of the death of Alexander Pope. The event culminated in Howard's delivery of the Warton Lecture, 'Pope and Slavery', to a packed and appreciative auditorium. That lecture, together with five other papers from the symposium, were subsequently published under his editorship as *Alexander Pope: World and Word*, in the *Proceedings of the British Academy*, 91 (1998).[2]

By the time that volume appeared Howard enjoyed an international reputation as one of the leading authorities on Pope. While at Swansea he had published a much admired edition of the *Horatian Satires and Epistles* (Oxford, 1964), but secured his academic reputation with *The Social Milieu of Alexander Pope: Lives, Example and the Poetic Response*, published to great acclaim in 1975. Donald Davie spoke for many when he remarked in the *Modern Language Review* that 'this is one of those rare books which truly deserve the description: humane learning … [Erskine-Hill's] book is a great achievement, and also a great pleasure. It is even in its sober way entertaining as well as instructive. I do not know when literary scholarship in England came up with anything so deeply satisfying.'[3] Based on the premise that 'a literary artist, like any other man, lives in a shared world', *The Social Milieu* presented an analysis, through six meticulously documented biographical studies, of 'Pope's society, and of the social poetry which, as a member of that society, Pope produced'.[4] Dismissing reports of the death of the author as greatly exaggerated, Howard emphasised the poet's agency, creative, moral and conflicted, by examining his complex engagement with the dynamics of contemporary political and social life. At the heart of his concern

[2] The other contributors were Hester Jones, Claude Rawson, Julian Ferraro, David Nokes and Thomas Keymer.
[3] D. Davie, 'Review of *The Social Milieu of Alexander Pope*', *Modern Language Review*, 73 (1978), 407.
[4] H. Erskine-Hill, *The Social Milieu of Alexander Pope: Lives, Example and the Poetic Response* (New Haven, CT, 1975), p. 1.

was the relationship between history and exemplarity, and the ethics of using, and abusing, living persons to point literary morals. Pope's heroes he identified as John Kryle, the celebrated 'Man of Ross', John Caryll, the Jacobite peer, William Digby, fifth Baron Digby of Geashill, and Ralph Allen, the model for Fielding's Squire Allworthy. His villains were Peter Walter, Fielding's Peter Pounce, and Sir John Blunt, of South Sea Bubble fame, or infamy. The distinguishing criterion Howard credits Pope with using was philanthropy, understood as the socially responsible use of material resources. By investigating hitherto neglected archives he brought the whole gallery of rogues and heroes to life, contextualising the poetry as never before. If the work had a fault it was a failure adequately to recognise the inevitable gap between reality and representation. There is a lot more to the psychology of satire than just 'the strong antipathy of good to bad', and one suspects that Pope's motives were often less impartial, and even less lucid, than Howard suggests.[5] Nevertheless, he succeeds magnificently in elucidating the materials from which the myths were fashioned.

The Social Milieu was intended as the first of a two-part study and the project was completed in 1983 with the appearance of *The Augustan Idea in English Literature*, a massive exploration of the relationship between poetry and power from the ancient world to the eighteenth century, gauged through varying responses, from the hostile to the celebratory, to the 'idea of the Augustan'. Howard's basic contention was that this 'idea' was plural and relentlessly self-reflexive:

> The word 'Idea' in my title is not intended to suggest that the English reception of Rome's Augustan Age involved one idea alone, as it might be for example, of peaceful empire, or of enlightened patronage of poets. 'Idea' must perforce stand for a shifting pattern of ideas, some diametrically opposed, if pressed to their extreme forms. The grateful view of Virgil and Horace; the penetrating and hostile view of Tacitus; and the Christian providential view of Eusebius, each quite different from the others, are the major components of what may for the sake of brevity be termed the Augustan Idea. Separated out, they formed the arguments in a debate about the nature of Augustan Rome. Drawn together they composed a compound image in which compatibility was more evident than contradiction.[6]

Amongst the study's most innovative features is the recognition of 'Augustan' elements in political iconography and courtly literature long before the Restoration in the writings of Donne and Jonson. But Howard's main interests lay in the eighteenth century and the work culminates in a subtly nuanced set of essays on Pope's imitations of Horace, mingling acutely close readings of the texts with minute attention to the political circumstances in which they were written.

---

[5] 'Epilogue to the Satires: Dialogue 2', l. 198.
[6] Erskine-Hill, *The Augustan Idea in English Literature*, pp. xi–xii.

The introduction to *The Augustan Idea* provides the clearest, and for some the most provocative, articulation of Howard's critical philosophy: 'Evidence has been presented and conclusions based on that evidence. I acknowledge the principle of truth as the end of scholarship, and have no interest in the production of subjective myth in the guise of criticism, or in the mere multiplication of readings none of which has any greater probability than the rest.'[7] No one is mentioned by name but a former colleague, detecting a personal slight, took immediate umbrage—not unlike Pope's Belinda. In the course of a somewhat bilious critique in the *Kenyon Review* Frank Kermode professed to find Howard's comments 'quite deplorable', particularly from 'so pedestrian an author'.[8] It was a foretaste of intellectual battles to come. Yet Kermode's response hardly came as a surprise; there was bad blood there already, owing to previous protracted disputes in the English Faculty. On hearing news of Kermode's imminent departure to the United States in 1981, Howard confided to his Commonplace Book the opinion that 'nobody has done such disservice to his subject and to our Faculty. I should like the church bells of Cambridge to ring to celebrate his going.'[9] In a highly Popean manner policies had become personalised and persons politicised. The antagonists had far more in common than they imagined, but neither could see it. And the silence of the bells was ominous. While welcoming the advent of Christopher Ricks as Chairman of the Faculty Board the following year Howard admitted, 'I still can't stop myself disagreeing with him.'[10] But why should he? Whether he knew it or not, such disagreements were the engines of his intellectual life.

Beginning with Niall Rudd's warm appraisal in the *London Review of Books*,[11] the general reaction to *The Augustan Idea* was, pace Kermode, highly positive. According to Paul Hammond, for example, 'Dr Erskine-Hill has not only brought alive a significant intellectual tradition, but also shown that the key texts which are located at the critical moments of that tradition are more careful, complex, and, in the end, costly achievements than we had realized.'[12] The most prevalent criticism of the work, best articulated by Emrys Jones, was not to its content but its structure. In the second half, Jones observed, 'the author seems at some points distracted into side-issues, at others over-attached to some of his favourite themes, such as Horatian influence or imitation. The problem is partly that, by the final sections of the work the Horatian has, in

---

[7] Ibid., p. 13.

[8] F. Kermode, 'Review of *The Augustan Idea in English Literature*', *The Kenyon Review*, n.s. 6 (1984), 132–5.

[9] Commonplace Books, 31 December 1981.

[10] Ibid., 6 November 1982.

[11] N. Rudd, 'Review of *The Augustan Idea in English Literature*', *London Review of Books*, 4 August 1983, 22–3.

[12] P. Hammond, 'Review of *The Augustan Idea in English Literature*', *The Review of English Studies*, n.s. 36 (1985), 604–5.

a sense, displaced the Augustan—an outcome that would undoubtedly have pleased the poet if not the *princeps*.' But Jones concluded that he had 'learned a great deal, and have been made to think about a large and important complex of ideas. I will certainly return to *The Augustan Idea* for further stimulus and enlightenment.'[13]

It was adherence to the principles that so offended Frank Kermode that led Howard to oppose the proposal to confer an honorary degree on Jacques Derrida at Cambridge in 1992.[14] What was at stake, in his view, was nothing less than the validity of truth itself, a concept Derrida appeared to disable, thereby rendering evidentially based research impossible. To honour the man, he argued, was to endorse the methodology and undermine the educational standards to which students and teachers should aspire. The flysheet he composed with the eminent philosopher Hugh Mellor charged that 'the major preoccupation and effect of [Derrida's] voluminous work has been to deny and to dissolve those standards of evidence and argument on which all academic disciples are based'. According to the opposed camp, Derrida was attempting 'to reveal the links between thought, language, and the world'. In the Senate House on 21 March 1992, Howard, together with Ian Jack, Hugh Mellor and Raymond Page, cried 'non placet' against the proposed award, thereby triggering a debate in Congregation some weeks later. In the meantime the controversy reached the national press. For those unacquainted with Latin *The Times* helpfully translated 'non placet' as 'roughly, you must be joking' and quoted Howard as saying that,

> The heart of the matter is that Derrida does not seem to have a theory of knowledge in which one can distinguish probability from non-probability or truth from falsehood. His theory does not recognise the touchstones which allow us to distinguish the likely from the unlikely ... It is not good enough to argue that because someone is influential he is worthy of an honorary degree. (*The Times*, 9 May 1992)

Howard drew particular comfort from the support of so many international philosophers, remarking that 'throughout the campaign professional philosophers inside and outside Cambridge supported the non placet side. In particular, the letter from nineteen philosophers all over the world, published in *The Times* on 19 May 1992, including the name of Willard van Orman Quine, made it clear that there was international opposition to what Cambridge was proposing to do on the part of those best qualified to judge.' The issue was debated in Congregation on 16 May, with eventual victory to the proposers by a margin of 336 votes to 204. The opponents had not necessarily expected to win. As Howard explained, 'our goal was something more

---

[13] E. Jones, 'Review of *The Augustan Idea in English Literature*', *Modern Language Review*, 80 (1985), 423–6.

[14] For a full account of the matter see H. Erskine-Hill, 'Viewpoint', *The Cambridge Review*, 113, no. 2319 (December 1992), 173–7.

important: to deny anyone the possibility of claiming that Derrida now represented an orthodoxy in Cambridge. We wished to put down a marker that would make it clear to all who had not much considered the issues, and especially junior members, that there was plenty of intellectual space for the development of their own views and that the controversy concerning the value of Derrida was very much alive.'[15] Nonetheless, the outcome dismayed him for he saw it as tantamount to 'symbolic suicide' on the part of the university (*Guardian*, 18 May 1992). Or, as he later put it somewhat more colourfully, Cambridge had appointed 'a pyromaniac to the post of chief fireman'.[16] Resentments lingered for many years, worsening an already fractious atmosphere within the English Faculty.

Although the politics in which Howard interested himself were primarily those of the state, he focused upon personalities. For him, public life was the stage upon which principle was tested and he was fascinated by the various acts of courage, cowardice and betrayal it produced, particularly as represented in poetry and drama. His work in this area culminated in the simultaneous publication in 1996 of the two companion volumes *Poetry and the Realm of Politics* and *Poetry of Opposition and Revolution*, dealing between them with the politics of literature from Shakespeare to Wordsworth. In the introduction to the first volume Howard best articulated the critical principles that informed not just the current publications but his lifelong aims:

> The chief contention of this book is that there is a political comment, often involving contemporary political ideas and historical circumstance, in some of the most powerful poetic works of sixteenth- and seventeenth-century English literature, works which have in the past been usually read for their aesthetic achievement and generalized wisdom. I argue that this political component is an eventual part of their aesthetic life, and that that, in its turn, is part of that wider historical culture which it is the vocation of scholarship to explore with as much imagination and disinterestedness as it can.[17]

A particular strength of the two-volume project is its analysis of the ways in which various writers such as Milton, Dryden, Pope, Dr Johnson and Wordsworth struggled with experiences of defeat, disaffection or disappointment. For private as well as professional reasons, Howard was always fascinated by the lost cause, the missed opportunity, the road not taken, a feature of his writing that is particularly evident in his frequent recourse to Jacobite history, and the fine analysis of Wordsworth's *Prelude* that concludes *Poetry of Opposition and Revolution*.[18] But it was Pope, a selection

---

[15] Ibid., pp. 174, 175.
[16] See B. Peeters, *Derrida: a Biography* (Cambridge, 2013), p. 433.
[17] H. Erskine-Hill, *Poetry and the Realm of Politics: Shakespeare to Dryden* (Oxford, 1996), p. 1.
[18] H. Erskine-Hill, *Poetry of Opposition and Revolution: Dryden to Wordsworth* (Oxford, 1996), pp. 169–247; Howard described the *Prelude* as 'a kind of poetic companion of my life' (p. viii).

of whose letters he edited in 2000, and whose biography he was writing at the time of his death, who remained to the end the centre of his scholarly attention.[19]

In the absence of romantic attachments, close literary friendships, notably with the poets Donald Davie and John Holloway, and his many pupils and colleagues, provided the emotional ballast of Howard's life.[20] With Davie he developed a particularly close bond, cemented by the poet's dedication to him of 'Reminded of Bougainville', a meditation on the Falklands War inspired by a late-night conversation in Cambridge. On receiving the typescript, Howard records that,

> I wept for some minutes. Why should this be? I think these were tears of release. Partly that a poet I admire so much should inscribe a poem to me—thus, gratified self-importance on my part. Partly, and perhaps more relevant, that in this tenuous way I was linked with an episode which so stirred my imagination, and with this expedition in which I so much longed to have been included, absurd as such an idea might seem.[21]

A further instance of appreciation occurred in 2008 with the appearance of the Festschrift *Literary Milieux: Essays in Text and Context, Presented to Howard Erskine-Hill* edited by David Womersley and Richard McCabe with contributions from Alastair Fowler, Tom MacFaul, David Nokes, Paul Hammond, Julian Ferraro, Niall MacKenzie, George Rousseau, Robert Mayhew, Hester Jones, Robert Douglas-Fairhurst, Claude Rawson, Valerie Rumbold, Thomas Keymer and Peter MacDonald. Commenting on the collection the editors noted that,

> the pervasive concern with intellectual and political context evident in our essays reflects Howard's own scholarly approach, but their chronological range [from Spenser to Wordsworth] falls far short of his. The bibliography of his writings supplied at the close of this preface attests to the astonishing scope and depth of his interests and also to the diversity of his readership. His works range from the most magisterial of research monographs to the most accessible of student introductions and the two categories are intimately related. In Howard the teacher and the scholar are one.[22]

And the bibliography is truly astonishing in charting not just the intellectual life of an indefatigable scholar but also, in the section headed 'Letters', a lifelong commitment to asserting and defending personal principles. The final category, 'Poetry', is misleading in listing only one item, some verses from a sequence on Augustus contributed to *Pembroke Poets*, edited by Robert Macfarlane and David Quentin (Cambridge, 1997). In fact, Howard wrote poetry throughout most of his life as a means of exploring the

---

[19] H. Erskine-Hill (ed.), *Selected Letters: Alexander Pope* (Oxford, 2000).
[20] See Howard's obituary of John Holloway, *The Independent*, 9 September 1999.
[21] Commonplace Books, 12 February 1983.
[22] D. Womersley and R. McCabe, 'Preface', in D. Womersley and R. McCabe (eds.), *Literary Milieux: Essays in Text and Context, Presented to Howard Erskine-Hill* (Newark, DE, 2008), p. 7.

intricate relationships between his work, his friendships and his attitudes to the wider world.

The letters Howard directed to various newspapers and politicians chart his changing political views from militant Labour and the Campaign for Nuclear Disarmament, via the Tories, to the United Kingdom Independence Party (UKIP). The transition was difficult. Much as he admired Mrs Thatcher's stance over the Falklands, news of an election in 1983 filled him with doubt. 'Who can I vote for?', he asked himself on 12 April, 'four years ago I had no hesitation in giving my vote to Mr Callaghan and Labour. Now I cannot easily vote Labour … If you believe in democratic procedure and in defence, you cannot vote Labour this time. If you believe in government support for the economy and unemployment, you cannot vote Tory.'[23] As time went on, however, he became increasingly antagonistic to the European Community and ever more supportive of Mrs Thatcher's euro-scepticism. On 12 May 1991 he wrote to the then former Prime Minister, dissuading her from stepping down from the House of Commons so that she could lead opposition to the European project. 'I am originally a Labour voter who came over to the Conservatives during your premiership', he explained, 'your record on the Unions, and your example on the Falklands War, converted me; and I have subsequently written to you to express support for your policies: when you gave the USA landing rights for its Libyan raid, when you departed for the Madrid summit, and on the resignation of Sir Geoffrey Howe.' This was just the introduction: he had a particular point to make, and one that is very resonant today:

> Shortly before you resigned you seemed to envisage the possibility of holding a referendum on entry into a federal EC. I wrote to the papers to support this (the *Independent*, I think, published a letter) and I am still convinced that an honest and open referendum is the only way in which the United Kingdom can properly decide whether to support closer European integration, without shattering one or both of the main parties. Country should in any case come before party on this issue: neither side of the dispute can welcome the centuries of frustrated nationalism which are likely to ensue if a British Government joins a federal EC without the wholehearted support of the British people.

After Thatcher left the Commons, dissatisfaction with her successors, and anxieties over what he regarded as the progressive loss of national sovereignty, eventually led Howard to UKIP.

Howard's religious views underwent a transformation no less radical than his politics. Despite (or because of?) his Methodist schooling he spent his student years as an atheist and maintained essentially the same outlook into middle age. But shortly

---

[23] Commonplace Books, 12 April 1983.

after Brian Watchorn became Dean and Chaplain of Pembroke in 1982 Howard started to appear at Sunday Evensong in Chapel. He relished the stylistic elegance of the Book of Common Prayer and regularly read the First Lesson from the Old Testament of the King James Bible. If asked to read from the New Testament, he often came close to tears. Yet the Church of England was fated not to be his final destination. Unhappy at the ordination of women as priests, he was eventually received into the Roman Catholic Church. But although the Catholic chaplaincy, Fisher House, became his spiritual home, he by no means abandoned College Chapel, continuing to attend evensong on Fridays and Sundays, before proceeding to dinner in Hall. On the demise of the antique gong that had traditionally summoned Fellows to dine he drew on his command of mock epic to extract a humorous memento mori:

> Aeneas, Hector, captains all,
> Great Agamemnon, all did fall,
> Princes and Pawns shall pass away,
> *Timor mortis conturbat me…*
> Now Time's fell hand it hath done wrong,
> To Pembroke Senior Parlour's Gong
> Resounding bronze must age decay
> *Timor mortis conturbat me…*

The gong was restored.

On New Year's Eve 1981, having recently migrated from Jesus College to Pembroke, Howard recorded in his Commonplace Books, 'not a bad year. I am happy at Pembroke, more than I could have been at any other Cambridge College'. That happiness was to last and, in the years following his mother's death, take on an ever deepening significance. At his home in Chesterton, shared with a feisty little Dachshund named Bounce (named, naturally, after Pope's favourite dog), he gathered a considerable collection of antiquarian books, prints and Jacobite medals and memorabilia. There also he received special friends and entertained in remarkably generous style. But college life provided the wider society that, especially in the final years, served as an antidote to the encroaching loneliness of age. After several months of decline, exacerbated by a bad fall, he slipped away peacefully on 26 February 2014 at the Cambridge Manor Care Home in Brian's company, and was buried, according to Catholic rites, with his mother in the churchyard at Fen Ditton. As well as providing for Fisher House, Howard left the bulk of his estate to Pembroke, including his personal collection of pictures. He had previously secured for the college the substantial collection of his friend. Monica Partridge, firming up the creation of a college Fine Arts Committee which, it is hoped, will stand as a memorial. Perhaps his best epitaph, as both scholar and teacher, was written by his favourite poet:

Blessed with a taste exact, yet unconfined;
A knowledge both of books and human kind;
Generous converse, a soul exempt from pride;
And love to praise, with reason on his side.
(Pope, *Essay on Criticism*, II. 639–42)

Note on the authors: Richard McCabe is Professor of English Language and Literature at the University of Oxford, and a Fellow of Merton College, Oxford; he was elected a Fellow of the British Academy in 2007. Revd Canon Brian Watchorn is the former Dean of Pembroke College, Cambridge.

MICK MORAN

Michael Moran

13 April 1946 – 3 April 2018

elected Fellow of the British Academy 2004

by

DAVID SANDERS

Fellow of the Academy

Michael (Mick) Moran was W. J. M. McKenzie Professor of Government at the University of Manchester from 1990 until his retirement in 2011. At Manchester, he was variously both Head of Department and Faculty Dean. He was a member of the RAE Politics and International Relations panel in 2001 and of the equivalent sub-panel in 2008. He edited two of the major UK academic politics journals – *Political Studies* (1993–9) and *Government and Opposition* (2000–6). Moran was one of Britain's foremost analysts of the modern regulatory state, making particularly important contributions in *The Politics of Banking* (1989) and *The British Regulatory State* (2003).

Biographical Memoirs of Fellows of the British Academy, XVIII, 15–29
Posted 8 April 2019. © British Academy 2019.

MICK MORAN

Michael (Mick) Moran was born in Smethwick, Birmingham, the son of immigrant working-class parents who returned to their native Ireland soon after his birth. He spent much of his early life in County Clare, living on his family's smallholding on Scattery Island in the mouth of the Shannon Estuary and in the nearby town of Kilrush. He was educated at the local Christian Brothers' school, an experience that subsequently allowed him to joke with authority about his *Angela's Ashes* upbringing. His family returned to Smethwick in 1959, where he attended the Cardinal Newman secondary modern school.

Mick always drily acknowledged that he had been brought up in considerable poverty. He also stressed that he considered himself fortunate to have lived at a time when educational opportunities were such that, notwithstanding his background, he was able to attend university. Having self-started his own education in Smethwick Public Library, he secured a place at the newly established University of Lancaster where he studied Politics, Economics and Mathematics, graduating in 1967. He went on to take an MA at Essex where he met Anthony King, who encouraged him to stay on for a PhD under his supervision. Mick completed his doctoral thesis, an in-depth study of the Union of Post Office Workers (UPW), in 1973. Even before the completion of his PhD—in 1970—he had secured a Lectureship at the then Manchester Polytechnic, where he was promoted to Senior Lecturer in 1974. In 1979, he moved to Manchester University's Department of Government where he remained until his retirement in 2011. He became W. J. M. McKenzie Professor of Government in 1990 and a Fellow of the British Academy in 2004.

Mick spent most of his adult life living in Glossop, Derbyshire, where he was an active member of, and fund-raiser for, Glossop Mountain Rescue. He was a passionate family man who was devoted to, and immensely proud of, his wife and two sons. His colleagues at Manchester, together with generations of his undergraduate and graduate students, benefited enormously from his wisdom, humour and kindness. He was a thoughtful and charming host to the many visitors to the Manchester Department, who were frequently invited back to Mick's home in Glossop to sample the wonderful Derbyshire countryside and local beer.

Mick was a modest man who had very little to be modest about. He was a brilliant teacher, well known both at his own university and through his lectures at the annual North-West A-level Conferences organised by Bill Jones and others. At Manchester, he was variously both Head of Department and Faculty Dean. He was a member of the Research Assessment Exercise Politics panel in 2001 and of the equivalent sub-panel in 2008. He edited two of the major UK academic politics journals—*Political Studies* (1993–9) and *Government and Opposition* (2000–6). As a scholar, he made an enormous contribution to our understanding of the workings of modern British government.

Mick's first book, deceptively entitled *The Union of Post Office Workers: a Study in Sociology* (London, 1974), was based on his doctoral thesis. The book was in fact much more than a modest case study of the workings of a single trade union in the 1960s and 1970s—as might have been suggested by its title. Rather, Moran assembled a huge amount of original source materials, including interviews with local and national officials, surveys of UPW members and a wide range of union documents to test a general theory of organisational effectiveness. The theory, which reflected the prevailing orthodoxy in organisational theory at the time, was tested systematically against the experiences of the UPW in the post-war period. Its core claim was that organisational effectiveness is greatest when there is 'congruence' between members' motivation for involvement and leaders' primary goals and actions. The ideal congruent trades union, for example, would be composed mainly of members who had instrumental, pecuniary motives for joining and would have a leadership focused on remunerative goals.

Moran's counter-intuitive central finding was that the UPW was effective *despite* being 'non-congruent' in the sense that the leadership was far more focused on the promotion of Labour's political creed than the rank-and-file membership, which was concerned primarily with remuneration. Moran identified two reasons for the UPW's effectiveness. The first involved the work of local branch officials—unpaid but committed volunteers—who frequently represented individual workers when they had grievances against management. Members' typical response to these representation efforts was a strong sense of personal loyalty to local officials, which the latter were able to mobilise when members voted on matters of national union policy. The second reason for the UPW's effectiveness was members' general ignorance of and apathy towards the union's national-level policies. This largely translated into indifference towards the union's national goals and activities, as long as sufficient national effort was put into securing suitable remuneration arrangements for members.

In the book's conclusion, Moran was not afraid to acknowledge that his core initial hypothesis had been wrong. The UPW was not 'congruent' as an organisation, yet it was effective both in delivering suitable remuneration for its members and in supporting Labour Party policies nationally, even though many rank-and-file members were indifferent to Labour's fortunes. At a time when British political science was seeking to find its epistemological feet—and when a large part of the UK profession appeared neither to accept nor even understand the importance of the Popperian principle of falsification—Moran's efforts to introduce scientific rigour into what, on the face of it, was a 'simple case study' represented an important innovation. Indeed his analysis of the UPW embodied two features that were to characterise all his later work: the location of detailed case study materials within the context of wider theoretical interpretations and claims; and his insistence on the need to challenge existing orthodoxies, using the weapons of careful theorising and the systematic application of empirical evidence.

Moran continued his adoption of deceptively modest titles for his books with his second monograph, *The Politics of Industrial Relations: the Origins, Life and Death of the 1971 Industrial Relations Act* (London, 1977). This was no dry description of the Heath government's failed attempt to redesign Britain's industrial relations landscape. Rather, it was a penetrating analysis of trades union legislation since the mid-nineteenth century. It traced the industrial relations policies of successive governments and analysed the changing balance of the three main industrial policy traditions—market liberalism, voluntary collectivism and forced collectivism. Moran showed how the first two dominated, in varying combinations, in the period between 1870 and 1970. The Parliamentary Acts of 1871, 1875 and 1906 effectively reduced the role of law in industrial relations to a minimum—and for decades thereafter business, unions and government were largely content to maintain that position.

By the 1960s, however, there was a widespread sense that the incidence of strikes was increasing significantly, even though the actual figures on strike rates were both difficult to interpret and easily distorted by a single, unusual strike event. Nonetheless, there developed a near universal view among politicians across the political spectrum that the UK had 'a serious strike problem'.

At the heart of Conservative Party concerns about industrial relations policy was the problem of the enforceability of union–business agreements on pay and conditions. In the Tory view, because workers failed to honour agreements—as indicated by the high level of 'unconstitutional' strikes—the country's collective bargaining laws must be reformed; hence the 1971 Act. The Conservatives' policy paper, *Fair Deal at Work*, which they produced while in opposition in 1968, was subsequently used as a blueprint for reform by Robert Carr when he became Secretary of State for Employment in the Heath government in June 1970. As Moran observed, the detailed working out of policy provisions while in opposition was and remains a relatively rare practice in British politics. At the same time, Carr knew that he needed to consult widely on *Fair Deal*, and particularly with the unions and the Confederation of British Industry (CBI). After all, Labour's failure properly to consult in 1969 over Barbara Castle's similar set of proposals for industrial reform, *In Place of Strife*, had been crucial in their collapse.

The consultation on the *Fair Deal* proposals, however, included a list of conditions —all to be overseen by a National Industrial Relations Court (NIRC)—which the government indicated were non-negotiable. These included: the right of an individual to join or (critically) not to join a union (which would end closed shops); the compulsory registration of unions; the introduction of legally binding agreements; the restriction of existing legal immunities enjoyed by trades unions; provision for strike ballots and cool off periods; rights for union recognition; and machinery to define bargaining units and to establish rights of representation. Within a very short time, the Trades Union Congress (TUC) General Council had rejected all of these conditions and committed itself to doing all it could to destroy the proposed Act. The TUC's withdrawal meant that the consultation was largely limited to government departments and the CBI—and even the CBI were concerned about the proposed ending of the closed shop on the grounds that this could seriously damage union–business relations. However, the government rejected the CBI's arguments in the Bill that was presented to Parliament. Given that the Conservatives enjoyed a majority in both the Commons and the Lords, very few amendments were passed—though the government did compromise on trade union registration, which remained 'recommended but voluntary'. Unsurprisingly, Labour tried to protract the process of the Bill's passage, as the Labour left vigorously tried to expose it as 'class legislation designed to strengthen employers and weaken unions' (p. 99). The formal Labour position, however, was heavily laden with irony. Labour's claim that 'law has no place in industrial relations' rang very hollow given that Labour's *In Place of Strife* had tried to impose legal rules on industrial relations only two years earlier. In spite of a strong extra-parliamentary campaign mounted by the TUC, involving mass demonstrations, strikes and intensive advertising, the Bill was passed and the Act was given Royal Assent in August 1971.

TUC resistance did not stop with the passage of the Bill, however. It switched its focus to union non-registration, which was not required under the terms of the Act. The difficulty with this approach was that unregistered unions were subject to exactly the same restrictions as their registered counterparts—and yet they enjoyed none of the potential benefits of the legislation in terms of obliging employers to stick to agreements. The key drivers behind the failure of the Act, however, were two-fold. First, many individual unions were fully prepared to threaten or indeed to take mass strike action, even in the face of fines and asset sequestrations imposed by the NIRC. The decisive second factor was a Court of Appeal ruling that quashed a test case fine on the Transport and General Workers' Union (TGWU) which had been imposed in March 1972 as a result of dockers in Hull, London and Liverpool refusing to handle containers. The Court of Appeal ruled in the TGWU's favour on the grounds that the union's rule book gave no authority to its shop stewards to initiate unofficial action and so the TGWU could not be held responsible for the dockers' actions; if the NIRC wanted to take action against the dockers, it would have to prosecute individuals rather than the union itself. Even though the Law Lords overturned the Appeal Court decision in July 1972, the legal and political confusion surrounding the dockers' case, together with similar confusions that arose from other related cases, significantly damaged the credibility of both the NIRC and the legislation that had underpinned it. When Labour was re-elected in February 1974 it introduced the Trade Unions and

Labour Relations Act 1974—thereby abolishing most of the institutions and measures connected with the 1971 Act. As Moran notes, however, the 1971 Act did mark the passing of the dominant tradition of voluntary collectivism that had been practiced more or less continuously since 1870. Labour's 1974 legislation confirmed that the law was to play a crucial role in the development of industrial relations in Britain—a principle that was subsequently to be reinforced by Margaret Thatcher and Norman Tebbit in the 1980s.

By the time Moran wrote *The Politics of Banking* in 1984 (London; a second revised edition appeared in 1989), his work was providing an exemplar of how good policy research should be conducted. Moran's intellectual humility, however, could not prevent him from disparaging the very analytic genre that he had embraced. In the introduction to *The Politics of Banking*, Moran observed:

> Academic case studies of public policy are in disrepute. Their faults are obvious: they lack the immediacy of journalism, the authority of history or the analytical scope of conventional social science. (pp. 3–4)

Moran's natural modesty was misplaced. His case studies were always much more than the narrow accounts of developments in a particular policy sphere that characterises so much policy analysis. Moran's work invariably used carefully formulated theory to inform his discussion and to disentangle the complexities of the frequently contradictory thinking displayed by different individual and institutional actors. His work also consistently located contemporary policy developments in their correct historical context. In so doing, his work showed precisely how good case study analysis can provide real enlightenment in murky policy debates. Indeed, Moran's case studies, though highly readable, avoided the central weaknesses of the three other approaches that he complimented in the above quotation: unlike much journalism, his work was never over-simplified or lacking in depth; unlike much historical analysis, it avoided an emphasis on 'interpretation' and instead focused on providing causal explanations; and unlike vast swathes of conventional social science, his work never reified (often statistical) technique as a substitute for theoretically informed and systematic empirical analysis.

The Politics of Banking focused on how the relations among the Bank of England, the major banks and bankers, and successive governments produced policies on *Competition and Credit Control*, which became the focus for UK financial reform in the 1970s.

Moran identified three key features of the UK finance sector. The first was that, because industry in the UK developed earlier than the banking sector, banking and industry in the UK were *separated* in ways that contrasted strongly with the position in the USA and Germany. It was only in the mid-1970s that UK bankers 'shed their dislike of long terms and became entangled in the affairs of their industrial customers' (p. 12). The second feature was the *concentration* of financial ownership and power within the traditional UK elite—until 1980, for example, fully two-thirds of directors appeared in *Burke's Peerage*. The third was the predominance of financial *cartels* centred on the Big Five banks. After 1918 cartel practices were widespread across the UK financial sector, underpinned by the 'club' social unity associated with ownership concentration.

Competition and Credit Control was actually the title of a consultation paper published by the Bank of England in May 1971, which was intended 'for discussion with banks and finance houses'. A revised version of the paper was issued as a set of regulations in September 1971 that would determine the way in which the Bank regulates banks' competition and credit control. Crucially, the new rules removed the previous ceiling on how much banks could lend; instead the price of lending in the form of interest rates would now become the key mechanism of control.

The result of the reforms was a massive increase in bank lending, which significantly increased M3, the then preferred measure of the UK money supply. This in turn fuelled the inflationary pressures that were already growing globally as a result of the US decision to fund the Vietnam War through deficit spending—pressures that were further reinforced by the oil price hike of October 1973. As Moran noted, the immediate practical effect of the credit expansion of 1971–3 was to turn the control of the money supply into a major political issue. This was in part because much of the new lending after the removal of the ceiling went into property: property-based lending increased by 400 per cent compared with only a 50 per cent increase in industrial lending. In addition, too much lending based on questionable security guarantees caused a property price bubble that was transformed into a financial crisis in late 1973 as the government, aiming to control the growth in M3, significantly increased interest rates. In Moran's view, the major failing in all this was the government's disposition to 'place excessive trust in the independent capacity of bankers to act prudently' (p. 85: shades of 2007–8). A secondary problem was the tendency of regulators to have the wool pulled over their eyes by 'the more ingenious of the regulated' (p. 85).

The Bank of England's response to the 1973 crisis, supported by the Heath government, was to rescue ailing banks and finance houses, in order to ensure the survival of confidence in the banking sector more generally. This was merely the continuation of a policy trajectory that had been followed since the late nineteenth century—similar approaches had been adopted with the Overend Gurney crash in 1866, with the Baring crisis of 1890 and with the prolonged recession crisis of 1929–33. As Moran noted, the Bank of England—and the world at large—had come to regard the taking of prompt and decisive action to prevent loss of confidence as one of the essential roles of a central bank. (p. 98)

Moran's key analytic contribution in *The Politics of Banking* was his examination of the debate over deregulation as a device for dealing with the problems of policy complexity and the propensity of regulated actors to contrive self-interested strategies that enable them to avoid, evade or circumvent the effects of regulation. As Moran observes, all experience shows that the self-interested regulatee—the 'sophisticated opportunist'—will always find ways of subverting any system that regulators can contrive. In these circumstances, how can policy best be developed? Neo-liberals argue that deregulation is the obvious answer. Competition, along with its implication of business failure for some, is the only sensible long-run solution: let the state do less and allow the market to produce optimal equilibrium outcomes. Moran rejected this view. He argued that the state has an important role in regulation, even if perfect regulatory regimes are unachievable: 'If people are to live tolerably with complexity, opportunism must either be tightly controlled, or it must be harnessed, or its influence must be diminished by appealing to more altruistic motives.'

In Moran's view, governments need to balance these three possible solutions and they have three possible strategies for doing so. One option is *more technical rationality*: governments need more effective instruments of surveillance and control. The problem here, of course, is how this can be achieved in specific and frequently rapidly changing circumstances. Having possession of the right information at the right time is clearly difficult to achieve in any sector and is perhaps especially difficult in the complex high-stakes world of banking—as the subsequent financial crisis of 2007–8 demonstrated. A second option is *more competition*. As Moran notes, this may work in the private sector as long as business failure does not result in rescues or bailouts. Sadly, in the public sector more competition can too easily be subverted by opportunism. Here, more competitive self-interest serves largely to encourage the manipulation of public information and (damagingly) 'lessens the restraints exercised by professional values' (p. 157). The final strategy Moran identified was for government to *place more trust in the organisations that it seeks to regulate*. The paradox here, however, is that this would require behaviour to be constrained by moral codes which themselves are typically undercut by increased competition.

The policy implications of Moran's work were fairly clear—even if they failed to be followed through by subsequent governments. In the private sector, more competition was a good thing as long as private failure was not met by government bailout. In the public sector, competition was only worthwhile if it could be maintained at a level commensurate with the maintenance of professional values that would temper the subverting tendencies of competing self-interested actors. If Moran's implicit policy advice had been followed after the publication of the second edition *The Politics of Banking* in 1989, the history of the UK banking sector—and that of health and education in the public sector—might have been very different. Moran himself, of course, was typically modest about the direct policy implications of his work. Academics, he pointed out, often conclude that policymakers need better-defined objectives and better information about the projected and actual effects of policies. Citing Charles Perrow, he noted that:

> Every remedy brings its own disease, every benefit a painful loss … Decisions are rarely produced by careful thought; they are invented half-consciously in the often desperate effort to cope with immediate dangers … or in calmer times they come out of the bovine power of custom. Thus do we all try to live with complexity or at least to survive it. (pp. 161–2)

Moran refined and extended his ideas on regulation in his *The British Regulatory State* (Oxford, 2003). From the 1970s onwards, UK policymaking was characterised by liberalisation, privatisation and the reconstruction of the public sector. Moran points out that in this period the UK developed the largest and most complex institutional apparatus for regulating privatisation and privatised industries in Europe. Before the 1970s, Britain had relied primarily on self-regulation in its domestic markets for labour, services and goods. However, the relative stagnation of the British economy during the 1950s and 1960s, combined with the disastrous liberalisation of the financial sector and rapid retrenchment (with the introduction of a command-like prices and incomes policy) in the early 1970s, led to an economic policy crisis that lasted throughout the 1970s.

The response, under Margaret Thatcher, was policy innovation. Moran offers three 'images', prevalent in UK policymaking circles in the early 2000s, of the changes in UK governing arrangements that occurred after 1980. The first was that the state withdrew from grand interventionist projects, such as attempts to effect comprehensive slum clearance. On this account, the emphasis in policy was now on 'steering not rowing': the role of government was to make strategic decisions about the shape and direction of the state rather than to engage directly in delivering services. The second image was that the changes during the 1980s were dominated by the creation of regulatory agencies—for privatised industries; for the impact of human activity on the environment; and for the expansion of regulation inside government. The third image was that the changes were largely a response to the crisis in Keynesian economics of the 1970s—to the failure of an economic strategy based on large-scale public ownership and purposive economic management aimed at maintaining full employment. For this image, the new approach after 1980

> created systems of rules that were then implemented elsewhere ... it focused on the task of remedying market failures rather than the more ambitious interventions of the Keynesian era ... the command modes of which it rejects. (p. 6)

Moran argued that these three images told only a part of the story of the changing UK policy world of the 1980s. In his view, the turn towards a more regulatory mode significantly extended the range of UK social and economic life that was subject to direct political power. He also suggested that the hyper-innovation in UK policy-making after 1980 was a response to two crises rather than to one. The first was the crisis in Kenynesianism referred to above. The second was the crisis of *club* government that had first been described by David Marquand: 'the exhaustion of an historically ancient project ... [that had preserved] ... oligarchic government in the face of democratic institutions and a democratic culture' (p. 7). On this account, the UK 'club state' that evolved during the course of the nineteenth century was based on an oligarchic elite who shared a set of common values, experiences, education and even gentlemen's club memberships. The corollary of the club system was the principle of self-regulation of the professions and of the City, combined with Inspectorates that monitored performance and investigated abuse or failure. By the 1970s, it was clear that these traditional institutions were failing to deliver the sort of economic efficiencies and innovations that were required if UK plc was to thrive in the modern world.

The new regulatory state of the 1980s, in these terms, was a vehicle for coping with the economic policy crisis of the 1970s *and* of reconstructing the institutions of government on the ruins of the club system by adopting a new approach to regulation itself. Under the new system, a large range of policy domains became the target for innovative methods of regulation: central banking; the physical environment; food safety; health and safety at work—new agencies were established that were intended to be free from partisan political control, where policy implementation was guided by technical imperatives.

For Moran, the new UK approach to regulation from the 1980s meant downplaying one of the traditional functions of the modern state: redistribution. In its place, greater emphasis was placed on economic stabilisation and on using regulation to promote efficiency by remedying market failure. This placed the UK somewhat at odds with the developing regulatory state model encouraged by the European Union. In contrast to the subsidiarity model favoured by the EU, where decisions are devolved to lowest possible level of governance, the UK regulatory state increasingly colonised new policy areas (such as the regulation of the professions and of privatised markets) and increasingly used command law as an instrument of that colonisation. In addition, in the UK there was no real retreat from hierarchy in favour of management through dispersed networks. On the contrary, in the UK, institutional formality and hierarchy were maintained, while too much of the available investment resource, most obviously in health and education, was directed to strengthen the reach and grip of bureaucracies in order to secure front-line service compliance with centrally determined standards and targets. Returning to themes that he had developed in his analysis of banking, Moran showed how this new regulatory 'command' approach was subverted by its own contradictions. The regulated used 'creative compliance' to circumvent regulatory directives; and rational self-interested actors reshaped and distorted the effects of regulation. All of this meant that by the late 1990s the new regulatory state, which had been intended to involve government steering self-regulated networks, ended up with a plethora of supposedly self-steering systems that were in fact subject to tight, centrally determined hierarchical control.

Moran developed these ideas in *The British Regulatory State* through a series of case studies in the fields of transport, finance, health and education. In his analysis of the regulation of privatisation and of private industries, he accepted that privatisation improved several things that would be expected in a modern liberal democracy —accountability, transparency and plurality of representation—in ways that were superior to what had happened under the post-war system of nationalised industries. As he also noted, however, the new approach did not depoliticise the newly privatised sector. Rather, it entangled it in an increasingly complex system of regulation imposed both by national government and by the EU that far too frequently resulted in policy failure or even disaster. In the remaining areas of the public sector, what had begun as the New Public Management (NPM) approach in the late 1980s had by 2000 seen the creation of over one hundred agencies. These new institutions replaced the direct line-of-command relationships between government and service deliverers with an elaborate system of charters and performance indicators that required a massive increase in the resources allocated for monitoring and for regulation itself. For Moran, the outcome failed comprehensively to deliver the aimed-for flexibility and distancing of service delivery from political control. On the contrary, NPM's main consequence was the maintenance of hierarchical control combined with the micro-management of service delivery by the metropolitan, central government elite. To complicate the position further, NPM also failed to prevent the capture by traditional elites of the institutions and processes that had been designed to secure tighter central managerial oversight and control. The result was a contradictory mishmash of centrally determined targets and standards, implemented by bureaucrats whose practices were strongly influenced by the circumventory and subversive aims of rational, self-interested front-line service deliverers. It was small wonder in these circumstances that the six 'policy fiascos' investigated in some detail by Moran—the Millennium Dome, Rail Privatisation, the Poll Tax, the collapse of Barings Bank,

BSE and the long list of government IT failures—should have occurred in the decade or so after Next Steps.[1]

In addition to his wide-ranging research contributions, Moran also found time to write three major textbooks which are familiar to generations of students studying at both undergraduate and graduate levels in British, European and North American universities. In *Politics and Society in Britain* (London, 1985 and 1989) Moran provided a comprehensive political sociology of British political institutions, mass and elite political behaviour, and the character and functioning of the British state. In *Politics and Governance in the UK* (Basingstoke, 2005 and 2011) he provided a wonderfully clear and comprehensive account of British politics in all its facets and manifestations. It was, and remains, widely used as an introductory text for both A-level and undergraduate students across the UK—and deservedly so. His *Business, Politics and Society: an Anglo-American Comparison* (Oxford, 2009), although publicised and presented as a textbook, was rather more than that. Rather, it was a model of how to conduct cross-national comparisons between similar political systems, in order both to evaluate general theoretical claims and to enhance understanding of differences and similarities across and within the different countries analysed. In many respects, it offered a definitive analysis of the (many) failures and (limited) successes of financial and business regulation on both sides of the Atlantic.

In his final book, *The End of British Politics?* (Basingstoke, 2017), intended for both students and the general reader, Moran reflected on the current condition of the UK, particularly in the light of the continuing pressures for Scottish Independence and the divisions in popular opinion deriving from the Brexit referendum result. His analysis, as always, was both theoretically informed and grounded in substantive historical knowledge and understanding. The abandonment of empire after 1945 ushered in a new social democratic project in the 1960s that in turn foundered on the stagflation crisis of the 1970s. The neo-liberal Thatcherite turn towards markets strengthened the service sector (especially the finance sector) whilst at the same time producing a significant centralisation and extension of the regulatory state, a tendency that was reinforced by the Blair governments after 1997. In Moran's view, these marketising and centralising tendencies had played an important role in damaging the UK's social and political fabric. Indeed, the UK's current political difficulties and tensions could probably be addressed effectively only by a radical decentralisation of

---

[1] The Next Steps initiative was an administrative reform introduced by the Thatcher government in 1988. It involved devolving the operational delivery of various civil service functions to a new set of supposedly lean and efficient public agencies with their own strategies, staff and leadership structures. For review, see https://www.instituteforgovernment.org.uk/sites/default/files/case%20study%20next%20steps.pdf (accessed 24 January 2019).

power. He was pessimistic that such a radical decentralisation could re-establish the social contract that thirty years of marketisation had broken—though he admitted to a 'glimmer of hope' that it might.

Michael Moran was always consummately professional in his presentation of arguments and evidence. With most of his writing, across most of his career, it would be difficult to discern his own 'political position'. In retirement, however, his passionate lifelong objections to inequality, and especially the role of neo-liberalism in increasing it, certainly revealed themselves in all their glory. In his final paper,[2] prepared for a conference at Essex on the character and origins of contemporary authoritarian populism, Mick was unequivocal in identifying where he thought the responsibility lay for so many of the difficulties we currently face:

> The deregulation of financial markets (in New York in 1976, and in London a decade later) was a choice, made because economic and governing elites sensed advantage in the act. That choice set free the forces of Financialization; led to the world of maximised shareholder value; enriched beyond the dreams of avarice those corporate managers who could deliver that maximised value; and thus brought to birth income inequality and the new plutocracy. Choice created deregulated labour markets and often—as in the case of the miners in the UK—led the state to destroy whole working class occupations. Choice fashioned taxation systems to enrich plutocrats. Choice positioned the UK as a post-industrial service economy in the international division of labour, where the most important enterprises were branch subsidiaries of foreign enterprises. Choice sold over one and a half million social housing units, and thus created the conditions for the appearance of 'generation rent.' Choice on both sides of the Atlantic opted for the light touch deregulation of financial markets that led to the catastrophe of the Great Financial Crisis and the decade of austerity... different choices across Europe produced very different levels of income inequality from those in the Anglo-American world.
>
> The proverb says: 'you can turn an aquarium into fish soup, but you cannot turn fish soup back into an aquarium'. In the decades after 1980 elites made fish soup of the post-war settlement. Now they are living with the consequences. They are right to be anxious. They have a lot to lose. In many discussions of populism the 'problem' that is posed is assumed to lie in the attitudes and behaviour of 'ordinary' (read 'normal') citizens rather than in elites. In the most recent anxious despatch from an elite institution (Harvard) the solution offered is to subject the population to civic education. But the betrayal in the broken contract suggests that the problem lies not with 'ordinary' people but with abnormal elites. It is elites, not 'ordinary' people, who need re-education. But the scale of the problem suggests that re-education alone will not do the job.

[2] M. Moran, 'Populism and social citizenship: an Anglo-American comparison', in I. Crewe and D. Sanders (eds.), *Authoritarian Populism and Liberal Democracy* (Basingstoke, 2019).

Mick never got to deliver his paper. He died two weeks after he sent it to me as conference organiser. I read it for him in his absence. It was the highlight of the conference. UK political science will miss his wisdom and his calm judgements enormously.

Note on the author: David Sanders is Emeritus Professor of Government at the University of Essex. He was elected a Fellow of the British Academy in 2005.

RANDOLPH QUIRK

Charles Randolph Quirk

12 July 1920 – 20 December 2017

elected Fellow of the British Academy 1975

by

DAVID CRYSTAL
Fellow of the Academy

RUTH KEMPSON
Fellow of the Academy

Randolph Quirk, Baron Quirk of Bloomsbury from 1994, was Vice-Chancellor of the University of London (1981–5) and President of the British Academy (1985–9). A specialist in English language studies, he became Professor of English at University College London, where he instituted the Survey of English Usage in 1960, innovative for its focus on spoken as well as written usage, and went on to lead a team of grammarians to produce the two main reference grammars of English in the second half of the twentieth century, *A Grammar of Contemporary English* (1972) and *A Comprehensive Grammar of the English Language* (1985).

Biographical Memoirs of Fellows of the British Academy, XVIII, 31–48
Posted 8 April 2019. © British Academy 2019.

RANDOLPH QUIRK

Randolph Quirk was born on the family farm at Lambfell, near Peel, on the Isle of Man on 12 July 1920, the youngest child of Thomas and Amy. The Quirks had farmed that land since the seventeenth century; and it was a source of some pride to RQ (as many colleagues would later refer to him, from his distinctive abbreviated signature) that his heritage was a mixture of Celtic and Norse. The name Quirk, in that spelling, is a distinctively Manx variant of a Gaelic form, seen also in O'Cuirc or MacCuirc—son of Corc, a fifth-century Irish king. He was educated at nearby Cronk y Voddy primary school and then at Douglas High School for Boys (today the upper school of St Ninian's), where he became the first member of his family to get to university. In the only personal interview he ever gave—a contribution to an anthology made for the Philological Society, *Linguistics in Britain: Personal Histories* (Oxford, 2002), from which all quotations in this memoir are taken—he reflected on how his upbringing in a farming family led him 'to be obsessively enamoured of hard work and to be just as obsessively sceptical about orthodoxies, religious or political'. His family was 'a mixture of Catholic and Protestant, of Anglican and Methodist, in an island community where self-consciously Manx values cohabited uneasily with increasingly dominant English values'. And he reflected wryly, 'if I'm an eclectic pluralist, it may simply be that the Manx in general are', recalling his fascination with the Scandinavian as well as the Celtic history and archaeology of the Isle of Man.

He was referring to one of the adjectives often used to describe his approach to linguistics: *eclectic*—by which he meant a reluctance to espouse any single theory of language, but to take bits from any theoretical approach that would be useful in his description of English grammar. It was a position very different from the linguistic climate of the times, when researchers were routinely identified by a particular school of thought—one might be a Bloomfieldian, a Firthian, a Hallidayan, or a Chomskyan, for example. While RQ had lived through all these eras, and indeed had worked with scholars from each of these traditions, he distanced himself from all of them. As he commented, 'The nice thing about eclecticism is, as its etymology proclaims, that you can choose freely and widely what you need for a particular purpose, without boxing yourself into any single (and doubtless inevitably flawed) theoretical position. It's a matter of taste and personal intellectual bent, I suppose, but I have always found it liberating to be unconstrained by the very idea of an orthodoxy.' It is a non-conforming and heterogeneous philosophy that earned him some criticism later from scholars who maintained the need for a strongly theoretically coherent approach.

It is possible to see the origins of this intellectual bent in the earliest days of his scholarly career. At secondary school he was especially drawn to the sciences, but the pull of history, language (evidence of Manx was everywhere, though not much spoken) and thus linguistic history, caused him to switch to the arts. His strong interest in language(s) is not only documented by his school performance in languages, but also by his school prizes. At the ages of fifteen, sixteen and eighteen he opted for book prizes: in 1935 *The Concise Oxford Dictionary of Current English*; in 1936 *Cassell's Latin Dictionary*; in 1938 *The Oxford Companion of Classical Literature* (as his choice for the Latin prize) and also that year *The History of England during the Reign of Victoria (1967–1901)*—his choice for the French Essay prize! Then in 1939 he gained the Northern Universities Higher School Certificate in English, French, Latin and History, with distinction in English, and also won the Isle of Man Education Authority's Scholarship of £80 p.a. for four years (in fact held for three years only). When he obtained a place at University College London (UCL) in 1939, he opted for English precisely because of the historical and linguistic emphasis in the curriculum there: Gothic, some Old Saxon and Old High German, a lot of Old Norse, and even more Anglo-Saxon, all in the wider context of Germanic philology, the history of the language, and palaeographical study from runes to court-hand.

The year 1939 was hardly the best time to commence a degree course, and it was soon interrupted: in 1940 he began a period of five years in RAF Bomber Command, during which he became so deeply interested in explosives that he returned to his school interests, and started an external degree in chemistry through evening classes at what is now the University of Hull. During the RAF years he was also employed as an evening instructor in English and Economics (one of the books of this period was T. S. Eliot's *Collected Poems 1909–1935*). He was also employed for three years as an instructor for explosives to air crews. Fortunately for English language studies, in 1945 he resumed his English course, spending some time in Aberystwyth (where the UCL department had relocated during the war), learning some Welsh, getting into local socialist politics and supplementing his minimal Manx grant by playing the clarinet in a local dance band. During his final two years he studied phonetics with Daniel Jones, encountered the subject of linguistics at the School of Oriental and African Studies with J. R. Firth, and became enamoured with the thought of doing research. He married Jean Williams in 1946, and they had two sons, Eric and Robin.

He graduated from UCL in 1947. In 1946 he had already been awarded the Elsie Hitchcock Prize for the most distinguished work in English philology in the Department. With his graduation he won the Early English Text Society's prize for his work on Medieval English Language and Literature. He also won the John Marshall Prize in Comparative Philology, and was given an engraved medal in silver. This is his first academic medal, going back seventy years, so UCL, which was to become his beloved college, awarded him a medal at the very beginning of his academic career! The distinction was such that he was also offered the Rouse Ball Open Research Scholarship (tenable at Trinity College, Cambridge), of £300 p.a. for three years to read for a PhD, which he declined, electing to stay at UCL. He was also invited by the Folkuniversitetet in Stockholm to spend a year (1947–8) in Sweden to lecture, but he declined this as well.

UCL offered him an Assistant Lectureship in the English Department (he became Lecturer in 1950) and the chance to write an MA thesis under the supervision of Professor A. H. (Hugh) Smith. He chose an aspect of Germanic philology that was exercising scholars at the time: whether the vowels in such Old English words as *heard* 'hard' or *feoh* 'cattle' were really diphthongs or just simple vowels plus diacritics indicating consonant qualities. He completed his MA thesis in 1949: 'Interpretation of Diphthongal Spellings in Old English with Special Reference to the Phonological Problems Presented by the Fracture Spellings in Cambridge University Library MS Ii.1.33'. And he began lecturing, his undergraduate classes including medieval literature, the history of the language, Old English and Old Norse. The teaching had an interesting side-effect: it brought home to him the realisation that traditional Germanic philology was of little assistance to students wanting to learn Old English, whereas the neglected areas of syntax and lexicology would, he felt, be much more beneficial. So for his PhD he switched to syntax, completing a thesis that was published by Yale University Press in 1954: *The Concessive Relation in Old English Poetry.* The choice was serendipitous. It coincided with a proposal by Professor C. L. Wrenn at Oxford to write an Old English grammar. Up to that point, such grammars traditionally covered only pronunciation and word structure (phonology and morphology), and Wrenn wanted this book to be different, with as full an account as possible of Old English syntax as well as word-formation. The result, *An Old English Grammar*, published by Methuen in 1955 (an enlarged edition with S. E. Deskis appeared in 1994), became a standard course book for students of Old English, at home and abroad, referred to as 'Quirk and Wrenn'.

In the meantime, there was a development that would put RQ into close contact with most leading English language scholars of the mid-twentieth century. In 1951 he was awarded a Harkness (formerly Commonwealth) Fellowship that took him first to Yale, where he met Bernard Bloch and Helge Kökeritz, visited Columbia, Brown, and Harvard (he especially valued meeting Roman Jakobson) and then to Ann Arbor, where he participated in the Middle English Dictionary project that was headed by Hans Kurath and Sherman Kuhn, and co-wrote two papers on Old English phonology with the latter. The immediate motivation was to work lexicographically on the UCL *Piers Plowman* project that had been started many years before by Professor R. W. Chambers, but of far greater importance for RQ's subsequent development was the close contact he had there with the leading Michigan linguists of the time, such as Charles Carpenter Fries, Albert Marckwardt, Kenneth Pike and Raven McDavid. It allowed him to become more acquainted with the historical and contemporary relations between American and British English and (especially through seminars that took place in Fries's home) with modes of working empirically on the syntax of unedited speech. It brought home to him the importance of the tape recorder, and the kind of naturalistic data that could be collected especially when speakers did not know they were being recorded (through a judiciously placed hidden microphone). The technique would raise some eyebrows in these modern privacy-sensitive times, but in its day the recordings provided an invaluable corrective to what people imagined the syntax of everyday informal spoken English to be like.

On his return from the USA in 1952 he felt he needed a change from London, and two years later took up a post as Reader in the small English department at Durham, where he was responsible for developing the language courses, which hitherto had been focused on the cultural and textual history of Anglo-Saxon England. This was the period when he developed an approach to the relationship between language and literature. An early instance of this relationship is his translation of an Icelandic saga for his students, published in 1957: *The Saga of Gunnlaug Serpent-Tongue*, edited with an introduction and notes by P. G. Foote. It led to a series of insightful papers in the developing area of stylistics, focusing on Shakespeare, Swift, Wordsworth, Dickens, T. S. Eliot and other literary greats, most of whom had never received any kind of linguistically informed analysis. He became a professor in the Department in 1958. His inaugural lecture, 'Charles Dickens and Appropriate Language', was held on 12 May 1959 and published in the same year.

The focus on the linguistic side of the relationship between language and literature and the teaching of the mother tongue came to the attention of the BBC, who invited him to give a series of broadcast lectures. This involved frequent weekend trips to London, where the BBC gave him a desk and access to its tapes and transcriptions of spontaneous speech in numerous discussion programmes. Like many linguists with a family, his children did not escape, producing data that were put to good use in the broadcasts. These lectures, where listeners often raised questions on current English usage, just as his students did in classes, made him aware of the rather unusual situation that there was no scholarly handbook on contemporary English grammar. England did not have its *Bon Usage* as the French, or a *Duden* as the Germans. Henry Sweet's *A New English Grammar Logical and Historical*, published at the turning of the twentieth century, was very dated. The modern English grammar then used as the standard reference book was R. W. Zandvoort's *A Handbook of English Grammar*. It had originally been written for Dutch students and was bilingual, but because of the great demand for a modern English grammar, a monolingual English edition was produced which came out in 1957. At that time, English grammar-writing was then in solid foreign hands, with the Netherlands and Sweden as leaders. These multi-volume works, written in English, all claimed to describe the modern language (Etsko Kruisinga's *A Handbook of Present-Day English*, Hendrik Poutsma's *A Grammar of Late Modern English* and Otto Jespersen's *A Modern English Grammar on Historical Principles*), but they were far from being so, being based on literary texts and having started publication in the first decades of the twentieth century.

As a consequence, during his years at Durham, RQ began to think seriously about the grammar of present-day and especially spoken English, both as an object of study and as a goal in teaching. The dual emphasis is seen in the collection of essays he edited with Hugh Smith in 1959 (London, revised 1964), *The Teaching of English*. There were so many variables to take into account that he early on saw the necessity of the computer and took a programming course with Ewan Page at Newcastle. Durham provided modest seed money for basic recording and analysis facilities, and RQ devised a long-term project for the description of English syntax. Several publishers were interested in supporting the proposal for a 'Survey of English Usage', especially Longman, and provided some basic funding for a research assistant. When in 1960 RQ moved back to UCL, as professor (1960–8, then Quain Professor, 1968–81), what he called his 'infant Survey' progressed rapidly, thanks to support from UCL provosts, the British Council (funding postgraduates and visits from senior scholars from abroad), the Ford Foundation (who brought over such scholars as Jim Sledd and Nelson Francis), the research councils and the major charities (such as Leverhulme), who were more than once called upon to help solve a Survey financial crisis. Longman set up a fellowship to fund visits from postdoctoral students, so they could use the Survey research to produce English-teaching materials when they returned home. The plans for the Survey were formally reported in a paper to the Philological Society in 1960. Annual reports on Survey progress were made thereafter, and are available for consultation in Survey archives and online: http://www.ucl.ac.uk/english-usage/ archives/index.htm (accessed 28 January 2019).

Several of the research assistants who worked on the Survey in those early years would later become known in various fields of linguistics, including the two authors of this memoir. David Crystal became the lead partner with RQ in devising the scheme by which the multiple systems of prosodic and paralinguistic features of speech were recognised, categorised and transcribed (*Systems of Prosodic and Paralinguistic Features in English*, The Hague, 1964); and RQ's collaborations with Jan Svartvik, Sidney Greenbaum and Ruth Kempson resulted in studies of psycholinguistic elicitation techniques and the notion of acceptability—aspects of the Survey that he felt significantly complemented the corpus analysis that was its central preoccupation (with Greenbaum, *Elicitation Experiments in English*, Harlow, 1970; with Svartvik, *Investigating Linguistic Acceptability,* The Hague, 1966; with Kempson, 'Controlled activation of latent contrast', in *Language*, 47 (1971), 548–72). The computational analysis became more sophisticated, with many nocturnal hours spent on off-peak access to the large Atlas machine in Gordon Square.

RQ directed the Survey from 1959 to 1983. The aim was to compile and analyse a databank, or corpus, of both written and spoken British English—an enterprise that went against the fashionable view of the time, with Noam Chomsky and other generative linguists arguing that personal intuition was all that was necessary for linguistic analysis. For RQ, this was not enough: to obtain a reliable account of all variations in the language, he believed one needed a wide sampling of authentic, observed language in use. Today, with corpus linguistics a major branch of the subject, it is easy to forget how daring this pioneering enterprise was, going as it did against the prevailing orthodoxy of the time—typical Quirk. And it was revolutionary in its scale: one million words—200 texts each of 5,000 words—including dialogue and monologue, and writing intended for both reading silently and reading aloud. In the modern world of Big Data, with online linguistic corpora of billions of words now routine, it is again easy to forget the enormous challenge of achieving a million-word target in a pre-digital era along with detailed accompanying annotations. The transcription of the spoken language required a huge investment of time, using heavy reel-to-reel tape recorders and repeaters, with the transcription painstakingly typed up onto small slips of paper and filed in storage cabinets while awaiting full grammatical and prosodic analysis.

The Survey took up the bulk of RQ's time in the 1960s and 1970s. His first major publication in London, making use of his BBC broadcast series, was *The Use of English* (London, 1962, enlarged edition 1968, with supplements by A. C. Gimson on English phonetics and Jeremy Warburg on notions of correctness). It was a truly ground-breaking work that stimulated innumerable readers to develop an interest in English language and language studies. Many of them (like the first writer of this memoir) would come to be able to quote from it by heart, and retell its anecdotes with impressive accuracy.

In 1972, the first large-scale work, based on the Survey's database of spoken and written contemporary English, appeared: *A Grammar of Contemporary English* (London), in collaboration with Sidney Greenbaum, Geoffrey Leech and Jan Svartvik. Its successor, *A Comprehensive Grammar of the English Language* (London, 1985—with the same team and twenty-five years of joint scholarship), had a hugely increased data and research basis. Both works proved—according to unanimous scholarly acclaim—to be RQ's chief linguistic legacy. They were the first reference grammars of present-day English to be published in the twentieth century that were based on insights from modern linguistics; and the thirty-plus obituaries and personal tributes brought together on the Survey's 2018 website (https://uclsurveyofenglish.wordpress.com/2018/01/02/in-memory-of-randolph-quirk (accessed 28 January 2019)) repeatedly acknowledge the role these two books played in the writers' world, with adjectives such as 'monumental' a recurring theme. When the first grammar came out, Longman dictionary editor-in-chief Della Summers wrote on that website: '*A Grammar of Contemporary English* was added to our reference library and immediately became the essential arbiter on any question of grammar, so much so that its approach to grammatical description was used in the new *Longman Dictionary of Contemporary English*, and indeed it was to echo Randolph's work that the word 'contemporary' was put into the title of the dictionary.' Michael Swan similarly acknowledged the role these works played in informing the wider ELT (English Language Teaching) world: 'In producing these monumental reference guides, Randolph and his collaborators did a very great service not only to practitioners like myself, but directly and indirectly to the whole English-teaching profession.'

In the same year, 1972, RQ completed another major service to the nation. From 1969 to 1972 he was Chairman of the Committee of Enquiry into Speech Therapy Services: its Report would revolutionise the profession, not least by making it an all-graduate career and emphasising the importance of having language at the core of the speech therapist's discipline. Public recognition was overwhelming, and in 1975 he was elected a Fellow of the British Academy on the basis of 'his sustained demonstration in his published works of the significant relation between linguistics and literature, by which the study of both subjects has been furthered; his initiation and expert direction of the Survey of English Usage at University College London; his service to national welfare as chairman of the Committee of Enquiry into Speech Therapy Services; his acknowledged international standing as a linguistician'.

After the publication of *A Grammar of Contemporary English* and its derivative works, the Survey of English Usage became a leading destination for scholars of the English language because of its new approach. The international impact caused queues of linguists from abroad eager to access the Survey material. Postgraduates from the Netherlands, Belgium, France, Germany, Sweden, and elsewhere came to use the data for their dissertations. Professors of English Language visited, wanting to familiarise themselves with this new project in order to inform their students. Researchers spent time at the Survey to explore whether they might set up a similar research project in their own countries (and produce a grammar).

Many of the younger generation of researchers described the Survey atmosphere as unique: the help provided by the 'Survey gang' was generous, and RQ's presence was inspiring and encouraging. Every day there was a tea/coffee break when work stopped for half an hour. All moved to RQ's office (Survey staff with their own mugs, and spare mugs for visitors), brought their 5 or 10p for the tin box, and the Prof himself prepared the beverages. He returned to his desk, everyone else sitting around the table, and for (exactly) half an hour anything could jointly be discussed. At the end of the day, to clear the mind, squash was encouraged, with RQ playing anyone who could be persuaded to take him on. A close network was established, and many of the young linguists from abroad became university chair-holders of English language in their respective countries (such as Liliane Haegeman, Sylviane Granger, Wolf-Dietrich Bald, Svetlana Terminasova and Ranko Bugarski). An international group of Surveyists came into being which in the European tradition would have been referred to as a 'school' or 'circle' (as in the Prague Circle or the Geneva School of Linguists).

At the same time as developing the Survey, RQ was taking a keen interest in the development of linguistics at UCL, and it was largely due to him that the subject grew there to become the major force it is today. During the 1960s he was part of a project to form a Communication Research Centre, and this led to 'a spot of energetic head-hunting in Edinburgh'. The result was the addition to the English department of a linguistics section headed by Michael Halliday and including Bob Dixon, Rodney Huddleston, Dick Hudson and Eugene Winter. Later, this section moved out of English and ultimately joined Phonetics to become the Department of Phonetics and Linguistics. The influence of Halliday on RQ's approach to grammar should be acknowledged at this point, as should some of the important consequences of Halliday's appointment: a large-scale project on linguistics in English teaching involving a large team of linguists and teachers during the 1960s, initially funded by Nuffield and later the Schools Council, and which had RQ's strong behind-the-scenes support; and Huddleston's project on the grammar of scientific English which ran alongside the Nuffield project between 1964 and 1967.

The international success of *A Grammar of Contemporary English* made the publisher Longman want to revitalise its dictionary publications. To this end a committee, Linglex, was set up which RQ was to chair for the best part of forty years. Della Summers describes him as 'the most formidable chair you could imagine, always nailing the point, always practical in finding a solution'. Linglex gave RQ the opportunity to stimulate and influence the study and description of vocabulary. With his knowledge of English, French, Latin, Icelandic and Swedish he had always been interested in the lexicon, semantic change and etymology, and especially in the way different languages lexicalise similar concepts. It was an interest that can be seen very early on, in his work on the *Middle English Dictionary* in Ann Arbor in the 1950s, and in the *Old English Grammar*, which includes a description of word-formation that was a new approach at the time. He taught lexicology at UCL for many years. His two major reference works are not only grammars: both *The Grammar of Contemporary English* and *A Comprehensive Grammar of the English Language* include an Appendix on modern English word-formation—the first overview of this subject produced by a native speaker. He was a member of the Oxford Advisory Committee for the *Third Edition of the Oxford English Dictionary*, and was instrumental in securing financial support for the *Historical Thesaurus of the English Language* (1965–2009).

As Chairman of Linglex he was able to bring his interests in grammar, the lexicon and teaching together. When the *Longman Dictionary of Contemporary English* came out in 1978, it was hailed as a revolution in lexicography for ELT. Until then, Oxford University Press had held a quasi-monopoly position with A. S. Hornby's *Advanced Learner's Dictionary of Current English*. The new Longman dictionary developed a fresh approach that challenged Oxford's primacy, introducing a Quirkian grammatical description into the entries and using a defining vocabulary—a restricted set of some 2,000 lexical items—for the definitions. C. K. Ogden's influence (*Basic English*) is here clearly recognisable (he and C. K. Ogden were good friends).

Despite a heavy teaching and administrative load, RQ produced a steady stream of books and articles. He never forgot the need to make research available to a wider readership, and each of the big grammars was soon supplemented by an abridged text, written with Sidney Greenbaum: *A University Grammar of English* (Harlow, 1973) and *A Student's Grammar of the English Language* (Harlow, 1990). He enjoyed collaboration, evidenced by *A Common Language* (with A. H. Marckwardt, London, 1964), *Systems of Prosodic and Paralinguistic Features in English* (with David Crystal, The Hague, 1964), *Old English Literature: a Practical Introduction* (with Valerie Adams and Derek Davy, London, 1975), *A Corpus of English Conversation* (with Jan Svartvik, Lund, 1980), *English in the World* (with Henry Widdowson, Cambridge, 1985), and two books written with his second wife, German linguist Gabriele Stein (whom he married in 1984, his first marriage having been dissolved in 1979): *English in Use* (Harlow, 1990) and *An Introduction to Standard English* (Tokyo, 1993). The breadth of his interests is evident from these titles: his early historical fascination is still there, along with literary, linguistic and stylistic themes, and an increasingly global perspective on the language. Several collections of papers provide further illustration, notably *Essays on the English Language: Medieval and Modern* (which begins with a paper on Old English metrics and ends with one on grammatical acceptability, Harlow, 1968), *The English Language and Images of Matter* (London, 1972), *The Linguist and the English Language* (London, 1974), *Style and Communication in the English Language* (London, 1982) and *Words at Work: Lectures on Textual Structure* (based on the series of lectures he gave in Singapore as Lee Quan Yew Distinguished Visitor, 1985–6: Harlow, 1986).

In the 1980s his personal output slowed down, though his influence on the work of others continued throughout this period and beyond—he continued working at his office in the Survey until well into the 2000s—and his insights about gradient acceptability are still being revisited today. There were two very good reasons for the reduction in quantity. Firstly, most of his writing time was devoted to preparing the *Comprehensive Grammar*—a difficult task, given that the 'gang of four' were geographically separated—Leech in Lancaster,[1] Svartvik in Lund—and of course in those days drafts of chapters had to be circulated by mail. And secondly, he was appointed Vice-Chancellor (VC) of the University of London in 1981, a position he held for four years ('another job, like my very first, that I didn't apply for and was in this instance very reluctant to accept'). The appointment did have one linguistic benefit, though: it meant that the occasional meetings of the four collaborators could take place in a spacious office in Gordon Square.

Why reluctant? He had been a member of the University of London Senate since 1970, and of the Court since 1972, but those were the austerity years of the Thatcher government when all universities faced severe cutbacks—in the case of London, a funding reduction of 17 per cent spread over three years—and RQ took up the role of VC in 1981 at a time when funding for universities in the UK was under continuing acute pressure. As events turned out, he was the last genuinely effective VC of London University, being as it was then still a properly functioning compound unit, with Boards of Studies approving the assignment of examiners and examination results at all levels, ensuring conformity of standards right across the institution. Moreover, since this was a time when VCs of Oxford and Cambridge were only of two-years duration and generally little more than a senior title without academic functionality, RQ was very influential and effective in the UK university sector as a whole, keeping the profile of humanities and social science high despite difficult financial circumstances. Furthermore, his tenure of the VC role was just at a time when Imperial College and UCL were urging their independence, with heavy pressure coming from the sciences; and arguably he showed considerable prescience in seeing that the only way to protect the colleges as viable units was to merge some, so that a move superficially implementing severe cuts, in the spirit of the time, had the reverse effect of ensuring the now very successful independent institutions of Queen Mary University of London (QMUL: the result of merging Queen Mary and Westfield Colleges) and Royal Holloway University of London (RHUL: the result of merging Royal Holloway and Bedford Colleges), with the School of Slavonic and East European Studies as a notable further follower of this pattern, remaining very active and identifiable after its merger with UCL.

His period as VC ended with a knighthood (1985), an accolade that supplemented a CBE he had been awarded in 1976, and which would in turn be eclipsed by becoming a life peer in 1994, when he sat as a cross-bencher in the House of Lords, taking a special interest in educational issues. This concern had begun while he was VC. He records a meeting with the then Secretary of State for Education, Sir Keith Joseph:

> In one of my chilly confrontations in the Senate House with Sir Keith, he told me

[1] See G. Myers, 'Geoffrey Neil Leech 1936–2014', *Biographical Memoirs of Fellows of the British Academy*, 16 (2017), pp. 147–68.

bluntly that if his department had the kind of money I was seeking, he wouldn't give it to me but to where it was infinitely more badly needed. 'When were you last in any of our inner city comprehensives?' he asked. The following week he took me to one for a couple of hours, and the scales fell from my eyes. In all my years as a university teacher, I was ashamed to realise that I had never bothered to find out what sort of quality education the majority of schools meted out. Ever since, I've been trying to make restitution in whatever way I could.

As President of the British Academy (1985–9), and in the House of Lords, this is precisely what he did. In his own words:

> When I was President of the British Academy, I worked (as in so much these days, along with my wife, Gabriele Stein) at radically improving the new National Curriculum so as to ensure a better schooling 'for the many' as New Labour would say, without disrupting the kind of education expected of the growing numbers of students coming into the universities. We had some success in eradicating the emphasis on trivial aspects of grammar (such as the split infinitive) and introducing more serious attention to vocabulary, in the course of exposing the misplaced disdain for Standard English affected by many in the educational establishment.

His term as President of the British Academy coincided with an important phase in the institution's history, in which he played a key part. He was the first President to make the Academy, then in Cornwall Terrace, Regent's Park, his principal academic base, becoming in effect an additional member of staff, taking over its small library as his office, and involving himself with trademark force and vigour in all its affairs. This was the more remarkable in that he assumed the presidency soon after major heart surgery (a quadruple bypass)—an event that caused great consternation among his colleagues—though the concern was replaced by amazement at the extraordinary rapidity with which he recovered, throwing himself into Academy activities ignoring all fears for his health. His presence proved immensely valuable in the daily conduct of business and in interactions with staff—he was always ready to try out and react to ideas in a wholly unbuttoned way. Interactions with members of staff and Council ranged from arguments as to the best way forward, which he didn't always win, to staff finding themselves recruited in linguistic experiments: he delighted the Secretary's daughter by treating her as an informant on teenage argot.

The period of his presidency covered the years when, with inimical conditions in the university sector, the absence of a Humanities Research Council was being increasingly felt, and though the Academy was encouraged by the government to regard itself as the next best thing, it could not offer the range or size of awards that, for example, its nearest equivalent, the Economic and Social Research Council, did in the social sciences. The Academy had already begun to assume wider responsibilities—in 1984 taking over from the Department of Education and Science the administration of the national scheme for postgraduate studentships in the humanities, and it had begun to shape future policy in this area—and it was being called upon to involve itself more in national discussions on research policy and resource allocation, eventually to become fully integrated in the system. RQ's relations and standing with successive Secretaries of State and within such bodies as the University Grants Committee and the Advisory Board for the Research Councils were much to the Academy's advantage as he steered the institution through choppy waters.

These years also saw internal reorganisation and a major expansion in the Academy's activities, with RQ always a driving force. Apart from postgraduate studentships, there was a notable coup (1985) in the publicly funded scheme for three-year postdoctoral fellowships which, further expanded, remains to this day a principal element in the Academy's programmes. (RQ was fond of pointing out that three-quarters of the Academy's public grant went on the 'under thirties'.) To this was added a mid-career Research Readership programme—a submission to fund a top layer, as it were, of Research Professorships was unsuccessful, and had to await a later day—and a start was made in supporting what was then called 'group research', to complement the schemes for individual personal projects. These were publicly funded, an achievement in itself, but successful approaches were also made to private funders, not merely research foundations such as Wolfson and Leverhulme (which initiated support for group research projects), but also British Gas, Swan Hellenic (which agreed to finance research posts) and individual sponsors, notably Dr Marc Fitch. (One approach, which came to nothing, was to Robert Maxwell, who startled RQ initially by proposing to grant him a personal retainer as President of the Academy.) Structural change was also taking place within the Academy, as the recommendations of a review of the Section structure were implemented, intended to make the Academy more comprehensive ('representative' was the term of use) in its membership, particularly in the social sciences, and more sensitive to changing fields of scholarly enquiry, with a committee structure more closely articulated with work in universities and other institutions of higher education. The work and scope of the overseas (mainly archaeological) schools and institutes that were historically linked to the Academy also came under scrutiny, and there was a considerable growth in the Academy's international relations and contacts.

As Baron Lord Quirk of Bloomsbury, RQ joined the House of Lords in 1994, in whose activities, as ever, he combined wit with intense commitment. As he said in the Philological Society interview:

> Since entering the House of Lords, I have still further extended my interest in general educational issues to take up the disgracefully neglected matter of education and training for prisoners and 'young offenders'—the vast majority of them male and (even compared with our grossly under-educated population at large) disproportionately illiterate. In this respect too, I'm trying to make up for a happy, lucky life in the charmed circles of academia, though in another respect it's a return to an interest I indulged when I was in Durham. The Chief Constable was Alec Muir, brother of another friend Kenneth, who was Professor of English in Liverpool. Alec persuaded me to give a course of lectures for lifers and the like in Durham Gaol. I've never had more attentive and appreciative audiences!

He became a member of the House of Lords Select Committee on Science and Technology in 1998. His commitment to Upper Chamber work included the valuable support he provided in the setting up of the All-Party Parliamentary Group on Modern Languages in 2008, to which he went on to contribute actively, seeking to enrich children's literacy and language skills within the educational system, and doing everything possible to sustain a focus on how essential modern language skills are in economics, diplomacy, export growth—indeed, every aspect of UK life. Working behind the scenes he also made a contribution to the reciprocal health agreement between the Isle of Man and the United Kingdom in 2010.

His interest in educational matters of national importance in fact antedated both his British Academy and House of Lords days. He served on a committee looking into school examinations (the Lockwood Report was published by HMSO in 1964). He was seen as a hidden force behind the influential report of the committee headed by Sir John Kingman into the teaching of English (1988), whose impact would be seen a few years later in the National Curriculum for English. He was passionate in his advocacy of the need for young people to learn about their mother tongue, but was cautious about the teaching of grammar in schools. Grammar, he felt, should be taught well or not at all. What he really believed was missing in schools was the study of vocabulary, and it is thanks to him and his wife (also a lexical researcher) that the National Curriculum for English strongly and repeatedly emphasises the acquisition of a differentiated command of the vocabulary.

He was also very active in his ongoing support of the Wolfson Foundation, where he was a trustee (1987–2011), serving as Chairman of its Arts and Humanities Panel for many years, during which time a great deal of its investment in education matters was shaped by his energy and insight. During his chairmanship, not only was there ongoing support for history research through its Wolfson History Prize, but substantial sums were given for the care and restoration of historic buildings (notably St George's Hall in Liverpool), cathedrals (in particular, the transept of St Paul's,

London), churches (such as St Martin-in-the-Fields, London), major public gardens (such as the one at Kenilworth Castle), and libraries (including the London School of Economics, Queen's University Belfast and the British Museum for its Centre for Conservation). He also acted as a member of its Schools Panel, reflecting his deep interest in secondary education. The Academy in particular benefited from the leading role he played at Wolfson in supporting Humanities programmes over an extended period.

His reputation as a linguist made him much in demand by national bodies over and above the Academy and the Wolfson Foundation, and somehow he managed to find time to be an active presence in all of them. They included being a governor of the British Institute of Recorded Sound (1976–80) and the English-Speaking Union (ESU, 1980–5), and then vice-chair (the chairman was the Duke of Edinburgh) of the ESU's English Language Council. He chaired the A. S. Hornby Educational Trust (1979–93), the Anglo-Spanish Foundation (1983–5), and the British Library Advisory Committee (1984–97), and had periods as president of the Institute of Linguists (1982–5) and the College of Speech Therapists (1987–91) and as vice-president of the Foundation for Science and Technology (1986–90). He was a member of the Royal Academy of Dramatic Art's Council (1985–2004) and of the Board of the British Council (1983–91) for whom he undertook many foreign tours, returning with detailed commissioned reports on the language situation in the countries specified. His lecture visits took him to China, Japan, Korea, Russia, South America, the USA, such Commonwealth countries as Australia, Fiji, Ghana, India, Malta, New Zealand ('in the only spell of sabbatical leave I ever had, 1975–6'), Nigeria, Singapore, South Africa, Tonga, and closer to home to Austria, Belgium, the Czech Republic, Finland, France, Germany, Greece, Iraq, Italy, the Netherlands, Poland, Romania, Spain, Switzerland, Sweden and Yugoslavia. In him, English had an international voice.

Academic accolades were numerous. He was elected a member of Academia Europaea, the Royal Belgian Academy of Sciences, the Royal Swedish Academy, the Finnish Academy of Sciences and the American Academy of Arts and Sciences. He was an honourable bencher at Gray's Inn, and was made an honorary fellow of the College of Speech Therapists, the Institute of Linguists, and most of the constituent colleges of the University of London. He was the recipient of many honorary doctorates: Aston, Bar Ilan, Bath, Brunel, Bucharest, Copenhagen, Durham, Essex, Glasgow, Helsinki, Leicester, Liège, London, Lund, Newcastle upon Tyne, Nijmegen, Open, Paris, Poznan, Prague, Queen Margaret, Reading, Richmond, Salford, Sheffield, Southern California, Uppsala and Westminster. The three other members of the 'gang of four'—Sidney Greenbaum, Geoffrey Leech and Jan Svartvik—edited a Festschrift for him, *Studies in English Linguistics* (London, 1980), in which his eclecticism is well reflected in its thirty international contributors, including Noam Chomsky, Michael Halliday, Dwight Bolinger, Josef Vachek, Archibald Hill and Sven Jacobson—linguists who would be very unlikely otherwise to rub shoulders in the same volume.[2]

We can perhaps put RQ's achievements in perspective by recalling an earlier giant in the history of the English language. When the lexicon had developed to such a degree that there was a general public demand for an authoritative dictionary, Dr Johnson compiled the *Dictionary of the English Language* (1755) for the nation. Some three hundred years later, when English was on its way to becoming the world lingua franca, RQ produced what was needed: he gave the nation an authoritative grammar. As Vice-Chancellor of the University of London, Trustee of the Wolfson Foundation and a member of the House of Lords, he seized all the opportunities which presented themselves to raise the profile of the humanities and social sciences in their vital role for society. The devoted service which he gave to his country was exemplary.

When the news of his death was announced, on 20 December 2017, the public accolades were numerous, and a remarkable consistency emerged in the personal tributes listed on the UCL memorial page (https://www.ucl.ac.uk/english-usage/about/quirk-memorial.htm (accessed 28 January 2019)). There is unanimity that he revitalised the scientific study of English grammar in the UK in the twentieth century, after almost half a century of academic neglect, and pointed the way towards the integrated study of language and literature. Students remember him as a charismatic, energetic and energising lecturer, recalling his clarity of expression, his wit and his gift for the apt and memorable example of language in use—characteristics reflected in the elegance of his writing. Junior colleagues recall his unfailing and enthusiastic support for whatever research topic they broached with him, generous with his time, giving them all his attention, offering incisive comments, and often following them up with a handwritten note. He launched the careers of many linguists, both in the UK and abroad, including the two writers of this memoir.

In a letter in 2000, RQ wrote to Keith Brown, at the time compiling an anthology of mini-autobiographies for the Philological Society: 'I have become increasingly convinced that my own personal history would not be worth reading and that, by writing one, I would be implying that I thought it was.' He reluctantly agreed to be interviewed, and much of the information in this memoir comes from that. The refusal to write his own autobiography was the only bad decision he ever made.

[2] That Festschrift also contains a list of his publications up to 1980, compiled by Valerie Adams.

Note: A memorial event in RQ's honour was held on 9 July 2019, hosted by the Academy.

Note on the authors: David Crystal is Honorary Professor of Linguistics, University of Bangor; he was elected a Fellow of the British Academy in 2000. Ruth Kempson is Professor Emerita, Philosophy Department, King's College London; she was elected a Fellow of the British Academy in 1989.

JOHN A. BURROW

John Anthony Burrow

3 August 1932 – 22 October 2017

elected a Fellow of the British Academy 1986

by

THORLAC TURVILLE-PETRE

John A. Burrow was Winterstoke Professor of English at the University of Bristol from 1976 until his retirement in 1998, and Dean of the Faculty of Arts from 1990 to 1993. He was the leading authority on medieval English literature of his generation, author of many books and essays, including *A Reading of Sir Gawain and the Green Knight* (1965), *Ricardian Poetry* (1971), *The Ages of Man* (1986), *Langland's Fictions* (1993), *Gestures and Looks in Medieval Narrative* (2002) and editions of Thomas Hoccleve's *Complaint and Dialogue* (1999) and William Langland's *Piers Plowman: the B-Version Archetype* (2018).

Biographical Memoirs of Fellows of the British Academy, XVIII, 49–61
Posted 8 April 2019. © British Academy 2019.

JOHN A. BURROW

John Anthony Burrow, who died at the age of eighty-five on 22 October 2017, brought new grace and sensitivity to the understanding of medieval English literature and was one of the most influential literary scholars of his generation. He wrote with clarity and wit, and had no time for the narrow professionalism that characterises so much academic writing. He was born and brought up in Loughton, Essex, the only child of William Burrow, an accountant, and his wife, Ada (née Hodgson), a teacher. He went to Christ Church, Oxford, in 1950 to study English. Looking back on his experience of Oxford after fifty years, he wrote:

> Oxford English in the 1950s offered three alternative courses. Courses I and II concentrated on early English writings, philology, Old Norse, and the like, but most undergraduates, including myself, followed Course III. The outline of that more general programme was determined by a set of required Finals papers which extended over all periods of English from Anglo-Saxon and Middle English up to 1830.[1]

Even the 'general programme' leant rather heavily towards philology.

In 1953 he met the girl who was to become his wife, Diana Wynne Jones, later to become a celebrated author of fantasy novels for young readers. She later recalled meeting a group of students:

> One of them said, 'Diana, you know John Burrow, do you?' I sort of looked. Not properly. All I got was a long beige streak of a man standing with them in front of the old Arthur Ransome cupboard. And instantly I knew I was going to marry this man.[2]

They married three years later, while he was an assistant lecturer at King's College London. In 1957 they set up house in Iffley Road, Oxford, with John lecturing for Oxford colleges. Appointed Fellow of Jesus College in 1961, he collaborated with his friends John Carey and Christopher Ricks to breathe much-needed fresh life into the English syllabus. He describes this time:

> Among the lecturers on Middle English subjects were such distinguished names as J. A. W. Bennett, C. S. Lewis, and J. R. R. Tolkien, but some of us thought that, in the medieval work as elsewhere, too little attention was paid to the qualities of the writings as literature.[3]

The Burrows moved out of Iffley Road into a college house off the Cowley Road. Diana gave a memorable description:

> In 1967, the new house was ready. It had a roof soluble in water, toilets that boiled periodically, rising damp, a south-facing window in the food cupboard, and any

---

[1] J. A. Burrow, 'Should we leave medieval literature to the medievalists?', *Essays in Criticism*, 53 (2003), 278.
[2] D. Wynne Jones, *Reflections: on the Magic of Writing* (New York, 2012), p. 292.
[3] Burrow, 'Should we leave medieval literature to the medievalists?', 278.

number of other peculiarities. So much for my wish for a quiet life. We lived there, contending with electric fountains in the living room, cardboard doors, and so forth, until 1976, except for 1968–9, which year we spent in America, at Yale. Yale, like Oxford, was full of people who thought far too well of themselves, lived very formally, and regarded the wives of academics as second class citizens.[4]

Diana was not fond of Oxford and was delighted when in 1976 John was appointed to the Winterstoke Chair of English Literature at Bristol, though his arrival was delayed for some months by a horrific car crash in which he managed to save his family by turning the wheel at the last minute, at the cost of severe injury to himself. At Bristol he served as Head of Department and as Dean of the Faculty of Arts (1990–3). He inevitably had to deal with a number of difficult situations and was deeply troubled when the University imposed a series of staff cutbacks, which however he handled with great compassion: 'His was intellectual leadership of a really meaningful kind, rather than of the sort often invoked in manuals of management technique,' one colleague writes. Though he was greatly admired as a humane administrator, his first loves were teaching and writing, and somehow he continued to do both throughout. As a great believer in the idea that critical writing should be informed by the experience of teaching, he wrote a wonderfully lucid and concise introduction to medieval authors during this period.[5] He was an outstanding teacher, as I myself remember, his demands for high standards always moderated by kindness and humour. He once asked a student whether she had learnt her Old English paradigms. 'Do you mean', she replied defensively, 'parrot-fashion?' He sucked his pipe ruminatively and asked, if she had not learnt them in the fashion of a parrot, how she had learnt them: 'Sieve-fashion?'

Burrow's first book, *A Reading of Sir Gawain and the Green Knight* (1965), focused precisely on 'the qualities of writings as literature' that he found lacking in earlier studies. It remains an essential guide to a remarkable poem.[6] It takes the reader through the text, fit by fit, examining in detail precisely what the poet means, analysing action and guiding interpretation, in a fashion quite different from anything earlier critics had attempted. There is a danger of undervaluing Burrow's critical approach, for he made it all look so easy. Every sentence he wrote is pellucid, every judgement he made is so persuasive, that readers forget that the ideas were new until they read them. The argument of *A Reading of Sir Gawain and the Green Knight*, expressed methodically, logically, and with precise clarity, is that the poem is about *trawthe*, which has a sense much wider than 'truth'; the key section of the book is Burrow's analysis of

[4] Wynne Jones, *Reflections*, p. 292.

[5] J. A. Burrow, *Medieval Writers and their Work: Middle English Literature 1100-1500* (Oxford, 1982, 2nd edn 2008).

[6] J. A. Burrow, *A Reading of Sir Gawain and the Green Knight* (London, 1965).

trawthe in the description of the pentangle painted on Gawain's shield. This is the passage dismissed in the standard edition of the poem with the complaint that 'the pentangle itself is not even mentioned by name after the elaborate account of it'.[7] This uncomprehending comment quite missed the point, for Burrow showed that the pentangle hangs over the action and over our evaluation of Gawain's conduct throughout the poem. His perceptive interpretation of detail is everywhere apparent, as when he notices that the third time Gawain and his host meet to exchange what they have gained during the day, the occasion on which the hero withholds his winnings, Gawain is dressed in a blue coat and hood: 'For his one act of duplicity Gawain wears *blue*— the traditional colour of faithfulness, occurring here and nowhere else in the poem.'[8]

The same close reading characterised *Ricardian Poetry* published six years later, a study of four contemporary writers, Chaucer, Gower, Langland and the *Gawain*-poet.[9] Critics, and there were many, called it 'formalist', a description which Burrow rejected.[10] Reviewers were sharply divided on the merits of the book. The best account of its reception is by Charlotte Morse in the Festschrift presented to Burrow on his retirement. She explains:

> In publishing *Ricardian Poetry* John Burrow offered the term 'Ricardian' as a replace-ment for the familiar 'Age of Chaucer'. As much as any recent theorist of literature, Burrow had a political agenda within English studies. By elevating Chaucer's three major contemporaries to something like parity with him and perceiving these four major Middle English poets as constituting a period, Burrow hoped to enhance the status of medieval English literature in the larger field of English literature.[11]

Burrow unashamedly restricted his discussion to 'high art', and critics objected that these four exceptional writers were, by definition, not representative of the Ricardian age. They also complained that wider considerations—politics, the author in society, manuscript contexts, philosophy, theology, art and architecture, and so on—were not addressed. Morse distinguished between British and American critics of the time, the former relying on criteria based on taste, the latter 'bemused by a kind of British criticism that offers leisurely commentary, marked by sometimes brilliant *aperçus*, but no argument'.[12] Burrow himself acknowledged that in *Ricardian Poetry*:

[7] *Sir Gawain and the Green Knight*, ed. J. R. R. Tolkien and E. V. Gordon, revised by Norman Davis (Oxford, 1967), p. xxi.
[8] Burrow, *A Reading of Sir Gawain and the Green Knight*, p. 112.
[9] J. A. Burrow, *Ricardian Poetry* (London, 1971).
[10] Burrow, 'Should we leave medieval literature to the medievalists?', 279.
[11] C. Morse, 'From Ricardian poetry to "Ricardian Studies"', in A. J. Minnis, C. Morse and T. Turville-Petre (eds.), *Essays on Ricardian Literature* (Oxford, 1997), pp. 316–17.
[12] Ibid., p. 324.

the four poets were considered and compared synchronically, with little regard for the historical circumstances from which they arose or to which they might have made reference. In recent years, however, the interest of literary scholars in the Ricardian period—and in the Lancastrian period that followed it—have taken a sharp turn towards history.[13]

He remarks tartly of some of these scholars: 'Were it not for the quotations, [readers] might not notice that the texts under consideration were poems at all.'[14] But it was not historicist criticism to which he objected, for, after all, good historicist explorations inform and guide the reading and appreciation of texts. Rather his complaint was that critics neglected literary qualities in order to mine texts for some other purpose.

Indeed, when reviewing critical fashions such as 'the death of the author', he wrote: 'Texts without authors are often no more reliable guides to their own meaning than authors without texts.'[15] Yet it is just such a situation that often faces the medievalist, and in the same year he studied an extreme instance of the problem in the case of the Rawlinson Lyrics, precariously surviving on a narrow strip of parchment in a guardbook of fragments. They had attracted fanciful criticism, and in 'Poems without Contexts' Burrow argued that in the regrettable absence of external information about them, it is important to identify the genres to which they belong as some sort of control over interpretation.[16] On the other hand, with Thomas Hoccleve we have a wealth of information, with records from his service in the Privy Seal and indeed from autobiographical passages in his poetry describing a mental breakdown.[17] Hoccleve's Victorian editor, F. J. Furnivall, took these at face value, as a self-portrait of a 'weak, sensitive, look-on-the-worst side kind of man'.[18] More sophisticated critical approaches saw such comments as absurdly naive. These self-references, it was argued, are merely conventional, references not to the author but to the fictional 'author'. To believe otherwise is to fall prey to the 'autobiographical fallacy'. In his British Academy Gollancz lecture, 'Autobiographical poetry in the Middle Ages', Burrow characterised the 'conventional fallacy', whose victims 'combine a learned and sophisticated awareness of literary convention with an apparently naive and reductive notion of what real life is like—naive and reductive because they talk as if non-literary experience were not itself shaped by conventions'.[19]

[13] Burrow, 'Should we leave medieval literature to the medievalists?', 280.

[14] Ibid., 280–1.

[15] J. A. Burrow, 'Alterity in medieval literature', *New Literary History*, 10 (1978–9), 388.

[16] J. A. Burrow, 'Poems without contexts', *Essays in Criticism*, 29 (1979), 6–32; reprinted in J. A. Burrow, *Essays on Medieval Literature* (Oxford, 1984), pp. 1–26.

[17] For the Hoccleve life-records see J. A. Burrow, *Thomas Hoccleve, Authors of the Middle Ages 4* (Aldershot, 1994).

[18] F. J. Furnivall (ed.), *Hoccleve's Works: The Minor Poems*, EETS ES 61 (London, 1892), p. xxxviii.

[19] J. A. Burrow, 'Autobiographical poetry in the Middle Ages: the case of Thomas Hoccleve', *Proceedings*

Autobiography in poetry was a subject to which he would return, as indeed he returned to Hoccleve, securely establishing him as a significant poet, one to be added to 'the canon of the good and the great' as he put it in a polemical essay 'The sinking island and the dying author'.[20] Previously Hoccleve had been greatly undervalued and misrepresented. Burrow quotes one critic who described Hoccleve as 'a bungler, misfit, and perpetual also-ran'.[21] His job as a privy-seal clerk may mislead us into imagining him as a lowly functionary, but Burrow shows us that it would be closer to the mark to think of him as a courtier, in day-to-day contact with the great officers of the royal court and on intimate terms with some of them, and depicted as presenting a copy of *The Regiment of Princes*, his work of guidance for good rule, to Henry Prince of Wales.

Burrow also did much to establish Hoccleve's text and promote a new understanding of it. Hoccleve's poetry holds a very special interest for an editor, since there are three holograph manuscripts containing a total of 7,000 lines of verse, though one of these manuscripts, Durham University Library MS Cosin V. iii. 9, has lost the first two quires containing Hoccleve's *Complaint* and the first 252 lines of the *Dialogue*, which only survive in scribal copies.[22] These holographs provide a unique opportunity to study Hoccleve's orthographic and metrical practices, uncovering significant details that had not previously been noticed. Burrow shows, for example, that Hoccleve employed the *punctus elevatus* to mark questions, but only questions of a certain sort. In modern English *yes/no* questions end on a rising pitch, whereas *wh-* questions generally do not. It is the former that are marked by the *punctus elevatus*, not the latter, which also indicates that Middle English questions had the same intonational pattern as they do today.[23] Burrow also confirmed that Hoccleve's decasyllabic verse obeys a strict syllable-count, as French verse but unlike Chaucer's, which led him to secure conclusions about the circumstances in which final *-e* and *-es* counted as a syllable.[24] These conclusions contradict the accepted view among philologists of the

of the British Academy, 68 (1983), 389–412; reprinted in J. A. Burrow (ed.), *Middle English Literature: British Academy Gollancz Lectures* (Oxford, 1989), p. 228; and reproduced in J. A. Burrow, *English Poets in the Late Middle Ages* (Farnham, 2012), Essay V, p. 228.

[20] J. A. Burrow, 'The sinking island and the dying author: R. W. Chambers fifty years on', *Essays in Criticism*, 40 (1990), 19; reprinted in Burrow, *English Poets in the Late Middle Ages*, Essay III.

[21] J. A. Burrow, 'Hoccleve and the "Court"', in H. Cooney (ed.), *Nation, Court and Culture: New Essays on Fifteenth-Century English Poetry* (Dublin, 2001), n. 16; reprinted in Burrow, *English Poets in the Late Middle Ages*, Essay XVII.

[22] The holographs are reproduced in J. A. Burrow and A. I. Doyle, *Thomas Hoccleve: a Facsimile of the Autograph Verse Manuscripts*, EETS SS 19 (Oxford, 2002).

[23] J. A. Burrow, 'Hoccleve's questions: intonation and punctuation', *Notes and Queries*, 49 (2002), 184–8, reprinted with revisions in Burrow, *English Poets in the Late Middle* Ages, Essay XX; and J. A. Burrow, 'Intonation and punctuation in the Hoccleve holographs', *Notes and Queries*, 60 (2013), 19–22.

[24] See J. A. Burrow, 'Some final -es in the Hoccleve autographs', in M. Calabrese and S. H. A. Shepherd

historical development of these sounds. Still further, it became clear to Burrow that Hoccleve's spelling system was highly regular, so that a text that survives only in scribal copies may confidently be restored to its original Hocclevian forms in all its detail. This is what he set out to do in his edition of the *Complaint and Dialogue* for the Early English Text Society, in which the reconstructed text is printed side by side with the scribal copy in Bodley MS Selden Supra 53.[25] For twenty-three years, from 1983 to 2006, Burrow served as the Director of the Early English Text Society, chairing the meetings of Council with his usual urbanity and grace, and steering many editions through to publication.

Piers Plowman was an abiding preoccupation. He had begun a never-to-be completed postgraduate thesis on the poem, an offshoot of which was an early essay, 'The action of Langland's second vision',[26] recently described as 'one of the most influential essays ever written on the poem'.[27] In it Burrow uncovers the structure of the second dream, previously seen as a succession of brilliant vignettes—the seven deadly sins, the ploughing of the half-acre, the tearing of the pardon—revealing a well-organised plot, following the sequence from sermon, confession and pilgrimage, and ending with pardon; following, that is to say, the Church's standard penitential scheme. Burrow argued, though, that Langland polemically substitutes St Truth for St James, so that the pilgrimage is the good work of ploughing and *anything but* a literal pilgrimage.

Burrow kept returning to Langland throughout his career. A book that has perhaps not been as celebrated as it deserves is *Langland's Fictions*. What is particularly striking is the willingness to accept that at times Langland got things wrong and let his imagination run away with him, as in the Tree of Charity episode in the B text where Piers attacks the devil (who is scrumping the fruit) with one of the three props, the one representing God the Son—an episode that leads up to Langland's account of the Incarnation. 'Yet', says Burrow, 'nothing that Piers represents can possibly be supposed to have initiated the Incarnation,' so Piers is written out of the C text revision. This 'illustrates Langland's tendency to treat his earlier imaginings rather ruthlessly, as if they no longer held his interest; but in this particular case surely something had to be

---

(eds.), *Yee? Baw for Bokes: Essays on Medieval Manuscripts and Poetics in Honour of Hoyt N. Duggan* (Los Angeles, CA, 2013), pp. 45–53.

[25] J. A. Burrow and A. J. Doyle, *Thomas Hoccleve's Complaint and Dialogue* EETS OS 313 (Oxford, 1999). Burrow sets out the arguments for reconstruction in J. A. Burrow, 'Scribal mismetring', in A. J. Minnis (ed.), *Middle English Poetry: Texts and Traditions. Essays in Honour of Derek Pearsall* (Woodbridge, 2001), pp. 169–79, where he compares Chaucer's practice.

[26] J. A. Burrow, 'The action of Langland's second vision', *Essays in Criticism*, 15 (1965), 247–68; reprinted in Burrow, *Essays on Medieval Literature*, pp. 79–101.

[27] R. Hanna, *The Penn Commentary on Piers Plowman* 2 (Philadelphia, PA, 2017), p. 48.

done to clear up the mess'.[28] This is part of Burrow's discussion of 'Fictions of history', where he contrasts Langland's imaginative version of biblical history with the standard 'historical' retellings such as that in a probable source, Deguileville's *Pèlerinage de Jhesucrist*. The question of Langland's self-representation is taken up in the chapter 'Fictions of self?'. The question mark is significant. As with Hoccleve, the poet describes his life and gives his opinions in his own voice, but since we know almost nothing about William Langland except from the poem, his real life is much more in doubt than Hoccleve's, whose autobiographical statements are backed up by documentary evidence. Thus many critics regard the 'autobiographical' passages as a fictional creation of 'Long Will'. Burrow argued that this is not a simple alternative between truth and fiction, since in life individuals create and project a variety of self-representations: 'The right starting-point, rather, is to recognise that, when Langland imagines himself as Long Will, he is doing something which everyone does all the time anyway.'[29] That is, he is creating a self-image, his 'writer self', one who is constantly being questioned about the value of such a time-wasting occupation as writing *Piers Plowman*, and so he is confronting 'some of the difficult moral issues involved in that creation'.[30] This anxious self-questioning is, after all, one of the forces driving the poem.

We had previously worked together happily on *A Book of Middle English*,[31] and so, convinced by Burrow's earlier exercise in the reconstruction of Hoccleve's text, I asked him to join me in reconstructing the archetypal text of the B Version of *Piers Plowman* for the Piers Plowman Electronic Archive. In other respects he seemed an unlikely editor of an electronic text, having set his face resolutely against using the internet or even email. But as committed recensionists, we both wanted to challenge the conclusion of the editors of the Athlone text that 'the B version of *Piers Plowman* would be the despair of a recensionist'.[32] In fact we were convinced that the establishment of the stemma of the manuscripts of the B Version was reasonably straightforward, and we thought we could present a fairly secure reconstruction of the archetypal text from which all the surviving witnesses descended, accompanied by annotations justifying our choice of reading. We were able to take advantage of the technology so that, in addition to the reconstructed archetype, we could present in parallel the lines from the

[28] J. A. Burrow, *Langland's Fictions* (Oxford, 1993), p. 75.
[29] Ibid., p. 90.
[30] Ibid., p. 91.
[31] J. A. Burrow and T. Turville-Petre, *A Book of Middle English* (Oxford, 1992, 3rd edn, 2005).
[32] G. Kane and E. Talbot Donaldson (eds.), *Piers Plowman: the B Version* (London, 1988), p. 62. For Burrow's view see J. A. Burrow, 'The Athlone edition of *Piers Plowman* B: stemmatics and the direct method', *Notes and Queries*, 61 (2004), 339–44.

ten important witnesses.[33] To set all this up electronically relied upon a team of technical experts with skills of a high order which neither of us possessed. Resulting from this close work with *Piers Plowman*, Burrow wrote eighteen notes and short articles on cruces in the poem, excavating new interpretations from this much-studied text.

In three books, *The Ages of Man*, *Gestures and Looks in Medieval Narrative*, and his last book, *The Poetry of Praise*, Burrow takes a single theme and explores it in relation to particular Middle English poems. Anticipating *The Ages of Man* were two classic studies of the three-age scheme (youth, middle age and old age) in Langland and in Chaucer.[34] As in Dante's *Divine Comedy*, Will, the narrator of *Piers Plowman*, undergoes a mid-life crisis in which he realises how far he has wandered from the direct path. Will is forty-five, at the end of middle age according to this scheme; Burrow argues that this is to be read as autobiography, expressing Langland's own uncertainties about the value of his life to date. The essay on Chaucer's 'Knight's Tale' shows how the story was constructed upon the three-age scheme of youth (Emily and the two lover knights), middle age (Theseus as mature ruler of Athens), and old age (Thesius' father Egeus, who offers sententious maxims on the inevitability of death), with their corresponding gods. *The Ages of Man* begins by tracing the development of the various age-schemes that were adopted by medieval writers: the four ages that Bede relates to the humours and the seasons, the six ages that Augustine links with the ages of the world, the seven ages that Ptolomy associates with the planets.[35] The second half of the book shows how these ideas are taken up in different ways in works such as *Beowulf*, *The Owl and the Nightingale*, and a number of *The Canterbury Tales*.

Once again we can marvel at his mastery of close reading. Here he is in *Gestures and Looks*, analysing 'the minute notation of non-verbal behaviour' when Troilus first sets eyes on Criseyde in the temple (Chaucer, *Troilus and Criseyde*, I. 288–94):

> She was previously (before Troilus saw her) said to be taking up only a small amount of temple space, 'in litel brede', standing near the door 'ay undre shames drede'; and the downward direction of her present look matches that description, conforming to familiar images of female 'shame'. But the look also serves to appropriate some of her small standing-area insofar as it is directed 'a lite aside' from the vertical, for gaze is one way of defining and indeed defending personal territory.[36]

[33] *The B-Version Archetype*, *The Piers Plowman Electronic Archive*, vol. 9 (2014); http://piers.chass.ncsu. edu/texts/Bx. A printed edition has now been published: J. A. Burrow and T. Turville-Petre, *Piers Plowman: the B-Version Archetype (Bx)* Society for Early English and Norse Electronic Texts (Chapel Hill, NC, 2018).

[34] J. A. Burrow, 'Langland *Nel mezzo del cammin*', in P. L. Heyworth (ed.), *Medieval Studies for J. A. W. Bennett, Ætatis Suæ LXX* (Oxford, 1981), pp. 21–41. J. A. Burrow, 'Chaucer's *Knight's Tale* and the three ages of man', in Burrow, *Essays on Medieval Literature*, pp. 91–108.

[35] J. A. Burrow, *The Ages of Man* (Oxford, 1986).

[36] J. A. Burrow, *Gestures and Looks in Medieval Narrative* (Cambridge, 2002), p. 129.

In *The Poetry of Praise* Burrow explains that 'the study of praise in medieval poetry grew out of the observation that modern critics and readers (myself included) commonly find it hard to come to terms with the many varieties of eulogistic writing that are encountered there. So we either turn our eyes away from this "poetry of praise" or else look into it too eagerly for such ironies and reservations as may accommodate it to modern tastes and values.'[37] He traces the theme back to early masters of eulogistic writing, 'the superlative manner known to Greek rhetoricians as "auxetic"',[38] a term which Burrow revives to cover praise of everything from a hero to a bowl. Roman rhetoricians from Cicero onwards divide the epideictic mode into *laus* and *vituperatio*, praise and dispraise, and these terms were a fundamental way of analysing poetry in the Middle Ages. From a popular thirteenth-century Latin version of Aristotle's *Poetics* he cites: 'Every poem and every poetic utterance is either blame or praise.'[39] This is so different from modern ways of understanding literature that we are prompted to find ironic intentions in such praise. Is Beowulf a flawed hero, preoccupied with his own valour at the expense of the safety of his people? Is Chaucer's Knight a brutal killer who hides his savagery in a cloak of Christian chivalry? Burrow argues that such ironic readings are misplaced, and that where a writer intends irony it is clearly signalled.

The idea for the book probably originated in an essay published a year earlier, in which Burrow introduced the work of the late medieval Scottish poet William Dunbar.[40] Having outlined Dunbar's life and career, he notes that 'the surviving corpus of mostly quite short poems exhibits such a wide variety of types that it is hard to give a synoptic account of them'.[41] It is here that he hits upon the notion of dividing them into *laus* and *vituperatio*, since 'these two modes played a large part in the work of earlier poets, not least those with court connections like Dunbar'. This approach works wonderfully well to encompass the extraordinarily aureate praise of the *Ballat of Our Lady* as well as the humorous *Flyting of Dunbar and Kennedie* savaging Walter Kennedy: 'He and his mistress go begging at the mill for scraps with nothing to their name but lice and long nails. Dunbar gleefully imagines him being pursued through the streets of Edinburgh by a rabble of boys and dogs.'[42]

This essay encouraged Burrow to devote further attention to Dunbar. 'Dunbar's art of asking' analyses the many artful ways the poet tried to prise open James IV's

[37] J. A. Burrow, *The Poetry of Praise* (Cambridge, 2008), p. vii.
[38] Ibid., p. 2.
[39] Ibid., p. 8.
[40] J. A. Burrow, 'William Dunbar', in P. Bawcutt and J. Hadley Williams (eds.), *A Companion to Medieval Scottish Poetry* (Woodbridge, 2006), pp. 133–48.
[41] Ibid., p. 135.
[42] Ibid., p. 142.

purse, in poems contrasting the long-term value of his services as court poet with the contribution of other craftsmen, shipwrights and glaziers, or likening himself to a faithful old horse neglected by his royal master.[43] In 'Dunbar and the accidents of rhyme' Burrow explores the ways in which searching for the rhyme drives a poem in a certain direction, particularly in refrain poems where the same rhyme-sound occurs multiple times: Dunbar's poem on the court official James Dog provides a notable case in point ('frog' 'hog', 'clog', 'bog', 'Magog', 'schog').[44] From Dunbar Burrow turned to his English contemporary, John Skelton, with an article reinterpreting Skelton's 'Collyn Clout' as an attack on Cardinal Wolsey, and finally, as one of his last essays, a substantial survey of Skelton's satires and invectives, thus neatly combining an earlier interest with a new subject.[45] In this essay he is delighted to discover Rap, comparing the tradition of flyting to modern dissing, and Skeltonics, the verse form Skelton uses for invective, to lines of Rap.

In the preface to *Langland's Fictions* Burrow records that the four chapters formed the Alexander Lectures given at Toronto in 1989, and that chapters were also read at Hakone in Japan and Alcala de Henares in Spain. Some years later we travelled together to a memorable *Piers Plowman* conference at Asheville in North Carolina in the beautiful foothills of the Blue Ridge Mountains, where he lectured on the significance of winking in *Piers Plowman*.[46] However, he was not, it must be said, a keen traveller. An early boating holiday on the Norfolk Broads ended in near disaster, knocking a fisherman flying and nearly drowning Diana. Later family holidays were regularly taken with less drama in the Lake District, usually staying in Troutbeck. In what turned out to be his last serious walk, he and I got up very early to avoid the unaccustomed heat, and walked up Ill Bell and along the ridge.

After Burrow's retirement in 1998, he and Diana continued to live in the Polygon in Clifton, in a wonderful Georgian house on five floors, in which the ground floor was filled with copies of Diana's books, and John's study was up several flights of stairs. The house was always lively and full of visitors. He was left bereft by Diana's death in 2011. He expressed his grief in a poem both witty and moving, entitled 'Diagonal', quoting from *Tristram Shandy* Walter Shandy's verdict on his brother's impending marriage: 'Then he will never be able to lie *diagonally* in his bed again':

---

[43] J. A. Burrow, 'Dunbar's art of asking', *Essays in Criticism*, 65 (2015), 1–11.
[44] J. A. Burrow, 'Dunbar and the accidents of rhyme', *Essays in Criticism*, 63 (2013), 20–8.
[45] J. A. Burrow, 'The argument of Skelton's *Collyn Clout*', *Chaucer Review,* 51 (2016), 469–77; J. A. Burrow, 'Satires and invectives', in S. Sobecki and J. Scattergood (eds.), *A Critical Companion to John Skelton* (Cambridge, 2018), pp. 88–101; this volume is dedicated to John Burrow's memory.
[46] Published as J. A. Burrow, 'Gestures and looks in *Piers Plowman*', *Yearbook of Langland Studies*, 14 (2000), 75–83.

Some passer-by had snapped the sapling off
With nothing but a thread of wood and bark
To join it to the root. We bound it up,
My wife and I, with strips of cloth and twine
And saw it grow into a 'forest giant'
Just like the tree-book said it ought to be,
Taller than any other tree around.

But it was Diana, not the tree, that died,
So I may watch its branches from the house
Diagonal in bed as I do now.

Sadly, for a man who enjoyed walking in the woods around Bristol and in the Lake District, the polio from which he had suffered as a boy hit back at him in later life, and he became increasingly disabled. Though he could no longer leave the house, he accepted his confinement with remarkable stoicism, and continued writing and publishing prolifically to the end, leaving his last essay completed on his desk at his death.

Acknowledgements
I am indebted to Colin Burrow, David Devereux, David Hopkins, Ad Putter, Pat Rogers and Myra Stokes for information and advice.

Note on the author: Thorlac Turville-Petre is Emeritus Professor, Faculty of Arts, University of Nottingham.

JACK HAYWARD

Jack Ernest Shalom Hayward

18 August 1931 – 8 December 2017

elected Fellow of the British Academy 1990

by

EDWARD C. PAGE

Fellow of the Academy

Jack Hayward was Professor of Politics at Hull (1973–93 and 1999–2017) and Oxford (1993–9) universities. He contributed greatly to the professionalisation of political science in Britain through his work in the Political Studies Association of which he was Chair and later President in the 1970s. He chaired the British Academy Political Studies Section between 1991 and 1994. A specialist in French and European politics and public policy as well as French social and political thought, his *The One and Indivisible French Republic* (1973) became a standing reference for scholars and students of France in the 1970s and 1980s. His later work additionally explored broader comparative themes in European public policy and European integration. He played a significant role in the campaign for the fair treatment of civilians interned by the Japanese during the Second World War.

Biographical Memoirs of Fellows of the British Academy, XVIII, 63–91
Posted 18 April 2019. © British Academy 2019.

JACK HAYWARD

While this account of Jack Hayward's intellectual work and scholarly approach will reprise the main contours of Hayward's life and career, let me start with a puzzle.[1] One of Hayward's books begins with a question about Fifth Republic France: 'Why did it take two monarchies, two empires, the Vichy regime and five republics … before France was able to reconstitute a government capable of giving democratic leadership through an elected head of state?'[2] The puzzle is this: how was it possible for Hayward to give a convincing answer to this question about contemporary France in the form of a book looking at six French thinkers, of whom the most recent died in 1881? This puzzle deepens when one considers that Hayward did not have any marked affection for the past and was vehemently dismissive of arguments and ideas he felt were backward-looking. One of his often-used phrases, usually said when trying to steer a colleague away from being preoccupied with defunct ideas or theories, was 'let the dead bury the dead!'.

At first glance one might just see this enduring preoccupation with nineteenth-century social and political thought as the consequence of Hayward being a scholar who started off in political theory never quite letting go of his intellectual roots as he became a leading specialist in contemporary French and European politics and public policy. There was much more to it than this. There is a clear and consistent intertwining of empirical analysis, in the sense of examining contemporary political and social phenomena, along with social and political thought throughout all his writings. In some the empirical analysis tends to dominate, in others the political theory, but both are usually present. Both are part of a method of analysis he used to explore contemporary politics. For Hayward political and social theory was an empirical tool, and to solve the puzzle we need to understand how he used it.

Jack Hayward played a leading part in shaping the British study of political science in the post-war era, especially in its period of rapid growth in the 1970s and 1980s and not only through his writings. Consequently, and because his background and experiences offer important insights into his work, this account begins with a brief outline of his life and career. Then we can go on to look in the second section at the first

[1] Hayward's life and career are remarkably well covered in a range of biographical, autobiographical and other sources. See especially J. E. S. Hayward, 'Between France and universality: from implicit to explicit comparison', in H. Daalder and E. Allardt (eds.), *Comparative European Politics: the Story of a Profession* (London, 1997), Chapter 13; PCA (Parliamentary Commissioner for Administration), *A Debt of Honour: the Ex Gratia Scheme for British Groups Interned by the Japanese during the Second World War.* 4th Report Session 2005–2006 HC 324 (London, January 2006); W. Grant, *The Development of a Discipline: the History of the Political Studies Association* (Chichester, 2010); J. E. S. Hayward and R. Bridge, 'British Identity Theft: an Official Far Eastern Fiasco' (unpublished manuscript, 2010); J. E. S. Hayward, 'Beyond France: from implicit to explicit comparison', *French Politics*, 13 (2015), 110–19.
[2] J. E. S. Hayward, *After the French Revolution: Six Critics of Democracy and Nationalism* (London, 1991), p. xi.

appearance of the approach to political theory as empirical methodology explicitly discussed (albeit not using the terms I use here) in his PhD thesis.[3] While his later work in the 1960s still contained the kind of theoretical/empirical mix outlined above, these writings tended to emphasise the more empirical aspects—the description of, say, how the Economic and Social Council in France worked around the mid-1960s—though even here some of the discussion points to his understanding of French politics being based on an appreciation of the sometimes diverse political traditions developed and reflected in the works of the major theorists.[4] The earliest striking elaboration of such an understanding was published in his *The One and Indivisible French Republic* in 1973,[5] discussed in the third part. I then go on to look in the fourth part at this approach to political theory as methodology and in the fifth to how he used it to characterise France after de Gaulle in a range of studies including his last main book on the subject, *Fragmented France*.[6] In his later work on France the balance swung more toward empirical analysis than theory, especially his work on economic policy and policy coordination. Jack Hayward's intellectual contribution also came in the form of a series of collective works, above all on methodology and the European Union but also including the work he did leading to the posthumous completion of Samuel Finer's *History of Government*.[7] I look at these in the seventh section before going on in the eighth to discuss his unpublished work arising from his treatment (and that of many others) by the UK government arising from his imprisonment by the Japanese during the Second World War. I conclude with a reflection on some of the dominant themes of his work.

Jack Hayward's life and career

Jack was born in Shanghai in 1931 and brought up in a family of four sisters and two brothers. His father, Menachem Hayward, a British national orphaned at an early age and brought up by his aunt in Hong Kong, was in charge of a warehouse dealing in exports to and from the UK for the Sassoon family firm. Menachem married an Iraqi, Stella David, shortly before the outbreak of war in 1914, having earlier anglicised his surname. Jack got his first name from an uncle, an athlete living in China and mur-

---

[3] J. E. S. Hayward, 'The Idea of Solidarity in French Social and Political Thought in the Nineteenth and Early Twentieth Centuries' (University of London PhD thesis, 1958).
[4] J. E. S. Hayward, *Private Interests and Public Policy: the Experience of the French Economic and Social Council* (London, 1966).
[5] J. E. S. Hayward, *The One and Indivisible French Republic* (London, 1973).
[6] J. E. S. Hayward, *Fragmented France: Two Centuries of Disputed Identity* (Oxford, 2007).
[7] S. E. Finer, *The History of Government*, 3 vols (Oxford, 1997).

dered in training, his middle names Ernest and Shalom from his parents' love of the Oscar Wilde play and the desire to give him a Jewish name—his mother's uncle was Chief Rabbi of Shanghai. The concession was very British, with the children attending local English schools, becoming wolf cubs, brownies and guides and taking part in school productions of Gilbert and Sullivan. The family moved to Hong Kong in 1937 when the Japanese attacked Shanghai, returning there after six months. In 1943 the family, with the exception of the eldest sister who was in England for the duration of the Second World War, was interned by the Japanese following the invasion of Shanghai. Jack, his parents and three sisters were sent to Yangchow camp, his older brother interned in a separate and even more severe camp. The brutality, semi-starvation, malnutrition and hardship he and his family endured are briefly covered in his account of his life in the camp.[8] 1945 brought release from internment and in January 1946, at the age of fourteen, Hayward was sent to London, was welcomed by his eldest sister whom he had not seen since 1937 and went to live with an aunt. After boarding school in Staffordshire he studied Government at the London School of Economics (LSE) between 1949 and 1952 and went on to do a doctorate there. National Service in the Royal Air Force (he became an Education Officer in it) interrupted his doctoral studies and he finished his PhD in October 1958 (awarded in 1959) with what he described as an excessively long (1,129-page) thesis on the concept of solidarity (discussed below).[9]

Hayward linked the choices he made at the start of his academic career to his earlier experiences. He had wanted to study history at university, but his schooling did not include the necessary qualification in Latin; his school in England, unusually for the time, taught economics and he became converted to a set of beliefs he described as Thatcherism 'avant la lettre … that free trade at all times … was the only sensible way of avoiding short-sighted, mutually impoverishing attempts to "beggar one's neighbour"'.[10] He developed an aversion to the rather insular approach to the study of politics he saw in Britain in general and the LSE in particular. He wanted to go beyond treating the study of politics in any one country as a subject in its own right and make comparisons. Since he had learned French at school and become interested in French life through contact with the French concession in Shanghai, Britain and France were to be the proposed comparators and the research was to examine how social thinkers reconciled individualism and collectivism in the two countries. However, the topic on which he actually wrote his thesis was not explicitly comparative and he hit on it by chance. A shortage of British thinkers to include in the proposed Franco-

---

[8] Hayward and Bridge, *British Identity Theft*, Chapter 2.
[9] Hayward, 'Between France and universality', p. 143.
[10] Ibid., p. 140.

British comparison and a chance reading of Léon Bourgeois' *Solidarité* in a Parisian bookshop led him to abandon a direct comparison and concentrate on, as the title of his thesis puts it, 'the idea of solidarity in French social and political thought in the nineteenth and early twentieth centuries'.[11] Michael Oakeshott supervised his dissertation, but Hayward points out that his involvement in the thesis was 'nominal' and he wrote the thesis 'with no guidance to speak of'.[12] Hayward certainly does not appear to offer a glowing report on his LSE days; apart from some 'lively lectures' on French political institutions by William Pickles '[t]he only other series of lectures on France I attended were by Ralph Miliband on the French Revolution, but what I remember was a single seminar by Isaiah Berlin on Joseph de Maistre in which he had arrestingly argued that what alone kept a state intact was the Public Executioner'[13]—a point he reiterated in his speech on receipt of the Isaiah Berlin Prize for a Lifetime Achievement in Political Studies in 2011.

Hayward worked as an assistant lecturer, then lecturer, in Sheffield University between 1959 and 1963 during which time he produced several articles arising from his PhD thesis and an article closely linked to it,[14] but also pointing to a developing concern with the study of interest groups; 'Educational pressure groups and the indoctrination of the radical ideology of solidarism, 1895–1914'.[15] He moved to Keele University in 1963 where Sammy Finer was the 'presiding genius'.[16] His work on French interest groups, economic policy and economic planning developed here. He also wrote *The One and Indivisible* while at Keele. This book covered French politics, institutions and public policy in such breadth, and in such amenable language, that it served as the main textbook on France for any politics student in the 1970s and 1980s. Its breadth is indicated by the influences on its writing he cites: Stanley Hoffmann, Catherine and Pierre Grémion, Jean-Claude Thoenig and Michel Crozier. He always regarded his work as 'implicitly comparative' in the sense that it is impossible to understand what is distinctive about France unless one has some point of comparison.

---

[11] L. Bourgeois, *Solidarité* (Paris, 1896).

[12] Hayward 'Between France and universality', p. 143.

[13] Hayward 'Beyond France', 111.

[14] Including J. E. S. Hayward,. 'The official social philosophy of the French Third Republic: Léon Bourgeois and solidarism', *International Review of Social History*, 6 (1961), 19–48; J. E. S. Hayward,. 'Solidarist syndicalism: Durkheim and Duguit: Part I', *The Sociological Review*, 8 (1960), 17–36; J. E. S. Hayward, 'Solidarity: the social history of an idea in nineteenth-century France', *International Review of Social History*, 4 (1959), 261–84.

[15] J. E. S. Hayward,. 'Educational pressure groups and the indoctrination of the radical ideology of solidarism, 1895–1914', *International Review of Social History*, 8 (1963), 1–17.

[16] Hayward, 'Between France and universality', p. 147.

He started to develop his interest in explicit and systematic comparative work in the 1970s, with a collaborative comparative study of planning in Europe.[17]

By this time Jack Hayward had moved to a chair at Hull University where he served variously as Head of Department and Dean of Faculty at periods between his arrival in 1973 and the time he left for Oxford in 1993. He and Dr Margaret Hayward, a scholar of French literature specialising in Balzac whom he had met and married in Paris while studying for his PhD, had two children, Clare and Alan. They lived in Kirk Ella, just outside Hull's city boundaries. Colleagues and visitors to Hull will remember happy and collegial parties there at which Jack Hayward would share some of the rare wines that he had accumulated over the years. His knowledge of wines made him the Wine Fellow who supervised the purchase, acquisition and cellaring of wines when he later moved to St Antony's, Oxford. Hayward built up a very strong and successful department that was at the top of the early rankings for university politics departments (including an international set of rankings from *Le Monde*).

During his time at Hull Hayward also spent periods teaching outside the UK, including the Institut d'Études Politiques in Paris, the universities of Paris II, Paris III, Bordeaux, Grenoble, Rennes, Bilbao and British Columbia. In 1984, he visited the University of Baroda in India (at the invitation of his close friend and Hull colleague Bhikhu Parekh who served as Baroda's Vice Chancellor in the early 1980s) to deliver six talks in the Tagore Memorial Lecture series. These lectures formed the basis of his book *After the French Revolution* from which the puzzle set out in the opening paragraph of this account is drawn.

It was in the mid-1970s that Hayward's name became more widely known throughout the profession as he was one of the key figures in what is described as the 1975 'coup', or the 'Oxford-led insurgency'.[18] Led by Brian Barry, the immediate focus of the enterprise was to replace the existing Political Studies Association (PSA) Executive Committee with a completely new team in the election in spring 1975. Hayward convinced Barry of the need for a manifesto—a programme of reform. In the election the 'Old Guard was decisively routed by a slate of Young Turks',[19] and Hayward became chairman of the PSA in a change that was widely seen as 'reinvigorating' it and giving 'the discipline [of political science] a more effective Association which was trying to think systematically about the challenges it faced and how they might be met'. He served as Chairman until 1977, as its President between 1979 and 1981, and Editor of its journal, *Political Studies*, between 1987 and 1993.

[17] M. Watson and J. E. S. Hayward, *Planning, Politics and Public Policy* (Cambridge, 1974).
[18] Grant, *Development of a Discipline*, Chapter 4.
[19] Robert Goodin, quoted in Grant, *Development of a Discipline*, p. 73.

Hayward moved to Oxford in January 1993 and became the first Director of Oxford University's European Studies Centre, formerly the West European Centre,[20] an outfit not noted for harmonious relations among those attached to it, and Jack Hayward managed to achieve greater harmony in this respect. His intellectual work at Oxford was dominated by his collaboration with Vincent Wright on an ESRC-funded project on coordination in 'core executives' and through his work on the completion of the ambitious three-volume *History of Government from the Earliest Times* left unfinished by the death of its main author, Sammy Finer, in 1993.

After retirement from Oxford in 1998 he returned to Hull—the Haywards had kept their Kirk Ella house—where Hull University gave him the title of research professor and an office. He resumed his influence over the development of the Politics Department at Hull in a variety of ways. He participated actively in departmental meetings, he played an influential role in Hull's Centre for European Union Studies (CEUS), gave lectures on France to undergraduate students and acted as informal supervisor for undergraduate dissertations on French politics until shortly before his death. Jack always had time for students as long as he was convinced that they put in their best possible effort. He took the lead on a range of projects such as his co-edited *Leaderless Europe* and *European Disunion* books, the latter co-edited with Rüdiger Wurzel, a colleague who directed CEUS and became a close friend when Jack rejoined the Hull department.[21] In his later stint at Hull Hayward also brought to fruition the project on coordinating 'core executives' started at Oxford with Vincent Wright, another very close personal friend and intellectual companion whose death in 1999 affected him greatly. It was during this period that he became involved in the campaign surrounding compensation for those held prisoner by the Japanese during the war discussed in detail below.[22] What was at stake for Hayward was a proper recognition of the suffering of those imprisoned and his understanding of 'what it means to be British and what it means to have an identity as someone who is British. I happen to regard it as having inestimable value.'[23] The suggestion that he and others in his position were not properly 'British' because they lacked a 'blood link' to the United Kingdom caused 'anger and outrage'. The muddle, mess and cover-up that ensued angered him even more. As he said, 'The Japanese ... did not enquire of my family,

---

[20] C. Nicholls, *The History of St Antony's College, Oxford, 1950–2000* (Basingstoke, 2000).

[21] J. E. S. Hayward (ed.), *Leaderless Europe* (Oxford, 2008); J. E. S. Hayward and R. Wurzel (eds.), *European Disunion: Between Sovereignty and Solidarity* (Basingstoke, 2012).

[22] For an excellent account of the episode and its consequences see also J. Lunn. *Ex-Gratia Payment for Far East POWs and Civilian Internees*, Standard Notes. London: House of Commons Library, 2009.

[23] Public Administration Select Committee, *A Debt of Honour, First Report for the Session 2005-6*, HC735, 19 January 2006, London: House of Commons, Oral Evidence, Q19.

myself, and others like me what our blood links were with the United Kingdom.'[24] While enraged, the experience did not put him off his stride—he was writing, among other things, his *Fragmented France* at this stage.

Hayward's achievements were recognised in a variety of ways. He was elected to the British Academy in 1990, given two French national honours (made a *Chevalier de l'Ordre Nationale de la Mérite* in 1980, and a *Chevalier de la Légion d'Honneur* in 1996), a Lifetime Achievement Award from the Political Studies Association in 2003, and the Isaiah Berlin Prize from the Political Studies Association in 2013. A Festschrift was written in his honour in 2005,[25] and he was awarded an honorary doctorate in 2013 from Hull where he had done so much for the department, all those who had passed through it and for the profession at large.

Jack Hayward was an active and influential Fellow of the British Academy. He chaired its Political Studies Section (S5) between 1991 and 1994. Along with Brian Barry and Archie Brown he edited for the Academy *The British Study of Politics in the Twentieth Century*, himself contributing the opening chapter on 'British approaches to politics: the dawn of a self-deprecating discipline'.[26] Published in 1999, the volume was the first in the British Academy Centenary Monographs series, which aimed to demonstrate the vitality of British scholarship in the run-up to the Academy's Centenary in 2002. Between 1998 and 2005 Hayward chaired the China Selection Panel (which oversaw the Academy's China programmes, including exchange schemes jointly administered with the Economic and Social Research Council), and in this period he also served on the Academy's Overseas Policy Committee, overseeing all the Academy's international relations activities. His international roles in the Academy brought him to visit China for the first time since the end of his internment in 1945. He was in a group of leading international scholars in the social sciences and humanities invited to Beijing by the Chinese Academy of Social Sciences. His report on the visit for the Academy included some characteristic dry scepticism: the final meeting of the Beijing visit was filmed and shown on national television 'persuading some participants that it indicated the high standing of our disciplines in China with the powers that be'.[27]

---

[24] Ibid.

[25] A. Menon and V. Wright (eds.), *From the Nation State to Europe: Essays in Honour of Jack Hayward* (Oxford, 2001).

[26] J. E. S. Hayward, 'British approaches to politics: the dawn of a self-deprecating discipline', in J. E. S. Hayward, B. Barry and A. Brown (eds.), *The British Study of Politics in the Twentieth Century* (Oxford, 1999), Chapter 1.

[27] J. E. S. Hayward, 'A social scientist's sojourn in Beijing: retrospective reflections', *British Academy Review* 4 (July–December 2000), 37–8.

Solidarity and the relationship between thought and practice

Hayward's PhD thesis, and especially its introduction which was published as a separate article,[28] makes it clear that this is not a straightforward analysis of the development of ideas surrounding the notion of solidarity but a wider study of the relationship between thought and practice.

> Our discussion of the role of the concept of solidarity in France is an appraisal of the social history of an idea rather than the history of a social idea. It is intended to be not merely the chronological description—or even the logical analysis—of the development of this idea; it is an attempt to elicit its social significance, its direct influence upon French society and its indirect implications for the social organization of humanity.[29]

France was a particularly interesting place to look at this relationship between thought and political practice in large part because of the 'notorious French addiction to deductive reasoning from first principles' and the tendency for 'programmes of social, political and economic reform being placed under the aegis of one or more ideas'.[30] Solidarity was such a potentially fruitful subject because it sought to understand the ideological (in a non-Marxist sense, we would probably use the word 'ideational' in contemporary social science jargon) underpinnings of state intervention through economic and social policies. In particular, the concept of solidarity was an attempt to build a philosophy of state action and social intervention.

> Just as the eighteenth century witnessed in France the development into a dominant position of the idea of unfettered personal liberty, coupled with the institution of civil and political justice for the defence of individual rights, the material and intellectual circumstances of the nineteenth century promoted the progressive prominence of the idea of social solidarity, associated with the establishment of economic justice for the protection of 'social' rights.[31]

In exploring the construction and nature of ideas about solidarity one is examining the creation of 'new foundations for the social and political order to replace the discredited *"ancien régime"* by new principles of social integration'.[32]

The variety of ambiguities involved in defining 'solidarity' (whether the social interdependence that underpins it is voluntary, involuntary; conscious and rational, unconscious and irrational; harmonious, disharmonious among many other

---

[28] Hayward, 'Solidarity: the social history'.
[29] Hayward, *Idea of Solidarity*, p. xxiv.
[30] Ibid., p. xxv.
[31] Ibid., p. vii.
[32] Ibid., p. iv.

possibilities) gives rise to myriad versions of the term that Hayward treats in three broad, roughly chronological, groupings (the naturalistic foundations including de Maistre, Saint-Simon, Comte and Blanqui among others; the 'moralistic criticism' covering Proudhon and Renouvier; the 'neo naturalistic reformulation' including Walras, Durkheim and Duguit, and the 'eclectic official dogma' of Léon Bourgeois). Hayward sees the notion of solidarity as having achieved the significant function of providing the ideological underpinnings of forms of 'associational and legislative activity which have left an enduring mark on French social institutions, orientating them in the direction of the "Welfare State"',[33] and as most influential during the period of Radical ascendancy at the start of the twentieth century. The interpretation of the role of ideas so far appears fairly conventional. What marks Hayward's approach as distinctive is his understanding of the consequences of the failure of the concept to provide a coherent vision of state intervention in social and economic life. The 'fluidity and vagueness' of the concept 'concealed far too many unsolved problems for it long to withstand successfully the degeneration into political bombast to which it has largely succumbed at the present day'.[34] After the First World War its 'heroic phase was over' although it continued to make its mark in, for example, the preamble to the Fourth Republic's constitution in 1946 and the Social Security Act of the same year.[35]

Towards the very end of his thesis Hayward quotes Alfred Fouillée, the French philosopher writing in 1900: 'Les idées incomplètement formulées et mal pratiquées par la France prendront leur revanche dans la seconde moitié du XXe siècle, qui, selon toute apparence, sera un siècle d'inspiration social et de réformes sociales.'[36] Unlike Britain and Germany, which had developed public philosophies and practices that enabled collectivist projects on the scale of the construction of a welfare state, 'France is characterised by economic and social institutions of a tenaciously individualist character.' The tension between ideological aspiration and reality is especially problematic in France with its enormous 'if somewhat baroque, efforts made to formulate principles from which could be deduced practical ways of harmoniously reorganising a society which had undergone the crises of industrial and political revolution',[37] and, as noted above, the 'notorious French addiction to deductive reasoning from first principles—programmes of social, political and economic reform being placed under

---

[33] Ibid., p. 590.

[34] Ibid., p. lii.

[35] Ibid., p. 621.

[36] 'Ideas that are poorly conceptualised and put into practice in France will have their revenge in the second half of the twentieth century, which looks very much like it will be a century of social inspiration and social reform', quoted in Hayward, *Idea of Solidarity*, p. 630.

[37] Ibid., p. xxiii.

the aegis of one or more ideas'.[38] One of the legacies of the failure is the status as bombast and the complacency that the concept of solidarity engenders in French public life; 'regarding the intractable deviations from the juridical norm as transitory aberrations, the legally trained French politicians have been all too often content to reaffirm principles rather than embark upon the painful business of implementing them'.[39]

A second legacy of the failure is the inability to provide a 'civic sense of self-discipline'. '[P]ersonal and group egoisms, religious, political and personal animosities, exacerbated class conflicts [and a] temperamental hostility to compromise' render France 'a constant prey to authoritarian *coups d'état* and plebiscitary dictatorship'. Third, the status of solidarity as a cherished but vacuous slogan has produced attempts to introduce what might be termed 'solidarist' solutions by coercive means (Hayward earlier having distinguished between Jacobin and Girondin approaches to solidarity):

> France has oscillated between self-assertive liberty and coercive solidarity, feverishly inventing, establishing and demolishing a wealth of grandiose and ingenious constitutional expedients, none of which have provided more than temporary relief for this tormented nation from the inner tensions that threaten imminent rupture of its fragile political structure, based upon illusory juridical forms that merely paper over the fissures in French society.[40]

While such discussion of the role of ideas does not occupy a large portion of the thesis, the broad insight into the role of nineteenth- and early twentieth-century ideas in shaping the French political history of the twentieth century through the legacy of what such ideas did not achieve, and what they became after they had failed to achieve their promise, formed the basis of his later writing, above all *The One and Indivisible French Republic*. Hayward's bemusement at being honoured by the French state for his writing on France is understandable given that the thrust of his approach was not flattering to contemporary French politics or politicians. When he got a letter from the French government proposing he become *Chevalier de l'Ordre Nationale de la Mérite* he replied that he would like the designation of 'agricultural merit, third class' (the government office concerned wrote to refuse this request on the ground he was not qualified for it). Some years later he joked he could not even ride a horse when he was made a *Chevalier de la Légion d'Honneur*.[41]

[38] Ibid., p. xxiv.
[39] Ibid., p. 611.
[40] Ibid., p. 612.
[41] Hayward, 'Beyond France', 114.

The One and Indivisible

In *The One and Indivisible* the distinctive insights into the shortcomings that ideas might have as a basis for political action and constitutional organisation were developed in the context of an even bigger concept than solidarity: sovereignty. The development of the argument is also fundamentally different. This is not simply the difference between a 1950s PhD (with its untranslated French quotes, some of them very lengthy, and 400 pages of notes and appendices) and a 1970s textbook. This was contemporary France through the lens of the idea that both dogged and defined much of its public life. Hayward had already written a book on contemporary French government, or rather one part of it, the Economic and Social Council, which, although it included in its prologue some brief reference to some of the syndicalist views covered in the doctoral thesis, located itself in the field of interest group theory and had the more empirical aim of studying how the Council 'works in practice, in the hope that it will shed some light on the … impact of interest group representation …'.[42] In his 1973 book the blending of theory and empirical description was more consciously pursued and to even greater effect than in his earlier work.

The One and Indivisible's title is an ironic joke that Hayward felt not enough people seem to have got.[43] It is a joke because the central thesis is that France is highly fragmented and the notion of indivisibility is a fiction, but a fiction that has consequences for the institutional and political structures of contemporary France. Debates about the notion of sovereignty and where it is located produced two broad answers. One was that it resided in the executive or, in the caesarist-Napoleonic version, the head of the executive. The other, associated with Abbé Sieyès, was that it resided in the legislature. The 'unresolved problem of the location of sovereign power has continued to bedevil French attempts at creating an effective and acceptable form of government' with systems veering between 'parliamentary omnipotence' and 'executive dominance'.[44] The 'attitude of the French political élite towards politics has been dominated by a belief in the need for a strong, unified, centralized authority, capable of containing the centrifugal forces that constantly threaten the integrity of the state'. This is matched by an alienation of citizens and groups from state power characterised by occasional inconclusive protest but more common mass apathy and distrust of authority. Together they produce an 'immobilist symbiosis between the liberal-representative and the authoritarian-administrative traditions'.[45]

---

[42] Hayward, *Private Interests*, pp. 5–6.

[43] J. E. S. Hayward, *Governing France: the One and Indivisible French Republic* (London, 1983), Preface; Hayward, *Fragmented France*, p. v.

[44] Hayward, *One and Indivisible*, p. 7.

[45] Ibid., p. 10.

The main thesis is sustained first in the examination of the relationship between Paris and the provinces, where the doctrine of a standardised pattern of government paralyses any decentralised decision-making. The French form of centralisation encourages, as the Crozier/Thoenig school in the 1960s and 1970s set out so clearly,[46] a collusion between prefects as representatives of the central state in the locality and mayors of towns and villages to make 'large and irresponsible demands' of Paris. But the power of the thesis extends throughout the system. Parliament in the Fifth Republic lost a large amount of the power that it had in the Fourth and interest groups are important mediators between state and society. Yet the executive, or more specifically the relatively closely knit group of top administrators and politicians at the top, the 'techno-bureaucratic executive', dominates the decision-making process. Top executive officials and politicians can select which interests they listen to and can play one part of the fragmented interest group world off against another—making such groups pressured rather than pressure groups.[47] A strengthened executive had led to an erosion of civil liberties in France in the Fourth and Fifth Republics, although France remains at heart a liberal democracy with a stubborn libertarian tradition of resistance to authority. Its budgetary process is fragmented and chaotic, characterised by an executive dominance of the whole process with side payments to legislators for their pet projects to make sure the budget passes. The consequences of the French approach to state sovereignty specifically in the field of economic management, especially the system of economic planning, can be seen in patterns of policy-making common to those found in other policy areas. However, in economic policy-making, Hayward acknowledges 'the political and administrative architects of public policy have served their country well',[48] as suggested by the high levels of economic growth since 1945. In foreign and European policy 'alliances were seasonal, dictated by the opportunism of a government determined to preserve the sovereignty of the state in an international environment which threatened foreign penetration and domination'.[49]

Political thought as empirical methodology

Hayward's *The One and Indivisible* was not an argument about an unchanged or unchanging pattern of French politics. The political demise of de Gaulle as well as the

[46] Among the most well-known writings from this school are J.-P. Worms, 'Le Préfet et ses notables', *Sociologie Du Travail*, 8 (1966), 249–75 ; M. Crozier and J.-C. Thoenig, 'The regulation of complex organized systems', *Administrative Science Quarterly*, 21 (1976), 547–70.
[47] Hayward, *One and Indivisible*, p. 58.
[48] Ibid., p. 189.
[49] Ibid., p. 228.

changing international, especially European, political and economic environment and France's own economic modernisation feature strongly in the book. Before we go on to consider his account of change in France since the text came out in 1973 we might begin to answer the puzzle set at the beginning. Understanding how a political concept, such as sovereignty or solidarity, is handled within a country offers an important and fruitful way of understanding that country's politics. Why the concept should generate significant debate in the first place illustrates the empirical political problems—of diversity and consent in the case of sovereignty, of a basis for state intervention in the case of solidarity—that it is supposed to address. The norms that such ideas produce have two sorts of impacts: in the observance and in the breach. In the observance they produce laws and policies that appear to conform to them—the solidarist welfare legislation of the Radicals in the early twentieth century or the centralised constitution of the Fifth Republic. They also constrain debates about options and possibilities for reform since they become limited to include only those which easily conform to the idea. In the breach they affect the form that public hypocrisy takes: the fiction that the state never listens to interest groups or that the highly individualist economic and social institutions are nevertheless solidarist. The form such hypocrisy takes is important since it cuts off some of the possibilities of addressing problems and limits the acceptable solutions to be found to them.

To some degree Hayward alludes to this methodology in his inaugural lecture at Hull when he mentions his 'old addiction to the insights into the normative presuppositions of decision makers afforded by the history of ideas'.[50] We see this methodology at work most clearly in his *After the French Revolution*. His assessment of the enduring impact of the French Revolution focuses on the thought and legacy of six thinkers who all died before the start of the twentieth century. Joseph de Maistre, the ultraconservative Catholic thinker, is handled first. As already noted, de Maistre was of particular interest and furthermore occupied a key place in Jack Hayward's writing ever since his 1958 PhD. He is the first thinker covered in his thesis and makes several appearances throughout; he is mentioned in *The One and Indivisible* and features prominently in his last main book on France in 2007, *Fragmented France*. With help from de Maistre's criticisms of the vacuity of the claims to base a society on liberty, equality and fraternity and his Catholic authoritarianism based on the primacy of Rome, Hayward traces the origins and enduring importance of the clerical-anticlerical cleavage that remained so potent in France until the latter part of the twentieth century. The portrait of Saint-Simon underpins a culture of elitist technocracy that has long characterised the French state and the 'appeal to knowledge rather than

---

[50] J. E. S. Hayward, *Political Inertia* (Hull, 1975), p. 6.

popularity as the non-democratic source of public power in France'.[51] Through Constant and de Tocqueville we can see the difficult progress of political liberalism in France since the Revolution. Through Proudhon he develops an understanding of some of the distinctive features of French trade unionism (including a syndicalist anti-statist bias) and through Blanqui he examines the organisational form of revolutionary socialism of parties of the left.

France after the Revolution

The key question of *After the French Revolution* was whether the French Revolution appeared to be at last over, in the sense that the key questions of legitimacy arising from it no longer produced political instability. In response Hayward argued that now 'the French no longer quarrel ardently over the legitimacy of their political regime and have settled for a lukewarm, liberal democratic constitutional relativism'.[52] The conclusion of *After the French Revolution* is that it took until the Fifth Republic and the arrival of de Gaulle, Pompidou and Mitterrand to develop some sort of consensus on the issues that drove the controversies these thinkers, among others, addressed.

The wider thesis Hayward developed was that the political economy of France began to change after 1945, and the Fifth Republic appeared to give France a level of political stability that it had not enjoyed for a sustained period in its history: 'It took the Second World War to shake France out of its economic lethargy … and the Algerian War to give it stable institutions.'[53] Yet there remained distinctive features of elite predispositions that shaped the rhetoric of its leaders and the reality of government processes and institutions. *Fragmented France*, his last book-length look at the topic, highlights three main enduring features of the legacy of the conflicts arising from the ideological conflicts of the past: first, an 'Anglo-American counter-identity' which defines French identity in terms of its relationship with the English-speaking world,[54] above all the United States; second, a lack of acceptance of its diminished role in world affairs since 1945 characterised both by 'paralyzing self-doubt and its nostalgic illusion of selfless superiority';[55] and third, the domination of the state and its consequent crowding out of pluralist-liberal politics. Indeed, the three are somewhat

[51] Hayward, *After the French Revolution*, p. 100.
[52] Ibid., p. 299.
[53] Hayward, *Fragmented France*, p. 372.
[54] Ibid., p. 38.
[55] Ibid., p. 373.

related because 'the pluralist, Anglo-American anti-model has proved instinctively repugnant' in France.[56]

To sustain and develop this argument in the post-de Gaulle era Hayward again examines the thought of influential post-war thinkers including Raymond Aron, Stanley Hoffman, Michel Crozier and Pierre Rosanvallon. A renewed interest in liberal ideas coincided with a revival of interest in de Tocqueville, but this was something of a 'false dawn'.[57] Despite the efforts of politicians such as Michel Rocard, Jacques Delors and Jacques Chaban-Delmas, the forces of economic liberalism did not challenge the fundamental premise among political leaders that the state must 'protect or compensate the various losers of market competition' and that 'top-down state intervention' is the dominant form of economic policy design.

Nevertheless, a common theme of Hayward's later writing on France is a concern with a range of political changes, not least the developing European Union, experiences of cohabitation (i.e. government where the presidency and the legislative majority are held by different parties), and changing patterns of party competition, that have added to the other factors stressed in his earlier work suggesting the declining distinctiveness of the French state. This leads to a second theme that comes to the fore even more in his later works: the disjuncture between French elite perception and reality. He acknowledged how all the social, economic and cultural changes of the past forty years had served to make France less 'exceptional' and, in his very last published words, he writes 'in comparative context, the French state remains somewhat exceptional in its norms and impulses, even more than in its behaviour'.[58]

The pathologies Hayward identifies in the French political system are becoming increasingly matters of a dissonance between, on the one hand, elite self-perception, official ideology and constitutional thought, and, on the other, the realities of power, influence and politics in a modern industrial state. For several years, and without success, Hayward tried to convince the editors of the journal *Pouvoirs* to commission a special issue not on the *l'état de droit en France* (the *Rechtsstaat* or, more freely, the rule of law in France) but on the *l'état de passe droit en France* (the state based on turning a blind eye to the law).[59] This was, he argued, a characteristic and ignored feature of modern French politics. He points to some of the key areas where such dissonance can be observed and where 'the traditional state culture's assumptions are

[56] Ibid., p. 365.
[57] Ibid., p. 344.
[58] J. E. S. Hayward, 'The state imperative', in R. Elgie, E. Grossman and A. G. Mazur (eds.), *The Oxford Handbook of French Politics*, vol. 1 (Oxford, 2017), p. 58.
[59] Hayward served on the editorial board of *Pouvoirs* for many years. He took his responsibilities as editorial board member on this and the other boards on which he served (including that of the *British Journal of Political Science*) very seriously, making a point of attending their meetings.

not valid';[60] the belief in an economic sovereignty that is unsustainable and unsustained in an open international economy; the monomaniacal belief that the Presidency embodies the Republic, 'trying to subject all to his fiat' and yielding to the 'urge to place his personal imprint upon the country and the world';[61] the 'championing of the nation state' in the European Union and other international forums; the growing adoption of forms of delegation to organisations not directly controlled by the state through 'new public management' processes and reforms of the territorial government system more generally marking a break from the assumed 'one and indivisible' traditions of French constitutional law; '[d]espite lip service to equality, France has systematically institutionalized educational, cultural, social, economic and political inequality'.[62] The distinctive features of French politics and government are present, and some of them still maintain a potent practical effect (the centrality of the state and the characteristics of the Presidency as main examples) but their effect is increasingly taking the form of giving structure to France's official hypocrisy rather than to its policies and practices.

The (more conventional) empirical contribution

The use of political thought to explain the behaviour of political elites in France requires an understanding of French political and policy practice as well as an understanding of its political thought. This was something Hayward developed not just by maintaining and expanding his wide range of contacts with key research institutions, scholars and friends in France, by having an encyclopaedic knowledge of French history, by carefully working through the Paris newspaper *Le Monde* to which he was a subscriber since the 1950s (he only gave up his subscription to the satirical magazine *Le Canard enchaîné* a couple of years before he died) and by listening to French radio, but also by his own research.

His first book, *Private Interests and Public Policy*, was a study of the Economic and Social Council (ESC) in France, and the focus is on the ESC as a forum for interest group politics. In fact, Hayward's first main study of the role of groups,[63] his article on the Ligue de l'Enseignement in the development of 'solidarist' education policies in the Radical governments of the late nineteenth and early twentieth centuries, suggests this focus on interest politics may have been stimulated by his historical work.

---

[60] Hayward, 'The state imperative', p. 57.
[61] Ibid., p. 55.
[62] Hayward, *Fragmented France*, p. 372.
[63] Hayward, 'Educational pressure groups'.

Private Interests discusses the development of the Council from 'ineffectual obscurity into influential limelight'.[64] It draws upon his earlier theoretical work. He contrasts, for example, the Proudhonian aspiration for workers' control with the 'Saint-Simonian reality of expertise applied to the organization of economic growth' as part of the dynamic explaining the behaviour of those involved in it.[65] But most of the book was a careful study of the Council based on interview and documentary evidence. One way the ESC increased its role was through its involvement in economic planning. Hayward wrote an article on the French approach to economic planning (in French— his French was flawless) in the *Revue Française de Sociologie*,[66] and a range of other contributions to the field followed.[67] The interest in planning was sustained by his co-editorship of two books looking at planning (including wider policy and land-use planning) in other European countries.[68]

Hayward also wrote many articles and book chapters looking at the French approach to policy-making, often focusing on economic policy-making. He contributed a chapter on France to the influential edited collection that sought to determine distinctive national 'styles' of policy-making.[69] Moreover, his work in this field was brought together and developed in his *State and the Market Economy: Industrial Patriotism and Economic Intervention in France*.[70] If one looks at *The State and the Market Economy* some of the familiar leading figures in Hayward's developing understanding of France are there—Proudhon and Saint-Simon get a few mentions—but the distinctive contribution of the work is that it sets out the decision-making of a 'concerted economy' with its characteristic features framed by the broader processes he identified in earlier work, above all the role for a techno-bureaucratic state and its close relationship with business. Within this broad description he sets out the practices of government techno-bureaucratic entrepreneurialism and the political strategies of the different groups involved in economic decision-making. This account includes his

[64] Hayward, *Private Interests*, p. 85.

[65] Ibid., p. 91.

[66] J. E. S. Hayward, 'Le fonctionnement des commissions et la préparation du Ve Plan. L'exemple de la Commission de la Main-d'œuvre', *Revue Française de Sociologie*, 8 (1967), 447–67.

[67] Including J. E. S. Hayward, 'State intervention in France: the changing style of government-industry relations', *Political Studies*, 20 (1972), 287–98; J. E. S. Hayward, 'National aptitudes for planning in Britain, France, and Italy', *Government and Opposition*, 9 (1974), 397–410: J. E. S. Hayward, 'The politics of planning in France and Britain: the transatlantic view', *Comparative Politics*, 7 (1975), 285–98.

[68] J. E. S. Hayward and M. Watson (eds.), *Planning, Politics and Public Policy* (Cambridge, 1975); J. E. S. Hayward and O. A. Narkiewicz (eds.), *Planning in Europe* (London, 1978).

[69] J. E. S. Hayward, 'Mobilising private interests in the service of public ambitions: the salient element in the dual French policy style', in J. J. Richardson (ed.), *Policy Styles in Western Europe* (London, 1982), Chapter 5.

[70] J. E. S. Hayward, *The State and the Market Economy: Industrial Patriotism and Economic Intervention in France* (Brighton, 1986).

characterisation of French interests as pressur*ed* groups and thus not fitting neatly into conventional understandings of pluralist decision-making; it also covers the national and local management (and mismanagement) of economic decline, nationalisation and the policy of 'national champions'. Here in economic policy the characteristic assumptions held by French policy elites are, as elsewhere, important explanatory factors. His judgement of French socialism, for example, is that

> on the relatively rare ... occasions, such as 1936 or 1968, when the Left has briefly occupied or approached power ... there has been a romantic tendency to consider that 'everything is possible'. This is one variant of an assertive and active French policy style which emphasises the will of the actor rather than the inertial constraints that inhibit innovation. Its pretensions may and often do exceed the capacity to attain its objectives, leading to humiliation when the gap between them is publicly exposed.[71]

His last major interview-based research project was part of a collaborative effort conducted under the auspices of the Economic and Social Research Council's Whitehall Programme.[72] It was a joint project led by Hayward and Vincent Wright. They were also to do the work on France and several other colleagues were supposed to cover Germany, Italy, the Netherlands, Austria and Spain. Wright and Hayward published a short report covering all the countries in the project which raised many questions but actually answered few and contained little by way of empirical detail. The authors conceded they had 'struggled to deal with rather than resolve the ... major conceptual and methodological problems ...'. This imposed 'significant limitations on the general and specific findings at which we arrived' and they suggested these findings 'will be set out in further detail in a series of volumes both national and comparative'.[73] Separate volumes on each of the countries in the project were planned (and indeed listed as published by Macmillan) along with an overview volume to be edited by Hayward and Wright. However, the only volume that appeared in print (published by Oxford University Press) was the Hayward and Wright volume on France *Governing from the Centre: Core Executive Coordination in France.*

The quality of this work on France leads one to regret the unfinished work of the collaborators as a sorely missed opportunity. Written effectively by Hayward after Wright's death, the book examines the concept of coordination. It contrasts on the one hand the aspirations to, and claims of, achieving comprehensive consistency and cohesion in policy development with the reality of decision-making where competing

---

[71] Ibid., p. 213.

[72] See R. A. W. Rhodes, 'A guide to the ESRC's Whitehall Programme, 1994–1999', *Public Administration*, 78 (2002), 251–82.

[73] V. Wright and J. E. S. Hayward. 'Governing from the centre: policy co-ordination in six European core executives', in R. A. W. Rhodes (ed.), *Transforming British Government*, vol. 2: *Changing Roles and Relationships* (Basingstoke, 2000), pp. 27–46.

power centres pull in different directions, where communication is poor and where pressures external to state institutions as well as external to France exert strong constraints. They start by setting out the 'normative framework' of coordination, and in many ways offer an enrichment of the thesis at the heart of *The One and Indivisible* by outlining the institutions (*cabinets*, inter-ministerial committees and the like) supposed to achieve singleness and indivisibility as well as the traditional forces (such as departmentalism, ministerial ambition) that have challenged it. Then, using four broad 'case studies' (coordination of EU policy, budget coordination, privatisation, and immigration), they examine how the normative framework and its institutions have worked in practice since 1981. The conclusions are detailed and sector specific, but they also have a strong bearing on the broader themes Hayward emphasises in his other work on France—the *dirigiste* tradition, the domination of the executive, the nature of relations with regional and local government and parliamentary weakness all shape the style of coordination; how it is attempted or not attempted, how potential conflicts are avoided and the form in which coordination, where attempted, succeeds and fails. Yet in substantive terms France is much like any other European state. Overall the 'flattering image of an integrated state disintegrates' and 'to the extent that it was formerly exceptional, France has increasingly ceased to be so' as it faces the same sorts of pressures of 'polycentric complexity' that face all modern states: 'anachronistic symbolic shibboleths are being remorselessly prised apart by intrusive substantive pressures'.[74]

Collaborative comparisons

Hayward described his intellectual development in an autobiographical note as a movement 'from implicit to explicit comparison'.[75] We have already mentioned his early conviction of the value of the comparative method of research. Comparison can, as he explicitly recognised, take a variety of different forms. His PhD was comparative, even though there were few pages devoted to experience or thought outside France, in the sense that the distinctiveness of French approaches to solidarity and their impact on policy and political development can only be appreciated with reference to patterns elsewhere (in this case mainly England but with some reference to Germany). His following books on France were all based on a recognition that French political thought, institutions and practices displayed distinctive features, which he contrasted through often brief references to other countries. More generally he argued

[74] J. E. S. Hayward and V. Wright, *Governing from the Centre* (Oxford, 2002), p. 271.
[75] Hayward, 'Between France and universality'.

against the belief that the *only* form of valid comparison was conducted on the basis of the identification, and preferably measurement, in several jurisdictions of an array of key independent variables with a bearing on a key dependent variable and performing some sort of regression—whether statistical, impressionistic or something in between: 'To dismiss the historically grounded studies of foreign politics as casual and amateurish because they are inductive, qualitative, and only implicitly comparative, is to assume that the quantitative American deductive approach is the only sound one.'[76] His preferred style of more elaborate and explicit comparison was, he said, citing Peter Mair approvingly, 'the bringing together of micro case-sensitive, context-sensitive groups of studies which, through team effort, and collaborative group effort, can genuinely advance comparative understanding, and can genuinely contribute to the development of comparative politics'.[77]

Hayward had already pursued this collaborative form of comparison in a series of contributions on planning, already discussed. He used the edited book format to address questions, mainly comparative, that he did not feel were addressed in the British political science literature; he also had a very good sense for emerging issues of central political importance and used this format to explore them.[78] He had highlighted the need for all-Europe comparisons before the Iron Curtain fell in a comparative edited collection with another Hull colleague, Bob Berki,[79] and at Hull he edited a special issue of a journal looking at the changing role of trade unions in Europe.[80] The 150th anniversary of the abolition of slavery and his role in Hull's celebration of Wilberforce's part in it generated *Out of Slavery*.[81] At Oxford he produced edited comparative volumes including one on industrial policy and European integration,[82] another on populism in Europe,[83] and with a close former Oxford colleague he edited a collection of comparative essays on contemporary European government which

---

[76] J. E. S. Hayward, 'Beyond Zanzibar: the road to comparative inductive institutionalism', in C. Hood, D. King and G. Peele (eds.), *Forging a Discipline: a Critical Assessment of Oxford's Development of the Study of Politics and International Relations in Comparative Perspective* (Oxford, 2014), pp. 227–8.
[77] Ibid., p. 243.
[78] When editing books Jack tried to include a mix of established and junior researchers. For such edited books he would generally organise a workshop (in Hull sometimes these were on shoe-string budgets) which, he made sure, would run exactly according to the planned timetable. Few, not even notorious latecomers, dared to be late either for the workshop sessions or in submitting draft/completed chapters. He told tardy collaborators that he would publish without them and name and shame them. He probably would have done, but I know of no case where he did.
[79] R. N. Berki and J. E. S. Hayward (eds.), *State and Society in Contemporary Europe* (Oxford, 1979).
[80] In a special issue of *West European Politics*, 3 (1980).
[81] J. E. S. Hayward (ed.), *Out of Slavery: Abolition and After* (London, 2013).
[82] J. E. S. Hayward (ed.), *Industrial Enterprise and European Integration: from National to International Champions in Western Europe* (Oxford, 1995).
[83] J. E. S. Hayward (ed.), *Elitism, Populism, and European Politics* (Oxford, 1996).

became the most cited of his edited books.[84] Shortly after the end of the division of Europe he recognised that many of the politics texts would be out of date and this led to *Governing the New Europe* which I had the privilege of coediting with him.[85] He produced two books on the methodology of political research, or rather how scholars approach the study of politics.[86]

Working on Sammy Finer's *History of Government* was a different kind of collaboration. As described by Finer's widow and Hayward himself this was a collaborative effort.[87] Sammy Finer died in 1993 having completed most of the work on thirty-four of the projected thirty-six chapters of this monumental work that started with the Sumerian city-state in the third millennium BCE and finished with the present day. Finer had left behind a set of notes for anybody editing his work were he to die before its completion. The editing involved sending the chapters, all in varying states of incompletion, to other scholars whom Finer had consulted while working on the book. These colleagues checked, completed and corrected different chapters, while Hayward was 'responsible for orchestrating the collective effort'. There was 'no attempt to interfere with Finer's own interpretation of events and developments'.[88] One can see why Hayward took on this large task. He begins his own account of accepting the challenge with the point that he made to all his colleagues, especially junior ones, at Hull (and probably everywhere else) quoting the nineteenth-century economist Léon Walras: 'if you want quick results, plant lettuce; enduring results take longer'.[89] Spending a long time on a big project that matters is infinitely more attractive than going for a speedy publication. Apart from his long-standing admiration for Finer, as well as 'paying the intellectual debt that he owed him',[90] Hayward's enthusiasm for working on his unfinished text was clear:

> Who other than Sammy Finer, in this era of professional prudence in which most of us retreat into the stultifying specialization that was profoundly repugnant to him, would have had the breath-taking boldness, the exuberant breadth of sympathy and the imaginative energy to embrace government throughout recorded history as well as throughout the world?

[84] J. E. S. Hayward and A. Menon (eds.), *Governing Europe* (Oxford, 2003).

[85] J. E. S. Hayward and E. Page (eds.), *Governing the New Europe* (Cambridge, 1995).

[86] J. E. S. Hayward and P. Norton (eds.), *The Political Science of British Politics* (Brighton, 1986); J. E. S. Hayward, B. Barry and A. Brown (eds.), *The British Study of Politics in the Twentieth Century* (Oxford, 2003).

[87] K. Jones Finer and J. E. S. Hayward, 'Preface' to S. E. Finer, *The History of Government*, vol. 1 (Oxford, 1999).

[88] Ibid., pp. v–vi.

[89] J. E. S. Hayward, 'Finer's comparative history of government', *Government and Opposition*, 32 (1997), 114.

[90] Hayward, 'Between France and universality', p. 149.

The volumes he edited in the ten years before his death reflected, perhaps more strongly than earlier ones, his disappointment and irritation with contemporary European politics, especially politics in Britain. These books also returned, in their different ways, to the concept of solidarity with which Hayward's intellectual career began. *Leaderless Europe* seeks to address the question of the failure of the European Union to live up to its promise and initial expectations: 'How did initial imaginative innovation give way to lacklustre, routine indecision',[91] amongst other things paving the way for populist appeals likely to undermine it? The conclusion was not entirely pessimistic—inertia and routine can be a way of keeping things tolerably together as long as they are done well and the prize of more 'heroic' leadership styles does not slip entirely away. *The Withering of the Welfare State*, which started from a despair at the reversal of solidarist values, pointed to the 'squalid consequences of liberty without solidarity', and expressed Hayward's fears over the 'headlong regression of countries that were once at the forefront of the welfare state', 'moving back from citizen solidarity, based upon self-respect grounded on a social recognition of equal worth, to self-serving inequality'.[92] His last edited book offered more than a nod to his earliest academic work in its title, *European Disunion: Between Sovereignty and Solidarity*. It focuses on the question of 'how much distrustful divergence the European Union can contain without degenerating into ineffectiveness and fragmentation'.[93]

Reflections on British citizenship

A very great personal disappointment, one which angered and disgusted him, was the treatment of British citizens who had been imprisoned by the Japanese during the Second World War and whose Britishness was denied by a capricious and offensive administrative decision that appeared to be based initially on the mercenary motive of limiting the extent of the government's financial liability. The episode also displayed a range of systematic problems with the British government, and Hayward, together with Ron Bridge, Chairman of the Association of British Civilian Internees Far East Region (ABCIFER), wrote this up in a book.[94] The book highlighted the campaign by ABCIFER and others to secure recognition and compensation for internees' suffering at the hands of the Japanese. After unsuccessful attempts to secure compensation

[91] J. E. S. Hayward (ed.), *Leaderless Europe* (Oxford, 2008), p. 1.
[92] J. Connelly and J. E. S. Hayward (eds.), *The Withering of the Welfare State: Regression* (Basingstoke, 2012), p. 16.
[93] Hayward and Wurzel, *European Disunion: Between Sovereignty and Solidarity*, p. 12.
[94] Hayward and Bridge, *Identity Theft*. Hayward approached several publishers with the manuscript, but did not manage to get it published.

from the Japanese, a quiet demonstration during the May 1998 state visit of the Japanese Emperor to London (which involved a candlelit vigil during which the protestors turned their backs to the Queen and Emperor as they drove in a carriage down the Mall) helped put the issue on the British government's agenda and eventually, in late 2000, after more pressing and mobilising parliamentary and public support, the prisoners' groups got a promise of 'a single *ex-gratia* payment' of £10,000 to each of the surviving ex-prisoners of the Japanese. The War Pensions Agency (WPA), part of the Ministry of Defence, in developing the details of the scheme, limited the eligibility for the payment to those British citizens at the time of imprisonment with a 'bloodlink' to Britain. This, as interpreted by the WPA, ruled out many people, including Hayward, who held British passports at the time.

The term 'bloodlink' has racial connotations and those it discriminated against in practice made it a racialist policy: it disproportionately excluded from the scheme Jews, Catholics of Irish descent born outside Britain, Eurasians who could not prove having a grandparent born in the United Kingdom and women who had become British through marriage.[95] The limitation appeared to be justified by a rather muddled argument that opening up the civilian scheme would lead to huge numbers of claims from ex-Indian army prisoners. There followed a long and hard-fought campaign, led by ABCIFER, and its chairman Ron Bridge in particular, in which Hayward played a significant role. Most notably Hayward complained to the Parliamentary Commissioner for Administration (PCA, often termed 'ombudsman') who eventually took up his case. In its report, *A Debt of Honour*, the PCA found maladministration, cover-up and misrepresentation stemming from the Ministry of Defence's wilful refusal to admit its mistakes, its incompetence and its obfuscation and obstruction when faced with claims for compensation.[96] The clear and strong PCA findings of maladministration were rejected by the Ministry of Defence, but, following further ABCIFER pressure and a parliamentary select committee's condemnation, the Ministry changed course significantly and invented a new rule to include some of those formerly excluded (the '20-year rule' by which those who had lived for twenty years in Britain up to 2000 also had a special link to the UK and were thus eligible). One of the defence ministers involved was Tom Watson, a former student in Hull's Politics Department whom Hayward had taught. A threat of court action by ABCIFER led to some improvement in the application of the twenty-year rule, and ABCIFER decided to accept the unsatisfactory revised scheme on the ground that the longer it dragged on the fewer surviving beneficiaries would be around to benefit from the scheme. Nevertheless, the progress of assessing and awarding the

---

[95] Ibid., Chapters 3 and 4.
[96] PCA, '*A Debt of Honour*'.

payment was very slow and still had its inconsistencies. Thus, while Hayward got his payment (which he immediately gave to a hospice) 'of two surviving Hayward sisters, one qualified under the 20-year rule and the other did not although all three had suffered exactly the same internment'.[97]

For Hayward the experience brought out the worst of British policy-making and politics. He had made implicit and less implicit comparative observations about the character of British policy-making across a range of his works, which tended to emphasise its conservatism, its passivity with respect to interest group pressure, its timidity and irresolution.[98] Where he might have been able to see some small positive elements in this in his earlier work, such considerations are hard to find here—*Identity Theft* concludes with a chapter entitled 'Maladministration: the unlearned lessons of an instructive fiasco'. This was a 'systemic failure that tells us much about the wilful amnesia of an administrative elite that had ceased to understand much less discharge what the then Prime Minister called "a debt of honour"'. Britain had retreated into a pettier form of self-identity: 'the expansive, imagined identity of an assertive Greater Britain shrank in the second half of the twentieth century into the defensive identity of a Lesser Britain'. There was a 'systemic incapacity of public servants to serve the public with standards of competence they are entitled to expect', a failure to carry out policies agreed by politicians and a failure by politicians to ensure that they are carried out; a confusion of responsibilities with inconsistent procedures and 'cultures' across government departments suffering from very rapid turnover in ministerial incumbents. The analytical core of the book is characteristically strong, yet the insult Hayward felt for himself, his family and his fellow internees and his anger with the way parts of the British politico-administrative system handled the matter helped ensure that the book could not be a commercial proposition for an academic publisher—and it remained unpublished.

The impatience with British policy-making and administration can be seen in his later work and was confirmed and magnified by Brexit. His commitment to remaining in the EU led him to propose and help organise events at Hull University, including arranging for Alan Johnson, the leader of 'Labour In for Britain', to give the Jean Monnet Lecture in 2016 with the title 'Involvement or isolation: the choice facing Britain'. Jack despaired of the referendum campaign, the vote and the political and administrative mess that followed. The title of a Hull University session arranged shortly after the referendum was unmistakeably his: 'Britain beyond European Union: causes and consequences of self-ejection'.

---

[97] Hayward and Bridge, *Identity Theft*.
[98] Hayward, *Political Inertia*, pp. 11–12.

Conclusion: inertia

Hayward's inaugural lecture at Hull in 1975 might at first might be taken as a specific reaction to his immediate environment. It has a characteristically jokey introduction:

> There are many sorts of chairs: bath chairs, deck chairs, electric chairs, push chairs, rocking chairs, to name but a few. Having been appointed to a second chair, it occurred to me to inquire what the holder of the first chair had spoken about at his inaugural and to choose a topic that was complementary to it. Professor Dodd … had elected to speak about political change … it seemed appropriate that I should select political inertia as my subject.[99]

However, the concern with inertia went deeper than gentle mockery of a colleague. Hayward often referred to inertia and his inaugural lecture; the term features explicitly in some of his writings and implicitly in almost all of them. He used it in two ways: as pluralist incrementalism or 'muddling through' on the one hand and on the other as political processes that never seem to be able to stop following characteristic and long-established patterns. 'Characteristic' did not, however, mean 'predictable'.[100] In his Beijing talk in 2000 he

> emphasised institutionally induced inertia and resistance to change. Because, in government, as in most other established institutions, the organisational equivalent of biological death was missing, the result was that the organisation triumphed over its function. Extrapolation from past tendencies as a basis of forecasting the future was likely to lead to futurological false prophesy.[101]

In his writing on planning, he makes the distinction between two different ways of making policy: a humdrum and a heroic.[102] Humdrum policy-making follows the pattern of pluralistic 'muddling through'; it is a diffuse and unstructured process where 'unplanned decisions are arrived at by a continuous process of mutual adjustment between a plurality of autonomous policy makers operating in the context of a highly fragmented multiple flow of influence'. Planning is an heroic form of policy-making involving the 'ambitious assertion of political will by government leaders'. Britain could never embrace effective economic planning in the postwar years because of 'a powerful but immobilist administration and politicians preoccupied with short-term manoeuvres within a party framework'. France would seem to have been well

[99] Ibid., p. 3.
[100] C. E. Lindblom, 'The science of "muddling through"', *Public Administration Review*, 19 (1959), 79–88.
[101] Hayward, 'A social scientist's sojourn in Beijing', 38
[102] Hayward, 'National aptitudes for planning in Britain, France, and Italy', 399.

placed to develop economic planning, but its success in coordinating a fragmented set of institutions, albeit more marked than in Britain, has been overstated as decisions have reflected a more fragmented and piecemeal approach. The concern with this form of inertia is found in his later writing on the EU where aspirations of 'heroic statecraft' are swamped by concern for the 'humdrum coordination of conflicting interests'.[103]

Yet his understanding of inertia did not just cover the notions of inaction and drift, but also inertia in responding to challenges and change. Thus he refers to Lampadusa's 'dynamic conservatism' where change is pursued by elites so that things can remain the same. He cites Kepler's definition of inertia as 'that property of matter by virtue of which it continues in its existing state, whether of rest or uniform motion in a straight line, unless that state is altered by external force'.[104] For Hayward it is institutions and the characteristics of the decision-making process, including its 'institutionalised values', that constitute the inertia shaping political decisions. Thus, in the second edition of *The One and Indivisible*, when considering the possibility for major change following the rise to power of the left for the first time in the Fifth Republic, he argues 'prudence suggests that once the dust has settled, the traditional routines favouring centralization, incrementalism, *dirigisme* and managerial control will reassert themselves'.[105]

The main theme of Hayward's work on France is the impact of the legacy of past conflicts, as seen through the window of political and social theory, on the institutions, processes and attitudes that make up the inertial pressures of contemporary politics. In this conception of inertia, it is not 'heroic' forms of political leadership that bring about change, much as Hayward acknowledged the role of political-bureaucratic 'innovators' in French planning such as Monnet, Bloch-Lainé and Delors.[106] Hayward emphasises that such inertial tendencies become modified when conditions change and they become increasingly difficult to sustain. Developments in the international economy system forced changes on France after the Second World War, but it was not until the Fifth Republic was well advanced that the legacy described in *The One and Indivisible* started to fade in the political system. Nevertheless, it remains still quite strong through the lasting impact of the fiction of indivisibility and the pre-eminence given to the state as a solver, if not preventer, of market failures. The past potency and present impact can be seen in the hypocritical contortions that

---

[103] J. E. S. Hayward, 'National governments, the European Council and Councils of Ministers: a plurality of sovereignties. Member State sovereigns without an EU sovereign', in Hayward and Wurzel, *European Disunion: Between Sovereignty and Solidarity*, p. 68.

[104] Hayward, *Political Inertia*, p. 7.

[105] Hayward, *Governing France*, p. 279.

[106] Hayward, 'National aptitudes', 405; see also Hayward, *The State and the Market Economy*.

French political debates go through to maintain these fictions even if the reality suggests a less distinctive pluralist liberal polity. If and when these fictions eventually fade further in France, the more generic 'muddling through' inertia of humdrum policy-making in pluralist systems will have nothing to hide it.

Note on the author: Edward C. Page is Sidney and Beatrice Webb Professor of Public Policy at the London School of Economics. He was elected a Fellow of the British Academy in 2001.

J. CLYDE MITCHELL

James Clyde Mitchell

21 June 1918 – 15 November 1995

elected Fellow of the British Academy 1990

by

SUSAN J. SMITH

Fellow of the Academy

J. Clyde Mitchell was one of the finest anthropologists of his generation. An early recruit to the Rhodes-Livingstone Institute, he became its fourth Director in 1952, overseeing a remarkably productive period and a tum to urban research. An advocate for case and situational analysis, he also had a feeling for numbers that was unique for the time. His anthropological 'standards' include *The Yao Village* and *The Kalela Dance* (both published in 1956), while a fascination with human relations and agency made him a pioneer of social network analysis. From 1955, Mitchell occupied the first Chair in African Studies at the University College of Rhodesia and Nyasaland (now the University of Zimbabwe). A decade later, the Unilateral Declaration of Independence in Southern Rhodesia propelled him to the UK, where he renewed his association with 'The Manchester School', before completing his career in Oxford, where he was the first anthropologist elected to the fellowship at Nuffield College.

Biographical Memoirs of Fellows of the British Academy, XVIII, 93–133
Posted 8 April 2019. © British Academy 2019.

J. CLYDE MITCHELL

Introduction
'Social anthropology is disappearing as a discipline ... '[1]

James Clyde Mitchell (Clyde to those who knew him) was one of the finest anthropologists of his generation. Born in Pietermaritzburg in 1918, the fourth of seven children (all boys) of a Scottish rail worker, he moved with his father's job from place to place in what was then Natal Province (now KwaZulu-Natal). Growing up in the shadow of colonialism, Clyde spoke Zulu from childhood. He felt keenly the winds of political change and anchored his life's work on how they shaped the course of African urbanisation.

Initially struggling both to afford, and to win, access to a university education, Clyde settled into life as a civil servant, as a hospital clerk monitoring the cost of treating infectious diseases. To break out of this, which he felt he must, he pursued a part-time degree in social studies (by evening class) mounted in 1938 by the University of Natal, then a College of the University of South Africa. Apparently he had social work in mind as a new career. However, he excelled in sociology and psychology, and this opened up a whole new world. Intellectually, he found his niche as an anthropologist, though he was ambivalent about the label and eschewed the disciplinism it implied.[2]

By the time Clyde graduated in 1941, the Western world was at war, and he joined the air force, initially as a pilot. It is rumoured that he flew round the Mediterranean with sociological texts propped up on his map table.[3] Whatever the reason, he soon discovered that his métier lay in navigation and it is tempting to organise his intellectual journey—his myriad projects and his, for the time, prodigious output of twelve books and seventy or so articles—in similar geographical vein.

Clyde's academic career began in Africa, at the then-Rhodes-Livingstone Institute (RLI),[4] after a brother stationed in Durban saw an advert at the local university. Clyde

---

[1] In a letter to A. L. (Bill) Epstein in the early 1950s, Mitchell wrote 'I think that social anthropology is disappearing as a discipline and that the future lies in modern studies' (28.5.1951). At the time, ironically, he was busy transforming the subject in ways that, in the end, would help secure its future.

[2] In the earlier part of his career Clyde, like a number of his colleagues, notwithstanding their disciplinary credentials, used the appellation 'sociologist'. This gave their subject a more 'scientific' feel while signalling affinity to a style of anthropology designed explicitly to escape the charge of 'Othering' (Robert Gordon, pers. comm. 28.8.2018).

[3] Clyde spoke little about his distinguished war record (despite keeping his log books for many years). He reputedly flew without doors, enabling swift, and therefore safe, take-off immediately after landing. His passengers included wounded men, refugees, and emissaries, one of whom was apparently a lieutenant sent by Tito for discussions with Churchill about the future of Yugoslavia (John Goldthorpe, pers. comm. 29.8.2014).

[4] Established in 1937 in Livingstone as the first social research institute in Central Africa, the RLI became the Institute for Social Research/Centre for African Studies between 1966 and 1971, and the Institute for

accepted the position of Research Officer (assistant anthropologist) in 1946 and studied for a doctorate under the supervision of Max Gluckman. He stayed for nine years, assuming the role of Senior Sociologist from 1950, and becoming the Institute's fourth Director from 1952 (working from a field site in Luanshya, before moving with the Institute from Livingstone to Lusaka the following year).[5]

His next move was to Salisbury (Harare) in 1955 into the first Chair in African Studies at the University College of Rhodesia and Nyasaland (UCRN, now the University of Zimbabwe) where he stayed for a decade before being propelled to Britain by Rhodesia's Unilateral Declaration of Independence (UDI) in 1965. From 1966, he occupied the Chair in Urban Sociology at Manchester University, making his final move to Nuffield College Oxford in 1973, which had never before elected an anthropologist. As if to underline this disciplinary homecoming he simultaneously accepted an honorary fellowship in the Department of Social Anthropology at University College London. He nevertheless remained in Oxford for the rest of his life, retiring in 1985, just a decade before his death.

If this implies a singular journey, however, it is an illusion. Clyde's DPhil was registered at the University of Oxford where he was a student at St Catherine's College, living in the precincts for the requisite three terms. Throughout that period, he was continuously employed at the RLI, interleaving even that with lengthy fieldwork excursions to Nyasaland (Malawi). From 1953 and throughout his Directorship of the RLI he was also a Senior Research Fellow at Manchester University, straddling two institutions and narrowing the gap between them with a sense of common purpose. All the while, his work ranged back and forth in space and time; indeed, his final authored book, *Cities, Society, and Social Perception* (1987) made new sense of his earliest research at the RLI, and his final published paper (Mitchell, 1994) was a reworking of data that first appears in the book of his DPhil thesis (Mitchell, 1956a). Mitchell may have journeyed extensively during a highly productive career, but all the time he was steeped in Oxford anthropology, integral to the Manchester School, and spliced to his African roots.

In the end, neither Mitchell's work nor his life fit neatly into geographical, historical or even intellectual categories, and I feel sure he would not have wanted to compartmentalise them in that way. My guess is that he would have preferred to think of himself as part of an extensive interdisciplinary network, spanning three-quarters of a century and stretching across the globe. He would not have placed himself at the heart

---

African Studies from 1971 to 1996. Since 1996 it has been known as the Institute for Economic and Social Research (INESOR) at the University of Zambia.
[5] After Godfrey Wilson (1938–41: the first Government-appointed anthropologist in the region), Max Gluckman (1941–7) and Elizabeth Colson (1948–51).

of it nor willingly turned a spotlight on the corner that he anchored. This may be why, despite the radical originality of his contribution, his ideas are less explicitly acknowledged or profiled than those of some predecessors, peers and successors.[6] In truth, however, without his influence an extensive and enduring web of anthropological and sociological scholarship would be far less intellectually remarkable than it is; it would be less dense, less coherent, less vibrant, and would lack the warmth and generosity of spirit that Clyde infused into its life and work.

Bearing all this in mind, I have chosen to profile, in no special order, five facets of Clyde Mitchell's intellectual contribution. They are his unswerving commitment to empirical research (it is probably fair to say that all his key ideas were wrested from close encounters with human subjects); his fascination with numerical techniques; his methodological and conceptual innovations around case, situation and network analysis; his substantive contributions to debates on African urbanisation; and his highly personal political position. These items are in no special order, because in Clyde's work, and indeed in his life, they were inseparable and interleaved.

Empirical foundations
'the laboratory in the field'[7]

As a research student Clyde was swept into a unique anthropological collaboration anchored by the RLI, under its second Director, Max Gluckman. Mitchell's doctorate, which he embarked on in 1946 and secured in 1950, slotted into an ambitious multi-centre seven-year research plan which aimed to document the changing times of Central Africa, spanning what are now the national territories of Zimbabwe, Zambia and Malawi (Gluckman, 1945).[8] The scholars Gluckman assembled regarded their work as an exercise in empirical observation, their field as a 'laboratory'. Schumaker (2001, 84) writes engagingly about this collaboration, noting that 'the concept of the field laboratory helped to structure the research and standardize

[6] Reflecting on the legacy generally of the RLI-based south-central African anthropologists, Werbner (1984, 190) observes that notwithstanding the enduring relevance of their work, it is too often underestimated 'or even neglected as if it were hopelessly out of date'. Referring specifically to Clyde's position, in the foreword to Mitchell's last, capstone, book, Kapferer (1987a, xv) explains: 'He is generous with ideas in the extreme and in the most marvelous way. Thus while he generates ideas in others he always seems to impart the impression that these ideas are those of his students or colleagues rather than his own.'

[7] This phrase, used as a chapter heading by Schumaker (2001), alludes to an essay published by Max Gluckman (1946) in a short-lived monthly magazine; it positioned Central Africa as a laboratory for those 'scientific' studies of social life referred to in the RLI statement of aims.

[8] A second seven-year plan, running from 1950, was developed by the Institute's third Director, Elizabeth Colson, who also facilitated the RLI's move from Livingstone to Lusaka (Schumaker, 2001, 119).

the researchers' individual approaches … [it also] aided the emergence of a shared work culture among the team members, not unlike the unique styles that develop in physics and biology laboratories'. In the end, the RLI programme rolled out in two ways.

On the one hand, Mitchell himself inspired a series of social surveys, whose design and execution owe much to the skills he brought to the group. He in fact drove this part of the agenda. Colleagues embarking on rural ethnographies were persuaded to carry census cards with them, while Clyde himself directed the larger-scale 'socio-graphic' surveys of the towns.[9] He saw this style of fieldwork as essential for its conceptual value ('a way to refine and deepen' generalisations, or 'bring to light regularities which might otherwise have escaped notice'); equally he promoted it for pragmatic reasons, because census type materials were not, on the whole, yet available in the African countries (Mitchell, 1966, 39). Others, including Max Gluckman, who had previously tried to recruit a demographer to the RLI, embraced this quantitative turn for the scientific credibility it brought to the group.[10]

The main survey project (reported in Mitchell, 1987) was, moreover, truly innovative for its time. A carefully stratified sample of around 12,000 people, interviewed over five years in all the major Copperbelt towns, answered a range of questions that went far beyond a simple census to create a rounded 'social profile of the people'. The schedule covered quality of life in urban versus rural settings, occupational status, perceptions of regionalism and ethnicity, and more. Administering it, however, was a drawn-out process. In a series of letters to John Barnes in the early 1950s, Mitchell writes (20.12.1951) 'whatever [i]nthusiasm I have had for the Copperbelt has died from marasmus. The sociographic survey drags its uninspired feet month after month—nothing emerges from it;' later he seems resigned to failure, noting that: 'The history of the Copperbelt study was a sad one' (22.11.1952). Yet, the survey kept going, and although Clyde was dreading having to check and prepare the data, the results have endured thanks mainly to his own dogged determination not only to complete the work at the time, but also to transfer the data onto 80-column punched cards once computers were installed in universities—a challenge that apparently took five years to complete (Mitchell, 1987, xvi). Notwithstanding sample bias and other challenges highlighted retrospectively by Mitchell (1987) and others (e.g.

[9] Thanks to Richard Werbner (pers. comm. 31.7.2018) for this insight, and for the observation that because Gluckman, though much-influenced by Mitchell's convictions, was not wedded to social surveys (and perhaps did not have the skills to handle them), the quantitative programme stood somewhat apart from the RLI's anthropological tradition except through the persona of Mitchell himself.

[10] Robert Gordon (pers. comm. 28.8.2018) pointed this out and goes as far as to suggest that Gluckman saw statistics as a kind of 'magic bullet' in this respect.

Peil, 1988), it was the most systematic contemporary data resource assembled around the zenith, and in the wake, of colonialism in Africa.

Max Gluckman's overarching plan, on the other hand, which is more widely documented, was anchored in a comprehensive programme of detailed ethnographies whose completion rested on a unique division of intellectual labour. This equally systematic effort formed the core anthropological project of what was later known as the Manchester School (whose impact is profiled by Werbner, 1984, and forthcoming). Although it was (thanks largely to Clyde's powers of persuasion) de facto interleaved with the survey effort it was the area of work in which Clyde initially felt least at home. In the end, however, he would take a lead, conceding that intensive approaches—or 'anthropological methods'—tend ultimately to generate the most 'fruitful hypotheses' (Mitchell, 1966, 42). He was, indeed, Director of the RLI when some of the more important 'Manchester' fieldwork was done (Kapferer, 1987a).

Gluckman's original idea was to assign each researcher to a different 'tribe' or ethnic group,[11] in settings strategically selected to illuminate particular questions or problems.[12] While the programme—with its ambitious aim of gaining a comprehensive, even total, understanding of the region—was never (and probably never could have been) completed, the result was series of complementary monographs and articles, much as had occurred under the tutelage of Robert Park in Chicago a quarter of a century before. The early African effort was initially and in part collected as *The Seven Tribes of British Central Africa* by Colson and Gluckman (1951). As time went on, however, most studies turned into at least one book and the collaboration became, as Hannerz (1980) has observed, a 'school' whose size and scope—with the arguable exception of its Chicago counterpart—no other single localised complex of ethnographies has matched.

The cumulative, comparative and collaborative character of the fieldwork was established from the start. In that sense, it stood in marked contrast to the more individualised model of anthropological endeavour that prevailed at the time.[13] Clyde has described in person and in print the way he, John Barnes, Elizabeth Colson and Max Marwick formed the 'early team' under Max Gluckman, their common approach informed by an initial training programme and followed up from time to time when

[11] Mitchell later distanced himself from the label 'tribe' though it was in common use during the 1940s and 1950s; see footnote 35.

[12] For example, Chewa (Max Marwick), Lozi (Max Gluckman), Luapula (Ian Cunnison), Mambwe (William Watson); Ndembu (Victor Turner), Ngoni (John Barnes), Shona (Hans Holleman), Lakeside Tonga (Jaap van Velsen), Plateau Tonga (Elizabeth Colson), and so on. Mitchell's study was of the Yao villages of Nyasaland (Malawi).

[13] Though in practice and as time went on, neither the RLI project nor the Manchester School more broadly were (as Werbner, 1984, points out, citing Mitchell as a source) as unified internally as they may have seemed from the outside.

they were called in (often from sites hundreds of miles distant) to spend a week discussing progress and problems.

The seminars thus spawned are legendary. Everyone would present a paper covering the data they had secured, their first attempts to make sense of it all, their thoughts about fieldwork and their ideas of how to go on. Such meetings were critical in helping those who struggled with fieldwork—Mitchell very much among them.[14] By providing an opportunity to exchange ideas, work out differences, develop a structured approach to fieldwork and a shared understanding of the importance of detailed documentation, the seminars wrested synergies from the group and were 'the crucial method of building us into a team' (Mitchell, interview with Bernard, 1990). Maps, censuses and systematic record-keeping were, at Gluckman's insistence, essential ingredients of the process, whose field notes (which Bruce Kapferer, pers. comm., 8.2.2016, describes as 'frightening' in their meticulous detail) had to be accessible to others, and were eventually lodged in the library.

In short, the ethnographic programme at the RLI called for high standards and painstaking documentation. Some seminars, apparently, are still archived, as are the reams of correspondence that culture of openness and exchange encouraged. This not only enabled team members to travel (Barnes to Norway, Epstein to Papua New Guinea, and so on) without losing a sense of connectedness but produced vigorous exchanges of letters around research ideas and achievements that kept the group in close (if uneven) contact with one another and added to their collective conceptual edge. In Clyde's case there is a particularly notable exchange of long, inspiring letters in the late 1940s and early 1950s with Gluckman (whose supervisorial role soon evolved into collegiality and friendship), Barnes (a close friend, fellow mathematician, and ally among peers),[15] and Epstein (a research student-turned-partner in a collaboration that Richard Werbner, pers. comm. 31.7.2018, suggests forms 'the very heart of Mitchell's Copperbelt contributions and project').[16]

Mitchell's earliest original (doctoral) contribution to this collaborative effort was a study of the Yao, a Bantu-speaking matrilineal Muslim community in rural Nyasaland (now Malawi) with whom he worked in two phases from September 1946 to September 1947, and from September 1948 to June 1949, with an interlude in

---

[14] This struggle is scattered across Mitchell's correspondence, for example in his letter to Max Gluckman on 25.3.1949, reporting that 'fieldwork languishes as usual'.

[15] On 20.3.1949, for example, Clyde sent seven pages of closely typed notes to Barnes offering a critique and elaboration of his marriage paper (later a book).

[16] Interestingly, but not especially unusually for the time, they rarely published under joint names, except perhaps for pragmatic reasons. Mitchell, for example, reflecting in a letter to Epstein on a rare joint work (Mitchell and Epstein 1959) indicates: 'I am glad we have got the stuff out—I hate to see material lying around not made use of' (15.1.1956).

Oxford from May 1947 to fulfil the DPhil residence requirement. The work adopted a now classic, then innovative, mixed methods approach, combining historical analysis, a village-by-village census and survey, mapping exercises, case studies, use of local tax records and more.

Such work was fraught with problems. Some were practical (the challenge of living in tents, with few amenities, far from home), others were financial (Clyde reports living from hand to mouth when his children were young). Many hurdles were bureaucratic, and most, of course, were political (see later), including being treated with suspicion by all parties. As an exercise in anthropology, moreover, working from his nomadic base in a tent, he struggled to find a niche: 'Each day I set out with good intentions ... and each day end up by discussing witchcraft' (letter to MG 25.3.1949) (a topic he felt was already well explored by Evans-Pritchard and Gluckman himself).

Although Clyde's CV is peppered with outputs from this project (whose substantive significance is considered later), the book of his thesis remained unpublished until long after he had left the Copperbelt for Salisbury. As he notes in the opening chapter: 'the hardest part of fieldwork is writing it up' (Mitchell, 1956a, 7). This is another lament that he carried throughout his working life. My own notes, having read a cross-section of his letters, read 'JCM spends his whole career struggling to write everything up ... '.[17] So it was September 1954 before he reported to Barnes that 'the Yao Book is posted off', and 22 June 1956 before the published version—*The Yao Village*—came out, just in time for Clyde's proud father (to whom, together with the memory of his mother, it is dedicated) to see it before he died.

It is interesting to note that so pervasive was the collaborative ideal, that in the acknowledgements even of this most individualised of treatises—his doctorate—Mitchell (1956, ix) wrote 'the book is as much my colleagues' as my own'. He also acknowledged that his first wife, Edna, had 'the major share' in the book's preparation. They refused to be separated by the demands of the project and she shared with him the difficulties of life in the field. Indeed, hers and their first (at the time only) son Donald's presence clearly helped Clyde integrate into village life. Among professional colleagues, he acknowledges Max Gluckman as the person to whom he owes the most. Gluckman, at the same time (while lamenting that more of the ethnographic material had not been packaged into it), described the pre-publication

---

[17] Though it did not prevent him building up a remarkable CV. For example, by 1954, while Director of the RLI, Clyde reported being 'thoroughly browned off and doing nothing at all in the way of getting any of my stuff out' (letter to Barnes 6.1.1954)· yet by September he had managed to post off the manuscript of the book of his DPhil (*The Yao Village*). Similarly, a year later, he wrote, 'I have got nowhere with writing anything except letters' (to Epstein 16.8.1955), even though just months later *The Kalela Dance* was published, again to great acclaim.

manuscript as 'magnificent, a notable contribution, well-argued and very interesting
to read ... a great book' (letter 9.11.1955); later, on 24.1.1957, Gluckman wrote of
the book itself: 'I have just been lecturing on it for two hours, and it is perfect. It left
me feeling not only humble but also envious.' The work is described by a contemporary reviewer as 'an outstanding example of the recent attempt by social
anthropologists working in Africa to document their findings statistically (Fallers
1957, 731). As for one or two cooler reviews, Gluckman's observation (writing to
Mitchell 28.5.1957) was that: 'It was too good for the present state of Anthropology.'
Later, of course, it would become a classic; perhaps the first original use of the
extended case study in the discipline.

   If *The Yao Village* was a classic of one type, exemplifying the systematic survey
strand of the RLI endeavour, Clyde's other classic—*The Kalela Dance*, possibly the
best, most original piece of contemporary anthropology—embraced and enlarged the
ethnographic tradition that the Manchester School was best known for. It was a for-
tuitous encounter; an accident of location described both in interview with Russell
Bernard (1990) and by Shumaker (2001). Based with his family in Luanshya in a house
provided by the RLI, Clyde was drawn by the noise of the drums on a Sunday afternoon to the nearby municipal African township. There he witnessed a tribal, or ethnic,
dance which—unlike its counterparts further South—was not ablaze with extravagant
costumes and exotic colour but was performed by young African men dressed in
European suits 'shuffling around in a circle'. More notable still, given that 'tribal'
dances were generally attracting rather small audiences in urban settings, the Kalela
was 'packed thick' with spectators. Clyde's curiosity was piqued and, together with
field assistant Sykes Ndilila (who also translated the song), he embarked on what
was to become one of anthropology's seminal works, tracing out in minute detail
the structure and form of the dance, together with the fourteen-stanza song embedded in it.

   Clyde's engagement with practical fieldwork was in some senses (and measured
by the scale of the project) cut short when he moved to the Chair at the University
College of Rhodesia and Nyasaland (UCRN). Like so many scholars steeped in
fieldwork, the teaching and administrative burdens he encountered as his career
developed, together with the urge to write up the data he already had, might well
have curbed his travel. He also had a large and growing family (a daughter and three
sons—Gillian, Donald, Keir and Alan), all under the age of ten when he moved to
Salisbury, where he also lost their mother, his first wife Edna, to leukaemia. By then,
however, he had assembled as much material as any anthropologist of his generation and more than enough to complete his career, the majority of which was
devoted to analysing and publishing his Copperbelt materials. There might also
have been a shift in his thinking about the nature of empirical research and analysis

around this time; one of his sons recalls a growing interest in numerical techniques and a renewed determination to define his subject as 'sociology' (D. Mitchell, pers. comm. 22.5.2018).

In her assessment of the work of the Manchester School, Shumaker (2001, 256–7), concludes that the book of the Copperbelt project—a much hoped for and talked about 'final jointly written volume on the industrial revolution in central Africa'—was never realised. It is possible, however, that Clyde's last book (Mitchell, 1987) was his own attempt to see this through, albeit drawing, by then, primarily on his own materials.[18] It was not the last word, of course: the impact of the Manchester School, and in particular of Max Gluckman as the individual most associated with it, continues to fascinate scholars (its momentum most recently assured by Gordon, 2018, and Werbner, forthcoming). That, however, is (mostly) another story.

These empirical underpinnings stayed with Clyde throughout his life, as did the collaborative spirit they nurtured and which, for Mitchell, was one of the defining features of the Manchester School. He certainly took this ethos to heart when he, in turn, became director of the RLI, using it as a platform from which to launch a new and wide-ranging programme of self-consciously urban research. Always hungry for new material, he had even hoped to apply some elements of the RLI model when he moved to Manchester University and was involved in a programme of linked studies funded by the ESRC to chart the social impacts of the growing conurbation.[19] He certainly remained a stickler for regular contact with students in the field to stimulate ideas and reduce isolation. As he notes in an afterword to a collection of essays assembled in his honour: 'One lives through the research experience of one's students as they are conducting their enquiries … I required them to write to me once a month even if they had little to report because I know how lonely anthropological research can be' (Mitchell, 1995, 335).

---

[18] As early as the mid-1950s, Mitchell wrote to Barnes indicating that he had taken on the mantle of writing a final work, noting that he was spending 'much of my time now working on the Copper Belt material which promises to be [a] huge volume' (JCM to JB June 1955). Much later, in the early 1980s, I recall Clyde speaking to me, and possibly to others, about the responsibility he felt to bring to fruition the ideas and materials that he and his colleagues had assembled. He apparently held a contract for such a book for many years (though not with the publisher he eventually used for *Cities, Society and Social Perception*).

[19] This is referred to in his papers, though not contained in the e-searchable ESRC archives (which do not go back that far). Richard Werbner has some memory of a project on social stratification (pers. comm. 31.7.2018) and there may therefore be records in Manchester (e.g. among the papers of Max Gluckman) or in hard copy reports to what would then have been the SSRC.

Feeling for numbers
'The only person I knew who had unbounded enthusiasm
for my data and statistical problems'[20]

In an interview in July 1990 in the garden of his Oxford home, Mitchell, speaking to Russell Bernard, describes in passing how he spent his spare time while training for the air force in the 1940s. He took the opportunity to calculate chi-square values for illegitimacy and religion among the Zulu on a slide rule! This self-defining moment sums up a key element of his intellectual legacy: an insatiable appetite for using formal descriptive tools to illuminate the substance of social life.

Clyde's fascination for numerical techniques anticipated, embraced and survived the so-called quantitative revolution of the 1960s, just as his systematic collation and organisation of empirical data of all kinds presaged the advent of cumulative social science and the turn to 'big data'. Throughout his career his receptiveness to—indeed demand for—new empirical material was more than matched by his passion for making the most of it analytically. Moreover, his early sense that there would always be new analytical possibilities—a feeling for numbers perhaps—influenced the way he approached even his ethnographic data collection. His early recognition that prestige was a salient social marker, for example (see later), drove him not only to observe and describe the deference the Yao villagers paid to the 'Headman' but equally to 'make a special effort to collect as much quantitative data relating to these indicators of prestige that I could' (Mitchell, 1994, 267).

Clyde's letters over the years are peppered with this appetite for numbers. When Max Gluckman sent him a correlation chart in the late 1940s, he described it as a masterpiece. 'I am', he writes, 'hanging it in the house in place of my Cézanne', following up, wryly, with the observation: 'There is an arithmetical approach to the same problem that would have taken up less space' (JCM to MG 18.5.1947). His letters are full of phrases like 'I think I have worked out a survival table for Yao marriages' (JCM to MG 25.3.1949); or that he had done 'a little algebra' on Epstein's PhD data on the decline in Union membership 'for fun' (JCM to AE, 16.8.1955). It is no surprise to find that when Max Gluckman tried to tempt Clyde to move to Manchester in the early 1950s, he wrote as a PS to his letter of 6.5.1949: 'I should add that Manchester is stiff with calculating machines! and that in our faculty statistics are taught!' Neither is it unexpected to find that Clyde's last published paper (whose proofs he checked during his last admission to hospital) contains a reanalysis of data collected during

---

[20] Part of a tribute from the late Professor Ceri Peach read at a memorial service for J. Clyde Mitchell held at Nuffield College (1996).

his doctoral fieldwork in a Yao village 'using techniques which have become available since' (Mitchell, 1994, 268).

In the intervening years, Clyde devoted a great deal of time and many publications to exploiting the new calculating power that pre-computers and then a generation of mainframe machines brought to his fingertips. He thought it important, and he delighted in it. He initially managed to analyse his early census work at the RLI, for example, by securing the use of a Hollerith machine owned by Anglo-American Copperbelt mines; he was also drawn to the mining companies' own punch-card database of staff records. During a gap with no director at the RLI in 1951, when Mitchell was the heir apparent and the wheels were grinding slowly, he was consoled by writing about 'indices of urbanisation'.

In September 1954 his dismay at the plodding role of the Directorship he had now assumed at the RLI was temporarily alleviated by news that the Trustees had allowed him to buy a Powers-Samas tabulating machine (a device that read punch-cards mechanically). By the following year, he had embraced the move to Salisbury, with the caveat that 'The University are taking so long to let me have a calculating machine that I can't get out the short statistical pot-boilers I have almost ready' (letter to Epstein 16.8.1955). One of these potboilers was apparently a factor analysis of the mining staff records mentioned above; this would have been among the earliest substantive applications of the technique in the social sciences.[21]

As the years went by, Clyde was increasingly fascinated by the range and complexity of the numerical techniques available to social research, and he played a key role in stimulating their use in social anthropology. His interest and impact grew through the 1970s and culminated in a wide-ranging edited collection (Mitchell, 1980), which did 'a fine job of demonstrating the substantive value of mathematical approaches' (Robbins, 1983). Notwithstanding the inscription he wrote in my copy—'some dull reading for a light afternoon'—and belying its paltry twenty-three Google Scholar citations, it is a path-breaking collection with an engaging editorial introduction, introducing some less well-known but substantively illuminating approaches that have since become standards.

While 'Numerical techniques' is perhaps his best-known intervention in this area, it is notable that, in response to a request I sent to colleagues for memories of Clyde and his work, his feeling for numbers was a recurring theme.[22] Commenting on his

---

[21] I have not been able to track down every paper on Clyde's publication list, but as far as I can see, this analysis was never published. His landmark round-up of the causes of labour migration (Mitchell, 1959) contains phrases and conceptualisations that are entirely appropriate to a factor analytic approach but it is based on secondary sources.

[22] Even his family reported this to me. For example, in the early years, he had a hand calculating machine that one of his sons, recalling his childhood, describes as 'a combination of levers and number barrels

time at Nuffield College, his friend and colleague John Goldthorpe noted, 'One remarkable thing was how much quantitative analysis Clyde did in those days—when computers were still difficult and user non-friendly beasts—on a hand calculator. I recall him once telling me that in fitting a particular statistical model he had to carry out twenty-seven iterations of an algorithm in this way before getting a satisfactory convergence!' (pers. comm. 29.8.2014). Peter Jackson reflecting on the 1980s noted that 'his enthusiastic engagement with each project he supervised' extended in his, Jackson's, case to 'undertaking a smallest space analysis of some of my housing data' (pers. comm. 27.8.2014). Vaughan Robinson, writing to Clyde's wife Jean shortly after his death, told the story of how, at a particularly tedious College meeting, Clyde appeared to be dozing, but was in fact leafing surreptitiously through a wedge of computer printout—balanced on his knees under a table—containing the results of his latest efforts at multi-dimensional scaling.

I am guessing that practically all his students, and most of his colleagues, have a story of this kind to tell. Eleanor Kelly's work on the length of stay of homeless families in temporary accommodation is a case in point. Rather than simply setting out the characteristics of the sample and speculating on the variable (always slow) rate of rehousing into the social sector triggered by various priority needs, Mitchell found a way to quantify the data and conduct a multivariate analysis to show that, ironically and counter-intuitively, length of stay was longest for those *most* eligible for rehousing (Kelly et al., 1990).

Even the co-supervisor (with Clyde) of my own DPhil was drawn into this pattern, when Clyde spotted that by using multidimensional scaling techniques to classify indices of similarity, and logistic regression techniques to analyse the results, it would be possible to resolve a longstanding debate around segregation and intermarriage. Peach and Mitchell (1988) thus established that spatial separation reduced the odds of intermarriage between ethnic groups in San Francisco (in 1980) to a greater extent than either educational difference or social distance. This numerical imperative did not, of course, flow in just one direction. Across the top of an offprint he gave me of a paper using generalised procrustes analysis to cast light on processes of social stratification (Mitchell and Critchley, 1985), Clyde has written '[a] very useful technique this, that Frank introduced me to'.

Mitchell could, in short, be relied on to draw everything possible from the fragments of social life that fieldwork captures from the chaotic melée that makes up

---

driven by something similar to a sewing machine handle'. From time to time, around bedtime, 'teddy' might fall into this machine and be shredded into a thousand tiny bears. Clyde would apparently recount with mirth and pleasure how the micro-bears spread anxiously in a swarm searching for a suitable integration function enabling them to reassemble into the original toy (Don Mitchell, pers. comm. 22.5.2018).

the world. He had a feeling for numbers—an intuitive understanding of what quantitative techniques could achieve for knowledge. To be clear, however, his fascination
with the numerical was not with the power of technique or the clever manipulation of
statistics for their own sake (he describes having to teach the methods course at
Manchester as 'absolute hell'). He was concerned rather with what the advent of new
ways of handling, manipulating, and analysing social and anthropological data added
to his conceptual and substantive interests. The only restriction he placed on contributors to his book on numerical techniques (Mitchell, 1980, 2–3), for example, was 'that
each paper should relate to a substantive ethnographic or anthropological problem'.

In short, Mitchell was an advocate of numerical reasoning in the broadest sense,
not of number crunching as an end in itself. Craig Calhoun describes it as the difference between 'caring about what people do in their lives and what happens in their
lives', on the one hand, and 'relatively abstract intellectual puzzles', on the other (pers.
comm. 29.11.2015). Kapferer (2010, 7) puts it more formally: 'The study of statistical
analysis was, in Mitchell's view, thoroughly dependent on ethnographic work that was
alive to social variation and its situated production.' This is more than evident in the
ideas we turn to next.

Epistemological energies
*'In Manchester School anthropology, fieldwork materials and conceptualisation
shape and use one another, producing recurrent epistemological surprise'*[23]

The RLI model of working produced broadly comparative studies across the so-called
Copperbelt. This early leaning to comparability in qualitative as well as quantitative
observation underpinned the development of two epistemological ideas that Clyde
would play a major part in advancing across his career. Both challenged dominant
wisdoms relating, first, to generalising from unique occurrences, and second to the
conceptualisation of social life itself. They are, case and situational analysis on the
one hand, and network analysis on the other.

Case and Situation
*'It is always good to advance theory and empirical analysis at the same time, but in
practice very difficult to move on both fronts at once'.*[24]

The case study approach which Clyde encountered through his early social work
training became central to the operation of the Manchester School. Its epistemological

---

[23] Evans and Hendelman (2006, ix).
[24] Memorable advice offered by Clyde to his research student, Craig Calhoun (pers. comm. 29.1.2015).

significance is set out in a seminal paper (Mitchell, 1983) that was once envisaged as a book. The appeal of the case study—an abstraction from a wider situation made to illustrate a theoretical point—is that it offers a means by which the rigour of qualitative methods can be established in its own right, rather than set against (or positioned as lacking in relation to) standards applied to test the significance of quantitative social and scientific research.[25] To that end, Mitchell (1983, 192) defined the concept of 'case study' quite tightly, and certainly as very much more than an exercise in bounded description. He positions it, rather, as 'a detailed examination of an event (or series of related events) which the analyst believes exhibits (or exhibit) the operation of some identified theoretical principle'. Mitchell's main interest was in the possibility to use such material to generalise, not by analogy with statistical inference (which would imply standard questions administered to random samples), but by invoking a logical inference in which 'the validity of the extrapolation depends not on the typicality or representativeness of the case but upon the cogency of the theoretical reasoning' (p. 207). His point is that what happens in one case study may (probably will) be unique; but that does not mean that it will not allow general principles about particular social phenomena to be drawn out.

Logical inference is a serious undertaking which demands intensive knowledge of the context from which case materials are drawn. Its value for Clyde was that 'it forced one to appreciate the complexity of behaviour of people even when operating within, say, the framework of a lineage system' (Mitchell, 1986a, 17). So, case study research is integral to, and inseparable from, the situational approach that is more particularly seen as a hallmark of the Manchester school.

'The starting point in situational analysis', for Mitchell (1987, 8), 'is the assumption that social behaviour exists as a vastly complex set of human activities and interactions about which any one observer can appreciate only a limited part.' Characteristically, in developing this idea, a great many of the most pertinent ideas were exchanged and sharpened up in an exchange of letters. A letter from Clyde to Max Gluckman on 2.11.1948 following the death the previous year of American sociologist W. I. Thomas remarks: 'He is the person that I get the situational approach from and it is an approach which I think holds quite a lot of answers to our difficulties.' He was especially engaged by Thomas' interest in 'defining the situation', a conversation he took up with Barnes in correspondence early the following year (e.g. Barnes to Mitchell 20.3.1949). It retained his fascination through to the conclusion of his last book: 'The importance of this idea was that it located the reality of norms and customs in the perceptions of the actors in a social situation' (Mitchell,

---

[25] This is an interesting take on the scientific aims of the RLI: the 'laboratory in the field' established its own rules of the game for securing generalisations from ethnographic data that had their own validity.

1987, 289). This is a further reminder of the lasting influence the early American sociologists, especially those based in Chicago, had on the Manchester School. It is a signal too that while it is easy to attribute a set of ideas to a single person—Gluckman, for example, is generally credited, not least by Mitchell himself, as the originator of the situational approach developed at the RLI, and his idea, in turn, was much-influenced by Evans-Pritchard (Kapferer, 1987b)—the truth about scholarly ideas is that they arise in a community of interest.

To epitomise the situational perspective he advocated, Mitchell often referred—even in his later years—to Gluckman's (1940) essay on the opening ceremony for a bridge in 'Zululand'. In the mid-1950s he urged Gluckman to reprint the paper 'because I feel there is a certain freshness in the approach which I think you will never be able to capture again with this material' (2.11.1956). Mitchell wrote an introduction to the reprinted paper which Gluckman found 'not only flattering, but also most charming—it touched me deeply' (28.5.1957). Mitchell went on, however, to publish a paper that, for some, would eclipse this classic, and would in its turn become what Kapferer (2005, 101) describes as 'one of the best examples of the situational approach'. It is an in-depth study of one set of enactments of the then-widely performed Kalela dance. The impetus this gave to the qualitative research tradition in the RLI was noted earlier, and its substantive significance is considered later. Epistemologically, however, this thoroughgoing case study is at the heart of a research tradition that 'loses sight neither of the complexities of social life through time nor the importance of theorizing these' (Evans and Hendelman, 2006, ix). It is an important precursor of what would later be described as an anthropology of generic moments (Meinert and Kapferer, 2015; Kapferer, 2010).

There is a sense in which advancing the case for situational sociology could be seen as Mitchell's core project. The first chapter of his last book is an extended, thirty-three-page, essay on the topic. It is a theme he returned to time and again to argue not just for the practice but also for the absolute necessity of 'the intellectual isolation of a set of events from the wider context in which they occur in order to facilitate a logically coherent analysis' (Mitchell, 1987, 7). That is, of course, a contestable position, especially in the light of more recent innovations in participatory research, but its potential for making sense of complexity, and especially for understanding that analytical concepts (such as 'class struggle') are not necessarily recognisable in everyday life, has endured. As Kapferer (1987, x) puts it in his forward to the book: it is 'a method whereby the meanings in use can be systematically unravelled, their perceptual texture peeled away, and the social processes which generated them examined concretely'. Most importantly, Mitchell's situational analysis embraced both 'a practice of structure' and 'a structure of practice' (p. viii); it recognised that a prevailing political-economic order can be unsettled by actors who have agency and creativity, even if neither the potential nor the limitations of that are immediately obvious in the lived experience of daily life.

It is easy to argue (and indeed has been argued) that the situational perspective lacks critical, structural edge, but it is hard to find a basis for this in a close reading of Mitchell's work. From very early days, Mitchell spoke and wrote of the distinction between, and interleaving of, structural, categorical and personal relations (e.g. his letter to Epstein dated 12.2.1958) and, as he himself points out (Mitchell, 1987, 313), a situational perspective is impossible without reference to, and understanding of, a wider structural setting. So what Mitchell's project achieves—with its insistence on tackling the naivete of some styles of qualitative research—is certainly not reductionist. In truth, it offers a radical departure in anthropological reasoning; a way of organising and interpreting social data that Max Gluckman among others described as key for the next generation.

Linked in

'The founder, if anyone, of social network analysis'[26]

Clyde Mitchell was a central figure among a group of scholars who, during the 1950s, were dissatisfied with anthropological functionalism, wary of the turn to structuralism, unhappy with institutionalism, and deeply interested in the articulation of micro-social processes with the political-economy of urbanisation. Mitchell was particularly concerned with a disconnect between theoretical expectations about structural change, on the one hand, and the fruits of ethnographic observations on the other. This drove his search for alternative—or more properly complementary—frameworks to account for the extent to which, under colonialism and industrialisation, traditional institutions were breaking down, while newer ones struggled to establish themselves. The case study approach, with its emphasis on complexity, was a step in the right direction, but Mitchell soon realised that he 'needed some other method of formal analysis to understand what was going on in a systematic way' (Mitchell, 1986a, 17).

That 'other method' had to do with wresting order from the character, form and content of social networks. 'It was', observed Mitchell, speaking in 1990 about his fascination with the concept, 'the minutiae … people doing things in relation to one another which fascinated me.' The process-orientated concept of a web, mesh or network of social relations was attractive from the start. It probably has its origins in 1930s psychology, or even earlier (Freeman, 2004), and the broad idea quickly found

---

[26] Discussing Mitchell's influence by telephone Barry Wellman, then co-Director of Toronto University's NetLab (http://groups.chass.utoronto.ca/netlab/barry-wellman/) identified Mitchell as '*the* founder, if anyone, of social network analysis' (pers. comm. 31.3.2016).

its way into a wider literature during the decade that followed. Mitchell's côterie, however, were the first to use networks conceptually and analytically in the social sciences more broadly, and they were publishing on it at a time when few others were.

Barnes (1954) is usually credited with the first anthropological use of networks as more than metaphorical—as both a conceptual and an analytical tool. Mitchell (1969, 4) himself drew a distinction between earlier studies informed by formal question-naires, and Barnes' interest in working with networks 'based predominantly upon participant observation'. These early experiments were nevertheless part and parcel of the collective that was the Manchester School. That is what helped Elizabeth Bott (1957) reshape her research on marital relations in London into what Mitchell (1990, in interview) regards as the first publication in which the idea of network was used substantively as an analytical tool to explain behaviour.

Thinking with networks offered a way to lay bare the array of linkages—the flows of information and ideas, of goods and services, of beliefs, values and expectations, of power and influence—that underpin, indeed help realise, the structures of social life; structures which may or may not fit within conventional abstractions such as norms, institutions, class or ethnic divides. The appeal of this is apparent in Mitchell's own earliest writings. In a letter to Epstein (12.2.1958), for example, he talks of social rela-tionships being ordered in three kinds of ways 'depending on the intimacy or face-to-face contact required of them': these are—categorical 'where the contact is superficial and people react to symbols or uniforms'; 'structural' 'whereby people interact consist-ently within an institutional framework'; and 'network type relations' which applied to the more personal relations of kinship and friendship which 'are unique for each person and ramify across the community'. By the end of his inaugural lecture at UCRN Mitchell (1960, 30) had arrived at a conception of societies as 'complex retic-ulations of social relationships in which people are linked and cross-linked by numer-ous ties and bonds', whose contents and characteristics were key to understanding the conflicts and continuities of plural societies.

It is hardly surprising that when, during the mid-1960s, Mitchell convened a field-work seminar (continuing a longstanding tradition) for a new generation of urban anthropologists at the UCRN, networks were high on the agenda. The result was an edited collection (Mitchell, 1969) that one contemporary reviewer regards as 'the first major work to explore systematically the utility of network analysis of sociological field materials' (Aronson, 1972, 476), and another describes as 'a pioneering work of theoretical significance to social anthropology in any ethnographic context' (Gulliver, 1971). It includes an editorial introduction that Carrigan and Scott (2011) recognise to be 'one of the earliest summaries of a formal social networks methodology'. This lengthy essay sets out the concept and use of social networks and puts flesh on the bones of morphological descriptors like anchorage and reachability, and of interactional features like content and durability. In subsequent years, as well as taking on the associate editorship of the journal *Social Networks* (launched in 1978), Mitchell made numerous interventions in this interdisciplinary paradigm shift, laying the foundations of what would become a new anthropology of complex systems.

As might be expected, Clyde warmly embraced the quantitative turn that some of this literature took, often writing his own computer programs, and securing research council grants to facilitate this.[27] However, he was also wary of a growing disparity between 'the underlying assumptions and therefore the characteristics of networks taken to be significant by those interested in network analysis algorithms' on the one hand, and matters of concern to 'those interested in substantive issues' on the other (Mitchell, 1979, 438). Although he ventured at least one essay on the untapped potential of key techniques for which data in appropriate formats had yet to be collected, more usually he was worried that innovations in the numerical were outstripping both theoretical and substantive advances, and the fieldwork required to operationalise them (Mitchell, 1974, 279). He thus used a keynote lecture in the USA (Mitchell, 1986a) to insist on the merits of fieldwork—of securing qualitative, ethnographic data—in network research, arguing that while formal analytical procedures may be essential, it is the quality of the observational data driving them that is key. The real objective of such work was, he urged, to illuminate social life not push the boundaries of statistical or mathematical technique. That, he believed, required analysts not only to 'draw on more extensive information about the people involved' but also to become familiar with 'the overall social context in which these people happen to be located' (Mitchell, 1986b, 91).

That is probably what prompted Kapferer (2005, 112) to recognise that a key merit in Mitchell's approach to network analysis was 'to attend to individual agency without losing the significance of larger structural forces'. It was also a way to explore the impact of large-scale social processes without losing their connection with lived experiences. It could indeed be said that Mitchell's aim in invoking the concept of networks was to explore the ongoing realisation of the social, of humanity itself; and this, as Kapferer (2014b) recognised much later, is one of a number of links and complementarities between what he describes as 'Mitchellian' and 'Latourian' notions of networks. There are, to be sure, gaps that neither of them fill: Kapferer talks about values, and Strathern (1996) about lengths, cuts and stopping points; the literature has moved on. Yet, it might still be said that Mitchell's take on performativity was prescient of Latour's, and that it is Mitchell who spearheaded the approach which, in Boissevain's (1979, 392) words, 'opened a door to permit the entry of interacting

---

[27] One of the doctoral students funded in this way, Martin Everett, became co-founder in 1977 and President of the International Network for Social Network Analysis (INSNA).

people engaged in actions that could alter and manipulate the institutions in which they participated'.

It is not surprising in light of all this that, in 1986, Mitchell received the Simmel Award for major advances and achievements in the study of social networks; it may indeed have been the flourishing of this strand of work that finally (and belatedly) sealed his election in 1990 as a Fellow of the British Academy. There is, however, something of a discontinuity running through the world of networks. On the one hand, Clyde's books and articles on networks account for by far the majority of his citations.[28] As Hannerz (1980, 181) observed nearly forty years ago, Mitchell's approach to networks probably inspired 'the most extensive and widely applicable framework we have for the study of social relations'; morphological and interactional qualities together providing 'an idea of what is potentially knowable and what would be needed for something approaching completeness in the description of relationships'. On the other hand, given the wide-ranging contemporary impact of his ideas, and their resonance with the cutting edge of post-social science, Hannerz has more recently observed that 'as network analysis has spread in the social sciences, the foundational work of Clyde and his colleagues is seldom given the recognition it deserves' (pers. comm., 25.8.2014).

Where this oversight occurs, it partly reflects the massive growth of the field in recent years and its appeal to very many different disciplines, each with their own histories and traditions. It also reflects the enormous potential of the idea, its rapid spread in popularity,[29] and a certain disciplinary 'stickiness' in some areas. It may also reflect the fact that few contemporary commentators are either as generous as Kapferer who, when billed as 'one of the founders of social network analysis', used that keynote specifically to describe a movement inspired 'most notably by Clyde Mitchell', or as vocal as Barry Wellman, who not only featured Clyde's influence in his later works (Rainie and Wellman, 2012; Wellman and Berkowitz, 1988) but identified Mitchell as '*the* founder, if anyone, of social network analysis' (pers. comm. 31.3.2016), who 'did more than any other person to put network analysis on the map (Wellman, Ties and Bonds, n.d., 13).

Certainly in his later years Clyde was most in demand for this aspect of his work and was, thanks to his third wife, Jean, able to travel and teach on it in retirement

[28] Alan and Don Mitchell estimate that 75 per cent of Clyde's citations and licensing (ALCS) fees are accounted for by networks.
[29] Rogers and Vertovec (1995), for example, introducing a collection of essays assembled essentially as a festchrift for Clyde, identify four ways in which the idea could transform even one field of urban studies: documenting the rural-urban spectrum empirically; exploring the interleaving of the social with the spatial; charting the flow of information and resources; and capturing the agency involved in social change.

despite various challenges to his health.[30] As time went on, then, networks were what tied Clyde most explicitly into the ongoing international, interdisciplinary and intellectual adventure that had been his life's work. Viewed in the round, it is the positioning of networks as an analytical tool that is arguably the most influential of his intellectual legacies. It is fitting, then, that the UK's world-leading centre for social network analysis is based at Manchester, rooted in the work of the Manchester School and 'named after and dedicated to Clyde, in memory of his foundational role for the development of social network analysis'.[31]

Substantive challenge
'the best anthropologist of the new generation'[32]

From his earliest work at the RLI to his final few publications, Clyde Mitchell was pre-occupied with understanding the political-economy and cultural politics of African urbanisation. This forced him to think about the drivers of urban-industrialism, the residualisation of rural life, and the processes of labour migration that linked the two.[33] The context was time- and space-specific and his substantive project was, at heart, about getting to grips with the lived experience of colonialism or, as he put it, of 'colonial social orders of different kinds' (Mitchell, 1987, 312). His spotlight fell on the process and practicalities of social change: the conflicts and alliances inspiring it, the networks and mobilities that channelled it, and the identities, beliefs and behaviours of those least able to control it. He thereby illuminated many substantive themes, often—albeit fortuitously—challenging the intellectual status quo.[34]

Initially, like his peers, Mitchell worked in a rural setting and was engaged in an intense study of a single 'tribe' or people.[35] His main substantive interest, after an

[30] Clyde lived for many years with diabetes.

[31] http://www.socialsciences.manchester.ac.uk/mitchell-centre/about-us/clyde-mitchell/.

[32] In an exchange of letters with Mitchell about the prospects of him moving to Manchester, Max Gluckman referred to the mix of 'intellectual quality' and 'sociological insight' that positioned Mitchell as 'the best anthropologist of the new generation' (14.7.1959).

[33] The details of Clyde's work on labour migration merit more space than this memoir allows; his early paper (Mitchell, 1959) on that theme has been described as 'a classic contribution to which all subsequent scholars of African migration have been indebted' (Cohen, 1990, 609).

[34] Mitchell was not drawn to scholarly combat; quite the opposite, as he wrote to Max Gluckman in the late 1950s: 'one wants to seek happiness and contentment and peace with life and fly in the face of ambition doing it' (letter to MG 7.7.1959).

[35] In the third printing of his first book, Mitchell substituted the appellation 'Malawian People' for 'Nyasaland Tribe' in the subtitle both to reflect the creation of the independent state of Malawi in 1964 and to accommodate the fact that the label 'tribe' had taken on 'social and political connotations I did not imply when the book was first published' (Mitchell, 1956a: 1971 reprint, x). In this vein I have also,

early fascination with kinship[36] and a tactical eschewal of witchcraft, was in social stratification.[37] He regarded the Yao Villages that were the subject of his doctoral project as internally differentiated material and social structures; concentrations of huts occupied by people 'who recognise their social identity against other groups' (p. 3). He located each such assemblage as 'a unit in a larger field of political relations' (p. 2), shaped by the imposition of a colonial administration. Amid the tension between these scales or orders he identifies myriad struggles for recognition. He documents, for example, the changing character of the 'Chiefdoms', the jostling for position (or rank) of Headmen, the cross-cutting effects of kinship and clanship, and the complex confrontations of matrilinearity, uxurilocality[38] and patriarchy occasioned by the catastrophe that colonial rule (and some earlier dislocations) had inflicted on Malawian rural life.

In this way, *The Yao Village* posed a challenge to grand theories of the exploitation of labour by capital; not because such exploitation was of marginal interest, but because, for Mitchell, demonstrably in the empirical world so much more was implied by, and required to appreciate, the impacts of colonialism. This drew him not only to scrutinise the social trappings of production and consumption but also to embrace the struggle to control symbolic as well as material rewards. Even viewed from the rural edge of what Mitchell would eventually cast as a process of urban change, the messiness of the real world drew him to regard prestige or status as a crucial modality through which the contradictions of colonialism were lived.

In this, he nodded towards Max Weber,[39] for whom the acquisition of status has to do with struggles over life chances and resources that are occasioned or mediated by 'a positive or negative social estimation of honour' (Weber, 1968, 187). The idea of status fascinated Mitchell because it enabled him to engage with the heterogeneity of African societies, attending to the complexities of a political-economy held together by *multiple* oppositions and confrontations, including a 'competition for various symbols of prestige' (Mitchell, 1956a, 76). This possibility that the social and political structures of colonial societies were powerfully expressed through status is the Ariadne's thread linking Mitchell's DPhil thesis to his wider lexicon. It runs from an early much laboured-over paper on occupational prestige in the late 1950s (Mitchell

---

except in direct quotations, tended to use alternative labels—village, ethnic, kin-group and so on—for Mitchell's references to subjectively understood communities of descent in publications from that time.

[36] A topic that Max Gluckman persuaded him to set aside in the late 1940s.

[37] See, for example, his letter to Epstein on 15.1.1956.

[38] Systems in which a married couple resides with or near the wife's parents.

[39] Clyde never cited Weber's work, though he talked about his ideas and was interested in Schutz's elaboration of them (as well as Simmel's input to them); the point here is that Mitchell was aligned with a body of thought that recognised the importance of a variety of subjectivities as the basis or framework for action.

and Epstein, 1959) to his final full paper, which in the mid-1990s revisited the ordering of a wider range of symbolic markers (Mitchell, 1994).

There is, however, a second game-changing thesis embedded in the Malawi study. Already, in this, Mitchell was adopting what Norman Long might term a 'processional view of village politics' to explore the encounter of traditional and modern forms of political authority under colonialism. This encounter, to Mitchell's eye, testified not just to the resilience of traditional patterns of social life (itself a radical idea, in the face of colonial rule) but also to their vitality—to their creative adjustment to external shocks and influences.[40] The study thus offered important early insights into the truism that people are never bound into fixed categories but are linked into boundary-crossing networks that can draw them in different directions. In his 1959 inaugural lecture as Professor of African Studies at the University College of Rhodesia and Nyasaland in Salisbury, Mitchell positioned this manouverability as key to social change under colonialism (Mitchell, 1960, 30). He gave two examples of what that key could unlock, both highlighting the actancy of African people caught in the contradictions of colonialism.

First, he tells the story of an individual (William) who to all intents and purposes had long abandoned traditionalism in favour of the trappings—diet, dress, habits and appearance, at home and at work—of a Western-oriented townsman. Professionally, however, William was a *ng'anda*—a traditional medical practitioner whose success depended not on the rational application of scientific principles (though he was not averse to invoking these when required) but on the veracity of magic. Magic featured in his printed brochures, worked for his regular patients, and won him office in a professional association of *ng'andas*. In short, he readily operated in a setting in which 'quite disparate systems of belief may co-exist and be called into action in different social situations' (Mitchell, 1960, 19). William was inventive, and in that sense powerful, eliding the traditional with the modern to define his professional niche.

A second example picks up on a foundational interest of the RLI—the labour migrations required to support the Northern Rhodesian copper mines. This was the project of founding director Godfrey Wilson, who struggled with authority and bureaucracy to pursue it (Morrow, 2016, chapter 8). For many years, labour negotiations were funnelled through a system of consultation with village elders. This broke down over time, in favour of more conventional systems of wage bargaining. Wilson interpreted this as an aspect of 'detribalisation' and lamented the loss of cultural

---

[40] The novelty of this is signalled in a contemporary review by Mary Douglas (1957); in later years (the early 1970s) she went further, expressing considerable admiration for Mitchell's work and explicitly attributing the processual turn in the study of African local politics to *The Yao Village* (Richard Fardon, commenting on a lecture he attended in 1972–3, pers. comm. 31.7.2018).

heritage it represented. Mitchell, however, argued that the shift was more complex, and was not entirely (or even) about the proletarianisation of Africans who had severed their rural ties. In fact, Mitchell's account shows that the mineworkers were able actively to embrace modernity as industrial employees without sacrificing more traditional (ethnic) relationships and (village-specific) orientations in other areas of their lives. That is, two seemingly intermeshed spheres—one rooted in rural life, the other a route to urban industrialism—flourished without either precluding, much less subsuming, the other.

These examples offer one illustration of how traditional identities dovetailed with the world of work through a period of political and economic upheaval. Both question the idea that the colonial order inspired a steady process of 'detribalisation', and in this they enlarge on the findings of Mitchell's earlier more widely cited study of the Kalela Dance (Mitchell, 1956b). This foundational piece is, however, the touchstone for myriad other innovative theses.

In an era when *urban* anthropology was at best in its infancy, at worst marginal to the discipline, the Kalela Dance presaged the comprehensive urban research programme that the RLI embraced under Mitchell's directorship. That programme drew attention to the lived experience of crisis and change 'at a time in the history of anthropology when such topics were more an afterthought than the major focus of interest' (Kapferer, 2006, 86). It also recognised, from the start, that there was little value in essentialising towns or cities; that the focus should not be on what Mitchell (1966, 44) called 'historic change' as labour migrants adapt their behaviours to immutable urban institutions, but rather on 'situational change' effected through urban encounter as 'new institutions and patterns develop out of old'. *The Kalela Dance* also established Mitchell as a pioneer in the anthropology of ethnicity—a term he favoured as time went on to refer to people's affinity with (in Max Weber's terms) a 'subjectively believed community of descent' (Weber, 1968, 309).

Although, as noted earlier, Mitchell was indebted to Weber for his interest in the status order, he had a different view about how ethnicity—as a particular realisation of the distribution of power—fitted into this. While Weber regarded ethnicity as a very specific, somewhat irrational and probably transient, element of the status order, Mitchell positioned it more centrally. He recognised it to be as powerful and enduring a force as occupational prestige, and a crucial mediator of social relations in public life. In this, he was influenced by the Urban Sociology of post-depression USA, which set the scene for a round of empirical urban research sensitive to markers of difference other than class (Hannerz, 1980). In the US context these cleavages were generally labelled race or ethnicity, the first applying to African-Americans, the second to European immigrants. Both were obstinate in the face of expectations around integration and assimilation. This resilience might have shaped Clyde's thinking as he approached the Kalela Dance, but by the time the work was complete, he had laid the foundations of a much more radical theory of society.

Mitchell used the Kalela dance—enacted before a crowd of onlookers by Bisa labour migrants in the suburbs of Luanshya—as a lens through which to view the structure of social relationships (the 'whole social fabric') among Africans on the Copperbelt. As an exercise in case and situation analysis, a first important observation was that its location, its segregated setting, and other features of its performance—that it was limited to Sundays and holidays in the absence of European officials, drew large crowds because the drums reached easily across a swathe of densely packed municipal housing, and so on—testified to the way *all* social relations in the Copperbelt were powerfully framed by colonialism; by 'the general system of Black-White relationships in Northern Rhodesia' (Mitchell, 1956b, 1).

Drawn to the Kalela partly because of this, Mitchell found, nevertheless, that the dance was not primarily about those oppositions; indeed it did not directly reference them at all. That social life on the Copperbelt would be enmeshed by colonial regulation (laws enacted to circumscribe the lives of town-dwellers) and industrial transformation (economic imperatives that unsettled traditional social ties) was, both for Mitchell and for those performing the Kalela Dance, axiomatic. Dancers and author alike might have been enmeshed in the 'Othering' that a binary opposition between 'Western' and 'African' implies, but the Kalela Dance was, in practice and in performance, about very much more.

Mitchell's starting point, in fact, is a paradox: the Kalela Dance—by far the most popular traditional dance enacted across the Copperbelt—was ostensibly about ethnic distinction (Bisa identity), yet it eschewed all the trappings of a conventional 'tribal' dance. To be sure, it gathered dancers—primarily young unskilled male workers—from a variety of regional backgrounds, but they did not disrupt the world of colonial urbanism with exotic costumery, flamboyant gesture or rural reference. On the contrary, the team of nineteen youths was dressed in 'well-pressed grey slacks, neat singlets and well-polished shoes', and mounted a performance that was surprisingly unobtrusive, 'almost prosaic'. It took the form of a shuffle rather than a display of athleticism or authenticism, made no reference to traditional themes, was far from ostentatious and included none of the key roles (e.g. village headman, or elders) that a Bisa village might contain. Rather it revolved around a committee with a chairman, secretaries, treasurers and other officials, who 'conduct their business on the same lines as any European association does'. It seemed wholly 'ethnic' in spirit yet was strikingly 'modern' in look and feel. For Mitchell, therefore, the defining qualities of the Kalela were 'drawn from an urban existence'—an act of self-definition that was in and of a space that many believed to be structured specifically to submerge traditional identities rooted in villages, kin and clan.

Eager to account for this and attentive to every nuance of lived experience, Mitchell turned to the songs. Sung in Bemba using an urban lingua franca that would have been lost on an outsider, they were full of witty, topical verses 'composed in towns for the amusement of people in towns'. In performance the songs served primarily to define and underline the unity of one ethnic group, the Bisa, and set it against a heterogeneity of others, but there was nothing to suggest that village ties and the identities rooted in them were homogenised, suppressed, dissolved or absorbed by the transformations of colonial-industrial life. Rather key points of commonality and distinction were underlined through the use of Bisa self-praise (a method of identification), and by the construction of stereotypes to depict and categorise 'rival' groups, mainly through the vehicle of ridicule. In fact, the whole dance, as Mitchell recognised, could be cast as a kind of 'joking relationship'.[41] It thus testified to the veracity and diversity of ethnic affiliation, yet was a parody of tradition rather than a means of enacting or preserving it.

This, in a sense, is what resolved the paradox. The Kalela was neither about 'detribalisation' nor was it a manifestation of traditionalism *sensu stricto*. It was positioned somewhere between the two. It neither facilitated the assimilation of labour migrants into a colonial urban order, nor transplanted 'a complete tribal system' (of kinship, clanship or village membership) into the city. The categories used to organise lived experience—in a setting where the economic order was broadly individualising—could reasonably be described as ethnic or 'tribal', but they were not primordial or 'essential'. In the suburbs of Luanshya, where labour relations were not so structured as around the mines, the message the Kalela delivered was about the *creation of something new*.

As Mitchell put it himself, 'the set of relationships among a group of tribesmen in their rural home is something very different from the set of relationships among the same group when they are transposed to an urban area' (Mitchell, 1956b, 44). Labour migrants' social lives were structured through colonial-industrialism, but with inventiveness and imagination African peoples resisted the fracturing of identity—the anomie or alienation—this might imply. Performing (and witnessing) the Kalela thus offered both incumbents and audiences a way to understand self and categorise others amid the multiple and mutable social orders of the city. In that sense, the dance might reasonably be cast as a political resource, or at least as a point of resistance against the idea that heterogeneity was on the wane and that entire social structures would yield to the values and organisational requirements of colonial industrialism.

---

[41] A new generation of urban anthropologists would show more explicitly how 'joking relationships' masqueraded for (but by no means detracted from) the dynamic interplay of politics with culture (e.g. Cohen 1993).

Certainly Bisa people, like others inhabiting a new urban order, sought to, and did, shape their own way of life even under the conditions of high colonialism that Mitchell positioned at the heart of his analysis.

It was probably insights such as this—and Clyde spent a great deal of time labouring over them—that secured him the award of the Rivers Memorial Medal by the Royal Anthropological Institute in 1960.[42] He continued to develop the 'performativity' thesis (though he would never have called it that) across a quarter century or more, recognising the absolute irreducibility of ethnicity to traditional institutional or structural forms (kinship, class and so on) and using his last substantive writings explicitly to conceptualise its emanant qualities, casting ethnicity as 'not a pervasive element in social relationships but one which emerges in particular social situations' (Mitchell, 1987, 241).

There are two other themes from the Kalela that Mitchell took up in later years. First, for a work so attentive to process and a thesis so wedded to futures still-to-be-made, the Kalela Dance makes surprisingly frequent reference to what might be called a 'categorical imperative'. Although Mitchell roundly resisted the formal classification of social structures and their gathering into bounded functional wholes, he did recognise that social life is shot through with alliances and oppositions which encourage social life to settle out into recognisable if mutable shapes. Ethnicity is a case in point, arising out of what Mitchell thought of as 'the alignments and interests of the actors in specified situations in which [ethnic] cues and signs *take on* meanings and are used to define the stances that actors adopt to one another in that interaction' (Mitchell, 1987, 241).

In urbanising Africa, for example, Mitchell observed that many lines of cleavage, such as clanship, which might have been important in the villages, were downplayed in favour of visually recognisable characteristics, mainly for pragmatic reasons: 'a way of simplifying or codifying behaviour in otherwise 'unstructured' situations' (Mitchell, 1966, 53). A whole section of *The Kalela Dance* is devoted to this point. Describing the dilemma facing a stream of labour migrants, Mitchell wrote 'their own ethnic distinctiveness which they took for granted in the rural areas is immediately thrown into relief by the multiplicity of tribes with whom they are cast into associations. Its importance to them is thus exaggerated and it becomes the basis on which they interact with all strangers.'

Second, while this kind of boundary-building might, through the Kalela Dance, have been played out with jocular nuance, in essence it is a method of confrontation.

---

[42] Clyde was the 40th recipient of the Rivers Medal, which was first awarded in 1924; among anthropologists associated with the RLI he was preceded in winning this honour by Audrey Richards, Monica Wilson, Max Gluckman and John Barnes, and succeeded by Victor Turner and Elizabeth Colson.

Mitchell's analysis of the Kalela Dance is one nudge in a direction—inspired not least by the work of Georg Simmel—that inclined him very distinctly towards a conflict theory of society. He tilted at this in his 1959 inaugural lecture at UCRN observing that consensus exists 'only among those people who happen to be acting jointly in one particular situation, in other circumstances there may well be conflicting valuations and hence dissent among the same people' (Mitchell, 1960, 30). As his ideas developed, he was increasingly conscious of how readily shared cues could turn into divisive markers; that social life was structured through oppositions as well as alliances; and that networking could be as much about enacting difference as building consensus. This set him apart from prevailing (acculturationist, assimilationist and integrationist) views of African urbanisation and positioned the status order that preoccupied him as just one realisation of an irresolvably uneven distribution of power in urban settings shaped by colonial rule.

Finally, it is worth noting that although Mitchell's empirical eye inhabited a space outside categories like capital, labour and class, he readily acknowledged their veracity as structuring principles. He did not write extensively about them, but he did engage with them. He recognised, for example, the complexities of articulating the structures that constrain lived experience (the impact of urban industralism in a colonial setting, for example) with the agency he observed in the field (the capacity of central African people to shape their lives and futures). He also understood the significance of a disconnect between lay meanings and experiences—ideas that people could articulate and engage with—and the operation of wider, structural, forces which might not be accessible to, or appreciated within, the conduct of everyday life. This is as far in the direction of 'grand theory' that he ventured, but he did take some steps to formalise his position.

In a mid-1970s paper on perceptions of ethnicity and ethnic behaviour, Mitchell (1974, 2) voiced a concern that analysts tend to use ethnicity 'either as a structural category, that is, as a general principle that illuminates the behaviour of persons in specified social situations', or 'as a cultural phenomenon, that is, as a set of attitudes, beliefs and stereotypes that people hold about persons identified by some appropriate 'ethnic' label'. The elision is common today, and Mitchell's worry was that it prevented the relationship between these two sets of ideas being properly conceptualised, understood or acted on (whether by politics, policy, or publics).

Addressing this, Mitchell collated a range of material from the RLI projects to illustrate, graphically and quantitatively (by way of an hierarchical cluster analysis), the four 'levels of abstraction' that he felt could account for the different ways that actors and analysts might conceive of the world. It was a slightly unwieldy formulation,[43] but

---

[43] It differentiated (broadly speaking) between, first, commonsense perceptions of cues embedded in

his typically painstaking attention to detail does explain why 'structural' and 'interpretative' approaches to the same data might lead analysts to different, seemingly irreconcilable, conclusions. Later he simplified the argument, identifying two orders of data (Mitchell, 1987, 243): 'The first relates to the way in which the actors see the situation' (and thus how they account for and rationalise what they think and do); 'The second relates to the abstract structural or morphological characteristics of the settings which derive from the theoretical perspectives adopted by the analyst' (and which the average actor is unlikely routinely to engage with, and may never easily relate to).

There are many ways of unpacking this but the important point is that Mitchell embraced the challenge that the critical theorists were starting to pose, and sought to locate his own work within that frame. The labels 'first' and 'second' when referring to 'orders' of data are, nevertheless, to my eye significant. Whatever else they achieve, these essays surely are Mitchell's way of signalling that while it is essential to understand how colonialism defined the parameters of African urbanism, analysts could and should also trace out and valorise the agency of subjugated peoples as they struggle to create and shape their lives and futures. That conviction was the heart of Mitchell's own life's work.

The personal and the political
'a man of fathomless courage'[44]

Clyde Mitchell was, as noted above, an early recruit to the Rhodes-Livingstone Institute where he spent the first decade of his academic career. The period (the mid-1940s to mid-1950s), the place ('Rhodesia'), and the name of the institution, all position him at the lip of British imperialism. A left-leaning liberal, Clyde's politics were lived rather than written, but his work and his life were powerfully sculpted by the struggles of the time.

The idea for the RLI was mooted by the then-Governor of Northern Rhodesia, Hubert Winthrop Young, who, in the wake of a mineworkers' strike, and with the world economy in recession, recognised that the pace of urban-industrial change in the Copperbelt had outstripped the administration's ability to handle it. An Institute tasked to secure a systematic, independent, anthropologically informed, understand-

---

everyday life, and behaviours associated with these cues, and second, analysts' constructs of cultural variabililty (based on common sense perceptions) and analysts' interpretation of structural differentiation (based on observed behaviours).

[44] In a tribute written for his memorial service, Kapferer (1996) observes that 'Clyde was a thoroughly tolerant man and a man of fathomless courage'.

ing of Africa and its people was the response. It was viewed with suspicion from the outset by a variety of constituencies, not least for its engagement with social change and its problem-solving brief (Morrow, 2016). Even its name tapped into a more complex mix of local sentiments in the run up to the Rhodes Jubilee and Livingstone Centenary than might be imagined (Schumaker, 2001). In its later years the Institute might, for a time, have become a front for government interests but in the early days it operated with a distinctly radical edge.

Every early Director insisted on the political and commercial independence of the Institute's research agenda;[45] all were resistant to the racially exclusionary appointment policies favoured by its Trustees; without exception they assembled teams that were self-consciously pro-African and, for the most part, they were not afraid to act accordingly. Wilson, for example, resigned when the Trustees tried to limit fieldwork if it involved mixing with, and visiting the homes of, African mineworkers: 'it is said you have been sitting on a box with a native on a chair' (cited in Morrow, 2016, 190).[46] His successor, Max Gluckman, favoured the same anti-racist, anti-colonialist tradition, to the disappointment of the provincial commissioners (Musambachime, 1993). Elizabeth Colson, who followed, sought funds for African researchers, though her tenure was short.[47]

When Mitchell took over, the scene was set fully to involve properly paid and trained African researchers in both quantitative and qualitative research. Mitchell was keen for African scholars to advance and to publish, and arguably his directorship marked 'the first time in the history of anthropology that a large number of indigenous researchers worked together for a lengthy period of time doing studies of their own communities and society' (Shumaker, 2001, 152). That their main involvement initially was in the administration of surveys is an important caveat (Richard Werbner, pers. comm. 31.7.2018). However, Shumaker goes on to trace the life paths and careers of some of these scholars, demonstrating their engagement in the co-production of postcolonial knowledges, and documenting their involvement in renewed debate about tribalism, nationalism, and indigenous identity in Zambia.

Recruitment practices were one element of a more sweeping trajectory. Not only did the RLI stand out in this period as one of the few non-racial institutions in the Federation (that was Shumaker's point, above), but by the early 1950s it had become, and was generally seen to be, 'the most politically critical branch of a discipline otherwise not especially noted for its radicalism' (Kapferer, 2014b, 148). At its zenith,

[45] Partly reflecting their confidence in social *scientific* (impartial, objective) inquiry.
[46] Wilson may equally have resigned because the Trustees objected to his pacifism.
[47] During her short Directorship, Colson was instrumental in relocating the RLI from Livingstone to Lusaka, but left for health reasons in 1951.

under Mitchell (who presided over its most productive period), the RLI had, far from acting as an agent of colonial rule, become thoroughly Africanised both by virtue of the mixed constituencies that shaped its fieldwork and 'through its adaptation to the landscape of Africa itself and to the material constraints and opportunities it found there' (Shumaker, 2001, 6-7). Its pragmatic, even anti-intellectual, edge was widely recognised and reflected in the pride its male members took in being dubbed 'the cloth cap boys' of academia (Epstein, in Yelvington, 1997).

Mitchell did not greatly enjoy the Directorship, shot through, as it was, with politics and bureaucracy. His tenure was correspondingly short. 'It is impossible' he wrote to Barnes 'to describe the inanities I have to commit as Director of this show' (22.11.1952); and two years later: 'Life out here is even more bloody than usual ... it is a long and dismal tale of an uphill struggle against obscurantism' (6.1.1954). He was particularly candid in his correspondence with Max Gluckman, with whom he shared the frustration and the stress of 'running a liberal research institute in an illiberal atmosphere' (JCM to MG, 9.2.1955). By June that year (1955), Mitchell was ready to leave. He and Gluckman were increasingly disaffected with the Institute, its governance and its productivity as an academic centre. Before long, their doubts about its direction, independence and critical edge were leading them to sever all remaining ties. 'The R.L.I. as we knew it', wrote Mitchell (17.6.57) 'no longer exists'; 'it seems quite clear to me' replied Gluckman two months later, 'that the RLI is going to become an adjunct to government' (8.8.1957). Deliberating at what point her own account of the work of the RLI should stop Schumaker (2001, 227) summed it up: 'One could end with Mitchell's resignation and use that endpoint to stress that academically minded anthropologists no longer controlled the Institute and its research agenda.'[48]

Political frustration did not, of course, ease with Mitchell's move to Salisbury (Harare) and the Chair at UCRN, where he was initially happy, maintaining the critical, problem-oriented spirit of the RLI despite duties that prevented him working on the Copperbelt materials.[49] One such duty was teaching, which was not his first love.[50] At the time, however, it was proving increasingly difficult for Africans to obtain higher

---

[48] Shumaker did not, in the end, conclude her analysis with Mitchell's move to Salisbury, partly because she felt his influence endured, partly because she was interested in the ongoing role of the RLI as a field centre, and mainly because she wanted to recognize the first appointment of an African director, Philip Nsugbe, in 1968.

[49] Werbner (1984, 161) identifies this emphasis on 'relevance of the problems to the people themselves' as a dominant strand of the Manchester School, writing in the preface to his own contribution that 'Clyde Mitchell, my fieldwork supervisor at the University College of Rhodesia and Nysaland, did his best to get me to appreciate the impact of state intervention on the people's lives—he urged me to study current social problems' (Werbner, 1991, vi).

[50] Though, ironically, he was always sought after and valued for his teaching, especially by his research students.

education, and Clyde saw the opportunity to change this by creating a learning environment that taught African Studies without objectifying African people. As he notes in interview with Russell Bernard, with the help of grants from the Ford Foundation he transformed a dominantly white degree programme into one with more balanced (50/50) participation.[51]

As an academic administrator his work was, nevertheless, increasingly compromised. Although he successfully attracted scholars like Kingsley Garbett and Jaap van Velsen (who extended the radical implications of some of his work) to join him as colleagues, together with PhD students such as Bruce Kapferer, David Boswell, Peter Harries-Jones and Richard Werbner—all resistant to the principle of white rule—his attempts to create opportunities for African scholars were often thwarted[52] and his bid to employ A. L. (Bill) Epstein was blocked.[53] When Epstein wrote on 10 February 1956 declaring that anyway he felt himself shrinking increasingly away from the field situation, Mitchell replied (28.2.56) 'I appreciate very keenly, of course, your concerns about staying in Africa. Who with any conscience has not had them?' These concerns quickly increased, and as the 1960s gathered pace the pressures became intolerable.

Among Mitchell's papers in the Bodleian library is a news clipping from the *Sunday Mail* of 13 September 1964. The headline is 'Smith's great gamble'.[54] It rules out 'one man, one vote' and promises instead to consult 'people who have made a lifetime study of African custom and African law' to find out how best to take into account the views of the African people. This explicit attempt by Ian Smith to hijack professional anthropology to legitimise his decision to disenfranchise black Africans was the last straw for Mitchell who (as he later wrote in response to a 1975 inquiry from UNESCO), as the senior anthropologist in the country at that time, could categorically state that: 'Mr. Smith had not consulted me or any of my colleagues' (letter to Mrs. O'Callaghan 2.5.1975). Within a week, Mitchell had assembled a group of scholars to argue publicly for the democratic rights of Africans. Their position, set out

[51] He took an number of initiatives in this respect, including sending a life changing letter to Gordon Chavunduka who, after working with Mitchell as a sociologist in Salisbury/Harare, studied for two degrees (at UCLA and Manchester University) and later became Vice Chancellor of the University of Zimbabwe (http://www.colonialrelic.com/biographies/dr-gordon-chavunduka/, accessed 1.8.2018).

[52] In a personal communication (31.7.2018) Richard Werbner has described how a potential African research assistant had to run for his life in the night, after leading an anti-government protest; Werbner himself later became a prohibited immigrant under the Smith regime.

[53] Epstein had tried to study the social and organisational life of migrant African labourers in the towns of the Copperbelt and was cast as pro-Union and subversive: he had, as Rew (1999) writes in his obituary, 'dared to act as an anthropologist in towns rather than in a rural location'.

[54] This refers to Ian Smith's bid for Rhodesian independence to prevent the transition from colonial rule, and a shift to full enfranchisement.

on page 1 of the 22 September 1964 edition of the *Guardian* was that 'No other method [than the right to vote] can give valid results'. 'We are', the group is quoted as saying, 'utterly opposed to the idea that there is something peculiar to Africans that makes it impossible to test their opinions by normal procedures.' For this they were roundly attacked by the government, with several signatories to the *Guardian* letter (including Mitchell's second wife, Hilary Flegg-Mitchell) apparently banned from re-entering the country.

Undeterred, Mitchell kept a close eye on the censoring of academic freedom, and in 1965 wrote another letter to the *Rhodesia Herald* complaining of ministerial inter-ference—in this case the removal of items from a reading list at the Teachers Training College. Elsewhere among Mitchell's papers—files he must have kept for years—is a list of Council members for the University College of Rhodesia and Nyasaland dated 30 March 1965; he has written at the bottom 'No African member of College Council since break-up of federation (1963)'. Speaking to Russell Barnard (1990) he tells of his growing outrage as the government populated the lay memberships of University committees with its own sympathisers, and of his fears for the future. In his initial response to the UN inquiry mentioned above, he describes this process as spanning the entire period 1957-65 in which 'there was a slow infiltration of people with Rhodesian Front sympathies into lay positions on the various administrative councils and they began to make their influence felt in many ways particularly in respect of the political activities of members of staff and students of the College' (letter to Mrs O'Callaghan, 14.3.1975).

In early December 1965, shortly after the declaration of UDI, Mitchell wrote to the Principal of the University setting out the principles of operation of an inde-pendent University. Independence rests, he argued, 'squarely on the freedom of the scholars who constitute it—staff and students alike—to be able to criticise current social, economic, political, religious, philosophical, ethical, scientific or any other type of thought'. This was impossible, he felt, 'where government is exercised by a minority whose justification to govern rests upon ideologies which cannot withstand the cold analysis of trained minds'. He then lists the ways in which the University could respond to maintain its independence. It is a lengthy, thoughtful and construct-ive letter; the reply from the then-principal is a single, platitudinous line. On 21 December 1965, Mitchell left Africa for the UK.

There is a scattering of materials in Mitchell's papers testifying to the extent to which he remained engaged in post-UDI politics, including letters from 1967 that suggest he had raised funds to meet the defence costs of African political detainees and prisoners. He was so steeped in all this that when in the mid-1970s he was approached by a UNESCO enquiry into how social scientists like him had seen their work in Rhodesia, it was only in the follow up correspondence that he was forced to make the blindingly obvious statement that underpinned his entire life's work: 'The major impact on African social structure was undoubtedly their military conquest by Europeans' (to Mrs O'Callaghan, 2.5.1975). The fact that he regarded this as self-evident—as the catastrophe at the heart of every anthropological inquiry or social study he engaged in—was not always appreciated.

For two decades, Mitchell's work had been located at the centre of a 'perfect (political) storm' whipped up by colonialism, dispossession, racism and segregationism. He saw these forces as central to the lived experience of everyday life, and he resisted such oppressions with every fibre of his being. He was devastated, therefore, when both his role and his work were roundly criticised by Bernard Magubane (1969, 1971), who cast anthropology in Africa as a handmaiden of colonialism. Mitchell's and Epstein's ethnographic work came under particular scrutiny, first for taking the colonial system for granted (i.e. assuming that its general characteristics were known) and second for dwelling on the trivial materialities of dance and fashion (symbols of 'acculturation') rather than on the fundamentals of oppression and inequality. More generally, the Copperbelt anthropologists were charged with ethnocentrism, bias and 'a pragmatic propagandisation of certain ideals in the guise of sociological analysis' (Magubane, 1971, 430).

There followed robust debate (with all positions represented in the twelve replies to the 1971 critique published by *Current Anthropology* (volume 12 (4)).[55] It was not resolved then (though it was much-debated by subsequent RLI directors) and is unlikely to be concluded now. In part, it was about a much wider post-colonial critique of traditional anthropology, which was quickly politicised and soon embraced geography, sociology and more. In part it reflects an enduring intellectual struggle between grand theory and small stories, between structure, agency and more. Either way it informed a new generation described by Shumaker (2001, 230) as 'largely non-African anthropologists and historians' who were involved 'in a territorial move for the displacement of British social anthropology from the African field'.

Whatever the wider ramifications of this exchange,[56] as a specifically political debate with Mitchell, Magubane's intervention, though thoroughly distressing, and unsettling (notwithstanding the fact that Clyde was well aware of his awkward

[55] Mitchell was not enamoured by the cut and thrust of the academic mainstream. Explaining in a letter to Max Gluckman (7.7.1959) why he could not move to Manchester at that time he wrote 'Heaven knows, I am insecure enough as it is in intellectual circles—to face up to hostility (as I am absolutely certain I shall have to) would knock me up completely.' Rightly or wrongly, he experienced Magubane's critique as a personal attack, all the more upsetting because his demonstrably critical opposition to the regime was not recognised (Kapferer, pers. comm. 24.7.2018).
[56] It is certainly the case, as Werbner (1984, 159) observed, that, for a variety of reasons, during the 1970s 'the great stream of fieldwork and fieldworkers, primarily in Zambia, dried up to a trickle, as did the stream of monographs'.

positionality), was less than convincing even in its own terms. A central concern that 'the colonial social order worked to limit every aspect of African life' (Magubane, 1971, 420) is one that Mitchell clearly shared; and the argument that more should have been done explicitly to conceptualise, document and resist that system will always be true. Mitchell was mortified by Magubane's tendency to leap from reasonable critique (e.g. 'there is no image of the colonial social structure') to sweeping conclusions (e.g. that implicitly, therefore, those anthropologists believed 'in the rightness of the white conquest of the African'). As a scholar, moreover, Mitchell could not agree that studies of ethnicity and social status could be reduced to the analysis of class.[57] He was concerned that Magubane misread his use of 'tribalism', criticising him for arguing that tribal values from rural areas were relevant in town when Clyde was suggesting the opposite, namely that tribalism in towns was, as Kapferer puts it, 'a radical construction within modernity' (pers. comm. 24.7.2018). Finally, Mitchell never accepted that 'taking for granted' the extent to which African urbanisation in the post war years was shaped by a colonial order—that is, actively positioning colonialism as the context or setting for a series of studies—amounted to condoning or supporting that regime.

Ironically, Mitchell himself felt that, during his time in Africa, his role as an anthropologist was justifiably viewed with suspicion—not because he was courting government, but because of the challenge his team posed to the regime by virtue of the fact that 'we were all supporting the blacks against the whites' (interview with Russell Bernard, 1990). To be sure, some—a lot—of his written work might reasonably be construed as apolitical, reflecting his interest in the scientific credibility of social research, and his attentiveness to small-scale social processes. But taken together, and as works of their time, his research and publications are distinctive for the extent to which they recognise and harness the agency of African subjects. As Schumaker (2001, 7) puts it: 'As terrible in its consequences as colonialism was ... [in this programme of research] colonial actors never exercised complete domination and colonial subjects never behaved solely as passive victims.'

On balance, it is hard to see how a close reading of Mitchell's lexicon as a whole, much less an assessment of his life 'in the round', could cast him or his scholarship as in any way uncritical of colonialism. Indeed, many regard his contribution as explicitly anti-colonial (see Brown, 1973; Hannerz, 1980, 157–62; Shumaker, 2001, 239–41). The cautionary tale this inspires is elegantly recounted by Jeffrey Prager (1982, 99). Charting the course of racisms and oppressions through time, Prager notes that what

---

[57] Nor did he alter a view expressed in his inaugural lecture at UCRN that anthropological teaching and intervention were important because 'it is a subject which deals in abstract terms with custom and belief, and these are perhaps the first aspects of African life to understand' (Mitchell, 1960, 6).

is radical and progressive is itself situated in time and place. To look back and recognise yesterday's mistake is not always to assume a position of strength tomorrow. Each generation, observes Prager, is inclined to label the work of their predecessors with phrases like 'Theirs was a racist reaction; ours enlightened'. Mitchell—undoubtedly radical, for his time enlightened, and always a modest, generous scholar—entirely avoided that conceit.[58]

Acknowledgements
Heartfelt thanks to Jean Mitchell for her warmth, generosity and patience, and for her permission to quote from Clyde's letters and papers. Thanks, too, to Don Mitchell for co-ordinating helpful feedback from the Mitchell family, and to Erica Flegg for our fleeting exchange. I am grateful to Tim and Peter Gluckman for permission to quote from Max Gluckman's unpublished letters to Clyde and for insightful comments on (and corrections to) the text.

Bruce Kapferer has an incomparable feel for Clyde's intellectual contribution. His published insights already eclipse most of what I have written, and his feedback has been invaluable; I greatly enjoyed our conversations and hope I have done them justice. Special thanks, too, to John Goldthorpe who opened a window onto Clyde's time in Oxford and at Nuffield College, and to Richard Werbner for a lively and constructive exchange.

Many other scholars responded to my request for information and conversation about Clyde's life, work and influence, and (where needed) gave permission for me to include their replies. They are: H. Russell Bernard, Craig Calhoun, Frank Critchley, Martin Everett, the late A. H. (Chelly) Halsey, Ulf Hannerz, Peter Jackson, Michael Keith, Sir James Mirrlees, Clive Payne, Ceri Peach, Alistair Rogers, and Barry and Bev Wellman. Among scholars who took on the full draft, or key sections thereof, in addition to some of those mentioned above, I am especially grateful to Felix Driver, Richard Fardon, Robert Gordon and Marilyn Strathern for their close reading and thoughtful comments. It is heartening to know that my own experience of Clyde as a kind, generous, self-effacing yet formidable scholar with a strong sense of justice is so widely shared, and to be reminded of his humour, his hobbies (he was a keen birdwatcher) and his love of a good curry.

I am indebted to the Bodleian Library for help in accessing relevant collections and in particular to Senior Archivist, Lucy McCann. Any errors or oversights are, of course, my own. I hope, given Clyde's own struggle to write up, that he would not be too alarmed—and might even be amused, in a frustrated kind of way—that this

---

[58] Many of his students will have notes and letters like those he wrote to Epstein (29.1.1951), about a lecture he is giving in Kitwe 'I have suggested that you might attend—if you want some light amusement'.

memoir is published so long after his death, and so long after even I (not the first person to take it on) had aimed to deliver it. As one of his many research students, I knew him well for a while, yet I am not sure that I ever properly thanked him for the extraordinary lengths he went to in order to support my career. Above all, I am grateful that Clyde shared with me, as he did with countless others, what his own friend and mentor Max Gluckman describes as 'a quality of imaginative adventurousness' (letter to JCM, 15.1.1951) that is undiminished by the passage of time.

Note on the author: Susan J. Smith is Mistress of Girton College, and Honorary Professor of Social and Economic Geography, at the University of Cambridge. She was elected a Fellow of the British Academy in 2008.

References

Aronson, D. (1972) 'Review of Mitchell (ed.) *Social Networks in Urban Situations*', *American Journal of Sociology*, 78: 476–8.

Barnes, J. A. (1954) 'Class and committee in a Norwegian island parish', *Human Relations,* 7: 39–58.

Bernard, H. R. (1990) Video Dialogues in Anthropology: Clyde Mitchell and H. Russell Bernard (recorded 19 July, held in the Human Studies Film Archive at the Smithsonian Institution). https://siris-archives.si.edu/ipac20/ipac.jsp?uri=full=3100001~!218883!0&term=#focus; and https://www.youtube.com/watch? reload=9&v=Q-zWvgUfOy4 (accessed 23 January 2019).

Boissevain, J. (1979) 'Network analysis: a reappraisal', *Current Anthropology*, 20: 392–4.

Bott, E. (1957) *Family and Social Network* (London).

Brown, R. (1973) 'Anthropology and colonial rule: Godfrey Wilson and the Rhodes-Livingstone Institute'. In T. Asad (ed.), *Anthropology and the Colonial Encounter* (New York), 173–98.

Carrington, P. J. and Scott, J. (2011) 'Introduction'. In P. J. Carrington and J. Scott (eds.), *The Sage Handbook of Social Network Analysis* (London), 1–8.

Cohen, A. (1993) *Masquerade Politics: Explorations in the Structure of Urban Cultural Movements* (Berkeley and Los Angeles, CA).

Cohen, R. (1990) 'Review of Zegeye and Ishemo, *Forced Labour Migration. Patterns of Movement within Africa*', *African Affairs*, 89: 609.

Colson, E. and Gluckman, M. (eds.) (1951) *The Seven Tribes of British Central Africa* (Manchester).

Douglas, M. (1957) 'Review of Mitchell, *The Yao Village*', *Africa,* 27: 290–2.

Evens, T. M. S. and Hendelman, D. (eds.) (2006) *The Manchester School. Practice and Ethnographic Praxis in Anthropology* (New York and Oxford).

Fallers, L. A. (1957) 'Review of Mitchell, *The Yao Village*', *American Anthropologist*, 59: 731–2.

Freeman, L. C. (2004) *The Development of Social Network Analysis: a Study in the Sociology of Science* (Vancouver, BC).

Gluckman, M. (1940) 'Analysis of a social situation in modern Zululand', *Bantu Studies*, 14: 1–30.

Gluckman, M. (1945) 'The seven year research plan of the Rhodes-Livingstone Institute', *Journal of the Rhodes-Livingstone Institute*, 4: 1–32.

Gluckman, M. (1946) 'Human laboratory across the Zambesi', *Libertas*, 6: 38–49.

Gluckman, M. (1959) 'Ethnographic data in British social anthropology', reprinted in T. M. S. Evens and D. Hendelman (eds.) (2006), *The Manchester School. Practice and Ethnographic Praxis in Anthropology* (New York and Oxford), 13–22.

Gordon, R. (2018) *The Enigma of Max Gluckman: the Ethnographic Life of a 'Luckyman' in Africa* (Lincoln, NE).

Gulliver, P. H. (1971) 'Review of Mitchell, (ed.) *Social Networks in Urban Situations*', *Bulletin of the School of Oriental and African Studies*, 34: 199.

Hannerz, U. (1980) *Exploring the City: Inquiries Toward an Urban Anthropology* (New York).

Hansen, K. T. (1988) 'Review of Mitchell (ed.), *Cities, Society and Social Perception*', *Journal of Southern African Studies*, 15: 116–18.

Holland, P. W. and Leinhardt, S. (eds.), *Perspectives on Social Network Research* (New York).

Kapferer, B. (1987a) 'Forward'. In J. C. Mitchell (ed.) *Cities, Society and Social Perception* (Oxford), v–xv.

Kapferer, B. (1987b) 'The anthropology of Max Gluckman', *Social Analysis. The International Journal of Social and Cultural Practice*, 22: 3–21.

Kapferer, B. (2005) 'Situations, crisis and the anthropology of the concrete', *Social Analysis. The International Journal of Social and Cultural Practice*, 49: 85–122.

Kapferer, B. (2010) 'Introduction'. In the event—toward an anthropology of generic moments', *Social Analysis. The International Journal of Social and Cultural Practice*, 54: 1–27.

Kapferer, B. (2014a) Mitchell and Latour: two approaches to networks. Presented to the conference *50 Years of Sociology at Manchester* (Mitchell Centre, Manchester, October). https://www.youtube.com/watch?v=PyCnqF_wPOA (accessed 23 January 2019).

Kapferer, B. (2014b) 'A note on Gluckman's 1930 fieldwork in Natal', *History in Africa*, 41: 147–54.

Kelly, E., Mitchell, J. C. and Smith, S. J. (1990) 'Factors in the length of stay of homeless families in temporary accommodation', *Sociological Review*, 38: 621–33.

Magubane B. (1969) 'Pluralism and conflict situations in Africa: a new look', *African Social Research*, 7: 529–54.

Magubane B. (1971) 'A critical look at the indices used in the study of social change in colonial Africa', *Current Anthropology*, 12: 419–45.

Matsuda, M. (1989) 'Review of Mitchell, *Cities, Society and Social Perception*', *The Developing Economies*, 27: 214–18.

Meinhert, L. and Kapferer, B. (eds.) (2015) *In the Event: Toward an Anthropology of Generic Moments* (New York).

Mitchell, J. C. (1956a) *The Yao Village. A Study in the Social Structure of a Nyasaland Tribe* (Manchester, reprinted 1971 with a revised subtitle: *A Study in the Social Structure of a Malawian People*).

Mitchell, J. C. (1956b) *The Kalela Dance: Aspects of Social Relationships Among Urban Africans in Northern Rhodesia* (Manchester).

Mitchell, J. C. (1959) 'The causes of labour migration', *Bulletin of the Inter-African Labour Institute*, 6: 12–46.

Mitchell, J. C. (1960) *Tribalism and the Plural Society: an Inaugural Lecture Given to the University College of Rhodesia and Nyasaland on 2 October 1959* (London).

Mitchell, J. C. (1966) 'Theoretical orientations in African urban studies'. In M. Banton (ed.), *The Social Anthropology of Complex Societies* (London), 37–68.

Mitchell, J. C. (ed.) (1969) *Social Networks in Urban Situations: Analyses of Personal Relationships in Central African Towns* (Manchester).

Mitchell, J. C. (1971) 'Response to Magubane', *Current Anthropology*, 12: 434–6.

Mitchell, J. C. (1973) 'Networks, norms and institutions'. In J. C. Mitchell and J. Boissevain (eds.), *Network Analysis: Studies in Human Interaction* (The Hague), 15–36.

Mitchell, J. C. (1974) 'Social networks', *Annual Review of Anthropology*, 3: 279–98.

Mitchell, J. C. (1979) 'Networks, algorithms, and analysis'. In P. Holland and S. Leinhardt (eds.), *Perspectives on Social Network Research* (New York), 425–51.

Mitchell, J. C. (ed.) (1980) *Numerical Techniques in Social Anthropology* (Philadelphia, PA).

Mitchell, J. C. (1983) 'Case and situation analysis', *The Sociological Review*, 31: 187–211.

Mitchell, J. C. (1985) 'Configurational similarity in three class contexts in British society', *Sociology*, 19: 72–92.

Mitchell, J. C. (1986a) *Ethnography and Networks*. Keynote Address to the Sunbelt Social Network Conference, Santa Barbara, CA (manuscript copy held by author).

Mitchell, J. C. (1986b) 'Network procedures'. In D. Frick and H.-W. Hoefert (eds.), *The Quality of Urban Life* (Berlin), 73–92.

Mitchell, J. C. (1987) *Cities, Society, and Social Perception: a Central African Perspective* (Oxford).

Mitchell, J. C. (1994) 'The marks of prestige of Yao village headmen', *Zeitschrift für Enthnologie*, 119: 267–72.

Mitchell, J. C. (1995) 'Afterword'. In A. Rogers and S. Vertovec (eds.), *The Urban Context* (Oxford), 335–45.

Mitchell. J. C. and Critchley, F. (1985) 'Configurational similarity in three class contexts in British society', *Sociology*, 19: 72–92.

Mitchell. J. C. and Epstein, A. L. (1959) 'Occupational prestige and social status among urban Africans in Northern Rhodesia', *Africa: Journal of the International African Institute*, 29: 22–40.

Morrow, S. (2016) *The Fires Beneath. The Life of Monica Wilson* (Cape Town).

Musambachime, M. C. (1993) 'The University of Zambia's Institute for African Studies and Social Science Research in Central Africa, 1938-1988', *History in Africa*, 20: 237–48.

Peach, C. and Mitchell, J. C (1988) 'Marriage distance and ethnicity'. In C. G. N. Mascie-Taylor and A. J. Boyce (eds.), *Human Mating Patterns* (Cambridge), 31–46.

Peil, M. (1988) 'Review of Mitchell, *Cities, Society and Social Perception*', *Urban Studies*, 15: 263–4.

Prager, J. (1982) 'American racial ideology as collective representation', *Ethnic and Racial Studies*, 5: 99–119.

Rainie, L. and Wellman, B. (2012) *Networked: the New Social Operating System* (Cambridge, MA).

Rew, A (1999) 'Obituary: Professor A. L. Epstein', *The Independent*, 19.11.1999. http://www.independent.co.uk/arts-entertainment/obituary-professor-a-l-epstein-1127117.html (accessed 4 January 2018).

Robbins, M. C. (1983) 'Review of *Numerical Techniques in Social Anthropology*', *American Ethnologist*, 10: 181–2.

Rogers, A. and Vertovec, S. (eds.) (1995) *The Urban Context: Ethnicity, Social Networks and Situational Analysis* (Oxford and Washington, DC).

Schumaker, L (2001) *Africanizing Anthropology: Fieldwork, Networks, and the Making of Cultural Knowledge In Central Africa* (Durham, NC, and London).

Weber, M. (1968) *Economy and Society* (trans. G. Roth and C. Wittich) (New York).

Wellman, B. and Berkowitz, S (1988) *Social Structures: a Network Approach* (Cambridge).

Werbner, R. P. (1984) 'The Manchester School in south-central Africa', *Annual Review of Anthropology*, 13: 157–85.

Werbner, R. P. (1991) *Tears of the Dead: the Social Biography of an African Family* (Edinburgh).

Werbner, R. P. (forthcoming) *Anthropology after Gluckman: Manchester School Transformations* (Manchester).

Yelvington, K. A. (1997) 'An interview with A. L. Epstein', *Current Anthropology*, 30: 289–99.

Unpublished sources

The Academic Papers of James Clyde Mitchell are held in the Commonwealth and African Studies collections, Weston Library, Bodleian Library, Oxford. The citations in this Memoir are referred to by date, type and, in the case of letters, initial of recipient or sender (e.g. James Clyde Mitchell is JCM), and are from:

Correspondence with other members of the RLI, B-H, 1946-60 (MSS Afr. s. 1998, box 4), specifically
Correspondence with John Barnes (JB), 1946-60, 4/1
Correspondence with Arnold L. Epstein (AE) 1950-59, 4/3
Correspondence with Max Gluckman (MG), 1946-61 (MSS Afr. s. 1998, box 5), specifically:
Correspondence with Max Gluckman, 1946-51, 5/1
Letters to Max Gluckman, 1958-61, 5/2
RLI correspondence with Max Gluckman 1952/8 (not labelled)
Newspaper cuttings, correspondence and papers 1951-83 (MSS Afr. s. 2468, box 42)
Working data, research notes and correspondence 1955-83 (MSS Afr. s. 2486, box 32)
Items notified to me verbally, by letter or by email are cited, with permission, as 'pers. comm.' followed
        by the date of receipt of communication.

DONALD CAMERON WATT

Donald Cameron Watt

17 May 1928 – 30 October 2014

elected Fellow of the British Academy 1990

by

KATHLEEN BURK

Donald Cameron Watt gained a first-class degree in PPE at the University of Oxford in 1951, where he developed an interest in the origins and progress of the Second World War. After a brief period as a documents' editor—an activity he continued throughout his academic life—he joined the London School of Economics in 1954 to teach international history, where he remained for the rest of his career; he was promoted to a chair in 1972 and became Stevenson Professor in 1981. He published widely in contemporary history, emphasising the roles played by key individuals, for example by exploring decision-making within the various levels in the British foreign policy-making elite. His magnum opus, *How War Came: the Immediate Origins of the Second World War 1938–1939*, appeared in 1989 and won him the Wolfson History Prize in 1990; his other books included *Personalities and Policies: Studies in the Formulation of British Foreign Policy in the Twentieth Century* (1965) and *Britain and the Suez Canal* (1956).

Biographical Memoirs of Fellows of the British Academy, XVIII, 135–154
Posted 6 August 2019. © British Academy 2019.

DONALD CAMERON WATT

Donald Cameron Watt, Stevenson Professor of International History at the London School of Economics and Political Science from 1981 to 1993, was in one sense a figure of continuity, but in another a figure who developed and propagated a new approach to international history. He worked in a field which had traditionally been seen as one of importance, that of the interrelationship of states, but he emerged in an historiographical period when that field was seen as of less interest than others. Furthermore, much more emphasis was placed on historical forces and less on the free will of historical figures. His approach could perhaps be summed up by the title of his inaugural lecture, 'What About the People?' He did not deny that there were forces beyond the control of an individual or a government or a country, but he felt strongly that forces were the context, not the determining aspect, of decision-making, and that more emphasis should be placed on the ideas, backgrounds, relationships, misconceptions and misperceptions of decision-makers. He thought it vital that multiple archives should be used and, indeed, that as wide a range of sources both public and private were necessary in order even to approach whatever was the truth. Importantly, he had the humility to believe that his students and colleagues should challenge his ideas: he believed neither in schools of history nor in the desirability of acolytes.

Watt was born on 17 May 1928 at 9, Horton Crescent, Rugby, Warwickshire. His father, Robert Cameron Watt, was a housemaster at Rugby School, an independent boys' school, and later Rector of Edinburgh Academy.[1] His mother, Barbara Hannah, was Canadian and the daughter of the Bishop of Ontario. She and Robert met in 1926 at the Christmas Ball at the Royal Military College in Kingston.[2] Watt called his father an inspirational teacher, who was 'renowned for his remarkable ability to inspire pupils in spite of the illegibility of his handwriting on the blackboard and the almost inaudible manner in which he mumbled his way through lessons'.[3] Although Watt's own blackboard skills were never really tested, he certainly inherited his father's habit of inaudibility when speaking to groups. He ran an innovative MA on the Law of the Sea, which was massively oversubscribed, and when he mumbled, the students complained that they could not hear him. A microphone was brought in and attached to the lectern; he took one look at it, announced that he never used them, and moved to the side so that it could not pick up his voice.[4] It is unclear why he thought that it was irrelevant that many could not hear what he was saying.

During his entire career, Watt was driven by the need to understand the breakdown of Europe after Versailles, the rise of Nazi Germany and the origins of the Second

---

[1] He is not listed as an alumnus on Rugby's website—nor, for that matter, on Wikipedia's.
[2] M. G. Fry, Jr. (ed.), *Power, Personalities and Policies: Essays in Honour of Donald Cameron Watt* (London, 1992), Foreword by Fry.
[3] *The Times*, 4 February 2015; not the actual words of Watt but summing up his feeling.
[4] Brian Holden Reid to the author, 22 November 2018.

World War. This had its origins at Rugby, as he wrote in the Preface to his masterpiece, *How War Came: the Immediate Origins of the Second World War 1938-1939:* 'the drive to write this book began on September 2 and 3, 1939, when, as an eleven-year-old schoolboy, I helped my father and his colleagues fill sand-bags in one of the great sand quarries outside Rugby… . It grew enormously in strength two years later when, lazing in the summer on the banks of the school close, with the scent of new-mown grass in the air, I read for the first time an account of the British retreat to Dunkirk. How could a British army have come to find itself in so near-disastrous a position? How could things have been allowed to go so far?'[5]

When he was conscripted after the end of the war, he was driven to know more, and he 'wangled, connived, volunteered and out-competed' his fellow conscripts to win a posting to Austria as a member of the Intelligence Corps, where he became an acting sergeant in Field Security, concerned with de-nazification and 'with keeping an eye on the wilder and madder edges of the political spectrum, firstly among the inhabitants of Styria, [and] then among the tides of refugees from south-eastern Europe'.[6] What he learned from these experiences was that Central European politics produced a wide range of attitudes, both admirable and vicious, that he could not have imagined in his schoolboy days. He met all types of people, from a Croat deeply ashamed of the wartime activities of men claiming to represent Croatia to an ultra-nationalist doctor from South Tyrol to a village gendarme who called a plague on the houses of all politicians, no matter for which side they claimed to act. He also discovered a keen interest in official documents. His primary duty was to assess Nazi documents, and at one point he posted some secret documents to himself, presumably to save them from destruction, although one kind soul suggests that this was an early symptom of his chronic absent-mindedness.[7] In any case, the documents were intercepted by army security and, as a result, he was court-martialed. Luckily, he was only reprimanded and not reduced in rank.

In 1948 he went up to Oriel College, Oxford with a scholarship to read Philosophy, Politics and Economics, taking a First in 1951. Twentieth-century history was not yet recognised in Oxford as a fit subject for study by undergraduates, with the most modern Special Subject entitled 'Great Britain and the Making of the Ententes 1898–1907'. He felt himself lucky to have tutors who had had service experience in the war, whether in the Special Operations Executive or at Bletchley Park, which housed the work of the decrypting of German official messages. In particular, he was grateful to

[5] D. C. Watt, *How War Came: the Immediate Origins of the Second World War 1938–1939* (London, 1989), p. ix.
[6] Ibid.
[7] B. Holden Reid, 'Watt, Donald Cameron 1928–2014', *Oxford Dictionary of National Biography*, https://doi.org/10.1093/odnb/9780198614128.013.108084 (accessed 23 January 2019).

Christopher Seton-Watson, who had been elected to a Tutorial Fellowship in Modern History and Politics at Oriel even before completing his undergraduate degree at Oxford (he received a 'war degree'). Seton-Watson, who was ten years older than Watt, had served in the Royal Artillery in Belgium and France (he was evacuated from Dunkirk), Greece, Egypt and Italy, ending the war with a Military Cross and Bar. His specialty was late nineteenth- and early twentieth-century Italian politics, writing the classic book *Italy from Liberalism to Fascism 1870-1922*,[8] in which he dealt with some of the questions for Italy—why and how came Italy to Fascism?—that Watt would want to understand for Germany. The hours spent discussing the beginning and end of the war as well as the general history and politics of modern Europe with Seton-Watson were intensely stimulating.

It must be said, however, that his Oxford period was not all work. He was and remained interested in poetry, writing some himself, and in 1950 he co-edited *Oxford Poetry* with J. B. Donne, which was published by Blackwell in 1951. It is also likely that he sang. He had spent part of his schooldays as a boy chorister at King's College School, Cambridge, and later, a fine baritone, he auditioned for both Sadler's Wells and Covent Garden, but was unsuccessful. In later years he sang at friends' parties, reportedly everything from opera to musical theatre and, rumour whispered at the time, to country and western.

Instead of a musical career, then, he began one as an editor of documents. He joined for a three-year stint the team organised and run by Sir John Wheeler-Bennett as assistant editor of *Documents on German Foreign Policy, 1918-1945,* containing the captured archives of the German Foreign Ministry, which he helped to screen and then to edit for publication; the British team worked alongside French and American editorial teams. He was the first historian to read the German Foreign Ministry archives for 1933–1937 (later to be Series C). He also 'devilled' on the volumes covering March to September 1939. It is certainly the case that he had a deep bath in documents which would form the basis of much of his future work. Indeed, he got more than an inkling as to how inadequate his Oxford education had been when trying to understand what had happened. After his three years, he wanted a permanent post, and he was appointed Assistant Lecturer in International History at the London School of Economics and Political Science (LSE) in 1954, where he spent his entire academic career. (In 1954, International History at the LSE consisted only of the Sir Daniel Stevenson Professor of International History, W. N. Medlicott, and two junior lecturers, one of whom was Watt.) He was promoted in due course to Lecturer, Senior Lecturer and then Reader in 1966. In 1972 he took up a chair in International History, and in 1981 succeeded to the Stevenson chair, probably the premier chair in the field in the UK.

[8] C. Seton-Watson, *Italy from Liberalism to Fascism 1870–1922* (London, 1967).

One reason why he wanted a permanent position was that he was married. He had met Marianne Ruth Grau, a Jewish refugee from Germany and a schoolteacher, at the Oxford Operatic Society and, after the completion of his degree in July 1951, they were married in Oxford on 20 December. They had a son, Ewen; but however the marriage began, it deteriorated. Marianne could never escape from the traumatisation of her experiences in Germany. Divorce proceedings were begun, but in 1962, before they were completed, she committed suicide. Later the same year, on 2 December, Watt married Felicia Cobb Stanley, an American librarian whom he had met whilst studying in Washington. By all accounts she brought stability, as well as a stepdaughter, Cathy, and a multitude of cats, into his life.

Professor W. N. Medlicott was the convenor or head of department when Watt joined it. Watt thought highly of him, writing in the short biography that he wrote for the *Oxford Dictionary of National Biography* that 'Medlicott became the leader in Britain of that transformation of the history of foreign policy and of diplomatic history into the discipline of international history... . He was a pioneer in the widening of old-style diplomatic history to include issues of trade, [military] strategy, and economic warfare.'[9] He very much encouraged Watt to write a book, but the latter was diverted into other and, in this context, less productive directions. Months after the Suez Crisis in November 1956, he edited *Documents on the Suez Crisis* (he had already published *Britain and the Suez Canal*).[10] From 1961 to 1972 he edited the Survey of International Affairs for the Royal Institute of International Affairs at Chatham House. From 1985 to 1997 he was general editor of the multi-volume *British Documents on Foreign Affairs* that published the complete 150 years of the Foreign Office Confidential Print Series; he himself dealt with seven of the eventual thirty-five volumes. In 1978 he had accepted a commission to write the Official History of the Ministry of Defence after 1945, on which he worked at the same time, but this was a fiasco. The public story, repeated in most obituaries, was that Watt was intensely frustrated by the reluctance of Whitehall to give him access to the documents that he wanted to see and so he decided to quit. This may well have been the case, but there is an additional layer. Instead of one volume he produced three, including one entirely off the subject, a volume on the Committee of Imperial Defence. (The Committee of Imperial Defence—CID—had been formed in 1902; when the War Cabinet was established on the outbreak of war in September 1939, it absorbed the CID.) It was thought that parts of his history could be rescued, but the historian who read it thought that

[9] D. C. Watt, 'Medlicott, William Norton (1900–1987)', *Oxford Dictionary of National Biography*, https://doi.org/10.1093/ref:odnb/66374 (accessed 23 January 2019).
[10] *Documents on the Suez Crisis, 26 July to 6 November 1956*, selected and introduced by D. C. Watt (London, 1957); D. C. Watt, *Britain and the Suez Canal* (London, 1956).

publishing it would damage Watt's reputation, not least because it was written in a very tedious style. Watt asked a colleague in the field whether he could rescue it, but it was not thought possible, and the matter was dropped.

It is worth noting at this point, because it supports the argument of Watt's intense frustration with the Ministry of Defence, that Watt was one of the group of historians in the campaign, successful in 1967, to convince the Wilson government that the fifty-year rule against access to government archives should be reduced to a thirty-year rule.[11] By its implementation, archival research into the 1930s became possible, clearly of great benefit to Watt himself (at least until he tried to work on material which officials considered should be kept secret). I myself indirectly benefited from this access a decade later. Whilst writing a DPhil thesis on the First World War, there was only one occasion when a file that I wanted to read was already out to another researcher. Rather, most of those with whom I talked at the Public Record Office (now The National Archive) seemed to be working on the 1930s or the Second World War, partly because reading these newly-opened files encouraged the hope of making exciting discoveries, every research student's dream.

During Watt's early years as a lecturer, he did produce a number of articles, dealing with three separate countries, amongst which were 'Anglo-German naval negotiations on the eve of World War II',[12] 'Die bayerische Bemühungen um die Ausweisung Hitlers, 1924',[13] 'German strategic planning and Spain, 1938–1939',[14] 'The Rome–Berlin axis, 1936–1940: myth and reality',[15] and 'American strategic interests and

---

[11] The effort was begun in 1963 by a group of senior historians, many connected with the Cabinet Office or the Historical Branch of the Foreign Office Research Department, to obtain a revision of the 1958 Public Records Act. The campaign was fuelled by the apparent ease with which ex-ministers could gain access to the papers arising from their own periods in office to produce what were widely believed to be partial, if not partisan, defences of their official activities. Their individual protests were so abruptly rejected by Macmillan before his retirement from office in 1963 that the historians were driven to lobby the Cabinet Office collectively. The subsequent debate within the government and the Cabinet Office took place against the background of two general elections, and any such change was dependent upon the agreement of the committee of Privy Councillors drawn from all three parties. Debate lasted for four years, until the Public Records Act of 1967 changed the fifty-year rule to a thirty-year rule: D. C. Watt, 'Foreign affairs, the public interest, and the right to know', *Political Quarterly,* 34 (1963), 121–36; D. C. Watt, 'Contemporary history in Britain, problems and perspectives', *Journal of the Society of Archivists,* 3 (1969), 515–25; D. C. Watt, 'The historiography of appeasement', in A. Sked and C. Cook (eds.), *Crisis and Controversy: Essays in Honour of A. J. P. Taylor* (London, 1976), p. 120 for the lobbying.

[12] D. C. Watt, 'Anglo-German naval negotiations on the eve of World War II', *Journal of the Royal United Service Institute,* 103 (1958), 201–7.

[13] D. C. Watt, 'Die bayerische Bemühungen um die Ausweisung Hitlers, 1924', *Vierteljahreshaft für Zeitgeschichte,* 4 (1958), 270–80.

[14] D. C. Watt, 'German strategic planning and Spain, 1938–1939', *Army Quarterly*, 80 (1960), 220–7.

[15] D. C. Watt, 'The Rome–Berlin axis, 1936–1940: myth and reality', *Review of Politics*, 22 (1960), 519–43.

anxieties in the West Indies, 1917–1940'.[16] But he also produced two articles which attracted the terms 'seminal'[17] and 'watershed',[18] and which were seen as transforming the study of appeasement: 'Appeasement reconsidered: some neglected factors',[19] and 'Appeasement: the rise of a revisionist school?'[20] It was the second of these articles in particular that encouraged research on British policy in the 1930s to follow new directions.

To begin, Watt set out the 'orthodox' view: first of all, Hitler had come to power with certain long-term aims, and his actions betrayed 'a considered and premeditated drive to achieve German hegemony in Europe', and, secondly, that 'an England upset by Hitler's initial actions [was] determined after the summer of 1934 on taking the nationalist steam out of the grievances believed to inspire Hitler's policy by a policy of concessions'. He pointed out that the two theses had been advanced, and defended, by nearly all Britain's leading historians who happened to be interested in the recent past. He also pointed out that each part of the thesis depended on the veracity of the other. Since 1960, he continued, both parts of the thesis had come under critical attack, singling out the relevant publications of Medlicott and A. J. P. Taylor.[21] He accepted large parts of both of their arguments, although he also set out where he thought that they were wrong. But importantly, he argued that what was needed was much more evidence: he listed what historians and journalists did not know and made clear what this lack implied.[22] This was published in 1965, and it is clear from this article, if no other evidence were available, just what drove him to take part in the attempt to change the fifty-year rule. Indeed, he wrote that he had in fact begun in the late 1960s to write the book which, twenty years later, was published as *How War Came*, but that he then put that draft aside. His reasons then were that there was no serious French evidence, that it was impossible to make sense of the activities of the Soviets, and that he was completely dissatisfied with the received version of American policy.[23]

---

[16] D. C. Watt, 'American strategic interests and anxieties in the West Indies, 1917–1940', *Journal of the Royal United Services Institute*, 108 (1963), 224–32.

[17] S. Aster, 'Appeasement: before and after revisionism', *Diplomacy and Statecraft,* 19 (2008), 443–80, quote on p. 451.

[18] R. J. Caputi, *Neville Chamberlain and Appeasement* (Selinsgrove, PA, 2000), p. 99.

[19] D. C. Watt, 'Appeasement reconsidered: some neglected factors', *Round Table*, 53 (1963), 358–71.

[20] D. C. Watt, 'Appeasement: the rise of a revisionist school?', *Political Quarterly*, 36 (1965), 191–213. This was first read at the Anglo-American Conference in London in 1964. Watt, 'The historiography of appeasement', p. 126, fn 1.

[21] W. N. Medlicott, *The Coming of War in 1939* (London, 1963); and A. J. P. Taylor, *The Origins of the Second World War* (London, 1961). See pp. 199–207 of Watt, 'Appeasement: the rise of a revisionist school?', for his assessment of their arguments.

[22] Watt, 'Appeasement: the rise of a revisionist school?', pp. 192, 193, 194, 197, 213.

[23] Watt, *How War Came*, p. xi.

Of equal importance with his work in setting out a different way of looking at the period of the 1930s was his development of a new methodology to do so. He first presented it in September 1960 to a conference of the European Association of American Studies in Italy, then took it home, extended it, polished it, entitled it 'America and the British foreign policy-making elite from Joseph Chamberlain to Anthony Eden, 1895–1956' and published it in January 1963 in the American journal, *The Review of Politics*.[24] Watt's rationale for his new approach was that when looking at British attitudes to the USA, he noticed that they fell into two main divisions, both of which had drawbacks. First of all, there were studies, usually by American historians, of movements in British mass public opinion; secondly, there were studies of the radical and politically 'non-conformist' elements in British political society.[25] Both were inadequate to the task of understanding various developments in Anglo-American relations, the first because the 'social structure' of British political power does not rate mass opinion very highly and the second because in the sixty-one years covered by the article, radical elements controlled British foreign policy for only eight years and disputed its control for only another six. In any case, what he was interested in was not so much the ideas and activities of A. J. P. Taylor's 'proponents of an alternative foreign policy':[26] he wanted to know about the proponents of the orthodox foreign policy, the one that those in charge developed and implemented.

So, if his focus is the British foreign policy-making elite, who are they? How does he define them? Briefly, as members of a social group defined by its political functions; that is, what are the political processes by which foreign policy is made in Britain, and which organs and offices of government are involved in it? And then, who inhabits each position? First of all, there is the political level, the relevant members of Cabinet and their subordinates. Below the political level is the administration, in particular the senior personnel. First in importance is the Foreign Office, with its hierarchy in London and the Embassies. If there are strategic considerations, the Ministry of Defence and the three Services are relevant, whilst for economic and financial considerations, the official group must include the Treasury, Board of Trade, and Bank of England. After 1931 there was the Dominions/Commonwealth Relations Office, and until 1947 the India Office. His information came from British political and diplomatic

---

[24] D. C. Watt, 'America and the British foreign policy-making elite from Joseph Chamberlain to Anthony Eden, 1895–1956', *The Review of Politics*, 25 (1963), 3–33.

[25] An example of the first was A. Rappaport, *The British Press and Wilsonian Neutrality, 1914–1917* (Palo Alto, CA, 1951); an example of the second was H. Pelling, *America and the British Left, from Bright to Bevan* (London, 1956).

[26] A. J. P. Taylor, *The Trouble Makers: Dissent Over Foreign Policy, 1792–1939* (London, 1957), is cited by Watt, but he neglects to give a page reference for the quote, and I have been unable to locate it without re-reading the entire book.

memoirs, British and American diplomatic documents, *Who's Who* and the *Foreign Office Lists*. Then there are outside pressures: party foreign policy-discussion groups and ginger groups, both inside and outside Parliament; the editors and principal writers of the 'quality' press; and the Crown and its most intimate advisers.

The importance of this particular article of Watt's is not necessarily his arguments with regard to the content; rather, it is that it began his development of a new way of deconstructing the foreign policy world to see what made it tick, and then to use this analytical structure to study British and others' foreign policy. His methodology demonstrated much further development in his first book, *Personalities and Policies: Studies in the Formulation of British Foreign Policy in the Twentieth Century*, which was published in 1965.[27] It is really a book of thirteen essays, rather than a continuously organised and argued book, but it begins with a stronger analysis than the article as to what he is writing about, stating that the first two essays in fact develop the ideas that he had first discussed in the article. His thesis is that Britain is essentially an oligocratic society—not oligarchic, since the point is the exercise of power, not its possession. This is a society in which power is exercised by a minority of citizens grouped together in a cluster of smaller groups, which groups are consistent enough over time to be treated as both political and social phenomena and for the characteristics of their social organisation to be an essential element in the manner in which they perform their social functions. In any state, even in direct democracies, the nature of the exercise of power ensures that it is only exercised by a few. In Britain, they form a continuous and recognisable grouping. Their hallmark is the limitation of membership by approval.

It is notable, according to Watt, that this grouping is a good deal less responsible to and responsive to the main movements and currents of mass public opinion than are their counterparts in other countries. This aspect of his argument is of its time. First of all, he says that the major organs of communication are the correspondence columns of the 'quality press', the clubs and institutes of London's intellectual political society, and the BBC's Third Programme, which included substantial talks as well as classical music, but which became Radio 3 in 1970, in the process losing the talks. But the most obvious recent change in the relationship of the elite with mass public opinion, and in the felt need to take account of it, has been the rise of a tumultuous social media. Watt, sadly, did not live long enough to include them in his argument, as he would surely have done.

Watt divides this elite into four categories in a more structured manner than in the article. The first category is the Political, which is made up of the elected politicians

---

[27] D. C. Watt, *Personalities and Policies: Studies in the Formulation of British Foreign Policy in the Twentieth Century* (London, 1965).

(and presumably peers?) who participate in the making and selling of foreign policy. These remain those whom he listed in the article. The second category is the Diplomatic, which is primarily the Foreign Office (soon to be the Foreign and Commonwealth Office), where the flow of work both up from the junior levels to the senior and down from the senior to the junior unites these two levels in a way seldom replicated in other departments; the embassies and legations abroad are also intertwined with the Foreign Office itself. These officials are then united with their political heads. Not surprisingly, this is normally the most powerful group in this particular elite. The third category is Bureaucratic, which interweaves, depending on the topic, the primary officials. For example, for economic or financial topics, the members might be the Permanent Under-Secretary to the Treasury, the Cabinet Secretary, and the senior officials of the Treasury, the Bank of England and the Board of Trade; for the post-1945 period, a number of other positions are important whilst some were eliminated. Finally, the fourth category is the Military; this is of importance particularly in wartime coalitions or peacetime alliances. The sources of external pressure on the above remain as set out in the article: the quality press, foreign policy discussion and ginger groups, from both inside and outside Parliament, and the Crown and its advisers.[28]

His suggested method is to read as widely and deeply as possible in all available public and private papers, biographies and memoirs, newspapers and magazines such as *The Listener*, and to talk to people. He tries to see, almost person by active person, what they thought, how and with whom they spoke, what the personal as well as the institutional reactions were, what ideas and suggestions were being exchanged and by whom, and what, if any, were the results. This all takes place within the general political and international context. A problem, of course, is that asserting that this is the best, the only, method does not make it so, but it is certainly plausible. It is also ferociously labour-intensive—how could one deal with a war in this manner, for example? It does depend on the availability of public and private papers for research, so that it relegates very contemporary history to the margins—or, as historians a generation ago used to insist, the results were journalism, not history. His defence is that, whilst of course the results would be tentative, nevertheless there is no better way, because it 'approximates more than any other to the reality of the processes by which foreign policy is formulated in the open oligocracy that is Britain'—and besides, the so-called definitive study is an 'academic fantasy'.[29] Indeed, the best is the enemy of the good.

In 1982, Watt succeeded to the Stevenson chair. The following year, he gave his inaugural lecture, 'What About the People? Abstraction and Reality in History and the Social Sciences', in which he clearly set out his approach to the writing of

---

[28] Watt, *Personalities and Policies*, pp. 1–15.
[29] Ibid., p. 15.

international history to a wider academic audience. First of all, he points out that diplomatic and then international history arose out of 'disaster studies', i.e., the detailed studies, based on published government documents, of the Franco-Prussian War, the First World War, and then the failure of appeasement. As such, he points out, this approach was 'bedeviled by the search for "guilty men"'.[30] (He had earlier referred to this as the 'sin theory of international relations', in that, to understand the problems of a given foreign policy, it is enough to diagnose the underlying sins of those who had conducted that policy: once the sinner was identified, the remedy became clear'.[31]) With the rise of the social sciences, there are political and inter-national historians, such as he himself, who look to them for aid. But these historians do not turn to social scientists who base their work on quantification, on those who count, but rather to those who are concerned with the behaviour of the individual in society, with his immediate social environment, with the conventions and modes which govern the social behaviour of the individual, and with the individual's relations with, and perceptions of, external events and phenomena. Fundamentally, the social scientists try to find generalities, whilst historians are necessarily interested in partic-ularities. As he wrote, 'the historian of international relations, particularly when concerned with the disaster studies aspects of his field, engages himself in studying in depth, over time and in the round, the character and mind of those certain personal-ities who have been identified as playing key parts in the chain of events and circumstances leading up to the moment of disaster'.[32]

It can be extremely misleading, he suggests, to depend only on official documents, particularly when they look to be comprehensive. The historian has to differentiate between the decision-makers in title and based on constitutional rules and regulations and the decision-makers in reality. He has to look closely at the people involved, going beyond these documents. In sum, 'history without real people is a distortion of reality'.[33]

All of this, his long-standing interest in the origins of the Second World War and the new methodology he had developed, came together in his masterpiece, *How War Came: the Immediate Origins of the Second World War 1938-1939*, which was published in 1989. He makes his approach to the subject immediately clear:

[30] D. C. Watt, 'What About the People? Abstraction and Reality in History and the Social Sciences', An Inaugural Lecture (London, 1953), p. 4.
[31] Watt, 'The historiography of appeasement', p. 111.
[32] Watt, 'What About the People?', p. 5.
[33] Ibid., p. 18.

This is not a story of men whose activities are determined by large, impersonal forces.[34] The forces are there, but the stuff of history is humanity. Impersonal forces only figure in this narrative in so far as they formed part of the perceptions of the individual actors. History is lived through and, for the fortunate, survived by people. Their actions, their failures to act, their hesitations, their perceptions, their judgments, their misunderstandings, misperceptions and mistakes act and interact upon each other across political, social and cultural divisions.[35]

Over nearly two decades, he had worked to understand what had happened. He assiduously compiled documents from every government involved, small as well as big. He tried meticulously to ascertain the personal qualities and flaws of diplomats and their superiors. He read virtually every political, diplomatic, military and press biography or memoir that he could find. He made detailed calendars as a means of discovering what his actors were doing, where, when and with whom. He made flow charts. He wrote and re-wrote. He made it clear that 'people count in history as individuals and are not puppets jerked about by impersonal forces'.[36] They are responsible. And when he had finished, he had produced a book of stunning breadth and depth, one written in such prose that reading it is a pleasure. It is a classic of international history.

One reason that the book reads so well is that he followed his own advice as given to his PhD students, which was to read detective stories as guides to good writing. His own favourites included the political thrillers and spy novels of Eric Ambler. One of his former research students wrote that Watt 'compared the work of the international historian to that of the detective. Both involved the careful reconstruction of elaborate timetables and decision-making flow charts and an analysis of the behavior of people under stress.' Both should provide a compelling narrative 'studded' with rich personality portraits. This, he said, was the most suitable way to write international history.[37] Certainly *How War Came* does just that, setting the scenes, sometimes day by day and hour by hour, analysing people and sometimes groups of people, how they

[34] As Joseph Maiolo notes, he was 'critical of Marxist historians such as Timothy W. Mason, who portrayed Hitler's decision to attack Poland in 1939 as a "function" of a larger socio-economic regime in "crisis" rather than the fulfillment of an ideologically framed intention'. J. Maiolo, 'Personalities, policies, and international history: the life and work of Donald Cameron Watt', *Diplomacy and Statecraft*, 26 (2015), 207.

[35] Watt, *How War Came*, p. xiii.

[36] Harvard historian Gaddis Smith, in his review of *How War Came*—*New York Times*, 3 September 1989. Elsewhere, Watt suggested that 'Since the historian is usually concerned not with a single individual but with the interplay between a limited but identifiable group of individuals, the approach employed must be multibiographical or prosopographical': D. C. Watt, *Succeeding John Bull: America in Britain's Place 1900–1975* (Cambridge, 1984), p. 4.

[37] Maiolo, 'Personalities, policies, and international history', p. 207.

looked, what they wrote and said, how they interacted. He was not afraid of casting aspersions or praise where they were, in his opinion, deserved. The Hungarians caught many of the former:

> Contempt for the Magyars among the great powers and fear among the minor ones made an odd reward for individuals so determinedly proud, so exclusively ethnocentric as the Hungarian leadership. But watching their single-minded obsession [with Romania] throughout the summer of 1939, their discussions of possible bacteriological warfare against Romania, and the constant menace of war their troops represented in a Europe filled with tender of all kinds, it is difficult not to feel that the destruction by the war of the social system on which their power rested was richly deserved.[38]

Indeed, he could get very personal, as when he refers to 'the restless peregrinations of Count Csàky, the Hungarian Foreign Minister (who, like some small-time crook, sure that a major criminal operation was about to occur somewhere, kept rushing around trying to edge his way into the deal)'. He had total contempt for Ribbentrop, the German Foreign Minister, and gives many examples of his ego and incompetence.[39] On the other hand, he admired the Turks.[40]

But Watt also cautioned against 'the illusion of certainty and completeness ... No scholar is free from biases and social conditioning. No set of sources is complete. The mountains of files in twentieth-century government archives obscure the yawning gaps in the record as well as the importance of what was not recorded in official sources and, indeed, what was not recorded at all.' And in international relations as they are conducted, what is causation? 'Disorder, instability, result not from the malfunction of a single component but from a change in one or more relationships.'[41] Is this likely to be recorded in all of its aspects in the official record? The idea that one can produce the definitive work in a subject based on all the evidence, whatever that means, is, Watt asserted, 'Germanic dogma'.[42]

His conclusion was that 'In the end the war was Hitler's war. It was not, perhaps, the war he wanted. But it was the war he was prepared to risk, if he had to. Nothing could deter him.' The inhabitants of the states of Europe which fought suffered horribly because of Hitler and his obsession to start and win a war and continually to expand the power and glory of Germany. The belligerent that suffered the least was the United States, 'the only untrammelled victor' in the war. This, given his analysis of

---

[38] Watt, *How War Came*, p. 283.
[39] Ibid., p. 470 for the quote; the anti-Ribbentrop theme runs throughout the book.
[40] Ibid., pp. 275–6.
[41] D. C. Watt, 'Some aspects of A. J. P. Taylor's work as diplomatic historian', *Journal of Modern History*, 49 (1977), 21.
[42] Ibid., 29.

President Roosevelt, was not altogether due to Roosevelt's leadership. On the contrary, at least in the period of appeasement,

> Lacking a clear lead, American opinion remained divided and confused. Roosevelt, apart from infrequent outbursts of public oratory, had done nothing practical to rally his allies, to win over the waverers or to remove the deep distrust which a majority of Congressmen, already aware that there was nothing to stop him running again for President in 1940, so great was his domination of his party, felt towards him. He was a man who preferred stealth to openness, who encouraged division even among his own supporters, and who looked for and complained of the lack of courage and leadership in Britain and France; in the field of American foreign policy he had yet to supply or demonstrate these qualities himself.[43]

As he summarised the relevance of Roosevelt's character on the international system, 'It does not bode well for the peace of the world when the President of the United States allows himself to be manoeuvred into appearing as an inept and ignorant fool.'[44] Few leaders escaped Watt's criticisms. They, not 'forces', bore the greatest responsibility for the outbreak of the war. In the 1980s, 'most historians regarded diplomatic/international history as an intellectual backwater' which had relatively little to contribute to new questions about and new ways of writing history.[45] Watt hoped that his book would change some minds.

The book was, in fact, an academic as well as a popular success. In 1990 it won the Wolfson History Prize, awarded annually for the book which best combines excellence in historical research with readability for a general audience. The same year, he was elected to a Fellowship of the British Academy. In the USA, the book was the *New York Times*' Book of the Year in 1990. All in all, for Watt it was a gratifying year. That, however, was the last monograph that he produced; in fact, it was the last book of his own. In 1965, he had published his first book, *Personalities and Policies*; the same year came *Britain Looks to Germany: a Study of British Opinion and Policy since 1945*;[46] in 1968 came *A History of the World in the Twentieth Century. Part I: 1899–1918* (Parts II and III were produced by others);[47] in 1975 he published *Too Serious a*

---

[43] Watt, *How War Came*, p. 268.

[44] Ibid., p. 264. A number of American historians might contest Watt's assessment, or at least Roosevelt's sole responsibility for his actions or lack of them. One who thought that this was the case was Gordon Wood, who wrote in his review of the book that 'Aside from being another example of Watt's weakness for the all-purpose put-down, this seems at the very least ungenerous': 'Making way for Hitler', *New York Review of Books*, 12 October 1989.

[45] Maiolo, 'Personalities, policies, and international history', 207.

[46] D. C. Watt, *Britain Looks to Germany: British Opinion and Policy towards Germany since 1945* (London, 1965).

[47] D. C. Watt, *A History of the World in the Twentieth Century. Part I: 1899–1918* (London, 1967).

Business: European Armed Forces and The Approach to the Second World War,[48] which was very closely based on the Lees Knowles Lectures he had given in 1973 at Cambridge; in 1984 came *Succeeding John Bull: America in Britain's Place 1900-1975. A Study of the Anglo-American Relationship and World Politics in the Context of British and American Foreign-Policy-Making in the Twentieth Century*,[49] largely based on the 1981 Wiles Lectures in History which he had given in Queen's University, Belfast, with the addition of three further essays, each based on a separate case study; and finally, *How War Came* in 1989.

What about further research and writing? He seemed to be a bit at sea, but this is not unusual in an historian who has spent a substantial proportion of his or her career on a single period and has finally written the book as always planned. He thought about extending his book on Anglo-American relations, *Succeeding John Bull*, but this did not happen. However, he was not idle. One must not forget the work on *British Documents on Foreign Affairs*, on which he worked until 1997. He also wrote many articles, essays, conference proceedings and reviews on a range of topics. Importantly, he was crucial in establishing the new field of intelligence history. He set up an Intelligence Study Group at the LSE, a very important forum since the subject 'was still in its infancy and needed nurturing'; it remains active and strong, although it now meets at the Royal United Services Institute. A major factor is that it combines both academics and practitioners, the latter predominantly former members of MI5 and MI6, which was 'an incredibly adventurous format in the 1980s'. There was something of a crackdown in 1986–7 after the trial over the publication of *Spycatcher* in Australia, 'but the essential format did survive and intelligence practitioners continued to write and then even speak'.[50] I myself took along a friend who, passing as a diplomat, had been the station chief in Kenya and then in Iran in the 1970s, and he was rather appalled at what was being revealed. Had he known, Watt would probably have been delighted.

What did upset him was his reluctant part in the trial of David Irving, which took place in London from 1996 to 2000. The American historian Deborah Lipstadt had published in 1994 her book *Denying the Holocaust: the Growing Assault on Truth and Memory* in which she had labelled Irving a 'Holocaust-denier', and Irving sued her for libel.[51] Irving argued that he was 'an honest, serious and objective historian', claiming

---

[48] D. C. Watt, *Too Serious a Business: European Armed Forces and the Approach to the Second World War* (London, 1975).

[49] D. C. Watt, *Succeeding John Bull: America in Britain's Place. A Study of the Anglo-American Relationship and World Politics in the Context of British and American Foreign-Policy-Making in the Twentieth Century* (Cambridge, 1984).

[50] Professor Brian Holden Reid to the author, 4 December 2018. Christopher Andrew was also involved from the beginning and Richard Aldrich joined soon after the Group was established.

[51] D. Lipstadt, *Denying the Holocaust: the Growing Assault on Truth and Memory* (London, 1994).

that he 'had shown, through the application of the usual methodology of historical investigation, that, among other things, Hitler had no knowledge of the Holocaust'.[52] In 1965, Irving had collaborated with Watt in the publication of a lengthy German intelligence document on British policy during the twelve months leading up to the outbreak of the war, and Watt had been very impressed with his work, later describing Irving as having an 'encyclopedic knowledge' of German wartime documents.[53] Because of their earlier collaboration, Irving called on Watt to give evidence as to his high quality as an historian; when Watt refused, he was subpoenaed. Watt told the court that 'as the author of *Hitler's War*, Irving deserved to be taken seriously'.[54] Nevertheless, he gave evidence against Irving at the trial, saying that some of Irving's assertions were prejudiced and not based in fact, that 'he can be seduced by the notion of conspiracies'.[55] Watt found the whole experience distressing.

What was Watt like as a man? The answer is, complicated. An historian who knew him well summed him up as 'formidable but kind'.[56] The following description rings absolutely true for those who knew him as more than a byline: by 1972, when Watt took up his chair in international history,

> [H]is persona had assumed its inimitable form. He dressed smartly but always unconventionally, with longish hair, large prominent spectacles, and a taste for bright colours and startling ties emblazoned with all manner of wildlife or kaleidoscopic patterns.[57] [The invitation to his Memorial Service on 11 February 2015 stated that 'In view of Donald's distinctive taste in neckwear the dress code on this occasion is bright tie or scarf'.] His speaking voice sounded thin and dry, emitted from a slight movement of the middle lips. He was an imaginative though demanding teacher who did not spare sharp criticism, and some students were frightened of him. He supervised a large cohort of research students [in one random year, he took on fourteen new ones in addition to the veterans], and the most able were devoted to him; but he could be maddening, dismissive, or neglectful. He was nevertheless convivial company, and a warm humorous heart beat beneath the formidable exterior.[58]

[52] 'Slugging through the mud', *The Economist*, 15 April 2000.
[53] D. C. Watt, 'History needs David Irvings', *Evening Standard*, 11 April 2000. Watt's argument here is that he, Watt, 'knew the Holocaust happened. I grew up among those who were fortunate to escape it. But what happens when the witnesses are all dead, if the reality had not been thrashed out? The truth needs an Irving's challenges to keep it alive.' See also http://aaargh.vho.org/fran/polpen/dirving/esdw000411.html (accessed 7 February 2019).
[54] R. J. van Pelt, *The Case for Auschwitz: Evidence from the Irving Trial* (Bloomington, IN, 2002), p. 437. Van Pelt was a Dutch architectural historian who had testified that Auschwitz did indeed have gas chambers.
[55] Watt, 'History needs David Irvings'.
[56] Fry, *Power, Personalities and Policies,* Foreword.
[57] The writer of the obituary in *The Times*, 4 February 2015, remembers peacocks and fish.
[58] Holden Reid, 'Watt'.

Watt's 'soporific chairing of seminars was legendary: sometimes snoring, his body would plunge forward but never quite tumble onto the floor; he always awoke as the speaker finished, however, and always asked a challenging question'.[59] I myself was a victim of this habit. Fellow postgraduate research students had warned me of it, and one offered to drop her briefcase on the floor to wake him up. He fell asleep about five minutes into my paper, snored but not too loudly, woke up just after I finished, and asked a question, although I cannot remember whether it was brilliant or banal. (One of his former research students thinks that Watt suffered from narcolepsy, since he would drift off during supervisions and then realise and ask a question, and that he remained aware during the session.[60]) In my case, after the seminar was finished he apologised to me, with the explanation that he was taking tablets for a medical condition.

Another real problem for seminar or lecture convenors was Watt's propensity to drone on seemingly forever. One such occasion took place at the German Historical Institute in London when it was headed by the German historian Wolfgang Mommsen. After about fifteen minutes of Watt's comments, very little of which could be heard by some of us, Mommsen finally said, 'Donald, you have spoken quite long enough. Now be silent.' Another occasion took place in Oslo, during the International Congress of the Historical Sciences in 2000. There was a session held to celebrate Watt, and he was invited to speak about his work. Two and a half hours later, by which time he had shown no sign of finishing, I crept out the back.

Tales of his treatment of his students abounded. One found himself in a curious situation during his PhD viva. The organiser of the viva tried to shuffle Watt over to a comfortable chair in a corner in the hope that he would fall asleep, but instead, Watt insisted that he sit next to his student. From this vantage point, he answered virtually all the questions put to the student by the Examiners, until the latter gave up.[61] The story of another PhD viva was more menacing. He had a bullying side, and students were sometimes the victims. Some years ago at a seminar at the Institute of Historical Research in London, a foreign student gave a paper on British intelligence in the 1920s. At that point, there were few papers in the relevant archive. The student said that he could produce a breakdown of the structure of the Secret Intelligence Service; Watt said that that was impossible, because the information did not exist. The student insisted that it did: in an impressive piece of lateral thinking, he had found such a breakdown in the Treasury papers. Watt was not pleased. When the occasion of the viva came, Watt was one of the Examiners and he gave the student a brutal time. He

[59] Ibid.
[60] Professor Joseph Maiolo, discussion with the author, 21 December 2018.
[61] Ibid.

told the External Examiner that he wanted to fail the thesis, and the External replied that if they did so, they would have to fail every other thesis ever written. The thesis was later published as a book, and the student later became a professor.[62]

Yet it is also the case that he wanted his students, both then and later as academics, to follow their own routes and to challenge him as they wished; as are many academics, he was proud when his students showed such independence of mind, as long as their research was thorough and the evidence intelligently analysed.[63] He did, however, set a bad example in that his desk, and indeed his room, in the LSE resembled a particularly messy archeological site, with layers of papers, files and books sitting on every surface, including much of the floor. It was memorable watching him frantically trying to locate the telephone as it rang and then finally ceased ringing. He was an owl rather than a lark, often working until 4 am, which might partially account for his tendency to nod off during the day.

He followed his own historical interests wherever they led him, and this was in many different directions, a fox rather than a hedgehog. This can influence the reputation of such an historian, since the theoretical mastery of one field of history is often more celebrated than the ability to walk confidently in more than one. Furthermore, his work in editing and publishing German and British documents, which was vitally important in enabling other historians to plunge into a field, arguably commanded less attention and approbation than ought to have been the case. The conundrum was well expressed in the entry on Watt written for the *Oxford Dictionary of National Biography*: he was 'a remarkably gifted and wide-ranging historian with an encyclopedic knowledge of twentieth-century history. He not only displayed breadth and depth but an astonishing exactness on detailed points. But he over-committed himself. He was a dominating authority and a fine historian who might have been a great one if he had directed his energies in one direction rather than scattered them over a broad front.'[64] It is likely, however, that the sheer quality of *How War Came* will ensure that the memory of him as a great historian will not be wholly lost.

[62] Professor David French to the author, 30 December 2018. Professor French was not the student; another professor, who was there, insisted on the veracity of the story.
[63] Professor Brian McKercher to the author, 3 January 2019, and others in conversations.
[64] His publications include six books, six pamphlets, nine edited books, twenty-three documentary publications, some comprising multiple volumes, and dozens of articles, essays, conference proceedings and reviews on a vast range of subjects: see Fry, *Power, Personalities and Policies*, pp. 299–320 for a detailed list.

Acknowledgements

I am very grateful for help from Professors Richard Aldrich, David French, Brian Holden Reid, Joseph Maiolo and Brian McKercher. Richard Aldrich and Joseph Maiolo went beyond discussions and read the draft for me.

Note on the author: Kathleen Burk is Professor Emerita of Modern and Contemporary History, University College London.

GUSTAV JAHODA

Gustav Jahoda

11 August 1919 – 25 January 2012

elected Fellow of the British Academy 1985

by

IVANA MARKOVÁ
Fellow of the Academy

ANDREW JAHODA

Born in Vienna, Gustav Jahoda arrived in the UK during the Second World War from France as a refugee. After the war he graduated from Birkbeck College London and obtained lectureships in psychology at the University of Manchester, the University College of the Gold Coast in Ghana and the University of Glasgow. In 1964 he became the founding Professor of the Department of Psychology at the University of Strathclyde in Glasgow. As a cross-cultural and a cultural psychologist he studied the development of mental processes and solutions to practical problems in children and young adults in Ghana, Scotland and European countries. Jahoda made transdisciplinary theoretical contributions in human and social sciences which he formulated in numerous books and articles, for example, in *Psychology and Anthropology* (1982), *Crossroads Between Culture and Mind* (1992) and *Images of Savages: Ancient Roots of Modern Prejudice in Western Culture* (1999).

Biographical Memoirs of Fellows of the British Academy, XVIII, 155–174
Posted 6 August 2019. © British Academy 2019.

GUSTAV JAHODA

Life

Gustav Jahoda was born in Vienna. He grew up in a turbulent period and his worldview was strongly influenced by the hunger and poverty he witnessed on the streets of Vienna during the economic collapse of the 1920s. However, he enjoyed his school education and recalled being taught mathematics at his Gymnasium by a Nobel Prize Winner. He discovered his Jewish background when the authorities expelled him from his secondary school with the rise of Fascism. Subsequently, he spent a year at school in Paris, where he lived with his aunt and uncle. Gustav recalled having had to learn French very quickly as he was initially bullied as a foreign pupil with no knowledge of the language. Later, after the Anschluss, the family moved to Paris just before the outbreak of the Second World War. Gustav enrolled in a civil engineering course. Once again, his studies were interrupted, this time by the outbreak of the war. He joined the French army and when the French front collapsed he escaped to the UK by leaving his unit and reaching St Nazaire, where the last of the British Expeditionary forces were being evacuated. Gustav was fortunate to choose to embark on the *Royal Ulsterman* and not the *Lancastria*, which was sunk with the largest single-ship loss of life in British maritime history. His parents and his younger brother made their way separately to New York and Gustav lost contact with them until after the war.[1]

Gustav arrived in Britain as a refugee and was always grateful for the tolerance and openness he met. He spoke no English and his grasp of the vernacular came from his time in the Pioneer Corps, the only unit of the British army prepared to admit enemy aliens. The Corps carried out various construction tasks under the supervision of the Royal Engineers, perhaps not taxing his civil engineering skills. However, he was later invalided out of the British army after suffering an extremely serious ankle break when training for D-Day. His subsequent war work was carried out under the auspices of the Official Secrets Act, which he steadfastly refused to discuss. When he was asked one final time, before he died, he did reveal that the work had been 'rather boring'.

After the war he studied part-time at Birkbeck College London, whilst working as a photographer and conjurer to finance his studies. When he graduated he obtained lectureships at the University of Manchester, the University College of the Gold Coast (Ghana), and the University of Glasgow. In 1964 he became the founding Professor of the newly established Department of Psychology at the University of Strathclyde in Glasgow.

---

[1] For further details of Gustav Jahoda's life and work see P. R. Dasen and G. Vermes, 'In memoriam: Gustav Jahoda', *Alterstice – Revue Internationale De La Recherche Interculturelle*, 6 (2) (2017), 7–11; J. Deregowski, 'In memoriam. Gustav Jahoda: a life', *Journal of Cross-Cultural Psychology*, 48 (2017), 455–60; I. Marková (ed.), 'Special issue: across culture, mind and history', *Culture & Psychology*, 24 (2018).

Gustav's experience in Ghana, where he had a lectureship in sociology, profoundly influenced his thinking and the approach to his work. He combined a scholarly interest in theory with a hands-on practical interest in applying research methods in a real-world context. For example, in Ghana children's names reflected the weekday of their birth, which were seen as having different characteristics. It was rumoured that the Ghanaian politician Nkrumah, who then became the President of Ghana, changed his name to Kwame, which means Friday, as it was associated with being auspicious. Monday's child was supposed to be placid while the child born on a Wednesday was likely to be aggressive. Gustav explored these beliefs by painstaking scrutiny of Juvenile Court Records. He discovered that children born on Mondays were significantly under-represented as offenders while Wednesday's children were significantly over-represented in offences against the person. Gustav saw this as early empirical evidence for labelling, while the traditionalists viewed it as vindication of the truth of the name values! Gustav and his economist friend Walter Birmingham carried out a very early electoral poll for the first election in the Gold Coast that brought Nkrumah to power. They predicted the result with great accuracy, leading to suggestions of witchcraft. Gustav spoke of the sampling having been very carefully carried out. People were polled at their homes and in private settings and Gustav saw that public utterances did not always reflect voting behaviour.

In the early 1960s Gustav took part in the activities of European social psychologists to establish their own vision of the discipline, and he was one of the founders of the European Association of Experimental Social Psychology (EAESP). He was a member of the first Planning Committee, together with Serge Moscovici, Henri Tajfel, Mauk Mulder and Jozef Nuttin. He built collaborations with psychologists across Europe and offered a fresh perspective which challenged some of the dominant views from North America. Perhaps what marked him out was the breadth of his knowledge and interests; he was a polymath with an extraordinary ability to retain information. In his interview with Sandra Schruijer in 2012 he observed that,[2] 'although EAESP has done much for the emancipation of social psychology in Europe and the introduction of European thinking into the USA, over time it became to resemble American-style social psychology more and more'.[3] Schruijer comments:

> Reflecting on the origins of EAESP and his role in it he said that although he was enthusiastic about the whole endeavor, he had some skepticisms as he saw himself more as a cultural psychologist and as a listener… the Americans wanted to convince the Europeans that social psychology should be experimental. "There was a wish to

[2] Y. H. Poortinga and S. G. L. Schruijer, 'Gustav Jahoda: the art and science of constructive scepticism', *Culture & Psychology*, 24 (2018), 368–81.
[3] Ibid., p. 376.

see social psychology as a science just like physics". Experimentation was associated with science. Gustav had his reservations. "There is an inverse relationship between the rigor of an experimental method and the relevance to real life phenomena".

In 1972, the International Association for Cross-Cultural Psychology was founded in Hong Kong and Gustav served as its first full-term president. In 1988 he was elected a Fellow of the British Academy, at that time into the section of Social Studies. Later on, when the British Academy diversified, he joined the Anthropology as well as Psychology sections. In 1993 he was elected a Fellow of the Royal Society of Edinburgh.

After he retired in 1985, Gustav spoke of his move from the field to the library. He continued to dedicate himself to learning and writing and publishing his research. Most of his work concerned the history of psychology. However, he maintained a keen interest in recent developments. In addition to reassessment of historical thinkers, he often identified themes or concepts with which those thinkers had grappled, and which continue to resonate in contemporary debates. Gustav himself sought to explore the origins of some psychological concepts that had been taken for granted. For example, he thoroughly explored the evolution of the term 'empathy' which, in the eighteenth century, was effectively a synonym of 'sympathy'.

Those who knew him might have been surprised to learn that he greatly missed the contact with students in his later years. He took genuine pleasure in the successes and achievements of colleagues or students. Though keen to encourage students' original thinking, he had no hesitation in taking issue with established figures when he believed their contentions were unsound. While his arguments were carefully constructed and telling, his criticisms were never personal.

Gustav's zest for knowledge and driven engagement with the world of ideas lasted until his final weeks and days. Up to the end of his last year he engaged with new ideas and developments in science, art and politics, and he was captivated by the measurement of gravitational waves. He continued publishing and planned new subjects for papers, making the trip by train to his office at the University of Strathclyde three days a week until his 94th year. He refused medical treatment when he realised that he faced a high level of dependence, discomfort and indignity, with the prospect only of further physical deterioration, and when his scope for active and independent intellectual functioning was going to drastically reduce or disappear.

In his last few weeks, when the members of his family asked him what academic endeavours he was most proud of, he said that it was his work to challenge lazy assumptions about cultural superiority.

'In order to become a really good social psychologist,
I ought to experience life in a greatly different culture'

Gustav Jahoda belonged to the generation of social scientists who had an unprecedented influence on the growth of human and social sciences after the Second World War. The horrors of Nazism and Communism led to vast migrations of scholars and scientists from their native lands to other European countries and to the United States. Having had their personal experiences of political and cultural distress, migrants within Europe developed their individual academic and practical styles by perpetuating the heritage of European philosophy, and of human and social sciences, in their new homes. Their migration had a profound effect on the broadly based intellectual cultivation of these disciplines, among them social psychology. As migrants, they had to struggle to be accepted, to establish themselves, and to make careers in their new countries. Some of the scholars who made highly significant contributions to the development of European social psychology after the war included Marie Jahoda, Henri Tajfel, Serge Moscovici, Hilde Himmelweit, Rudolf Schaffer and, of course, Gustav Jahoda.[4]

From the beginning of his career, Jahoda's scholarly work was very broadly based, crossing several human and social sciences, such as social and developmental psychology, anthropology, history, sociology and cultural studies. He was convinced that the human mind must be conceived in and through interdependent relations between humans and their socio-cultural and historical environments, in which they develop knowledge in transforming their ideas and concepts. In one of his last papers, entitled 'Seventy years of social psychology: a cultural and personal critique', Jahoda reflected on the advancement of social psychology after the war.[5] Believing that through new experimental developments, social psychology 'was really becoming scientific!', he had listened to a scholar from New Zealand, Ernest Beaglehole, who carried out anthropological and psychological research in the Pacific. Gustav Jahoda recalled: 'He advised me that in order to become a really good social psychologist, I ought to experience life in a greatly different culture.'

Cross-cultural psychology was becoming a new and stimulating field of study, and Gustav set off with his family to the Gold Coast, now Ghana, in West Africa. His aim was to replicate there the social psychological experiments that the well-known American social psychologist Theodore Newcomb had described to him. Thus, during

[4] I. Marková and A. Jahoda, 'Across culture, mind and history', *Culture & Psychology*, 24 (2018), 266–81.
[5] G. Jahoda, 'Seventy years of social psychology: a cultural and personal critique', *Journal of Social and Political Psychology*, 4 (2016), 364–80.

the years that followed, Jahoda carried out wide-ranging studies in Africa. These included research on the relation of Ashanti names and personality, geometrical illusions and environment, topological and Euclidean spatial features noted by children, factors influencing orientation errors in reproduction of Kohs-type figures, among others. The research and experience of living in Africa was deeply revealing, because Jahoda failed to obtain results similar to those found in the USA. Just like some other researchers, he concluded that the data obtained from US college students in experiments on social cognition, influence, conformity, group dynamics and other phenomena were not generally applicable across diverse populations internationally.[6]

The fact that children and young adults in African countries responded to Western experimental tasks differently than Westerners was often viewed by researchers as an inability by Africans to think abstractly. Jahoda insisted, however, that those researchers who wrote about the concrete and rigid mental capacities of Africans were not aware of their own limitations in thinking by using tests designed for Western cultures and 'comparing' results with those in African cultures. Tests do not operate in a vacuum and they have different meanings for people in different cultures. Not only did Western psychologists ignore the role of the environment in which individuals lived, but they also disregarded knowledge of neighbouring disciplines such as developmental psychology, history, anthropology and sociology. Above all, Jahoda was strongly influenced by anthropology that was 'hardly ever mentioned in social psychology texts'. In his classic book, *Psychology and Anthropology*, he traced the origins of culture-related psychology and ideas about the uniqueness of culture and mind.[7] He drew attention to the historical perspective that showed that these two disciplines, psychology and anthropology, emerged from common roots. They are both concerned with a number of fundamental topics such as personality, socialisation, social behaviour, systems of explanation and reasoning, classification and symbolism. Jahoda documented his understanding of the interface between psychology and anthropology by providing concrete examples of social activities such as customs, myths and the use of symbols. Given the complexity and richness of the phenomena studied from psychological and anthropological perspectives, Gustav was particularly scrupulous in approaching them with a clear elaboration of the conceptual and methodological strengths and limitations of each discipline.

Jahoda was a ferocious critic of the narrowly conceived experimental social psychology as it was established in the United States after the Second World War and transported to Europe. This kind of psychology fragmented humans into elements and studied their behaviour in terms of dependent and independent variables, ignoring

[6] Marková and Jahoda, 'Across culture, mind and history'.
[7] G. Jahoda, *Psychology and Anthropology: a Psychological Perspective* (London: 1982).

their dynamic nature and their environment. Jahoda emphasised that, without paying attention to the cultural and historical contexts of social conduct, the findings of experimental social psychologists reflect no more than contemporary fashions and current social norms. They are unlikely to reveal universal social processes and, instead, they masquerade the study of nature by presenting it as the study of social processes.[8] Jahoda was well aware that his critiques were not new, and that previous generations of scholars over many decades had expressed views similar to his own. However, naïve presuppositions of the static and universalistic features of humans that allegedly conformed to 'scientific' assumptions were resistant to questions about their truthfulness and, therefore, to any possibility of change.

Children's thinking is manifold and heterogeneous: Gustav Jahoda versus Jean Piaget

After his return from Africa in 1956, Jahoda took up a lecturing position at the University of Glasgow. Child psychology was one of his foremost interests, and he was particularly attentive to the study of practical problems and culture-related topics. Among the first empirical studies he undertook after his return was research on children's ideas about nationality. These studies were inspired by research of the renowned Swiss child psychologist Jean Piaget, with whom Jahoda disagreed—but whom he admired.

Jahoda's disagreement with Piaget became particularly apparent in his analysis of Piaget's research on children's understanding of Swiss nationality. Specifically, after the war, national stereotypes were extensively studied and in this context Piaget and Weil carried out a study into children's ideas about their homeland.[9] They found that children up to the age 10–11 did not understand class inclusion, that is, they did not comprehend that someone could be at the same time both Swiss and Genevan.

With his methodological rigour and ingenuity, Jahoda showed in his own study that the abstract concept of 'nationality' as a logical class, with its ill-defined boundaries, was likely to be responsible for the child's errors and confusions. Jahoda showed that young children could make category inclusions if they were familiar with the concepts in question, and if they were aware of class boundaries between them. For example, very young children could understand that someone could be at the same

---

[8] M. Billig, 'Those who only know of social psychology know not social psychology: a tribute to Gustav Jahoda's historical approach', *Culture & Psychology*, 24 (2018), 282–93.

[9] J. Piaget and A.-M. Weil, 'The development in children of the idea of the homeland and relations with other countries', *International Social Science Bulletin*, 3 (1951), 561–78.

time a schoolboy, a pedestrian, a human being, a son; and that something could be both a leek and vegetable.

Piaget studied a variety of forms of children's thinking such as the acquisition of causality, religion, science and morality, among others. Jahoda highly regarded Piaget's ingenuity and novel ways of studying child development. Piaget used the method of free and in-depth conversations to explore children's thinking, which was also used by anthropologists in explorations of interactions between humans and their cultural contexts. Nevertheless, there were fundamental differences between the theoretical presuppositions of Piaget and Jahoda. Piaget's universalistic approach to child rationality and genetic epistemology affected his observations and experiments that he and his teams carried out first in Neuchâtel and then in Geneva. His studies involved children from relatively homogeneous environments of middle-class Swiss families. The study of biology, philosophy and logic were leading disciplines on the basis of which Piaget constructed his coherent theoretical system. The beliefs in autonomy and freedom of the individual gave direction to Piaget's ideas of the ontogenetic and universal development of children's judgement and rationality.[10]

In contrast, Jahoda's intellectual background, his life in Austria, France and the UK, and in particular his experience in Africa, orientated him towards conceiving the child's thinking as heterogeneous, based not only on cognitive capacities but also as being interdependent with the child's social experience in family, peers and the life in community. Therefore, Piaget's universalistic approach to the child's cognition was totally at odds with Jahoda's presuppositions concerning child development. Piaget's epistemology presupposed that mental maturation of the child was uniform across age and culture. Jahoda particularly disagreed with Piaget's assumption that logi-co-mathematical operations were applicable to all kinds of children's thinking.

Jahoda's numerous and diverse cross-cultural experimental results during the 1950s and 1980s showed that a child's thinking takes manifold and heterogeneous forms and that it cannot be viewed as a mental capacity developing in a rigid and pre-established order. He abundantly explored children's ideas about nationality, economic institutions, markets and many other topics that influenced the development of their thought.[11] Children in different 'cultures' learn different things and acquire

---

[10] A.-N. Perret-Clermont, 'Epilogue: Piaget, his elders and his peers', in A.-N. Perret-Clermont and J.-M. Barrelet (eds.), *Jean Piaget and Neuchâtel* (Hove and New York, 2008), pp. 202–31.

[11] Among many studies of these topics, for example: G. Jahoda, 'Sex differences in preferences for shapes: a cross-cultural replication', *British Journal of Psychology*, 47 (1956), 126–32; G. Jahoda, 'Children's concepts of time and history', *Educational Review*, 15 (1963), 87–104; G. Jahoda, 'The construction of economic reality by some Glaswegian children', *European Journal of Social Psychology*, 9 (1979), 115–27; G. Jahoda, 'Development of Scottish children's ideas and attitudes about other countries', *The Journal of Social Psychology*, 58 (1962), 91–108; G. Jahoda, 'The development of children's ideas about country and nationality. Part I: a conceptual framework', *The British Journal of Educational Psychology*, 33

different kinds of experience which they apply in their relevant contexts. Jahoda's studies of children in Ghana, Scotland, and other European countries provided him with knowledge of the ways they acquire social concepts, that is concepts they learn about in their daily experience from parents, peers, or other people, rather than in formal schooling. These concepts include economics, money, banks, time and history, alcohol, national symbols, myth and magic.

In a pioneering study for the Scottish Home and Health Department in the early 1970s, Jahoda was faced with the challenge of evaluating young children's recognition of and attitude to the effects of alcohol. Innovative ideas included hiring a young actor to depict various states of inebriation on film. Jahoda's findings that children at the age of six years understand what it is to be drunk and that it is something negative led in Scotland to a recommendation, radical at the time, that primary school children should be taught about alcoholism.[12]

The novel feature of his studies was Jahoda's holistic perspective with respect to the child's understandings of concepts and phenomena in daily life. For example, Jahoda's research into socio-economic understandings of activities in shops and banks showed that it was necessary to find out whether the child comprehended basic principles of operations carried out in such establishments. Concerning shops, it was important to consider the child's knowledge of interpersonal relations—for example, between customer and shop, between shop and shop assistants and between shop and factory.[13] Equally, the understanding of functioning of the bank was dependent on the child's knowledge of concepts such as 'profit', 'loan', or 'interest'. The child obtains such knowledge mainly in family and in daily encounters. Different spheres of social thinking involve different kinds of practical knowledge and a range of interpersonal relations.[14] Jahoda was convinced that social psychology as a developmental

---

(1963), 47–60; G. Jahoda, 'The development of children's ideas about country and nationality. Part II: national symbols and themes', *The British Journal of Educational Psychology*, 33 (1963), 143–53.

[12] G. Jahoda and J. Cramond, *Children and Alcohol* (London, 1972); G. Jahoda, J. B. Davis and S. Tagg, 'Parents' alcohol consumption and children's knowledge of drinks and usage pattern', *British Journal of Addiction*, 75 (1980), 297–303.

[13] I. Marková and J. C. Jesuino, 'Social psychology as a developmental discipline in the dynamics of practical life: Gustav Jahoda's pioneering studies on children's social thinking', *Culture & Psychology*, 24 (2018), 343–57.

[14] Jahoda, 'The construction of economic reality by some Glaswegian children'; G. Jahoda, 'The development of thinking about economic institutions: the bank', *Cahiers De Psychologie Cognitive*, 1 (1981), 55–73; G. Jahoda, 'The development of thinking about socio-economic systems', in H. Tajfel, C. Fraser and J. M. F. Jaspars (eds.), *The Social Dimension*, vol. 1: *European Developments in Social Psychology* (Cambridge and Paris, 1984), pp. 69–88; G. Jahoda, 'Levels of social and logico-mathematical thinking: their nature and interrelations', in W. Doise and A. Palmonari (eds.), *Social Interaction in Individual Development* (Cambridge, 1984), pp. 173–8.

discipline must study the dynamics of practical life. Numerous examples of his research illustrate this point. For example, children in Zimbabwe and in Scotland had different kinds of experience concerning the socio-economic concept of 'profit'. While Scottish children below the age of 10 had no idea how to respond to the question about profit, children in Zimbabwe, who often helped their mothers in the market, could easily provide answers to such questions.[15]

From cross-cultural to cultural psychology

After the Second World War anthropologists and psychologists, more than ever before, were keen to explore similarities and differences of human psyche across the globe and therefore interest in cross-cultural and comparative studies, including Piagetian studies,[16] was rapidly growing. Yet despite its fast development and diversification, Jahoda emphasised that some dominant topics of this newly flourishing field showed a considerable continuity with, and repetition of, well-known historical themes that had been explored over the past two or three centuries. His cultural-historical sensitivity brought attention to the main and mutually opposing epistemological presuppositions within cross-cultural and cultural studies that were built into diverse views of human nature throughout its long past.[17]

First, there was an epistemological presupposition of continuity in the development of human species. This was implied by Darwin's assumption that all species could be placed on an upward continuum and that, as pre-humans gradually acquired reason and language, they progressed to humans.[18] Jahoda and Krewer were critical of the idea which implied that cultures were at different stages of development and that they gradually achieved higher intellectual powers:

> The dominant model of man as a natural creature endowed with reason corresponds in many ways to the basic model of cross-cultural psychology. From this perspective human diversity was conceptualised as a variation on the same theme, and it was this

[15] G. Jahoda, 'European "lag" in the development of an economic concept: a study in Zimbabwe', *British Journal of Developmental Psychology*, 1 (1983), 113–20.

[16] P. R. Dasen, 'Cross-cultural Piagetian research: a summary', *Journal of Cross-Cultural Psychology*, 3 (1972), 23–40; P. R. Dasen and A. Heron, 'Cross-cultural tests of Piaget's theory', in H. C. Triandis and A. Heron (eds.), *Handbook of Cross-Cultural Psychology*, vol. 4: *Developmental Psychology* (Boston, MA, 1981), pp. 295–342.

[17] G. Jahoda and B. Krewer, 'History of cross-cultural and cultural psychology', in J. Berry, Y. H. Poortinga, and J. Pandey (eds.), *Handbook of Cross-Cultural Psychology*, 2nd edn, vol. 1: *Theory and Method* (Boston, MA, 1997), pp. 1–42.

[18] T. Ingold, 'Beyond biology and culture: the meaning of evolution in a relational world', *Social Anthropology*, 12 (2004), 209–21; A. O. Lovejoy, *The Great Chain of Being* (Cambridge, MA: 1936).

theme that constituted the focus of interest. Evidence of how to up-to-date such an approach is … plea to peel the onion called culture.[19]

This is the model of Enlightenment according to which the human being is a composite of levels, each superimposed upon those beneath it and underpinning those above it. As one analyses humans, 'one peels off layers after layer' and finds the underlying structural and functional organisation.[20] Underneath psychological layers one finds biological foundations such as anatomical, physiological and neurological, of the human edifice.[21]

> This edifice of human life had to be unravelled by the scientific quest to understand both nature and human nature by assuming a determinism governed by natural laws. It was the attempt to transfer the successful Newtonian model from physics to human affairs that led to a machine-like, mechanical understanding of human beings as prototypically realised in La Metrie's (1748) *L'homme machine*.[22]

Among the ancestors of cross-cultural psychology Jahoda and Krewer included Francis Galton, Wiliam Halse Rivers, Richard Thurnwald and Frederik Bartlett. These scholars were involved in invaluable empirical and/or theoretical work across cultures.

When the newly developing field of cross-cultural psychology quickly diversified after the war, it followed the methodological strategy of mainstream psychology, focusing on inductive data collection, measurements and statistical analyses. Its approach was basically ahistorical, aiming at the discovery of universals. Jahoda and Krewer maintained that cross-cultural psychology united itself by its goal to internationalise the empirical basis of psychology by studying similarities and differences among citizens in different parts of the globe.[23] It defined itself above all by its methodology, rather than by epistemological, theoretical or content-bound concerns. They quoted from John Berry who explicitly expressed the priority of methodology in cross-cultural studies: 'It is our methodology that we must turn to in order to seek our identity as a discipline.'[24]

---

[19] Jahoda and Krewer, 'History of cross-cultural and cultural psychology', pp. 14–15.

[20] Y. H. Poortinga, F. J. R. Van de Vijver, R. C. Joe and J. M. H. Van de Koppel, 'Peeling the onion called culture', in C. Kagitcibasi (ed.). *Growth and Progress in Cross-cultural Psychology* (Amsterdam, 1987), pp. 22–34.

[21] C. Geertz, 'The impact of the concept of culture on the concept of man', in E. Hammer and W. Simmons (eds.), *Man Makes Sense* (Boston, 1970), pp. 44–65.

[22] Jahoda and Krewer, 'History of cross-cultural and cultural psychology', p. 15.

[23] Ibid., p. 3

[24] J. W. Berry, 'Introduction to methodology', in H. C. Triandis and J. W. Berry (eds.), *Handbook of Cross-Cultural Psychology*, vol. 1 (Boston, 1980), pp. 1–28.

The opposite kind of epistemological presuppositions in relation to cultural studies stemmed from socio-historical perspectives,[25] and Jahoda and Krewer viewed these as indicators for the emergence of cultural psychology. These perspectives had their origin in the Renaissance, showing a profound effect of the diversification of knowledge in various spheres of scientific and artistic concerns, as well as in daily life. Within these perspectives, social knowledge proved to be eminently relevant to the study of the human mind and culture as the dynamic and ever-changing processes of human history. The emphasis on language and communication became part of this process. Humanity could not be understood solely as constituted by natural dispositions but, equally important, as being shaped and as self-created in history and social development. Predecessors of cultural psychology included Giambattista Vico, Johann Gottfried Herder, Wilhelm Humboldt, Moritz Lazarus, Hermann Steinthal and Wilhelm Wundt, among others. Their ideas were part of the social, political and economic climate, in particular in Germany and in surrounding Central European countries, where debates for and against the formation of modern nations took place. Studies of their languages, communities and their histories, as well as of the collective spirit of people, were widely discussed.[26] As Jahoda argued, the beginnings of social anthropology, social psychology and ethnology were intermingled.[27] Complex mental processes and products of communities required a historical and comparative analysis. That was possible only in and through anthropology and psychology conceived as a historical-comparative study and a diachronic study of languages, myths and customs.[28]

During the 1990s debates at the International Association of Cross-Cultural Psychology concerning diversity within cross-cultural psychology took place,[29] and the socio-cultural tradition obtained the new title of 'cultural psychology'. Whilst 'cultural psychology' was not a unitary domain, its diverse sub-branches shared certain epistemological presuppositions about the human mind and its socio-cultural development.

Later in his life, Jahoda conceded that, just like many others, he started his career as a cross-cultural psychologist. Empirical research was a vital component of his cross-cultural commitments. At the same time he was convinced that the manipulation

---

[25] Jahoda and Krewer, 'History of cross-cultural and cultural psychology'.

[26] For example, R. Diriwächter, 'Völkerpsychologie', in J. Valsiner (ed.), *The Oxford Handbook of Culture and Psychology* (New York and Oxford, 2012), pp. 43–57; Jahoda, *Psychology and Anthropology: a Psychological Perspective*; G. Jahoda, *A History of Social Psychology: from the Eighteenth-Century Enlightenment to the Second World War* (Cambridge, 2007); E. Klautke, 'The mind of the nation: the debate about Völkerpsychologie, 1851–1900', *Central Europe*, 8 (2010), 1–19.

[27] Jahoda, *Psychology and Anthropology: a Psychological Perspective*.

[28] I. Marková, *The Dialogical Mind: Common Sense and Ethics* (Cambridge, 2016).

[29] Jahoda and Krewer, 'History of cross-cultural and cultural psychology', p. 1

of independent variables does not exert an effect on the development of knowledge in any simple and direct manner. The manipulation of variables cannot adequately explain complex processes of socialisation and social interactions.[30] Instead, these processes 'take place within an overarching cultural framework, and to ignore this is to be guilty of gross oversimplification'.[31] He critically referred to his own earlier work that was 'misguided' by what he called a less extreme model of simplistic cross-cultural research. However, he did not deny the valuable work that has been carried out within that tradition, but emphasised its limitations.

Gradually, he started to refer to his conversion from a 'merely "cross-cultural" to a wider "cultural" psychologist', often referring to the elusive concepts of culture.[32] For a great connoisseur of German cultural scholarship of the nineteenth and early twentieth centuries, such as Johann Herbart and Wilhelm Wundt, among others, Jahoda's move was not surprising. Moreover, whilst the cultural tradition had a rich spectrum of ancestors from Vico to Wundt, the discovery of the socio-cultural approach of Soviet psychologists Vygotsky and Luria was for Jahoda a new encounter, brought to his attention by Michael Cole.[33]

Jahoda acknowledged that cultural psychology made a radical break from mainstream experimental psychology and from its epistemological basis, because the kind of focus it followed could not be explored in and through ahistorical experiments. It did not mean that cultural psychology would abandon the empirical basis, but it followed a different path.[34] Nevertheless, Jahoda concluded that the two concepts of culture, 'those of cross-cultural versus cultural psychologists, are so divergent that it is hard to see how they could be reconciled'.[35] However, despite the difficulty to reconcile their differences, Jahoda viewed the work of cross-cultural and cultural psychologists as complementary.[36]

[30] G. Jahoda, 'The colour of a chameleon: perspectives of concepts of culture', *Cultural Dynamics*, 6 (1993), 277–87.
[31] Ibid., 280.
[32] Ibid., 281
[33] M. Cole, *Cultural Psychology: a Once and Future Discipline* (Cambridge, MA, 1996).
[34] Jahoda, 'The colour of a chameleon', 281
[35] Ibid., 282
[36] For more details about this division see W. J. Lonner and J. Adamopoulos, 'Culture as antecedent to behavior', in J. Berry, Y. H. Poortinga, and J. Pandey (eds.), *Handbook of Cross-Cultural Psychology*, 2nd edn, vol. 1: *Theory and Method* (Boston, 1997), pp. 43–83.

Culture, Mind and History

Throughout his broadly conceived scholarship, Jahoda's oeuvre was dominated by his focus on the interdependence between Culture, Mind and History. In his classic book *Crossroads between Culture and Mind* he compared these three concepts with another triad, that of Biology, Race and Mind.[37] He suggested that throughout the history of humankind, these two triads of concepts defined two fundamental themes, closely related to one another as they kept persistently returning: first, 'what are the boundaries between the human and the non-human?'; and second, 'how do we define the differences between 'us' and 'others''? These themes have not only a theoretical significance but also, above all, they determine relations and interactions among humans. These themes preoccupied Jahoda throughout all his work, because they implied the existence of racist attitudes which, from his early career, he intensely attacked.

First, Jahoda repeatedly posed the question: 'what does it mean to be a human being?' On the one hand, humans have biologically determined features that are not part of culture, such as giving birth, dying, breathing, and so on. These biological features humans share with non-humans. However, humans create themselves in history, through the interdependent relations between the culture and mind. And yet, already in human pre-history, 'we' and 'they' relations were fundamental to life. The preference for one's own group is very deeply and unconsciously entrenched in the human mind. It is difficult to reflect upon it and it is even less possible to eradicate it. 'We' identify with our group, nation or language, and are ready to distance ourselves from 'others' who are associated with danger, threat and risk, or at least who are not considered as valued beings.

In a number of studies Jahoda persistently analysed the views of racist ethnologists who asserted that non-Europeans, and especially Africans, were biologically incapable of ever functioning at the same intellectual level as Europeans. Racist ethnologists also distinguished between supposedly 'superior' and 'inferior' races within Europe, often on the basis of the shapes of their skulls. Since his initial career Jahoda published studies on political and racist attitudes.[38] His first book, entitled *White Man*,[39] was devoted to this pervasive issue, and was based on his early research in Ghana. Jahoda turned round the commonly studied white people's perceptions of black people and instead explored how white people were perceived by black Ghanaians.

[37] G. Jahoda, *Crossroads between Culture and Mind* (New York, 1992).
[38] G. Jahoda, 'Race differences and race prejudice', *Biology and Human Affairs*, 16 (1951), 138–44; G. Jahoda, 'Political attitudes and judgments of other people', *Journal of Abnormal Psychology*, 49 (1954), 330–4.
[39] G. Jahoda, *White Man: a Study of the Attitudes of Africans to Europeans in Ghana before Independence* (London, 1961).

This book resulted from diaries that he had kept during his work in Ghana, noting images that Africans had of other Europeans and even of himself. Attitudes towards Europeans referred to the past slave trade, missionary activities and to colonial rule. While illiterate villagers were subservient, educated people tended to behave in a more egalitarian manner. However, many Africans expressed the view that they were regarded as subhuman beings and this, Jahoda maintained, was 'one of the most significant findings' of his study. The widespread tendency to differentiate themselves from unwanted 'others' remained Gustav's theme throughout his work. In a historically conceived book, and conceptualised with high originality, *Images of Savages* strove to uncover the 'ancient roots of modern prejudice in Western Culture', in which the 'image of the savage as childlike' goes back a thousand years.[40] These images still manifest themselves as racial prejudices, showing that boundaries between the human and the non-human are still part of contemporary social and political life.

The theme of supposedly 'superior' and 'inferior' races also featured in Jahoda's recurrent analyses of Jean Piaget and Lucien Lévy-Bruhl.[41] These culminated in Jahoda's article devoted specifically to Piaget's alleged misinterpretation of Lévy-Bruhl.[42] Jahoda documented that, for Piaget, the work of Lévy-Bruhl was a source of inspiration. Piaget believed that Lévy-Bruhl had proposed 'analogies between the child and the primitive at every step'.[43] Jahoda accentuated that comparison between 'primitives' and children was a common theme in ninetenth-century literature, and that it was even supported by 'scientific' theories of the time. However, Lévy-Bruhl 'never directly compared primitives with children' and indeed he very rarely referred to children; when he did, 'he explicitly objected to such comparisons' which Jahoda verifies by numerous examples.[44] It appears that Piaget's misunderstanding was related to Lévy-Bruhl's terms such as 'participation', 'mystical mentality', 'magical thinking' and 'pre-logical thinking'. As Jahoda observed, due to numerous critiques, later in his life Lévy-Bruhl gave up his term 'pre-logical thinking', which had led to much confusion concerning his proper views.

More generally, Jahoda argued that the denigration of Lévy-Bruhl adopted by many scholars was unwarranted and based on inaccurate simplifications. In paying enormous attention to historical detail and accuracy of reading and the understanding of texts, Jahoda emphasised that Lévy-Bruhl attempted to explain different modes

---

[40] G. Jahoda, *Images of Savages: Ancient Roots of Modern Prejudice in Western Culture* (London, 1999).

[41] For details see Marková and Jesuino, 'Social psychology as a developmental discipline in the dynamics of practical life'.

[42] G. Jahoda, 'Piaget and Lévy-Bruhl', *History of Psychology*, 3 (2000), 218–38.

[43] J. Piaget, *The Child's Concept of Physical Causality* (Totowa, NJ, 1972), p. 88.

[44] L. Lévy-Bruhl, *La mentalité primitive* [How Natives Think], trans. Lilian A. Clare (Princeton, NJ, 1985 [1922]).

of thought due to cultural differences and that this point was crudely misconstrued. He insisted that Lévy-Bruhl's terms 'pre-logical' and 'logical' did not refer to an evolutionary point of view according to which the original 'pre-logical primitives' develop into rational beings. Instead, Lévy-Bruhl adopted the perspective according to which humans lived in different social and cultural environments and their rationalities were expressions of collective representations suited to those environments. Lévy-Bruhl's perspective, therefore, rejected the criterion of a fixed universal rationality and instead proposed multiple rationalities as processes that developed in accordance with the requirements of cultures in which humans live.

Jahoda observed that Lévy-Bruhl's ideas were misunderstood both by scholars adopting the egalitarian ethos of the late nineteenth century as well as by social anthropologists after the Second World War when the concept of cultural differences, of universal rationality, its growth in individuals, societies, and cultures, had been widely discussed. While all scholars attempted to hold the presupposition of the mental unity of mankind, the contents of these debates intermingled the social scientific issues with political agendas arising from the fact that different cultures, languages and minds of others can be understood only within their own idiosyncratic socio-historical situations, rather than universally.

Gustav Jahoda as a person

Gustav Jahoda was a very modest person, never emphasising his scholarly achievements and he was very uncomfortable with the general habit of academic self-promotion.[45] He had the deepest sense of personal integrity and he was very frank in expressing his views, whether to acclaimed authorities or to his friends and colleagues, paying no attention to personal loyalties. For these characteristics he was both an admired scholar and a formidable opponent in academic controversies. Although we could choose a number of examples of such incidents, let us refer to one. Poortinga remembered that he and his collaborators asked Jahoda to write a foreword for their textbook *Cross-Cultural Psychology: Theory and Applications.*[46] He accepted on condition that he could express his honest opinion. The authors were happy to accept this, but Jahoda's text, while expressing some positive aspects, 'outlined in some detail what he saw as an important shortcoming (basically insufficient attention to culturalist

---

[45] Billig, 'Those who only know of social psychology know not social psychology'.
[46] Poortinga and Schruijer, 'Gustav Jahoda'; J. W. Berry, Y. H. Poortinga, M. H. Segall and P. R. Dasen, *Cross-Cultural Psychology: Research and Applications*, 2nd edn (Cambridge, 2002).

approaches)'.[47] As a result, the authors wondered whether they should ask him for a preface in the second edition.

> Fortunately, in this case principles of open communication in science trumped the egos of the authors, but it is telling that there was a discussion, even after a balanced argument with more favorable than unfavorable comments.[48]

Gustav's energy and working spirit were relentless. Sandra Schruijer recalls her discussion with him,[49] seven years after he published his book on the history of social psychology.[50] One of the reviewers was hoping for a volume 2, probably not being aware that Gustav was 86 years old when the book was published. Sandra Schruijer refers to a mail with Gustav, who was then 92: 'I'm lacking in energy these days. What little I have is usually confined to work, which I'm determined to continue as long as I can.' But a few lines later he writes 'It occurred to me that we might discuss the possibility of some joint work, since we have similar interests – what do you think of that?'

Gustav Jahoda's legacy

Gustav Jahoda's long life and work brings to focus an exemplary case of a scholar who created and re-created his theories and empirical research in and through inter-dependent relations with the socio-cultural and political environments in which he lived. Conditions during and after the war, optimism in the possibility of scientific achievements of psychology, in the study of the human mind across the globe, guided his talent and energy 'to become a really good social psychologist', and 'to experience life in a greatly different culture'. At the same time he implicitly adopted presuppositions that guided research in social psychology in the postwar period. These implicit presuppositions became explicitly formulated and became the source of problems when Jahoda realised that social psychology was trapped in the search for universals using ahistorical and mechanistic approaches in its struggle to imitate natural sciences. For the rest of his academic career he faced the problem of how to reconcile his trans-disciplinary perspective, enabling him to explore the human mind and culture, with his meticulous search for clarity of concepts and methods. We see again and again Jahoda's attention to highly sensitive issues concerning the views of anthropologists and psychologists with respect to the unity of mind, and social scientific, political and ideological issues surrounding this domain.

[47] Poortinga and Schruijer, 'Gustav Jahoda', 373.
[48] Ibid.
[49] Ibid., 377.
[50] Jahoda, *A History of Social Psychology*.

In appreciating Jahoda's legacy, Dasen, Mishra and Wassmann emphasise the importance of his early work that was concerned with validity and reliability in cross-cultural research, confronting methodological problems, including his own.[51] Carl Ratner esteemed Jahoda as 'perhaps the first modern cross-cultural psychologist. He has done pioneering research that plumbed important methodological issues.'[52] Robert Serpell brings to attention the importance of Jahoda's influence on ethnolinguistic, disciplinary and historical approaches in pedagogical practices in Africa.[53] This is particularly important in child development, to combine indigenous traditions with pedagogical innovation. He appreciates Jahoda's fluent knowledge of several languages and his sensitivity to, and limitations of, translations of social scientific terminology. He maintains that over a period of a long time 'Jahoda provided the international community of academic scholarship with a dazzling array of insights into how different disciplines within which human development has been investigated in Africa has influenced the practices of different research cultures.'[54] These insights influenced the practices of different research communities, as well as led to the development of new concepts, theories and methods within and beyond those disciplines.

In re-appreciating Gustav Jahoda's work, Poortinga and Schruijer recall 'the prophets in the old testament of the bible who issued grave warnings'.[55] While they may not have been fully welcome in their own time and context because their admonitions were not appreciated by those at whom they were directed, 'Gustav rarely directed his arrows at insignificant issues' and 'being the target of Gustav's criticisms can be seen as a mark of distinction' because the issue was thought to be of some influence. Jahoda was always concerned with important themes, directing attention to the possibilities of the genuine theoretical and methodological development of social sciences. In his evaluation of Jahoda's oeuvre, Jaan Valsiner appreciates Gustav Jahoda as a deeply critical and constructive mind, someone who did not try to assemble followers of his theories in the busy academic life: 'Yet, he was always there … an honest scholar for whom all institutional absurdities of the games universities play were foreign. He was a Thinker in its own right. This is the highest appreciation any scholar of today can get.'[56]

---

[51] P. R. Dasen, R. C. Mishra and J. Wassmann, 'Quasi-experimental research in culture sensitive psychology', *Culture & Psychology*, 24 (2018), 327–42.

[52] C. Ratner, 'Jahoda, Gustav', in R. W. Rieber (ed.), *Encyclopedia of the History of Psychological Theories* (New York, 2012), chapter 28.

[53] R. Serpell, 'Situated understanding of human development in Africa: systematic inquiries at the nexus of psychology, social science and history', *Culture & Psychology*, 24 (2018), 382–97.

[54] Ibid., 383.

[55] Poortinga and Schruijer, 'Gustav Jahoda', 378.

[56] J. Valsiner, 'Culture, mind and history: building on the contributions of Gustav Jahoda', *Culture & Psychology*, 24 (2018), 398–400.

Acknowledgements

We are grateful to Sandra Schruijer for providing Gustav Jahoda's photo that she took in 2007 during her interview with him. We also thank Paul, Colin and Catherine Jahoda for helping us with information and comments on Gustav's life.

Note on the authors: Ivana Marková is Professor Emeritus in Psychology at the University of Stirling and Visiting Professor in the Department of Psychological and Behavioural Science at the London School of Economics; she was elected a Fellow of the British Academy in 1999. Andrew Jahoda is Professor of Learning Disabilities in the Institute of Health and Wellbeing at the University of Glasgow, and an Honorary Consultant Psychologist at NHS Greater Glasgow and Clyde.

IOAN LEWIS

Ioan Myrddin Lewis

30 January 1930 – 14 March 2014

elected Fellow of the British Academy 1986

by

WENDY JAMES

Fellow of the British Academy

Ioan M. Lewis originally studied chemistry, then moved into social anthropology at Oxford, focusing on the Horn of Africa. Intensive fieldwork followed from 1955, with his wife Ann Elizabeth Keir, in the British Somali Protectorate; and to a lifetime's interest in the wider regions of Somali speakers, their oral literature, and later their radio and other international communications. After a brief period at the Rhodes-Livingstone Institute, Lewis taught at Glasgow University and University College London before being appointed to the Chair of Social Anthropology at the London School of Economics in 1969. Dedicated to strengthening academic exchanges, especially across Africa, from his *A Pastoral Democracy* (1961) onwards he remained a prolific writer well beyond retirement.

Biographical Memoirs of Fellows of the British Academy, XVIII, 175–195
Posted 6 August 2019. © British Academy 2019.

IOAN LEWIS

Ioan Lewis is remembered for his life-long academic energies and intense commitments to the post-war strengthening of the more systematically observed, objectively presented and rationally argued side of social anthropology—but even more so for his life-long commitment to the Somali peoples of north-eastern Africa. Very few other anthropologists have maintained the decades of active interest, and indeed direct involvement, in the people and politics of the regions where they conducted their original fieldwork. Lewis embarked on his research in what was then the British Protectorate of Somaliland at the age of 25, became Professor of Social Anthropology at the London School of Economics (LSE) at 39, maintained links with the wider Somali-speaking regions of north-eastern Africa through decades of political upheaval and went on publishing his ideas in print and online until he was over 80. Some of his later public exchanges concerning Somali affairs, perhaps especially with the younger generation of more gender-conscious anthropologists and Somali-speaking scholars growing up world-wide, could be quite sharp. At the same time, from his early years he devoted a good deal of time to maintaining regular contact with a wide range of colleagues through attending and organising international conferences, chairing scholarly institutions and publishing widely on varied topics, occasionally in French and German, but especially Italian. The most complete bibliography of Lewis's writings I am aware of was compiled for *Milk and Peace: Drought and War*, a Festschrift devoted to Somali culture, society and politics in 2010.[1]

I first met Ioan Lewis in the mid-1960s, shortly after taking up my first post teaching social anthropology in the University of Khartoum, where Ian Cunnison was continuing as the first professor of our department since it was launched in 1958. Of course we deliberately used a good deal of ethnographic material relating to north-eastern Africa in our teaching, and I remember being a little nervous talking to a class about Azande witchcraft. I need not have worried; a couple of northern Sudanese students, one of them a woman, made a laughing comment on these lines: 'Oh, that makes sense. We have quite a few ideas like that in my home village!' But on another occasion, when I was using some of Ioan Lewis's descriptive accounts of the differences between northern (mainly pastoralist) and southern (mainly agricultural) Somalia, and how this ecological contrast had an impact on the forms of Islamic institutions and practice in the two regions, the students went distinctly quiet. Before I had quite finished, a young man stood up and asked how I could think that Islam would be affected by a small difference in geographical circumstances. It was clear from his tone of voice that I was in no position to teach such things (and I did not argue, but quietly put my papers together and left a little early).

[1] M. V. Hoehne and V. Luling (eds.), *Milk and Peace: Drought and War: Somali Culture, Society and Politics. Essays in Honour of I. M. Lewis* (London, 2010). For the Bibliography, see pp. 403–22.

Ioan Lewis came through the department at least twice during my five years there, once as our external examiner, and then as one of many global participants in a major conference held at the University in 1968 on the theme of 'Sudan in Africa'. The majority of the contributions in the resulting volume concerned history, politics and law, but one section contained three social anthropology papers. Professor Cunnison and I each presented papers discussing our respective fieldwork in the country, and Ioan Lewis gave a paper investigating the extent of spirit possession across north-eastern Africa, a topic which he had already started exploring world-wide. His well-known *Ecstatic Religion* was soon to appear (in 1971);[2] while the Khartoum conference volume appeared a year later (1972).[3] However, Lewis's own survey-style paper published there was itself re-published by the LSE in 1999, and again by Berg in 2004, as part of a collection representing key papers of his entitled 'Arguments with Ethnography'. There were virtually no changes in the later editions, apart from slight variation in the title and the insertion of a few subtitles; but there was one, rather long, extra footnote. This drew attention, very reasonably, to some more recent work done on spirit possession in the Sudan, especially by Janice Boddy, of the University of British Columbia, among the women of the northern Nile valley. However, echoing some of his more general disagreements which had deepened over the years about the properly objective character of ethnography, Lewis distances himself from her 'cognitive' approach, suggesting that through refocusing or reframing the experience of possession, women are able to 'confront and transcend the socio-cultural categories which constrain them'. He clearly disagrees with her claim that, thus enabled to think and feel differently, they are empowered to experience 'more felicitous outcomes in their encounters with others'. Lewis goes to on suggest that this claim 'is, unfortunately, undocumented and remains hypothetical. Space which might have been devoted to exploring how this bold hypothesis might be tested, is instead given up to a "post-modernist" account in which the author's literary and other sensitivities are projected onto the Sudanese women concerned, without the adducing of any evidence that the latter share them.' Lewis's criticism is then extended, retrospectively, to a key work of mid-twentieth-century Oxford anthropology: 'In this respect, Boddy's account can be seen as an elaboration of similar tendencies to ethnographic over-writing present in a more subtle and less intrusive form in Lienhardt's (1961) well-known study of Dinka religion.'[4] Of course anthropologists always have a hard

---

[2] I. M. Lewis, *Ecstatic Religion* (London: 1971); 2nd edn, *Ecstatic Religion: an Anthropological Study of Spirit Possession and Shamanism* (London, 1988).

[3] I. M. Lewis, 'Spirit possession in North-East Africa', in Y. F. Hasan (ed.), *Sudan in Africa: Studies Presented to the First International Conference sponsored by the Sudan Research Unit, 7-12 February 1968* (Khartoum, 1972), pp. 212–26.

[4] I. M. Lewis, 'Present and past in North-East African spirit-possession', in I. M. Lewis, *Arguments with*

time in combining what they hope will serve as a straightforward account of human behaviour on the one hand with what they often feel to be an equally important capacity on the other to sense, and engage at least partially, with the self-consciousness of others. In his personal work, Lewis maintained a distinctive perspective: his style was to take a clear, pragmatic approach to the description and comparison of the forms of social organisation. He rarely engaged with those philosophical or qualitative ambiguities of human consciousness, reason, emotion and mutual communication that have come to inspire more recent anthropology in the UK (often, admittedly, derived from the Continent).

Over subsequent decades, I met Ioan every now and then, whether at large conferences, small seminars, annual general meetings of Africanists or anthropologists and so on. His contribution to the oversight and welfare of such official bodies was very substantial, quite apart from editing books and journals such as the wide-ranging *Journal of the Royal Anthropological Institute*, then known as *Man*, for thirteen years at a time of social anthropology's expansion (1959–72). This was also a key period in the consolidation of his own career, following his lecturing positions in Glasgow, then in London at University College where he was promoted to Reader; and then as early as 1969 his appointment as Professor of Social Anthropology at the LSE. Sally Healy, a former colleague of Lewis's in the Africa Educational Trust, has pointed out that while the 1960s saw a burgeoning growth in African studies generally, Somalia received scant attention at that time, and 'Lewis emerged as the leading British scholar in a badly neglected field. He was a vigorous advocate of Somali causes and a regular guest on the BBC World Service and the BBC's Somali Service, which he campaigned successfully to save from closure. He saw his advocacy as fulfilling a debt to the Somalis, on whom he depended for his work as an anthropologist.'[5]

Early years

Offspring of a Welsh family on his father's side, Ioan Myrddin Lewis was destined to spend a good part of his younger life in Scotland. His father, John Daniel Lewis, started his career as a professional journalist, soon moving to Iraq where he became editor of the *Mesopotamian Times*. It was there that he met and married Mary Stevenson Scott, whose family was based near Glasgow. The couple then made their

Ethnography: Comparative Approaches to History, Politics and Religion (London, 1999), chapter 6 (reprinted Oxford, 2004), pp. 80–96; see footnote 7, p. 96, referring to J. Boddy, *Wombs and Alien Spirits: Women, Men, and the Zar Cult in Northern Sudan* (Madison, WI, 1989) and G. Lienhardt, *Divinity and Experience: the Religion of the Dinka* (Oxford, 1961).
[5] S. Healy, 'Lewis, Ioan Myrddin (1930–2014)', *Oxford Dictionary of National Biography*, in press.

home in London, where his experience included work on the *Sunday Times*—and also a brief period as editor of the *Daily Mirror*. It was not long before they were expecting a child. Mary moved briefly up to Scotland to be back in her parental home for the birth (which took place on 30 January 1930), returning to London with baby Ioan soon after. I was most fortunate in 2018 to have the chance of some extended conversation with Ann Lewis, Ioan's widow, and their elder daughter Joanna, in Shropshire, where part of the family then lived.[6] I learned that the original Lewis family still live in the Lampeter area of Wales, and still speak Welsh. Ioan's father spoke it too, and talked of teaching it to his son one day; but sadly he died when Ioan was only 7 years old. His mother then moved with the boy back to the Glasgow area, where Ioan was brought up, spent most of his school years, entered university life and confidently embarked on what was to become a remarkable academic career. In a recorded interview conducted by an organisation based in Somaliland but devoted to cultural and historical preservation across the whole of the Somali-speaking regions in 2010, Ioan was asked what had helped him become a writer. He replied 'My father was a journalist and my parents and grandparents valued literature and poetry', before outlining his scholarly training and mentioning the inspiration he received from Somalis in London 'who jointly inspired me' among others.[7] He was also known for observing occasionally that the Somali people were themselves responsible for making him the person he was; but while his forebears clearly had a role here too, his own career was indeed formed in due course with the help of an extremely supportive family of his own who shared much of his long-term commitment to the region and the people. It was not long after Ioan had embarked on postgraduate studies in Oxford that he met Ann Elizabeth Keir; they married, left together for the British Protectorate of Somaliland (where the first of their four children was born) and, very shortly after, to Rhodesia, where their adventures continued.

From chemistry in Glasgow to anthropology in Oxford

Ioan came into anthropology from an unusual starting point, as he was completing his four-year BSc at Glasgow University in chemistry in 1951. His attention was

[6] I was able to make contact with Ann Lewis through friends who had known the family for some years, and in addition to the personal conversations we were able to have at her home on 17–18 June 2018 we remained in touch through a number of letters and emails.

[7] 'An interview with Professor I. M. Lewis' was conducted by the Farshaxan group, established to share and disseminate historical and cultural memories of the Somali region generally. See the online article of 6 October 2010, about the interview: http://www.somalilandhorta.com/news/2010/oct /news2010oct6_5 Article.htm (accessed 12 April 2019).

caught by a Nuffield Foundation scheme offering to fund students in the natural sciences who wished to cross over into the human sciences. He was given advice by a former British administrator in Burma who had studied briefly with E. E. Evans-Pritchard in Oxford (this must have been Henry Noel Stevenson, who had since moved to Glasgow University in order to set up a programme in Third World studies and social anthropology). He encouraged Lewis to apply to Oxford. According to a very engaging personal interview recorded decades later with Charles Geshekter, an American colleague, the young Lewis had started looking at some reading he suggested on trams and buses around Glasgow. When interviewed for the Nuffield scheme in London, he was asked what sort of things he had read; what did he think of Evans-Pritchard's book on Azande witchcraft? Reflecting back half a century, Lewis remembered feeling rather vague and answering something like 'a bit boring...'. The interview panel fell about laughing; unknown to the students, Evans-Pritchard himself was a member of it. But Lewis was offered a grant; and shortly afterwards received a kind letter from Evans-Pritchard saying 'Although you were so rude about me, I'm pleased to tell you...'.[8]

Thus it was that Ioan Lewis settled into Oxford as a graduate student member of St Catherine's Society in the autumn of 1951 (five years later it would be formally integrated as a full College of the University). He attended the Institute of Social Anthropology for most of his lectures and tutorials. Shortly after E. E. Evans-Pritchard's appointment to the Chair in 1946, the Institute had acquired its own premises (separate from the geographers) at E. B. Tylor's former home, Museum House in South Parks Road, which is where Lewis would have first studied.[9] However, that handsome building had to be demolished in 1952 because of the expansion of the science buildings in the area, and the Institute as a whole moved to a nearby address at 11 Keble Road (by 1965/66 being moved again to 51–53 Banbury Road). During his first academic year studying for the Diploma in Anthropology Lewis was no doubt surprised at the philosophical questions anthropologists often liked to ask about the materials of basic ethnography. One of his tutors for this year was Franz Steiner, a refugee originally from Czechoslovakia with many languages and several years of research experience in different countries. Steiner had been given some money by the International African Institute and was engaged in compiling a bibliography of sources on the Somali and related peoples, but his health was failing and he had not written up the required text for them. He suggested that Lewis could act as his assistant and use the material

---

[8] C. Geshekter, 'Interview with Professor Ioan Lewis at his home in London', *Bildhaan: an International Journal of Somali Studies*, 1 (2008), 52–4. See https://digitalcommons.macalester.edu/bildhaan/vol1/iss1/7 (accessed 12 April 2019).
[9] A photograph of the building appears in P. Rivière (ed.), *A History of Oxford Anthropology* (New York and Oxford, 2007) p. 37.

during 1952–3 for his BLitt thesis (today the equivalent of a Master's degree) which often followed the Diploma year. Franz Steiner thus became his research supervisor, during an interesting time at which Steiner himself was evidently giving priority to his reflective analysis of belief, emotion and ritual in the book *Taboo*.[10] Unfortunately he died from a heart attack in November 1952, but Lewis decided to continue the project; Evans-Pritchard took over his supervision, and the thesis was finished the following year. This led directly to an invitation from the International African Institute's *Ethnographic Survey of Africa* to submit the work for a volume focused on the Somali and other peoples of the Horn of Africa (which duly appeared in 1955 and has remained in demand; the latest reprint emerging as recently as 2017).[11]

For Lewis, as for many students at the time, life in Oxford was busy and eventful. Regular gatherings of anthropologists, mainly on Friday evenings after the weekly seminar for visiting speakers, were already well established in the Lamb and Flag pub in St Giles. Students of all kinds were in the habit of dropping in to join friends on the upper floors of the Kemp Café on Broad Street, opposite Balliol College. In my conversations with Ann Lewis, she explained that this was where she first met her future husband, introduced by a mutual friend, the economist Roland Artle, probably towards the end of 1951.

Ann herself had arrived in Oxford a little earlier, joining St Anne's College in 1949, in parallel with the appointment of her father, Sir David Lindsay Keir, as Master of Balliol College. The family had come from Belfast, where her father had been Vice-Chancellor of Queen's University. Rather in parallel with her future husband, Ann had developed interests in science at school, but like other undergraduate science students coming to Oxford at that time, including medics, had to spend her first year on various topics in the humanities. She initially embarked on a degree in Politics, Philosophy and Economics (PPE), but was 'truly turned off by the Economics' and after the first year transferred to Psychology, Philosophy and Physiology (PPP)— pointing out to me that the School of Psychology on Banbury Road was the first department in Oxford to have computers. Ann completed her BA in 1952; her main tutor throughout had been the relatively young Iris Murdoch, recently appointed to the College. I did ask Ann whether she had ever met the anthropologist Franz Steiner, who had led Ioan Lewis to his research interests in the Horn of Africa, and whose relationship with Iris Murdoch was already quite well known before his unfortunate death in late 1952. She had not met him, but was half aware of him, and explained how surprised she had been in St. Anne's one day to see three obviously grief-stricken men in black clothing outside Iris Murdoch's study door.

---

[10] F. B. Steiner, *Taboo, Truth and Religion* (London, 1956).
[11] I. M. Lewis, *Peoples of the Horn of Africa: Somali, Afar and Saho* (London, 1955).

Soon after completing his BLitt Lewis moved to London and began work as a research assistant to Lord Hailey (of the famous *African Survey*) at Chatham House. Partly because of his knowledge of the relevant literature and history, he then secured the first grant ever to be awarded under the Colonial Development and Welfare Fund for fieldwork in the British Somaliland Protectorate. In this he was supported by John Beattie, a former colonial officer who had left the service in order to take up social anthropology at Oxford, starting with the Diploma in 1949, pursuing research in East Africa and later taking up a lectureship back in the Institute.[12] Meanwhile Ann had joined Lewis in London; their engagement was announced in September 1954, and the wedding took place soon after, on 30 December. Among the documents the family showed me was a letter written by Evans-Pritchard from All Souls, addressed 'Dear Ioan', thanking him for the invitation to the wedding but apologising for the fact that he and his wife would not be able to come, because they themselves had a new baby and the travel would not be easy.

One might think that the imminent fieldwork which the newly married couple were planning would not be particularly easy either. But they were able to gather plenty of advice in London. There even happened to be two Somalis living next door to their flat in Gloucester Road. Lewis had recently become fascinated by the Somali language, especially from meeting Bogumil Andrzejewski (often nicknamed Goosh), a Somali language specialist who by then was teaching at the School of African and Oriental Studies (SOAS). In an interview recorded by Dr Gorge Kapchits in 2015 with his widow, Sheila Andrzejewski, Goosh had graduated from Oxford in 1947 with a degree in English language and literature and an existing knowledge of several other languages. He was eventually offered a job in British Somaliland, not to teach but to make a study of the language with a view to creating an alphabet: 'We knew nothing of the country but he accepted the job with joy!'[13] On his appointment in 1948, Andrzejewski joined SOAS as a postgraduate scholar in the Department of Linguistics and Phonetics, and was introduced to the Somali friends mentioned. They already had experience advising the late phonetician Lilias E. Armstrong of University College London (UCL), who had pioneered the study of tone in Somali and Kikuyu as well as her comparative work on European languages.

In the 2008 interview conducted by Charles Geshekter, Ioan Lewis mentions some of his own first encounters in London: 'I met various Somalis, notably Musa Galaal.

[12] John Beattie's support for the initial grant, and for subsequent contacts with the colonial authorities in the British Protectorate of Somaliland, are gratefully acknowledged in the Preface to Lewis's first major work, *A Pastoral Democracy* (Oxford, 1961) p. vii.
[13] G. Kapchits, 'The traveller to legendary lands', interview of 31 January 2015, with Sheila Andrzejewski, Goosh's widow. See: https://wardheernews.com/traveller-legendary-lands-wardheernews-interview-sheila-andrzejewski/ p. 3 (accessed 12 April 2019).

I also met an intriguing character, and he must have been the first Somali I met, called Abdi "Telephone" who was in charge of various security telephones in government offices in central London. I don't know if he was actually in charge but he worked with the scrambling machines for various telephones in government offices in central London. He was an intriguing, flamboyant character.' And on his later meeting with Goosh Andrzejewski, with whom he became life-long friends: 'I became a pupil of his as far as linguistic matters were concerned … I was in the market looking for fields that were interesting, exciting, and relatively unexplored from the point of view of the subject of social anthropology, which was the case with the Somali scene. I had met an archaeologist who had done some work there during the Second World War. I came across other people who had been there in the British military administration, as well as some people who had served after the War in the Somaliland Scouts, as it was then called … I met a little caucus of people, a little network would perhaps be a more accurate description, who were either Somalis or concerned with Somali Studies.'[14] He then applied for funding to carry out research in the British Protectorate. It was quite a fraught time, as by 1954 there were Somali delegations in London to protest against the British decision to transfer the region of the Haud, in the north-western corner of the country, which had been largely a Somali grazing area, to Ethiopia. Nevertheless, once Lewis arrived, despite his worries about being treated as 'an adopted client' of the British administration (and perhaps because of the excellent contacts he had been able to make in London), nobody tried to interfere with his work. The fact that he had delved already into the study of the language, and the various modes of transcription then under discussion, would no doubt have impressed both the British and Somalis he was meeting.

To Somaliland

The Lewises left for the Somaliland Protectorate (in those days by sea through the Suez Canal) in September 1955, returning in June 1957, only three years before the country gained its independence. During their twenty months, spent mainly on fieldwork, Ioan met several men already very knowledgeable about Somali affairs as a result of their wartime experience followed by service in the colonial administration. These included John Drysdale (later Oriental Secretary at the British Embassy in Mogadishu), who was among those acknowledged in the Preface to Ioan Lewis's first major book, *A Pastoral Democracy* of 1961. He later contributed the opening chapter to Lewis's substantial Festschrift of 2010, providing a sense of continuity between

---

[14] Geshekter, 'Interview with Professor Ioan Lewis at his home in London', pp. 55–6.

many aspects of Somalia's earlier history and international connections.[15] The authorities would have recognised that Lewis was an unusual researcher in that he had thoroughly read the older literature relating to the region, and was ready to pursue his own enquiries and concentrate on his own agenda. They gave Lewis a good deal of freedom to do his own travelling and investigations; he was evidently trusted, and even welcomed into ex-Italian Somaliland. At the same time, we have to admit that unlike many postgraduate anthropologists he would not have had much opportunity before or during his fieldwork to ponder what fellow researchers were doing elsewhere in Africa, or the debates developing within UK anthropology at the time.

For the first months, Ioan and Ann enjoyed the opportunity for travelling together, through the wide semi-desert landscapes and mobile communities of pastoralists across the country. They had an early Bedford truck, a driver, a cook, an assistant cook, and various hangers-on, along with tents, chairs and so on. Their first base was at the religious settlement of Sheikh, not far inland from Berbera on the coast, after which they moved on to the small town of Burao a little further south. However, because they were expecting their first child they had to establish a home in Hargeisa, the capital, on higher ground to the north-west, where most of the colonial officials lived and there was a hospital. After Joanna's birth, Ann stayed on there while Ioan resumed his excursions, often travelling by camel (sometimes with live chickens attached), to visit the nomads' camps. When I asked Ann whether she herself had picked up any of the Somali language, she laughed and replied 'Oh, just kitchen Somali!'—at home she had a cook, and a cleaner. Overall, the field research was obviously more of a co-operative project than many such expeditions, or than most anthropologists would have set up for themselves.

Clearly Ioan must have been extremely efficient in the way he observed life in the field, making use of the extensive reading he had already done in conducting his enquiries. He must have started organising his material for the planned DPhil thesis well in advance of returning to London in June 1957. The long vacation was just starting in Oxford, so Lewis evidently devoted most of the summer in London to writing up his thesis. Arrangements were made in Oxford for its submission early in the autumn, and a successful oral examination took place in October 1957. The internal examiner was John Peristiany, who had received his Oxford DPhil on the Kipsigis people of Kenya in 1938, and then became a Mediterranean specialist, taking up a lectureship back at Oxford in 1950. The external examiner was Ian Cunnison, who after his own doctoral research for Oxford in Northern Rhodesia had undertaken work in the early 1950s, at Evans-Pritchard's suggestion, for the Sudan government on

[15] J. Drysdale, 'Reflections, 1943-1963', in Hoehne and Luling, *Milk and Peace: Drought and War*, pp. 19–33.

the Baggara nomads of its northern deserts. Cunnison then joined Manchester University in 1955.

I understood from conversation with Ann Lewis that the reason for the haste over completing the DPhil was that they had no money, so Ioan needed to get a job, and was looking to see what was available. For the Lewises, Ioan's success in gaining the DPhil no doubt helped raise their profile again in Oxford. One piece of welcome news was that the Master of Balliol offered two places at the College for Somali students, and invited Ioan to suggest whom he might consult about potential candidates.

Teaching in Rhodesia, Glasgow and UCL

The first opening that came Ioan's way was at the University College of Rhodesia and Nyasaland, where he was offered a position as Lecturer in African Studies. The foundation stone in Salisbury had been laid by Elizabeth the Queen Mother in 1953. The British government formally adopted the institution by Royal Charter in 1955, and the following year saw the setting up of a special relationship with the University of London. Lewis became one of the founding members of the new University—now the University of Harare. There were strong links with British anthropology already, through the Rhodes-Livingstone Institute (RLI) where Max Gluckman had played a key role. Others, including Ian Cunnison, and Clyde Mitchell who had served as its Director from 1952 to 1955, had helped raise the profile of the RLI and worked towards its integration into the new university. No doubt they were among those encouraging Lewis to consider applying in the first place. The Lewis family set out by ship, leaving in December 1957 via Cape Town and Durban, reaching Salisbury in time for Christmas. It was not long after they arrived that they heard news of a new department of Social Anthropology being established in the University of Khartoum, along with the appointment of someone to lead it. Ioan applied for this post, and was disappointed when someone else was chosen—Ann herself remembers that Ian Cunnison was in fact the person appointed.

Lewis was kept very busy teaching in Salisbury, though he found time to publish on general topics in the field of African Studies (the *Journal* of the RLI published an article of his in 1959 on the classification of African political systems[16]). But the main outcome of the couple of years he spent in Salisbury was the progress made towards his major book, *A Pastoral Democracy* (1961), which emerged from the doctoral thesis. In the Preface, Lewis generously acknowledged Mitchell's interest and

---

[16] I. M. Lewis, 'The classification of African political systems', *Journal of the Rhodes-Livingstone Institute*, 25 (1959), 59–69.

comments during the time he was preparing the book. It inevitably took many leads from his extensive reading of earlier literature on the region for his BLitt thesis and the *Horn of Africa* volume based on it, including many sources in Italian. However, the main aim was to present live accounts of the workings of Somali social and political organisation among the pastoralist communities of the then British Protectorate of Somaliland. A key theme running through the chapters on ecology, the organisation of grazing movements, encampments and occasional cultivation is the preeminence of the principle of agnatic (or patrilineal) descent in the male line; this gives coherence to clans, in their subdivisions and their wider groupings, their contractual relationships, feuds, and ultimately feeds into national administration and party politics of what was still then a colonial state. Relations established through marriage, whether of an inter-personal kind or a matter of inter-group collaboration or rivalry, were rarely on a significant scale. His supervisor, E. E. Evans-Pritchard, initially through his own work among the Nuer of the southern Sudan, had drawn the attention of a wide range of anthropologists to the model of a 'segmentary lineage system' as a way of grasping how inter-communal politics could work outside the framework of central institutions such as traditional chiefship.[17] Lewis was certainly able to draw inspiration from this direction, and generously acknowledged his continuing debt to Evans-Pritchard. But being steeped already in historical studies of the Somali, with their Islamic background, market centres for trading, rivalry with neighbours such as those based in Ethiopia and encounters with international figures from Asia and Europe, he sought to convince readers of the relative solidity and permanence of their clans and clan structures. The book offered a rich picture of how a relatively self-sustaining traditional way of life could be accommodated into the purview of late colonial rule as a 'Protectorate'. Of course, British Somaliland gained its independence in June 1960, and within a week was joined by the newly independent Italian Somalia to form the Republic of Somalia. From many points of view, the publication of Lewis's book in 1961 was a happy event all round. And despite the cataclysmic political turmoil and conflicts of the coming years in the Somali region, the book remained a staple in the growing field of Somali Studies for decades, republished twice in English and translated into Italian.

In 1960 Lewis returned from Rhodesia and took up a lectureship in anthropology at Glasgow University. He then moved back to London in 1963, having secured a position at UCL. During these years he embarked on an extremely productive publishing career, exploring some new topics throughout but maintaining his interests in the Somali people and managing to visit the region quite often. His *Pastoral Democracy*

---

[17] E. E. Evans-Pritchard, *The Nuer: a Description of the Modes of Livelihood and Political Institutions of a Nilotic People* (Oxford, 1940).

remained, however, the key framework of his rational, pragmatic approach to the nature of human society, which itself led to a remarkable array of extended enquiries into social and cultural practices over his lifetime.

It was not long after Lewis had returned to the UK from his time in Rhodesia that he also moved into active participation in various academic organisations and international networks. For example, he contributed a paper on comparing unilineal descent to the major decennial meeting of the Association of Social Anthropologists (ASA) of the Commonwealth in 1963 (The 'Anglo-American' conference), held in Cambridge, with a volume following in 1965.[18] By January 1964 he found himself organising quite a complicated conference for the International African Institute, 'Islam in Tropical Africa' held at Ahmadu Bello University, in northern Nigeria. The resulting publication of 1966 soon became a classic work;[19] and that same year Lewis chaired the annual meeting of the ASA at Edinburgh University, on the theme of history and anthropology, and introduced the resulting volume of 1968.[20] However, managing such conferences and the editorial responsibilities that followed did not detract from his key interests in the Somali language and oral literature, which had continue to expand from his postgraduate days in Oxford and London and which he then pursued further in the field.

Ventures into Somali language, poetry and broadcasting

Over a century before, Richard Burton had described from the Somali coast a country teeming with 'poets', 'the fine ear of this people causing them to take the greatest pleasure in harmonious sounds and poetical expressions, whereas a false quantity or prosaic phrase excites their violent indignation.... Every chief in the country must have a panegyric to be sung by his clan...'[21]

The partnership which had already developed between Andrzejewski and Lewis before he embarked on his fieldwork turned out to be long-lasting and highly productive. By the early 1960s, Lewis re-established a creative relationship with Oxford, where Evans-Pritchard and other colleagues, including the linguist Wilfred Whiteley, were preparing to embark on a series of volumes on African Oral Literature with the

---

[18] I. M. Lewis, 'Problems in the comparative study of unilineal descent', in M. Gluckman and F. Eggan (eds.), *The Relevance of Models in Social Anthropology* (London, 1965), 87–111; republished, without revision, under the slightly different title 'Deconstructing descent', in Lewis's retrospective collection—Lewis, *Arguments with Ethnography*.

[19] I. M. Lewis (ed.), *Islam in Tropical Africa* (London, 1966).

[20] I. M. Lewis (ed.), *History and Social Anthropology* (London, 1970).

[21] R. Burton, *First Footsteps in East Africa* (London, 1894), vol. 1, p. 82.

Oxford University Press. In 1964 the first volume of selected oral and written prose appeared, compiled by Whiteley; and the same year saw *Somali Poetry: an Introduction* by Andrzejewski and Lewis. These, plus a further two volumes of what was clearly an important series, were favourably reviewed by myself for *Sudan Notes and Records* in 1965; in the same year Lewis published a couple of warm reviews of introductory books on anthropology by colleagues in Oxford.[22]

The central importance Lewis himself gave to language and poetry as a part of his Somali research is reflected in tones rather evocative of Burton's. He reported a personal memory nearly forty years on from his early fieldwork, having met the itinerant man of religion Aw Jama Umar Ise. Of a somewhat 'fundamentalist disposition' he was extremely suspicious of Lewis and his activities among the nomads, 'seeking information about their customs and institutions and writing down their genealogies … his initial assumption was that I was a British spy, and I found him somewhat menacing in early encounters I had with him.' Some years later they met again: 'Sheikh Jama had become a self-taught oral historian and was busy collecting the poetry of Sayyid Mohammed Abdile Hassan' (already well-known to the Brits as the 'Mad Mullah'). He had received encouragement and equipment in the form of a tape-recorder from a much-respected commander of the Somali police force (later, incidentally, to become a major figure in the political upheavals of the whole Somali region). Aw Jama explained to Lewis that he had closely observed his ethnographic activities, and decided he was harmless; but the work would be better done by a native Somali speaker familiar with the religious background—'I had thus inadvertently made a convert and we became friends and colleagues.'[23] Over the years, especially when he was able to revisit the networks of Somali friends he had come to know, Lewis provided encouragement to a number of Somali scholars and creative writers, including poets. And his own pioneering efforts, especially on the artistic side of the Somali language and culture, helped spread interest internationally among a new generation of scholars; extending for example into women's perspectives and memories, as beautifully represented by Lidwien Kapteijns with Maryan Omar Ali, *Women's Voices in a Man's World,* focusing on the northern Somali region, published in 1999.[24] Kapteijns's work pursued further analyses of social and political events, not simply

---

[22] B. W. Andrzejewski and I. M. Lewis, *Somali Poetry: an Introduction* (Oxford, 1964). See review by W. James of *The Oxford Library of African Literature* (vols. 1–4), in *Sudan Notes and Records*, 46 (1965), 176–80. See also reviews by I. M. Lewis of G. Lienhardt, *Social Anthropology,* and John Beattie, *Other Cultures: Aims, Methods and Achievements in Social Anthropology* in *Man* (1965, pp. 158 and 202 respectively).

[23] I. M. Lewis, 'Afterword', in I. M. Lewis, *A Pastoral Democracy*, 4th edn (Oxford, 1999), pp. vi–vii.

[24] L. Kapteijns with M. O. Ali, *Women's Voices in a Man's World: Women and the Pastoral Tradition in Northern Somali Orature, c. 1899-1980* (Portsmouth, NH, 1999).

from women's perspectives but evaluating the re-shaping of the traditional 'clan' factor in recent Somali history.[25]

To the LSE, 1969

After his very active six years at UCL, Lewis's appointment as Professor of Social Anthropology at the LSE led to a further round of travels, including regular visits to the Somali regions throughout the 1970s and 1980s. He continued to write extensively about Somali society, as well as extending his comparative ideas about social organisation, using a variety of examples from across the world. He became honorary director of the International Africa Institute from 1981 to 1988, and consultative director thereafter. He was elected a Fellow of the British Academy in 1986. This is not the place to delve into the appalling events and suffering inflicted on the Somali regions during the later decades of Lewis's career, but it is important to recognise Lewis's efforts during these years to support successive periods of peace-making, educational institutions, and international communications between the world's increasing number of dispersed Somali communities. He had long been aware of the way the Somali in the old days were very attached to the radio, even as they travelled around on their camels. He claimed to have always found Somalis extremely cosmopolitan, and this partly explained their interest in radio broadcasting, particularly as news programmes in Somali became available around the world (no doubt following the dispersal patterns of Somali-speakers as a result of political developments).

Lewis has vividly described (in the Geshekter interview of 2008) an experience he had in the later part of his career, on the Jubba in southern Somalia when he was doing some work with an NGO development agency. They were looking at refugee settlements across the river in Somalia and waiting for the ferryboat.

> There was a quite impressive Somali family with livestock standing, waiting for the ferry, as well. The man was diverting himself, making good use of the time by frolicking in the river and he kept shouting to me 'Why don't you come and join me?' I said, 'Well, that's very kind of you but, unfortunately, I'm afraid of crocodiles. You obviously aren't, but I am.' I got talking to his wife, who had a huge transistor radio, a 'block blaster', whatever they call it, a huge one on the back of a burden camel. I asked her what were her favorite programs. She said she liked Radio Ethiopia for music, the BBC for truth, and Radio Mogadishu for news. She was really very funny.

---

[25] L. Kapteijns, 'I. M. Lewis and Somali clanship: a critique', *Northeast African* Studies, 11 (2004–10), 1–24.

Lewis added, 'I've met many Somalis who listened to Peking or Soviet transmitters all over the place or any available broadcast in Somali and, to some extent, in Arabic.'[26] He concluded that, obviously, these were people whose experience of the world was not limited to their locale.

I have mentioned Sally Healy's description of Ioan Lewis's role as a vigorous advocate of Somali causes, and a regular guest on the BBC World Service and the BBC's Somali Service. She mentioned also his part in saving the station from closure after a period of complicated challenges from different factions in the Somali-speaking area.[27] Lewis himself did recount how, in the latter days of the rule of General Muhammad Siad Barre, the political opposition often relied on oral poetry, either recorded on cassette tapes or broadcast through the Somali language service of the BBC, to voice their dissent. When the British considered closing the Somali language service down for financial reasons, a delegation of prominent Somali leaders met with the British, and argued that 'much as they appreciated the ambassador personally, it would be better to close the British embassy rather than terminate the BBC broadcast!'[28] Mary Harper, a BBC journalist who followed events in Somalia for two decades, has provided a very readable account of her experiences, both in the field and back in London.[29] She has emphasised that Somalia may be 'one of the most conflict-ridden countries in Africa; but it was one of the first to develop a mobile phone system'—and internet use is another modern phenomenon, connecting Somali communities who keep in touch with each other not only for political gossip, which they love, but also for maintaining their complicated trading links and financial dealings across the world. It is a refreshing read, with several references to the help that Professor Lewis provided her and the BBC over contacts and so on over the years. Thanks to a short review available online we do know that he appreciated this lively and very positive account of how the people of Somalia and Somaliland are seeking the best ways of surviving the ongoing struggles in their part of the world, at least in part through their own cultural exchanges: 'Harper claims to have not sought to produce a work of scholarship, but in fact she provides the most accessible and accurate account available of the contemporary Somali world—pirates and all ... Finally, a striking and pleasing feature of Harper's approach throughout this book, is the sympathy and empathy she displays towards her subjects, without romanticising them.'[30]

---

[26] Geshekter, 'Interview with Professor Ioan Lewis at his home in London', pp. 65–6.

[27] Healy, 'Lewis, Iaon Myreddin'.

[28] I. M. Lewis, *A Modern History of the Somali* (Berlin and Oxford, 2002), p. 251.

[29] M. Harper, *Getting Somalia Wrong? Faith, War and Hope in a Shattered State* (London and New York, 2010).

[30] See I. M. Lewis's review at http://mary-harper.blogspot.com/2012/03/somali-expert professor-im-lewis-writes.html (accessed 12 April 2019).

Other perspectives on Somali history and politics were emerging from research carried out primarily in the southern, more densely populated and largely agricultural parts of the Somali-speaking area, where history had seen many population movements and interactions, and where there were continuing levels of internal conflict, international refugee flight and settlement. Lewis was not always sympathetic to this new tide of research, and in some cases became known for his critical commentaries and reviews; one exchange of 1998 which led to widespread comment began with an article by him roundly criticising some of Catherine Besteman's earlier work on political crises and human suffering in the southern Somali regions. She replied effectively to this rebuff, and the following year a major book was published, relating the modern problems of the Somali regions in part to the legacy of slavery.[31]

Anthropological arguments beyond the Somali

In the earlier part of his career, Ioan Lewis rarely entered into direct arguments with colleagues over general anthropological issues in the way he, or they, interpreted ethnographic findings. But he held on to a very straightforward way of describing social activity and institutions, rather than speculating on what alternative meanings they might reveal if looked at from other angles. His initial two years at Oxford, after doing well in his chemistry degree from Glasgow, were rather fully taken up with assisting Steiner and then taking over his careful library research on the Horn of Africa. He has left us little of his response to the rising interest in French anthropology among his teachers and fellow students, despite his friend Ian Cunnison being invited by Evans-Pritchard to contribute a translation of Marcel Mauss's *Essay on the Gift*. This appeared in 1954 as the first of what became a long series of translations of creative essays from the French school of Durkheim by Oxford anthropologists, reaching well into the new age of Lévi-Strauss.[32]

By the time Lewis moved back to London in 1963, specifically to UCL, he would have encountered some major anthropological exchanges taking place between colleagues—some of which he took up in his Inaugural Lecture 'Anthropology's Muse' after being appointed as Professor of Anthropology at the LSE in 1969. One of these references has interested me specially, as it raises major criticisms of anthropological theorising by citing Mary Douglas's analysis of animal symbolism among the Lele

---

[31] C. Besteman, *Unraveling Somalia: Race, Violence and the Legacy of Slavery* (Philadelphia, PA, 1999).
[32] Ian Cunnison is well remembered for having launched the focus on translations from French anthropology with his original English version of Marcel Mauss's 1925 *Essay on the Gift* (London, 1954).

people of the Congo (first presented in an early article of 1957).[33] The Inaugural Lecture, delivered in 1972, opens with 'the role and meaning of field-work in social anthropology'; 'I hope ... to suggest a more realistic assessment than is generally acknowledged at the moment of the anthropologist's debt to those he studies.'[34] He also pays tribute to the 'tradition of brilliant empirical research' pioneered at the LSE by Malinowski—and indeed we could all endorse that claim, even in respect of the young Evans-Pritchard, who as a new history graduate abandoned Oxford in 1924 for the sake of pursuing the study of anthropology there with experienced fieldworkers, such as Malinowski and Seligman. Lewis offers some major examples of how field-workers can read too much into the explanations of their informants, as Mary Douglas uses her 'over-fertile' imagination to explore the symbolically 'anomalous' character of the small scaly ant-eater, a pangolin, which plays a part in a fertility cult—leading to her own associations with 'matter out of place' and 'biblical abominations'. 'Those who disagree with her views may feel that the Lele have much to answer for!'[35] I believe Mary Douglas had only one chance to return to the Congo following her original research, because of political insecurity, and never had another opportunity to pursue pangolins. But her interest in questions of ritual and symbolism expanded seriously, perhaps owing much to the inspiration she gained from Franz Steiner (whose well-known work *Taboo* appeared posthumously). Her fellow-student Ioan Lewis gained a rather different inspiration from him perhaps—the opportunity to soak himself in the literature on the Somali and thus make a very effective start to his career.

The particular issue of the pangolins lasted on the margins of anthropological discussion for nearly thirty years after Lewis's Inaugural. Close to his retirement in 1993, he decided to bring it out firmly into the open. In 1991 he published a paper in *Man* entitled 'The spider and the pangolin': 'Douglas bases her famous analysis of the "anomalous" pangolin on one type [*the smaller*] and rather passes over the other [*the larger*] ... this offers a unique opportunity to test the validity of theories of symbolisation. A fully satisfactory interpretation should be able to explain the circumstances in which one of the pair is chosen at the expense of the other.'[36] Lewis takes into account a variety of comparative situations from various different linguistic groups across the Congo basin, several studied by Luc de Heusch, and emphasises various ecological factors, such as the prevalent conditions of forest or of open water, which might help explain why one pangolin rather than another is seen as special; or how it

[33] Reference is made to a specific early article by M. Douglas, 'Animals in Lele religious symbolism', *Africa*, 27 (1957), 46–57, but Lewis does not make any mention of Douglas's later monograph devoted to a full-length study of the same people: M. Douglas, *The Lele of Kasai* (Oxford, 1963).
[34] I. M. Lewis, *'The Anthropologist's Muse', an Inaugural Lecture* (London, 1973), pp. 1–2.
[35] Ibid., p.17.
[36] I. M. Lewis, 'The spider and the pangolin', *Man*, 26 (1991), 513–25.

might be understood as bringing together animals, humans, and spirits in such a way as to justify the ritual attention brought to it. The argument is then set in motion by contrasting a parallel situation in southern Italy, especially Apulia, where two varieties of the tarantula spider are found—one smaller, with a bite sometimes lethal to men working in the fields, while the larger and more scary-looking one is able to possess women (mainly) and make them dance, in the context of a cult associated also with St Paul.[37] The original article was followed in 1993 by a debate in the same journal, 'Hunting the pangolin', consisting of a threesome: Luc de Heusch providing a Comment, Ioan Lewis offering a reply, and Mary Douglas defending herself. She rubbished Lewis's failure to see that the distinctions of western natural science could never match what species might be highlighted as ritually special in one or another cultural context, where animal categories most often arose from or echoed local understandings of *social* relations. This was followed immediately by further exchanges on 'Spiders, pangolins and zoo visitors' between Richard Fardon and Lewis in the next issue, Fardon pointing out that 'anthropology without speculation' (whether on the part of the anthropologist or the Lele) would be 'dull indeed'. Lewis's rejoinders mainly seem to continue the ongoing circles of the debate, though he ends on a slightly teasing jab at one of Fardon's comments which 'hardly does justice to the force of Professor Douglas's Durkheimian logic'.[38] The contrasting tarantula spiders appeared at least once more in Lewis's public lectures, specifically an address in Italian which took place in Rome and Naples in late 1995 in honour of Ernesto De Martino, the ethnologist who had originally written about their unusual qualities in 1961 (his analysis, according to Lewis, enabling us 'to see how Douglas's argument is seriously flawed').[39] In Lewis's collection of essays, *Arguments with Ethnography* (1999), he included a fairly recent Italian tribute to Martino, in English translation.

The relationship between Lewis's approach and that of younger anthropologists at Oxford seemed to fade over the years. Arguments were developing quite widely in the discipline, not specifically concerned with the Somalis, but with Lewis's pragmatic realism towards human life and experience in general. Soon after his *Ecstatic Religion* was first published in 1971 a rather sour review of it appeared in the *Journal of the Oxford Anthropological Society* (1972), with occasional barbed comments redirecting the reader rather more favourably towards Lévi-Strauss or even Wittgenstein. The piece was anonymously signed by 'Two Diploma Students', who clearly felt they were speaking for their generation's views at the time. When the collection of Lewis's repub-

---

[37] E. de Martino, *La Terra del Rimorso* (Milan, 1961).

[38] 'Hunting the pangolin', Comments by L. de Heusch and M. Douglas, with reply by I. M. Lewis, *Man*, 28 (1993), 159–66. See also R. Fardon, 'Spiders, pangolins and zoo visitors' and reply by I. M. Lewis, *Man*, 28 (1993), 361–3.

[39] Lewis, *Arguments with Ethnography*, p. 30.

lished papers brought out by the LSE in 1999 appeared, the Bulletin of SOAS carried a review by David Mills, a former student of the Oxford Institute. He commented that it was a 'brave scholar … who stands up for the potentials of "functionalist" thinking within the discipline of anthropology'. While suggesting that there is rather more to appreciate in this collection itself, including Lewis's own efforts to place the variations of the idea of 'function' that historically anthropologists have sought, Mills suggests 'The undisguised sub-text is of course a critique of dilettante theoretical arrivistes.' At the same time, he is fully supportive of what Lewis calls the 'fieldwork mode of production', one aspect of which could be referred to in a much more widely acceptable way as the 'situated' nature of knowledge.[40]

Ioan Lewis retired from regular duties at the LSE in 1993, after being diagnosed with heart failure. But over the next two decades, before his death on 14 March 2014, his activities scarcely seemed to cease. His interest in the Somali peoples continued, as he took up a range of activities connected with their future welfare in general, as well as continuing to publish new academic work (and some new presentations of older material). From 1995 to 2005 he was Chair of the Africa Educational Trust and initiated support for the restoration of education in various parts of Somalia. He received a lifetime achievement award from the Commission on Nomadic Peoples of the International Union of Anthropological and Ethnological Sciences (2003). The Festschrift presented to him in 2010, mentioned at the start of this memoir as containing the fullest available bibliography of his work, brings together a very impressive set of contributors belonging to different nationalities, age-groups and disciplines, while the chapters focus very much on Somali themes of the kind he had fostered through most of his life.

Note on the author: Wendy James is Emeritus Professor of Social Anthropology, and Fellow of St Cross College, University of Oxford. She was elected a Fellow of the British Academy in 1999.

---

[40] D. Mills, 'Review of *Arguments with Ethnography*', *Bulletin of the School of Oriental and African Studies*, 63 (2000), 326–7.

ANGUS MacKAY

Angus Iain Kenneth MacKay

28 August 1939 – 29 October 2016

elected Fellow of the British Academy 1991

by

ROGER COLLINS

Angus MacKay was the foremost British historian of late medieval Castile, a period even neglected in Spain when he first worked on it in his doctoral thesis. In the University of Edinburgh in the 1970s and 1980s he produced a remarkable body of books and articles focusing on social and economic topics, and above all on the complexities of frontier relations between Castile and the Nasrid kingdom of Granada. He also collaborated frequently with other scholars and his own numerous research students in what remains ground-breaking research and publication.

Biographical Memoirs of Fellows of the British Academy, XVIII, 197–216
Posted 6 August 2019. © British Academy 2019.

ANGUS MacKAY

The Neolithic stone circle known as the Calanais or Callanish Stones stands on a ridge overlooking Loch Roag, on the western side of the Isle of Lewis, where it has patiently endured the annual Atlantic storms since the first half of the third millennium BC.[1] The family of Angus Iain Kenneth MacKay may not have lived in its neighbourhood for so long a time, but this is where their roots can be traced, to the nearby Gaelic-speaking crofting communities of Breasclete, Achmore, Carloway, Garynahore and Callanish, all in the civil parish of Uig. It is perhaps unusual in a memorial of this sort, particularly one aimed at highlighting the academic achievements of its subject, to begin with what may seem like a lengthy focus on his family and antecedents. But in that Angus MacKay was a remarkable scholar with a very unusual background and early life experience, some attention to these is required if sense is to be made of his achievements and character as an historian.

While the ancient stones of Callanish were a striking physical presence in this landscape, the dominant local historical memories that would influence Angus's own intellectual and political development derived from the hardships faced by the crofters at the hands of a succession of absentee landlords and their factors, or land agents, who collected the rents.[2] Several of these were remembered by name in family tradition that reached back to the 1840s, along with the details of the evictions of tenantry and the clearances of townships for which they were held responsible. Lewis suffered particularly from these processes, and was the scene of a short-lived crofters' revolt.[3] Although the worst of the abuses were eliminated by the work of the Crofting Commission that reported in 1884 and the ensuing Crofters Act of 1886, the recollection of what had previously been endured lived on in a community with strong oral traditions, though no access before 1873 to more than a primary level of education, and it was passed on to Angus by his relatives.

However, although his Lewis inheritance would always exercise a powerful influence on him, he himself was born on the other side of the world, in Lima in Peru on 28 August 1939. He was the second son of Dr Neil Angus Roderick MacKay (1908–1987) and of his wife Mary MacAulay, and was always know to his family as Iain, though to most of the rest of his acquaintance as Angus.[4] The perhaps surprising connection with South America had begun with the previous generation. In the early

[1] P. Ashmore, *Calanais: the Standing Stones* (rev. edn. Edinburgh, 2002), pp. 6–17.

[2] Though the stones were not forgotten: Angus's father wrote a play about them in September 1933, while teaching in Harlow. For the definition of a croft: 'A small rented farm, especially one in Scotland, comprising a plot of arable land attached to a house and with a right of pasturage held in common with other such farms': Oxford Dictionaries, https://en.oxforddictionaries.com/definition/croft (accessed 30 May 2019).

[3] T. M. Devine, *The Scottish Clearances: a History of the Dispossessed* (London, 2018), pp. 134–5, 235–7 and 321–4.

[4] His son, Angus John, indicates in the very moving funeral eulogy on his father that he was always 'Gus' to his wife.

1900s Angus's grandfather, Neil MacKay (1875–1914), who came from Carloway, had moved with his new wife, Christina MacIver, to Patagonia in Chile, to work as a hand on a sheep farm located on the Strait of Magellan.[5] Neil was the second youngest of seven or more siblings, the children of Neil MacKay (1834–1899) and Catherine Morrison (1836–1904). As his father was himself one of an extended family, whose original croft had already been divided in 1881 into several small parts, the chance of work in Patagonia offered better prospects than remaining in Lewis.[6]

The sad loss of their first son, due to the remoteness of the farm from the necessary medical facilities, led to Angus's father actually being born back in Lewis in 1908, but the family soon returned to South America, where Neil became the manager of another sheep farm, this time near the Rio Gallegos in Argentina, until forced to resign after contracting tuberculosis in late 1912. On the journey back to Lewis, their only daughter died of scarlet fever, and Neil himself followed in March 1914, aged only thirty-nine, while in medical isolation in an outhouse of his wife's family croft at Breasclete.

Left widowed with only one of her three children surviving, Angus's grandmother had to take work on the Scottish mainland as a cook and housekeeper for a succession of wealthy families, while her son remained with her family on Lewis. In 1921, an aggressive tumour, that had kept him out of formal schooling for nearly two years, resulted in the amputation of his left leg; a subject on which he later never spoke to his own sons. He always compensated very successfully for it by pushing himself extremely hard physically and was even able to ride long distances during his many years spent in South America later in his life. But for all the emotional and physical loss he had to endure in these early years, Neil Angus—Angus's father—then proved himself to be a remarkably able pupil in the Nicholson Institute in Stornoway, of which he became Dux in 1926/7, and then winner of the first Nicholson University Bursary, which enabled him to take up a place in the University of Edinburgh from 1927 to 1932.[7] There he began an Honours course in English, but switched to a broader degree covering a much wider range of subjects, from which he emerged with a prize medal

---

[5] I am indebted to the memoir of Dr Neil Angus Roderick MacKay written by his elder son Donald Neil MacKay, and kindly lent to me by Angus John MacKay for information on the early history of the wider family and on Angus's parents. Little or nothing seems to be known about the family or the early life of Angus's grandfather Neil (but see note 6 below), and it is his grandmother's MacIver family that dominates the historical memory of their descendants.

[6] The croft, in Garynahine, just south-east of Callanish, was divided on the death of Neil's grandfather, Norman MacKay (1798–1881), whose wife Margaret Morrison (1803–1869) had predeceased him. They had at least seven children. Neil MacKay (born 1875) may have had up to seven siblings; six are certain.

[7] The Nicholson Institute, or Sgoil MhicNeacail, was the first secondary school in Stornoway, founded by a donation from five brothers of the name of Nicholson and opening in 1873. The title of *Dux* is awarded in some Scottish schools to the highest achieving student in the sixth form.

in Latin and other prizes in Philosophy, Economics and Psychology and fourteen out of a possible sixteen First Class certificates.[8]

On the strength of his results and references, he was appointed to teach at Harlow College in Essex in 1933, a private school for about 180 boys. This had been founded in 1862 with the stated aim 'to provide a superior education for the sons of gentlemen and … to train at low charge, the sons of missionaries abroad, of clergymen similarly engaged at home, as well as orphan sons of gentlemen who have been reduced in circumstances'.[9]

It is not known if the ethos of Harlow College influenced Neil Angus's subsequent decision to look for employment as a lay missionary and teacher, or if this was a plan already long formed in his mind. Like his family and the majority of the population of Lewis, he was a committed member of the Free Church of Scotland, whose primary school he had attended. The choice of South America as his chosen place of service may have been the product of the memory of his own very early years there. Despite the loss of a leg, only manifesting itself visibly in a limp, he was accepted by the Foreign Missions Commission of the Free Church and assigned a five-year posting to the Colegio Anglo-Peruano in Lima, starting in January 1935. Founded by the Free Church in 1917, it began as a primary school but soon expanded to include a new secondary department in 1919.[10]

Neil Angus married Mary MacAulay (1899–1994), a member of another Breasclete family, whom he had long known, in the Methodist Central Hall in London on 12 January 1935.[11] They set out on the journey by sea to Peru, via New York and the Panama Canal, in September that year. It was here their two sons were born, Donald in 1936 and Angus on 28 August 1939. Their father's contract would have expired that year, but the outbreak of war in Europe in September of that year meant that he could not be replaced and had to remain in post until 1945.

Neil Angus, like his son Angus after him, drove himself hard. In addition to his work in the school, of which he also became headmaster in 1942, he worked for a

---

[8] This five-year, two-part, course, that no longer exists in Edinburgh, resulted in the award of two degrees: a Master of Arts and a Bachelor of Commerce; the latter was first introduced in the University of Birmingham in the early 1900s and is still offered in various universities in the Commonwealth, as well as in India and Hong Kong.

[9] http://www.oldharlovians.co.uk/history_harlow_college.html (accessed 30 May 2019). The school was forced to close in 1965, and the name is now that of a College of Further Education.

[10] For the history of the school see J. M. MacPherson, *At the Roots of a Nation: the Story of San Andrés School in Lima, Peru* (Edinburgh, 1993), especially pp. 59–91 for the period of Neil Angus's time there.

[11] There is a little uncertainty about her year of birth, as the UK Census of April 1901 includes her as aged three at the time, and the passenger manifest for the SS *Franconia* of 19 October 1946 records her age as forty-nine. Her grave marker in the cemetery in Dalmore on Lewis gives her age as ninety-five and date of her death as 21 June 1994.

doctorate on the philosophy of Alfred North Whitehead, a degree that he received from the Universidad de San Marcos in Lima, where he also served for a time as Professor of English Literature. He gave talks on the radio on reforms in British education and advised the Peruvian Ministry of Education on the adoption of new textbooks.[12] His Spanish was said to be fluent, and it is likely that Angus's own extraordinary command of the language was initiated in these years in Peru, when the family was unable to return to Britain.

Peru may have offered a little more tranquillity than Europe at the time, though it had fought a war with its neighbour Chile that had ended in 1929, before engaging in another with Colombia from 1932 to 1933, and yet another with Ecuador in 1941. Initiated by boundary disputes, they were all at least short-lived. Within the country, the position of a foreign run Protestant school was not always easy, while the costs incurred in maintaining it, although originally expected to be self-supporting, led to periodic threats of closure.[13] These and other problems were faced by Neil Angus, before he was able to take his first leave in a decade in July 1945.[14] Returned to Scotland, in weakened health and facing the question of the educational needs of his own two sons, he decided not to return as planned to Lima, and resigned his post in 1946. Instead he and his wife joined his mother in a house in Warrender Park Road in Edinburgh, just south of the Meadows and the medieval heart of the city along the High Street or Royal Mile. They also took Angus and his brother Donald for their first ever visit to their numerous relatives in Lewis. However, it was not long before they were heading back to South America, sailing from Liverpool in October 1946 to New York and thence to Colombia, where Neil Angus had been posted as the Representative of the British Council in Bogotá.[15] He would work for the British Council for the next twenty-three years.

This initial posting was short, as Neil Angus was hoping for a longer stay in the United Kingdom while his sons received their schooling. So, they returned to Britain in 1947, where Neil Angus was appointed Director of the Latin American Department of the British Council. The family took a house in East Barnet, and Angus was sent to a local primary school, while Donald went to Queen Elizabeth Grammar. Neil Angus, who, like his son after him, never did one thing if he could do two instead, also enrolled for an external BA degree in Spanish from the University of London. He was bored by routine, and complained of its effects on his health, only to be completely

---

[12] MacPherson, *At the Roots of a Nation*, pp. 81–2.

[13] For example, the change of name from La Escuela Anglo-Peruviano to the Colegio de San Andrés had been forced on it by the Peruvian government in 1942, when it forbade the institutional use of names with foreign connections: MacPherson, *At the Roots of a Nation*, p. 78.

[14] The family arrived in Southampton from New York on the SS *Aquitania* on 2 September 1945.

[15] The National Archives, Kew, reference BW24.

revitalised by a demanding trip on behalf of the British Council to the USA, Mexico, Cuba and six countries in South America in 1950.

The following year, feeling their sons were not getting the best out of their education, the family returned to Edinburgh after Neil Angus applied for the post of British Council representative in Scotland. Only after his sons' school education was complete did Neil Angus return to South America for a final posting as Representative in Argentina, based in Buenos Aires, from 1956 to 1969.[16] In the meantime, the two boys were entered as pupils in The Royal High School.

Then located in its Neoclassical building on the south side of Calton Hill, overlooking Waverley Station, the school claimed an institutional ancestry going back to the foundation of Holyrood Abbey in 1128. Certainly, the school formerly run by the abbey was put under the control of the city council following the Reformation. Angus seems to have thrived, gaining a Merit Certificate in his first year, when a member of Form I 'X'. Although he is not recorded as winning any more such certificates, he remained in the same stream throughout his years at the Royal High School. This is significant because 'the "X" class was very much for the elite academic pupils'.[17] His next recorded distinction was for another, less well-known aspect of his career, as a piper or player of the bagpipes. In 1956 he was both the School's Pipe-Major and the recipient of the MacKelvie Trophy for piping.[18] He kept up with his piping at the University of Edinburgh, where he sometimes played with the Lothian and Borders Police Pipe Band.[19]

He left the Royal High School at the end of his Fifth Form Year (or Lower Sixth in the English education system), as was often the case in the Scottish educational system when a student had gained admission for a four-year degree in a Scottish university. In Angus's case, it was to read history in the University of Edinburgh, for which he was awarded a First-Class degree in 1962. While the syllabus required chronological breadth, including both medieval and modern periods but with a rather lesser geographical extension (excluding Scottish history entirely and most Spanish), Angus's interests and experience might have been expected to make him focus particularly on more recent periods, perhaps with a South American dimension.

But it was to be medieval history, particularly that of the fifteenth century, that became the focus of his academic interests, largely thanks to the influence of Denys

---

[16] For details of Neil Angus's career with the British Council, I am grateful to Stephen Witkowski, of the Global Information Services of the British Council.

[17] Personal communication from Alastair Allanach, honorary archivist of the Royal High School Club. See also *Annual Report of the Royal High School* for 1951/1952, Prize List, p. 11.

[18] Ibid., for 1955/1956, Senior School Awards, p. 8. I am grateful to Alastair Allanach for these pieces of information and for photocopies of the documents.

[19] Information from the eulogy delivered on his father by Angus John MacKay, 9 November 2016.

Hay (1915–1994), who had come to the university in 1945, and became the first holder of the new chair of medieval history in 1954. He was fondly remembered by many who wrote about him as a remarkable teacher, as well as a productive and wide-ranging scholar. As one memorialist recalled, 'Hay brought deflation of pomposity, enthusiasm and intense stimulation'. [20] All these were characteristics that would not only have appealed to Angus but would become the hallmarks of his own teaching style. It is likely that the undergraduate course on 'European History, 1324—1449' was the one that most strongly influenced him, as it was to the latter part of this period that Angus turned when deciding upon a topic for doctoral research, and he acknowledged that it was also Denys Hay who suggested that he should make Spain his focus.

It was, however, an adventurous choice for several reasons. First, for a future academic career in a history department, Spain was a risky choice. Very little Spanish history appeared in the undergraduate syllabus of any university, and there were few books on any period of it written in English. In the 1960s, and for some decades to come, almost every historian of Spain, especially of the medieval period, in a British university was to be found in the Spanish or Hispanic Studies department and not in History. There was also the problem of inadequate library resources for Spanish history of any kind in most British universities outside Oxbridge and London; some-thing Angus would later remedy in Edinburgh. A few years later, he became one of the first Hispanists to find a permanent place in a university department of history, initially in Reading and then at Edinburgh.

The second potentially inhibiting factor might have been the political tenor of the government of Spain at the time, which was that of *El Caudillo*, Francisco Franco (d. 1975). Angus had developed strong views that remained with him throughout his life in favour of social equality and justice, in part deriving from the experiences of his family on Lewis and in part from his own reactions to the British politics of the 1950s. He was a committed socialist and supporter of the Labour Party, and he was not likely to find the Spanish regime of the time in the slightest degree congenial. However, it is one of the distinguishing features of his scholarship that he would put up with what might seem uncongenial in the interest of pursuing what he thought was important.

This is reflected in his choice of thesis topic, developed in consultation with Denys Hay. While his supervisor's interests and academic approach could be said to be more wide-ranging, synthesising and culturally oriented, Angus's focus was on what he regarded as the economic underpinning of the society that interested him, in this case that of fifteenth-century Castile. While clearly influenced by Marxist historians he

[20] J. Larner, 'Denys Hay 1915-1994', *Proceedings of the British Academy*, 90 (1996), p. 396.

had read, he did not become one himself, any more than he became a professional economic historian. If anything, it was the work of the French *Annales* school, then becoming more widely known to anglophone academe, that made the greatest impact on his choice of both topics and methodology. However, Angus was never an uncritical follower of any school or ideology, valuing independence of thought above everything. But for his first, broadly based foray into what would become his life's work, a thesis entitled 'Economy and Society in Castile in the Fifteenth Century' proved an ideal choice.[21]

In his selection of period, however much he may have enjoyed Denys Hay's lectures on a wider chronological and geographical scale, he made another risky decision. Outside the Italian Renaissance, very little in fifteenth-century Europe, particularly in the first three quarters of it, was then attracting much scholarly interest. It was a period of weakness of royal governments, endemic warfare, social upheaval and economic decline in many if not most parts of the continent. In Spain, in particular, where a narrative of *Reconquista*, the gradual recovery of the lands lost to Islam after the Arab conquest of the peninsula in 711, had long dominated not just the academic but also the popular understanding of the development of Spanish history across the medieval centuries, the weakness and internal divisions of the Castilian monarchy under the House of Trastámara (1362–1504) made it a period of national disgrace. Obviously, this was reversed under the joint rule of *Los Reyes Católicos*, Fernando and Isabel, under whom the whole programme of recovery and the elimination of Islamic would be brought to triumphant conclusion after a long period of stasis under their predecessors. Theirs was a period that attracted much scholarly interest, in the way that the earlier decades of the fifteenth century did not, except for a very small number of independent minded historians, amongst whom Angus would find some of his closest friends.

The thesis itself, which was accepted for the award of the degree of PhD in 1970, begins with a survey, 'the evidence and the problem', the latter identified as 'the inadequate nature of historians' knowledge of the Castilian economy and society in the fifteenth century'.[22] While not as polished a piece of writing as his later published works, it presented its author's arguments with absolute clarity. Even here, from the outset of his career as an historian, Angus's preoccupation with the acquiring and understanding of all available evidence stands out, as does his clear focus on recognising the terms on which it could be used to illuminate the question he was trying to

---

[21] Never published, the thesis in two volumes can be accessed via https://www.era.lib.ed.ac.uk/handle/1842/19953 (accessed 30 May 2019).
[22] A. MacKay, 'Society and Economy in Fifteenth Century Castile' (University of Edinburgh thesis, 1970), vol. 1, pp. 1 and 10–15.

answer. Ideologically inspired theory, of whatever kind, had no place in Angus's intellectual world, and this made him the superb historian that he was. He always gave absolute fidelity to the process of evaluating evidence, and never imposed a priori interpretations on it.

In his thesis he identified the key determinant of the politics of the Castilian kingdom in the fifteenth century as the attempts by rival families and groupings in the greater nobility of the kingdom to gain access to new sources of revenue through attempts to dominate the royal court, the Church and the towns, and then he asked 'Why, with such landed fortunes at their command, did the Castilian nobles seek so desperately to acquire royal revenues? What had happened to the Church and the towns?'[23] He recognised that the only way to answer such questions was to discover why the previous normal sources of wealth of this nobility were no longer able to sustain them, and why they were therefore driven into new forms of competition to compensate for the losses, with consequent damage to the political and social stability of the realm. For this he had to undertake a detailed study of hard economic data relating to price fluctuations, monetary devaluations and the decline of the agrarian economy. Much of what he discovered appears in a remarkable series of thirty-three appendices, providing tables of such things as the prices of barley, wheat and cloth in Seville, royal budgets, incomes and expenditure, urban corporate incomes, monastic revenues and much else besides.[24] Unlike his mentor Denys Hay, Angus relished archival work from the start, and it was always the basis for his most important discoveries.[25] Seville was a particular focus of his attention, because of the wealth of its surviving records, not least those of the Duques de Medinaceli, but his enquiries took him to Burgos, Valladolid and Santo Domingo de Silos, as well as the great Spanish central archives in Simancas and Madrid.

Although he never published the thesis in full, a reduced version of it appeared in 1981 as *Money, Prices, and Politics in Fifteenth Century Castile*, a volume in the Royal Historical Society Studies in History Series (no. 28). It stripped out most of the secondary elements in the thesis, so as to focus on the central arguments and provide an often very technical study of their evidential basis. A statement in the Introduction may be a warning to the unwary reader: 'I have constructed an equation which allows for the calculation of the price in maravedies of a mark of fine silver or gold by using the data available for the intrinsic content of coins. Thus $P = xy/z$ where "P" is the price of one mark of gold or silver in maravedies, "x" is the value of the coin in maravedies, "y" is the number of these coins minted from one mark, and "z" is the

---

[23] Ibid., vol. 1, p. 14
[24] Ibid., vol. 2, pp. 554–640.
[25] Ibid., vol. 1, pp. 5–10.

fineness of the coin relative to the maximum degree of purity of gold or silver.'[26] While the text is little over one hundred pages long, it is augmented by many of the tables and graphs generated by the original thesis and by an appendix of documents from his archival researches. It may not be for the general reader but is a remarkable piece of work.

The period in which he was working on his thesis, from 1963 to 1969, was marked by other important changes in his life. Most significant was his marriage to Linda Volante, whom he had first met while earning money on the side working as a waiter in her family's business, Ritchie's Tearooms in Cockburn Street in Edinburgh. They married in 1963 and immediately departed for Spain, for his archival work in Madrid; according to their son, Angus John, born in 1964, a story reached the local press that they had eloped together. Their daughter Ann-Marie was born in 1966. That Linda and her family were practising Roman Catholics also made explicit Angus's breach with the Free Church doctrines and practice in which he had grown up. Again, faith was probably not an area in which he could give unquestioning loyalty or to which he would sacrifice his independence of mind.

By this time a further change had occurred. Angus acquired his first academic position, as a lecturer in the History Department in the University of Reading in 1965. After four years there, he applied for and was appointed to a similar position in the University of Edinburgh. Here he joined a growing department, the medieval component of which was still under the leadership of Denys Hay, but with several new members of both medieval and modern sections being appointed in the 1960s. These included Anthony (A. E.) Goodman (in 1961), Harry Dickinson (in 1966), Gary Dickson and Rhodri Jeffreys-Jones (both in 1967), Robert Anderson (in 1969) and Michael Angold (in 1970). All of them would remain in the University of Edinburgh for the rest of their careers, and would there be joined by others, such as Robert Bartlett (from 1980 to 1986) and Tom Brown (in 1980), who contributed to the excellence of the department in this period. Angus's family enjoyed hearing his tales of the doings and sayings of his colleagues.[27]

1969 also saw the return of Angus's father from Argentina, following a complete collapse in his health brought on by overwork. In addition to his role as Representative for the British Council, he had served as honorary Cultural Attaché at the British Embassy in Buenos Aires, befriending Jorge Luís Borges (1899–1986), then Director of the Argentinian National Public Library, and other leading cultural figures in the Argentine. He was awarded the CBE in 1968, adding to a previous OBE. However, the pressures he placed on himself proved excessive, and he had to retire to Edinburgh in

---

[26] A. MacKay, *Money, Prices and Politics in Fifteenth-Century Castile* (London, 1981), p. 1.

[27] Angus John MacKay, eulogy on his father 9 November 2016.

1969. There, he became a leading lay figure in the governance of the Free Church, serving as a Member and often as the Convenor of several important Commissions and Committees relating to education, finance, and publications that were set up by the General Assembly between 1976 and 1986.[28] He also became closely involved with Angus's work, reading and re-reading drafts of his writing, and in the process 'saved me from many a blunder'.[29] The religious divide that had opened up between them never blunted the closeness of their relationship.

Angus's literary output was initially small, while he developed the courses he would teach, and he soon began work on his first book.[30] As one of his long-term colleagues said of him: 'Angus was devoted to teaching, his students and research.' He may have surpassed his own first source of inspiration, Denys Hay, as a charismatic lecturer, not least through his ability to talk fluently and clearly, however complex the subject, but without a single note. This was also the hallmark of his style when presenting academic seminar papers to his fellow Hispanists and other historians. A former student of Hispanic Studies, who only encountered him for a second-year half-course in Spanish History, recalls 'excellent and hugely informed lectures from which we came away with a really good coherent knowledge and clear and cogent notes. There was certainly never any danger of our not turning up at 9am on Monday. A stimulating start to the week!' Another remembers attending seminars, held in his room 'always full of research papers and books' that covered most of the chairs and even the telephone, and in which 'each time they went Angus asked them where they had got to the week before, and, once reminded, spoke for the full hour without recourse to any notes'.

As a colleague he is described as being 'always among the most lively, opinionated and open of the members of the Department. He could be choleric—I remember him storming out of a Department meeting because he considered the Chairman had been less than respectful to a colleague—but he was always collegial, intellectually stimulating and a very successful teacher (students noticed what a beautiful voice he had).' One of his former research students, from Spain, wrote 'what I personally liked most was his easy way of inspiring people to think, to be critical while being polite (his use of irony was famous and feared), and what I didn't like so much, but has helped me to

---

[28] *The Principal Acts of the General Assembly of the Free Church of Scotland, 1970-1979* (Edinburgh), pp. 91, 123 and 150, and *The Principal Acts of the General Assembly of the Free Church of Scotland, 1980-1989* (Edinburgh), pp. 10, 14, 31, 35, 64 and 112; see https://freechurch.org/resources/acts-of-assembly (accessed 30 May 2019).

[29] A. MacKay, *Spain in the Middle Ages: from Frontier to Empire, 1000-1500* (London and Basingstoke, 1977), p. vii.

[30] For a comprehensive bibliography of his work, see A. Goodman, 'A bibliography of the works of Angus MacKay relating to Medieval Spanish history and literature', in R. Collins and A. Goodman (eds.), *Medieval Spain: Culture, Conflict and Coexistence. Studies in Honour of Angus MacKay* (Basingstoke and New York, 2002), pp. xvii–xxi.

develop as a historian, was his famous sentence: "Go and read", a kind of mantra "do it yourself", which he repeated to me constantly while I was doing my PhD. Independent thinking is probably part of his legacy to his students.'

Something that attracted frequent comment, not least from native speakers, was Angus's extraordinarily good command of the Spanish language. This was not just a matter of grammatical proficiency or even of the remarkable purity of his accent, though this was a time in which even some highly learned and distinguished professors of Spanish did not think it necessary to speak like a Spaniard. The most arresting feature of Angus's command of the language was his ability to move at ease between different registers, from the earthy speech of the street and the bar to the most florid of academic discourses. One Spanish former student recalled 'his astounding knowledge of Spanish, in which he could talk and swear just like a native speaker, with almost no foreign accent', and a friend reported hearing stories from Angus himself about his years of graduate research in Spain 'where he lodged in houses of ill-repute, which further contributed to his colourful accent'.

His first published article 'Popular movements and pogroms in fifteenth century Castile',[31] which appeared in *Past & Present* in 1972, grew out of a paper he gave to the medieval history seminar that, after his retirement in 1980, would later be named in honour of Denys Hay.[32] This typified both the approaches already adopted in his thesis and the style of many of his future publications, by combining intense interest in popular movements, riots and disturbances with very specific analysis of hard economic data in the search to understand the motivation behind them. This also manifested itself in his skilful use of charts and maps to deploy those data, as in this case with a graph of fluctuating cloth prices in Seville *c.* 1400–1474, a distribution map of Jewish settlements as listed in Castilian tax assessments from 1450 to 1474, and tables of local violence and unrest and of crises of subsistence across these same decades. From this he created a masterful analysis of the social and economic pressures that led to the rise in Jewish conversion to Christianity, its consequences for the new *Conversos*, and the complex causes of the local reactions against them, triggered by the economic problems of the time and the weakness of royal government. Although his earliest publication, it remains one of his most important, as well as a signpost to the way his historical interests would develop, particularly directed at minorities and marginalised groups within this turbulent society.

---

[31] A. MacKay, 'Popular movements and pogroms in fifteenth century Castile', *Past & Present*, 55 (1972), 33–64. Thanks to a rogue spell-check, the title is given as 'Popular movements and programs' in Anthony Goodman's bibliography (see note 30 above), p. xvii.

[32] For an earlier and more general assessment of his publications see R. Collins, 'Angus MacKay and later medieval Spain', in Collins and Goodman, *Medieval Spain: Culture, Conflict and Coexistence. Studies in Honour of Angus MacKay*, pp. vii–xvi.

A much shorter article in the *English Historical Review* for the following year, 'A Castilian report on English affairs', typifies another feature of his scholarship: his relish for co-operation.[33] Written with his friend and colleague Anthony Goodman (1936–2016), a distinguished historian of later medieval England, this was the first of several collaborative articles; several of these were written with his research students. He also relished co-operating in publication of books, texts, and collections of essays.[34] One of the most novel of the latter was *Love, Religion and Politics in Fifteenth Century Spain*, in which he paired eight of his own articles with those written by Ian Macpherson, then Professor of Spanish in the University of Durham, thus combining both historical and literary topics.[35] Other such projects included the volume he edited with his former colleague Robert Bartlett entitled *Medieval Frontier Societies*, which focused upon one of his greatest interests, and grew out of a conference they organised in Edinburgh in 1987.[36] It included contributions focusing on Ireland, the Polish-German frontier, Anglo-Scottish and Czech-German relations, as well as several relating to Spain, such as Angus's own 'Religion, culture and ideology on the late medieval Castilian-Granadan frontier', one of his best articles on this topic.

The Atlas of Medieval History that he edited for Routledge with David Ditchburn was not published until after his retirement. It consists of short articles on a wide range of topics each accompanied by a map and covering the whole span of the medieval centuries from 395 to 1500, though with greater concentration on the last four of them. Many of these were contributed by Angus himself in the first edition, and he wrote in the Preface that he 'hoped that university undergraduates, senior school pupils and professional historians will find the atlas useful and rewarding', and that 'enlightened tourists' would also benefit.[37]

A similar need was met in his first published book, *Spain in the Middle Ages: from Frontier to Empire, 1000–1500*, that came out in 1977. It was the second volume in a series devised by Sarah Mahaffy of Macmillan and under the enormously genial and extremely helpful editorship of Denis Bethell (1934–1981). Of him Angus wrote that 'he devoted much time to helping me say what I meant, and the book has benefitted

---

[33] A. MacKay, 'A Castilian report on English affairs', *English Historical Review*, 88 (1973), 92–9.

[34] In *Historia de Juan II* (Exeter Hispanic Texts vol. XXIX: Exeter, 1981), he edited with Dorothy Sherman Severin the surviving manuscript evidence for an abridgement of a major fifteenth century Castilian chronicle.

[35] Published by Brill in Leiden in 1988. Angus contributed chapters I–III, VII–X and XII.

[36] R. Bartlett and A. MacKay (eds.), *Medieval Frontier Societies* (Oxford, 1989, corrected paperback edition, 1992).

[37] The original edition of 1997 has now been replaced by a much altered and enhanced second edition, edited additionally by David Ditchburn and Simon Maclean (Abingdon and New York, 2007), in which they note 'although Angus MacKay was not directly involved in revising this volume, it remains very much a monument to his own wide-ranging research and teaching', p. viii.

greatly from his constructive comments and advice'.[38] The result was a book that broke new ground and provided an English-speaking readership with a short but magisterial survey of the history of late medieval Spain; something hitherto entirely lacking. Indeed, there was nothing like it for a Spanish readership either, in the sense that it was using methodologies and pursuing interests that at the time were little known in Spain itself. It can also be said that in it he produced a remarkable and very readable overview of Spanish late medieval society that was dependent on much detailed and meticulous archival research on his part, which he did not parade in the book. As he wrote 'the use of extended references in a work of this size would be a luxury'.[39]

There are idiosyncrasies to be found in it, to be sure. Angus was not particularly interested in the period before c.1350, though he did his best to do justice to it in his own way. The greater prevalence in that period of ecclesiastical documents over the kind of texts he relished, such as tax assessments, tax data, and judicial records, explains his preference, and he was almost prejudiced against the even less well-endowed earlier medieval centuries. Though, as with many of his *obiter dicta*, it was never clear how far any of his casually expressed views were deeply held or merely intended to provoke the kind of intellectual argument he loved, and in which he was always a formidable debater. Such bold claims as the impossibility of a Hispanist being interested in cricket were intended to provoke, though they might just serve to give offence.

He also, intentionally or otherwise, always favoured Castile over Aragón or Navarre, as can easily be seen from the index entries for the individual monarchs of those realms. The Mediterranean-wide empire that was built up by the Aragonese is almost entirely missing from the book. But then he was far less interested in the narrative history of royal courts or their diplomatic entanglements than he was in the life of the streets or in the hard realities of making a viable living at whatever social level. Even within the kingdom of Castile itself, his personal enthusiasms always led him to cities rather than the countryside, as the archival records were better, and to Andalucia rather than the northern parts of the realm, such as the Asturias or Galicia, as this was home to the most vibrant and complex of frontier societies in the period he relished. The ambiguities in allegiances, conduct and motivation that he detected in his work on both sides in the frontier zone between the kingdoms of Castile and Granada led him to some of his best work, and to the warm friendship of like-minded Spanish scholars, such as Manuel González Jiménez and José Enrique López de Coca Castañer.

---

[38] MacKay, *Spain in the Middle Ages*, p. vii.
[39] Ibid.

Some of the topics touched on in his first book were pursued in a plethora of articles that followed the publication of *Spain in the Middle Ages*, and the fifteen years between 1977 and 1992 saw a remarkable body of work on his part, that in its originality and authority thoroughly justified his election as a Fellow of the British Academy in 1991. Colleagues in other areas concur; one writing that 'I would regard him as a major historian of Medieval Spain, at home with sources, allowing them to speak for themselves, but also a perceptive interpreter who understood the importance of establishing contexts', while another simply stated that 'Angus was one of the most original medievalists of the past thirty or forty years'.

At least forty-eight scholarly articles, several written in Spanish, were published by him in this period, with a handful more being written during this time but appearing in print a little later.[40] Some were contributions to collective volumes and conference papers. Amongst the most significant of them was a ground-breaking article 'The ballad and the frontier in late medieval Spain', which originated in a lecture to the annual Conference of Hispanists of Great Britain and Ireland, of which Angus was a regular attender. Just as his analysis of what was necessary to understand the social and political conflicts of fifteenth century Castilian society led him to engage with economic theory and make himself a master of it, so did his interest in the Castilian/Granadan frontier require him to come to a better understanding of one of the most distinctive products of the period, the ballad. His intention, successfully carried out, was to identify the value of such works, hitherto the preserve of literary scholars, as sources of evidence for his purposes. He showed, with the clarity and precision for which he became renowned, that these were not the products of a diffuse popular culture, but actually the favoured entertainment of the social elite, particularly on the frontier. From this he was able to deduce that 'the hostility between Christians and Moors ceases to be such a dominating theme in the oral tradition of frontier society', with important consequences for the understanding of what united rather than what separated the two sides.[41]

This would not be his only foray into the use of literary evidence, and he wrote articles on a variety of such sources across a span of time extending from the verse *Cantigas de Santa María* of King Alfonso X *el Sabio* of Castile (1252–1284) to the *La Lozana andaluza* of Francisco Delicado (*c.* 1475–1535), a picaresque tale in dialogue form that was intended to criticise the vices of Rome in the time of Pope Clement VII (1523–34). He used them to illuminate themes that interested him, such as antisemitism, and to illuminate the lives of sectors of society ignored in the chronicles and

---

[40] Goodman, 'Bibliography', pp. xviii–xxi, items 3 to 53 in the section headed 'Articles'.
[41] A. MacKay, 'The ballad and the frontier in late medieval Spain', *Bulletin of Hispanic Studies*, 53 (1976), 22.

court literature of late medieval Spain. The range of topics that he covered in the publications of these years is impressive for its breadth and for the consistency of his evidence driven approach to making sense of whatever he studied. As one of his former research students has written in assessment of him: 'His contribution to frontier studies in the Iberian Peninsula has been acknowledged by generations of Spanish historians who have learned with his books and articles. His study on money and prices in fifteenth-century Castile were a spearhead in the economic studies of the medieval period in the early days after Franco's regime.'[42]

A new project based on archival research led to the publication of a book in Spanish in 1985, that was followed by a smaller scale English version, given to one of the annual meetings of 'The Historians of Medieval Spain', and then published in a volume of essays in honour of his long-term friend R. B. (Brian) Tate.[43] In this he examined the evidence for the events themselves, in the form of various depositions and witness statements preserved in the archive of the Duques de Medinaceli, and then moved on to reveal the motivations and consequences of this short-lived uprising. It is a remarkable piece of detective work that uses very localised sources to illuminate the wider context and significance of what they describe. The English version provides a succinct account of his findings, but the Spanish original publishes the documents in full.

This productivity brought its rewards in the form of rapid promotion. He was appointed a Senior Lecturer in 1981, and then a Reader in 1982, before being given a personal Professorship of Medieval History in 1985. These in turn led to greater administrative burdens. From 1985 to 1991 he served as Dean of the Scottish Universities International Summer School, organising its annual event, to which he attached great importance. He even planned to open it to students from Russia with money from the British Council.

He was strongly committed to international co-operation. In a memorial to him in the University of Edinburgh's School of History, a close colleague recalled that 'he always saw Edinburgh University as a European university and wholeheartedly embraced the Erasmus Exchange Scheme, for which he created the Coimbra group. This brought together medievalists from the universities of Edinburgh, Vienna,

---

[42] Ana Echevarria, personal communication.
[43] A. MacKay, *Anatomía de una revuelta urbana: Alcaraz en 1458* (Albacete, 1985); A. MacKay, 'A typical example of late medieval Castilian anarchy? The affray of 1458 in Alcara', in R. Cardwell and I. Michael (eds.), *Medieval and Renaissance Studies in Honour of Robert Brian Tate* (Oxford, 1986), pp. 81–93. On Tate, see B. Taylor and A. Coroleu, 'Robert Brian Tate 1921–2011', *Biographical Memoirs of Fellows of the British Academy*, 16 (2017), 303–21.

Poitiers, Siena, Salamanca and Granada, becoming a force attracting European, and in particular Spanish, students to Edinburgh.'[44]

Equally demanding, if not more so, was his appointment as Head of Department in 1990. Unlike many faced with such a charge, Angus did not reduce his commitment to research and publishing, as his bibliography for these years indicates. Instead he tried to enhance his productivity, as he had done while working on his first book, when his son remembered him working into the early hours of the morning, to 2am or beyond.[45] It has to be said that his energy did not of itself make him a natural administrator. Like his father, he was bored by routine, and had little patience with the kind of bureaucratic culture that even then was becoming ever more entrenched in British universities. What he valued he did to the best of his abilities. What he did not value might not get done, perhaps to the despair of his extremely efficient secretary. The same attitude led him, wisely or not, to accept an invitation to give weekly lectures in the University of Seville, flying to and from Edinburgh to do so. He was also preparing to write a late medieval contribution for Blackwell's multi-volume History of Spain series that would be his largest project since the completion of his *Spain in the Middle Ages* of 1977.

Rare is the Hispanist for whom a convivial discussion of a topic cannot be facilitated by a good glass of wine, preferably Spanish, and Angus was no exception. A friend and colleague recalled that 'the only piece of serious advice he gave me was over how he tackled intractable historical questions. He opened a bottle of red wine and by the time he had finished it the problem was solved.' Unfortunately, this was not the solution to the whole weight of demands placed upon him or which he himself had embraced from the late 1980s. These had been made worse by the death of his father in 1987 which, as his son recalls, 'was something he struggled to come to terms with. In one of his books he had dedicated his work to his father whom he described as "my father and my friend". Being as much of a "Scottish man" as it was possible to be, he did not communicate well emotionally and I think this, his father's death and the subsequent pressure of a range of academic activities combined to bring him low.'[46]

The exact nature of this is not easily recaptured. A colleague remembers the strange atmosphere in the Department of History one Monday morning when word got out that Angus had failed to come in, and hurried and secretive meetings were called between senior members and the administrators. In practice he was not to

[44] M. Angold, 'Angus MacKay, Professor Emeritus of Medieval History – a conspectus' (published 10 November 2016), http://www.edinburgh.ac.uk/history-classics-archaeology/news/news-events/obituaries-tony-goodman-angus-makay/angus-mackay-a-conspectus (accessed 20 June 2019).

[45] Angus John MacKay's funeral eulogy on his father, 9 November 2016.

[46] Ibid.

return. A complete collapse in his health necessitated prolonged sick leave, and eventually formal retirement from his professorship nearly five years later in 1997. Looked after by his devoted family, and in particular by his wife, Linda, Angus effectively withdrew from the world of scholarship, other than providing a very brief prologue to the Spanish translation of his *Money, Prices and Politics in Fifteenth-Century Castile*.[47] His stamp collection, which he had formed over many years and which extended beyond just Hispanic issues, provided him with some intellectual stimulus.

In 2002 friends from Britain, Spain and the USA collaborated in a three-day conference in his honour in Edinburgh, though he himself was only able to attend the final ceremony, in which he was presented with the collection of essays they published in tribute to him.[48]

Verdicts on Angus the scholar are easier and more uniform than those on Angus the man. As an American friend and fellow Hispanist wrote in an obituary of him, 'Angus MacKay was a scholar of unique insights and generosity. He was also an engaging and selfless friend. His death on 29 October 2016 represents an immense loss to those who work on European medieval literature and history in general and that of the Iberian Middle Ages in particular. His absence is also one deeply felt by the many of us who knew him personally; who benefitted from his capacious intellect; and with whom he so gracefully shared his knowledge and bonhomie.'[49] Others recognised his learning and his great scholarly achievement but could find him 'difficult'. One perceptive colleague felt that Angus's originality 'required that he kept his distance'. In part this may have been prompted by his love of a good intellectual argument, pursued forcefully and vociferously; something with which some British academics are not entirely at ease. But this was integral to his personality. His son remembered 'his inability to distinguish between an academic debate to the death and a domestic discussion. He just wouldn't yield.'[50] This could make him seem threatening to those whose egos might be bruised by their favourite ideas or beliefs being assaulted. Apart from in the closeness and happiness of his home, he was probably most at ease in the company of congenial friends and his fellow Hispanists, though of not all of them did he approve. This could be at the annual Hispanist Association conferences or the more intimate setting of the yearly gatherings of 'The Historians of Medieval Spain'.[51] In

[47] A. MacKay, *Moneda, precios y política en la Castilla del siglo XV* (Granada, 2006), produced on the initiative of Manuel Gonzalez Jiménez, and furnished with an appreciation of Angus, pp. 13–15.

[48] Collins and Goodman, *Medieval Spain: Culture, Conflict and Coexistence*.

[49] T. F. Ruiz, 'In Memoriam Angus MacKay, 1939–2016', *La Corónica*, 45 (2017), 5–8.

[50] Angus John MacKay, funeral eulogy on his father, 9 November 2016.

[51] Founded by Peter Russell and Derek Lomax, this met originally in Oxford but subsequently became peripatetic around several British universities. Involving a small number of committed members, it involved four or five papers being given in just over twenty-four hours, with much time for discussion, wine and good fellowship.

particular, to be in Spain and in conversation with his close friends there was always a great delight.

In appearance, apart from a lack of concern about neatness that his family recognised as beyond remedy, he was for most of his adult life distinguished by a long, pointed beard that in repose might make him look like one of those stately Hidalgos, often Knights of the Order of Santiago, who stare enrapt out of the canvases of El Greco. But there the similarity ends, for Angus was never one for passive contemplation when there was work to be done, his eyes were rarely turned heavenwards, and his smile was more often mischievous or ironic rather than beatific.

Acknowledgements
I am very grateful for information, views and advice from Angus's family, particularly his son Angus John MacKay, and from many of his friends, and former colleagues and students. These include Mr Alastair Allanach, Professor Michael Angold, Professor Robert Bartlett FBA, Dr Tom Brown, Dr Gary Dickson, Dr Fran Dorward, Professor Ana Echevarría Arsuaga, Professor Manuel González Jiménez, the late Professor Anthony Goodman, Professor Richard Hitchcock, Professor Jeremy Lawrance FBA, Dr Peter Linehan FBA, Dr Judith McClure, Professor Teofilo F. Ruiz, Mr Stephen Witkowski, and Professor Roger Wright. Others invited declined to assist.

Note on the author: Dr Roger Collins is Honorary Fellow in the School of History, Classics & Archaeology, University of Edinburgh.

IAN STEWART

Bernard Harold Ian Halley Stewart

10 August 1935 – 3 March 2018

Elected Fellow of the British Academy in 1981

by

DONAL BATESON

Ian Stewart was elected a Fellow of the British Academy for his outstanding contribution to British numismatics. His areas of interest were the Scottish coinage, Anglo-Saxon and later medieval English coins. He published extensively, *The Scottish Coinage* and *English Coins 1180–1551* being standard works. Yet he never held an academic post. His collections of English and Scottish coins were outstanding. Stewart was a banker by profession but had a second career in politics, holding several ministerial posts in the 1980s. He was knighted and subsequently raised to the peerage as Lord Stewartby in 1992.

Biographical Memoirs of Fellows of the British Academy, XVIII, 217–240
Posted 16 October 2019. © British Academy 2019.

IAN STEWART   (1981, *Monitor Press Features Limited*)

Collectors often enjoy recounting details of their first acquisition. In the case of six-year-old Ian Stewart it was the finding of a double-headed coin—a copper half-penny of William and Mary—lurking in a jar on the local grocer's counter. Often such interest soon falls by the wayside or lacks real roots but in this case it was to bear extraordinary fruit. Ten years later, while still at school, he wrote what remains the standard introduction to Scottish coins and some fifty years on the classic work on the later medieval English coinage. Between, there appeared a multitude of numismatic publications which many academics would be pleased to have produced. Yet, he never held a university or museum post. In fact, he pursued two other successful careers, in politics and banking. He served as a Member of Parliament for eighteen years and held a number of ministerial posts before being elevated to the Lords where he was a working peer. He retired in 2015 and spent the last few years of his life in the Scottish Borders continuing to research on coinage and keeping in touch with the Upper House.

Bernard Harold Ian Halley Stewart was born on 10 August 1935—coincidentally in the same London nursing home as his future spouse. He used the name Ian, Halley being the surname of a maternal ancestor. Although born and bred in England he was immensely proud of his Scottish ancestry. There was a farming history with Stewarts from the Highlands settling in Atholl and Mar but the patriarch of the family was Alexander Stewart (1790–1874) born in Kirkcaldy in Fife. After an adventurous life at sea, including capture during the Napoleonic War, he settled in London where he became a popular and highly regarded minister in the Congregational Church.

His tenth child, Halley, was born in 1838. After working as a clerk he, too, felt the call of religion. At the same time a growing involvement with politics was encouraged by the Liberal victory under Gladstone in 1866. Three years later he went into business with his brother Ebenezer as manufacturers of superior cattle cake. Halley stood for Parliament and won a famous victory in the Spalding constituency in Lincolnshire in an 1886 by-election. At the end of the century the company was sold but in 1900 was replaced by a new venture in brick manufacture. In 1923 this became the London Brick Company. Twelve months later Halley retired and set up what is now the Sir Halley Stewart Fund. He was knighted in 1932. The company produced over 120 million bricks a year in Wootton Pittinge, Bedfordshire, which was transformed into a model village renamed Stewartby. It gave him great pleasure to baptise his latest great-grandson in 1935 Bernard Harold Ian Halley Stewart.

Ian's grandfather, Bernard Halley Stewart (1873–1958), Halley's youngest child, went up to Cambridge, to Jesus College, and obtained an Honours degree in Natural Science in 1896. He joined the family firm but his heart was not in business and in 1899 decided to study medicine. After qualifying he chose general practice.

Bernard and Mabel Stewart had three children of whom the eldest was Harold Charles (1906–2001). He, too, became a GP but was later appointed to a chair in Pharmacology at London University. Ian was his only son.

Born in August 1935 and baptised by his 97-year-old great-grandfather, Ian Stewart attended prep school at St Michael's, Tawstock. The first person he met on his first day was Tom King, who was to be a life-long friend and subsequently a political colleague. His Classics Master, R. M. Ashcroft, recognised his ability in that subject and guided him towards Haileybury which had an excellent Classics Department. He was also taught art by Wilfred Blunt, the brother of his later numismatic mentor and friend, Christopher. He flourished there and, unlike so many others at public school, enjoyed it. He excelled both academically and in sport and it was in his last years at Haileybury that his serious interest in numismatics developed.

Between 1954 and 1956 he did his National Service in the Royal Naval Volunteer Reserve. He won a scholarship to Jesus College, Cambridge, in Classics in 1956 and gained a Double First in his Classics Tripos three years later. However, sport was not neglected and he was a double blue in tennis as well as an admired batsman on the cricket field. After coming down his interest in the ancient world took a practical course when he went to the British School at Athens. Lord William Taylour had just taken over the directorship of the excavations at Mycenae from W. B. Wace and there Ian made his way to participate. Unfortunately, he caught a severe throat infection and was hospitalised in Corinth. His memorial eulogy recounted that, sporting a full beard and carrying a copy of the New Testament in Greek, Ian was mistaken for an Orthodox priest. However, he was to be neither priest nor archaeologist, deciding on a career in the City. After a brief period in a Discount House, he joined the private bank of Brown Shipley & Co Ltd in 1960.

It was there that he met his future wife, Deborah, who was employed as an intern. The Hon Deborah Charlotte Buchan was the daughter of the 3rd Baron Tweedsmuir. She is thus the granddaughter of John Buchan, politician, sometime Governor-General of Canada and best known as an author of histories and adventure novels of which *The Thirty-Nine Steps* is the most famous. Buchan's father was the minister of the Gorbals Parish Church in Glasgow. Ian's family, too, had a connection with Glasgow, a kinsman being responsible for bringing clean water to the city in the nineteenth century. There is some uncertainty as to how brief the courtship was, but a reliable source says the pair were engaged within the week. Ian and Deborah were married in 1966 in Ewelme Parish Church and it was there they returned to celebrate their Golden Wedding Anniversary in 2016 surrounded by their three children, Henry, Lydia and Louisa with their spouses, and their grandchildren, to all of whom he was devoted and immensely proud.

After National Service Ian served in the Royal Naval Reserve rising to the rank of Lieutenant-Commander. Every summer he would take a train to Newcastle for his two weeks active service. This took place on HMS *Northumberland* which was on mine-sweeping duty in the Tyne Division. However, on one occasion the ship made its way to Gibraltar where it was given an exercise to lay tracer fire on an incoming aircraft. Nothing happened for several hours but at last a Royal Air Force plane was spotted and duly 'fired' on, taking evasive action. It was only that evening when the officers attended a reception at Government House that another guest, a pilot in the RAF who had arrived with a number of sick personnel, was overheard to complain of being fired at as he came in over the island and having had to take swift action to the consternation of crew and 'passengers'. Fortunately, it did not become an incident. Ian was a navigation officer and maintained an interest in cloud formations for the rest of his life. He was awarded the Reserve Decoration but regretfully resigned on being appointed a government minister.

In the early 1970s Ian began to become interested in politics, believing there needed to be better links between the City and government. He was encouraged by Edward Heath to stand for parliament and in not unusual fashion was chosen to contest the unwinnable Labour seat of North Hammersmith, losing by over 6,000 votes. However, in the February 1974 general election he won Hitchin for the Conservatives with a majority of just over 4,000, and when Harold Wilson went to the polls a second time that year he held the seat. Jim Callaghan replaced Wilson in 1976, but after the winter of discontent was decisively beaten by the Conservatives under Margaret Thatcher in the general election of 1979. Ian held his Hitchin seat with a thumping majority of over 13,000. That year he was appointed Parliamentary Private Secretary (PPS) to the Chancellor of the Exchequer, Geoffrey Howe, a position he held for four years.

Early in 1983 he was promoted to Parliamentary Under-Secretary of State for Defence Procurement, when the Secretary of State for Defence was George Younger, in which role he served until October of that year. In June there had been a general election when he retained his seat, now re-named Hertfordshire North with slight boundary changes, with a majority of almost 10,000 and the Thatcher government won a formidable majority of 143 seats. In October he became Economic Secretary to Her Majesty's Treasury, then led by Nigel Lawson. During his tenure he was responsible for a number of important Acts including the Trustee Savings Bank (1985), Building Societies (1986) and Banking (1987) Acts, which together greatly changed the face of finance in the United Kingdom. He was also the British representative on the European Budget Council and on one occasion caused consternation by quoting Virgil's famous phase from the *Aeneid* (II:49), 'Beware the Greeks bearing gifts', except that he delivered it in Latin much to the surprise of the simultaneous translators most of whom removed their ear-phones in puzzlement. Alas the context has been lost.

Another general election was held in June 1987 when the Tory majority was still over one hundred and Ian's personal majority was increased to over 11,000. In the newly formed government he was offered the post of Minister of State for the Armed Forces under George Younger, the Defence Secretary. This he held for just under a year before being moved as Minister of State to the Northern Ireland Office, headed by Tom King. There he was responsible for Security, an arduous and, at the height of 'The Troubles', a dangerous brief and one resulting in the need for care and vigilance for many years after. The following summer he hurt his hip in a helicopter incident and had to resign from office. He was appointed to the Privy Council in 1989 and in the Queen's Birthday Honours List of 1991 he was made a knight. He decided against standing again in the 1992 general election by which time John Major had replaced Margaret Thatcher as Leader of the Conservative Party.

That year Sir Ian Stewart was raised to the Lords, taking as the title for his life peerage Baron Stewartby of Portmoak in the District of Perth and Kinross. This referred to both his English and Scottish heritage with Stewartby being the model village to the south of Bedford founded by the family firm and Portmoak a small village to the south-east of Loch Leven, where Alexander Stewart's family had a small farm. The dwelling still exists but is now the headquarters of the Scottish Gliding Club. Stewartby's coat of arms is based on that of his great-grandfather Halley who had obtained a grant of arms in 1922 as a 'Gentleman without title'. The shield is 'Or, a fess chequey and Argent between a Portcullis … And in base a lymphard, all within a border azure'. The fess refers to King Robert II, the portcullis to membership of the House of Commons and the ship probably to Alexander Stewart's time at sea. The Stewartby arms supporters are the Tweedsmuir Stag sinister and Lion proper dexter. This also possesses the coronet appropriate to a Life Baron and a peer's mantling and helmet—the crest on the latter again being a lymphard with a fleur-de-lys either side of the prow possibly referring to Alexander's unwelcome stay in France. Above is the family motto, 'THERE REMAINETH A REST' (Hebrews 4.9–16). Finally there is the addition of the cross of the Order of St John behind the shield and the pendent badge of a Knight Batchelor. The Lord Lyon noted that the pendent badges were not necessary and that £20 could be saved in the fee through their omission.

***

Alas the coat of arms bears no reference to numismatics which was such a major part of Ian's life. From that early encounter with the old coin on the grocer's counter (being collected for the war effort, but fortunately not compulsory as with iron railings, and replaced with another) his interest had grown and at its meeting on 27 February 1952 he was elected a Junior Member of the British Numismatic Society. Also elected to Junior Membership was Peter Spufford who was to have an eminent academic career at Cambridge as a medieval historian with strong numismatic interests. The most eminent British numismatist at that time was Christopher Blunt, who before and after the war was responsible for regenerating a somewhat moribund society. He was to remain at the forefront until his death in 1987. He was described as the 'mentor, friend and colleague of numismatists young and old' in his Fellow's memoir, appropriately written by Ian.[1] This indeed aptly describes the fruitful relationship between the two. Ian recounts that soon after joining the Society he purchased a run of back-numbers of the *British Numismatic Journal* for what seemed a modest sum and only discovered years later that he had been charged merely half price, the rest being paid for by Blunt.

Ian soon began to make his mark. In September 1952, lately turned just 17, he delivered his first lecture, entitled 'The attribution of the Thistle-head and Mullet groats' to the 'British', accompanied by an exhibition of relevant specimens. This was subsequently printed in the Society's journal for 1952–4 along with two other papers, 'The Heavy silver coinage of James III and James IV' and 'Double moneyers names on early Scottish pennies'. In 1954 the Royal Numismatic Society instituted the Dr Parkes Weber Prize, sponsored by its then longest-standing member who was a physician and a collector, who donated a large part of his collection to the British Museum, as well the writer of several numismatic publications. The prize was intended to encourage younger numismatists who had to be under twenty-three and submit an original essay of under 5,000 words on any aspect of coins, medals or tokens. The winner received ten guineas along with a specimen of Frank Bowcher's portrait medal of Weber. Ian submitted an essay, neatly written in a Haileybury exercise book, on 'Aspects of coinage and currency in medieval Scotland'. Although this did not win the prize it was runner-up with high commendation. He received an invitation to tea with the great man.

In his final years at Haileybury Ian was working on a somewhat larger project, namely a handbook on the coinage of Scotland. This had been completed before he left for National Service and the final corrections were addressed to Ordinary Seaman Stewart at Victoria Barracks, Portsmouth, in mid-October 1954. Although considered eligible to partake in battle, legally at nineteen he was not allowed to sign the publication agreement with Spink, the leading numismatic publishers in London. His father signed on his behalf at the end of October 1954. For some time little work had been carried out on the Scottish coinage. Edward Burns' magisterial three-volume *The*

---

[1] I. Stewart, 'Christopher Evelyn Blunt 1904–1987', *Proceedings of the British Academy*, 76 (1991), pp. 347–81.

Coinage of Scotland published in 1887 remains the standard reference work for the series. Yet it is often difficult to use, cannot easily be moved around and is expensive. As Ian succinctly observed in the preface of his new work, 'it is exhaustive and exhausting'. Thus, little had been added to the subject in the first half of the twentieth century and it needed to be updated and revised. With the post-war rejuvenation of British numismatics a condensed and reliable handbook was required for the student, researcher and collector. Thus B. H. I. H. Stewart's *The Scottish Coinage* admirably fulfilled this role. Its success was shown by the print run of 1,000 being sold out within a decade, with the author receiving royalties of £332.

Over the next sixty years, despite his other commitments, there was a steady stream of publications. Apart from books and special publications, these appeared mostly in the *British Numismatic Journal* and *Numismatic Chronicle*, with lesser notes in *Spink's Numismatic Circular*. There are several papers on 'Unpublished Scottish coins', among which 'Some Scottish ceremonial coins' (1965) is his sole contribution to the *Proceedings of the Society of Antiquaries of Scotland*. This included his discovery of the only recorded survivor of the touch pieces produced for the touching ceremony held after Charles I's Scottish coronation at Holyrood in 1633, which he identified in William Hunter's eighteenth-century cabinet in Glasgow.

He believed in the importance of publishing coin hoards and dealt with a number of these, assiduously describing the contents and interpreting their numismatic, historical and economic value. Several were joint papers for he was a ready collaborator with colleagues. These include the 1956 fifteenth-century Glenluce hoard; the 1961 fifteenth-century Rhoneston find (with R. B. K. Stevenson); the nineteenth-century Biggar (Crosscryne) find of thirteenth- and fourteenth-century sterlings; the 1963 Renfrew hoard of mainly pennies deposited a few years after Robert the Bruce recaptured Berwick and pointing to a date of circa 1320 for his coinage (with Peter Woodhead); the 1966 Loch Doon treasure trove of pennies probably hidden in the 1330s, used for the analysis of the hoards of this period (with Peter Woodhead and George Tatler); two nineteenth-century finds of later fourteenth-century issues from Dipple and Balgony; 'Some Edwardian hoards from Scotland' (1973); the 1900 hoard of Edwardian sterlings from Berscar (Closeburn), (1977); but few further after this latter date. Although there was but one joint output with Robert Stevenson, who was Keeper of the National Museum of Antiquities of Scotland with a strong interest in numismatics, there was a fruitful working relationship covering advice, discussion, exchange of information, encouragement and access to the National Collection of Scottish coins as well as new finds. Collaboration continued after Stevenson's retirement in 1987 until his death in 1992, especially on his publications of the bawbees and groats of James V.

In 1967 Spink published a revised edition of *The Scottish Coinage*. However, it is disappointing that they decided to print a facsimile of the first 1955 edition and to add the revisions as a single supplement instead of integrating these. There are some thirty additional pages (to the original 184) containing errata and corrigenda, changes to the text, lists, bibliography and the chart of mints, as well as an extra plate. Account is taken of recent published and unpublished work and 'new theories, identifications and material' incorporated. The year 2017 marked the fiftieth anniversary of its appearance and it is remarkable that it remains the standard introduction to the coinage of Scotland.

Also in 1967 there appeared a paper on unpublished coins of the early reign of James III written jointly with Joan Murray. This marked the start of twenty years of collaboration and friendship with Lt. Col. J. K. R. and Mrs J. E. L. Murray which produced a wealth of research and output on the Scottish coinage. Born Joan Clarke, she was an outstanding mathematician and after Cambridge was recruited in 1940 for the top-secret code-breaking work being carried out at Bletchley Park. There she met and became engaged to the brilliant Alan Turing but broke off their engagement. After the war she was employed at Government Communications Headquarters (GCHQ), where she met Jock Murray, late of the Indian Army. They married in 1951. The Murrays became seriously interested in collecting and researching Scottish coins in the early 1960s, and after meeting Ian in 1964 they formed a triumvirate on the series.

The trio happily complemented each other: Ian being especially interested in the early issues; Joan in those of the later fourteenth century and the Jameses; Jock in the later sixteenth- and the seventeenth-century coinages. Their work was meticulous and, making use of documentary sources, they greatly enhanced our knowledge and under-standing of the Scottish issues. Jock published outstanding surveys of the gold and silver coinages of Charles I for Scotland, Charles II's Scottish silver and, with Ian in 1972, 'The Scottish copper coinages 1642-1697'. A postscript in 1978 published a document which solved an outstanding problem with the turners of the 1640s and the 1660s. The II after the CR on the reverse was shown to refer to Charles II and not the value of twopence Scots, at last allowing these very common coins to be assigned correctly to the respective reigns. Joan's important work on the arrangement of the coinage of Robert II was the subject of her final talk to the British Numismatic Society in 1994. Colonel and Mrs. Murray died in 1986 and 1996 respectively. Ian published 'Mrs.Murray's arrangement of the coins of Robert II, 1371–1390' in 2015, a final tribute to an outstanding contribution to Scottish numismatics.

Meanwhile, in 1971, for the Festschrift in honour of Albert Baldwin, Ian contributed 'Scottish mints', a short title belying an extensive and in-depth examina-tion of the mints from the twelfth century to the Act of Union in 1707. This covered the location and function of the mints and the mint names, as they are found on the coins, followed by a comprehensive survey of the early sterlings (1136–95). Then came a discussion of the short and long cross sterlings (1195–1280), followed by the single cross sterlings (1280–1357). The latter did not bear a mint signature but he attempted to assign them, probably on the whole correctly, by counting the differing number of points found on the stars and mullets of the reverses. Next came the later Middle Ages (1357–1513) and the modern period until the end of the Scottish coinage early in the eighteenth century. He concluded with a study of the die-links between the mints, especially in the period 1136 to 1280. This monumental paper allowed him to move beyond *The Scottish Coinage* and to put forward his own ideas and interpretations, greatly contributing to the understanding of Scotland's coin output. It has, perhaps, not received the attention and use it deserves.

In 1969 the second large hoard, of long cross pennies, had been discovered in Colchester (the earlier being in 1902 of short cross pennies) and Ian was asked to write up the Scottish element containing just under 500 specimens, which was published in 1974. Burns had described the Scottish long cross issues, struck between 1250 and 1280 at the largest number of mints (sixteen) operating in Scotland for a specific issue, though he did this on a limited amount of material. Albert Baldwin presented a new arrangement based on approximately 1,750 included in the huge 1908 Brussels hoard in Part V of the celebrated Lockett Sale held in 1957. Two years later Ian conducted a review of this on the coins and notes still held at Baldwin's—'The Brussels Hoard: Mr. Baldwin's arrangement of the Scottish coins'—and in 1970 discussed 'The long voided sterlings of Alexander in Burns'. All this allowed him to give a well-considered and concise account of the issue in his 'Scottish mints' in the Baldwin Festschrift.

By 1977 academic interest in the Scottish coinage had developed greatly, not least due to Ian's work and enthusiasm, and a highly successful symposium was organised by the Ashmolean on the uses of coinage in medieval Scotland. This brought together numismatists, archaeologists and historians who discussed how coinage could contribute to the study of monetary matters. This produced a highly useful *Proceedings* in which Ian contributed the paper 'The volume of early Scottish coinage', a synopsis of what he said about a previously neglected aspect of the series but the lengthier content as presented at the meeting intended for another time did not emerge. There was a reduction in his numismatic output in the 1980s due to an increasing interest in the English coinages and his governmental commitments during that decade.

However, there were important papers in two special publications. The first, in the 1981 volume commemorating the bicentenary of the Society of Antiquaries of Scotland, was entitled 'Two centuries of Scottish numismatics with a biography of Scottish numismatics', and the second in the 1983 Festschrift in honour of Robert Stevenson, 'Coinage and propaganda: an interpretation of the coin types of James VI'. He also contributed an appendix to the 1987 *Sylloge of Coins of the British Isles* volume (*SCBI* 35) covering the Scottish coins in the Ashmolean and Hunterian collections on the unique Alexander III transitional short cross penny of 1249–50 struck at Glasgow, probably the earliest output of a mint there. It had surfaced in the Spurway Sale (1984) when it was purchased by Ian, who later generously passed it to The Hunterian.

The 1990s saw renewed emphasis on his English research and, apart from a few short notes, his major paper was the 'Classification of the single-cross sterlings of Alexander III'. This major and detailed work examined the most common of Scottish medieval coins, introduced shortly after its English prototype of 1279 and largely struck in the early 1280s. Also in 1990 the Edwardian sterlings in the Lochmaben, Blackhills and Mellendean hoards were looked at afresh and reclassified. Both papers were written in collaboration with J. J. North, the authority on Edwardian pence.

The year 2000 saw another collaboration, with Nicholas Holmes of National Museums Scotland who was working closely with Ian on several Scottish topics. 'Scottish coinage in the first half of the fourteenth century' was followed by 'The 1533 issue of James V placks' in 2008 and the classic work 'The coinage of John Baliol' in 2010. Another joint note in 2007, this time with Lady Stewartby, had a somewhat later subject but one to which others continually return to, Mary's ryals of 1565–7 with the palm and tortoise. This puts forward the novel theory that the design refers to the siege of Malta in 1565 rather than to the more usual, but dubious, Crookston Castle yew tree or to her husband Lord Darnley.

Ian returned to the Brussels hoard when he contributed a detailed section on the Scottish coins in the British Numismatic Society's special publication printed in 2012. A short note in 2013 confirmed the start of Alexander's single long cross pence in 1280 based on the re-examination of the contents of the 1873 Northampton hoard. His final paper, 'The saltire-stopped heavy groats of James III', was published in the *Numismatic Chronicle* in 2015.

****

Although Lord Stewartby made an outstanding contribution to Scottish numismatics, surprisingly only around a third of his published work relates to this coinage. He was also greatly committed to the English coinage, Anglo-Saxon and later medieval, in which areas he wrote a much greater number of papers. In the *British Numismatic Journal* for 1955–7, for example, he had two notes and a review on the issues of Aethelred II from the Stamford mint, the crux issue and the first small cross issue. These were followed by two papers on the Northumbrian Viking coins found in the Cuerdale hoard written jointly with Stuart Lyon, with whom he was to collaborate fruitfully, and a lengthy article, 'The coinage of Southern England, 796–840', again with Lyon and also Blunt. Alone he wrote on the meaning of the terms *moneta* and *mot* as used on the Anglo-Saxon pennies. Alongside these was a string of short, but insightful, notes on a spread of topics ranging from the mints at Lincoln, York, Peterborough, Wessex, Droitwich and Caistor to types of Aethelred II, Edward the Confessor and the Vikings. By the 1970s, however, he seemed to be developing a greater interest in the later medieval English series and though interest in the earlier series remained he moved from the later issues to those of the tenth century.

Over the years Christopher Blunt's interest had also moved, but from the later medieval period to the Anglo-Saxon and, in particular, the tenth century, looking at the unifying of the currency as the country was unified. Out of this emerged the classic study of the coins of Aethelstan published as a single volume (42) as a special publication of the *British Numismatic Journal* to mark his 70th birthday in 1974. His work on the preceding and subsequent reigns led him to the conclusion that the period should be dealt with as a whole for publication. Stuart Lyon was also interested in these coinages, as was Ian, and both were invited by Blunt to collaborate on a project which by 1976, after much thought, was to be nothing less than a comprehensive study. It was over a decade in the making, being published by the British Academy in 1989. It commences with the reign of Edward the Elder (899–924) and ends with Edgar's strategic reform of the coinage which probably occurred in 973. This authoritative work leaves students in Anglo-Saxon studies greatly indebted to these three scholars. Additionally, it was intended to be used in conjunction with the Academy's *SCBI* volume (34) by Marion Archibald and Blunt on the British Museum's holding of over 1,400 coins from Aethelstan to Edgar's reform, published three years earlier. Worked on in parallel, *Coinage in Tenth-Century England* provides the arrangement and referencing while *SCBI* provides a large corpus of specimens which would have not been feasible in the former alone. The latter handsomely acknowledges Ian's assistance.

This was followed by another major output in his section of *A New History of the Royal Mint*, edited by Christopher Challis, published in 1992. Ian wrote the first section covering the start of the English coinage in the seventh century to the end of the Norman issues in 1158, when Henry II introduced the Tealby penny. This consisted of a major overview of the entire Anglo-Saxon output along with that of the first century after the Conquest. The reviewer in the *British Numismatic Journal* lamented the lack of such a survey previously and described it as 'the first reputable modern survey of the history of coinage in Britain over the period as a whole' and added 'To the study of the coinage from the earliest times to 1158, which in other hands might have remained as confusing and amorphous as the raw material on which the historical narrative must be based, Lord Stewartby has brought an almost magical clarity and his remarkable gift for summarising the complexities of scholarly argument without either looking down to the reader or misrepresenting any essential point.'

Ian's first contribution to the later medieval English coinage consisted of a brief note in 1957, 'A new Norman forger', concerning a contemporary light penny of William I made from altered London dies by one of the mint's own moneyers. In the 1960s came two articles on die output in the fourteenth century and a further one on style. During the 1970s there appeared a series of notes on many diverse subjects ranging from Stephen, Matilda, William I and II and Henry I to Edward III, Richard II and Henry VII. A more in-depth two-part paper covered the later issues of John and the early issues of Henry III. Further notes appeared throughout the 1980s on various issues, mints and dies from William I to Henry VII. In 1988 he was invited to deliver the first Howard Linecar Memorial Lecture to the British Numismatic Society, choosing as his subject 'English numismatics—progress and prospects'. Ian had known Linecar as head of publications at Spink from his early teens when he first started acquiring numismatic books. This lecture covered many diverse topics including: the revival of English numismatics and the British Numismatic Society in the post-war years under Blunt's leadership; the appointment of Michael Dolley to the British Museum and the latter's work on Edgar's reform and the subsequent periodic re-coinages into the twelfth century; his own doubts on Dolley's thesis; the changed post-war market in coins; photographic recording by polaroid—which seems so dated now in the digital age; the increased discovery of coin hoards; imitations; and his dislike of the normalisation of moneyers names—the cause of much confusion. But he thought the Society could take pride in its achievements and was optimistic for the future.

Short articles on John's recoinage of 1208 and Henry I type xv followed. Freed of ministerial responsibilities, there was continuous output of material concentrated on the medieval period. They are too numerous to list but mention may be made of his substantial 1995 paper 'German imitations of English short-cross sterlings'. The single long cross imitations of the late thirteenth and early fourteenth centuries produced in the Low Countries had received much attention but the earlier copies of the short cross coinage (1180–1250), emanating chiefly from Westphalia in the first half of the thirteenth century, only now received a detailed study and catalogue.

However, all was leading up to Ian's *magnum opus* on the later coinage. Contemplated for forty years and written between 1994 and 2007, his eagerly awaited *English Coins 1180–1551* was published to wide acclaim in 2009—'nothing short of a masterpiece', 'an indispensable work of reference'. The author wrote that after a century of intense activity in English numismatics 'it seems timely to attempt a conspectus of the subject of our state of knowledge at the turn of the millennium'. His aim was 'to provide a general historical survey combined with a classified description of the coins' of use to numismatists, historians, collectors and the general user. The work begins with the major reform of the coinage by Henry II in 1180 when the short cross issue replaced the poorly produced products dating back to the civil war and ends with another major reform carried out by Edward VI in 1551 to replace his father's debased monetary system. The period is divided into nine chapters each containing the historical background and overview of the period followed by a clear, full classification of the coins. These are accompanied by sections on mint output and a calendar of relevant events. The first three chapters deal with the end of the period when the silver penny constituted the mainstay of the coinage. Next comes Edward III's attempt in 1344 to follow Europe in introducing a gold coinage. It required further modifications before the change was successful in 1351. In that year, too, the silver was expanded with a larger coin, the groat of fourpence. The second half of the book is then devoted to the development of this coinage. The main system is fairly simple in its limited number of denominations but complicated in the extensive use of privy marks. The latter are dealt with comprehensively but with clarity. Two major weight reductions in the silver allow splits in 1412 and 1464 and the seventh chapter leads to the reign of Henry VIII and his revaluation of 1526 by which time there was a greater range of coins—and real portraiture introduced by the Renaissance. Henry receives two chapters from 1526 and the last from 1544 to 1551 when he debased the coinage. This was reversed by Edward VI in 1551 thus opening a new and modern period for the English coinage.

There was to be one further medieval English paper, on the notorious 'dandyprats', which was published in 2012. These inferior quality halfgroats issued by Henry VII for use in his Boulogne campaign of late 1492 have engendered much debate. He suggested that the low weight halfgroats of London and York with a pellet and lozenge in the centre of the reverse could indeed be identified with the dandyprats, reviewing critically the counter-argument that the sequence of Henry VIIs initial marks did not allow this.

Two other lesser interests may be noted. The first was the Roman mint of London. This was opened by Carausius, the usurper who founded the first British Empire in 287, and continued to function until 325 when closed by Constantine the Great, though it was revived for a brief period in the 380s. In the late 1980s Ian published three notes in which he was able to confirm, with actual specimens, the existence of two previously dubious issues. The first is a bronze follis of Constantine the Great as Augustus with reverse Mars and the rather long legend MARTIPATRIPROPVGNATORI. The second is of Constantine as Caesar with the *Adventus* reverse dating to 307 and suggesting a first planned or actual imperial visit that year prior to those of 312 and 314. In 1992 he spotted in a sale lot another excessively rare follis of Constantine as Caesar with MARTI PATRI CONSERVATORI reverse, otherwise known only from a single specimen in the Vienna Cabinet. He returned to the extensive coinage of Constantine Caesar when he discovered a follis lurking unnoticed in the trays at the Fitzwilliam Museum with the *Virtus* type hitherto unknown as an issue of this emperor. The coin was recorded along with a detailed survey of the numerous tetrarchic issues from London of late 307 to 309 according to the three reducing weight standards.

Further research took him to two Lincolnshire finds of early tetrarchic folles recovered before the war at Market Stainton. The two hoards contained a combined total of over 700 bronze coins of Diocletian, Maximian, Constantius and Galerius, mostly from the London Mint. His final Roman paper appeared in 2011 and concerned a hoard found in Falmouth in 1865. Somewhat similar to the Market Stainton hoards, it appeared on the market in 1970 when it was acquired by Baldwin. Ian was able to examine those coins still in stock in 1991 and provided a further detailed corpus and discussion of London's tetrarchic issues.

****

Another interest lay in the history of numismatics. The history of collecting had become popular towards the end of the twentieth century culminating in the Enlightenment Gallery which opened at the British Museum in 2003, thus placing Ian among the first to work on this subject. Two substantial papers complement each other and provide a major insight into the collecting and research of Scottish coins over 300 years. The earlier is a contribution to the bicentenary volume of the Society of Antiquaries of Scotland in 1980. The Society had been interested in coinage from its foundation and in 1781 received the donation of 109 Scottish coins from Dr William Hunter and its collection continued to grow until transferred to the (now) National Museums Scotland in Edinburgh where it constitutes the national collection of the Scottish series. Its first President, the 3rd Earl of Bute, was a serious collector of coins. The paper covers the study of Scottish coins and currency noting that this tended to flourish when collecting was more active, as in the period 1850–90 and from the mid-1950s. It looks at the nature of coinage, the development of the Scottish coinage and the collecting of Scottish coins from the seventeenth century. Literature on the subject dates back to the early eighteenth century, culminating in the standard work *The Coinage of Scotland* by Edward Burns in 1887 but restarted with Ian's own handbook of 1955/1967. An appendix contains a useful bibliography of Scottish coinage.

His second paper, 'Scottish coin collectors', published in 1996, deals more specifically with collections, collectors and contents. Scottish coins are more often elements in larger cabinets of British and Classical coins formed mainly by the great and lesser English collectors. The number of collections of Scottish coins alone and formed by Scots in Scotland is limited. The paper is concise but comprehensive. The earliest collections date to the late seventeenth century with Scottish elements in those of the Earls and Dukes of Bridgewater and Archbishop Sharp of York while that of the Edinburgh botanist James Sutherland focused on Scottish issues. The great eighteenth-century collections included those of the Earls of Oxford and Pembroke and of Martin Folkes, Richard Mead and William Hunter—whose cabinet was one of the few not to end up in the saleroom but was bequeathed to the University of Glasgow. The early nineteenth century was less active but John Lindsay of Cork, who published *A View of the Coinage of Scotland* in 1845, owned over 600 Scottish coins. This was followed later in the century when R. W. Cochran-Patrick and Edward Burns wrote their outstanding works and also collected coins. However, the best collections of Scottish coins at that time belonged to two West of Scotland businessmen, Thomas Coats and James Wingate, that of the former being the basis of Burns' *The Coinage of Scotland* and ending in the Edinburgh museum. While the first half of the twentieth century was 'quiet', noteworthy were the Grantly, Ryan, Dakers and Lockett cabinets and sales. After 1950 there was simply one outstanding collection of over 6,000 carefully selected Scottish coins, that of Lord Stewartby.

In addition to these two works, there was a number of other historical contributions. An appreciation of Edward Burns, based on nine volumes of letters from the 1880s preserved by his descendants, appeared in 1987 to commemorate the centenary of *The Coinage of Scotland*, a 'great and enduring work' which 'set new standards in numismatic technique'. Making further use of this archive, Ian wrote a paper on the background to the Wingate sale—one of the great nineteenth-century Scottish collections sold at Sotheby's in 1975—and the part played by Burns which provides a 'fascinating and perhaps unique insight'. Two further papers along similar lines appeared in the centenary volume of the British Numismatic Society in 2003. Here he dealt with aspects of English numismatics which in the first half of the twentieth century received more analytical and specialised attention. An appendix to the first lists over fifty crucial papers, mainly in the pages of the *British Numismatic Journal*, including that of Lawrence on the short cross and long cross coinages, the Foxes on the long single cross Edwardian sterlings and Blunt and Whitton on Edward IV. Much of the basic work was carried out in the first half of the century with several scholars undertaking work on detail and refinement in the second half. The second paper arose out of a previously unknown obituary of J. G. Murdoch (1830–1902) who represented the earlier enthusiastic collector who did not research or publish. However, Murdoch built up one of the greatest collections of British coins which was sold at Sotheby's in 1903–4. A final short paper, 'Evans and the coinage', was contributed to the centenary volume *Sir John Evans 1823–1908*.

It may be appropriate to end this review of Ian's contribution to numismatic research by referring to an interesting and intuitive paper he wrote with Michael Metcalf in 2007 entitled 'The bust of Christ on an early Anglo-Saxon coin'. The coin is a small base silver sceatta belonging to Metcalf's Secondary series type Q assigned to the first half of the eighth century and to West Norfolk. The obverse depicts a facing bust with a cross behind—'a cross without a nimbus makes this unequivocally a portrayal of Christ and not a saint'. The reverse type of a bird and snake is suggestive of the battle between good and evil. One of Ian's lesser known pastimes was early Christian art, so it is an area he had some knowledge of. He had bought this otherwise unrecorded coin for his own collection but generously donated it to the Fitzwilliam Museum in 2017.

This academic contribution to numismatics was accompanied by a willing participation in the administrative side, both leading to election and appointment to many committees and the award of prizes and honours. His interests naturally led him towards the British Numismatic Society. He was elected to the Council in 1960 and served on it for over fifty years. He held the post of Director from 1966 to 1975 and was a Vice-President from 1980 until his death. In 1971 the Society awarded him the John Sanford Saltus Medal for his scholarly contribution to British Numismatics. He did, however, also join the Royal Numismatic Society, being elected a Fellow in 1956 and winning the Society's Parkes Weber Prize for that year. In 1996 he was presented with the Medal of the Royal Numismatic Society awarded annually to 'some person highly distinguished for services to Numismatic Science'. Cambridge recognised its alumnus by awarding him a LittD in 1978 while he was made an Honorary Fellow of Jesus College in 1994; he was appointed Honorary Keeper of Medieval Numismatics at the Fitzwilliam Museum in 2008. In 1981 Ian Stewart was elected to a Fellowship of the British Academy; the *Sunday Telegraph* for 12 July reported that he had received this high, and unusual for a politician, honour for distinction in numismatics—the first time a sitting Member of Parliament had been so honoured since Arthur Balfour and John Morley in the foundation list of 1902. He served on the Academy's *Sylloge of Coins of the British Isles* Committee from 1967 and was Chair for ten years from 1993 to 2003. The *SCBI* has been a particularly successful Academy project, producing some seventy volumes from 1958 to 2017. During Ian's chairmanship some ten volumes were published covering Anglo-Saxon, Norman and medieval English coins as well as seventeenth-century tokens in collections from Britain, the United States, Latvia, Estonia, Russia and Sweden. He was elected a Fellow of the Society of Antiquaries and served on its Council from 1974 to 1976. He was also elected a Fellow of the Society of Antiquaries of Scotland and a Fellow of the Royal Society of Edinburgh. Ian was the numismatic adviser to the National Art Collections Fund from 1988 and Chair of the Treasure Valuation Committee from 1996 to 2001.

****

The third area of Ian's working life was banking and he was frequently referred to as a 'banker by profession' or 'retired banker'. He spent almost fifty years in the City, broken only by his ministerial appointments. It is less easy to say a great deal about this aspect of his life—owing, no doubt, to banking discretion. He first entered a firm of bill brokers after coming down from Cambridge in 1959 but found his metier when he moved to Brown Shipley & Co. Ltd., a merchant bank where he worked from 1960 and was appointed a Director in 1971. He resigned in 1983 on his appointment to government. His experience and expertise were put to good use in seeing a number of banking related bills through Committee and Commons on to the statute book during his time as Economic Secretary to the Treasury.

After injury brought his ministerial career to a premature end in 1989 he returned to the City. He joined Standard Chartered plc in 1990, becoming Deputy Chairman in 1993 and chairing the Audit and Risk Committee. He was also Chairman of the Throgmorton Trust, Deputy Chairman of Amlin and a Director of Diploma plc. He served on the Financial Services Agency (formerly Securities and Investment Board) from 1993 to 1997. Ian retired from these various posts between 2004 and 2007.

Among other interests Ian had a close connection with the Order of St John, as had his father. He was made a knight of the Order in 1992. He served as County Vice-President of the St. John Ambulance for Hertfordshire from 1978 to 2007, when he became County President. He provided direction and wise advice in many ways over these years. A close relationship was maintained with his old school where he was a Life Governor and Member of the Haileybury Council between 1980 and 1995. His interest in Stewart history found an outlet in the Stewart Society of which he was Honorary Vice-President from 1989 and served as President from 2007 to 2010. In addition, he was a Trustee from 1978 before being made President of his great-grandfather's philanthropic trust, the Sir Halley Stewart Trust, in 2002.

His sporting activities continued throughout his life. He played tennis into his sixties and turned out for The Lords cricket team. Among his clubs was the MCC. The last quotation in the Order of Service for his Memorial Service at Jesus College made by Sir Clive Lloyd is worth repeating, 'We played a match last week, a former West Indies side against a team from the House of Lords and Commons. We won easily, but there was one batsman, the Lord Stewartby; we couldn't get him out—he played so straight.'

****

There remains something to be said on the Stewartby coin collection. Ian collected for pleasure and the increase of knowledge. He built up two outstanding collections: the first of English coins of the Anglo-Saxon and later medieval issues and the second his Scottish coins. The former was sold at auction over five days by Spink in 2016–17 with the specific title, 'The Academic Collection of Lord Stewartby'. Unfortunately, catastrophe had struck the Scottish cabinet in 2007 when the significant early portion of the twelfth and thirteenth centuries was lost to theft. Nevertheless over 5,000 specimens from the later thirteenth to the seventeenth century remained and were generously gifted to the University of Glasgow in 2017.

The English coins were auctioned in five parts, each accompanied by a fully illustrated catalogue which will be works of reference in their own right. Almost 3,700 coins, from the first half of the seventh century to the seventeenth century, when milled coinage replaced hammered a few years after the Restoration, made up 1,879 lots. They were meticulously provenanced, many from the great collections, and provide a fascinating insight into coin collecting in Britain over the last hundred years. The majority of the collection was purchased mainly from the leading London dealers and at auction and a small number were gifts. The terms rare, very rare, and exceedingly rare litter the catalogues. A few examples may be noted. The very first lot was a gold thrymsa or shilling of King Eadbald of Kent (616–640), one of only seven known examples and one of the two in private hands. There were two portrait pennies of Offa and another depicting his queen, Cynethryth, as well as a specimen of Alfred the Great's London penny of the early 880s. At the end of the first part there were Civil War pennies of the Yorkshire baron Eustace Fitzjohn and of Matilda struck at Bristol.

In Part 2 the academic aspect became more prominent with over 1,500 coins covering the Tealby (from 1158), short cross, long cross and single long cross (to 1333) of Henry II, Richard, John, Henry III and Edward I, II and III in myriad classes, subclasses, varieties, mints and moneyers.

Part 3 comprised the gold coins of which there were 153 commencing with a leopard or florin from Edward III's first unsuccessful attempt to introduce a gold coinage. Only five specimens are now known. Edward succeeded with a bi-metallic coinage in 1351. The coin was now the noble. Some twenty-six, from Edward III to Henry VI, were included showing it lived up to its name. Another splendid later medieval coin was the sovereign or pound depicting the monarch enthroned. Introduced by Henry VII it was issued in every reign to that of James I. A superb run was offered with those of Mary and James I being rare and choice. The triple unite of 1642 minted at Oxford, one of only four known, cannot avoid notice.

Returning to the silver, Part 4 contained over 800 coins running from the reform of Edward III in 1351. The groat and halfgroat were now supreme and the plethora of issues, mints and privy marks found to the end of this king's reign are well represented by some 350 coins. Likewise, the long and numismatically productive reigns of Henry VI and Edward IV were given considerable attention in Ian's collecting. He possessed smaller runs of the less numerous and rarer issues of Richard II, Henry IV and V and Richard III. Overall a remarkably complete picture is provided of a silver coinage which remained consistent in the issue of five denominations for well over a hundred years.

The last part of the English collection covered the Tudor and Stuart silver issues from Henry VII to Charles II's hammered coinage of 1660–2. The reigns of Henry VII and VIII and Edward VI were represented in greater numbers. Shortly after 1500 a Renaissance-style profile portrait replaced the old medieval stylised facing bust. The best example was a very fine and extremely rare halfgroat of London. Over 150 specimens traced the increasing debasement of the coinage in Henry VIII's reign. Edward VI set about remedying this and his introduction of the fine issue in 1551, of five values from crown to threepence, as well as the lesser pieces, marked another major reform of the English coinage.

It was at this point that Ian ended his book and drew back on his acquisitions. There was a very fine groat of Philip and Mary, with Mary's portrait only, but the number of coins from Elizabeth I's and James I's long reigns ran only to seventy-four and thirty-one respectively. There were over a hundred specimens of Charles I's prolific coin output among which were a rare Oxford pound of 1642, several examples of the issues of the provincial mints and a nice example of a Pontefract shilling of 1648 in the name of Charles II. The collection ended with a half-dozen of the hammered coins of 1660–2 which were replaced by the modern milled coins. The archives associated with the Stewartby English collection—along with his other papers—were deposited with Jesus College.

It is rightly said that the Stewartby collection of Scottish coins is the best of this series ever put together by a private individual. Its only rival in importance is that of National Museums Scotland. The main collection was made up of around 6,000 coins from the reign of David I, when the coinage was instituted in 1136, to the end of a separate Scottish issue following the Act of Union in 1707. It is mainly of silver though with many runs of billon and copper and a smaller group of gold lions, unicorns, riders, ryals and unites. It was a lifetime's work carefully constructed with a view to having as complete a representation as possible and used as the basis for much of the owner's extensive research and publication on Scottish coinage. Condition ranges from uncirculated through fine to poor, when such pieces filled a gap in the jigsaw.

It is tragic that such an outstanding collection suffered a major theft in 2007 when Ian was working on the early coinage—the pennies of the twelfth and thirteenth centuries—and had them at home in Broughton in the Scottish Borders. While Lord and Lady Stewartby were away in June the house was broken into and ransacked. The coins along with Lady Stewartby's jewellery—carefully concealed in the attic—were stolen. The thieves had the audacity to return at the end of the following year and removed a smaller group of coins from the end of the series. Despite a reward of £50,000 being offered nothing has been recovered. The theft greatly affected Ian, but he managed to complete and see through the press *English Coins 1158–1551.*

Unfortunately, the collection was not catalogued or photographed so the loss was doubly felt. Such a large and comprehensive collection of the early coins was extremely important given that no numismatic archives from that period have survived.

Early in 2017 Lord Stewartby gifted his Scottish coins to the Hunterian Museum at the University of Glasgow whose internationally important coin cabinet is based on the substantial eighteenth-century bequest of Dr William Hunter. The richness of this lies in his Classical coins but the Scottish element which, while good, is relatively small and is now immensely enhanced by the Stewartby coins. At the handover Lord Stewartby said, 'I am very pleased the Coin Cabinet of the Hunterian Museum felt able to accept my Scottish coin collection, built up over 75 years. The new Coin Cabinet [opened at the Kelvin Hall Hunterian Study Centre in 2016] is a fitting home for it where scholars and numismatists from all over the world may study the collection.' He hoped that the thieves might return the missing portion so that it could be re-united with his gift to make the collection complete as a 'full history of Scotland from David I to the Union told through coins'. Funding was generously provided to list and digitise the coins.

The collection now starts with the Second Coinage of Alexander III. Introduced in 1280 this is the Scottish equivalent of Edward I's long single cross penny which had appeared the previous year. There is a long run of almost 400 of these including a group of the new round halfpennies and farthings. Alexander's penny is the most common of Scottish medieval coins and Ian contributed greatly to its arrangement and interpretation. John Baliol and Robert the Bruce issued similar coinages from 1292 and 1320 respectively. All are rare but the collection possesses 112 pennies of the former and eleven of Robert as well a total of twenty-two of the lesser values.

After his release from captivity in England, David II added the larger groat and halfgroat to his coinage. The extended range was followed by Robert II and III and the half-century to 1406 is represented by over 1,000 specimens, mainly groats. The reigns of James I, II and III continued the groat as the main denomination but debasement of the smaller coins began early in the century and James III introduced a billon plack of four pence Scots—the £ Scots now increasingly diverged in value from the £ Sterling. Another innovation of James was the more natural depiction of his image in the renaissance style on his groat issues of 1471 and 1484—over twenty-five years earlier than Henry VII. The collection has forty-six groats and eight halfgroats of the former issue and fifty groats and ten halves of the latter. This richness may be compared with the total of twenty-four contained in the two major university cabinets at Oxford and Glasgow. The relief on the portrait coins is low thus often leading to a lack of detail through wear but many of the Stewartby examples still possess clear and pleasing portraits.

James IV reverted to the older stylised bust except for the groat struck for the Maundy Service of 1512. Unusually the image is bearded and the specimen included is an excellent example of an extremely rare coin. James V did not issue silver until 1526 but now used a proper profile portrait similar to that of Henry VII. He also introduced, in 1538, another billon piece called the bawbee of six pence Scots. This was to endure for a long time and would eventually be the equivalent of the English halfpenny. The 500 coins of Mary Queen of Scots are weighted somewhat towards her bawbee of which there are almost 200 specimens. Among the hundred examples of the new testoon or shilling is one of the rare issue of 1561 depicting the newly arrived widow. Mary also introduced the large crown-sized ryal represented by a dozen examples.

During his Scottish rule prior to the Union of the Crowns after Elizabeth I's death, James VI issued a great variety of types and denominations among which is a pleasing specimen of the rare two merks or thistle dollar of 1580 depicting the national emblem. Although Lord Stewartby was perhaps less interested in the seventeenth century, nevertheless he acquired over 400 coins from each of the reigns of Charles I and II and some twenty from the shorter rule of James VII. From later issues to the Union there are only twenty-six coins of William and Mary of the two highest values for the theft removed the rest.

The gold coins, of which there are 120, were kept apart and thus spared from the thieves. Gold only became a regular feature of the Scottish coinage at the end of the fourteenth century. The collection includes twenty-eight lions and demies from the reigns of Robert III and James I and II. There are two of James III's new unicorns and three of the riders. One of the half unicorns of James IV is an extremely rare variety. In his coinage of 1539 James V brought portraiture to the Scottish gold coinage. Ducats of 1539—the first Scottish coin to bear a date—and 1540 depict a handsome bust of the king wearing a jewelled bonnet. There is an example of each. Mary Queen of Scots struck gold issues up to 1560, the first being minted at Holyrood and hence known as Abbey Crowns. Again, there are two good examples of this rare coin. Only the three-pound piece and its half of 1555–8 bear the queen's image and both are represented.

Apart from David II's gold noble of 1357 of which the four known examples are in museums, the most valuable Scottish gold coin is the £20 piece of 1575 and 1576 bearing a magnificent half length figure of James VI wearing armour and holding a sword and olive branch. Ian had obtained a pleasing example of the earlier date. James minted several issues of gold up to 1604 including ducats, lion nobles, thistle nobles, hat pieces, riders and sword and sceptre pieces, all represented. After the Union of the Crowns the two coinages became similar in design and size albeit with minor differences to distinguish the London and Edinburgh output, but of different values. Thus, the respective unites were £1 sterling and £12 Scots. The latter and its lower values are well represented. These are shown by twenty-one examples including four unites of James VI/I and three of Charles I. The portrait is half-length bearing sword and orb and that of Charles I's third coinage of 1637–42, by Nicholas Briot, is particularly fine. The latter is the last issue of gold in Scotland bar the pistole or £12 Scots and its half produced in 1701. William II/III permitted gold dust obtained in Guinea by what is commonly known as the Darien Company to be minted into these. There is an example of each of these rare and historic coins, the last gold of the Scottish coinage which was soon to be extinguished by the Act of Union.

The collection is housed in small white envelopes in row upon row, carefully arranged by reign, metal, issue, class, denomination, mint and date. It arrived in two deed boxes but transferred to a museum cabinet it is an impressive sight clearly showing the huge amount of time and effort put into it. In a working collection more details can be given on envelopes and changes to order made more easily. On the back of each are the source and date of acquisition along with previous provenances. More recently the accompanying archive of the Scottish collection and his Scottish numismatic books have been deposited with the Hunterian.

****

Ian Stewart was a remarkable and talented person who contributed greatly to country, community and coin collecting. He was a banker, though his career in the City was in two parts as he had to step down from this during his ministerial career in the 1980s. He was a Director at Brown Shipley before and Vice-Chairman at Standard Chartered after. He retired in 2004. In the early 1970s he became seriously interested in politics and entered the Commons as a Conservative in 1974. He was courteous but firm at the hustings though he never had a cabbage thrown at him as had his great-grandfather at a Liberal party meeting. Ian was a diligent and conscientious constituency MP who maintained a large majority. His rise to office began with his appointment as PPS to the Chancellor, Geoffrey Howe, in 1979. He progressed to ministerial office at Defence, the Treasury, Defence again, and then became number two at the Northern Ireland Office. He suffered an injury on a helicopter journey in 1989 and soon after had to resign his post. He was knighted in 1991. He stood down from the Commons when the 1992 general election was called and was subsequently raised to the peerage. He then had another career in the House of Lords until he retired in 2015. But he was first and foremost a family man.

He was also one of that group of amateur scholars/coin collectors who have played an outstanding role in English numismatics for over a century. He was proud to be a member. Note may be made of the less obvious contribution to the study of the coinage by the main London dealers such as Baldwin, Spink and Seaby. Ian maintained a good relationship with each in expanding his collection and obtaining crucial and often new varieties. He was a distinguished scholar in English and Scottish coinage, producing a revised edition in 1967 of his 1955 *The Scottish Coinage*, making major contributions to *Coinage in Tenth-Century England* and *A New History of the Royal Mint* and successfully publishing his outstanding work *English Coinage 1180–1551* in 2009. It was his desire and intention to produce a similar in-depth study of the Scottish coinage but, alas, this was not to be. He was an active member and Chair of the Academy's *Sylloge of Coins of the British Isles* Committee. His numismatic work was recognised by the award of many honours from the major societies of fellowships and medals. His Scottish coin collection was generously handed over to the University of Glasgow where it is a valuable addition to Scottish heritage accessible to researchers and the public. Ian enjoyed coins, as he did so much else in life—Haileybury, Cambridge and Jesus, banking, politics, the Royal Naval Reserve and not least sport. He had a great respect for John Buchan, affectionately known as 'JB', his wife's grandfather. Lord and Lady Stewartby bought the old Buchan house in Broughton when it was put up for sale in the 1990s. This became their home though they journeyed to London frequently. For some years Ian suffered from Parkinson's Disease and after other complications died peacefully at home as the snow covered Broughton early in March 2018. He is buried in Ewelme churchyard.

Acknowledgements
I am extremely grateful to Lady Stewartby for kindly providing a wealth of material and discussion. Edward Buchan, Honorary Lay Canon, Bristol Cathedral, generously allowed me a copy of his eulogy delivered at Lord Stewartby's Memorial Service held in Jesus College on 1 July 2018. Nicholas Holmes, National Museums Scotland, provided many helpful comments on the draft. His 'Publications of Ian Stewart, Lord Stewartby', *British Numismatic Journal*, 88 (2018), 255–61, has been of immense help and should be referred to for full details of these publications. Jesper Ericsson, Curator of Numismatics, The Hunterian, read the draft scripts and made many corrections and useful comments. David Newton's *Sir Halley Stewart* (London, 1968) proved particularly useful for the Stewart family history.

Note on the author: Dr Donal Bateson is Honorary Research Fellow at the Hunterian, University of Glasgow.

ROBERT GOFF

Robert Lionel Archibald Goff

12 November 1926 – 14 August 2016

elected Fellow of the British Academy 1987

by

JACK BEATSON

Fellow of the Academy

Robert Goff, Lord Goff of Chieveley, will be remembered as a master of common law technique, a creative and original scholar, and for twenty-three years a judge of the highest distinction, latterly as Senior Law Lord at the apex of the UK's legal system. As a scholar, he, with Professor Gareth Jones, disinterred the law of restitution in England and Wales and in their 1966 book *The Law of Restitution* sought to place it on a principled basis. As a judge, he was involved in many fundamentally important decisions at all levels and was pivotal in the authoritative acceptance by the House of Lords in *Lipkin Gorman v Karpnale Ltd* of restitution as an independent branch of law founded on the principle of unjust enrichment.

Biographical Memoirs of Fellows of the British Academy, XVIII, 241–273
Posted 23 October 2019. © British Academy 2019.

ROBERT GOFF   (*Universal Pictorial Press & Agency Ltd*)

Overview

Robert Goff, Lord Goff of Chieveley, died on 14 August 2016 at the age of 89. He will be remembered as a master of common law technique, a creative and original scholar, and for twenty-three years a judge of the highest distinction, latterly as Senior Law Lord at the apex of the United Kingdom's legal system. As a scholar, he, with Professor Gareth Jones who died on 2 April 2016, disinterred the law of restitution in England and Wales and, in their 1966 book *The Law of Restitution*,[1] sought to place it on a principled basis. As a judge, he was involved in many fundamentally important decisions at all levels and was pivotal in the authoritative acceptance by the House of Lords in *Lipkin Gorman v Karpnale Ltd* of restitution as an independent branch of the law of England and Wales founded on the principle of unjust enrichment.[2] He worked hard and with dedication and was a devoted family man. He could at first seem formidably formal, perhaps because of his reticence and modesty, but his warmth, kindness and sense of fun (often accompanied by a giggle and a twinkle in his eye) very soon dispelled that impression.

Although, after the publication of the American Law Institute's *Restatement of Restitution* in 1937,[3] restitution was discussed in English courts[4] and law journals,[5] there was no comprehensive treatment of it and it was dealt with only briefly in contemporary books on contract.[6] Suggested definitions and underlying principles were controversial, either excluding cases that were, 'for want of a better name',[7] described as quasi-contracts, or including cases which were not.

The preface to Goff and Jones stated that 'the law of Restitution is the law relating to all claims, quasi-contractual or otherwise, which are founded on the principle of unjust enrichment'. The book analysed the cases on common law quasi-contractual obligations and those on equitable doctrines and remedies, both of a personal and a

---

[1] R. Goff and G. Jones, *The Law of Restitution* (London, 1966), hereafter 'Goff and Jones'.

[2] [1991] 2 AC 548.

[3] Its full title was the *Restatement of Restitution: Quasi-Contract and Constructive Trust*, and the reporters were Professors Seavey and Scott of Harvard.

[4] Notably *United Australia Ltd v Barclays Bank Ltd* [1941] AC 1 at 27–9 (Lord Atkin); *Fibrosa* [1943] AC 32 at 61, 64 (Lord Wright); *Nelson v Larholt* [1948] KB 339, 343 (Denning J).

[5] E.g. Winfield, (1937) 53 *Law Quarterly Review* 447, (1939) 55 *Law Quarterly Review* 161, and (1944) 60 *Law Quarterly Review* 341–2; Seavey & Scott (1938) 54 *Law Quarterly Review* 29; Allen (1938) 54 *Law Quarterly Review* 201, 202, 26–7; Holdsworth, (1939) 55 *Law Quarterly Review* 37; Lord Wright, *Legal Essays and Addresses* (Cambridge, 1939) and (1941) 57 *Law Quarterly Review* 200.

[6] The post-war treatment was fuller than it had been. The chapter in the 1945 edition of W. R. Anson, *Principles of the English Law of Contract* (19th ed.) (London, 1945) was nineteen pages long, and that in the first edition of Cheshire and Fifoot's *The Law of Contract* (London, 1945) was twenty-two pages long, whereas the chapter in the 1937 18th edition of *Anson* was six pages long.

[7] Anson, *Principles of the English Law of Contract*, pp. 422–3.

proprietary nature, and gain-based remedies. The relationship in English law of the various common law and equitable doctrines had not previously been considered in a systematic way. The authors acknowledged their debt to the scholarship of Professors Seavey and Scott, the Reporters of the American *Restatement*, but were determined that their work should, as far as possible, constitute 'an organic development of English case law and so be acceptable to the legal profession'.[8]

The book was an immediate success. Within two months of publication it was described as 'admirable' by Edmund Davies J.[9] In his review in the *Law Quarterly Review*, Lord Denning stated that the book was 'long-needed' and 'a creative work': the authors have 'done for Restitution what Pollock and Anson did for Tort and Contract … [they have] given us relevant principles which we can understand', and 'not hesitated to expose false doctrines'.[10] Other reviewers welcomed its clarity of style and analysis, the critical appraisal of the law as it then was, and the suggestions for future developments or reforms.[11] An observation in Bill Cornish's review highlighted the originality of the book. He said the book had caused some perplexity in academic circles; the library of one ancient university classified it as Criminal Law and the library of one Inn of Court refused to take it at all.

As a judge, apart from restitution, Robert Goff was involved in many significant decisions on commercial law, jurisdiction and tort. But his range was far wider. It included decisions raising profound moral and ethical questions about the end of life and the position of incapacitated adults. It also included important questions of public and private international law and policy such as those that arose in the *Pinochet* cases about whether a former head of state charged with acts of torture could be extradited, and cases about the boundaries of public and private law.

In his judgments he displayed careful creativity which was the product of a deep understanding of the law and an ability carefully and lucidly to reveal the principles underlying the result in individual cases and so to develop the law organically and incrementally. He described the process in his 1983 Maccabaean Lecture, 'The Search for Principle',[12] a process which led him to have regard for the contributions of gener-

---

[8] Robert Goff's speech at the dinner of the conference in Cambridge in January 1998 marking Gareth Jones's retirement from the Downing Professorship of the Laws of England which he had held since 1975 (hereafter 'Speech at dinner for Gareth Jones').

[9] *Chesworth v Farrer* [1967] 1QB 407, 417. Robert had been tipped off in advance and was present in court with his pupil Andrew Longmore, now a Lord Justice of Appeal, who described it as the judicial baptism of the book.

[10] (1967) 83 *Law Quarterly Review* 277–8.

[11] Harris, (1967) 25 *Cambridge Law Journal* 114; Cornish, (1966) 29 *Modern Law Review* 579.

[12] R. Goff, 'The search for principle', *Proceedings of the British Academy*, 69 (1984), pp. 285–308 (hereafter *The Search for Principle*). This reflected the maturation of ideas which can be seen in, for example, his 6th Lord Upjohn Lecture, R. Goff, 'The law as taught and the law as practised', *The Law Teacher*, 11 (1977), 75–88.

alists. Five years later he stated 'obviously the work of the generalist may appear shallow to the modern specialist; but generalists themselves have their own virtues which specialists often lack'.[13] In 1999, in a letter graciously declining an invitation to contribute to a Festschrift, he said 'although I can claim that my understanding of the law has become profound, my knowledge of the law is unsystematic and, unlike a professor of law I have no particular topics in mind which I can readily work up into a learned paper suitable for a Festschrift'.[14]   In his Maccabaean Lecture he had observed that a judge's vision of the law tends to be fragmented because he considers the point of law in relation to the particular set of facts in the case.

Professor Andrew Burrows' obituary stated that 'for many in the legal academy, Lord Goff was the greatest judge of all times', that 'his judgments were models of clarity and rigour and epitomised his oft-expressed aim of achieving principled "practical justice"'.[15] In difficult cases, in his search for principle he deployed insights from other systems, in particular German law, and the contributions of comparative lawyers, although he did not favour the development of a single European body of private law.[16]

In all that Robert did, he promoted what he described as 'the proper recognition of the contribution made by the academic world to the development of English law'. He valued their analyses in building up a systematic statement of the law on a particular topic in a coherent and principled way with criticism and suggestions for its beneficial development, something different from but complementary to the focus of judges on the facts of the particular case. He stated that it is the fusion of the work of academics and judges 'which begets the tough, adaptable system which is called the common law'.[17] In *The Spiliada,* in 1986, he described jurists as 'pilgrims with [judges] on the endless road to unattainable perfection'.[18] In a letter to Professor Peter Birks in 1999, he said that he did not know how far he succeeded in promoting proper recognition of the contribution of the academic world to the development of English law, but that, if he had, 'that alone will give me great satisfaction'.[19]

Family was fundamentally important to Robert Goff. He married Sarah Cousins in 1953. They had four children, Katherine, Juliet, William and Thomas. Tragically,

[13] R. Goff, *A Voyage around Holdsworth* (Birmingham, 1988), Presidential Address to the Holdsworth Club of the University of Birmingham, p. 12 (hereafter *A Voyage around Holdsworth*).
[14] Letter dated 22 February 1999 to Professor Schwengzer of the University of Basle, who was co-editing a Festschrift to mark the 70th birthday of Professor Peter Schlechtriem.
[15] (2016) *Society of Legal Scholars Reporter* 39.
[16] Letters dated 2 and 17 December 2001 to Professor Peter Schlechtriem and Lord Bingham.
[17] Goff, *The Search for Principle*, p. 171. For a more qualified view by a judge-jurist, see Rodger (1993-5) 28–30 *Irish Jurist* 1; (2010) 29 *University of Queensland Law Journal* 33.
[18] [1987] AC 460, 488.
[19] 28 November 1999.

William contracted viral meningitis at seven months and, despite Robert and Sarah's devoted care, died of its consequences when he was two. At Robert's funeral, Juliet's address captured the warmth of the atmosphere of the family home and the closeness of the family.[20] Robert and Sarah, who had survived the illness and death of William, had a relationship of absolute dependence and trust. Robert worked hard, not only at the law, but with Sarah, acquiring DIY skills, making their home a place of beauty and comfort, and nurturing the family. Robert spent a lot of time with the surviving children, being patient, taking them skating on Sunday mornings, and 'most of all' giving them music, which, although he loved his work, was what 'fed his soul and relaxed him'.[21]

Family background, childhood, school and war service

Robert was born in Perthshire on 12 November 1926. He was the second child of Lieutenant Colonel Lionel and Isobel Goff. His sister Josephine was a year older than him. His father was educated at Eton and the Royal Military Academy, Woolwich, and commissioned in the Royal Artillery in 1897. He fought in the Boer War, was badly wounded at the relief of Ladysmith, mentioned in despatches, and was brought back to Portsmouth on a hospital ship. He also fought in the First World War and was again wounded and mentioned in despatches. He remained in hospital until about 1921. In 1923 he married Isobel Higgon, née Denroche-Smith. Isobel was much younger than Lionel, and the widow of Archie Higgon, who was killed in action in September 1915. Isobel's father, Thomas, married her mother, Florence Bayley, after a very successful career in the Bengal Civil Service and they had four children. Their family home was Balhary, near Alyth, North Perthshire.

As a child Robert and his family lived at Monk Sherborne in Hampshire. He had a close relationship with his mother, who remained a passionate Scot. During his childhood and adolescence they spent many summer holidays at Isobel's family home in Perthshire, then lived in and owned by her brother Lewis. His relationship with his father was not as close. Robert did not share his father's principal interests of hunting, shooting and riding, and refused to shoot after his eighteenth birthday. His passion for music was not shared by his father.

Robert's first school was a Dame School in Basingstoke. From the age of eight he attended St Aubyn's, a preparatory school in Rottingdean, and he started at Eton in September 1939, the beginning of the war. His family say he regarded himself as

---

[20] St Mary's Church, Chieveley, 5 September 2016.
[21] Ibid.

fortunate there. He continued to concentrate on the classical languages and history but, save for some biology, he did no science. He was taught history by C. R. N. ('Dick') Routh and classics by Cyril Butterwick, who was also his housemaster. Routh and Butterwick greatly influenced Robert and may have been instrumental in turning him into a scholar. Dr Henry Lee, one of the organists who had played at George VI's coronation, taught him the piano and encouraged him. Robert became a very good pianist and his love of music stayed with him even after his health failed. Its importance to him is illustrated by his statement many years later that 'one can always tell whether people are musical from the way they talk'.[22] He also loved wild things. At some stage as a boy he made a scholarly and extensive collection of birds' eggs, which he kept for the rest of his life.

In December 1944 Robert left Eton. He had been offered a place at New College, Oxford, after completing his military service. An indication of how he was regarded at school is seen in a letter dated 13 December 1944 from Dick Routh to Nigel Wykes, who had succeeded Butterwick as his housemaster. Routh stated that Robert was 'very gifted and intelligent'. He referred to his 'sense of humour, shrewd judgement, and an almost fantastic modesty'. He, however, regarded the most attractive of Robert's gifts to be 'his sensitivity, the instinctive appreciation of everything which is Good, and the capacity not only to recognise it but to feel it deeply'. Routh considered that, although worth a scholarship, Robert was unlikely to win one because in his last half at school 'he has not been able to give that unremitting attention and whole-hearted absorption' to his studies and a large part of his time had been taken up with friends, and cultural, social and athletic activities.

Robert was called up in December and commissioned in the Scots Guards. He was told that he would be going to the Far East in September 1945 and trained for combat in that theatre, but the surrender of Japan that August meant that he was not sent there. After a period of Guard Duty at Windsor Castle he volunteered to go to Italy as part of a force to deal with the threat posed by Marshal Tito at that time. He travelled by train across Germany and via the Brenner Pass. His obituary in *The Times* refers to him being amazed by the beauty of the landscape and saying of the gushing waters of the River Adige and the sight of peach orchards in bloom that he thought someone had picked him up and put him in the Garden of Eden.[23]

He remained in the army and in Italy until July 1948. He spent periods of leave travelling and exploring northern Italy. He went skiing and pursued his musical and cultural interests when he could and introduced his men to them. While stationed at Windsor, he had been allowed into the Royal Art Collection with its Leonardo

[22] Goff, *A Voyage around Holdsworth*, p. 13.
[23] 23 August 2016.

drawings, and his time in Italy enabled him to nurture his love of Italian art, religious frescos and other monuments. He combined the task of setting up communications posts with visits with his men to see the art, including Michelangelo's *David* in Florence and Piero della Francesca's Polyptych in Perugia. In Venice, he stayed at the Hotel Danieli, which had been taken over by the NAAFI, and where those in the services could stay for a shilling a night. He was allowed to play two of the hotel's four pianos.

The reason Robert remained in the army and Italy after December 1947 when, having done three years' service, he could have been demobbed was that the place he was offered at New College for the two-year 'shortened' Final Honour Schools course for ex-servicemen started in October 1948. He was told that he could read either Greats, Law or History. He thought that History in two years would be no fun and decided to read Law, and then to qualify and practise as a barrister. He was able to pay for Oxford out of savings from his army salary.

John ('Jack') Butterworth, who later became the first Vice-Chancellor of Warwick University, was the Law Fellow and Robert's tutor. One of his other tutors was Wilfrid Bourne who 'weekended' there while starting at the Bar, but later joined the Lord Chancellor's Department and ultimately held the paired top offices of Clerk of the Crown in Chancery and Permanent Secretary to the Lord Chancellor. Teaching arrangements were then much more informal. Many tutors did not provide reading lists, leaving the undergraduates to identify the leading cases and any articles on a topic from the recommended textbook and any lectures or classes which they attended.[24] Robert used to contact Wilfrid Bourne during the week identifying the chapter of the relevant book on which he was preparing for the tutorial. Although clearly committed to his subject, Robert later stated he 'attended hardly any lectures on law', but that 'Cecil Fifoot's admirable lectures provided one great exception'.[25] He probably attended a joint New College/Queen's revision class given by Butterworth and Professor Tony Honoré, then a Fellow of The Queen's College but who, as a Rhodes Scholar, had done the graduate Bachelor of Civil Law degree at New College immediately after the war.[26] Robert won an outstanding reputation both as a potential

---

[24] The introduction of reading lists after the War is attributed to Dr John Morris, the Law Tutor at Magdalen from 1936, although before the War Stallybrass at Brasenose is said to have achieved the same result by simply telling his pupils what to read for the next tutorial: see P. M. North, 'John Humphrey Carlile Morris 1910-1984', *Proceedings of the British Academy*, 74 (1988), p. 443.

[25] Goff, *A Voyage around Holdsworth*, pp. 8–9.

[26] Honoré succeeded Butterworth as the law tutor at New College in 1964 and in 1971 became the Regius Professor of Civil Law. His successor at New College was Alan Rodger, later Lord Rodger of Earlsferry, another scholar judge and a Fellow of the Academy: see H. L. McQueen, 'Alan Ferguson Rodger 1944–2011', *Biographical Memoirs of Fellows of the British Academy,* 13 (2013), p. 361.

lawyer and as Steward (President) of the Junior Common Room and was awarded a distinguished first-class degree in 1950.[27]

Fellow and Tutor in Law, Lincoln College, Oxford 1951–5

The plan to go straight to the Bar changed soon after Robert's examination results came out. While at his mother's family home in Perthshire, he was telephoned by Keith Murray, the Rector of Lincoln College, who invited Robert to come to see him. At the meeting, the Rector offered him the fellowship and tutorship in law that had become vacant in 1949 when Harold Hanbury became the Vinerian Professor of English Law.[28] Robert said he was astonished and asked for half an hour to consider the proposal.[29] Although the Rector was apparently equally surprised that Robert needed to think about the offer, the half hour was given, after which Robert accepted provided he could first do the Bar exams and be called to the Bar.[30] He was called to the Bar at the Inner Temple in 1951, began teaching at Lincoln in October that year, and remained in the post until the end of the 1954–5 academic year.[31] As well as his teaching, he did his share of administrative duties, serving on a number of committees and as Dean in 1952–3 while the incumbent was on leave.[32]

Robert was very conscious of the fact that he had done the shortened Schools, which involved studying only six subjects and not in great depth. In his 2002 talk to law students at Oxford he said that he could tell them two things: 'first—taking six papers in Schools was a woefully inadequate preparation for the job: second—the best way of learning law is to know that you have to teach it!'[33] He described having to get up at 5.00 am to do 'some pretty hectic and thorough preparation for tutorials' but said 'at least I was not stale'. Whether or not Robert was inadequately prepared for the job at the outset, he became a very effective teacher. In the *Lincoln College Record* for 1954–5, after

---

[27] *Lincoln College Record*, 1954–5, p 3.

[28] At that time the teaching was done by Peter Webster, a College Lecturer who was determined to practice at the bar but agreed to stay on for a second year. The *Lincoln College Record*, 1950–1, p. 3, stated that Webster was 'an exceptionally fine tutor' and the 'pleasantest of colleagues'. He became a very successful commercial practitioner, chairman of the Bar, and a High Court judge.

[29] Talk to Law Students at Oxford, Hilary Term 2002.

[30] He was elected to the Law Fellowship for a probationary year commencing in October 1951: Lincoln College Governing Board Minutes, 6 November 1950.

[31] Lincoln College Governing Board Minutes, 24 October 1951 (admitted to Fellowship), 22 October 1952 (confirmation of Fellowship), 26 January 1955 (resignation from the end of the academic year).

[32] Lincoln College Governing Board Minutes, 6 May 1952 (Dean), 6 November 1952 (refurbishment of public rooms), 6 November 1953 (award of scholarships, improvements to the library, choice of artist to paint former Rector's portrait).

[33] Hilary Term 2002 (hereafter '2002 talk').

referring to the fact that when he was appointed to his Fellowship 'it was already clear that he was attracted by the idea of practice at the Bar', Sir Walter Oakeshott, then Rector of the College, stated that 'the quality of his teaching proved so good that there was widespread hope of his being content to go on as an academic lawyer, and by his departure law studies at Oxford, as well as the College, will suffer greatly'.[34]

As was usual at that time, Robert taught a wide range of subjects. They included Criminal Law and Roman Law, the last of which gave him a fund of jokes on legal occasions about 'the useful subject of manumission of slaves'.[35] As was also usual at the time, he had a network of exchanges, for example sending his Lincoln pupils to Robert Heuston at Pembroke for Constitutional Law and taking the Pembroke lawyers for Roman Law.

In his 2002 talk to law students Robert said that the numbers reading Law at Lincoln and the fact that all the third years needed two tutorials a week meant that his hours were very stretched.[36] The College allowed him to recruit a weekender, and between 1953 and 1955 his friend and contemporary Patrick ('Pat') Neill, then a Prize Fellow of All Souls,[37] fulfilled this role. Robert also gave joint classes with Tony Honoré, where he may have first met A. W. B. ('Brian') Simpson, one of Honoré's Queen's pupils, and Robert's successor at Lincoln. Robert enjoyed engaging with enthusiastic young minds. He stayed in contact with a number of his Lincoln pupils. One of them, Swinton Thomas (later a member of the Court of Appeal of England and Wales), became a lifelong friend and died two days before Robert.

Lecturer (CUF), University of Oxford 1953–5

In 1952 Robert was appointed to a Common University Fund (CUF) lectureship in law with effect from 1953.[38] The lecture lists published in the *University Gazette*

---

[34] *Lincoln College Record*, 1954–5, p. 3.

[35] For example, his speech to Nottinghamshire Law Society in 1987, the President of which was a former Lincoln pupil, Jeremy Ware.

[36] In that talk he stated that he had fifty-four pupils in his first year and in a letter dated 9 November 2001 to Lord Jenkins of Hillhead following a dinner in Lincoln College to mark the end of his tenure as High Steward of the University of Oxford stated that he inherited 'nearly 50' pupils. These numbers probably include those from other colleges who were 'farmed out' to be taught by him, but law was the largest single honour school at Lincoln between 1951 and 1953 with twenty-nine (16.7% of the total) reading Final Honours School Jurisprudence in 1952-3: *Lincoln College Record*, 1950–1, p. 10, and 1952–3, p. 11.

[37] Patrick Neill subsequently became a distinguished QC, Warden of All Souls, Vice-Chancellor of Oxford, and chaired many bodies including the Council of the Securities Industry, the Press Council, and the Committee on Standards in Public Life. He was ennobled as Lord Neill of Bladen in 1997.

[38] The University Statutes for 1953 stated his appointment was from 1953 until 30 September 1957.

between Michaelmas Term 1952 and Trinity Term 1955 state that he gave classes with Ronald ('Ronnie') Maudsley, the Law Tutor at Brasenose, on Restitution, also described as 'Unjustifiable Enrichment' and 'Quasi Contract',[39] and gave lectures on Defamation.[40]

As to restitution, in his 2002 talk to law students Robert said that he 'noticed at the end of *Anson on Contracts* a strange subject called Quasi-Contract—with rather weird headings' and 'surely' this needed attention. It was not on the syllabus, but he decided that he could build up a course of lectures.[41] The first edition of Cheshire and Fifoot's *Law of Contracts,* published in 1945, stated that 'the attempts made from time to time to tame the refractory material have provoked acute controversy' and that 'it may be that the ultimate solution will be to free the topic from its historical associations … and to merge it in a unique and generic doctrine of Restitution'.[42] It is not clear whether Robert picked this up from Fifoot's lectures. But, for whatever reason, Robert was attracted by the idea of trying to tame what was both unruly and undervalued and got together with Maudsley, who he discovered was also interested in the subject.

Because the subject was not on the syllabus, not many students came to the seminars, but those that did included some who became distinguished academic lawyers.[43] After an introduction to the subject, the seminars included one on proprietary claims, one on necessity, and one on mistake in contract and in restitution. They were joint seminars, but either Robert or Ronnie Maudsley took the lead. Robert said that in the seminar on necessity he was trying to create in English law something like the Roman law doctrine of *negotiorum gestio.* He described it as all very exciting and decided that it could become a book. Because the work would involve researching both common law and equity (Maudsley's principal speciality) they were a well-matched pair. Robert started work on the book that was to become *The Law of Restitution* in 1953 but the joint project with Maudsley later floundered.

As to defamation, the lectures probably focused on the important changes made by the Defamation Act 1952. It had implemented the recommendations of the Porter Committee *inter alia* on unintentional defamation, qualified privilege and the defence of justification.[44]

---

[39] In Michaelmas Term and Trinity Term 1953 and 1954.

[40] In Hilary Term and Trinity Term 1953 and Hilary Term 1955.

[41] 2002 Talk.

[42] Goff and Jones, *The Law of Restitution*, pp. 429 and 434.

[43] In his 2002 talk to law students Robert said they included Professor Tony Guest and Sir Peter North, both Fellows of the Academy. As Peter North only came up to Oxford in 1956, the year after Robert left full-time academic life, in his case this must have been when Robert was teaching on a part-time basis. Sir Peter North's memory is that Robert 'in his very learned but unassuming way, had the skill to engage us in debate without our feeling overawed': email dated 18 December 2018.

[44] Cmnd. 7536 HMSO 1948. In his 2002 talk to law students, Robert said that he was told that, in his first

Family life

Robert met Sarah at a 21st birthday party near his parents' home in Hampshire in the autumn of 1952, after his first year at Lincoln. She had read History at St Anne's College, Oxford, and at the time was starting a BLitt. They married in July 1953 and spent their honeymoon in Italy. After their return they rented an attic flat in 58 High Street from Magdalen College and Robert began preparing for his teaching.

They lived in the flat in the High Street until they left Oxford in 1955. Robert continued to work very hard on his teaching, and they enjoyed the social life of a young academic couple. This included music and dining with friends and with some of the more senior academics. Jack Butterworth and his wife entertained them, and Robert recalls visiting Maurice Platnauer, then Vice-Principal of Brasenose and a friend of his Uncle Lewis.[45] As a result of his interest in Italy and the history of art, Robert also came to know Tom Boase, then President of Magdalen College, with whom he got on very well.

After marriage, Robert began to think again about his plan to go to the Bar. He said that Oxford was a marvellous place to live and work, but he wanted to be at the centre of gravity for the common law. At that time that was not in the universities but in the courts. Great judges were responsible for some of the most remarkable developments of the common law. They stamped their mark on it and academic jurists were much less influential.[46] He was later to say that although he admired and valued the work of the jurists, he considered that judges were more important in the development of legal principles because the dominant element in such development should be professional reactions to individual fact situations rather than theoretical development of principles.[47] Robert left full-time academic life in 1955 and began to practise in Sir Ashton Roskill QC's Chambers in King's Bench Walk, a commercial and shipping law chambers now known as 7 King's Bench Walk.

---

year he would have to give a basic and factual lecture course on 'a new Criminal Justice Act' but that, after that, he could lecture on any aspect of the law that interested him. There is, however, no record of lectures by Robert on criminal law. The *University Gazette* states that between 1952 and 1955 lectures in that subject were given by Philip Landon, Reader in Criminal Law and Evidence, Fellow of Trinity College, and Rupert Cross, Tutorial Fellow of Magdalen College, and that in Hilary Term 1954 Landon also gave four lectures on the *Criminal Justice Act* 1948.

[45] Letter to Bill Swadling after the lunch on 27 November 1999 at which Robert was presented with W. Swadling and G. Jones (eds.), *The Search for Principle: Essays in Honour of Lord Goff of Chieveley* (Oxford, 1999)—hereafter Swadling & Jones, *The Search for Principle*. The lunch was in the rooms which Platnauer had occupied when Vice-Principal of Brasenose.

[46] 2002 Talk, in which he recognised the changes since then and the profound influence of many jurists, including Glanville Williams, Herbert Hart, and later Peter Birks.

[47] Goff, *The Search for Principle*, pp. 185–6.

Between 1955 and 1975, the family lived at 5 Holland Villas Road in Holland Park, London. Robert travelled to chambers on the tube and was often able to complete the *Times* crossword between Holland Park and Chancery Lane. In 1966 they bought a barn in West Penwith, Cornwall to convert into a cottage. After sorting out the granite shell, the family spent summers there, although Robert sometimes had to go to London for work. The location was idyllic and had extraordinary views. Robert loved the wild coastline and the sea. Juliet described herself and Katherine clinging onto him for dear life when he took them 'to bathe in the huge crashing waves of the Atlantic Ocean'.[48] But it was an eight-hour journey from London and its isolation meant that, when they decided to move out of London, one of their criteria was to find a house in a reasonably large village. They sold the barn in 1974 and in 1975 moved from Holland Villas Road to Chieveley House in Berkshire, between Newbury and Oxford. Their London base became a flat on the top floor of 12 King's Bench Walk in the Inner Temple.

Robert introduced Sarah to opera and they would often go to Covent Garden. Juliet remembers being woken up in the middle of the night on which her parents had been to *Parsifal*. They had enjoyed it so much that when they got home they listened to the whole opera again on the gramophone. The way Robert 'gave' music to the children was by encouraging them to play, accompanying them, arranging pieces for them to play, and listening to music on the gramophone with them. At his funeral, the music included an arrangement of 'Soave sia il Vento' from *Cosi fan Tuti*, one of the many pieces arranged by Robert for his children. The family's repertoire extended beyond Bach, Mozart and Tchaikovsky to Flanders and Swann and Fats Waller whose songs were sung on the long car drive from Holland Villas Road to West Penwith.

Practice at the commercial bar

Robert's pupil master was Basil Eckersley, from whom he learned precise and concise draftsmanship. After becoming a member of chambers, Robert was instructed in shipping matters by Ken Elmslie of Richards Butler and several solicitors at Botterell & Roche, which later amalgamated with Norton Rose. He drafted contracts and rules such as those of Protection and Indemnity Clubs, but he 'had a pretty lean time'. This was because at the time he started in practice there was very little small work for junior barristers at the commercial bar. It was, he said, 'mostly silk's work'. The silks, that is Queen's Counsel (QC), tended to have almost permanent juniors. For instance, Eckersley (who never took silk) was generally led by Ashton Roskill. Robert was only

---

[48] Juliet Jackson's funeral address, 5 September 2016.

led by Roskill on two occasions when Eckersley had pneumonia. He was hardly led by anyone else.[49] As a result, he did not particularly enjoy being a junior barrister, but he had time to continue to teach and to research the law of restitution.

Robert's great interest in students and encouraging the young, evident in his Lincoln years, continued after he went into practice. Because his Inn, the Inner Temple, at that time gave its bar students virtually no educational support, he and an Inner Temple friend, Ted Laughton-Scott, arranged for lectures to be given for them. The Goffs and the Laughton-Scotts prepared the room and brought coffee, milk and biscuits. The lecturers included Robert's former Oxford colleagues Rupert Cross, Cecil Fifoot, Peter Carter and Robert Heuston, and the historian Marjorie Reeves[50] (who happened to be Sarah's tutor at St Anne's) gave a talk on the courts at the time of Henry II.

This interest in encouraging young lawyers later produced an important legacy in the form of the Pegasus Scholarship Trust which supports exchanges of young lawyers in many common law countries, placing them with private practitioners, judges and government law offices. Robert created and chaired the trust between 1987 and 2001. Originally confined to the Inner Temple, it soon became a collaboration between all four Inns. Robert used his skill, charm and formidable networking skills to assist in marshalling resources and providing practical assistance in this and other countries. His group included a former Prime Minister, Lord Callaghan, and Lord Mackay, shortly to become Lord Chancellor.[51] Considerable financial and other support was secured from British Airways for travel and, for those who wished to take a degree, from the Cambridge Commonwealth Trust.

As to teaching, Robert 'weekended' at Lincoln. At some stage after 1962 he gave classes on restitution at the London School of Economics with Bill Cornish. He also continued his research on that subject in the library of the Inner Temple. One of his principal sources was the noted 1929 edition of *Smith's Leading Cases,* one of the three editors of which was the young 'Tom' Denning.[52] Robert later said that it was analysing hundreds of cases for the book for so many years that turned him into a decent lawyer. By 1959, when the project with Ronnie Maudsley floundered, he had a clear idea of the structure and shape he wanted for the book.

---

[49] There are exceptions; for instance, in *Schtraks v Government of Israel* [1964] AC 558, an extradition case, he was led by Leonard Caplan QC.

[50] A Fellow of the Academy. See the obituary by Ruth Deech, *The Guardian*, 13 December 2003, and G. Lewis, 'Marjorie Ethel Reeves 1905–2003', *Proceedings of the British Academy*, 138 (2006), pp. 309–18.

[51] Foreword to Swadling and Jones, *The Search for Principle*, p. v.

[52] *Smith's Leading Cases* (13th ed.), (London, 1929), the other editors were Thomas Chitty KC and Cyril Harvey.

While a junior barrister, Robert considered his practice was not large enough for him to take pupil barristers and he had only one pupil. Andrew Longmore, a graduate of Lincoln College, now Lord Justice Longmore, started with Robert in 1966 and spent nine months with him until Robert took silk in 1967.[53] Longmore says he learned a lot from Robert about life, music and the issues of the day as well as the law. Once in silk, Robert Goff's practice took off quickly. He appeared in many important and technically difficult commercial cases[54] and also in commercial arbitrations in the City of London. His first choice of junior in chambers was Brian Davenport, who had the room next to his and was a great friend.[55] He also led his former pupil master, Basil Eckersley, his former pupil, Andrew Longmore, and many from other commercial chambers who went on to have distinguished careers including Mark Saville, Nicholas Phillips and John Hobhouse.

Robert was in the habit of working early in the morning, often playing Mozart on his piano to clear his head for what he described to Andrew Longmore as the 'tyranny of 10.30' when court sat. But there was also time for fun. Sir Stephen Tomlinson, who became a member of chambers in 1975, the year Robert was appointed to the High Court Bench, recalls visits during his pupillage to the Temple Table, a coffee house at which Robert and others met friends from other commercial chambers and regaled each other and the youngsters with anecdotes about amusing encounters with judges and others.[56]

Goff and Jones

Robert's project with Ronnie Maudsley floundered after Maudsley spent an extended period in the United States and was not responsive to Robert's communications. The breaking point came one day in 1959 when Robert opened the *Law Quarterly Review*

[53] In 1965 Robert appeared in two reported cases; *Margaronis Nav. Agency v Henry W Peabody* [1965] 2 QB 430 and *Fidelitas SS Co. v VIO Exportchleb* [1966] 1 QB 650. In both his opponent was Michael Mustill, another scholar judge and a Fellow of the Academy: see S. Boyd, 'Michael John Mustill 1931–2005', *Biographical Memoirs of Fellows of the British Academy*, 16 (2017), pp. 281–99.

[54] Examples include *York Products v Gilchrist Watt* [1970] 1 WLR 1262 (liability of sub-bailees who were not in a contractual relationship with the owner of goods); *The Mihalis Angelos* [1971] QB 164 (classification of contract terms; anticipatory breach); *Comp Tunisienne de Nav. SA v Comp. d'Armament Maritime SA* [1971] AC 572 (private international law; effect of choice of law clause governing contract); *The Atlantic Star* [1974] AC 436 (unsuccessfully arguing for widening circumstances in which English proceedings would be stayed because of prior proceedings in another more appropriate jurisdiction); *The Brimnes* [1975] QB 929 (repudiation of contract; effectiveness of telex received during office hours but unread).

[55] *The Mihalis Angelos* was one of the many cases in which he led Davenport.

[56] Memorial Service, The Temple Church, 6 February 2017.

and saw what he believed was largely the material on proprietary remedies in restitution from their seminars.[57] Robert wrote to Ronnie again but, when he still heard nothing, he 'concluded he was signing off and didn't feel able to tell me'.[58] By then Robert's practice was growing and he realised that if what he described as 'a rather difficult book on Restitution was ever to see the light of day' he had to have a collaborator.

Brian Simpson introduced Robert to Gareth Jones, who had undertaken graduate work at the Harvard Law School, and was leaving a temporary post at Oriel College, Oxford, for a lectureship at King's College London.[59] They got on very well and worked successfully together. Robert described Gareth as 'the ideal co-author—hard-working, good tempered, and generous to a fault',[60] and thought they 'were both quite surprised at the way their thoughts met' and that their minds 'seemed to fit together like a pair of gloves'.[61]

In 1961, the year Gareth Jones moved to a Fellowship at Trinity College, Cambridge, and a lectureship in the Faculty of Law, an issue of the *Modern Law Review* devoted to law reform contained an article by Robert about the 'Reform of the law of restitution'.[62] This demonstrated the amount of work he had done by then and may be said to contain the essence of the approach later developed in Goff and Jones, his Maccabaean lecture, and his judgments on restitution. Not surprisingly, he considered that restitution was in too unsettled and undeveloped a state for codification. His approach to specific proposals to eliminate obvious injustices is telling. He stated that two principal temptations had to be resisted.[63] The first was 'to substitute a wide discretion for ascertainable legal rules'. The second was to avoid piecemeal reform. He considered the *Law Reform (Frustrated Contracts) Act 1943* to be an example of the failure to resist both temptations.[64] He stated that, although the Act had the merit of reducing the scope of the doctrine of entire contracts, it did so by vesting in the court a discretion so wide that it was difficult for a lawyer to give firm advice on the prospects

[57] 2002 Talk. See R. Maudsley, 'Proprietary remedies for the recovery of money' (1959) 75 *Law Quarterly Review* 234.
[58] Ibid.
[59] Simpson was a good matchmaker: he had already introduced Jones to his future wife, Vivienne. See C. McCrudden, 'Alfred William Brian Simpson 1931–2011', *Biographical Memoirs of Fellows of the British Academy*, 11 (2012), pp. 547–81.
[60] W. R. Cornish, R. Nolan, J. O'Sullivan and G. Virgo (eds.), *Restitution Past, Present and Future, Essays in Honour of Gareth Jones* (Oxford, 1998), p. vii.
[61] 2002 Talk.
[62] R. Goff, 'Reform of the law of restitution', (1961) 24 *Modern Law Review* 85.
[63] Ibid.
[64] He expressed his criticisms and grappled with some of the difficulties in *BP Exploration Co. (Libya) Ltd v Nelson Bunker Hunt (No 2)* [1978] 1 WLR 783, 799, 800 aff'd [1981] 1 WLR 232; [1983] 2 AC 352 (CA & HL), although see Paul Mitchell's critique of the case in C. Mitchell and P. Mitchell (eds.), *Landmark Cases on the Law of Restitution* (Oxford, 2006), ch. 10.

of a claim. Moreover, in only applying to contracts discharged by frustration, the doctrine was unaffected in contracts discharged for breach or some other reason. The criticisms were repeated five years later in the first edition of Goff and Jones when the 'cumbrous, discretionary provisions' of the 1943 Act were contrasted with 'the simplicity and clarity' of §468 of the American Law Institute's *Restatement of Contracts* and almost twenty years later when the first case on the Act came before him in the Commercial Court.

After Gareth Jones moved to Cambridge, Robert spent many weekends staying with him and his wife, Vivienne, at their house in Cavendish Avenue and working on the book in Trinity College. On other weekends Gareth came to work at Holland Villas Road. At the beginning of their collaboration, Robert produced more than Gareth. Later on, as Robert's practice at the Bar grew, Gareth produced more than him, especially during the final stages.[65] They reckoned that, overall, they had made equal contributions to what they regarded as a total collaboration. Robert said that whoever had produced the first draft of a chapter, they 'threaded [their] way through the minefields of legal argument in every chapter, during contented hours of debate and writing' as they hammered out the final text together.[66]

Robert gave a sense of their excitement with the project in an evocative after-dinner speech to mark Gareth's retirement from the Downing Chair in 1998. He acknowledged the great debt they owed to their predecessors, Lord Mansfield in the UK and, in the United States, Professors Keener and Woodward,[67] and the Reporters of the 1937 *Restatement*, Professors Seavey and Scott. But, casting aside his usual modesty at this celebration for Gareth, who he described as a good man to go tiger-shooting with, he said:

> Gareth and I may have been callow youths in those days; but we knew that we were pioneers, and we revelled in it. You have, if you please, to imagine a fitter Goff and a slimmer Jones, hacking our way through the jungle of precedents, liberating our chosen subject from the tyranny of false concepts, cutting logs and building shelters for rational principles, [and] bravely tackling a few ravening beasts, Lord Sumner among them ... and carefully nurturing some precious green shoots, the fruits of our analysis.[68]

Robert's growing practice and Gareth's academic commitments in Cambridge and elsewhere meant that, as often happens with a new work by busy people, it all took

[65] Speech at dinner for Gareth Jones in January 1998.
[66] 2002 Talk.
[67] W. A. Keener, *A Treatise on the Law of Quasi-Contracts* (New York, 1893) and F. C. Woodward, *The Law of Quasi-Contracts* (Boston, MA, 1923); see also J. B. Scott, *Cases on Quasi-Contracts* (New York, 1905).
[68] Speech at dinner for Gareth Jones in January 1998.

much longer than they had anticipated. Their publishers, Sweet and Maxwell, pressed them over finishing times and they eventually submitted the manuscript in the last part of 1964. The page proofs, which arrived in January 1965, contained many mistakes, and they also made many alterations to the text. The publishers made them pay for a second set of proofs. Robert said that, as a result, they made practically no money at all out of the first edition. He commented that Sweet and Maxwell 'appeared to understand nothing about writing pioneering books'.[69] The book was published in 1966. Robert maintained that it was one of the reasons he was appointed a QC in 1967.

The book had four parts.[70] At its core was the demonstration of the fictional nature of the explanation that the basis of recovery is implied contract, and a statement of the principle of unjust enrichment and the limiting principles marking its boundaries. Its discussion of the nature and place of proprietary claims in the law of restitution and, in the second part of the book, of the character of the benefit to a defendant (and the challenges posed in cases of non-monetary benefits) are also of importance.

The closeness of the authors' collaboration and their commitment to it is illustrated by the fact that when, on the basis of the first edition, they supplicated for higher degrees at their respective universities, they refused to differentiate between their contributions. Apparently the Oxford Law Faculty Board initially declined to consider Robert's application on this basis because it was necessary to know who had written which parts of the book. But an administrator in the University Registry who was Secretary of the Law Board pointed out that the statutes required the Board to appoint examiners and that the syllabus for the subject introduced in 1970 to the graduate BCL course consisted of chapter headings from the book.[71] Robert took his DCL in 1971 and Gareth his LLD in 1972. In 1975 Robert was appointed to the High Court and Gareth to the Downing Professorship of the Laws of England at Cambridge. They wrote two further editions jointly, which were published in 1978 and 1986, the year in which Robert was appointed a Lord of Appeal in Ordinary.

The prefaces of the three editions, which they wrote jointly, show how they kept the boundaries and shape of the subject under review. So, in the second edition several scenarios involving gifts and the restitution of stolen property were omitted on the ground that they were part of the law of property. There was a new chapter on benefits

---

[69] Ibid.

[70] The fourth part, on restitution in the conflict of laws, was dropped from subsequent editions because the authors considered they had little to add to its treatment in J. H. C. Morris, *Dicey and Morris on the Conflict of Laws* (9th ed.), (London, 1973).

[71] Speech at dinner for Gareth Jones in January 1998. In a letter to Peter Birks dated 27 September 1999, Robert stated that H. W. R. Wade was the prime mover and wondered 'how they managed to give Crick and Watson Nobel Prizes for the Double Helix'.

acquired in breach of confidence and a fuller analysis of proprietary claims, in particular for mistake, and the defences to such claims. Contracting out and illegality, originally in the part of the book on defences, were moved to the section on the limits to restitutionary claims as factors meaning that an enrichment was not 'unjust'.

The second edition rejected the previous 'free acceptance' analysis of *Craven Ellis v Canons Ltd.*,[72] where recompense was granted for services rendered under a void contract to a company with no qualified directors as 'manifestly erroneous'. It also re-analysed the difficulties posed where restitution is claimed for services rendered and the relationship of restitution and contract, and its treatment of subrogation, described as one of the most intractable subjects in the law of restitution, was revised. Subrogation is a good illustration of the effect of the book. The authors' attempt in the second edition to formulate principles which unite all categories of subrogation was undoubtedly a major influence on the work of other scholars[73] and the ultimate recognition by the House of Lords in 1998 that non-contractual subrogation is concerned to reverse or prevent unjust enrichment.[74]

In a note at the end of the preface to the fourth edition, published in 1993, Robert stated that the edition was the work of Gareth Jones alone because his work as a Law Lord and increasing calls on him to give lectures and chair bodies precluded him from fulfilling the role of an editor. As Gareth observed, Robert's contribution to the book nonetheless remained a real one, albeit in the form of the influence of his innovative and closely reasoned decisions which did much to mould the modern law and the text of the book. Gareth edited three further editions, in 1998, 2002 and 2007, after which responsibility for Goff and Jones passed to a new team[75] which produced the eighth edition in 2011, renaming it *The Law of Unjust Enrichment*,[76] and removing the discussion of gain-based remedies founded on wrongdoing on the ground that the relevant cause of action is a civil wrong not unjust enrichment.

---

[72] [1936] 2 KB 403. Compare 1st ed., pp. 269–71 and 2nd ed., pp. 303–5.

[73] Notably P. Birks, *An Introduction to the Law of Restitution* (Oxford, 1985), p. 93; A. Burrows, *The Law of Restitution* (Oxford, 1993) p. 92; C. Mitchell, *The Law of Subrogation* (Oxford, 1994), p. 4.

[74] In *Banque Financière de la Cité v Parc (Battersea) Ltd* [1999] 1 AC 221 Lord Steyn stated (at 228) that 'distinguished writers have shown that the place of subrogation on the map of the law of obligations is by and large within the now sizeable corner marked out for restitution'. See also 234 (Lord Hoffmann, with whom Lord Griffiths and Lord Clyde agreed) and 245 (Lord Hutton).

[75] Professors Charles Mitchell and Paul Mitchell, and Dr Stephen Watterson. The 9th edition was published in 2016.

[76] Peter Birks had done this in 2003: see P. Birks, *Unjust Enrichment* (2nd ed.) (Oxford, 2004).

The bench

After eight busy years as a Queen's Counsel, Robert was appointed a High Court judge in October 1975. He had been appointed a Recorder of the Crown Court in 1974. After seven years in the High Court, two as the Judge in Charge of the Commercial Court, he was appointed to the Court of Appeal in 1982 and to the House of Lords in 1986. He served as Senior Law Lord between 1996 and 1998 when he retired aged 72 but continued to sit on an occasional basis until his 75th birthday. He participated in over 300 cases in the House of Lords and 160 cases in the Judicial Committee of the Privy Council and gave many luminous, pathbreaking and painstakingly crafted judgments.

In the High Court he soon showed his qualities, particularly in commercial and other areas of private law. Once he became an appellate judge his qualities were seen in many new areas and I remember him telling me how stimulating he found his discussions with the other judges hearing an appeal. There are important judgments in criminal law,[77] although his extra-judicially expressed views about the mental element required for murder attracted academic criticism.[78] His formulation of the test for disqualification on the ground of bias or apparent bias as a 'real danger' from the perspective of the court in possession of all the relevant evidence clarified what had been a confusing body of authority,[79] and he gave an important judgment in *Pinochet (No. 2)* in which the rule of automatic disqualification for interest was extended to non-pecuniary and non-proprietary interests.[80] He also made important contributions in cases raising profoundly difficult ethical questions such as arose in the *Bland* case about the end of life of a young man in a persistent vegetative state,[81] and in filling

---

[77] For example, *R v Preddy* [1996] AC 815 (revealing a lacuna in the law of obtaining property by deception because the payee of a cheque obtains a different chose in action to the one the victim of the fraud has lost, on which see text to n.142 below); *R v Brown* [1996] AC 543 (retrieving information from computer screen was not the offence of 'using' data); *R v Morhall* [1996] AC 90 (provocation). See also *Collins v Wilcock* [1984] 1 WLR 1177 (rationalisation of defences to action for trespass to the person under a general umbrella of conduct which is generally accepted in ordinary life); *C v Eisenhower* [1984] QB 331 (rupture of purely internal blood tissues not a wound); *Whittaker v Campbell* [1984] QB 318 (no general principle of law that fraud vitiates consent).

[78] Compare Goff, (1988) 104 *Law Quarterly Review* 30 with Glanville Williams, (1989) 105 *Law Quarterly Review* 387.

[79] *R v Gough* [1993] AC 646.

[80] *R v Bow St. Metropolitan Stipendiary Magistrate, ex p. Pinochet (No 2)* [2000] 1 AC 119.

[81] *Airedale NHS Trust v Bland* [1993] AC 284 (doctors' conduct in discontinuing artificial feeding and supply of antibiotics to patient in persistent vegetative state is lawful because it can properly be characterised as an omission. Lord Mustill concurred but considered that the distinction was 'morally and intellectually misshapen').

apparent lacunae by using the principle of necessity in cases of lack of capacity.[82] There are also significant and sometimes high profile cases on public and private international law and policy, such as those in the *Pinochet* cases about whether a former head of state charged with acts of torture was immune from the jurisdiction of English courts,[83] and in cases concerning the jurisdiction of English courts where the defendant is not within their territory.[84]

When dealing with public law questions, he generally had a more cautious approach but there are important exceptions in judgments holding that there was unlawful sex discrimination in an area where there were fewer grammar school places for girls than for boys,[85] in the *Factortame* case disapplying the rule of national law barring injunctive relief against the Crown as contrary to European Union law,[86] and in the *Woolwich* case discussed below giving a right to the restitution of *ultra vires* payments received by public authorities. He did not favour allowing public law concepts to make it more difficult in practice to vindicate private law rights: his view that a person whose private law right (by claim or defence) involved challenging a public law act or decision was not required to proceed by way of judicial review with its very short time limit and other procedural disadvantages was endorsed by the House of Lords.[87]

In private law, as well as much cited decisions on sales and international carriage,[88] arbitration,[89] and the conflict of laws,[90] in tort he made his mark on the law governing liability in tort for pure economic loss and the complexities of fault and strict liability.[91] In one judgment he asked whether the fear of too much liability in such cases had a rational basis or was blind conservatism.[92] In *Muirhead v Industrial Tank Specialities*

---

[82] *Re F (Mental Patient: Sterilisation)* [1990] 2 AC 1; *R v Bournewood Community and Mental Health NHS Trust, ex p. L* [1999] 1 AC 458 (principle of necessity the basis for lawfulness of medical intervention or informal admission to hospital where it is in the best interests of the patient and court has inherent jurisdiction to declare that it is in patient's best interests).

[83] Discussed below.

[84] *Spiliada v Cansulex Ltd* [1987] AC 460; *Re Norway's Application (Nos 1 & 2)* [1990] 1 AC 723; *Seaconsar (Far East) Ltd v Bank Markazi Jomhouri Islami Iran (Service Outside Jurisdiction)* [1994] 1 AC 438 (jurisdiction and service out); *Kuwait Airways Corp. v Iraqi Airways Co (No 1)* [1995] 1 WLR 1147 (sovereign immunity).

[85] *R v Birmingham CC, ex p. Equal Opportunities Commission* [1989] AC 1155.

[86] *R v Secretary of State for Transport, ex p. Factortame Ltd (No 2)* [1991] 1 AC 603.

[87] *Wandsworth LBC v Winder* [1985] AC 461, at 480.

[88] For example, *The Pioneer Container* [1994] 2 AC 324 (ability of non-party to rely on contract); *Clough Mills v Martin* [1985] 1 WLR 111 (effect of retention of title clause on insolvency); *The Ocean Frost* [1985] 3 WLR 640 (ship purchase, bribery and corruption).

[89] For example, *The Leonidas D* [1985] 1 WLR 925 and *The Antclizo* [1988] 1 WLR 603.

[90] For example, *Coupland v Arabian Gulf Oil* [1983] 1 WLR 1136; *Amin Rasheed v Kuwait* [1983] 1 WLR 228 (aff'd [1984] AC 40).

[91] *Cambridge Water Co. v Eastern Counties Leather plc* [1994] 2 AC 264.

[92] *The Aliakmon* [1985] QB 350, 394–5.

Ltd., he grappled with the problems of principle and policy in such cases and identi-fied the underlying principle as a voluntary assumption of responsibility limited by a need not to undercut contractual allocations of risk.[93] In Lord Rodger's words, the principle then had a chequered history,[94] but was revived and developed, largely by Robert in three significant decisions of the House of Lords.[95] Robert also made important contributions to the understanding and analysis of fact situations which prima facie give rise to claims based on more than one branch of the law of obliga-tions. In the case of overlapping claims in contract and tort his view has been that, notwithstanding the apparent elegance of insisting that one claim should take prece-dence, there are advantages in permitting, as it is now clear that English law does, a claimant to choose which case to pursue, although he was always sensitive to the need not to allow the undermining of contractual allocations of risk.[96] That sensitivity was also apparent where the overlap was between claims in contract and in restitution: 'The existence of the agreed regime' was more likely to render 'the imposition ... of a remedy in restitution both unnecessary and inappropriate.'[97]

Robert Goff's willingness to develop the common law to meet wholly new situations involving difficult questions meant that other great judges sometimes took a different view.[98] This was particularly evident in three decisions—*Woolwich Equitable BS v IRC,*[99] mentioned above, *White v Jones,*[100] and *Kleinwort Benson Ltd. v Lincoln CC.*[101]—in all of which the House of Lords split 3:2. The first and the third were res-titution cases. *White v Jones* was one of the 'assumption of responsibility' cases. Although where opinions were divided Robert did not always prevail,[102] in these three cases he was in the majority and gave the leading speech. His speeches in these cases

---

[93] [1986] QB 507.
[94] *Customs and Excise Commissioners v Barclays* [2007] 1 AC 181 at [49]. It was not favoured in *Smith v Eric S Bush* [1990] 1 AC 831, 862, 864–5 and *Caparo Industries plc v Dickman* [1990] 2 AC 605, 628 and 637.
[95] *Henderson v Merrett Syndicates* [1995] 2 AC 145, 180, *White v Jones* [1995] 2 AC 207 and *Spring v Guardian Assurance Plc* [1995] 2 AC 296.
[96] See *Henderson v Merrett Syndicates* [1995] 2 AC 145, *White v Jones* [1995] 2 AC 207, and *Coupland v Arabian Gulf Oil* [1983] 1 WLR 1136.
[97] *The Trident Beauty* [1994] 1 WLR 161, 164. See also *The Evia Luck* [1992] 2 AC 152, 165.
[98] For example, in *White v Jones* Lord Mustill. In *Tinsley v Milligan* [1994] 1 AC 340, Nicholls LJ and Lord Browne-Wilkinson were more willing to develop the law.
[99] [1993] AC 70.
[100] [1995] AC 207.
[101] [1999] 2 AC 349.
[102] See, for example, *The Gladys (No 1)* 1990] 1 WLR 115 (was defendant a party to arbitration clause); *Tinsley v Milligan* [1994] 1 AC 340 (effect of illegality); *Westdeutsche Landesbank Girozentrale v Islington LBC* [1996] AC 669 (on award of compound interest); *R v Secretary of State for the Home Department, ex p Venables* [1998] AC 407 (whether special criteria needed when considering case of very young person convicted of murder); *R v Secretary of State for the Home Department, ex p. Pierson* [1998] AC 539 (fixing

and in other cases on liability in tort for economic loss referred to above deployed
powerful analysis of the authorities, the conceptual difficulties, and (where relevant)
the way common law principles and statutory regimes co-existed. He also considered
and used the position in other jurisdictions but did so with sensitive awareness of how
difficult and potentially misleading an exercise in comparative law can be when
conducted by an English judge.[103]

What do his judgments tell us about his approach to the common law, his view of
the role of the judges in developing it, and what he believed about the boundary
between legitimate development by judges and illegitimate trespass on the province of
the legislature? One way of examining this is to consider how his approach changed as
he rose in the judicial hierarchy and the extent to which he avoided what, in 1983,[104] he
would describe as the three pitfalls that lie in the path of those who seek to state legal
principle: the temptation of elegance; the fallacy of the instant, complete solution; and
the danger of an unhistorical approach to earlier authority. In important early first
instance decisions on the doctrine of *forum non conveniens* and the scope of sovereign
immunity, his search for principle of course respected precedent.[105] However, where
precedent produced what he saw as illogicality, he lucidly identified the difficulties, thus
laying the ground for future reconsideration of the precedent by a higher court.[106]

Two of his first instance judgments made significant contributions to the
development and understanding of the principle or principles of estoppel which pre-
clude those who have made a promise or representation which has been relied on from
resiling from it where it would be unfair or unjust to do so.[107] His first instance decisions

---

minimum period to be served under a life sentence); *Alfred MacAlpine (Construction) Ltd. v Panatown
Ltd.* [2001] 1 AC 518 (scope of exception to principle that a third party can recover damages only for its
own loss).

[103] See e.g. *White v Jones* [1995] AC 207, 263.

[104] Goff, *The Search for Principle*, pp. 174–5.

[105] In *MacShannon v Rockware Glass Ltd* [1977] 1 WLR 376 he followed *The Atlantic Star* [1973] QB 364
(which had rejected his submissions as counsel) and in *The Playa Larga* [1978] QB 500 he followed *The
Philippine Admiral* [1977] AC 353. In both cases although the House of Lords reversed his decisions it did
so by departing from the decisions which had bound him: see [1978] AC 795 and [1983] AC 244.

[106] In *MacShannon v Rockware Glass Ltd* the issue was the rule that proceedings in this country should
only be stayed where continuing them would be oppressive, where he considered (as the law now is) that
the principle is that a stay should be granted wherever there is another clearly more appropriate forum
overseas. In *The Playa Larga* the issue was having a qualified rather than an absolute principle of sovereign immunity only in actions *in rem,* which he described as illogical. See also Goff, *The Search for
Principle*, pp. 170, 177–8.

[107] *The Post Chaser* [1982] 1 All ER 19 (while not necessary to show detriment, absence of prejudice to
one may mean that it is not inequitable for the other to resile) and *Amalgamated Investments & Property
Co Ltd v Texas Commercial International Bank*]1982] QB 84, 105–6, (which first identified the relevance
of unconscionability in this context). See Lord Goff's discussion in *Johnson v Gore Wood & Co* [2002] 2
AC 1, 39 and Justice Handley (2007) 7 UQTLJJ 477.

on frustrated contracts,[108] payments made under a mistake,[109] and benefits conferred in anticipation of a contract which does not materialise[110] are important *hors d'oeuvres* to his major contributions to the law of restitution starting with the recognition by the House of Lords in *Lipkin Gorman* in 1991 that it is an independent branch of private law.[111] They are also illustrations of the way he deployed detailed textual analysis of untidy and sometimes illogical bodies of case law to deduce the underlying principles and their limits. In the case of mistaken payments causation replaced 'supposed liability' as the test, but principled limits, including that the payment discharged a debt, and that the payee had changed its position in good faith as a result of it were imposed. This style would also be seen in his appellate judgments.[112]

In 1978 the first case on the *Law Reform (Frustrated Contracts) Act 1943* came before him in the Commercial Court. His judgment contains a sophisticated analysis of the nature of the benefit conferred where services are rendered and seeks to weave what the Act required into the fabric of the common law, for instance as providing statutory recognition of the defence of change of position. His categorical statement that the Act was intended to reverse unjust enrichment and that the determination of the 'just sum' under it had nothing to do with loss apportionment has, however, been criticised as not borne out by the statutory language.[113] It is also possible his analysis of claims for the repayment of money and the fact that the Act did not limit recovery to cases of total failure of consideration may have influenced his later support for allowing recovery at common law for a partial failure of consideration where apportionment can be carried on without difficulty.[114]

These cases are good illustrations of Robert's approach. He considered that, in general, the most potent influence upon a court in formulating a statement of legal

---

[108] *BP Exploration Co (Libya) v Hunt* (No. 2) [1979] 1 WLR 783, aff'd [1981] 1 WLR 232, [1983] 2 AC 352.

[109] *Barclays Bank Ltd v WJ Simms Son & Cooke (Southern) Ltd.* [1980] 1 QB 677.

[110] *British Steel Corp. v Cleveland Bridge & Engineering Co Ltd.* [1984] 1 All ER 504.

[111] *Lipkin Gorman v Karpnale Ltd.* [1991] 2 AC 548, 578.

[112] For example, in *Attorney-General v Guardian Newspapers (No. 2)* about the publication of extracts from *Spycatcher,* a book by a former spy, a statement of 'the broad general principle' of when a duty of confidence arises (which Lord Goff did 'not in any way intend to be definitive') was followed by three limiting principles: (a) once information enters the public domain it cannot be confidential; (b) the duty does not apply to useless information or trivia; and (c) the public interest that confidences should be preserved may be outweighed by a countervailing public interest which favours disclosure: see [1990] 1 AC 109, 281–3.

[113] The Court of Appeal ([1981] 1 WLR 232, at 243) did not endorse his approach and the critics are Paul Mitchell in Mitchell & Mitchell, *Landmark Cases on the Law of Restitution*, ch. 10 and the editors of Goff and Jones, *The Law of Unjust Enrichment* (8th ed.), (Oxford, 2011), para. 15–41.

[114] *Goss v Chilcott* [1996] AC 788, 798 and *Westdeutsche Landesbank Girozentrale v Islington LBC* [1996] AC 669.

principle is the desired result or the merits of the particular case.[115] But they also show that he meant 'the perception of the just solution in legal terms, satisfying both the gut and the intellect'. This, he considered, was achieved by combining the impact of the practical experience of practising lawyers and using facts to develop principles in a pragmatic way, achieving principled practical justice but leaving 'wriggle room' to deal with unanticipated consequences. In a lecture in 1984 he summarised his view in vivid language:

> We have to be very careful indeed to avoid too precise a formulation of principles. Legal principles are perhaps best regarded as basking sharks, lying just beneath the surface of the water, perceptible, indeed recognisable, but undefined. Definition may not only lead to error or injustice, as new fact-situations, unperceived by the author, come to light. Definition may also preclude an adjustment, a re-drawing of the boundaries, a shifting of the marking buoys.[116]

It is for this reason that, despite his important role in identifying and developing the principle of 'assumption of responsibility', Robert would surely have agreed with the more recent statements that the principle must be used with care and does not provide a complete answer to all cases of pure economic loss.[117]

Robert's focus in *White v Jones* on 'practical justice' was criticised by Tony Weir as appearing to be ready to create what Lord Mustill in his dissenting speech in that case described as a specialist pocket of tort law in cases of negligently inflicted economic loss in a way which the dissenters (and Weir) considered was not reconcilable with principled law.[118] However, flexibility within a principled framework which did not deprive it of the stability that is needed to enable citizens to obtain advice, regulate their affairs and resolve their disputes was the essence of Robert Goff's view of the law. In 1983 he stated that the law is a kaleidoscopic mosaic 'in the sense that it is in a constant state of change in minute particulars'.[119] In 1986 he stated that 'although the framework within which we work today' was governed by 'fundamental legal principles', 'seen in the perspective of time all statements of the law ... are no more than

---

[115] Goff, *The Search for Principle*, p. 183.

[116] R. Goff, 'An innocent turns to crime' [1984] *Statute Law Review* 5 at 14–15.

[117] *Customs and Excise Commissioners v Barclays* [2007] 1 AC 181 at [4], [35]–[38], [52] and [87] (Lords Bingham, Hoffmann, Rodger and Mance).

[118] T. Weir, 'A damnosa heriditas', (1995) 111 *Law Quarterly Review* 357, 361. See Lord Mustill at [1995] 2 AC 207 at 291. This case and Lord Mustill's criticism of the distinction relied on by Robert in *Bland's* case (see n. 81 above) suggests he had a more rigid view of what principle required and was less attracted to what Robert described as 'practical justice'.

[119] Goff, *The Search for Principle*, p. 186.

working hypotheses'.[120] But Sir Andrew Longmore is surely correct to say that the words 'no more than' rather overstate the case.[121]

For Robert, seeing law in terms of rules rather than principles was 'the dogmatic fallacy'[122] but nor did he favour the development of the law by courts creating wide discretions.[123] He stated that, while hard and fast rules and discretionary powers are necessary in every legal system, 'neither is to be encouraged because the one lacks the flexibility, and the other the consistency, of legal principle'.[124] He would surely have approved of Dr. Johnson's statement that 'the more precedents there are, the less occasion is there for law; that is to say the less occasion is there for investigating principles'.[125] There is also some similarity with the approach of Ronald Dworkin,[126] and it was thus not surprising that, in *Lipkin Gorman v Karpnale Ltd.*, Robert stated:

> The recovery of money in restitution is not, as a general rule, a matter of discretion for the court. A claim to recover money at common law is made as a matter of right; and even though the underlying principle of recovery is the principle of unjust enrichment, nevertheless, where recovery is denied, it is denied on the basis of legal principle.[127]

In *Woolwich Equitable BS* he commented on the boundary traditionally understood to lie between legitimate development of the law by judges and legislation. It was that case in which English Law recognised that an *ultra vires* exaction by a public authority was itself a ground for restitution irrespective of whether the payor was mistaken or under duress. Robert stated that, while he was 'well aware' of the boundary, he was 'never quite sure where to find it': 'its position seem[ed] to vary from case to case'.[128] His reasons for concluding that development of the law by the judges in that case would not illegitimately trespass on the province of the legislature included the constitutional principle that taxes cannot be levied without the authority of Parliament, the inequality in the legal and factual positions of the state and the citizen, and the fact that the Law Commission was considering the various statutory regimes governing *ultra vires* payments to public authorities and could assess whether the common law defences to recovery sufficed or additional defences were needed.

[120] R. Goff, 'Judge, jurist and legislature', *The Denning Law Journal*, 2 (1987), 79–95.

[121] A. Longmore, 'Is law no more than a working hypothesis?', Lords Goff and Hobhouse Memorial Lecture, 25 February 2019: https://7kbw.co.uk/the-2019-lords-goff-and-hobhouse-lecture/ (accessed 10 July 2019).

[122] Goff, *The Search for Principle*, p. 183.

[123] See the discussion above of his 1961 *Modern Law Review* article.

[124] Goff, *The Search for Principle*, p. 181.

[125] J. Boswell, *Life of Dr Johnson LLD* (3rd ed.), (Oxford, 1976), p. 468.

[126] R. Dworkin, *Law's Empire* (London, 1986), pp. 226–7 and 400 (law as integrity).

[127] [1991] 2 AC 548, 578.

[128] [1993] AC 70, 173.

In *Kleinwort Benson,* Robert led a unanimous court in holding that there is no rule or principle precluding the recovery of money paid under a mistake of law. However, but for a change of mind by Lord Hoffmann after the hearing, he would have been in the minority as to whether a payment made in accordance with a settled and generally accepted view of the law at the time of payment the payer was to be regarded as mistaken. As it was, he also led the majority in holding that the declaratory theory of judicial decision-making as a matter of principle meant that such a payment was mistaken. He was not deterred by the fact that the Law Commission had reported and recommended denying restitution in such a case on grounds of policy. While such a limit might be justified in respect of overpaid taxes because of the numbers affected and the consequent effect on the public finances, it should be introduced by legislation because these policy factors did not apply to payments under transactions between citizens and standard restitutionary defences sufficed.

Kleinwort Benson was heard six months before Robert retired as Senior Law Lord and a full-time judge and handed down a month after he did so. Lord Hoffmann described Robert's speech in that case as 'one of the most distinguished of his luminous contributions to this branch of the law'.[129]

These are cases in which Robert considered that development of the common law was justified by principle. What of the role of discretion? Robert recognised that it is not always possible to avoid giving a court wide discretion, but he considered that this should not be by judicial development of the law. Despite some reservation about legislation in private law and a hostility to codes (not needed in a jurisdiction with treatises such as Dicey and Morris *on the Conflict of Laws* and *Bowstead on Agency*),[130] he considered that conferring wide discretion on a court was a matter for legislation rather than by developing the common law.

His dissenting judgment in *Tinsley v Milligan*[131] accepted that there were problems with the common law principle precluding a claim or a defence which relied on an illegal transaction but stated that reform by the introduction of a discretion (such as a 'public conscience' test favoured in the Court of Appeal in that case) should occur only after a full inquiry by the Law Commission and by legislation. His judgment suggested such a review and his response to the Law Commission's 1999 consultation paper on the topic reiterated his view that the topic is not suitable for judicial development of the law. [132]   Notwithstanding his general view, in the particular context of

---

[129] [1999] 2 AC 349, 357 and Lord Browne-Wilkinson, who dissented, stated that it contained 'yet another major contribution to the law of restitution'.
[130] Goff, *The Search for Principle*, pp. 173–4 ('the best code is one which is not binding in law').
[131] [1994] 1 AC 340, 363–4.
[132] Response to Law Commission, *Illegal Transactions: the Effect of Illegality on Contracts and Trusts,* Consultation Paper 154 (London, 1999) in a letter dated 6 December 1999 stating that this was because

illegality, had he been sitting when twenty-two years later the matter came before the Supreme Court in *Patel v Mirza*[133] he may possibly have joined the majority, which introduced a structured discretion to deal with the effect of illegality.[134] The Law Commission recommendations to this effect[135] were not going to be implemented and three Supreme Court decisions had left the law on illegality in further disarray.[136]

Public service and engagement

Robert had a profound sense of public duty and engagement throughout his career. He chaired many legal committees and bodies; these included the sub-committee of the House of Lords Select Committee on the European Communities dealing with law and institutions between 1986 and 1988 and the Court of the University of London between 1986 and 1991.[137] Between 1991 and 2001 he served as High Steward of Oxford University. He enjoyed these roles, particularly where they had a strong educational or international or comparative character. They could be time-consuming, involving strategic questions about financial priorities and appeals from disciplinary tribunals, but also relatively minor but sometimes sensitive matters where he had patiently to act as an intermediary between those in dispute.

On appointment to the Lords, he was concerned about the poor library and research facilities available and sought to get them improved. Later, and particularly after becoming Senior Law Lord, he worked hard to improve other administrative arrangements concerning appeals. He was concerned about the handling of petitions for leave to appeal which he considered 'too subjective and too superficial'.[138] As Senior Law Lord he also had to deal with the expectations of those qualified to sit in the House of Lords or the Privy Council by reason of their judicial office or former office who were not a Lord of Appeal in Ordinary and the financial and other barriers to them sitting except when there were insufficient Law Lords available.[139]

---

of the wholesale re-examination of contract, trusts and restitution and because long-standing rules of policy would have to be rejected and replaced by different principles, probably of a discretionary nature.
[133] [2016] UKSC 42.
[134] The contributions to S. Green and A. Bogg (eds.), *Illegality after Patel v Mirza* (Oxford, 2018) show that the decision to do this by common law development was controversial.
[135] Law Commission, *The Illegality Defence*, Report 320 (London, 2010).
[136] *Hounga v Allen* [2014] 1 WLR 2889; *Les Laboratoires Servier v Apotex Inc* [2015] AC 430; *Bilta (UK) Ltd v Nazir (No 2)* [2016] AC 1.
[137] He also chaired the Law Reform Committee of the Bar (1974–6); Council of Legal Education (1976–82); British Institute of International and Comparative Law (Chairman 1986–2000), President (2000–2008); and the Chartered Institute of Arbitrators (President, 1986–91).
[138] Letter to Lord Bingham dated 2 May 2000.
[139] On the position of Lord Cooke of Thorodon who expected to sit regularly during his visits to England, and the effect of an expressed wish from a source in New Zealand that he should not sit on New Zealand

Despite his hostility to codes, suspicion of legislation and preference for incremental development of the common law by judges, Robert was a strong supporter of the work of the Law Commission. He referred to the Commission's work in his judgments and was available to advise the Commissioner responsible for a project.[140] In 1992 he introduced and piloted through the House of Lords Bills implementing Law Commission reports on transfer of title in carriage of goods by sea[141] and filling the lacuna in the offence of obtaining property by deception in the Theft Act 1968[142] which had been identified by him in *Preddy*.[143]

He gave many public lectures to lawyers and students in the United Kingdom and many other parts of the world. These included two three-week tours of India where he gave four lectures and participated in smaller functions.[144] His range extended well beyond topics building on and relating to the theme of development of the common law by judges.[145] His Lionel Cohen Lecture in Jerusalem in 1987 dealt with the mental

Appeals, see P. Spiller, 'Lord Cooke of Thorndon: the New Zealand dimension', (2002) 10 *Waikato Law Review* 55, 63 and 'A Commonwealth judge at work: Lord Cooke in the House of Lords and Privy Council' (2003) *Oxford University Commonwealth Law Journal* 29, 48, 66.

[140] See Lord Mackay of Clashfern's Foreword to Swadling and Jones, *The Search for Principle*, p. vi: The Commissioners he assisted were Brian Davenport QC, Jack Beatson, and Andrew Burrows. In his early days in the Lords, some of his colleagues did not approve of him citing the work of the Commission, an attitude which he helped to dispel, and which, since the UK Supreme Court at present includes three former Chairmen of the Law Commission and two former Commissioners (one a Scottish Commissioner), seems extraordinary.

[141] *Carriage of Goods by Sea Act 1992*, implementing Law Commission, *Rights of Suit: Carriage of Goods by Sea*, Report 196 (London, 1991); Scottish Law Commission, *Rights of Suit: Carriage of Goods by Sea*, Report 130 (Edinburgh, 1991); and see also *Sale of Goods Amendment Act 1994*, implementing Law Commission, *Sale of Goods Forming Part of a Bulk*, Report 215 (London, 1993) and Scottish Law Commission, *Sale of Goods Forming Part of a Bulk*, Report 145 (Edinburgh, 1993).

[142] [1996] AC 815, see note 77 above.

[143] *Theft (Amendment) Act 1996*, implementing Law Commission, *Offences & Dishonesty: Money Transfers*, Report 243 (London, 1996).

[144] The tours to India in 1984 and 1986 were organised by Dr L. M. Singhvi, a jurist and Parliamentarian, and later the Indian High Commissioner to the UK.

[145] The lectures include: 'The Law as Taught and the Law as Practised', 6th Lord Upjohn Lecture, (Kings College London, 1977); 'The Judicial Ethic in the Administration of the Law' (University of Birmingham, 1980 and 1981); 'Force Majeure and Frustration' in La Vendita Internazionale, Milan: Giuffrè (1981) 301–25; 'An Innocent turns to Crime' (Statute Law Society's Conference, Institute of Advanced Legal Studies, 1983); 'The Commercial Court and Commercial Contracts' (Society of Public Teachers of Law, 1983); Presidential Address to the Bentham Club, 'A Visit from Jeremy Bentham' (1986); The Child & Co Oxford Lecture 1986, 'Judge Jurist and Legislature'; Talk at University of Chicago Law School Symposium on 'The Concept of a Constitution' to mark the Bicentennial of the Constitution of the United States (June 1987); the Lionel Cohen lecture, 'The Mental Element in the Crime of Murder' (Hebrew University of Jerusalem, 1987 and (1988) 104 *Law Quarterly Review* 30); Presidential Address to the Holdsworth Club, 'A Voyage Around Holdsworth' (University of Birmingham 1988); 'The Distinctive Features of the Common Law' and Goff Lecture on Arbitration, 'Future Imperfect' (Hong

element in murder and his Cassel lecture in Stockholm in 1993 addressed end of life issues highlighted in the *Bland* case and considered the relevance to those issues of the Hospice movement. His talk on *The Concept of a Constitution* at a Symposium organised by University of Chicago Law School in 1987 to mark the bicentennial of the Constitution of the United States showed the power of his analysis applied to a topic which was not his natural legal home. Robert also led judicial and legal exchanges with a number of civil law countries, in particular Germany, France and Italy.

I have referred to the Oxford DCL recognising his scholarship in *The Law of Restitution.* His distinction was recognised by honorary doctorates awarded by five British universities,[146] his election as a Fellow of the British Academy in 1987, and his honorary Fellowships at New, Lincoln and Wolfson Colleges, Oxford. On Robert's retirement as Senior Law Lord, friends and colleagues presented him with a volume of essays aptly entitled *The Search for Principle.* In the words of the editors, William Swadling and Gareth Jones, this was 'not simply to mark his retirement from high office, but as a tribute to the significant part he has played in the development of English law'.[147]

The later years

As Robert retired three years before the compulsory retirement age he continued to sit until shortly before his 75th birthday in 2001. Of the cases he heard after stepping down as Senior Law Lord and a full-time judge, *Pinochet Nos 2 and 3*[148] and *Dextra Bank & Trust Co v Bank of Jamaica*[149] are noteworthy. By the turn of the century he had started to shed his other responsibilities. In 2000 he stepped down as Chairman of the British Institute of International and Comparative Law and became its President. In 2001 he stepped down as High Steward of Oxford University and Chairman of the Advisory Council of the Oxford Institute of European and Comparative Law.

In *Pinochet (No 1)* a majority of the House of Lords held that a former head of state was not immune from arrest and extradition in the United Kingdom for alleged

---

Kong, 1990); The Cassel Lecture 'A Matter of Life and Death' (Stockholm University, 1993); The Wilberforce Lecture, 'The Future of the Common Law' (1997) 46 *International and Comparative Law Quarterly* 745 (28 November 1999).

[146] The Universities of London, Bristol, Reading, and Buckingham and City University, London.

[147] Swadling and Jones, *The Search for Principle*, p. vii.

[148] *R v Bow St. Metropolitan Stipendiary Magistrate, ex p. Pinochet (No 2)* [2000] 1 AC 119 and *(No 3)* [2000] 1 AC 147.

[149] [2001] UKPC 50, [2002 1 All ER (Com) 193.

acts in breach of the Torture Convention 1984 committed while he was head of state because the acts could not be regarded as within the official functions of a head of state.[150] Robert was not a member of the court but was in *Pinochet (No 2)*, where the earlier decision was set aside on the ground that Lord Hoffmann's connections with Amnesty International meant he was automatically disqualified for interest,[151] and in *Pinochet (No 3)* which reheard the appeal. Six of the seven judges who heard *Pinochet (No 3)* reached the same conclusion as the differently constituted court had in *Pinochet (No 1)*, albeit on very different reasoning. [152] Robert dissented. He rejected the suggestion that the customary rule of immunity of a head of state from the domestic courts of another state had been impliedly overruled by the Torture Convention as contrary not only to principle and authority, but also to common sense.[153] His judgment in what was at the time an area in which there was much confusion, has been described as exhibiting much moral courage and faithfulness to values inherent in the Rule of Law[154] and has the approval of Sir Robert Jennings, a former President of the International Court of Justice.[155]

In *Dextra Bank,* his very last case, Robert gave a joint judgment with Lord Bingham.[156] He had no doubts about the Privy Council's emphatic statement that the defence of change of position applies to changes in anticipation of as well as after the receipt of a benefit[157] or what he described in a letter to Lord Bingham as the rejection of ignorance as a ground for restitution.[158] But he stated that he was rather worried whether, buried in the complicated facts, there was, as commentators have subsequently argued,[159] a relevant mistake of fact as well as the misprediction which did not suffice as the ground for a restitutionary claim.

[150] *R v Bow St. Metropolitan Stipendiary Magistrate, ex p. Pinochet (No 1)* [2000] 1 AC 61.

[151] See above, text to note 80.

[152] See the summary in *R v Loma* [2017] QB 1729 at [25]–[39] of the differences between *Pinochet (No 1)* and *(No 3)* and of the disagreement among the majority in *No. 3* as to the basis of the decision.

[153] [2000] 1 AC 147 at 214, 219 and 223.

[154] G. Zellick, *Private Conscience: Public Duty,* Van der Zyl Lecture, London 8 May 2003, p. 12 (published in *European Judaism: a Journal for the New Europe,* 36 (2003), 118–31).

[155] R. Jennings, 'The Pinochet extradition case in the English Courts', in L. Boisson de Chazournes and V. Gowlland-Debas (eds.), *The International Legal System in Quest of Equity and Universality* (The Hague, 2001), pp. 677–98.

[156] Robert wrote the part of the judgment on restitution and Lord Bingham the part on bills of exchange.

[157] Letter to Peter Birks dated 5 December 2001. The letter also said he was relieved to have delivered his last judgment and that 'I tend to forget the judgments which I now feel were right; whereas the ones which I now think were wrong prey on my mind.'

[158] Letter to Lord Bingham dated 17 September 2001 stating that Peter Birks and Andrew Burrows would not be pleased by this. There is no express reference to 'ignorance' in the judgment but see [31]—[33].

[159] Burrows, *The Law of Restitution* (3rd ed.), p. 203; and J. Edelman and E. Bant, *Unjust Enrichment* (London, 2016), pp. 174–5.

In February 2002, three months after his 75th birthday, Robert's colleagues gave a dinner for him in the Inner Temple marking the end of his judicial sitting. In a letter to Tony Honoré, who could not be there, Robert said 'I have been very fortunate in my career; but am now more conscious of the judgments which I believe I got wrong than I am of the ones which I still think I got right. I expect that is true of many judges, particularly those who (like me) have stuck their necks out.' He also said that he had given up practically everything and looking back had a feeling that he 'took on too many commitments, and that they all suffered in consequence'.[160] That that feeling was clearly wrong is shown by the profound legal knowledge displayed in his judgments and lectures, which, as Lord Rodger stated in the Festschrift presented to him three years earlier, 'enriched us with a store of invaluable opinions'. He was a great judge not only because of the depth of his knowledge and the width of his interests, but because, in Lord Mackay of Clashfern's words, he 'did not come to any case with an entrenched point of view' and 'was willing to consider any reasonable and well-presented argument and to analyse it in a rigorous, very well-informed way'.[161]

By 2004 Robert's health had declined and in 2006 he and Sarah moved from Chieveley to Cambridge to live near their daughter Juliet. He remained in their home in Storeys Way until his death in 2016. In her funeral address, Juliet stated:

> And so we come to the last few years of his life, the last many years in which Dad's intellect faded. His ability to understand and to articulate words diminished. And yet, his essential nature remained: his love of music, the comfort he derived from being at home with Mum and his delight when family and friends came to visit. His kindness, his humour and his affection remained to the very end.

Acknowledgements

I have been greatly assisted by the addresses given by Juliet Jackson at Robert's funeral in St Mary's Church, Chieveley, on 5 September 2016 and by Sir Stephen Tomlinson at his memorial service in the Temple Church on 6 February 2017. My greatest debt is to Sarah Goff who generously provided me with information about Robert's family and the background to many events in his life, copies of many of the lectures he gave, and his correspondence about them, his work as Senior Law Lord, and with scholars and students in this and other countries. Dr Elizabeth Wells, Foreign, Comparative and International Law Librarian, Bodleian Law Library, helped track down the records of university lectures and classes given by Robert, and Lindsay McCormack, Archivist at Lincoln College, gave me access to material about his time at the College. I have also been greatly assisted by Professor Andrew Burrows, Sir Richard Buxton,

---

[160] 26 January 2002.
[161] Lord Mackay of Clashfern, 'Foreword', p. v.

Professor Bill Cornish, Sir Julian Flaux, Simon Gardner, Sir Nicholas Green (Chairman of the Law Commission), Professor Tony Honoré, Juliet, Sean and Rupert Jackson, Lord David Lloyd-Jones, Sir Andrew Longmore, Professor Charles Mitchell, Sir Peter North, Celia Pilkington and Professor Francis Reynolds. Some of these will find their words pillaged here, not always with proper acknowledgement.

Note on the author: The Rt Hon. Sir Jack Beatson is Visiting Professor at the University of Oxford, and Professorial Fellow at the University of Melbourne. He was a Lord Justice of Appeal from January 2013 to February 2018. He was elected a Fellow of the British Academy in 2001.

EDWARD TIMMS

Edward Francis Timms

3 July 1937 – 21 November 2018

elected Fellow of the British Academy 2006

by

RITCHIE ROBERTSON

Fellow of the Academy

Edward Timms, the pre-eminent authority on the Austrian satirist Karl Kraus, did much to shape the sub-disciplines of Austrian studies and German-Jewish studies. His many publications include a magisterial two-volume study of Kraus's work, life and milieu (1986, 2005). As a University Lecturer at Cambridge and Fellow of Gonville & Caius College, he co-founded the yearbook *Austrian Studies*. Having moved to the University of Sussex as Professor of German, he founded the Centre for German-Jewish Studies. His marriage to Saime Göksu gave him an intense interest in Turkey; together they wrote a biography of the poet Nazım Hikmet. Among much else, he had a talent for engaging with people and for promoting collaborative enterprises. He received many honours from Austria and Britain.

Biographical Memoirs of Fellows of the British Academy, XVIII, 275–287
Posted 23 October 2019. © British Academy 2019.

EDWARD TIMMS

Edward Francis Timms, who died at the age of 81 on 21 November 2018, was an academic who shaped two disciplines within Modern Languages: Austrian studies and German-Jewish studies. His academic work was inseparable from the personal journey which he recorded, near the end of his life, in his autobiography, an honest and detailed account of how, in Nietzsche's phrase, he became who he was.[1]

Edward was born on 3 July 1937, the third of eight children of the Rev. John Timms, Vicar of Buckfastleigh in Devon, and Joan Timms, née Axford; an older brother, born out of wedlock and given away for adoption, later came to light and was welcomed into the family. Like most of his siblings, Edward attended Christ's Hospital, which admitted children from lower-income families without a fee. In 1956 he started reading Modern Languages at Gonville and Caius College, Cambridge, where he soon decided to concentrate on German, taught first by E. K. Bennett and then by F. J. Stopp. With Stopp he took a comparative paper on satire, which included early modern texts such as Brant's *Narrenschiff* but also works by Swift, Pope and Pascal; its lasting effect is visible not only in the attention Edward would later pay to ironic techniques and satirical archetypes in Kraus's writing, but also in a remarkable, much later essay on the possibility of Christian satire.[2] After a year teaching in Nuremberg, he began a PhD thesis on Karl Kraus, supervised by the charismatic Peter Stern.

Edward would later become the world's pre-eminent Kraus scholar. How he came to Kraus is recounted in his autobiography. As an undergraduate at Cambridge he had scarcely connected literature with politics. His favourite topic, on which he was fortunately able to write in his final exams, was the depiction of nature by the out-wardly placid, inwardly complex Austrian author Adalbert Stifter. After graduating, however, his experience of modern Germany made him raise questions about the relation between present and past. A student teacher he knew in Nuremberg, Hans Keith, responded to his enquiry about critical authors by advising him to read Karl Kraus, along with the Weimar satirist Kurt Tucholsky. Kraus's opaque and intricate writings provided a challenge which Edward addressed, guided by Peter Stern, who owned a complete set of Kraus's satirical journal *Die Fackel*. It is probable that *Die Fackel*, nowadays available online, was not present at that time in any British library.

Undertaking a study of Kraus was adventurous. He still has an uneasy place on the margins of the German canon. Aside from some poetry, he did not write in familiar literary genres. Even his huge anti-war drama, *Die letzten Tage der Menschheit*

[1] E. Timms, *Taking up the Torch: English Institutions, German Dialectics and Multicultural Commitments* (Brighton, 2011).
[2] E. Timms, 'The Christian satirist: a contradiction in terms?', *Forum for Modern Language Studies*, 31 (1995), 101–16. See also 'Der Satiriker und der Christ - ein unvereinbarer Gegensatz?', in A. Schöne (ed.), *Akten des VII. Internationalen Germanisten-Kongresses Göttingen 1985* (Tübingen: 1986), vol. 2, pp. 201–8.

(The Last Days of Mankind) is *sui generis*, though its use of documentary materials has a partial precedent in Büchner's *Dantons Tod* (Danton's Death, 1834) and successors in postwar documentary dramas by Peter Weiss and Heinar Kipphardt. Most of Kraus's work consists of pamphlets and journalism, by its nature diffuse and difficult to master. *Die Fackel* alone contains some 22,600 pages, the vast majority written by Kraus. The twenty-volume scholarly edition published by Suhrkamp under the direction of Christian Wagenknecht started to appear only in 1986, while the carefully annotated three-volume edition of Kraus's pre-*Fackel* writings by Johannes J. Braakenburg dates only from 1979. There is as yet no complete edition of Kraus's letters, though individual correspondence has been published. In other words, the prior *Grundlagenforschung* or fundamental research, that one could rely on with a classic author such as Goethe or Lessing, had not even been attempted. Having begun this arduous task in 1960, he completed the thesis and was awarded the PhD in 1967.

Much more was happening in Edward's life meanwhile. In 1963 he was appointed an Assistant Lecturer at the newly founded University of Sussex, which offered great scope for innovatory and cross-disciplinary teaching. In his autobiography he also describes this period as formative for his personality. Unconventional and exciting new acquaintances such as the libertarian socialist and historian of science Brian Easlea helped to shake him out of his shyness and reserve. Sussex also provided an international and multicultural atmosphere such as he had not experienced in Cambridge or elsewhere. Through Brian Easlea he met Saime Göksu from Ankara, the only female research student in Theoretical Physics. Saime had already confronted many difficulties. As one of seven children (five girls and two boys) in a low-income family, she had had to work throughout her studies, and in her final year she was diagnosed with tuberculosis, which was only overcome by an expensive operation carried out in Germany. Not only her strong personality, but her family's secular political values, had their effect. Saime recalls:

> In those two years [1963–5] we ended living in the same square as Ted moved there from a room with a family far out of town. My room in Marine Square became a meeting-place where we discussed politics, the Vietnam War, the anti-nuclear campaign, British politics, the Arts and Science division, Marxism. Visitors to my room included Joe Townsend [a journalist], Gavin Wraith [a mathematician from the Physics Department], and Indian, Pakistani, African students. ...[3]

Returning to Cambridge as a University Assistant Lecturer and Fellow of Caius in 1965, Edward found this environment more restrictive but did his best to broaden the curriculum by lecturing on such subjects as Hegel, Marx and the Frankfurt School, and later by collaborating with colleagues on a highly successful course, 'Avant-Garde

[3] From an email to Ritchie Robertson, 15 April 2019. Cf. Timms, *Taking up the Torch*, pp. 114–15.

Movements in Europe 1900–1939'. His autobiography also mentions the course 'Culture and Society in Germany since 1965', inspired by the upheavals in German universities, where students were protesting, with some reason, against conservative academic structures and teaching materials. Even when most inclined to radicalism, however, Edward favoured a humane and reflective variety of Marxism, personified by Rosa Luxemburg and Jürgen Habermas and also, in his opinion, by the student leader Rudi Dutschke. When Dutschke was studying at Cambridge, Edward invited him to address students on his course, and was impressed by Dutschke's conception of 'the long march through the institutions' as an alternative to revolution. Dutschke and his family were soon afterwards expelled from Britain on the implausible grounds that they threatened national security.

In April 1966, under romantic and dramatic circumstances recounted in his autobiography, Edward married Saime, thus beginning a lifelong bond with Turkey. They adopted two Turkish orphan babies, Yusuf in 1974 and Daphne in 1976. In 1983 they enlarged their family by becoming guardians of the orphaned twelve-year-old Sebastian Tennant. Saime moved from physics to psychoanalysis, doing psycho-dynamic counselling in Cambridge and later in Sussex. This move matched a shift in Edward's focus of interest from political to psychoanalytic theory, from Marx to Freud. They had many discussions of psychoanalysis in which Saime evaluated the theories of Melanie Klein in opposition to what she (and not only she) considered Freud's too male-dominated outlook.

At one time Edward and Saime considered spending their lives in Turkey. In 1969–70 Saime taught at the Middle East Technical University in Ankara. Edward used six months' study leave from Cambridge to join her there; he taught courses on European intellectual history. It was by no means certain that once his period as University Assistant Lecturer expired in 1970 he would be appointed to a permanent post, so Ankara was a feasible alternative. However, Cambridge did reappoint him, albeit somewhat grudgingly. Reservations probably arose not only from his reputation for radicalism but also from his failure to publish anything apart from book reviews and reflections on left-wing thought, the latter in Cambridge organs such as *Granta* (though they may well have interested more people than many scholarly publications). Strange as it seems now, Edward was long a notorious non-publisher; his first academic paper appeared only in 1981.[4]

Edward's doctoral thesis was the seed of his first book, *Karl Kraus, Apocalyptic Satirist: Culture and Crisis in Habsburg Vienna*, published in 1986 by Yale (after Cambridge University Press had ill-advisedly refused to publish it except in truncated

---

[4] E. Timms, 'Hofmannsthal, Kraus and the "Theatrum mundi"', in W. E. Yuill and P. Howe (eds.), *Hugo von Hofmannsthal: Commemorative Essays* (London, 1981), pp. 123–32.

form). Tactfully described by a reviewer as 'long-awaited', it was worth the wait. Setting Kraus's satirical writings against the whole background of late Imperial Vienna, it offers perceptive analyses of difficult texts that often resist conventional critical methods, while bringing out Kraus's importance as a campaigner for social and sexual emancipation. Private aspects—Kraus's relationship with Sidonie von Nádherný, and his dealings, as a converted Jew, with the Roman Catholic Church—are treated with wonderful delicacy. The whole book has the attractive, unpretentious, understated lucidity which distinguished everything Edward wrote.

At the same time, the book brings out the political bite of Kraus's satire. It emphasises Kraus's lone campaign, through the journal *Die Fackel* which he founded in 1899, against a range of targets so wide—corruption in public life, philistinism in the media, hypocrisy in the legal regulation of prostitution, the excessive power of newspaper owners—that Kraus himself cannot be identified with any particular ideological standpoint. His problematic correspondence with the racist Houston Stewart Chamberlain, and his turn, after his conversion to Catholicism in 1911, to a conservatism recalling that of G. K. Chesterton and Paul Claudel, are treated in a cautious and nuanced way. Later in the book, the outbreak of the First World War provides an opportunity to reflect on the public responsibility of the intellectual. German and Austrian intellectuals who unquestioningly supported the war and the accompanying propaganda are contrasted with Kraus's sceptical analysis of patriotic speeches as a cover not only for militarism but also for economic imperialism. This leads up to an analysis of *Die letzten Tage der Menschheit*. Kraus worked on it from 1915 on, and successive versions reflect major shifts in his political views. When he began, he was still attached to his pre-war conservatism, which is still marked in the edition of 1919. His gradual disillusionment with the Austrian political class led him to support the Social Democrats, so that the revised and enlarged text published in book form in 1922 has a strongly socialist and republican thrust.

Though *Karl Kraus, Apocalyptic Satirist* extends only to 1918, after which Kraus would live and write copiously for another eighteen years, it was immediately recognised as towering over all other studies of Kraus. It was translated into German, and even made required reading in its English version in at least one Austrian university. A second volume was always envisaged, but took almost twenty years to write.

The method underlying both volumes on Kraus was interdisciplinary, though in the 1980s this term was not bandied about quite so much as it is now. To map the interactions among different cultural groupings in early twentieth-century Vienna, Edward devised a diagram which he labelled 'The Vienna Circles'. He describes in *Taking up the Torch* how he first presented it at a lecture given at the University of East Anglia in February 1978, in the presence of the Austrian specialists Cedric Williams and Max Sebald:

The great strength of the Viennese modernism, I suggested, lay in its internal organization. By analogy with the Vienna Circle of logical positivists, the whole structure of avant-garde culture could be pictured as a condensed system of microcircuits. This idea was illustrated by a diagram of 'Creative Interactions in Vienna around 1910', incorporating fifteen intersecting circles, each of them centred on a dominant personality: from Victor Adler and Rosa Mayreder through Freud, Kraus and Adolf Loos to Schoenberg, Mahler and Klimt.[5]

Thus the circle with Kraus at its centre overlaps on one side with Freud's, the overlap containing the name of the intermediary Fritz Wittels, whose memoirs Edward would later discover and publish. At the other end, Kraus's circle overlaps with the one centring on the modernist architect Adolf Loos, the overlap being occupied by their mutual friend the sketch-writer Peter Altenberg. A very much more elaborate version, illustrating the intricate cultural interconnections of the post-1918 period, appears in the second Kraus volume.[6] By this stage the diagram has approached the limits of what a representation in only two dimensions can achieve. It still provides a more helpful overview of complex cultural interactions than any merely verbal description could provide.

Edward's focus on Austria led to his starting an Austrian Study Group at Cambridge and eventually to the foundation of the yearbook *Austrian Studies*. His account of both can be found in the twenty-fifth anniversary issue of *Austrian Studies*.[7] Although Edward speaks generously of my share in this enterprise, I was in every way the junior partner, and learnt an immense amount both professionally and humanly. Initially I was too much in awe of other people's articles to make drastic editorial changes (how long ago it seems), but I learnt from Edward how to reshape an article so as to make it coherent, and to bring out an argument that was only latent in the original text. Humanly, I learnt much from Edward's tact, forbearance and diplomatic skills, honed no doubt in the exacting atmosphere of the Caius Senior Common Room, and invaluable in negotiating with the sometimes strongly held views of contributors.

Initially Edward wanted to call the journal *Meridian*, perhaps because he was so much impressed by Paul Celan's speech published under that title, but he was finally persuaded that such a title misleadingly suggested Southern Europe and that, as our

[5] Timms, *Taking up the Torch*, p. 183; the diagram appears on p. 182. A slightly simpler version is presented in E. Timms, *Karl Kraus, Apocalyptic Satirist: Culture and Catastrophe in Habsburg Vienna* (New Haven, CT, and London, 1986), p. 8.

[6] E. Timms, *Karl Kraus, Apocalyptic Satirist: the Post-War Crisis and the Rise of the Swastika* (New Haven, CT, and London, 2005).

[7] E. Timms, 'The founding of *Austrian Studies*: a collaborative enterprise', *Austrian Studies*, 25 (2017), 6–11.

eventual publisher Martin Spencer put it, 'penny plain' is better than 'tuppence coloured'. As Edward recounts, the journal was originally offered to Oxford University Press, but rejected after a number of negative remarks, mainly from historians. One, whom I afterwards identified by chance, expressed the suspicion that such a journal might become 'a cosy *Kaffeeklatsch*'; later, however, this very person became an enthusiastic and much valued contributor to *Austrian Studies*. In Martin Spencer, who, after transforming Manchester University Press had transferred his energies to Edinburgh, we were fortunate enough to find a gifted publisher who combined imagination with sound judgement. His sudden death at a tragically early age was a painful shock. Fortunately, his successor, Vivian Bone, continued to support *Austrian Studies*.

Becoming increasingly restless in Cambridge, Edward accepted the invitation to return to Sussex in 1992 as Professor of German. It took him and Saime some time to find a suitable house in Brighton. It was important for them both to live near the sea—not only because they were passionately fond of swimming, but because of the sea's wider, symbolic significance. When I suggested that they should find a house near some swimming-baths, Edward politely intimated that that was not the point at all. Eventually they moved into 4, The Cliff, a handsome house separated from the sea only by a long, sloping patch of grass inhabited by badgers. There they gave hospitality to many visitors, who had to sing for their supper by writing something memorable in the visitors' book. It was Edward's home for the rest of his life.

At the University of Sussex, with the support of Vice-Chancellors, Gordon Conway and later Alasdair Smith, Edward founded the Centre for German-Jewish Studies. Helped by a network of supporters from the Jewish community in London, Brighton and further afield, the Centre aimed to illuminate the history of Jewish emancipation, assimilation and persecution in German-speaking countries. Initially stimulated by a meeting at the London home of Diana Franklin, the Centre benefited from the support of a number of German-Jewish refugees who wanted to ensure that their parents' and grandparents' achievements in that brief period of German-Jewish 'symbiosis' were not overlooked or forgotten. At that time the Shoah was achieving its rightful place in the history of the 20th century with increasing numbers of academics and museums concentrating on the Holocaust. In parallel with this trend, individuals and organisations such as the Leo Baeck Institute and the Belsize Square Synagogue welcomed the chance to collaborate with the Centre in order to provide an academic and analytical perspective on the immense Jewish contribution to non-Jewish culture in pre-war Germany and Austria. Edward's ability to bring his English academic skills into this environment provided the Centre's supporters with a welcome academic home at Sussex and their relationship was secure enough for Edward to feel able to play the Horst Wessel song at a meeting of the Leo Baeck Lodge in Hampstead.[8]

[8] I thank Diana Franklin for the information in this paragraph.

The Centre held a number of major conferences, papers from which were published in book form, notably *The German-Jewish Dilemma; from the Enlightenment to the Shoah* in 1995 (Lewiston, NY). Besides forming its own archive of refugees' papers, it secured a large Arts and Humanities Research Council grant to compile a database of refugee archives in Britain. A particularly fascinating collection was the Arnold Daghani archive, which the University had had since 1987 without knowing its value: some 6,000 works of art and notebooks by a survivor of the Nazi slave labour camp at Mikhailovka. This gave rise to several publications, including *Memories of Mikhailowka: Labour Camp Testimonies in the Arnold Daghani Archive*, edited by Edward with the art historian Deborah Schultz (Brighton, 2007).

Fully aware of the need to encourage young scholars, the Centre set up the bi-annual Max and Hilde Kochmann summer school for doctoral students in European cultural history. With the support of the Association for Jewish Refugees the Centre initiated an annual Holocaust Memorial Day event at the University of Sussex. Both events continue. So does the Centre, though from March 2019 it forms part of a larger entity, the Weidenfeld Institute of Jewish Studies, established with help from the German government.

Although Edward had effectively transferred his energies to the sub-discipline now known as Exile Studies, Karl Kraus was not forgotten. The second volume of *Karl Kraus: Apocalyptic Satirist*, subtitled *The Post-War Crisis and the Rise of the Swastika*, appeared in 2005. Massive, encyclopaedic, with 550 pages of text and 57 pages of notes, it increasingly focuses on Kraus's exposure of the horrors of Nazism, especially in his great polemic *Dritte Walpurgisnacht* (Third Walpurgis Night) which was published only in 1951. There was, however, so much to be found out about Kraus's writings and activities in the 1920s and 1930s that the book necessarily deals with a vast range of topics. The cultural context is now no longer the Habsburg Empire but 'Red Vienna', where a socialist administration instituted many beneficial reforms in such areas as education, child-care and workers' housing. Some of its members, notably David Josef Bach, a little-known figure who is here rescued from virtual oblivion, were also committed to bringing high culture, particularly modernism, to the people at large (one might recall, as an analogy, the original mission of the BBC's Third Programme). Links are explored with Kraus's public readings, in which he declaimed passages from Goethe, Nestroy and Shakespeare (in the Schlegel-Tieck translation) to audiences of devotees.

A major theme is law: the complexities of legal citizenship for inhabitants of the rump state left behind by the fragmentation of the Habsburg Empire in 1918; Kraus's growing interest in international law as a means of keeping the peace in painfully divided postwar Europe; and his appeal to the law in his many campaigns against powerful people such as the press magnate Emmerich Bekessy (a prototype of Rupert

Murdoch) whom Kraus managed to get expelled from Vienna. Once again, therefore, the responsibilities of the citizen come under scrutiny.

The book has to address a particularly controversial topic, Kraus's support for the authoritarian Dollfuss government of Austria. Two days after the Nazi seizure of power in Germany, the Chancellor, Engelbert Dollfuss, suspended the constitution and governed by decree. His main target was the terrorist activities of Austrian Nazis. The National Socialist party was banned in Austria; many of its adherents were confined in a concentration camp. In February 1934, however, the left wing of the Social Democrats, fearing that Dollfuss would also suppress them, began an armed insurrection, which predictably was quelled within two days. Kraus bitterly criticised the Social Democrats for not supporting Dollfuss. His stance has often been seen as a grievous betrayal.[9] Patient examination of the issues leads here to a more balanced verdict. Kraus was right to insist that Dollfuss's government was very different from Hitler's, and that the Left was wrong to lump them together as 'fascism' (the term 'Austro-Fascism' is often used even today). But he failed to speak out when his voice could have strengthened Dollfuss's anti-Nazi stance, and he was unjust in denouncing the Social Democrats, since (although Kraus could not know this) Dollfuss had a secret agreement with Mussolini, in which Mussolini undertook to support him against Germany provided he eliminated all traces of Marxism from Austria. Without concealing Kraus's errors of judgement, this investigation defends him convincingly against the criticisms, amounting sometimes to defamation, which his reputation has suffered. The price of Kraus's individual stance was to fall (in the German phrase) between all the stools.

There is far more in this book than can be indicated here. I read many chapters in draft and heard some given as conference papers. It was exciting to follow its progress, but often very hard to see how such heterogeneous materials could be combined into a single overarching narrative. Unlike the first volume, it is a book to be consulted and read in chapters, rather than to be read through. It is a resource which Kraus scholars will find indispensable for many years to come.

Earlier, Edward had published *Freud and the Child Woman: the Memoirs of Fritz Wittels* (New Haven, CT, and London, 1995), using the manuscript autobiography of the unorthodox Freudian Fritz Wittels to explore how eroticism helped to power creativity in the Vienna of Freud and Kraus. And he and Saime jointly composed a biography of the Turkish poet Nazım Hikmet, *Romantic Communist: the Life and Work of Nazim Hikmet* (London, 1999), based on oral history: Saime interviewed some thirty-five people in Turkey who had known Hikmet, she and Edward checked their information against archival sources, and Edward digested these materials into a smoothly flowing narrative.

---

[9] See, for example, chapter 4, 'Charting February 1934: Karl Kraus, Anna Seghers, Friedrich Wolf, Alois Vogel', in A. Barker, *Fictions from an Orphan State: Literary Reflections of Austria between Habsburg and Hitler* (Rochester, NY, 2012).

These achievements are the more remarkable when one recalls that from about 2000 Edward was increasingly disabled by multiple sclerosis. He bore his affliction with extraordinary fortitude, as I saw when in February 2009 I accompanied him to Vienna. The president of the Austrian Academy of Sciences, Werner Welzig, hoped for an English translation of Kraus's *Dritte Walpurgisnacht*. Edward and I translated sample passages and presented them for discussion. At that time Edward was mostly in a wheelchair but could walk short distances very slowly; this was sometimes necessary, as Vienna was deep in snow. Nonetheless, thanks to some logistical planning, we managed to go to the theatre and to an exhibition of sculptures by Ernst Barlach and paintings by Käthe Kollwitz, and to meet up with several friends. Edward's intellectual and social energies were unabated.

Although the Academy's project never materialised, Edward, together with Fred Bridgham, accomplished another seemingly impossible translation, that of Kraus's monster drama *The Last Days of Mankind*, published by Yale in 2015. Kraus's daunting range of speech registers, plus parodies of literary and journalistic styles, and comic and serious verse, are rendered skilfully and imaginatively.[10] This accomplishment was awarded the Aldo and Jeanne Scaglione Prize for Translation by the Modern Language Association of America. Edward and Fred subsequently collaborated on another, even more daunting translation, that of Kraus's great anti-Nazi polemic *Dritte Walpurgisnacht*, which, as I write, has yet to be published.

Having retired from directing the Centre in 2003, and become Research Professor in History, Edward continued to write, including reviews for the *Times Literary Supplement*, down to late 2017. He published in 2013 a study of Viennese modernism entitled *Dynamik der Kreise, Resonanz der Räume: Die schöpferischen Impulse der Wiener Moderne* (Weitra), and in 2016 he edited further archival material as *Anna Haag and her Secret Diary of the Second World War: a Democratic German Feminist's Response to the Catastrophe of National Socialism* (Oxford). Some outstanding articles are to be reprinted by Legenda. Other papers remain unpublished, as well as a long-cherished but probably incomplete draft for a book, *Freud and the Aesthetics of the Dream*.

Many honours arrived from both Austria and Britain. Edward received the Austrian State Prize for the History of the Social Sciences in 2002, the Austrian Cross of Honour for Arts and Sciences in 2008, and the Decoration of Honour in Gold for Services to the Province of Vienna in 2013. He was awarded the OBE for services to scholarship in 2005 and elected a Fellow of the British Academy the following year.

Everyone who knew Edward will remember his unfailing humanity, self-control, patience, kindness and forbearance. The closest approach to irritation I saw in him was when he told me, I forget why, that I had strong defence mechanisms. It was true, and salutary; I realise now that Edward must have recognised a resemblance to his

[10] See my review in *Translation and Literature*, 25 (2016), 256–62.

own younger self. He and Saime encouraged me at least to say 'I feel' rather than 'I think'. Some very English emotional reserve, instilled by his upbringing, lingered, but was counterbalanced by his sociability and talent for friendship.

Edward loved collaborative enterprises and was a natural networker. In the 1980s he helped to bring large numbers of Cambridge colleagues together to plan and compose books of essays on themes arising from the 'Avant-Garde' paper.[11] Involvement in a collective enterprise was a refreshing break from the usual isolation of academic study, though the editors faced some unexpected difficulties. The introduction that Raymond Williams supplied for one volume had a page missing, and as Williams, who died in 1988, was by then too ill to be consulted, the editors had to write a page themselves in an imitation of Williams's style. Edward made a point of reaching out to people. Travelling with him in a Vienna taxi, I remember him chatting to the taxi-driver in the latter's native Turkish. This friendliness could bring unforeseen rewards. In his autobiography Edward tells how, during a conference at the Austrian Cultural Forum, he addressed a complete stranger, who turned out to be the exile writer Jakov Lind; as a result of their acquaintance, Edward arranged a symposium followed by a publication on Lind's work.[12] Part of the motivation for his turn to Exile Studies was, I am sure, the scope it offered for getting to know exiles and their families, all of whom had memories and in some cases written archives that needed to be preserved.

A sign of the wide affection Edward inspired was an event held at the Stadt- und Landesbibliothek in Vienna on 27 March 2019. At the formal opening of an exhibition on Karl Kraus, organised by Katharina Prager, words were spoken in Edward's memory by Hubert Christian Ehalt and Friedrich Stadler, honouring his achievements and recalling his unique personality.

From the family vicarage, after the fading of Christian belief, Edward retained a strong moral seriousness which shows in all his writing. He also had a distinctively modernist sensibility, finding in the clean lines and clear thinking of the European (especially Viennese) avant-garde a rejection both of fussy ornamentation and of outdated social prejudices. (The downside was an impatience with remote literary conventions; he once told me he could not take Schiller's *Wilhelm Tell* seriously.) He had a very strong visual sense and a deep knowledge and appreciation of painting: I remember a fine, still unpublished lecture he gave at Yarnton Manor, at that time the base for the Oxford Centre for Jewish and Hebrew Studies, contrasting the frank

---

[11] E. Timms and D. Kelley (eds.), *Unreal City: Urban Experience in Modern European Literature and Art* (Manchester, 1985); E. Timms and P. Collier (eds.), *Visions and Blueprints: Avant-Garde Culture and Radical Politics in Early Twentieth-Century Europe*, with a foreword by Raymond Williams (Manchester, 1988); E. Timms and J. Davies (eds.), *Modernism and the European Unconscious* (Cambridge, 1990).
[12] Timms, *Taking Up the Torch*, p. 249; E. Timms, A. Hammel and S. Hassler (eds.), *Writing after Hitler: the Work of Jakov Lind* (Cardiff, 2001).

eroticism of Viennese modernist painting with the comparatively buttoned-up sexuality of its Bloomsbury counterparts. A paper he did publish, on Kokoschka, deserves to be widely known.[13] His aesthetic sense was conspicuous in the illustrations to his books and lectures and even in the design of brochures and other details accompanying the conferences he organised.

Edward's moral commitment helps also to account for the liberating, un-academic quality of his scholarship. The preface to *Taking up the Torch* consists of a two-page list of questions that arose at different stages in his life, including 'How are children affected by the approach of war?' and 'How should settled citizens respond to the plight of refugees, and why are those lost at sea so easily forgotten?' These, and the others in the list, are not the kind of 'research questions' that you would expect to meet nowadays in a funding application. Nor is it immediately obvious how one would frame a research programme to answer them. Yet they have an obvious and compelling human importance. It is in fact possible to approach these questions through historical, biographical, archival and literary research, and, staying with these two examples, Edward did so by looking at the development of child psychology in the 'Red Vienna' of the 1920s and its transplantation by exiles to London, and at maritime disasters in which ships sank that were crowded with refugees—one case is the *Wilhelm Gustloff*, whose history Günter Grass examined in *Im Krebsgang* (2004).[14] His example shows that the best research is powered, sometimes indirectly, by deep personal concern and refined by well-tried research techniques and by the academic virtues of industry, judiciousness, distance and clarity. It can be said—as of how few academic publications—that everything Edward produced needed to be written.[15]

Note on the author: Ritchie Robertson is Taylor Professor of German at the University of Oxford. He was elected a Fellow of the British Academy in 2004.

---

[13] E. Timms, 'Kokoschka's pictographs—a contextual reading', *Word and Image*, 6 (1990), 4–17.

[14] See E. Timms, 'New approaches to child psychology: from Red Vienna to the Hampstead Nursery', in E. Timms and J. Hughes (eds.), *Intellectual Migration and Cultural Transformation: Refugees from National Socialism in the English-Speaking World* (Vienna and New York, 2003), pp. 219–39; E. Timms, 'Remembering refugees lost at sea: the *Struma*, the *Wilhelm Gustloff* and the *Cap Anamur*', in A. Stephens and R. Walden (eds.), *For the Sake of Humanity: Essays in Honour of Clemens N. Nathan* (Leiden, 2006), pp. 325–49.

[15] A full listing to 2007 can be found in R. Robertson, 'Edward Timms: a bibliography', in J. Beniston, R. Robertson and R. Vilain (eds.), *Austrian Satire and Other Essays. Austrian Studies*, 15 (2007), 6–14.

CLAUDE LÉVI-STRAUSS

Claude Lévi-Strauss

28 November 1908 – 30 October 2009

Elected Corresponding Fellow of the British Academy 1966*

by

JAMES J. FOX

Claude Lévi-Strauss was a major figure in anthropology. In 1959 he was appointed to the Chair of Social Anthropology at the Collège de France, a position he held, with considerable intellectual flourish, for twenty-three years. In a lifetime of over a century, he remained productive into his nineties, propounding a form of analysis that became popularly known as 'structuralism'. His publications included major works on the foundations of kinship, on systems of complex social classification and on the logic of myth. Elected to the Académie française, Lévi-Strauss eventually became Dean of the French Academy.

* Biographical Memoirs are not commissioned for Corresponding Fellows of the British Academy, but it was thought appropriate to mark the tenth anniversary of the death of Claude Lévi-Strauss in this way.

CLAUDE LÉVI-STRAUSS

When Claude Lévi-Strauss was elected to the British Academy in July 1966 he was recognised and acclaimed as the leading anthropologist in France. His reputation was based on a global recognition that extended well beyond anthropology. Born on 28 November 1908, he lived to be over 100 and continued writing well into his nineties. He was enormously prolific, writing some sixteen books and numerous papers that were, even by French standards, remarkably varied. He was a public figure who was frequently interviewed for his engaging opinions on diverse subjects and his academic career was indeed stellar. When he died on 30 October 2009, he had become Dean of the Académie française and its oldest member.

Lévi-Strauss came from a distinguished artistic family that originated from Alsace. During World War I he lived with his maternal grandfather who was the rabbi of the Versailles synagogue. After the war and the return with his family to Paris, his father, Raymond, saw that he was thoroughly steeped in the arts, especially in opera and classical music. For a time, he took lessons in violin. He studied first at the Lycée Janson-de-Sailly and then at the Lycée Condorcet and began a study of Law before being admitted to the Sorbonne to study philosophy, placed third in his agrégation in 1931. None of this early education signalled a career in anthropology.

A turning point in his life was an invitation from Célestin Bouglé, the then Director of the École Normale Supérieure, to join the French mission to Brazil. From 1935 to 1938 he became Professor of Sociology at the University of Sâo Paulo, during which time he organised various expeditions to the Mato Grosso and the Amazon. In 1939, he resigned his position to be able to conduct more extended research among the Nambikwara and other populations of Brazil's interior. Unlike British anthropologists of his generation, Lévi-Strauss carried out his investigations, not as a single fieldworker attempting, over an extended period of residence within a community, to master a language for essential communication, but as a member of a team with multiple goals and with relatively little local language skills.

On his return to France, Lévi-Strauss was mobilised to the frontline but was then released because of his Jewish heritage. For a time thereafter he taught in Montpellier in the south of France but in 1941 managed to flee to the United States where he took up a position at the New School of Research. At the New School, he met the linguist Roman Jakobson, whose theories of structural analysis in linguistics had a significant influence on him. In 1942 he became one of the founding members of the École Libre des Hautes Études (The Free School of Advanced Study) which was a university in exile of outstanding French intellectuals. He stayed on in the United States until 1947, serving as the cultural attaché to the French Embassy in Washington.

When he returned to France, Lévi-Strauss' academic career involved a succession of distinguished appointments. He submitted, defended and was awarded his doctoral degree in 1948. He became assistant director at the Musée de l'Homme from 1949 to

1950; then director of anthropological studies at the École Practique des Hautes Études from 1950 to 1974. In 1959, he was elected to the Chair of Social Anthropology at the Collège de France, which he held from 1959 to 1982. In 1973 he became a member of the Académie française and in the same year received the Erasmus prize. In 2009, at the age of 100, he became Dean of the Académie. Throughout his career, he produced an array of notable publications but as he grew older he could not but decry the sad destruction of the earth and its diversity, a theme he had already signalled in his early writings. Lévi-Strauss died on 30 October 2009.

Foundational work: 1945–62

Lévi-Strauss' opus is daunting, remarkably varied and extends well beyond any simple labels. His career can best be charted by a consideration of the major works in this formidable opus, each of which offered a distinct contribution to anthropology.

Lévi-Strauss' first publication in 1948 was a short monograph, *La Vie familiale et sociale des Indiens Nambikwara*, that compiled his ethnographic investigations on one of the tribal groups, the Nambikwara, on whom he had concentrated his attention while in Brazil.

His first major publication was his thesis, *Les Structures élémentaires de la parenté*, which appeared in 1949. This is a massive work conceived on a grand scale and executed with considerable flair across a range of issues. The study's broad ambitions are unmistakeable: its title invokes Durkheim's *Les Formes élémentaires de la vie religieuse,* locating it directly within the French sociological tradition; its dedication to Lewis Henry Morgan, the founder of comparative kinship studies, situates the work within an American tradition of anthropology while its substantial focus on addressing issues in Radcliffe-Brown's research places it squarely in the British social anthropology tradition. *Elementary Structures* is certainly the work that established Lévi-Strauss' reputation as a major anthropological figure.

Lévi-Strauss initiates his work as a study of universals with an extended discussion of the transition from nature to culture and of the 'problem of incest' recalling previous approaches including, in particular, Durkheim's long disquisition on incest in the first volume of the *L'Année Sociologique* (1898). At its core, however, is an application of Marcel Mauss' ideas of reciprocity and exchange, as developed in his *Essai sur le don* (1925; translation: *The Gift*) intelligently applied to the structuring of different forms of marriage. Lévi-Strauss begins with an interpretation of the incest prohibition as a positive rule to marry out and proceeds to define cross-cousin marriage as an 'elementary' structure of exchange, drawing a crucial distinction between systems of 'restricted exchange' requiring immediate reciprocity and systems of 'generalised exchange' that depend on an extended and thereby delayed reciprocity.

Lévi-Strauss begins his analysis with Australian marriage systems based on the work of Radcliffe-Brown. Most Australian systems, of which the Kariera and Aranda are good examples, are characterised by restricted exchange. A significant change, however, occurs at the northern end of Australia with the Murngin whose marriage is supposedly based on exclusive matrilateral cross-cousin marriage. This marriage system thus constitutes a structural transformation from restricted to generalised exchange. From Australia, Lévi-Strauss directs his analysis to Asia, focusing first on generalised exchange among societies in mainland Southeast Asia such as the Katchin, Lahker, Kuki and various Naga groups of Assam, then proceeding to forms of generalised exchange among the Gilyak of Siberia before considering the possibility of restricted exchange in ancient China and, more briefly, similar possibilities in India.

In his conclusion, Lévi-Strauss identifies an axis of generalised exchange extending from Burma to eastern Siberia with a variety of mixed systems in-between and forms of restricted exchange in China. For him, 'matrilateral marriage represents the most lucid and fruitful of the simple forms of reciprocity' (*Elementary Structures*, 1969, 451). Finally, after trumpeting the distinction between restricted and generalised exchange and tracing the distribution of these forms of marriage in Australia, Asia and elsewhere, Lévi-Strauss goes on to suggest a transition from elementary forms to complex forms, which, as it happens, constitute the majority of the world's systems of kinship and marriage.

It is this supposed transition that is highly questionable. (Lévi-Strauss relies on the different senses of 'elementary' as both logically simple and as prior in development.) There is, however, nothing simple about most of the terminological systems he describes and the exchange practices they require: they are sophisticated and elaborate and this applies especially as he advances his argument ever more speculatively into Asia. The book in fact deals with relatively few of the world's kinship systems, many of which could also be considered 'elementary'. Perhaps most interestingly is the fact that in this book and during the rest of his career Lévi-Strauss made no similar, serious incursion into the study of the variety of Brazilian systems of kinship and marriage.

One of the first and most significant early responses to *Elementary Structures* appeared in Edmund Leach's long essay, 'The structural implications of matrilateral cross-cousin marriage' (1951; reprint 1961). In his forthright fashion, Leach wrote:

> In the course of a long, thorough, rapid journey through the ethnography of all Australia and most of mainland Asia, Lévi-Strauss scatters in profusion analytical suggestions of the greatest brilliance. But too often these ideas are misapplied, either because of weakness of ethnographic detail, or because the author is in too much of a hurry to get on to bigger and more exciting things. (1961, 77)

In the case of the Katchin, who were Leach's special focus of analysis, Lévi-Strauss is accused of 'inexcusable carelessness'. Nonetheless, Lévi-Strauss' 'wholly original theoretical suggestions ... are of the utmost importance for a proper understanding of the Katchin situation' (1961, 78). Leach defends Lévi-Strauss' use of models as essential for comparative analysis but argues that a model is an interpretive vehicle that should not be confused with ethnographic reality. This in brief can be taken to epitomise what became a repeated British response to Lévi-Strauss' methods.

Another substantial response to Lévi-Strauss' treatise came from J. P. B. de Josselin de Jong, the professor of anthropology at Leiden University who held an ongoing seminar on Lévi-Strauss' ideas in 1950–1. The seminar, which was attended by Rodney Needham, who had recently finished his DPhil at Oxford, resulted in a long exegesis and critique of *Elementary Structures* entitled *Lévi-Strauss' Theory on Kinship and Marriage* (1952; reprint 1977).

Josselin de Jong, his students and colleagues had since the mid-1930s been engaged in developing their own distinctive ideas about marriage alliance or what they referred to as 'circulating connubium'. In his inaugural address, 'The Malay Archipelago as an ethnographic field of study' (1935), Josselin de Jong postulated a connubial triad of bride-giving clans linked in ceremonial exchange requiring each partner to provide 'male' or 'female' goods in opposite directions and with wife-givers taking precedence over wife-takers. Underlying these clan relations was supposed to be a combination of double unilineal descent coupled with a thorough-going dual cosmology.

In his dissertation, *Sociale Stuctuurtypen in de Groote Oost* (1935; translation: *Types of Social Stucture in Eastern Indonesia*, 1968), F. A. E. van Wouden, who was Josselin de Jong's principal student, recognised that: (1) cross-cousin marriage is the logical expression of a systematic communication of women among larger descent groups; (2) the 'lineality' of the descent groups is theoretically immaterial to forms of connubium; (3) 'ordinary' cross-cousin (MBD/FZD) marriage—what Lévi-Strauss later labelled 'restricted exchange'—and 'exclusive' cross-cousin (MBD) marriage—what Lévi-Strauss labelled 'generalized exchange'—represented two opposed systems of affinal relationships between groups; (4) exclusive marriage with the FZD would make a systematic ordering of affinal relationships between groups impossible; and (5) an integral system of affinal relationships based on exclusive cross-cousin marriage would number at least three clans but could also be composed of any larger number of clans linked in a 'closed chain of marriage connexions'.

Whereas Mauss' idea of reciprocity expounded in the *The Gift* was critical for Lévi-Strauss, a key source for the 'Leiden School' was Durkheim and Mauss' essay on primitive classification, 'De quelques formes primitives de classification' (1903; translation: *Primitive Classification*, 1963). Directed marriage, particularly exclusive cross-cousin marriage, was the social basis for the establishment of coherent systems of dual and tripartite classification. A concordance of social and symbolic systems in the form of local dual cosmologies was regarded as the critical feature of these connubial exchanges.

In *Elementary Structures*, Lévi-Strauss had skirted the Indonesian archipelago in his transition from Australia to mainland Asia. He was completely unaware of the work of the Leiden School—whose importance he later indirectly acknowledged by offering his paper 'Do dual organizations exist' in recognition of 'the daring and fruitfulness of Professor J. P. B. de Josselin de Jong's theoretical ideas' (1956, 99; 1967, 128).

The key linking figure in this equation was Rodney Needham who was critically important in interpreting Lévi-Strauss and the Leiden School to a wider English-speaking audience and in trying to reconcile these two distinctive approaches, especially in making available through English translations the sources of their ideas. His translations of Durkheim and Mauss' *Primitive Classification*, Van Wouden's *Types of Social Structure in Eastern Indonesia* and Lévi-Strauss' *Totemism* and *The Elementary Structures of Kinship*, in particular, were directed to these ends.

Like Leach, Needham was wary of the imprecision of many of Lévi-Strauss' propositions and analyses. He insisted that advances in the field came from the quality of one's analytic concepts. For Needham, the distinction between 'preference' and 'prescription' was crucial: prescription is defined categorically by a society's terminological system. Lévi-Strauss frequently used the term 'preferred' in reference to those marriage systems, for which there is an obligation to marry a particular category of cousin. For Needham, all these systems were 'prescriptive' whereas the term 'preferred' was reserved for strategic, selective and therefore optional forms of directed marriage. Restricted exchange based on bilateral cross-cousin marriage in Needham's terminology became symmetric prescriptive alliance; while generalised exchange based on matrilateral cross-cousin marriage became asymmetric prescriptive alliance.

Equally important for Needham is the recognition of levels. At different levels of conceptualisation and practice, systems can be both prescriptive and preferential. In an analysis of a 'Murngin type' society, the Wik-Mungkin, Needham argued that the terminology as a whole is symmetric, but at the level of exchanging groups there is a preference for the matrilateral cousin.[1]

---

[1] The Wik-Mungkin case was Needham's chief analytic venture (1963) into the study of Australian kinship but its importance prompted recurrent assessment (see Needham, 1971, xlix–lii). The combination of symmetry and asymmetry is of common occurrence in other marriage systems, as for example the Atoni Pah Meto of Timor who have a symmetric terminology but regularly contract strategic marriages asymmetrically (Fox, 1999).

A key study was *Structure and Sentiment* (1962) in which Needham encapsulated his early interpretation of *Elementary Structures*. The essay is also an extended examination of the matrilateral marriage system of the Purum of Manipur presented in 'Leiden mode', analysing the Purum terminology, alliance cycles and dyadic symbolic classification. In the end, Needham analysed more than a dozen other instances of what he defined as prescriptive alliance

However, in the Preface to the revised edition of his *Elementary Structures* (French, 1967; English translation, 1969), Lévi-Strauss made it clear that he rejected Needham's interpretation of his work, insisting that the distinction between prescription and preference was a matter of degree and *Elementary Structures* was intended to embrace both forms of marriage. As he himself points out, accepting Needham's understanding would render Leach's s critique a valid assessment. Leach's view of *Elementary Structures*, which Lévi-Strauss quotes, was wincingly to the point: 'Since the "elementary structures" which he discusses are decidedly unusual they seem to provide a rather flimsy base for a "general theory".' Leach's conclusion was that Lévi-Strauss' ambitious attempt at a universal theory delivered in a magisterial manner was 'a splendid failure'.[2]

By whatever interpretation it is judged, *Les Structures élémentaires* was a major comparative effort and established Lévi-Strauss immediately in the front ranks of contemporary anthropologists.

Compared with the technical demands of his *Elementary Structures*, Lévi-Strauss' *Tristes Tropiques*, published in 1955 (English translation: *Tristes Tropiques*, 1967), was an immediately accessible literary work—a personal account of Lévi-Strauss' discovery of anthropology as an intellectual discipline and his anthropological efforts to begin to understand several Brazilian Indian societies—the Nambikwara, Tupi-Kawahib, Cadiveo and Bororo—whom he encountered during his various expeditions into the interior of Brazil.

Particularly revealing is his account of his disillusionment with philosophy and how the study of geology, psychoanalysis and Marxism—what Lévi-Strauss called his "three mistresses"—all 'showed that understanding consists in the reduction of one kind of reality to another' (1967, 61). This quest for the structure beyond the structure—the pattern behind immediate empirical evidence—is a defining feature of Lévi-Strauss' methodology. A striking analogy that he used to explain this quest came in a reply to David Maybury-Lewis' (1960) criticism of his analysis of dual organisations. In his response, 'On manipulated sociological models' (1960), Lévi-Strauss castigates 'the naturalistic misconceptions which have so long pervaded the British school' in

---

[2] Leach (1965, 20), quoted in *The Elementary Structures of Kinship*, Preface to the Second Edition, 1969, p. xxxi.

which 'social structure is like a kind of jig-saw puzzle, and everything is achieved when one has discovered how the pieces fit together'. He then goes on to advance an analogy to hint at his own deeper methodological ambitions.

> But, if the pieces have been arbitrarily cut, there is no structure at all. On the other hand, if, as is sometimes done, the pieces were automatically cut in different shapes by a mechanical saw, the movements of which are regularly modified by a cam-shaft, the structure of the puzzle exists, not at the empirical level (since there are many ways of recognising the pieces which fit together): its key lies in the mathematical formula expressing the shape of the cams and their speed of rotation; something very remote from the puzzle as it appears to the player, although it "explains" the puzzle in the one and only intelligible way. (1960, 52)

Equally revealing, in his *Tristes Tropiques*, is his explanation of what a comparative social understanding requires. In his words, all human societies 'choose certain combinations from a repertory of ideas which it should be possible to reconstitute. For this one must make an inventory of the customs that have been observed ... [and] with all this one could eventually establish a sort of periodic chart of chemical elements, analogous to that devised by Mendeleir' (1967, 160). From the beginning, Lévi-Strauss' methodology was elemental, combinatorial, naturalistic and, above all, cerebral.

Anthropologie structurale (1958; English translation: *Structural Anthropology*, 1963), which, when it appeared, was taken as a manifesto of a new intellectual approach to the study of society, consists of seventeen key essays that can be considered to epitomise Lévi-Strauss' 'structuralist' programme. This collection includes papers originally published between 1945 and 1956 and, if read in retrospect, can be seen to set out the foundations for much of his later, more sophisticated investigations.

In 'Structural analysis in linguistics and in anthropology' (originally dating from 1945), for example, Lévi-Strauss reveals the source of his idea of structural analysis and the basis of the binarism he would notably promote. Written at the time of his close association with the linguist Roman Jakobson, Lévi-Strauss makes the grandiose assertion that 'structural linguistics will certainly play the same renovating role with respect to the social sciences that nuclear physics...has played for the physical sciences'. Quoting N. Trubetzkoy, 'the illustrious founder of structural linguistics', Lévi-Strauss identifies 'four basic operations' that Trubetzkoy set for structural linguistics: 1) a shift from conscious linguistic phenomena to unconscious infrastructure; 2) analysis based on relations between terms, rather than as individual entities; 3) the treatment of these relations as a system; and 4) the aim to discover general laws by either induction or deduction (1963, 41). On the basis of these criteria, Lévi-Strauss draws an analogy between the phoneme and basic kinship terms and then, in an analysis that is recognisably and remarkably his own, he goes on to illustrate these 'distinctive features' in what he defines as the 'atom of kinship' using simple valency markers (**+/-**) to structure his oppositions.

In 'The structural study of myth' (published originally in 1955), he proposes an analytic stance, which he would carry forward in his later mythological analyses, arguing that myth must be 'treated as an orchestra score'. His use of valency markers (**+/-**) continues but these markers are now applied to specific binary categories (gods/men; fibres/sinews, etc) that serve as the specific concrete operators in his analysis.

Another crucially important Russian influence was the master work by Vladimir Propp, *Morphology of the Folktale* (1958), which Lévi-Strauss encountered in English translation soon after it appeared and responded to in 'L'analyse morphologique des contes Russes' (1960) in an effort to distinguish his structuralism from Russian formalism.[3]

These early articles, possibly as bold and provocative as any of his later more extended analyses, are fundamental to understanding his subsequent development.[4] Structuralism is offered as a technique for tracing the transformation of relations among symbolic entities. As such, it is concerned with meaning as a relational concept. However, for a methodology that claims to be universal, it must ultimately be replicable. As critics have frequently noted, Lévi-Strauss' scintillating forays in analysis reflect an intellectual virtuosity that is difficult to repeat.

Continuing work: 1962–91

Le Totémisme aujourd'hui (1962; English translation: *Totemism*, 1964) and *La Pensée sauvage* (1962; English translation: *The Savage Mind*, 1968) can be considered together. Both were published in the same year and were directed to an examination of the logic of complex classification. In *Totemism*, Lévi-Strauss endeavours to dispel a categorical illusion in anthropology—the misconception that certain relations linking individuals, groups and their particular animal or vegetable species emblems constitute some unique form of classificatory arrangement. In attacking such conceptual distortions, he engages in an extended commentary on the diverse ethnographic

---

[3] It was Lévi-Strauss who recommended Propp's work to Roland Barthes, a gesture which is credited with giving rise to Barthes' notion of 'narrativity'.

[4] Lévi-Strauss' opus is a complex web of initial papers followed by multiple reconsiderations. For example, Lévi-Strauss gave further consideration to his 'atom of kinship' in a paper, 'Réflexions sur l'atome de parenté', published in *L'Homme* in 1973 (included in his *Structural Anthropology II*) and later in another paper, 'Discussion sur l'atome de parenté', in *Paroles données* (1984). As his opus grew, Lévi-Strauss increasingly became his own chief interlocutor.

approaches of generations of 'Anglo-Saxon' anthropology from Fraser, Malinowski and Radcliffe-Brown, Boas, Lowie and Kroeber, to Stanner, Strehlow, Elkin, Firth, Fortes and even Evans-Pritchard. For a work that some might say involved 'beating a dead horse', this book is an intellectual tour de force. Lévi-Strauss even manages to enlist both Rousseau and Comte in support of his basic argument.

La Pensée sauvage resumes the argument begun in *Totemism*. (Key chapters are 'The logic of totemic classification' and 'Totem and caste'.) A profusion of detailed ethnographic examples of systems of complex classification, drawn from around the world, is stunningly arrayed to support his argument that 'the savage mind' is intellectually and sophisticatedly engaged with understanding the world: it distinguishes, analyses, and classifies, making use of specific 'concrete' operators whose logic is productive and transformative. In Lévi-Strauss' words: 'The savage mind totalizes' (p. 245). His efforts at interpretation constitute a 'science of the concrete' and are ultimately intended to 'legitimate the principles of savage thought' (p. 269). The final chapter of the volume takes issue with Sartre's *Critique de la raison dialectique* (1960) by asking whether the savage mind also engages in dialectic reasoning as well as analytic reasoning.

In all Lévi-Strauss' work, there is a considerable degree of intellectual play. His French can be elusive and often his allusions and plays on words do not carry over well into English. A striking example of this occurs on the cover of the French edition of *La Pensée sauvage* which is illustrated with a large coloured drawing of a 'wild pansy' (*pansée sauvage*).

Lévi-Strauss' mythological researches occupied most of his life. His first myth analyses date from the mid-1950s; the beginnings of his extended research on South American mythology date from the early 1960s and these researches were extended through the mythologies of Americas to the Northwest Coast, whose split-representational art had been of special interest to him from the mid-1940s. The result was his grand *Mythologiques* quartet—*Le Cru et la cuit* (1964; translated as *The Raw and the Cooked*, 1970); *Du Miel aux cendres* (1966; *From Honey to Ashes*, 1973); *L'Origine des Manières de Table* (1968; *The Origin of Table Manners*, 1978); and *L'Homme nu* (1971; *The Naked Man*, 1981)—plus three *petits mythologiques*—*La Voie des masques* (1975; *The Way of the Masks*, 1982); *La Potière jalousie* (1985; *The Jealous Potter*, 1988); and *Histoire de lynx* (1991; *The Story of Lynx*, 1995). Together these books constitute an enormous intellectual construction representing an almost obsessive research effort spanning half a century.

Lévi-Strauss' *Mythologiques* (given the English designation: *The Science of Mythology*) can best be regarded as orchestral creation that takes as its score all of the Amerindian mythologies of South and North America. Volume I, *The Raw and the Cooked*, is the overture to this grand symphony. It begins with the examination of a

Bororo myth (M 1) on 'the origin of water' and then goes on to examine an aria of Gé myths on 'the origin of fire'; it carries on, with a further chorus, to M 137. Still focused on South America, Volume II, *From Honey to Ashes*, proceeds to M 353; Volume III, *The Origin of Table Manners*, ventures into North America and carries its myth analysis to M 528; while, finally, Volume IV, *The Naked Man,* moves through a host of North American myths, particularly from the Northwest coast, before returning to a final Apinayé myth, M 813, on 'the putrefied man'. This numbering does not give an adequate idea of the full extent of the myths that Lévi-Strauss actually analyses.

Many of the myths under consideration have numerous alternative versions: M 682 has alternate versions 'a' to 'e', as do M 687 and M 752. The intricacy of this analysis is enormous and demanding since it does not follow a linear progression. Lévi-Strauss regularly shifts his attention to myths that he has previously considered in earlier volumes. His technical analysis retains his basic valences (+/-) but expands to include notions of 'conjunction', 'disjunction', 'identity', 'difference' and, his most frequently used opposition, that of 'inversion'. In addition to the recurrent binary operators such as male/female, night/day, sun/moon, many of Lévi-Strauss' specific concrete operators are as startling as the myths from which they derive: raw/cooked, boiled/rotten, foetus/penis, hummingbird/woodpecker. Throughout the *Mythologiques,* fire, and with it cooking, is the transformative means that marks the transition from nature to culture. Besides the myths themselves, the most engaging feature of Lévi-Strauss' continuing presentation is the detailed ethnographical and ecological commentary that accompanies his myth analysis.

After the appearance of the first volume of the *Mythologiques*, Lévi-Strauss postponed any attempt to explain his work until the end of his efforts. The final volume, however, leaves much unexplained. He argues tentatively that his work was only possible because all the myths of the Americas constitute a single myth told and retold over millennia. What one is to make of the work as a theoretical whole is by no means clear.

Lévi-Strauss' *Mythologiques* is his masterwork and the culminating effort of a long intellectual trajectory. Although he continued to produce important work along with, and after, his Mythologiques,[5] this daunting and exuberant opus is a monument that may well entice future interpretation or simply be left undeciphered and possibly ignored.

---

[5] He published a second volume of *Anthropologie structurale* II (1973; English translation: *Structural Anthropology* II, 1977). Another work, *Le Regard éloigné* (1983; English translation: *A View from Afar*, 1985), offers retrospective reflections on his work beginning with a return to his earlier study, *Race et histoire* (1952).

***

Lévi-Strauss was a public figure who never ceased to explain himself and to offer commentary on his work in newspapers, op-ed articles and particularly in recorded interviews at different stages in his career. Two best-known interviews are George Charbonnier's *Conversations with Claude Lévi-Strauss* (1961; English 1969), which were recorded in 1959 and are concerned more with his methods, and Didier Eribon's *Conversations with Claude Lévi-Strauss* (1988; English 1991), which were recorded decades later and provide reminiscences of his involvement with major intellectual figures of his era.

Of his British contemporaries, Edmund Leach remained the most sympathetic to Lévi-Strauss' ideas, writing a short book, *Claude Lévi-Strauss* for the Modern Masters series (1970).[6] Sensibly and selectively directed to Lévi-Strauss' methods of analysis of myth and elementary kin relations, this is a readable and largely positive rendering of Lévi-Strauss' contribution to social anthropology. By contrast Rodney Needham's assessment, 'Anthropology's Pope', originally published anonymously in the *Times Literary Supplement* (1968) in the aftermath of his falling out with Lévi-Strauss, is less than flattering. Written as a review of a volume of the *Association of Social Anthropologists* offered as critical homage to Lévi-Strauss, *The Structural Study of Myth and Totemism* (Leach, 1968),[7] Needham's assessment allows him to survey his colleagues' understandings. Particularly pertinent is the 'Introduction' by Leach and papers by Kenelm Burridge, Mary Douglas, Peter Worsley and Nur Yalman, all of whom express varying degrees of questioning admiration and outright scepticism. Mary Douglas captures this sentiment with the observation: 'whenever anthropologists apply structural analysis to myth they extract not only a different but a lesser

---

[6] Commentary on Lévi-Strauss's work by his French colleagues, former students, and successors is considerable and notable. One important critical assessment is that by Maurice Godelier: *Claude Lévi-Strauss: a Critical Study of His Thought* (2018). Also worth mentioning is Michel Izard's *Lévi-Strauss* (2004). Perhaps most important because of its scope and the remarkable number of contributors is the two-volume tribute offered to Lévi-Strauss on his 60th birthday: Jean Pouillon and Pierre Maranda (eds.), *Échanges et communications: Mélanges offerts à Claude Lévi-Strauss* (1970). Substantial biographies are also available: E. Loyer, *Lévi-Strauss* (2015: English translation, 2018); P. Wilcken, *Claude Lévi-Strauss* (2010).

[7] The French equivalent of this work is *La function symbolique* edited by Michel Izard and Pierre Smith (1979) and dedicated to Lévi-Strauss, which includes fourteen papers by distinguished anthropologists, mainly French colleagues closely associated with Lévi-Strauss. It is, however, of interest that the two most prominent figures in anthropology in Paris, Lévi-Strauss and Louis Dumont, whose work overlapped significantly, barely acknowledged each other. Lévi-Strauss cited Louis Dumont as a 'competent colleague' in the Preface to the 2nd edition of his *Elementary Structures* and Dumont offered his analysis on Kariera kinship to the Pouillon and Maranda volume for Lévi-Strauss (1970, 1983) without ever referring to Lévi-Strauss' earlier work on Kariera marriage systems.

meaning.' In his conclusion, Needham quotes Leach: 'Lévi-Strauss often manages to give me ideas even when I don't know what he is saying' but Needham counters this attitude, characteristically, by arguing that 'scholars ought rather to demand the more sober, inconspicuous, and enduring accomplishments of clarity, exactitude and validity.'

Lévi-Strauss' work is the most extensive, intellectually versatile and subtly sophisticated of any anthropologist who has contributed to the discipline of anthropology. For this reason, it may be far too early to venture an assessment of his achievement. It can be said, however, that all his varied studies highlighted the central value of ethnography and his influence, particularly in France, contributed to the continuing pursuit of high-quality ethnographic research within the field of anthropology.

In late November 1962, I travelled from Oxford to Paris to hear Lévi-Strauss lecture. He was then at the height of his recognition with the publication that year of *La Pensée sauvage.* His 'structuralism' attracted enormous attention. After two previous failed attempts at appointment, he had been elected to the Collège de France and his lectures were given in one of the Collège's large lecture halls. I arrived early and was able to find a seat but by the time Lévi-Strauss began, the huge lecture hall was packed with students sitting in the aisles, on the windowsills and standing in the back.

His lecture was his introduction to the *Mythologiques*—the beginnings of the initial volume in the series, *Le Cru et le fruit*, replete with savage pigs, cunning jaguars and the origin of fire. The presentation was intense and spellbinding, though I hardly understood what he was doing or attempting to do. When the lecture was over, in foreigner fashion, I tried asking some of the French students who had been sitting with me if they had grasped what Lévi-Strauss had been presenting but I could find no one who claimed to have understood. It hardly seemed to matter. He had captivated his audience and his following lecture was just as crowded.

To this day, I remember those lectures for their ambience and impact. I can hardly imagine anyone else giving a series of lectures like that—barely intelligible to most of the audience—and yet able to maintain by force of presentation rapt attention and the apparent conviction that what was being expounded was indeed profound and relevant.

Lévi-Strauss clearly had the capacity to enthral. He generated an aura of wisdom with a delphic intelligibility. He was a great mythologist—the great mythographer! He partook of what he studied and made himself part of his own mythology. This is why *Tristes Tropiques* and the various volumes of interviews with him are so engaging. Mythology and autobiography merged, allowing him at times to explain pre-literate cultures by reference to himself.

If Lévi-Strauss was the great mythologist, he was also the great tempter. He posed for anthropology a goal that is probably all but unattainable. If it had been attainable, it would doubtlessly have transformed anthropology into an entirely different field. Nonetheless throughout his career, Lévi-Strauss continued to offer the temptation— the search for a code, formula, schema that existed behind human phenomena as they presented themselves.

Note on the author: James J. Fox is Professor Emeritus in the College of Asia and Pacific Affairs at the Australian National University.

Bibliography

Works by Claude Lévi-Strauss
La Vie familiale et sociale des Indiens Nambikwara (Paris, 1948).
Les Structures élementaires de la parenté (Paris, 1949).
Race et histoire (Paris, 1952).
Tristes Tropiques (Paris, 1955). *Tristes Tropiques* (New York, 1967) [also under the title, *World on the Wane*].
Anthropologie structurale (Paris, 1958). *Structural Anthropology* (New York, 1963).
'Les organisation dualistic existent-elles?' *Bijdragen tot de Taal-, Land- en Volkenkunde*, 112 (1956): 99–128 [English translation in *Structural Anthropology*, pp. 128–60].
'On manipulated sociological models', *Bijdragen tot te Taal-, Land- en Volkenkunde*, 116 (1960): 45–54.
'L'Analyse morphologique des contes Russes', *International Journal of Slavic Poetics and Linguistics*, 3 (1960), 122–49.
Le Totémisme aujourd'hui (Paris, 1962). *Totemism* (London, 1964).
La Pensée sauvage (Paris, 1962). *The Savage Mind* (London, 1968).
Mythologiques (1964–71)
    Le Cru et la cuit (Paris, 1964). *The Raw and the Cooked* (London, 1970).
    Du Miel aux cendres (Paris, 1966). *From Honey to Ashes* (London, 1973).
    L'Origine des manières de table (Paris, 1968). *The Origin of Table Manners* (London, 1978).
    L'Homme nu (Paris, 1971). *The Naked Man* (London, 1981).
Les Structures élementaires *de la parenté* [New Edition with Corrections] (Paris, 1967). *The Elementary Structures of Kinship* [Translation of the 1967 Edition] (Boston, 1969).
Anthropology structurale II (Paris, 1973). *Structural Anthropology* II (London, 1977).
La Voie des masques (Paris, 1975). *The Way of the Masks* (London, 1983).
Le Regard éloigné (Paris, 1983). *A View from Afar* (Oxford, 1985).
Paroles données (Paris, 1984).
La Potière jalousie (Paris, 1985). *The Jealous Potter* (Chicago, 1988).
Histoire de lynx (Paris, 1991). *The Story of Lynx* (Chicago, 1995).

Other works cited
Charbonnier, G. (ed.) (1961) *Entretiens avec Claude Lévi-Strauss* (Paris).
Charbonnier, G. (1969) *Conversations with Claude Lévi-Strauss* (London).
Dumont, L. (1983) 'The Kariera kinship vocabulary: an analysis' in his *Affinity as a Value* (Chicago, IL) pp.175–91 (originally published in J. Pouillon and P. Maranda (eds.), *Èchanges et Communications Mélanges offerts a Claude Lévi-Strauss*, The Hague, 1970, pp. 272–86).
Durkheim, E. (1898) 'La prohibition d l'inceste et ses origins', *Année Sociologique*, 1, 1–70.

Durkheim, E. (1912) *Les formes élémentaires de la vie religieuse* (Paris). *The Elementary Forms of Religious Life* (London, 1915; Glencoe, IL, 1947).

Durkheim, E. and Mauss, M. (1963) *Primitive Classifications*, translated from the French with an Introduction by R. Needham (Chicago, IL).

Eribon, D. (1988) *De Près de loin* (Paris).

Eribon, D. (1991) *Conversations with Claude Lévi-Strauss* (Chicago, IL).

Fox, J. J. (1999) 'Precedence in practice among the Atoni Pah Meto of Timor', in L. Aragon and S. Russell (eds.), *Structuralism's Transformations: Order and Revisions in Indonesia and Malaysia* (Tucson, AZ), pp. 3–36.

Godelier, M. (2018) *Claude Lévi-Strauss: a Critical Study of His Thought* (London).

Izard, M. and Smith, P. (1979) *La Fonction symbolique* (Paris).

Izard, M. (2004) *Lévi-Strauss* (Paris).

Josselin de Jong, J. P. B. (1935) *De Maleische archipelago als ethnologisch studieveld* (Leiden: *The Malay Archipelago as a Field of Ethnological Study* [English Translation in P. E. de Josselin de Jong, *Structural Anthropology in the Netherlands*, The Hague, 1977, pp. 166–82]).

Josselin de Jong, J. P. B. (1952) *Lévi-Strauss' Theory on Kinship and Marriage. Mededelingen van het Rijksmuseum voor Volkenkunde* No. 10. [Reprinted in P. E. de Josselin de Jong, *Structural Anthropology in the Netherlands*, The Hague, 1977, pp. 254–321.]

Loyer, E. (2015) *Lévi-Strauss* (Paris)

Loyer, E. (2018) *Lévi-Strauss: a Biography* (Cambridge).

Leach, E. R. (1965) 'Claude Lévi-Strauss—anthropologist and philosopher', *New Left Review*, 34: 12–27.

Leach, E. R. (1968) *The Structural Study of Myth and Totemism* (London).

Leach, E. R. (1970) *Claude Lévi-Strauss* (New York).

Mauss, M. (1925) 'Essai sur le don: Forme et raison de l'échange dans les sociétés archaïques' *Année sociologique*, ns1: 30–186.

Maybury-Lewis, D. (1960) 'The analysis of dual organizations: a methodological critique', *Bijdragen tot de Taal-, Land- en Volkunde*, 161, 17–44.

Needham, R. (1962) *Structure and Sentiment: a Test Case in Social Anthropology* (Chicago, IL).

Needham, R. (1963) 'The Wikmungkan mother's brother: inference and evidence', *Journal of the Polynesian Society*, 72: 139–51.

Needham, R. (1968) 'Anthropology's Pope', *Times Literary Supplement*, 2 May: 445–7.

Needham, R. (1971) 'Introduction', in R. Needham (ed.), *Rethinking Kinship and Marriage* (London), pp. xii–cvii.

Pouillon, J. and Maranda, P. (eds.) (1970) *Échanges et Communications: Mélanges offerts à Claude Lévi-Strauss*, 2 vols. (The Hague).

Propp, V. (1958) *Morphology of the Folktale*, edited with an introduction by S. Pirkova-Jakobson (Bloomington, IN).

Sartre, J. P. (1960) *Critique de la raison dialectique* (Paris).

Wilcken, P. (2010) *Claude Lévi-Strauss: the Poet in the Laboratory* (London).

Van Wouden, F. A. E (1935) *Sociale Stuctuurtypen in de Groote Oost* (Leiden).

Van Wouden, F. A. E (1968) *Types of Social Stucture in Eastern Indonesia* (The Hague).

DANIEL WALEY

Daniel Philip Waley

20 March 1921 – 26 May 2017

elected Fellow of the British Academy 1991

by

TREVOR DEAN

Daniel Waley was one of the leading medieval historians of the second half of the twentieth century: author of major, enduring textbooks on Italy and on Europe, he also produced a long series of studies of Italian cities, their governments and their armies in the thirteenth century. Exceptionally for such a productive medieval scholar, he also wrote impressive works on British modern history, and made a mid-career change, from lecturing at the London School of Economics to managing a department in the British Library.

Biographical Memoirs of Fellows of the British Academy, XVIII, 305–324
Posted 29 October 2019. © British Academy 2019.

DANIEL WALEY

'I was born in the house of my paternal grandmother in Notting Hill, London W11, but all my earliest memories are of Porters Hall, Stebbing, Essex, a big house, surrounded by a moat, where we lived from 1921 till 1926.' So opens an unpublished memoir of his childhood written by Daniel Waley in 2010; the memoir offers a set of character sketches of his parents and grandparents, of some of their servants, and of the sequence of houses in which they lived.[1] His father, Hubert, had failed at a succession of ventures (as a student at Oxford and at art school, as a lithographer) before inventing a continuous film projector and obtaining a post in the British Film Institute as 'technical director'. His mother, Margaret, had also dropped out, of Natural Sciences at Cambridge. His grandfathers were Philip Samuel Waley, a stockbroker prominent in London Jewish circles, who 'lived in a grand house in Gloucester Square' with countless servants, and David Frederick Schloss, a civil servant and member of the Fabian Society, who changed his name to Waley during the First World War. One aunt lived in 'a rather smart flat in Piccadilly', and uncles included Sigismund (David) Waley MC, a Treasury civil servant who was knighted, and Arthur Waley the distinguished orientalist and translator. 'The general milieu of my parents … might be described as situated in the extreme outskirts of "Bloomsbury"', Daniel wrote, characterising this as 'a general approval of everything French' and 'a marked lack of interest in clothes and food'. From these sketches of people and places, Daniel draws a memorable portrait of his personal and family background: a high-achieving, wealthy family; a cosmopolitan outlook; enduring cultural interests in art and literature; and an inherited 'fidgety tendency'.

Daniel's education started early: his grandmother taught him French, using *French without Tears*; his mother read poetry to him, mainly Shakespeare; at a preliminary school an early encounter with art history, and with Giotto in particular, remained a strong memory in later life. Daniel's first school was near Dorking, and it followed an unusual learning scheme, the pupils not being taught in classes but individually moving from room to room to complete a set of assignments in a range of subjects. Daniel recalled the History teacher as 'brilliant', a judgement surpassed by a fellow pupil and later historian (Professor Sir Michael Howard): 'Daniel, we were taught by a genius!' Daniel then went to boarding school, Dauntsey's near Devizes (1934–8), the school having been chosen, Daniel recalled, on the basis of a not entirely enthusiastic recommendation by some friends. 'The staff were not a particularly impressive lot': the French master's insistence on pupils reading a book in French every week caused time problems in other studies; and the History teacher 'seemed to have used up all his energy in getting a First at Cambridge'; what Daniel enjoyed most was the cricket

---

[1] All further unattributed quotations are to this memoir. I am very grateful to Daniel's daughter, Harriet Sogbodjor, for allowing me to see this document.

('slow bowler, even slower batsman'). Despite these deficiencies, Daniel won a scholarship to King's College, Cambridge at the end of 1938, and then went to Paris for six months to take the 'Cours de Civilisation Française' at the Sorbonne, and to improve his French. It was while he was there in March 1939, on his eighteenth birthday, that he met Pamela Griffiths, who had come to Paris from a school in Kent on a similar mission. They married in 1945, almost immediately on Daniel's return from Italy and while he was an undergraduate.

Pam played a large role in Daniel's career. She was an excellent linguist and a distinguished academic (she had learned Japanese as part of her war-work at Bletchley and had her own career as Lecturer in Hispanic and Italian languages at Westfield College, London). Daniel acknowledged her role in the prefaces to several of his books: 'I am indebted most of all to my wife, who has aided me constantly with advice and criticism' (*Medieval Orvieto*, Cambridge, 1952); and 'a quite overwhelming domestic debt' was acknowledged for reading and critiquing the whole manuscript of *The Papal State in the Thirteenth Century* (London, 1961). Daniel was also devoted to his children, and Pam wrote proudly in 2015 of the fact that they were an international family, Jewish, Welsh, with an African son-in-law and an Algerian daughter-in-law.[2]

After one year at Cambridge, Daniel volunteered for military service, and served in the Eighth Army, 1940–5, with periods in the Intelligence Corps (Field Security), and attachments to 'a strange cosmopolitan "private army" in Tunisia' in 1943, and to an Italian 'First Motorised Group' in 1944. In a memoir of his experience in Tunisia, Daniel described his 'totally undefined role', mainly as an interpreter, to a multi-national 'secret unit' of British, French, Spanish, Greek and Austrian soldiers.[3] The memoir mixes a historian's concern to categorise the unit's activities— punitive expeditions, patrolling no-man's-land, and raids behind enemy lines—and to assess its achievements, with a more personal and emotional reminiscence—his fear before going on raids, his relief at the cancellation of a raid which, he later discovered, would have been a death trap, and his witnessing of a war crime ('I made no protest at the time'; the incident later gave him nightmares, according to Christopher Whittick). He recounts one hare-brained spying scheme: 'One operation which was suggested was that I should be dressed as an Arab fruit vendor, with a donkey, and should visit some German positions. I had only a few words of Arabic, and I turned the idea down .... I thought it quite likely that this operation would have concluded by my being shot.' The tale of another near-miss was marked by the same detached, retrospective amusement: 'the nearest I came to being shot at was fire from the Bren gun of a nervous British infantry outpost'. He also recalled with pleasure his

---

[2] Christopher Wright, personal communication.
[3] Imperial War Museum, Document 21185, Private Papers of D. P. Waley.

friendships with fellow-soldiers, an evening with some dancing Arabs, and a day when they drove to visit the Roman ruins at Dougga. He also served in the Sicilian campaign in the summer of 1943, and in his memoir he recreates some memorable episodes: problems with his puncture-prone motorcycle, an order to teach Italian to other members of his unit despite his own limited knowledge based on recipes, his involvement in the rounding up of active Fascists ('I interrogated many and arrested quite a few') and his outbreaks of malarial fever, requiring treatment in a field hospital near Syracuse. From Messina, he also embarked on the allied invasion of the Italian mainland.

'My war experience had a big impression on me', but, like many veterans, he did not talk much about it: according to Caroline Barron, he made out that he had had a clerical war, doing nothing much but sign cheques and write chits. He left Italy in September 1945, initially on leave, then on discharge, and within weeks he was back in Cambridge, newly married, belatedly joining the Michaelmas term, and opting for just one further undergraduate year (under special regulations for service-men), studying medieval European history and 'St Francis and the early Franciscans', a special subject taught by David Knowles, who left strong impressions on his students for his lectures, 'quite beyond the effect of the words themselves', for their 'beauty of language and depth of thought'.[4] Daniel himself praised Knowles as 'a great teacher', 'mio maestro'.[5] So what was the 'big impression' that the war made on Daniel? Foremost must have been a new interest in Italian history: in a conference paper at Assisi in the 1970s Daniel recalled his first sight of that city in October 1944 when his army division was advancing along the main road, en route to the front in the Apennines.[6] Second, Daniel came to have an abiding historical interest in military strategy, recruitment and leadership: it was failings in these very fields that he recalled of his experience in Tunisia in 1943.

Once he had gained a first-class degree in 1946, 'research seemed the obvious next move ... and medieval Italy seemed equally obvious', especially as Pam was already studying for a PhD in Italian, while Daniel's special subject and his interest in Italy discovered during the war also must have contributed to the decision. Daniel consulted Previté-Orton, the recently retired Cambridge professor of medieval history, on possible research topics. Previté (as he was known) was a scholarly and source-focused historian of Italy in his own right, though he was better known for his textbooks of European history, the *Outline of Medieval History* (Cambridge, 1916)

---

[4] C. Brooke, '1896–1974', in C. Brooke, R. Lovatt, D. Luscombe and A. Sillem (eds.), *David Knowles Remembered* (Cambridge, 1991), p. 21.

[5] D. P. Waley, 'Le istituzioni comunali di Assisi nel passaggio dal XII al XII secolo', in *Assisi al tempo di San Francesco* (Assisi, 1978), pp. 69–70.

[6] Ibid., p. 69.

and the *History of Europe 1198–1378* (London, 1937).[7] They met in the Botanical
Gardens, where, 'alternating historical advice with some serious bird-watching',
Previté suggested studying the cities of either Lucca or Orvieto: 'I eliminated Lucca
perhaps foolishly because I doubted my competence to deal with Lucchese banking
and silk manufacture'. That left Orvieto. (Daniel later unsuccessfully pressed Sydney
Anglo to take on the PhD topic of Paolo Guinigi of Lucca, a fifteenth-century regime-
leader.) David Knowles was assigned as his supervisor. However, Knowles' appeal as
a lecturer was not matched by skills as a thesis supervisor. He had supervised only one
previous student, and his inexperience meant that students felt 'pretty much unaided':
'the sparseness of his comments on sections of written work … was legendary'.[8]
Daniel himself later recalled that, on telling Knowles that he had finished his thesis,
Knowles remarked 'Let's see, I was supposed to be in charge of your work at one
stage, wasn't I?' To get that far, Daniel had spent parts of the period since 1946 in
Italy, reading in the archives and libraries, mainly in Orvieto. 'Orvieto was such a
dreary, dirty place in the 1940s, rather dominated by depressed *recluti* [conscripts]
eating water melons, the only thing they could afford', Daniel once told me, though
work in the mornings-only archive was supplemented by a kind arrangement by which
a local schoolboy carried registers to the municipal library at lunch-time for Daniel to
continue reading in the afternoon. Daniel became addicted to archival work, and he
and Pam went to Italy every year: 'my passion for the *inedito* was something of a
drug', he wrote, and he recalled working through from opening time to closing time in
Siena, or getting dispensation to work in the Vatican Archives in the afternoons.
Daniel's dissertation won prizes and plaudits: it was awarded the Cambridge University
Prince Consort Prize, being selected as 'specially distinguished',[9] and one chapter was
submitted for the Royal Historical Society's Alexander Prize, awarded 'proxime acces-
sit', being read and published in the Society's *Proceedings* in 1950. Presumably with
the help of Knowles, it was also quickly selected for publication by Cambridge
University Press.

　　While waiting to submit his PhD thesis in 1950, Daniel had applied for two
lectureships, at the London School of Economics (a five-year assistant lectureship)
and at Nottingham. Daniel was offered and took the post at the LSE, cabling from
Arles where he was on holiday 'Accept post writing'.[10] Daniel was to stay at the LSE
until 1972. There he taught late medieval English and European history and the

---

[7] R. B. Dobson, 'Orton, Charles William Previté', *Oxford Dictionary of National Biography* online:
https://doi.org/10.1093/ref:odnb/35608 (accessed 11 January 2019).
[8] D. Luscombe, 'David Knowles and his pupils', in C. Brooke, R. Lovatt, D. Luscombe and A. Sillem
(eds.), *David Knowles Remembered* (Cambridge, 1991), p. 132.
[9] London School of Economics, Archive, personal file of Daniel Waley.
[10] Ibid.; Christopher Wright, personal communication; Imperial War Museum, Document 21185.

intercollegiate special subject on Florence in the Renaissance. He was one of a small group of non-economic historians in the Department of Economic History, and for a time the only medievalist.[11] He was confirmed as without-term lecturer in 1956, promoted to Reader in 1961 and to Professor of History in 1970. After eighteen years' service, in 1967–8, he was granted three terms' sabbatical leave, which he used to write *The Italian City Republics* (London, 1969). Looking back, Daniel listed the advantages and disadvantages of this phase in his career: on the one hand, he enjoyed teaching some excellent students, cultivating friendships with colleagues, and opening the batting for the staff cricket team; on the other hand, the History degree was peripheral, and eventually he tired of teaching 'the same bits of medieval history in the same college year after year'. The LSE was, in Peter Denley's estimation, 'not a dream place' for a medievalist, especially a lone medievalist. There was no stream of research students in medieval Italian history.[12] Nevertheless, Daniel's own dissatisfactions were not shared by all his undergraduate students: Sydney Anglo recalls that Daniel 'was very good at teaching political ideas, because he was very sceptical and resistant to hi-falutin ideas. He was superb as a special subject teacher, and as a tutor.'[13]

Nevertheless, dissatisfaction must have been one of Daniel's main motives in applying for the post of Keeper of Manuscripts in the British Museum (now the British Library). Things converged to change his direction. The Museum's Trustees were keen to appoint an outsider. Daniel was looking for a change; he was interested in manuscripts; his uncle, Arthur Waley, had been a curator in the British Museum's Department of Oriental Antiquities; his son was also there in Oriental Printed Books and Manuscripts. Moreover, Daniel had been disturbed by the recent student protests—his daughter recalls that in 1968 he made himself available at home to students who wanted to have tutorials but had difficulty getting physically into the LSE. Normal academic life there was seriously disrupted between 1968 and 1970, with occupations, closures, barricadings, disruption of lectures, teach-ins and confrontations with the police, as a result of student protests across a broad range of issues, from the Vietnam war and investments in South Africa, to the dangerous traffic in Houghton St; and this long period of repeated confrontation and conflict generated bans, suspensions, legal injunctions, disciplinary hearings against both students and sympathetic lecturers, and criminal prosecutions:[14] 'It was always believed in the Dept of MSS that he was a refugee from the troubles which engulfed the LSE after 1968.'[15]

---

[11] LSE archive, Waley file.
[12] Sydney Anglo, personal communication.
[13] Ibid.
[14] *The Times*, 26 Oct. 1968, 11 Jan. 1969, 31 Jan. 1969, 4 Feb. 1969, 8 Feb 1969, 17 Feb. 1969, 8 Mar. 1969, 17 Mar. 1969, 2 May 1969, 19 May 1969, 26 Sept. 1969, 4 Mar. 1970, 27 Nov. 1970.
[15] Christopher Wright, personal communication.

Despite Daniel's lack of experience in general archive administration or in staff management, the British Museum was sufficiently impressed by his academic expertise and his reputation for friendly efficiency to appoint him to the post. The career of his predecessor as Keeper, T. C. Skeat,[16] perhaps led him to think that the job would be more ivory tower than bed of thorns: Skeat had been at the British Museum for over forty years, in which time he had managed to publish nearly a hundred books and articles. This vision of the keeper-scholar surfaced in Daniel's review of a Festschrift to Richard Hunt, Keeper of Western Manuscripts at the Bodleian Library: commenting on the photograph of Hunt, Daniel claimed to detect 'symbolical significance in the relative position of the material to be seen on the keeper's desk, where a medieval manuscript lies open on top of proofs of the *Oxford Dictionary of the Christian Church*, while these in turn conceal the contents of a mundane communication clearly marked "Confidential"'.[17] If that was the new environment Daniel was expecting, he was soon disillusioned. 'I had a frigid reception from the Keepers of the other departments', because he was seen as an outsider who had not followed their standard career path. External appointments were not common practice at the British Museum, and Daniel 'may well have been the first Keeper to be appointed from outside'.[18] Considerable difficulty also came from assistant keepers in his own department, some of whom were 'laws unto themselves'. His daughter reports that he was struck by the different workplace culture, for example the lunch and tea breaks;[19] but routinised down-time was not even half of the problem—much more serious was the general workplace ambiance— 'like a Victorian public school', one former colleague recalls, 'all protocols, hierarchy, cubby-holes and clock', with people addressing one another by their surnames.[20] 'Everything ... spoke still of ancient custom', wrote another former colleague.[21] The Department of Manuscripts was inward-looking, had a long-established hostile relationship with the Department of Printed Books and was isolated from the wider intellectual world. Daniel 'was one of the first to attempt to change this'.[22] In part this was through a 'liberal style of management'—social events, celebrating personal successes, humanising one-to-one progress meetings; and in part it was through new strategies, such as a positive change in the department's attitude to exhibitions, in favour of fuller participation.[23] However, there was also the

[16] J. M. Gullick, 'Skeat, Walter William', *Oxford Dictionary of National Biography* online: https://doi.org/10.1093/ref:odnb/94840 (accessed 5 October 2018).

[17] *Times Literary Supplement,* 1 October 1976, p. 1234.

[18] Christopher Wright, personal communication.

[19] Harriet Sogbodjor, personal communication.

[20] Andrew Prescott, personal communication.

[21] Peter Jones, quoted in *King's College, Cambridge, Annual Report*, 2018, p. 122.

[22] Andrew Prescott, personal communication.

[23] Ibid.; British Library Corporate Archive, Derek Turner to R. T. Richnell, 6 August 1974.

broader institutional context, which became more difficult after 1979 under the Thatcher government. Apart from the cuts to funding and the effects of high inflation, which overshadowed the Library's budgeting, a major issue arose over an imposed re-grading of curatorial staff, which was opposed by the unions. There was also, Andrew Prescott recalls, a civil service staff inspection, to which the British Museum had never before been subjected, examining comparability of grades. Daniel, however, stuck at it: 'perseverance marked his term as Keeper'.[24]

Early in his term, Daniel reported to the British Library Board on the three problems faced by his department, and proposed his solutions to them: at a time of inflation, acquisitions were becoming more difficult and a central institutional fund was needed; the rise in the number of loans of British Library manuscripts to external exhibitions needed to be scaled back because it was hampering the cataloguing work, 'the most fundamental of our activities' as he later called it; and the thirty-year lag in publishing the catalogues of manuscripts could be addressed by publishing summary descriptions instead.[25] How far did he succeed in remedying these problems? He did oversee publication of the catalogues of manuscripts acquired between 1946 and 1950 (in 1979), and between 1951 and 1955 (in 1982)—but progress remained slow, and in 1982, when the backlog was rising again, he was still pushing his preferred solution of 'less elaborate and perfectionist methods of arranging and indexing our collections'.[26] It is not clear that Daniel was able, either, to stem the flow of loans to external exhibitions, as there were twenty-three in 1981–2.[27] Part of the continuing backlog in cataloguing was caused, contrarily, by perhaps the most significant of acquisitions during Daniel's term: the Blenheim papers, of the first duke of Marlborough and his wife, which had been accepted by the Treasury in lieu of estate duty in 1978. This was an unusually large acquisition of over 600 volumes, and 'the cataloguing took eight years and extra staff had to be recruited to help with it'.[28] In more normal years, acquisitions, whether by purchase, gift or in lieu of taxes, were much smaller in scale: whether single parchment leaves, account rolls, volumes of poetry, or collections of letters and papers from nationally significant figures such as Lytton Strachey or British ambassadors. Among the important acquisitions in these years were 'the unique manuscript of Malory's *Morte d'Arthur*', purchased from Winchester College; a fifteenth-century anthology of English verse and prose ('very rare ... must be regarded as a "national heritage" item'); and the Benjamin Britten archive, another collection received in lieu of taxes, but with the complication that its long-term loan to the Britten-Pears Library

[24] Andrew Prescott, personal communication.
[25] British Library Corporate Archive, British Library Board, 73/48; 82/36.
[26] Ibid., 82/36; *British Library Annual Report*, 1981–2, p. 23.
[27] British Library Board, 82/36.
[28] Christopher Wright, personal communication.

in Aldeburgh had to be negotiated, by Daniel.[29] Daniel also played a significant role in the acquisition of the North (Sheffield Park) papers, securing those of national importance in what he and Christopher Whittick described as 'an entirely proper but archivally disastrous auction' in 1981.[30] Was there any strategy behind this pattern of acquisitions? In a strategy document in 1976, Daniel stated a preference for 'building on strengths' rather than 'filling the gaps'—'the Department should not seek to acquire "one of everything" in the spirit of a stamp collection'—and was very hesitant about 'taking the initiative' in approaching owners to deposit papers.[31]

One manuscript deposit caused Daniel considerable trouble, as he later recounted in a letter to *The Times*.[32] In 1984, he recalled, he had been approached by a former colleague at the LSE acting for Anthony Blunt, the so-called fourth man of the Cambridge spy-ring, unveiled by the Prime Minister Margaret Thatcher in 1983. This intermediary proposed the deposit in the British Library of a memoir written by Blunt, but on condition that there be no access to it for twenty-five years. Daniel accepted it on that condition. 'It was then that the trouble began.' First there was a leak to the press. Then Daniel received 'an agitated visit' from the British Library Chairman, who demanded to see the manuscript (Daniel surmised that he had received a reproof from the Prime Minister). Daniel had to explain that 'neither he nor I … could read it'. Later, at a meeting of the executive committee, Daniel was reprimanded by the Director of the Reference Division, who implied that he should have consulted higher authority before accepting the deposit.

This incident aside, Daniel derived great satisfaction from his career at the British Library: he was popular with colleagues, and he managed to publish a number of smaller-scale pieces of research. His richly varied career achievements were recognised by his election to the British Academy fellowship in 1991, the year also of his retirement, when he and Pam moved to Lewes, East Sussex. Daniel had lived in Littlehampton for a time as a child, so knew the county, and his keenness for walking (long walking) on the Sussex Downs was obviously well known to his colleagues, who gave him a waterproof Ordnance Survey map as a leaving gift. At Lewes, Daniel began to re-draw his remaining scholarly interests, completing some Italian projects, but slowly moving his focus to his own locality, his passion for archives leading him to the East Sussex Record Office.

Daniel's many publications fall into six categories: studies of urban and papal government in central Italy in the thirteenth and fourteenth centuries; military history,

---

[29] British Library Board, 79/57, 79/81.
[30] D. P. Waley and C. Whittick, 'The earl, his daughter, her brother's housekeeper and the cat: the remarkable story of the Sheffield Park archives', *Archives*, 36 (2011), 62.
[31] British Library Board, 76/83.
[32] *The Times*, 17 Aug. 2009, p. 25.

mainly in medieval Italy; his two major textbooks on Italian city republics and later medieval Europe; articles and catalogue introductions relating to acquisitions and exhibitions and the British Library; essays and biographies on a range of topics of local Sussex history; and pieces on aspects of political thought. He also produced one book of modern British history, and Daniel was a frequent reviewer of new publications, which throw light on his style and method as a historian.

Daniel's PhD thesis, published unchanged in 1952, already shows some of his character as a historian: the hunting out of documents to investigate the history of towns or themes little studied or unreliably portrayed; privileging those documents that make it possible 'to glimpse between the lines something of the reality of ... [the] political scene', 'to catch something of the "flavour" of communal politics' (pp. 3, 10); outlining some 'basic features', such as physical position, social composition, and lasting political alliances and enmities, that shaped the long-term political narrative; and stressing continuity over short-term change. In the case of Orvieto, 'typical of a kind of commune that has been extremely little studied', this meant using the rich series of city council minutes (*Riformagioni*), giving weight to the city's large class of artisans and farmers, and the commune's long connection with the papacy and alliance with Florence. One chapter, published in 1950,[33] concerned the context and outcome of a 'scandalous' agreement between Orvieto and Pope Boniface VIII in 1293, to exchange some papal lands for a favour to the pope's family, which Daniel described as 'a vivid and typical example of Boniface's scheming', but matched by Orvieto's 'sheer cold-blooded opportunism' in exploiting the pope's weakness ten years later. This article was followed a few years later by papers publishing or analysing previously overlooked documents in the Vatican Archives on aspects of thirteenth-century papal government—remnants from the thesis perhaps, but also preparing the ground for a major study, which became *The Papal State in the Thirteenth Century*.[34]

This work opened with a characteristic and apologetic statement of authorial incapacity: having quoted Edouard Jordan's definition of papal rule in Italy as 'a series of obscure and monotonous conflicts', Daniel confessed that 'to make such a story interesting would need the genius of a Gregorovius'. Nevertheless, he believed the attempt valuable, as even unsuccessful rule was worthy of investigation, and as the papal state created in the thirteenth century lasted into the nineteenth. The essential question was how the popes sought to make a reality of their territorial claims in central Italy. The answer focused very much on the play of circumstances and

[33] D. P. Waley, 'Pope Boniface VIII and the commune of Orvieto', *Transactions of the Royal History Society*, 32 (1950), 121–39.
[34] D. P. Waley, 'An account book of the Patrimony of St Peter in Tuscany, 1304–6', *Journal of Ecclesiastical History*, 6 (1955), 18–25; D. P. Waley, 'A register of Boniface VIII's chamberlain, Theodoric of Orvieto', *Journal of Ecclesiastical History*, 8 (1957), 141–52.

opportunities, on relative strengths and weaknesses, on shifting cooperation with and resistance to government structures. Daniel's narrative is punctuated with insights of acute political realism: typical is his comment on Pope Innocent III's situation in 1201, 'his own resources were small, but his ... adversaries rarely worked in unison' (p. 44). Chapters of narrative alternated with chapters examining papal jurisdiction, the structure of government and resources (regarding his tentative conclusions on the fiscal balance sheet, he issued a 'reminder that ... the whole foundation of this chapter is quite unsure', p. 271). This work was well received by reviewers: 'nothing comparable has been attempted' since the nineteenth century, wrote one, while another foresaw that it would 'long remain the standard work'.[35]

Meanwhile, an article in the *Papers of the British School in Rome* in 1954 had announced a new and important theme in Daniel's work: military recruitment, organisation and techniques. This article examined how the Normans were able to transport their cavalry in their campaign to conquer Sicily. From the title ('Combined operations') to the envoi, the article seems inspired and animated by Daniel's own military experience, as he concluded that 'lessons in combined operations learnt on the shores of Sicily in 1060–1 were applied between Normandy and England in 1066, just as those learnt on the southern Sicilian coast in 1943 were applied ... to the [Normandy] landings of 1944'.[36] This first foray into military history—Daniel later regretted the 'little space' he had given to it in *Medieval Orvieto*—was followed by an article in the *English Historical Review* in 1957, studying the recruitment of papal armies from the towns of the papal state, noting the extent of evasion of military service, and the weak authority of papal governors, often reduced to apologetic pleading and seeing their commands treated as mere requests.[37] He also wrote about military institutions and military obligations in Assisi, in the area around Rome, and, belatedly, at Orvieto, in what he called his 'Italian swansong', stressing that historians' attention has mostly been on large conflicts, not on the much more numerous but smaller military undertakings, which Orvieto's almost constant warfare seems to have typified.[38] In a more general conference paper attempting to look at warfare 'as it was', he stressed the dominance, among modes of fighting, of destructive raids, along with sieges and skirmishes, he rated highly the technical and strategic capacity of command of the

---

[35] P. Partner, in *English Historical Review*, 78 (1963), 324; D. Douglas in *Times Literary Supplement*, 2 March 1962, p. 139.

[36] D. P. Waley, 'Combined operations in Sicily, A.D. 1060-78', *Papers of the British School in Rome*, 22 (1954), 125.

[37] D. P. Waley, 'Papal armies in the thirteenth century', *English Historical Review*, 72 (1957), 1–30.

[38] D. P. Waley, 'Le istituzioni comunali di Assisi' and 'L'esercito del comune medioevale di Orvieto', *Bollettino dell'Istituto storico artistico orvietano*, 48–9 (1992–3, but 1999), 55–80; D. P. Waley, 'La féodalité dans la région romaine dans la 2e moitié du XIIIe siècle et au début du XIVe', *Structures féodales et féodalité dans l'occident méditerranéen (Xe-XIIIe siècles)* (Paris, 1980), 515–22.

condottieri, but he concluded that 'the real victims of war were the *contadini*'[39]—this last observation being 'very influenced by his wartime experience in Field Security', according to Christopher Whittick, 'where he had to cope with *contadini* hoping to cross the front line in order to get to market or drive their animals to pasture'. Waley's most influential and insightful statements in this vein of his work came in two essays, one on Florentine armies, the other on early mercenary captains.[40] In the former, Daniel effectively dismantled the common view that the citizen militias of the twelfth–thirteenth centuries, an expression of 'civic zeal', had been eroded in the fourteenth century by 'apathy, economic specialization and the "cash nexus"', and replaced by the mercenary armies and *condottieri* for which later medieval Italy became infamous. He argued, contrary to this republican myth, that the citizen army was itself from the first a paid army, that the hiring of foreign mercenaries began early, and that the detailed Florentine army lists from 1260 show a high level of absenteeism. In his article on early *condottieri,* using military contracts from thirteenth-century Bologna and Siena, he presented mercenary soldiers and their commanders as part of the precariat, leading a 'hand-to-mouth' existence of short-term contracts and unpredictable lay-offs, and investigated their identities and activities. In this, Daniel was decades in advance of more recent scholarship treating military service as a kind of labour.

Daniel may well be most remembered for his two exceptionally long-lived textbooks, *Later Medieval Europe from St Louis to Luther* (London, 1964), and *The Italian City-Republics* (London, 1969), currently in their third and fourth editions respectively. Following his practice of first sketching in some basic features, *Later Medieval Europe* starts with common elements of medieval monarchical government—from composite structures to the varying extent and efficiency of 'bureaucratic machinery'—and the core of the book is formed by a series of chapters on Italy and France, though Germany and the eastern Mediterranean are not overlooked. The structure of presentation is well-suited to the student audience: a typical argument starts with the causes and nature of change, proceeds to the effects of change, and the importance of continuity, before drawing up a balance sheet. Waley was careful to insert challenges to the sort of common historiographical views that students of the 1960s might have picked up from other current reading: that 'overmighty subjects' could in fact provide a counter-balance to the 'overmighty official' (p. 56), that the stereotype of French lawyers serving the Crown is too much based on Nogaret, who was not typical (p. 60), that it is difficult to establish that warfare was more continuous

---

[39] D. P. Waley, 'I mercenari e la guerra nell'età di Braccio da Montone', in *Braccio da Montone e i Fortebracci* (Narni, 1993), p. 128.

[40] D. P. Waley, 'The army of the Florentine republic from the twelfth to the fourteenth century', in N. Rubenstein (ed.), *Florentine Studies* (London, 1968), pp. 70–108; D. P. Waley, '*Condotte* and *condottieri* in the thirteenth century', *Proceedings of the British Academy*, 61 (1975), pp. 337–71.

in the fourteenth century (p. 100), that the Medici were tyrants (p. 220) and the Renaissance nothing more than a 'highly adhesive label' (p. 165). Repeatedly there is a stress on continuity: the Black Death only accentuated an existing trend (p. 103), the Avignon papacy marked no sudden break (p. 116), and so on. Military history too gets good coverage, in terms of organisation (John Zizka's innovations), training and strategy (English attacks on France), and tactics (the French in the Hundred Years' War and at Nicopolis). The first edition does now, it has to be said, show its age: the literary references, to Stendhal, Mann and Cervantes for example, are redolent of 1960s modern-language syllabi, and the use of foreign terms (three Latin words on the first page) did not make the text as accessible as it could have been. Nevertheless, as Peter Denley, who revised it, contends, 'compared to what else is available, it holds up even today, partly because it is so difficult to write a text book covering 250 years single-handed'. 'Still one of the best introductory textbooks on the market', said John Larner in reviewing the second edition in 1986: 'To read this book is like an everyday meeting with an old friend: so much, over the past twenty years, has one become familiarized with its author's words and thoughts as précised, paraphrased and plagiarized in so many student essays'.[41] The ultimate accolade of a high citation index.

A similar judgement could well hold for *The Italian City-Republics* (my personal interest: I revised it in 2010). This must stand as one of the most successful textbooks on medieval history written in the twentieth century: it has been almost continuously in print for fifty years, has been translated into French, German, Italian, Spanish, Japanese and Turkish, and is still cited by Italian scholars. It was first published as part of Weidenfeld and Nicolson's 'World University Library', joining other titles that would become long-lived classics, such as W. G. Forrest's *Emergence of Greek Democracy* (London, 1966), and Lucy Mair's *Witchcraft* (London, 1969). It is difficult now to recover how students would have managed before *City-Republics* appeared. A reviewer of the first edition noted that this was 'the first general survey of the medieval Italian communes to appear in English in over sixty years', possibly referring to W. F. Butler's *The Lombard Communes* of 1906 or mis-datedly to M. V. Clarke's *The Medieval City State* of 1926, which Daniel told me 'held the field before I came along'. *Italian City-Republics* is concerned with the republican city-state in northern and central Italy, especially its political life, between the late eleventh and the early fourteenth century, from the emergence of collective action and communal institutions to the consolidation of urban lordships or regional states which spelled the end of many independent republics. As in previous books, he began with basic features of the population (classes, size, mobility), before dividing his study into three large sections on

---

[41] *History*, 71 (1986), 505.

the institutions and officials of the communes, their evolution and complexity; on the communes' external relations with their neighbours and with emperors and popes (included here was discussion of public buildings and infrastructure); and internal divisions (magnates, *popolo* and the inevitable Guelphs and Ghibellines, which Waley downplayed). Waley's treatment had some unifying and well-judged features: a resistance to clear definitions and simple evolutions, frequent reference to analogous experience among the ancient Greek city-states, and the use of modern parallels. Also valuable for students is the use of a wide range of documentary sources—tax assessments, lists of oath-takers, financial budgets, diplomatic documents, statutes—combined with narrative and literary material (chiefly Dante and Boccaccio), and brief introductions to a range of fascinating types of text unfamiliar to the modern reader, such as advice books, letter manuals and civic eulogies. The continued pre-eminence of this book was confirmed by the second edition in 1978, which included a new chapter, prompted by work on agrarian history such as that by Philip Jones. This second edition was hailed in the *Times Educational Supplement* as 'a little gem which radiates readable scholarship'.

In the 1980s and 1990s, Daniel continued to write intermittently on various problems and places in Italian thirteenth-century history: on the question whether the inhabitants of communal territories (*contadi*) were oppressed and overtaxed by the cities which ruled them (with specific reference to Siena); on a political experiment in power-sharing between Guelph and Ghibelline factions at San Gimignano; on the creation of knights by the commune of San Gimignano and its motivations; and on the use of sortition (random selection) and two-stage election processes in the appointment to internal offices.[42] These studies contained some characteristic Waleyan methods and conclusions: that repression of the *contado* is too general a judgement given the complexity of town–country relations and the state of the documentation; that there is value in looking outside Florence for more typical history ('the insularity of Florentine historians is amazing', he wrote to me in 1991); and that the purpose of the commune's grant of knighthood was military, to re-stock its cavalry force.

[42] D. P. Waley, 'A commune and its subject territory in the thirteenth century: law and power in the Sienese contado', in *Diritto e potere nella storia europea: Atti in onore di Bruno Paradisi* (Florence, 1982), pp. 303–11; D. P. Waley, 'Guelfs and Ghibellines at San Gimignano, c.1260- c.1320: a political experiment', *Bulletin of the John Rylands Library*, 72 (1990), 199–212; D. P. Waley, 'Chivalry and cavalry at San Gimignano: knighthood in a small Italian commune', in C. Richmond and I. Harvey (eds.), *Recognitions: Essays Presented to Edmund Fryde* (Aberystwyth, 1996), pp. 39–54; D. P. Waley, 'The use of sortition in appointments in the Italian communes', in J. E. Law and B. Paton (eds.), *Communes and Despots in Medieval and Renaissance Italy* (Farnham, 2010), pp. 27–33. Also in this group of publications is D. P. Waley, 'Il commune di San Gimignano nel mondo comunale toscano', in D. Ciampoli (ed.), *Il Libro Bianco di San Gimignano*, vol. 1 (Siena, 1996), pp. 11–44.

These continuing studies of Tuscan cities were given more extended form in Daniel's last Italian book, *Siena and the Sienese in the Thirteenth Century* (Cambridge, 1991). This too ran on some familiar lines. First, the overall aim: 'to give an idea of how the city was run ... and what it was like to live there' (p. xiii). Second, the themes chosen for the individual chapters, starting with the physical setting, then the people (work and wealth) and, most extensively, the government, its institutions, its oligarchical personnel, its revenue and expenditure, its assumptions, and its actions in relation to the problems of disorder and control of territory. Third, cautions regarding methodology, aggregation and classification: to use tax payments as an index of wealth 'is to take a very short cut indeed' (p. 15), 'families cannot be regarded as units except in the loosest sense' (p. 37), and 'the medieval Sienese would certainly not have accepted that part of their notions and activities could be contained within a discrete category bearing the label "religion"' (p. 127). Though in this book he eschewed engagement with recent research on other Tuscan cities, Daniel did take issue with William Bowsky's interpretation of the 'regime of the Nine', an allegedly new ruling group coming to power in 1287: Daniel stressed continuity between old and new ruling groups.[43] However, *Siena and the Sienese* cannot count as one of his best works. A study that aims 'to give a realistic portrait of Sienese society' (p. xiii) without giving much space or voice to women is laying itself open to obvious criticism.[44] The chapter on religion (a rare concession) is really about the church, with the occasional saintly biography. Finally, Daniel's suggestion, based on the lists of tax payments, that Siena lacked a numerically substantial middle class was one that he later revised, having been persuaded by a modern economic historian, as he explained to me in 2008, 'that comparable statistics about tax payments in 19th century England would give the same impression, but would be misleading [because] the middle element had their wealth in forms that escaped tax'.

In a small group of works, Daniel showed that he could also write modern history very effectively. In a book published in 1975 he assessed how and how successfully public opinion was mobilised in support of the campaign for international sanctions against Italy for its aggression against Abyssinia in 1935.[45] Memorable here is his forensic dismantling of the claim that it was a 'deluge' of letters to MPs that led to the campaign's one success, the resignation of the Foreign Secretary. One reviewer commented that this book 'should be prescribed reading for all operators in the media, all MPs, all who teach British politics, all organizers of pressure groups'.[46] Daniel's

---

[43] W. M. Bowsky, *A Medieval Italian Commune: Siena under the Nine, 1287–1355* (Berkeley, CA, 1981).
[44] See the review by E. English in *Speculum*, 69 (1994), 1295–7.
[45] D. P. Waley, *British Public Opinion and the Abyssinian War 1935–6* (London, 1975).
[46] D. Watt in *Times Literary Supplement*, 1 October 1976, p. 1259.

smaller-scale study of men from Lewes who served in the South African ('Boer') War evocatively depicts the atmosphere of imperialistic patriotism in the town, including the flag-waving, the torchlit processions and the burning of effigies of Kruger, and the disproportionate local-press reporting of the quasi-heroic actions of individual Volunteers, rather than those of the regular soldiery: 'So full of enthusiasm and enterprise, so deficient in scepticism', Waley comments.[47]

From the British Library, Daniel's essays on newly acquired manuscripts cover an interesting range of topics: some of Stanley Spencer's wartime letters from Salonika prompt the comment that 'the most memorable experience which twentieth-century British painting can provide is a visit to Stanley Spencer's masterpiece, the Sandham Memorial Chapel';[48] and Daniel's military interests were also evident in publishing a new account of the battle of Waterloo by one of the soldiers present ('must be rare indeed').[49] English literary and Italian interests were evident too: 'Not all great writers are great readers, but George Eliot was', is his introduction to a study of her 'blotter' or commonplace book, which he then analysed noting especially her love of Dante and the cosmopolitanism of her literary tastes.[50] He also showed his personal knowledge and appraisal of her novels in the introduction to a catalogue of a British Library exhibition marking the centenary of her death, which included her copy of Machiavelli's *Prince*.[51] His post-retirement commitment to the records and history of his adopted county of Sussex come to the fore in his article on 'the fate of the papers of the … earls of Sheffield of Sheffield Park, Sussex, … one of the saddest cases of the dispersal of an important family archive', and on that part of the archive later acquired by the East Sussex Record Society, the letters of Lord Glenbervie and his wife 1808–15, which Daniel amusingly surveyed.[52] He also calendared over fifty Italian medieval charters, brought back from the Grand Tour by one of the earls of Ashburnham.[53]

In reviewing other scholars' works Daniel, true to his 'archive first' approach, was often most exercised by the quantity, quality and use of primary sources. He could be harsh on works that betrayed a lack of proficiency in reading or interpreting documents, and he could be superlative in his praise of works that were saturated with archive know-how: he lauded Peter Linehan's *The Spanish Church and the Papacy* (Cambridge, 1971), as 'the product of an extraordinary feat of persistence, a sort of

---

[47] D. P. Waley, 'Lewes in the Boer War, 1899-1902', *Sussex Archaeological Collections*, 132 (1994), 191.

[48] D. P. Waley, 'Two Stanley Spencer letters from Salonika', *British Library Journal*, 3 (1977), 167–8.

[49] D. P. Waley, 'A new account of Waterloo: a letter from Private George Hemingway of the Thirty-Third Regiment of Foot', *British Library Journal*, 6 (1980), 61–4.

[50] D. P. Waley, *George Eliot's Blotter: a Commonplace Book* (London, 1980), p. 3.

[51] Ibid., pp. 3–5.

[52] D. P. Waley, '"My dearest cheaty meaty": papers of Lord Glenbervie at the East Sussex Record Office', *The Book Collector*, 60 (2011), 205.

[53] Christopher Whittick, personal communication.

prolonged one-man raid on the Spanish ecclesiastical archives'.[54] Some characteristic historiographical attitudes are also conveyed in these reviews. There is a concern about typicality and how to establish it, evident in his review of Philip Jones' 'powerful' essay on later medieval Italy in the Einaudi *Storia d'Italia*.[55] There is a hostility to religion and faithful church history, shown in his review of a study of a Tuscan monastery, where Daniel singles out the permeation of the monastery by the world and the monks' lack of zeal, or in his comment on Peter Partner's *Lands of St Peter* (London, 1972), that 'the viewpoint sometimes seems a strongly papalist one and papal officials tend to get the benefit of doubt'.[56] There is a preference for 'how things actually worked', shown in his criticism of Walter Ullmann's *Short History of the Papacy* (London, 1974), a vision of the papacy from the centre and from the pope's pronouncements without regard to the actual machinery of power or to the hostile local reception and limited implementation of papal policies.[57] Also, Daniel always kept his eyes open for titbits of military history: 'Notarial sources always yield the unexpected to a patient reader', he remarked, before noting some accounts of joustings in published Perugian notarial registers;[58] or, among the 'celebrated names' in a new volume of the *Dizionario biografico degli italiani*, he noticed 'the Socialist leader Leonida Bissolati (who, incidentally, joined the army as a sergeant in 1915 at the age of fifty-eight and was twice wounded)'.[59]

From over six decades, Waley's written output inevitably includes items that escape classification. Among these are the twenty or so entries that he wrote for the *Dizionario biografico degli italiani*, all with surnames in the range A–C. They included a fair number of bishops, papal officials and Orvietani, and a couple of surprises: the Castilian military captain active in fourteenth-century Italy, whose epitaph (I can see Daniel's sceptical smile as I write) was 'belli maximus auctor'; and the figure Ugo Belciampolo, who turns out to be an English mercenary soldier, Hugh Beauchamp, who fought for Perugia in the 1320s.[60] Daniel also wrote biographies of fellow-historian Nicolai Rubinstein and of Sussex luminary Sydney Buxton, who served as governor-general

[54] *Times Literary Supplement*, 15 October 1971, p. 1268.
[55] *English Historical Review*, 95 (1980), 886–7.
[56] *Journal of Ecclesiastical History*, 24 (1973), 73–4; and *Journal of Ecclesiastical History*, 42 (1991), 512–13.
[57] *Times Literary Supplement*, 7 April 1972, p. 396.
[58] *English Historical Review*, 91 (1976), 630.
[59] *Journal of Ecclesiastical History*, 85 (1970), 223.
[60] *Dizionario biografico degli italiani*, 7 (1965), p. 551; 8 (1966), pp. 87–9.

in South Africa, 1914–20.[61] As a rare foray into intellectual history, an essay on Machiavelli, regarding nostalgia for an age of simplicity, argued that Machiavelli's views of the virtuous 'roughness' of the Germans came partly from Latin authors' praise of simple virtues, and partly from Machiavelli's observations in the Tyrol.[62]

Though Daniel was, as he liked to say, 'entirely Jewish by descent', his paternal grandfather had 'given up the synagogue',[63] as had his mother, and Daniel's mentality was entirely secular. 'He once affected not to know what a bar-mitzvah was', according to Christopher Wright. Indeed, Daniel had, according to Peter Denley, a 'phobia of formal religion, and as a medieval historian was really not interested in religion at all'. Anti-Semitism appears, thankfully, to have passed him by. In a letter in 2012, he recalled 'the only totally overt anti-Semitic opinion that I have ever encountered': in 1943, panic at a suspected air-raid in London had caused scores of deaths in a crush at the entrance to Bethnal Green underground station; Daniel at this time was in Tunisia, on 'a brief (one-day) course on the use of explosives (how to blow up bridges, etc) ... During a break, I overheard an officer commenting to another officer: "Panic: East End Jews, no doubt".'[64]

Daniel's contribution to history had several rare qualities: his success in writing about both medieval and modern history; his skill in constructing durable, student-friendly syntheses broad in scope; his ability to combine deep archival research with knowledge of the wider scholarship. Over a lifetime, he created a body of work that displays consistent characteristics in its preference for investigating and showing the inner workings and actual experience of government and warfare, and for expressing scepticism about the gap between professed objectives and real achievements. He defended military history at a time when it fell out of scholarly favour. He was an admirer of Margaret Spufford and what one might call the 'resurrectionist' school of history, with which his hallmark aim to recover the 'real' experience of people is clearly allied (and open to the same criticism). He was exceptional for his personal generosity, for his interest in people and in cultivating and maintaining friendships, for a wealth of acquaintances and contacts, and for personal modesty and a strong sense of equality (he resigned from the MCC over its refusal to admit women as members). Fittingly, given Daniel's anti-religious views, his funeral in Brighton in June 2017 was a wholly

---

[61] D. P. Waley, 'Nicolai Rubinstein, 1911–2002', *Proceedings of the British Academy: Biographical Memoirs of Fellows III*, 124 (2004), pp. 313–32; D. P. Waley, 'Buxton, Sydney Charles, Earl Buxton (1853–1934)', *Oxford Dictionary of National Biography* online, 2006, https://doi.org/10.1093/ref: odnb/32224 (accessed 18 February 2019); D. P. Waley, *A Liberal Life: Sydney, Earl Buxton, 1853–1934, Statesman, Governor-General of South Africa* (Hassocks, 1999).

[62] D. P. Waley, 'The primitivist element in Machiavelli's thought', *Journal of the History of Ideas*, 31 (1970), 91–8.

[63] Private Collection, D. Waley to H. Jones, 9 May 2012.

[64] Ibid. He also reported this incident, slightly differently, in Imperial War Museum, Document 21185.

secular, celebratory affair, not without its moment of unscripted humour, when it was discovered that the readings—from George Eliot and Philip Larkin—had been left behind. Daniel departed the field for the last time to the sound of 'Soul Limbo', the signature tune to BBC radio's much-loved cricket commentary, Test Match Special.

Note on the author: Trevor Dean is Professor of Medieval History in the Department of Humanities, Roehampton University.

MARGARET ASTON

Margaret Evelyn Aston

9 October 1932 – 22 November 2014

Elected Fellow of the British Academy 1994

by

SUSAN BRIGDEN

Fellow of the Academy

The Hon. Margaret Aston was an historian who studied English religious life between the late Middle Ages and the Civil War. She was born into families of great distinction, dedicated to high public service and the arts. Her first study was of the career of Archbishop Arundel, and from it grew an abiding interest in heterodoxy and popular belief. In a series of articles, she reconstructed the mental and social worlds of the Lollards. She was fascinated by the relationship between the image and the word, and by art and its power and spiritual dangers; this became the principal focus of her work. Her *summa* was her great diptych, conceived in 1971, which occupied the rest of her scholarly life: *England's Iconoclasts I: Laws against Images* (1988) and *Broken Idols of the English Reformation* (2016). These are works of great depth and range, which transformed the understanding of the long Reformation in England. An independent scholar for most of her career, she was involved in many scholarly collaborations.

Biographical Memoirs of Fellows of the British Academy, XVIII, 325–336
Posted 31 October 2019. © British Academy 2019.

MARGARET ASTON

Margaret Evelyn Bridges—always known as Martha to her family and friends—was born at Campden Hill Square, Kensington, London. The fact that she was born into families of great distinction, dedicated to high public service and the arts, marked her life. She was the youngest of four children of Edward Ettingdene Bridges, later first Baron Bridges (1892–1969) and his wife Katherine Dianthe (Kitty) (1896–1986), daughter of Thomas Cecil Farrer, second Baron Farrer of Abinger (1859–1940), and the musician, Evelyn Mary, née Spring-Rice (1862–1898). Her paternal grandfather, Robert Seymour Bridges (1844–1930), was poet laureate from 1913 to 1930; her grandmother Monica (Mary) (1863–1949) was the daughter of Alfred Waterhouse, the leading architect of the Gothic revival. Dame Frances Margaret Farrer (1895–1977), her maternal aunt, was a civil servant and general secretary of the National Federation of Women's Institutes.[1] Both her father and mother had Quaker antecedents.

Edward Bridges was one of the greatest civil servants of the twentieth century. Secretary to the War Cabinet (1938–1945), he was described by Winston Churchill as 'an extremely competent and tireless worker, but … also a man of exceptional force, ability and personal charm, without a trace of jealousy in his nature'. Selfless, irenic and tireless at this period of exceptional crisis, Bridges managed to prevent the likely friction between civil and military staffs.[2] In 1945 he continued as Secretary to the Cabinet but was also Permanent Secretary to the Treasury and head of the Civil Service until his retirement in 1956. An historian, Bridges was elected a Fellow of All Souls College, Oxford.[3] To her father and mother, and to her father's memory, Margaret dedicated two of her books. His strict morality guided his own conduct and set a daunting standard for those close to him to follow. Margaret's fierce intelligence and toughness were his. Her schoolfriend, M. E. Batstone, judged that she 'inherited her father's strength and integrity, and her mother's tenderness and love of beauty'.

Margaret's childhood was spent with her siblings Shirley, Thomas and Robert in the family home, Goodmans Furze in Surrey, purchased by her father in 1934. High up on the North Downs at the back of Box Hill, the house has an 'idyllic location',

---

[1] F. Heal, 'Aston [née Bridges; second married name Buxton], Margaret Evelyn (1932–2014)', *Oxford Dictionary of National Biography*, https://doi.org/10.1093/odnb/9780198614128.013.108153 (accessed 9 September 2019); R. A. Chapman, 'Bridges, Edward Ettingdene, first Baron Bridges (1892–1969)', *Oxford Dictionary of National Biography*, https://doi.org/10.1093/ref:odnb/32063 (accessed 9 September 2019); C. Phillips, 'Bridges, Robert Seymour (1844–1930)', *Oxford Dictionary of National Biography*, https://doi.org/10.1093/ref:odnb/32066 (accessed 9 September 2019); J. Summers, 'Farrer, Dame Frances Margaret (1895–1977)', *Oxford Dictionary of National Biography*, https://doi.org/10.1093/ref:odnb/107094 (accessed 9 September 2019).

[2] W. S. Churchill, *The Second World War*, vol. 2: *Their Finest Hour* (London, 1949), pp. 17–18.

[3] Chapman, 'Edward Ettingdene Bridges, first Baron Bridges (1892–1969)'.

with commanding views over Headley Heath.[4] Her mother was the centre of the close-knit family, for their father was often away in London, where the War Cabinet Office was manned day and night. Whether a sense of the sublimity of church architecture was stirred in the future historian in Headley's parish church of St Mary may be doubted, for its nineteenth-century nave and chancel have been described as 'appalling'.[5]

Margaret went away to boarding school, to Downe House near Newbury. The school had been founded in 1907 by Olive Willis on clear principles. Pupils were allowed more leisure and were less regimented than in most girls' schools, enjoying freedom from all-encompassing rules.[6] Creativity was encouraged and there was a strong musical tradition; Dame Myra Hess gave wartime concerts there.[7] Margaret, like her father, began to play the clarinet. Invited to write a pastiche of Chaucer—to invent an extra pilgrim for the *Canterbury Tales*—she presciently chose a poor scholar, 'with his boke'. At Downe House Margaret was influenced by the brilliant new history teacher, Isabel Bewick, and became Head Girl.

In 1951 Margaret won a scholarship to read history at Lady Margaret Hall, Oxford, one of six scholars in a bumper year for historians. These were heroic years for women's education at Oxford, for after decades of open or covert opposition the women's colleges became fully self-governing in the early 1950s. To be in a woman's college at this time was to experience the successful assertion of women's claims to an equal education, though how far this impinged on undergraduate awareness is uncertain.[8] Margaret's memories of the College were of its post-war atmosphere, of the bone-chilling cold and of its irksome restrictions after her liberal school.[9] Her history tutors were Anne Whiteman and Naomi Hurnard; the Principal was the historian Dame Lucy Sutherland. 'Miss Whiteman', returned to Oxford after wartime service in the Women's Auxiliary Air Force, was the very best kind of tutor—wise, warm, witty and 'profoundly humane', dedicated to the study of history and to the guidance of her students.[10] It was Hurnard who particularly impressed Margaret's year, but it took some time for Margaret to impress her. Study of Latin began badly, with $\gamma\beta$ for a first

[4] Sale details, Knight Frank.

[5] I. Nairn and N. Pevsner, revised by B. Cherry, *The Buildings of England: Surrey*, 2nd edn (Harmondsworth, 1971), p. 312.

[6] A. Ridler, *Olive Willis and Downe House: an Adventure in Education* (London, 1967); M. Midgley, *The Owl of Minerva: A Memoir* (London, 2005), p. 58.

[7] *Downe House Scrap-Book, 1907–1957*, p. 66.

[8] A. Whiteman, 'Lucy Stuart Sutherland, 1903–1980', *Proceedings of the British Academy*, 69 (1983), pp. 611–30.

[9] Lady Margaret Hall, 2015.083.

[10] B. Worden, 'Anne Whiteman', https://www.history.ox.ac.uk/anne-whiteman (accessed 9 September 2019).

term's work marred by wild guesses. By the final year, Sutherland was writing that 'Miss Bridges grasps abstract arguments with ease, and applies them with courage and incisiveness', and May McKisack recognised that 'her grasp of texts ... is something quite out of the ordinary'.[11]

With a First-Class degree awarded in the Modern History Schools of 1954, Margaret began graduate work under the forbidding supervision of K. B. McFarlane of Magdalen College, the renowned, though then resolutely little published, historian of the late medieval English nobility—of the world of magnate affinities, service and patronage, of 'good lordship' and of the Lollard knights: 'His intellectual integrity and historical craftmanship inspired the generation whose research he supervised.'[12] The stern standards of archival scholarship that he imparted were evident in Margaret's 1962 DPhil thesis, 'The career of Thomas Arundel until his exile in 1397'. At a meeting of the Stubbs Society (scene of student romance as well as of ardent historical discussion), Margaret had met Trevor Aston (1925–1985), the medieval economic historian, and immediately upon graduating, on 7 August 1954, she married him.[13] The marriage did not last, ending in separation after four years and divorce in 1969, but she would publish some of her most influential articles in the journal *Past and Present*, which Aston edited, and she dedicated a book to his memory. In Oxford, Margaret began tutorial teaching and was Lecturer at St Anne's College between 1956 and 1959.

In 1960–1 Margaret, who was venturesome, eager to improve her languages and to travel, held the Theodor Heuss Scholarship in West Germany. Returning, she was elected to the Jenner Research Fellowship at Newnham College, Cambridge, which she held from 1961 to 1966. She acknowledged with gratitude the grant of freedom 'as Virginia Woolf defined it to the college Arts Society in 1928—"five hundred a year and a room with a lock on the door"'.[14] At Newnham she became 'absolute' friends with Barbara Everett, Fellow in English. Margaret, sophisticated and artistic, redecorated her college rooms with a dark purple ceiling, terracotta-coloured wallpaper and black carpet—distant from the demure aesthetic of a women's college of the 1960s—incensing the Domestic Bursary. Barbara Everett remembers Margaret the risk-taker, rowing in thunderstorms. At this point, her career took a significant turn: she applied for, but missed, the permanent University post in Cambridge that might have been hers. Instead of becoming a tutor at a women's college—for men's colleges would not

---

[11] LMH, ACA/1/22.

[12] K. Leyser, 'Memoir', in G. L. Harriss (ed.), *K. B. McFarlane: Letters to Friends, 1940–1966* (Oxford, 1997), pp. 9–37; G. L. Harriss, 'McFarlane, (Kenneth) Bruce (1903–1966)', *Oxford Dictionary of National Biography*, https://doi.org/10.1093/ref:odnb/41133 (accessed 9 September 2009).

[13] R. Evans, 'Aston, Trevor Henry (1925–1985)', *Oxford Dictionary of National Biography*, https://doi.org/10.1093/ref:odnb/41133 (accessed 9 September 2009).

[14] M. Aston, 'Foreword' to *The Fifteenth Century: the Prospect of Europe* (London, 1968).

admit women until more than a decade later—or a University lecturer, bound to the academic round of terms, essay-marking and examining, and to administration, which she might, after all, have hated, she set off for America. In 1967 she became Resident Fellow at the Folger Shakespeare Library and taught at the Catholic University of America in Washington, DC, between 1966 and 1969. In Washington, she met Elizabeth Eisenstein, historian of the printing revolution, who became a life-long friend. She also held a Research Fellowship at the Henry Huntington Library in San Marino, California.

From this extensive period of research, a series of books and articles began to appear. The book of her Oxford dissertation—*Thomas Arundel: a Study of Church Life in the Reign of Richard II*—was published in 1967 (Oxford). This is a scholarly study of Arundel's career, principally as Bishop of Ely, but the added chapter on Arundel and heresy presaged her lasting interest in unorthodoxy and the late medieval heresy of Lollardy. Her first, and perhaps most influential article, 'Lollardy and sedition, 1381–1431', concerning the heresy's double challenge to church and state, had been published in 1960.[15] After the more limited prospect of Richard II's reign, she widened her perspective to consider Christendom. *The Fifteenth Century: the Prospect of Europe* (London, 1968) was written for the general reader. In this collection of impressionistic essays, the accounts of popular movements and popular piety are the most convincing, for this was the direction in which her research now turned. An imaginatively illustrated history, it revealed her abiding interest in art and its power. She chose as epigraph—and for her epigraphs were always important—Alberti's reflection: 'I look upon a picture with no less pleasure … than I read a good history … The historian paints with words, and the painter with his pencil' (*De Re Aedificatoria*).

In Washington, Margaret was introduced to the diplomat Paul William Jex Buxton (1925–2009) by a fellow pupil of McFarlane, Michael Wheeler-Booth. In September 1971 they married. They moved to Rome, where they lived in Trastevere. The marriage, which Margaret described as one of 'pure contentment', brought three step-children, Charles, Tobias and Mary, and the joy of their own two daughters, Sophie, an artist, and Hero.[16] It was while she was living in Rome in 1971 that Margaret conceived her *summa*, the great diptych, *England's Iconoclasts: I: Laws against Images* (Oxford, 1988) and *Broken Idols of the English Reformation* (Oxford, 2016), which would occupy the rest of her scholarly life. To her husband, who always greatly admired and supported her work, she dedicated it, in the decent obscurity of an ancient language:

[15] M. Aston, 'Lollardy and sedition 1381–1431', *Past and Present*, 17 (1960), 1–44.
[16] M. E. Batstone, *Cloisters*, Downe House school magazine; M. Sheppard, *The Independent*, 14 December 2014.

PAULO
ADIUTORI ALACRI
<DIFFICILIORI LECTORI>
MARITO CARO

While her husband was at the Northern Ireland Office between 1974 and 1985, the family lived in a series of houses in County Down. In 1984 Margaret became an Honorary Research Fellow of Queen's University, Belfast, where John Bossy, fellow historian of the social history of religion, became her friend. With small children, it was, she said, hard to hold a continuous thought, but she was an 'unfathomably gentle and patient' mother; Sophie could not 'remember her getting angry with me or Hero even once'. Neither family life nor her husband's position as Under-Secretary for Northern Ireland, 1981–1985, at the height of the Troubles, were always conducive to the calmer life of scholarship. In the preface to *England's Iconoclasts*, Margaret referred passingly to 'one unexpected and forcible clearance of my desk beside Belfast Lough'. Their house was blown up by the IRA. With early warning, the family escaped injury. Margaret's scattered papers were saved after a providentially dry night. It is hardly without significance that the great historian of the veneration of images and of their destruction should have lived both in Trastevere, the heart of Rome, and in Northern Ireland.

Six of her most important papers on Lollardy, written between 1960 and 1982, were reprinted, together with two new essays, in *Lollards and Reformers: Images and Literacy in Late Medieval Religion* (London, 1984). Here she considered Lollardy from its beginnings to its afterlife in the writings of late sixteenth-century Reformation propagandists, spanning the Reformation divide, and found the Lollards moving from their academic roots to a popular theology and personal faith founded in the reading of scripture and vernacular literature. Her research cast bright light on the lives and beliefs of the men and women of the movement, reconstructing their mental and social world. Were there Lollard women priests? Was literacy necessary for biblical understanding? It was the initial study of the Lollard assault on images, their fears that the gilded saints would seduce the faithful believer and inspire idolatry, that would lead to Margaret's enduring study of the power of images and their danger. In 1993, encouraged by Martin Sheppard, publisher at the Hambledon Press and her friend, she published a further collection of essays in *Faith and Fire: Popular and Unpopular Religion, 1350–1600* (London, 1993). This richly illustrated volume demonstrated, again, the depth and originality of her research and its latitude, for the essays ranged from the Lollard arguments for church disendowment to the learning of the Northern Renaissance, from Huizinga's *The Waning of the Middle Ages* to iconoclasm in Rickmansworth. The spirit of destruction and the rites of violence by which radical iconoclasts sent images to the amending flame had become a central focus of her work.

In the same year, *The King's Bedpost: Reformation and Iconography in a Tudor Group Portrait* (Cambridge, 1993) appeared. Investigating the esoteric painting of *King Edward VI and the Pope*, the work constructs a complex story of iconoclasm, artistic exchange and political tragedy, and makes a mysterious image speak again. Here Margaret discovered that this was not, as was once thought, a contemporary depiction, but a history painting made in the reign of Elizabeth, looking back on earlier reforms and perhaps painted as a warning to potential idolaters: to the Queen herself or to the Duke of Norfolk to deter him from marrying Mary, Queen of Scots. Immersed in sixteenth-century print culture, Margaret discovered that the unknown painter had used prints by the Dutch artist Martin van Heemskerck as a source and she revealed, more generally, the close ties between England and the Low Countries in the visual arts. In *Panorama of the Renaissance* (London, 1996) she devised a way of portraying central themes through art and created a visual feast of more than a thousand illustrations.

Many of the papers published in *Faith and Fire* were written by invitation. For this most private private scholar the ideal of the community of scholars was real. Commending Margaret's scholarly generosity, Colin Richmond wrote that this 'was based on an attitude to scholarship that deems it, first and foremost, one of communal endeavour. The doing of history is a social enterprise.'[17] She willingly accepted requests to lecture and was endlessly involved in scholarly collaborations, writing papers for edited volumes which were gilded by her contributions. In 1997 she edited, with Colin Richmond, *Lollardy and the Gentry in the Later Middle Ages* (Stroud), the proceedings of a conference they had organised at Newnham College two years earlier. And for Richmond, in friendship, she and Rosemary Horrox not only edited but privately published a collection of essays based around particular documents: *Much Heaving and Shoving: Late-Medieval Gentry and their Concerns* (Chipping, 2005). In 1996 she became a member of the advisory committee of the John Foxe Project at the University of Sheffield. For 2000–1 she served as President of the Ecclesiastical History Society, choosing as the theme for the annual conference 'The Church and the Book'. All the while, she continued to review. If not, for most of her life, a teacher, she was intensely interested in other scholars and their work, and she wrote references for many who remain grateful for her help in advancing their careers. The testament of her inspiration to other scholars, and of their affection as well as admiration for her, was the conference held in her honour in March 2008. The papers read there were published

---

[17] C. Richmond, 'Margaret Aston: an appreciation', in L. Clark, M. Jurkowski and C. Richmond (eds.), *Image, Text and Church, 1380–1600: Essays for Margaret Aston* (Toronto, 2009), p. 7.

as a Festschrift: *Image, Text and Church, 1380–1600: Essays for Margaret Aston* (Toronto, 2009), which contains a full list of her publications to that date (pp. 257–68).

Returning from Ireland to live in England, the family had settled in Chipping Ongar, Essex, in the Buxton family home, Castle House. In the inner bailey of the Norman motte and bailey castle, next to the castle mound, William Morice, a fervent evangelical, began to build Castle House in the 1540s. Margaret—writing as Margaret Buxton—told the story.[18] This was a family enclave, with step-children, and Sophie and her partner Rob, and their three children, Reuben, Phoebe and Hester, Margaret's grandchildren, living adjacent. Hero died in 2002. In the attic, next to Hero's bed-room—imaginatively painted with birds and flowers by Sophie—was Margaret's study, crammed with tottering piles of books and papers, with archaeological levels of notes and with uninterrupted views of the Essex countryside from her window. Out of this seeming chaos, with extraordinary discipline, stoicism and dauntless determina-tion, through four decades, she wrote the history of England's broken idols. At Margaret's feet were a succession of Cavalier King Charles spaniels—Moth, Thisbe, and lastly, Peaseblossom—eager to sit on a lap or game for a walk, perfect compan-ions for a scholar. If, for all the deep pleasures of family life, there were longueurs in life in an Essex village, or sometimes a sense of isolation, there were always visits to libraries and lectures to give.

Iconomachy and iconoclasm are world historical phenomena, as the destruction of the Buddhas at Bamyan in Afghanistan as idols by the Taliban in 2001 and the assault on the Temple of Bel at Palmyra by ISIS prove. Margaret Aston's profound achievement was to understand, describe and explain the great reversal in England over the course of its long Reformation, as image-worshippers were transformed into image-haters or image-breakers. Her two volumes considered the vast, superhuman destruction of venerated images, disrupting a millennium of worship, and the price of this revolution—the suffering and bewilderment of the deprived, the loss of loved objects of beauty, the wrecking of history and community. The epigraph taken from Ernst Gombrich—'Our attitude towards the image is inextricably bound up with our whole idea about the universe'[19]—signals the amplitude of her enterprise, which was hardly imagined until she undertook it. The sympathies of a historian so attuned to the beauties of art could not lie with the radical iconoclasts—'It takes great spirit to destroy great things. But I do not think that the iconoclasts were great-hearted' (*England's Iconoclasts*, p. 19)—but it was her purpose to understand and explain the 'death-dealing' (as Luther put it) animus, and through two volumes and nearly 1,500 pages she did, maintaining a remarkable objectivity.

[18] M. Buxton, 'Chipping Ongar and the Morices', in M. Leach (ed.), *Aspects of Ongar* (Ongar, 1999), pp. 34–49.
[19] E. H. Gombrich, *Symbolic Images* (London, 1972), p. 125.

She described a battle between word and image, as faith became a matter for ears rather than for eyes, and the process of oblivion whereby the holy could no longer be served by art. As physical idols were cast down in parish churches, the radicals assailed the images remaining in the mind's eye of the believer. For them, to imagine God, the Ancient of Days, as an old man with a beard, or Christ suffering on the cross, was a primal sin; this was to erect idols in the mind, and the memory of such 'feigned' images must be excised. Idolatry began within, embedded in man's fallen being. Less absolute than Calvin, Luther questioned an extremity—comfortless and censorious—which seemed to be at war with what it was to be human. Now even the raptures of romantic love became suspect, for to 'worship' the beloved derogated from the worship due to God alone. 'To love, as Ben Jonson loved Shakespeare "this side idolatry", was to dare devotion on the knife-edge between the most sacred and most sinful' (*England's Iconoclasts*, p. 467). In the heady days of the Civil War, zealots were convinced that both idolaters and adulterers deserved the death penalty. *England's Iconoclasts* traced the gigantic shift in religious consciousness that involved changes in both divine and secular laws, including the elevation of the Decalogue's prohibition of images into a separate commandment. The depth and range of Margaret's research was prodigious, spanning centuries, from the pronouncements of the Church Fathers, to the icono-clastic dispute that divided the Eastern Church in the eighth and ninth centuries, to the Lollard opposition to images, the shifting official policies of the Tudor monarchs and the busy iconoclasts of the Civil War. All this research was conducted in librar-ies—often distant from her Chipping Ongar fastness—rather than online.

Not everyone who promises a second volume fulfils the pledge, but Margaret kept faith with the great project which she had conceived in 1971. *Broken Idols of the Reformation* was published posthumously in 2016 (Cambridge), a thousand pages brought through the press by her daughter Sophie, who had known the work all her life, and her great-niece Venetia Bridges. This is an examination of the practice and experience of iconoclasm through the long centuries of the English Reformation, and its consequences for English culture. For most people, it was only when they went to church that they saw sculpture, painting, stained glass or heard contrapuntal music, but the reformers condemned all this as idolatry, and parishioners might become exiled in their own churches. Even a sound might be idolised, so church bells were silenced and the Angelus no longer rang out. There was midnight and midday destruc-tion, legal and illegal—individual, vigilante acts of destruction, and official ones. Images might be smashed or burnt or turned into 'idol' toys for children. Some were hidden away 'against another day' when they could return, and illustrations of images that survive from the thousands upon thousands that were lost, poignant remnants of a lost world, illumine the text. The tetragrammaton might replace the hoary vision of God the Father, but iconoclasts could never prevent the Holy Ghost flying as a dove in the imaging mind. Crosses were most ubiquitous and dangerous of all—in churches, in homes, by the wayside, in the memory, made as gestures in the air, sketched with thumb on a baby's forehead—and must be 'down a'. But there were crosses everywhere in God's creation. As John Donne asked:

> Who can deny mee power, and liberty
> To stretch mine armes, and mine own Crosse to be?
> Swimme, and at every stroake, thou art thy Crosse
> …
> Looke up, thou seest birds rais'd on crossed wings:[20]

But a nation that vanquished idolatry in the church might still practise it in the state. No historian of the Reformation can think of it in the same way after this magisterial work.

All Margaret's immense learning was born lightly. She wrote with a quiet power, in elegant and lucid prose, expressing complex ideas simply. Her style, the image of character, was never polemical; rather, she wrote as if stitching a tapestry. Theory had its part—Neoplatonic art theory and the psychology of Jung, for images served a psychological need. Themes and characters recurred. Apt metaphors, vivid images and vignettes, and telling quotations were characteristic of her writing, and the epigraphs particularly revealed her eclectic reading. Her shelves at Castle House were full of modern poetry, and it was in her heart and head. She might as easily quote modern poets, or Corneille, Dante, Hardy or Marie Lloyd, the music hall legend—'I am one of the ruins that Cromwell knocked about a bit'—as Reformation ideologues. This monumental work could only have been written by a historian not only of the deepest learning but also of the widest human sympathy.

For this most modest scholar there were due honours: Fellowship of the Society of Antiquaries of London (1987) and of the British Academy (1994), an honorary doctorate of the University of York (2001) and in 2013 a CBE 'for services to historical scholarship'. But her principal distinction was of character. Her friends eulogised her in superlatives, remembering her 'noble, caring heart', as 'noble in her courtesy … gracious and generous in her relations with others', her 'human magnificence', her 'nobility of mind', her kindness. To know her even a little was to recognise these qualities. She was a life-enhancing spirit. I remember her eager quickness and delight as she and I drove—with my spaniels perched precariously, illegally on her lap—to see the Creed windows at the Cheyne family church of Drayton Beauchamp. She died on 22 November 2014, while walking by the castle mound at Chipping Ongar.

---

[20] H. Gardner (ed.), *John Donne: the Divine Poems* (Oxford, 1952), p. 26.

Note on the author: Dr Susan Brigden is Supernumerary Fellow at Lincoln College, Oxford; she was elected a Fellow of the British Academy in 2014.

DAVID LOWENTHAL

David Lowenthal

26 April 1923 – 15 September 2018

elected Fellow of the British Academy 2001

by

TREVOR BARNES
Fellow of the Academy

HUGH CLOUT
Fellow of the Academy

Belonging to a family of lawyers and professors, the polymath David Lowenthal hated disciplinary divisions. American by birth but British by inclination, he learned the practice of geography through wartime service in Western Europe. During a long and highly productive career, spent mainly at the American Geographical Society and then at University College London, he made important contributions to Caribbean studies, environmental history, landscape interpretation and cultural and historical geography. His later work on heritage informs mangement agencies across the globe. The ideas of the pioneering nineteenth-century environmentalist George Perkins March formed an essential touchstone for many aspects of his writing. In addition to scholarly articles and books (notably *The Past is a Foreign Country*), Lowenthal also wrote for a wider audience. His impact in the public realm was arguably as great as that among academics.

Biographical Memoirs of Fellows of the British Academy, XVIII, 337–363
Posted 31 October 2019. © British Academy 2019.

DAVID LOWENTHAL

David Lowenthal was an intellectual giant who worked with brilliance and originality across many fields of scholarly enquiry. American by birth, British by inclination, his span of expertise extended far beyond the disciplines of geography and history in which he was formally trained. At the convergence of the humanities and social sciences, his writings covered historical geography, environmental perception, Caribbean studies, landscape interpretation, environmental history, heritage studies and cultural history. Peter Seixas remarked: 'I marvelled at his breadth of knowledge. It gave me a sense of wonder. How did he manage to keep all those different sources in his head at the same time?'[1] Or again, Laura Watt said that I was 'so impressed by … his ability to play with material across centuries, and across disciplines. [It] was truly astounding … [His] polymath mind [was] quoting a Roman philosopher in one breath and discussing skateboarders or some recent film in the next.'[2]

In a very long career, sixty-plus years that were abidingly productive, David's essays and major books enjoyed significant academic and popular audiences. They were marked, first, by immense erudition, though worn lightly, never pedantic or stuffy, and, second, by considered judgement. He thought that the problem with many disciplines, including his own, geography, was their over-concern with present crisis, which allowed no time to think of anything else.[3] In contrast, he believed scholars needed time to ponder, to contemplate, to reflect. He adhered to Erwin Panofsky's argument 'In defense of the Ivory Tower'.[4] He did not remain cloistered in an Ivory Tower, however. He became increasingly a public intellectual, speaking out and influencing international and national public and private institutions concerned with issues of history, memory, conservation and above all heritage. Never a shrinking violet, he urged, 'Our heritage must be accepted in its totality, the vile along with the valiant, the evil along with the eminent, the sorrowful as well as the splendid. Consciously informed use of heritage is essential to civilized life.'[5]

[1] Peter Seixas interview with Barnes, 30 April 2019.
[2] L. Watt, 'David Lowenthal and the genesis of critical conservation thought', paper given at the annual meeting of the *American Association of Geographers*, Washington, DC, 6 April 2019.
[3] D. Lowenthal and Y. Hamilakis, 'A conversation with David Lowenthal' [on 28 January], *Annual Review of Anthropology*, 46 (2017), 1–18.
[4] E. Panofsky, *In Defense of the Ivory Tower* (Cambridge, MA: Harvard Alumni Bulletin, 1957).
[5] D. Lowenthal, 'Why the past matters', *Heritage and Society*, 4 (2011), 167.

The life

Early years and army service (1923–46)

David Lowenthal was born on 26 April 1923 in New York City, the eldest child of Max Lowenthal (1887–1971, b. Minneapolis, Minnesota) and Eleanor (née Mack; 1898–1965, b. New York City).[6] From a first-generation Jewish family from Lithuania, Max graduated from the University of Minnesota in 1909, and three years later gained a law degree from Harvard. In 1915, he established his own legal practice in New York City specialising in labour law, concerned particularly with the protection of workers' rights. By the 1930s he was 'a very wealthy New York lawyer', with a home on Central Park West in the heart of Manhattan.[7] Early on Max's work led him into politics and public service both within the 'New Deal' of Roosevelt and later government war work. Always an out-of-sight influence, he never ran for public office or electioneered. In the mid-1930s Max befriended then Senator Harry Truman who, after he became president (1945–1953), appointed him to a series of national counsels and committees. In 1946 Max was sent to Berlin to gather evidence for the restitution of property stolen by the Nazis and later he influenced Truman's 1948 decision to recognise the State of Israel. Because of his commitment to and defence of labour rights, along with his close relation to Truman, from 1947 Max came under the scrutiny of J. Edgar Hoover and the Federal Bureau of Investigation (FBI) he directed. Max's response was to write an exposé, *The Federal Bureau of Investigation* (New York, 1950), detailing egregious examples of the agency's spying, 'red-baiting' and harassment of radicals and foreigners. Inevitably, it made Max only more of a marked man. Subsequently, questions were asked about him at Senator Joseph McCarthy's House Un-American Activities Committee, ending his thirty-eight years as a public servant.

David and his younger brother, John (1925–2003, a lawyer and filmmaker), and sister Elizabeth ('Betty Levin', b. 1927, a children's novelist) thus grew up in an affluent, highly educated, socially well-connected, liberal reformist family. Their mother, Eleanor, had a degree in history and music from Radcliffe College. Her uncle, Julian William Mack (1866–1943), was a University of Chicago law professor and then US Court of Appeals judge, while Max's brother-in-law, James Gutmann (1897–1988), was a Columbia University philosophy professor. David recalled the dinner table conversation as 'dazzling'.[8] As befitting their social class, the family boasted an Irish nanny, a dedicated cook and a farmhouse holiday home at Bridgewater in the Litchfield Hills, north-west Connecticut. Other vacations were spent on the Massachusetts

[6] H. Clout, 'David Lowenthal, 1923–2018', *Geographical Journal*, 185 (2019), 127–8.
[7] Anon. 'Adele D. Bramwen, artist, 64, is dead', *New York Times*, 14 August 1964.
[8] D. Lowenthal, 'David Lowenthal: childhood, schooling, army' (undated typescript), 15.

island of Martha's Vineyard. At an early age, David was taught piano, and attended in New York first the Walden School and later the Lincoln School of Teachers' College, Columbia University. Founded in 1917, the Lincoln School was based on the educational methods of the well-known American pragmatist philosopher and educator John Dewey (1859–1952). Encouraging individual exploration, learning by doing and collaborative small-group work, David was in his element, freely indulging his passion for reading. Later in life, he described himself as a 'bookish voyager'.[9] Following Dewey, the school also emphasised the importance of public service, a responsibility to contribute to the larger social conversation, and a striking leitmotiv of David's later work as a scholar.

Such was the high reputation of the Lincoln School that David was not required to take the normal entrance exam for admittance to Harvard, where between 1940 and 1943 he read for a BS degree in History (he was denied a BA because he lacked Latin). To say he read for a History degree is misleading, however. At Harvard he designed his own academic programme avoiding specialisation, allowing him to read expansively. As he later remarked: 'I hate disciplines. Specialization has been the bane of education.'[10] Despite his free-form degree programme, he never took a geography class; in fact, he never even heard of Harvard's Department of Geography. He enjoyed a course in geology, though, and assisted the director of the university's meteorological institute drawing weather maps for the Joint Army-Navy Weather Agency. Furthermore, his final-year honours thesis was on a classic topic within political geography, the placement of a national border, in his case the New Brunswick (Canada)-Maine (United States) boundary dispute.[11]

Because of the war, he was among the many in his class of 1944 who completed the four-year degree in three years. In May 1943, within a week he went from Harvard Yard to army boot camp. He had been drafted into the US infantry. It was a radically different world.

> Twenty-five-mile hikes carrying 50-pound packs alternated with rifle instruction and bayonet assaults on stuffed dummies. From April to July we were based first at hot, dry, dusty Camp Phillips, Kansas, then at hot, wet, humid Fort Collins, Arkansas, and finally in the swampy mosquito-ridden marshlands of northern Louisiana, before boarding ship for France.[12]

[9] D. Lowenthal, 'Remarks upon receipt of the Victoria Medal', *Geographical Journal*, 163 (1997), 355.
[10] Lowenthal and Hamilakis, 'A conversation', 2.
[11] D. Lowenthal, 'The Maine Press and the Aroostook War', *Canadian Historical Review*, 32 (1951), 315–36.
[12] D. Lowenthal, 'From infantry to intelligence in wartime France, 1944–45' (an unpublished memoir updated by David in 2018), 1.

David arrived at Cherbourg in Normandy on 15 September 1944, some three months after D-Day. He was a rifleman in General Omar Bradley's First Army. Because of short-sightedness and an ability to speak some French, he was excused the usual duties of a GI, assigned instead to teach troops enough of the language to get along with the locals. But the locals 'had enough of soldiers in their midst, German or Allied, and wished to see the back of us as soon as possible', he later recalled.[13] To that end, 'they plied us with diarrhoea-inducing unripe camembert and with the rawest of calvados, swilled in such quantity as to blind many soldiers used to nothing stronger than beer'.

In October, David's company left Normandy and headed east toward the Vosges mountains. At first they encountered 'only tattered remnants of German forces'.[14] Each day armed forays led to the capture of a few wounded German teenage soldiers who had only recently been press-ganged into the *Wehrmacht*. With his command of German enhanced during infantry training, David was charged with interrogating them. It was a case of 'one terrified young man questioning another terrified young man', he later acknowledged.[15] The wounded Germans were desperate to get word back to their families. Years later, David admitted: 'Twice I promised dying boys this would be done, although I knew it could not. Those young lives ebbing away for some remote insane cause haunt me to this day.'[16]

As David's company continued eastward, now over rough terrain and in appalling weather, it met major resistance. Asked-for reinforcements never came, and his company began to run low on food and water. Unable to advance, David and his comrades dug in, confined to foxholes that were soon wet, boggy and waterlogged. In turn, days of enforced immobility produced 'trench foot', a fungal infection due to booted immersion. When relief finally arrived, trench-foot invalids, including David, had to be carried to field camp, then sent by train to the coast. Once across the Channel, he was transported by hospital train to Taunton, Somerset. There his feet were elevated, left uncovered until the swelling subsided and he could walk again. That stay in England proved pivotal. To recuperate, David took walking trips into the Somerset countryside, provoking an 'immediate affection for England'.[17] That feeling never dissipated. He found a new home.

In December 1944 David was reassigned to military intelligence at the London outpost of the Office of Strategic Services (OSS), forerunner of the CIA. At first, using Baedekers and other travel guides, his assignment was to count lavatories in German castles to ascertain if there were an appropriate per capita number for

[13] Ibid., 1.
[14] Ibid., 2.
[15] D. Lowenthal in conversation with H. Clout.
[16] Lowenthal, 'From infantry to intelligence', 2.
[17] Ibid., 2.

occupying Allied officers. A month later, he was dispatched to Paris to work on the OSS's Intelligence Photographic Documentation Project (IPDP), 'a grand and never completed mission to survey and catalogue the whole of western Europe's terrain and built environment' in preparation for any future military conflict.[18] Working officially now as 'a geographer', David went to France, Belgium, Luxembourg, eastern Germany and Bohemia. In this role, he acquired the geographical skills he had not received at Harvard. His discharge papers disclosed at OSS that he carried out 'geographic survey and fieldtrips . . . Wrote reports on military geography, with relation to industrial installations, topography, communications, transportation, and other social and economic features, [and] briefed air photo intelligence teams on the above areas.'[19]

David believed his assignment to IPDP was because of a recommendation from the French geographer, Jean Gottmann, FBA (1915–94), who was related to his philosopher uncle, James Gutmann (Lowenthal 2007).[20] In 1941, Gottmann, who was Jewish, fled to the United States to avoid the Vichy regime and the Nazis. Max Lowenthal supervised him when Gottmann then worked as an advisor to the US Board of Economic Warfare. It was also during that period David first met the French geographer.[21] After Gottmann returned to France in 1945 on a mission for the French government, the two resumed their friendship: Gottmann was twenty-nine, David twenty-one. In Paris, Gottmann took David to several small select gatherings of French academics, including André Siegfried (1875–1959), who discussed especially the forthcoming shape of the postwar world.

For the IPDP, geographers worked with photographers in two-person teams travelling by jeep to areas to be surveyed. David and his photographer, Joe Bucolo, took and annotated tens of thousands of photographs. Their text and images were edited and printed in Paris, then sent back across the Atlantic. Their final mission was in southern Belgium in late summer 1945. There, however, while directing Bucolo who was driving, David fell off the jeep's roof and fractured his wrist. Sent back to America, he was discharged from the army in September 1945, but continued to work on issues of military intelligence in the State Department for another twelve months. In the end, neither the landscape photos nor descriptions he compiled were ever used. The entire body of IPDP's texts and images went up in flames in a warehouse fire outside Washington, DC.

[18] Ibid., 3.
[19] Ibid., 3.
[20] D. Lowenthal, 'Mémoires de temps de guerre et de la paix', in *L'Orbite de la Géographie de Jean Gottmann, La Géographie* 1523bis (2007), 190–4. On Gottmann, see H. Clout and P. Hall, 'Jean Gottmann 1915–1994', *Proceedings of the British Academy*, 120 (2003), pp. 201–15.
[21] L. Muscarà, 'David Lowenthal's past and our foreign present', paper given at the annual meeting of the *American Association of Geographers*, Washington, DC, 6 April 2019.

Although the fruits of David's wartime labour were destroyed, the efforts themselves, as David said shortly before his death, were 'formative and hugely important. [It was] through military intelligence work I became a geographer.'[22] He learned how to undertake field surveys; to depict and to interpret natural and human-made landscape features; to use photography and writing to represent different forms of terrain and the built environment; and finally, to know and to appreciate European regional landscapes, especially those of Britain, which were markedly different from those in the United States.

Graduate school and the American Geographical Society (1946–72)

In autumn 1946, rather than studying geography when he entered graduate school at Columbia, David took pre-med courses including psychology.[23] Gottmann changed that. Now teaching at the Johns Hopkins University in Baltimore, Maryland, Gottmann met David on several occasions. In 1947, he helped him secure a summer internship at the American Geographical Society (AGS) in Manhattan, and then persuaded him to transfer to the graduate programme in Geography at the University of California, Berkeley, shaped and run by perhaps America's most famous twentieth-century geographer, Carl Ortwin Sauer (1889–1975: America's 'Dean of geographers' as the *New York Times* called him in his obituary). Sauer was another polymath and like David was suspicious of disciplinary boundaries. The two were made for one another. David fell under his influence, recognising Sauer's 'intellectual curiosity and drive [that] embraced every epoch and every aspect of the ever-changing interplay between humans and their earthly home'.[24] David could not speak Spanish, however, so he was unable to carry out fieldwork in Mexico or in many parts of South America, the usual research sites for Sauer's students. He was given two weeks to find an alternative field location.[25] Given his facility in English, German and French, he selected the three Guianas—British, Dutch and French—during their colonial period and defined by the use of African slave and Asian indentured labour.[26] It led David to be interested in the larger Caribbean region, particularly the islands of the West Indies, and it remained a research interest throughout his career.

---

[22] Lowenthal and Hamilakis, 'A conversation', 2.

[23] H. Clout in conversation with Mary Alice Lowenthal, 15 November 2018.

[24] D. Lowenthal, 'Foreword', in M. Williams with D. Lowenthal and W. Denevan, *To Pass on a Good Earth: the Life and Work of Carl O. Sauer* (Charlottesville, NC, 2014), pp. vii–xi, vii.

[25] Watt, 'David Lowenthal and the genesis of critical conservation thought'.

[26] D. Lowenthal, 'Colonial experiments in French Guiana, 1760–1800', *Hispanic American Historical Review*, 32 (1952), 22–43; D. Lowenthal, 'Population contrasts in the Guianas', *Geographical* Review, 50 (1960), 41–58; D. Lowenthal, 'The range and variation of Caribbean societies', *Annals of the New York Academy of* Sciences, 83 (1960), 786–95.

For his doctoral research, Sauer and his colleague, John Leighly (1895–1986), encouraged David to study the life and work of the early American environmentalist George Perkins Marsh (1801–1882).[27] Rather than remain at Berkeley, however, David undertook that topic at the University of Wisconsin, Madison. Initially intending to enter the Geography Department, in the end he decided History was more intellectually congenial. His supervisor was Merle Curti (1897–1996), with geographers Richard Hartshorne (1899–1992) and Andrew Hill Clark (1911–1975) members of his supervisory committee. David's subsequent dissertation demonstrated that Marsh's experiences in his native Vermont and later during his diplomatic career in Turkey and Italy had profoundly shaped his depiction of the adverse impact of humans on the natural landscape of the Alps and Mediterranean Basin. In this sense, the dissertation was a case study of what David would soon call 'environmental perception', showing in this case how the life of Marsh had fashioned his environmental attitudes, allowing him to perceive the pernicious effects of human action on nature. But the thesis was also an account of the beginning of the idea of American nature conservation. Going against the nineteenth-century grain of the advocation of a rapacious destruction of nature, Marsh in *Man and Nature* urged its protection and preservation.[28] In effect, David's thesis anticipated the concerns of the environmental movement that were to become so prominent during the next decade and culminating in Earth Day (1970).[29] In early summer 1952, David presented a paper from his thesis at the International Geographical Union conference in Washington, DC and impressed three British geographers from University College London (UCL) who were in the audience: Henry Clifford Darby, FBA (1909–1992), William Richard Mead, FBA (1915–2014) and Eric Brown (1922–2018).[30] It was to become an important encounter for his later career.

In autumn 1952, David was hired as Assistant Professor of Geography at the then all-women Vassar College, Poughkeepsie, New York. He later said that the mostly women faculty members were collectively one of the most impressive group of

[27] B. Clark and J. B. Foster, 'George Perkins Marsh and the transformation of Earth', *Organization & Environment*, 15 (2002), 164–9.

[28] G. P. Marsh, *Man and Nature, or Physical Geography Modified by Human Action* (New York, 1864); D. Lowenthal, 'George Perkins Marsh and the American geographical tradition', *Geographical Review*, 43 (1953), 207–13; D. Lowenthal, 'George Perkins Marsh on the nature and purpose of geography', *Geographical Journal*, 126 (1960), 413–17.

[29] D. Lowenthal, 'Eden, Earth Day and Ecology: landscape restoration as metaphor and mission', *Landscape Research*, 38 (2013), 5–31.

[30] Lowenthal, 'George Perkins Marsh and the American geographical tradition'; D. Lowenthal, 'George Perkins Marsh and Scandinavian studies', *Scandinavian Studies*, 29 (1957), 41–52. On Darby see M. Williams, 'Henry Clifford Darby 1909–1992', *Proceedings of the British Academy*, 87 (1995), pp. 289–306; on Mead see H. Clout, 'William Richard Mead 1915–2014', *Biographical Memoirs of Fellows of the British Academy*, 14 (2015), pp. 383–408.

colleagues with whom he ever worked.[31] Apart from offering new courses on modern imperialism and the geography of underdeveloped areas, he arranged for Vassar to be a depository of the US Army Map Service and to receive a collection of US Geological Survey maps. While there David also revised his thesis for publication, retitled *George Perkins Marsh: Versatile Vermonter*.[32] He dedicated it to Merle Curti, acknowledging also editorial assistance from his first wife, Jane (1916–2002), whom he met at Vassar. There had never been anything quite like that book published in geography, a study combining painstakingly researched biography with a sophisticated political and social argument for environmental conservation. Clarence J. Glacken (1909–1989), the great Berkeley geography scholar of the history of the idea of nature, and who within a decade would publish his own magnum opus, *Traces on the Rhodian Shore*, called David's book 'satisfying, deeply human, and extremely interesting [and] a fitting memorial to Marsh and a great credit to its author'.[33]

Even before David's book was published, he was talent-spotted by the Director of the AGS, Charles Baker Hitchcock (1906–1969). In 1956, along with two other brilliant young men—William Warntz (1922–1988) and Calvin John Heusser (1924–2006)—Hitchcock appointed David as an AGS Research Associate, giving him the luxury of pursuing any research interest with no teaching obligation. David initiated two research projects, both building on his graduate work. The first was on the islands of the Caribbean. The very same year David started at AGS he was awarded a Fulbright Fellowship (1956–7) at the University College of the West Indies in Jamaica. It allowed him to continue working on the Caribbean and the ecologies and societies of islands more generally. A Rockefeller Foundation grant (1960–2) further consolidated that interest resulting, first, in the edited collection *The West Indies Federation: Perspectives on a New Nation* and, later, the single-authored tome, *West Indian Societies*.[34] A central element in both books was the issue of race, leading David to work sporadically for more than a decade in London for a non-profit think tank, the Institute of Race Relations (1961–72).

The second was to integrate environmental perception, environmental history and cultural landscape in studies of the meaning of place. This line of inquiry partly emerged from his study of Marsh, but it was also inspired by John Kirtland Wright (1891–1969), David's mentor at the AGS, who earlier developed the idea of 'geosophy',

---

[31] Lowenthal and Hamilakis, 'A conversation', 5.

[32] D. Lowenthal, *George Perkins Marsh: Versatile Vermonter* (New York, 1958).

[33] C. J. Glacken, *Traces on the Rhodian Shore* (Berkeley, CA, 1967); C. J. Glacken, 'George Perkins Marsh: Versatile Vermonter', *Geographical Review*, 49 (1959), 437–8.

[34] D. Lowenthal (ed.), *The West Indies Federation: Perspectives on a New Nation* (New York, 1961); D. Lowenthal, *West Indian Societies* (New York, 1972).

defined as 'the study of geographical knowledge from any or all points of view'.[35] In David's case his question was how place, environment and landscape were perceived differently by different people. He answered it in one of his most celebrated academic papers, 'Geography, experience, and imagination: towards a geographical epistemology', published in the discipline's flagship journal, the *Annals of the Association of American Geographers*.[36] David concluded that essay:

> Every image and idea about the world is compounded of personal experience, imagination, and memory. The places that we live in, those we visit and travel through, the worlds we read about and see in works of art, and the realms of imagination and fantasy each contribute to our images of nature and man. All types of experience, from those most closely linked with our everyday world to those which seem furthest removed, come together to make up our individual picture of reality.[37]

Over the rest of the 1960s, David continued work on environmental perception, often at interdisciplinary meetings held at the AGS under the aegis of the American Association for the Advancement of Science. He also received grants to pursue the topic from Resources for the Future Inc., and a prestigious Guggenheim Fellowship (1965–6). His work attracted much attention not only in geography but also in architecture, planning, landscape design and urban studies, with numerous invitations to present talks and to take up visiting professorships including at Berkeley, Columbia, MIT and Harvard.[38] One of those invitations came from geographers at UCL, a result in part because of the paper he gave on Marsh at the 1952 IGU in Washington, DC. The Head at UCL Geography, the esteemed historical geographer, Clifford Darby, wrote the invitation. At UCL, David collaborated with historical geographer Hugh Prince (1927–2013), developing a remarkably fruitful investigation of the characteristics of English landscapes, their perception and appreciation.[39] David cherished the partnership, saying it engendered 'an extraordinary sense of togetherness [and] was too enjoyable to give up'.[40] But he didn't have to. Because of increasingly acute money

---

[35] J. K. Wright, 'Terrae incognitae: the place of imagination in geography', *Annals of the Association of American Geographers*, 37 (1947), 12.

[36] D. Lowenthal, 'Geography, experience, and imagination: towards a geographical epistemology', *Annals of the Association of American Geographers*, 51 (1961), 241–60.

[37] Ibid., 260.

[38] D. Lowenthal, 'Fruitful liaison or folie à deux? The Association of American Geographers and the American Geographical Society', *Professional Geographer*, 57 (2005), 472.

[39] D. Lowenthal and H. C. Prince, 'The English landscape', *Geographical Review*, 54 (1964), 309–46; D. Lowenthal and H. C. Prince, 'English landscape tastes', *Geographical Review* 55 (1965), 186–222; D. Lowenthal and H. C. Prince, 'English façades', *Architectural Association Quarterly*, 1 (1969), 50–64; D. Lowenthal and H. C. Prince, 'Transcendental experience', in S. Wapner, S. Cohen and B. Kaplan (eds.), *Experiencing the Environment* (New York, 1976), pp. 117–31.

[40] D. Lowenthal, 'Reminiscences', talk given at UCL in 2002.

problems at the AGS—he was the last remaining Research Associate on the payroll—
David moved permanently to UCL in 1972, taking up the Chair of Geography vacated
by Asian specialist, Paul Wheatley, FBA (1921–1999).

University College London and after (1972–2018)

David Lowenthal was not the first choice, however. Colleagues in the UCL department
were almost unanimous that Wheatley's successor should be a model builder or a
quantifier. Three distinguished geographers of that persuasion were approached by
the head of the College, but each declined to apply. It was then that David was
considered. The Head of the Department, William Mead, wrote to UCL's Provost,
Noel Annan (1916–2000), to justify David's candidature: 'We are looking first and
foremost for a distinguished scholar, [someone] excellent with post-graduate students
. . . The very last thing we are looking for is an administrator.'[41] With a firm commitment that administration would never come his way, which he saw as 'a real blessing',
David accepted the offer.[42] The special dispensation was not revealed to junior
colleagues, however.

Over the next thirteen years at UCL, David taught undergraduate courses about
the West Indies, environmental perception (with Jacquie Burgess), and latterly conservation and preservation (with Hugh Prince). During 1977–8, one of the authors of
this essay, Barnes, was in David's upper-year environmental perception course. He was
a superb lecturer, the best that Barnes had as an undergraduate; each of his presentations was lucid, witty and erudite, with stunning visual illustrations, impeccably timed,
always ending with some biting take-home point despite a beguiling grin and carefree
shrug. David's intellectual sophistication and deep learning made us afraid of him,
though. He was so unlike any of us mere undergraduate mortals. He was the only
American that Barnes knew, however, so when he received during his third year a
clutch of offers from US Geography graduate schools, as nervous as he was having
never spoken to him before, he knocked on David's office door seeking advice. He
could not have been more generous and welcoming. Pouring glasses of sherry from a
bottle stored in a top filing cabinet and quickly perusing the offers, David said: 'You
must go to Minnesota. My father was from Minnesota, and he was a good and true
man. Go there.' Barnes did, never regretting it, forever grateful for the unreserved
good and true guidance. In 1971 David had taught the spring term in Minnesota,
where he enjoyed a lively discourse with his colleagues in geography.

---

[41] UCL Archives, Letter from N. Annan to R. W. Steel, 6 May 1972.
[42] Lowenthal and Hamilakis, 'A conversation', 5.

But not only undergraduates were intimidated by David; postgraduates and junior faculty were too. Despite Mead's justification to the Provost, David supervised only one doctoral student to completion during his tenure at UCL (although he ran many training sessions for postgraduates). It was hard not to feel overawed, to cower under David's encyclopaedic knowledge, capacious razor-sharp memory and flawlessly formed rounded sentences. It was unfortunate, though, given David's also great generosity and hospitality. For example, he hosted many distinguished North American scholars at departmental seminars, accommodating them in his home, holding Saturday evening parties for them with his wife Mary Alice (née Lamberty) at their large rambling house at Harrow-on-the-Hill. He was a gregarious, welcoming man, with a fondness for puns and an anecdote for every occasion, but these qualities were sometimes concealed when he took on the formal scholarly persona of the distinguished Professor David Lowenthal. He especially missed at UCL interaction with Master's students, an opportunity afforded him within North American universities, but not in Britain during the 1970s and early 1980s. To compensate he looked to the wider intellectual community within and beyond the University of London, where he gave myriad guest seminars to advanced scholars in anthropology, archaeology, architecture and design, art history, planning, heritage studies and landscape architecture. He also used long vacations to make new academic contacts around the world.[43]

In early autumn 1985, when British universities were under severe financial constraint, David's position at UCL came to an end. His plan was to take up an adjunct professorship at Berkeley, and to that end he and his wife purchased a house in the Berkeley hills. The professorship materialised but he decided against taking it up because Europe had so many intellectual possibilities. Nonetheless, he kept the house and after 2002 lived there about a third of each year—Berkeley was 'not really America' he once said.[44] London remained his base, first at Harrow-on-the-Hill, later a flat in Marylebone, central London, close to Wigmore Hall where he and wife frequently attended concerts (David never listened to recorded music or watched television). Even though he had no permanent academic job, he continued to hold short-term visiting professorships both in the UK and the USA, organise seminar series, give prestigious named lectures, contribute to scholarly societies and institutions, and especially to advise heritage organisations and to engage in public debates about heritage. He was fulfilling Dewey's charge to participate in the social conversation.

[43] D. Lowenthal, 'Perceiving the Australian environment', in G. Seddon and M. Davis (eds.), *Man and Landscape in Australia: Towards an Ecological Vision* (Canberra, 1976), pp. 357–65; D. Lowenthal, 'Australian images: the unique present, the mythical past', in P. Quartermaine (ed.), *Readings in Australian Arts* (Exeter, 1978), pp. 84–93; D. Lowenthal, 'Mobility and identity in the island Pacific: a critique', *Pacific Viewpoint*, 26 (1985), 316–26.
[44] G. Seddon, 'David Lowenthal: a tribute', *Journal of Australian Studies*, 27 (2003), 1.

Among the many organisations he advised included UNESCO, the International Council on Monuments and Sites, the International Council of Museums, the Getty Conservation Institute, the World Monuments Fund, the Council of Europe and English Heritage. In the public media he contributed notably to the disputes around the Parthenon sculptures ('Elgin marbles'), and the Cecil Rhodes statues in Cape Town and Oxford.[45]

While doing all these things David also managed to keep his nose to the grindstone of writing, turning out matchless prose in the form of a continuous production line of academic papers and single-authored books (four after 1985). The most well known, *The Past Is a Foreign Country*, appeared just a month after he left UCL.[46] Lavishly illustrated, about landscape, history, memory and heritage, it was a doorstopper, just shy of 500 pages. It kept on selling and was reprinted continually (three times alone in 1988). Thirty years later, a new version appeared, enlarged by a third with 3,000 footnotes, *The Past is a Foreign Country—Revisited*.[47] In 2016, this version won the British Academy Medal in recognition of its 'landmark academic achievement which has transformed understanding in the humanities and social sciences'. Not bad for a 93-year-old.

Central to David's prodigious output was his wife, Mary Alice, a former editor at the AGS. She was, as Neil Silberman puts it, 'David's sounding board, editor, and overall enabler of his continuing research and travel'.[48] Certainly, Lowenthal, as David Livingstone avows, was one of the 'discipline's great writers … [defined] by the richness of his vocabulary, the grace of his prose, and the elegance of his rhetoric'.[49] But that writing was fashioned in part by Mary Alice's 'sharp editorial pen', as Kenneth Olwig observes.[50] He adds that while 'the ideas are Lowenthal's … it is the skill of the editor that makes a key difference in the reading value and shelf life of a manuscript'.[51]

[45] D. Lowenthal, 'Classical antiquities as national and global heritage', *Antiquity*, 62 (1988), 726–35; D. Lowenthal, 'On arraigning ancestors: a critique of historical contrition', *North Carolina Law Review*, 87 (2009), 901–66; D. Lowenthal, 'Facing up to the deplorable past', *Perspectives on History*, 12 May 2016.

[46] D. Lowenthal, *The Past is a Foreign Country* (Cambridge, 1985).

[47] D. Lowenthal, *The Past is a Foreign Country—Revisited* (Cambridge, 2015). In 2011, David Lowenthal and Simon Jenkins had discussed 'Prizing the past for the present and the future' at the British Academy, subsequently written up in *British Academy Review*, 18 (Summer 2011).

[48] N. A. Silberman, 'David Lowenthal, 1923–2018', *International Journal of Cultural Property*, 25 (2018), 242.

[49] D. Livingstone, 'George Perkins Marsh: prophet of conservation', *Social and Cultural Geographies*, 3 (2002), 351–2.

[50] K. R. Olwig, 'In memoriam: a consummate scholar, David Lowenthal (26 April 1923–15 September 2018). A personal memory', *Landscape Research*, 44 (2019), 115.

[51] Ibid.

Throughout, David maintained a relentless schedule of travel long into 'retire-ment'—attending conferences, presenting talks, acting as a heritage consultant, jour-neying to new islands and revisiting old ones.[52] *Quest for the Unity of Knowledge*, his last book, the proofs of which he planned to begin reading the day he died, fittingly brought together the major themes of David's elongated and illustrious scholarly life.[53] They included the environment, human perception, race and religion, the past and present, heritage, conservation, landscape, geography and history, and island life. As Sverker Sörlin writes, 'These are themes that have been lived [by David] as much as they have been researched.'[54] David died in his sleep on 15 September 2018 in his ninety-sixth year, survived by Mary Alice and his daughters Eleanor and Catherine.

The works

The sheer volume and polymathic character of David's writing makes it difficult to identify neatly separated corpuses of work. In his remarkably long career, he produced eight single-author books, a dozen edited volumes, over 150 substantial articles and numerous brief reports, encyclopaedia entries and book reviews.[55] His writings tend to run into one another, making any categorisation only approximate. With that caveat, we organise David's principal interests under four headings: heritage, environment and perception, landscape and the West Indies.

Heritage

The latter part of David's career after he left UCL was best known for his writings on heritage. Indeed, he is usually taken as the originator, the founding father of heritage studies.[56] His 1985 book, *The Past Is a Foreign Country*, was seminal, becoming the canonical text in the field. In their bibliographic analysis, Gentry and Smith found that it is 'the most heavily cited book on heritage ever published, and is held by four times as many libraries globally than the next most popular work'.[57] Thirty years after

---

[52] D. Lowenthal, 'Islands, lovers and others', *Geographical Review*, 97 (2007), 202–29.

[53] D. Lowenthal, *Quest for the Unity of Knowledge* (London, 2019).

[54] Personal communication, Sverker Sörlin, 4 December 2018.

[55] H. Clout, 'David Lowenthal, 1923–2018', in E. Baigent and A. Reyes Novaes (eds.), *Geographers Biobibliographical Studies*, 39 (2020), contains a substantial list of David's publications.

[56] H. Clout, 'David Lowenthal, scholar who established heritage studies', *The Guardian*, 27 September 2018.

[57] K. Gentry and L. Smith, 'Critical heritage studies and the legacies of the late-twentieth century canon', *International Journal of Heritage Studies* (2019), doi 10.1080/13527258.2019.1570964.

The Past Is a Foreign Country was published, a much-revised version, *The Past Is a Foreign Country – Revisited*, appeared.[58] It was almost two-hundred pages longer, reorganised into twelve chapters under four sections rather than seven chapters under three sections in the previous edition. Yet more examples were added, replacing those that were out of date, as were more footnotes (now running to over 110 pages). In both books, the prose took a narrative form, with the argument made illustratively through layers of examples on a single page, with semicolons neatly separating each. The range of sources was astonishing, from the Bible and classics to an Alan Jay Lerner song and an episode of *South Park*.[59] As Neil Silberman observed, 'David was a master of the vivid antiquarian anecdote, the cultural detail, [and] the obscure newspaper clipping.'[60]

Several commentators noted that neither book needed to be read sequentially to be appreciated. They were perfect for serendipitous dipping, dropping the reader at one compelling case or another they probably knew little or nothing about. That Horace Walpole and Walter Scott built gingerbread houses; that English Heritage placed a blue plaque on a house in Soho London commemorating 'Jacob von Hogflume Inventor of time travel 1864–1909 [who] lived here in 2089'; and that the cigarette hanging from the bottom lip of the American bluesman Robert Johnson was airbrushed out of his photo for the US 29 cent stamp.[61] There was not only the startling variety of sources, but the elegant and exact prose that bound them. Luca Muscarà calls David's 'lexical precision . . . extraordinary', while Gentry and Smith evoke his use of multiple encrusted examples to label his style 'thick description' after the anthropologist Clifford Geertz.[62]

David's interests in history and heritage were there from the very beginning of his career as a geographer, which began when he worked for the IPDP at the end of the Second World War identifying buildings and landscapes of strategic significance in Western Europe.[63] It linked to his doctoral research on George Perkins Marsh around environmental preservation and conservation. And it was there in his joint writings with Hugh Prince on the distinctive qualities of the English landscape. It became more systematic and focused during the 1970s as David became a frequent keynote speaker at conferences and workshops on historic landscapes and valued environments. It was also during that same period that he began to work out how the past was

---

[58] Lowenthal, *The Past is a Foreign Country—Revisited*.

[59] Ibid., 315, 491.

[60] Silberman, 'David Lowenthal, 1923–2018', 242.

[61] Lowenthal, *The Past is a Foreign Country – Revisited*, pp. 191, 433, 545.

[62] Muscarà, 'David Lowenthal's past'; Gentry and Smith, 'Critical heritage studies'.

[63] Lowenthal, 'Mémoires de temps de guerre et de la paix'.

deliberately used to shape the meaning of a given place and space in the present.[64] He insisted that the connection between historical fact and heritage designation was often tenuous, brilliantly illustrating this point in his essay on the American Bicentennial celebrations.[65]

David was not, of course, arguing that we should dispense with the past. He thought it fundamental to our individual and social lives. There was not just one past, however. Different aspects of the past became more or less important as social interests changed. As he put it in the introduction to a 1979 lecture he gave at Syracuse University:

> Awareness of the past is essential to the maintenance of purpose in life. Without it we would lack all sense of continuity, all apprehension of causality, all knowledge of our own identity. [But] the past is not a fixed or immobile series of events; our interpretations of it are in constant flux … Today's past is an accumulation of mankind's memories, seen through our own generation's particular perspectives … The changing present continually requires new interpretations of what has taken place.[66]

Consequently, what counts as heritage is also in flux. The same heritage object—a memorial, a statue, a historical plaque—will take on different meanings over time. In some cases, the meaning may shift so dramatically that the object rather than being revered becomes reviled, requiring even its removal (as happened with statues of Cecil Rhodes at the University of Cape Town, South Africa).

Again, David did not then think that heritage should be suppressed. Heritage is vital and necessary, acting as a mnemonic device helping us to remember and connect to the past. It serves a crucial function. But David's argument was that the past invoked by heritage is never true history. We must remember that heritage expressed as displays, exhibitions, monuments, buildings, neighbourhoods, plaques, ceremonies and a host of other forms, is never the past as it was. It is a past always coloured by agendas of the present. The myriad illustrations in both editions of *The Past is a Foreign Country* repeatedly demonstrate this thesis: heritage is not bad, but it is not history. Sometimes the past that is invoked by heritage is patently bogus, as when it has been Disneyfied, or when subject to extreme political ideology as under Nazism or Stalinism. In other instances, it is not so obvious, more hidden. David deals with both overt and covert cases. Ultimately, all forms of heritage whether apparent or not will present warped versions of the past.

---

[64] D. Lowenthal, 'Past time, present place: landscape and memory', *Geographical Review*, 65 (1975), 1–36.
[65] D. Lowenthal, 'Environmental perception: preserving the past', *Progress in Human Geography*, 3 (1979), 549–59; D. Lowenthal, 'Age and artefact: dilemmas of appreciation', in D. W. Meinig (ed.), *The Interpretation of Ordinary Landscapes* (New York, 1979), pp. 103–28.
[66] Lowenthal, 'Age and artefact', 103.

To determine how warped, David appealed to the acid test of the historical method. It provided a 'testable truth', as he put it. That method still might not reveal the past as it really was, but he believed that it separated the wheat of more credible accounts of the past from the chaff of less credible ones. Historical truth could at least be approximated if not fully revealed. As Peter Seixas expressed it, David believed that while one 'could not recreate the past as it was, nevertheless there were better and worse ways of getting at it'.[67] Heritage did not, while the historical method did.

David's belief in the touchstone of history put him at odds with what Gentry and Smith identify as second-generation heritage studies known as critical heritage studies (CHS).[68] Aligned with various forms of post-structuralism, CHS supporters dispute that the historical method renders a more credible version of the past than any other method. For them, the historian's account is as fictional as Walt Disney's. Both are full of biases, erasures, leaps of logic and value judgements. These critics suggest David might have realised this if he had been more theoretically self-conscious and astute. Instead, he was overly taken by his many examples that became ends in themselves, missing the larger picture, with both books 'lacking sustained argument and critical substance'.[69] For example, Comer Vann Woodward reviewing the 1985 version of the book criticised it for its 'helter-skelter commingling'.[70] Stuart Piggott was harsher, saying about the same edition, 'detail is piled upon uncritical detail ... Professor Lowenthal goes down, not waving but drowning, under the dry but relentless wave of his own Dead Sea of index cards'.[71] David retained the same approach for the 2015 version, adding even more examples, leading David C. Harvey in his review to say: 'We end up revisiting a world of scholarship that, although impressive in its fermentation over a seventy-year career, hasn't really evolved for three decades.'[72] Other criticisms coming from CHS included David's geographical narrowness (his foci were primarily Western Europe and North America); his frequent reliance on examples involving anglophone dead-white-men; his patrician view from above; and his lack of political engagement, specifically a failure to recognise the hegemonic character of heritage that according to critics is bent on tricking subordinate social classes into supporting a system that is an anathema to their interests.

In 1996, David followed up the first edition of *The Past is a Foreign Country* with *Possessed by the Past: the Heritage Crusade and the Spoils of History* in the USA

---

[67] Peter Seixas interview with Barnes, 30 April 2019.
[68] Gentry and Smith, 'Critical heritage studies'.
[69] Ibid.
[70] C. V. Woodward, '*The Past is a Foreign Country*', *History and Theory*, 26 (1987), 346–52, 347.
[71] S. Piggott, '*The Past is a Foreign Country*', *Antiquity*, 60 (1986), 152–3.
[72] D. C. Harvey, '*The Past is a Foreign Country—Revisited*', *The AAG Review of Books*, 5 (2017), 208.

(titled *The Heritage Crusade and the Spoils of History* in the UK).[73] About two-thirds the size of the earlier book, but with no illustrations, it doubled down on his earlier claim about the importance of the distinction between history and heritage:

> The historian, however blinkered and presentist and self-deceived, seeks to convey a past consensually known, open to inspection and proof, continually revised and eroded as time and hindsight outdate its truths. The heritage fashioner, however historically scrupulous, seeks to design a past that will fix the identity and enhance the well-being of some chosen individual or folk.[74]

So, while history and heritage are both necessarily inflected by the present, history is open to revision, seeking always better representations of the past. History may never realise its ambition to describe the past as it was but it is able to discriminate between more reliable and less reliable accounts. In contrast, the open-endedness of history is denied by the project of heritage that fixes the past, closes it down, 'conserving and celebrating national and local legacies'.[75] It is less about holding up a mirror to the past than making it 'congenial', intentionally comforting the interests of the present.[76]

Environment and perception

David's wider interest in the environment was sparked by his reading of nineteenth-century American environmentalists including David Henry Thoreau (1817–1862), John Muir (1838–1914) and, most pertinent, George Perkins Marsh (1801–1882). Like David, Marsh was a polymath and was against disciplinary specialisation. Marsh had served first as a US diplomat in the Ottoman Empire during the 1850s and then for twenty-one years as the US Ambassador to the new kingdom of Italy (1861–82). As one of his many side projects, Marsh compiled a trove of original sources—he could read in twenty languages—documenting the destructive consequences of human action in the Alps and on the Mediterranean Basin, from the Ancient Greeks onward. Published as *Man and Nature* (1864), Marsh unusually for the time blamed humanity for debasing the Earth, not original sin, the cause normally singled out. In particular, he faulted material avarice and ecological blindness that became only more entrenched—at least within the USA under its regime of frontier industrial capitalism

---

[73] D. Lowenthal, *Possessed by the Past: the Heritage Crusade and the Spoils of History* (New York, 1996); D. Lowenthal, *The Heritage Crusade and the Spoils of History* (London, 1997); D. Lowenthal, *The Heritage Crusade and the Spoils of History* (paperback) (Cambridge, 1998).
[74] Lowenthal, *The Heritage Crusade*, p. xi.
[75] Ibid., p. 247.
[76] Ibid., p. 148.

and associated avaricious appetite for natural resources. As remedy, Marsh advocated environmental conservation that not only cut against the grain of then prevailing opinion but then later 'shap[ed] the course of conservation history in the US and elsewhere'.[77] One hundred years after its original appearance, David edited and introduced a new edition of *Man and Nature*.[78]

Study of the environment had long been part of the definition of geography as a field. David's dissertation on Marsh was different from mainstream disciplinary concerns, partly because of its biographical approach, and partly because of its focus on conservation. The emphasis on the latter, particularly after the thesis was published as *George Perkins Marsh: Versatile Vermonter* (1958), made it a perspicacious forerunner of 1960s American environmentalism. One of that book's reviewers, the well-known sociologist Lewis Mumford (1895–1990), very much appreciated the focus on Marsh, whom he described as the 'fountain head of the conservation movement'.[79] He was less keen on the volume's subtitle, however, believing it diminished and parochialised Marsh's achievements.

Maybe partly to make amends, David significantly rewrote his book, republishing it in 2000 with a new subtitle, 'Prophet of Conservation'.[80] As with the revised version of *The Past is a Foreign Country*, the new edition of *George Perkins Marsh* was all but a brand-new volume. The historical geographer William Cronon, who commissioned the book, said it went 'well beyond what is ordinarily even called a "revision"; it would be a new biography'.[81] While David recognised that the environmental problems that *Man and Nature* tackled—deforestation, soil erosion, desertification—were no longer now uppermost in many minds—instead they were global warming, biodiversity, rising sea levels—the important point was Marsh's identification of the primary cause of environmental devastation, humans, and more recently reinforced by the idea of the Anthropocene.[82] As David said in his introduction, the first biography was by a young man and the second was by an old man, with some forty more years of experience and with the world an entirely different place.

David's doctoral dissertation and the associated later books argued Marsh's life experiences gave him an ability to perceive the catastrophic damage humans wrought on the physical environment. Termed environmental perception, it was codified in

---

[77] W. Cronon, 'Foreword: look back to look forward', in D. Lowenthal, *George Perkins Marsh: Prophet of Conservation* (Seattle, 2000), pp. ix–xiii, x.

[78] D. Lowenthal (ed.) *Man and Nature by George Perkins Marsh* (Cambridge, MA, 1965).

[79] L. Mumford, *The Brown Decades: a Study of the Arts in America, 1865–1895* (New York, 1971), p. 35.

[80] D. Lowenthal, *George Perkins Marsh: Prophet of Conservation* (Seattle, 2000).

[81] Cronon, 'Foreword', p. xii.

[82] Lowenthal, *George Perkins Marsh: Prophet*, p. 423; D. Lowenthal, 'Origins of Anthropocene awareness', *Anthropocene Review*, 3 (2016), 52–63.

David's formative 1961 paper, 'Geography, experience, and imagination: towards a geographical epistemology'.[83] It drew inspiration from J. K. Wright's presidential address to the Association of American Geographers on 'geosophy', which concluded that 'the most fascinating *terrae incognitae* of all are those that lie within the minds and hearts of men'.[84] David took that phrase to heart making his own purpose to 'consider the nature of these *terrae incognitae*, and the relation between the world outside and the pictures in our heads'.[85] To do so he drew on a dizzying array of disciplinary sources, from philosophy, psychology, anthropology, linguistics, history and geography. He argued that we never perceive the world as it really is. Instead, we are stuck in the bubble of our own past experiences, imagination, memories, social norms and cultural expectations that collectively determine the pictures of the world we carry around in our heads. To understand human action and its effects on the outside world it is vital to identify those pictures, our *terrae incognitae*. As he later put it:

> I was concerned to show that it was not only environmental realities, but our perceptions of them, forged by experience and preconception, colored by taste and preference, and reshaped by memory and amnesia, that guided our environmental judgements and actions. All environmental behaviour, individual and group alike, was grounded in intention and feeling. These topics took me down psychological and other pathways hitherto unfrequented by geographers, notably the malleable mechanisms of long-term memory and surreal landscapes of dreams and visionary experiences.[86]

The link David forged with psychology was especially productive, triggering within human geography the new approach of behavioural geography. It came in both softer and harder versions. The softer form was concerned with examining the shaping effects on an individual's geographical perception of a person's culture, history and social position. It was the variety that David was most intellectually inclined towards, related to the humanities. The harder type was rooted in clinical psychology and behavioural science, focused on cognitive processes underlying spatial reasoning, decision-making and behaviour. Here formal mathematical models were invoked and rigorously tested against statistical data. Perhaps the best example of that research tradition was work on so-called mental maps, perceptual cartographies individuals supposedly stored in their brain and called forth to talk about or to travel in the world. Following David's argument, they were not the world as it 'really' was but only as it was mentally constructed in the mind of the perceiver. They were *Geographies of the Mind*.[87]

[83] Lowenthal, 'Geography, experience, and imagination: towards a geographical epistemology'.
[84] Wright, 'Terrae incognitae', 15.
[85] Lowenthal, 'Geography, experience, and imagination', 260.
[86] D. Lowenthal, 'Environmental perception: an odyssey of ideas', *Journal of Environmental Psychology*, 7 (1987), 338.
[87] D. Lowenthal and M. J. Bowden (eds.), *Geographies of the Mind* (New York, 1976).

Landscape

David's fascination with landscape intersected with his concerns in heritage, environment and perception, forming in effect a tightly merged complex of interests. Possibly his concern with landscape was the primary spark for the other elements. Interpreting landscape through photographs and written words was his first task as a professional geographer when he served in the OSS during the Second World War. It is unlikely that when he undertook that task he drew on any larger conceptual landscape scheme. That came in graduate school, first at Berkeley, then at Wisconsin. Drawing on the German tradition, Carl Sauer at Berkeley made landscape (*landschaft*) the central plank of his geographical science. Landscape was conceived as a cultural product, the consequence of a historical mutual relation between humans and their physical environment. In Sauer's words, 'culture is the agent, the natural area is the medium, the cultural landscape is the result'.[88] For Sauer, the purpose of geography was to reconstruct different historical cultural landscapes through fieldwork and archival research.

At Wisconsin, however, David received a very different argument about landscape, albeit also from someone steeped in the Germanic geographical tradition, Richard Hartshorne. He contended that the term was incoherent because it contradictorily meant both a restricted area and its opposite, an unlimited spatial vista. For that reason, Hartshorne thought landscape had 'little or no value as a technical or scientific term' and should be thrown on to the intellectual rubbish heap of geography.[89] Olwig contends that David's doctoral research on Marsh in effect had been his attempt, contra Hartshorne's, to rescue and revivify landscape as a central geographical idea; to demonstrate that it was profoundly useful, indispensable in understanding ourselves within an explicitly geographical world.[90] Rather than abandoned, landscape should be celebrated as one of geography's motherhood and fatherhood terms like space and place. In his work on landscape, David followed some of Sauer's precepts, making field and archival work foundational, taking as axiomatic that landscapes were sodden with cultural values, generating meaning and significance. But he also parted ways. Sauer was interested primarily in rural, pre-modern and representative landscapes, whereas David's concerns were often with modern, everyday and vernacular landscapes, both rural and urban. David had an ally here, another come-lately geographer from Harvard who also fought in the Second World War with the American

---

[88] C. O. Sauer, 'The morphology of landscape', *University of California Publications in Geography* 2 (2), 46.

[89] R. Hartshorne, *The Nature of Geography* (Lancaster, PA, 1939), p. 158.

[90] K. R. Olwig, 'Landscape: the Lowenthal legacy', *Annals of the Association of American Geographers*, 93 (2003), 871–7.

army in France, John Brinkerhoff Jackson (1909–1996). In 1951, Jackson founded the journal *Landscape*, devoted to the interpretation of the same ordinary and locally inflected landscapes that fascinated Lowenthal (and who published frequently in its pages). Another difference between Lowenthal and Sauer on landscape was that Lowenthal wanted to make judgements about the cultural landscapes he interpreted, including the values of its inhabitants who gave them expression. To do so required scholarship and rigour. It wasn't just mere opinion, something made up on the spot, but entailed considered evaluation and assessment, historical and social knowledge, and an aesthetic sensibility and training.

All those qualities were found in the collaborative work David undertook on the English landscape with Hugh Prince in the early 1960s. A little later, David used his Guggenheim Fellowship (1965–6) to travel to various parts of America—mainly the west coast from Mexico to British Columbia—to capture examples of ordinary, vernacular buildings and landscapes on black and white film, rather as he and Joe Bucolo had done in Europe for the IPDP.[91] Some of these images appeared in his books and articles. Most fittingly, though, the year before he died, his landscape prints were shown in an exhibition in Montpellier, France, which appropriately also included photographs taken by that other celebrator of ordinary landscape, J. B. Jackson.[92] Jackson was one of five others whose work focused on the ordinary landscape, both urban and rural. More generally, David's passion for the idea of landscape helped keep it alive within geography in the face of Hartshorne's critique, allowing it later to become one of the core notions of a 'new cultural geography' that took hold within the discipline from the 1980s. A little later, a selection of David's essays on landscape was brought to a wider audience in French translation by Marianne Enckell.[93]

The West Indies

David's interest in the West Indies was in some sense orthogonal to these other previous three bodies of work. Originally derived from his Berkeley MA thesis on the Guianas, he said in his last interview that West Indian societies had 'tremendously

---

[91] D. Lowenthal, 'Public attitudes on environmental quality; assumptions behind the public attitudes', in H. Jarrett (ed.), *Environmental Quality in a Growing Economy* (Baltimore, MD, 1966), pp. 128–37; D. Lowenthal, 'The American scene', *Geographical Review*, 58 (1968), 61–88; D. Lowenthal, 'Recreation habits and values: implications for landscape quality', in P. Dansereau (ed.), *Challenge for Survival: Land, Air, and Water for Man in Megalopolis* (New York, 1970), pp. 103–17; D. Lowenthal, 'Finding valued landscapes', *Progress in Human Geography*, 2 (1978), 373–418.

[92] Pavillon Populaire, *Notes sur l'asphalte, une Amérique mobile et précaire, 1950–1990* (Montpellier, 2017).

[93] D. Lowenthal, *Passage du temps sur le paysage* (Gollion, 2008).

excited' him.[94] He was intrigued especially by the sharp differences across the relatively geographically compact set of Islands. Indeed, the idiosyncrasies of island life contin-ued to fascinate him throughout his entire career, explaining his relentless island travel into his ninth decade. Barbuda in the Caribbean and later on Sark in the Channel Islands were special favourites.[95] David spent the academic year, 1956–7, at the Institute of Social and Economic Research at the University of the West Indies (Jamaica—UWI). The Institute comprised a dozen or so scholars from various social sciences 'all working on small islands and encompassing so-called different subject matter'.[96] This was the beginning of David's long association with the UWI, where he taught American history and served as a consultant to the vice-chancellor. He trav-elled to many West Indian islands and published on countless Caribbean insular themes.[97] In 1960, he received a two-year grant from the Rockefeller Foundation to further his studies, and edited *The West Indies Federation: Perspectives on a New Nation* for the AGS.[98] With financial support from the Institute of Race Relations (London), David then undertook archival research and worked on a monograph, *West Indian Societies*.[99] He explained:

> Islanded among continental giants are eleven million West Indians in some fifty societies, each distinct from the others, yet all different from the Anglo-American and Latin American leviathans that frame the Caribbean. This book chronicles the like-nesses and differences of these societies, their insularities and common bonds, and their citizens' efforts, in the wake of the hemisphere's longest history of slavery and

[94] Lowenthal and Hamilakis, 'A conversation', 3.
[95] D. Lowenthal and C. G. Clarke, 'Slave breeding in Barbuda: the past of a negro myth', *Annals of the New York Academy of Sciences*, 292 (1977), 510–35; D. Lowenthal and C. G. Clarke, 'Island orphans: Barbuda and the rest', *Journal of Commonwealth and Comparative Politics*, 18 (1980), 293–307; D. Lowenthal, 'The scourging of Sark', *Island Studies Journal*, 10 (2015), 253–8.
[96] Lowenthal and Hamilakis, 'A conversation', 6.
[97] D. Lowenthal, 'The population of Barbados', *Social and Economic Studies*, 6 (1957), 445–501; D. Lowenthal, 'The West Indies chooses a capital', *Geographical Review*, 48 (1958), 336–64; D. Lowenthal, 'The range and variation of Caribbean societies', *Annals of the New York Academy of* Sciences, 83 (1960), 786–95; D. Lowenthal, 'The social background of West Indian Federation', in D. Lowenthal (ed.), *The West Indies Federation: Perspectives on a New Nation* (New York, 1961), pp. 63–96; D. Lowenthal, 'Race and color in the West Indies', *Daedalus*, 96 (1967), 580–626; D. Lowenthal, 'Post-emancipation race relations: some Caribbean and American perspectives', *Journal of Inter-American Studies and World Affairs*, 13 (1971), 367–77; D. Lowenthal, 'Black power in the Caribbean context', *Economic Geography*, 48 (1972), 116–34; D. Lowenthal and C. G. Clarke, 'Caribbean small island sovereignty: chimera or convention', in U. Fanger (ed.), *Problems of Caribbean Development* (Munich, 1982), pp. 225–76; D. Lowenthal and L. Comitas, 'Emigration and depopulation: some neglected aspects of population geography', *Geographical Review*, 52 (1962), 195–210.
[98] D. Lowenthal (ed.), *The West Indies Federation: Perspectives on a New Nation* (New York, 1961); Lowenthal, 'The social background of West Indian Federation'.
[99] D. Lowenthal, *West Indian Societies* (New York, 1972).

colonialism, to transform vitality, elan, and creativity into a viable sense of identity.[100]

In doing so, he acknowledged: 'In the West Indies, as elsewhere, there are indeed things only an insider can know, approaches only an insider can take, errors only an outsider is prone to make.'[101]

Colin Clarke found David's writing 'imaginative, flexible, evocative but always penetrating and beautifully crafted. He allows West Indians to speak for themselves through contemporary poetry and prose ... This material is backed up with an astonishing depth of reading and maturity of understanding which few Caribbeanists can equal.'[102] Roger Abrahams praised David's 'brave book. It attempts—and generally succeeds—in bringing together very diverse reports from over fifty insular societies and making some sense out of them', but he regretted that David's 'generalizations all too often are derived from studies of the island elites or middle class'.[103] That last criticism was further elaborated by Susan Craig, who bitterly complained: 'The book is written in true "expert" tradition—the author might have learnt from the writings of others; certainly he has nothing to contribute' apart from 'the massive bibliography'.[104]

Together with anthropologist Lambros Comitas, David then edited four volumes of essays under the collective title *West Indian Perspectives*.[105] Of the seventy-two items in the four volumes, forty-five came from West Indians and the remainder from North American or British scholars. Anthony Bryan stated that this was 'a decent start' but argued that 'future collections ... may be enhanced by relying even more on Caribbean sources and less on metropolitan scholarship'.[106] Donald Innis found the volumes 'valuable' but lamented that their essays reflected 'middle-class views of West Indian problems. Too many authors seem to assume that the poorest and blackest people are some kind of inchoate proto-humanity with no viewpoint of their own.'[107] Back in the UK, David was instrumental in founding the Society for Caribbean Studies, to whose members he was guide, friend and source of inspiration for many years.

[100] Ibid., p. xiii.
[101] Ibid., p. xv.
[102] C. G. Clarke, 'West Indian Societies', *Geographical Journal*, 138 (1972), 503–4.
[103] R. Abrahams, 'West Indian Societies', *Hispanic American Historical Review*, 53 (1973), 355–6.
[104] S. Craig, 'West Indian Societies', *Social and Economic Studies*, 23 (1974), 138.
[105] D. Lowenthal and L. Comitas (eds.), *West Indian Perspectives* (4 vols) entitled: *Slaves, Free Men, Citizens*; *Consquences of Class and Color*; *Work and Family Life*; and *The Aftermath of Sovereignty* (New York, 1973).
[106] A. Bryan, 'West Indian Perspectives', *Hispanic American Historical Review*, 55 (1975), 329–30, 330.
[107] D. Q. Innis, 'West Indian Societies', *Geographical Review*, 64 (1974), 437.

Appreciation

As well as writing, teaching and giving conference presentations, David served as advisor to a wide range of national and international heritage organisations and museums, especially during his retirement years. The heritage organisations included UNESCO, the International Council on Monuments and Sites, the National Trust (UK), the National Trust for Historic Preservation (USA) and the National Trust Australia, while connections with museums included the International Council on Museums, the Getty, London's Science Museum, the Victoria and Albert Museum (1990–5) and the British Museum. Just as importantly, through his works and lectures David also influenced cohorts of heritage and museum staff.

His books earned David a run of distinguished prizes. The Association of American Geographers gave him awards for both the original 1958 version of *George Perkins Marsh: Versatile Vermonter* and the 2001 revised version, *George Perkins Marsh: Prophet of Conservation*. The 1985 edition of *The Past is a Foreign Country* received both The University and Professional Publication (UK) Award and the Historic Preservation (USA) Prize, while the 2015 revised version of the book was given the British Academy Medal (2016). In addition to these prizes, David was the recipient of many professional accolades that included the Victoria Gold Medal of the Royal Geographical Society in 1997, the Cullum Geographical Medal of the American Geographical Society (1999) and the Royal Scottish Geographical Society Medal (2004). In 2001, David was elected a Senior Fellow of the British Academy.

John Western characterised David as 'urbane, erudite, a conversationalist, a man of humour. He brought renown to academic geography.'[108] Of course, his target audience was broader than geography and history, as befitted a scholar who 'hated disciplines' and was 'constantly crossing boundaries'.[109] After being informed of David's death, Jacquie Burgess replied: 'I shall always remember him as one of the most erudite and witty people I've ever met. And his wicked grin! Especially after a couple of his martinis which could easily blow your head off.'[110] His friend, art historian Charles Saumarez Smith, declared: 'David Lowenthal was old and wise, unbelievably well read on every topic, and fascinatingly unclassifiable as a man of learning—like his books.'[111] His insatiable curiosity, incisive analysis and critique, wit as a storyteller and unfailing kindness will be sorely missed by friends around the world. Polymath David insisted: 'Discussion is vital: for the world to be sustainable, it must first be

[108] Personal communication, John Western, 11 November 2018.
[109] Personal communication, Sverker Sörlin, 4 December 2018.
[110] Personal communication, Jacquie Burgess, 10 October 2018.
[111] Charles Saumarez Smith, message 19 September 2018.

conversable.'[112] In the very last essay he wrote, David reflected on the evanescence of all things both animate and inanimate: 'All of us, not only curators, confront mortal dissolution ... Yet efforts to overcome entropy are fleeting and fugitive.'[113] Be that as it may, David used enormously well the scrap of time given to us all, his efforts less fleeting and fugitive than those of many.

Acknowledgements

For advice and information we are most grateful to Jacquie Burgess, Colin Clarke, Claudette Edwards, Peter Seixas, Sverker Sörlin, John Western, members of the Lowenthal family on both sides of the Atlantic, and especially Mary Alice Lowenthal who generously read and commented on the final draft of this essay. A long interview with archaeologist Yannis Hamilakis was recorded in David's London home on 28 January 2017; it is transcribed at Lowenthal and Hamilakis (2017) and is available as a video at https://vimeo.com/246465145 (accessed 20 September 2019). David's early years are presented in an unpublished manuscript, revised in 2018: 'David Lowenthal: childhood, schooling, army.' His wartime experiences are described in that text and in a second manuscript: 'From infantry to intelligence in wartime France, 1944–45.' A third manuscript, 'Jean Gottmann: war and peace memories', was published in French.[114]

Note on the authors: Trevor Barnes is Professor of Economic Geography, University of British Columbia; he was elected a Corresponding Fellow of the British Academy in 2014. Hugh Clout is Professor Emeritus of Geography, University College London; he was elected a Fellow of the British Academy in 1997.

[112] D. Lowenthal, 'Postscript [to the Lowenthal Papers]', *Annals of the Association of American Geographers*, 93 (2003), 885.
[113] D. Lowenthal, 'A sea-change rich and strange', in H. Hölling, F. G. Bewer and K. Ammann (eds.), *The Explicit Material: Inquiries on the Intersection of Curatorial and Conservation Cultures* (Leiden, 2019), p. 17. The editors dedicated their book to David Lowenthal, 'with gratitude for his wisdom and friendship'.
[114] Lowenthal, 'Mémoires de temps de guerre et de la paix'.

MARGARET SPUFFORD

Honor Margaret Spufford

10 December 1935 – 6 March 2014

elected Fellow of the British Academy 1995

by

ANN HUGHES

Margaret Spufford was one of the most original and influential social and cultural historians of early modern England active over the last century, despite never completing a first degree or having an established academic job until she was almost sixty. She was the author of a pioneering comparative study of inheritance practices, economic change and popular belief in three Cambridge villages, and of many fundamental studies of the education, religion, reading and clothing of the 'common people' of early modern England. All this was achieved despite her own ill-health, and the genetic disorder and early death of her daughter.

Biographical Memoirs of Fellows of the British Academy, XVIII, 365–385
Posted 21 November 2019. © British Academy 2019.

MARGARET SPUFFORD

(Honor) Margaret Spufford ranks amongst the most original and influential historians of her generation, yet her career was unconventional, even wildly improbable. She was the author of one of the most significant works of early modern English social history, *Contrasting Communities* (Cambridge, 1974), and the supervisor and inspiration of a remarkable cohort of graduate students, despite having no first degree in history (or indeed in any other subject) and no established academic post until her appointment as Research Professor at Roehampton Institute (later Roehampton University) in 1994, when she was almost sixty. Spufford's career was marked by her own ill-health and that of her mother; it was overshadowed by the tragedy of her daughter's genetic disorder, chronic illness and early death; but overall her life was one of scholarly achievement and personal fulfilment, enriched by a notably happy marriage and by her talent for enduring friendships.

Margaret Spufford was born in Hartford, Cheshire on 10 December 1935 into a comfortable middle-class home, with maidservants and a uniformed nursery nurse. This was a serious household of a scientific bent, where both parents had trained as chemists. Her mother, born Mary Johnson, one of the first women chemists at Cambridge University, and a Fellow of Newnham College from 1922 to 1925, had given up an academic career on becoming engaged; at the time of Margaret's birth her father, Leslie Marshall Clark, was Director of Research at ICI Alkali at Winnington near Northwich. Margaret's sister Jean, some seven years older, took a more conventional path to an academic career. Both Margaret and Jean were initially home-schooled by their mother, but when the family moved to St Asaph in North Wales during the Second World War, Jean attended Howell's School in Denbigh, moving from there to Newnham where she graduated with a degree in Geography in 1948. She was Director of Studies in Geography and Fellow of Girton from 1960 to 1994. For the younger Margaret, things were less straightforward, particularly after she witnessed her mother's serious stroke in 1945: 'The securities and tenderness of my childhood were shattered when I was ten', she wrote in 1989.[1] Margaret's father, absent in Cheshire throughout the week, was a distant figure and her earlier home schooling proved a mixed blessing when her mother's disability ushered in a succession of difficult schools and unsympathetic carers, before a more congenial and productive period at Cambridge High School for Girls. In Cambridge, Margaret lodged with the family of the distinguished archaeologist of Africa [Charles] Thurstan Shaw; Shaw's wife Ione was a crucial early influence, fostering a profound commitment to the Anglican church. The sudden death of her father in 1953 meant the loss of the family home in Cheshire and brought Margaret at eighteen significant responsibilities for her mother who also moved to Cambridge, where Jean was by now married with a growing family.

[1] M. Spufford, *Celebration* (London, 1989), pp. 25–6.

Somehow in these difficult early years Spufford acquired her stubborn vocation as a historian. She insisted that she had not 'the faintest idea' how this happened, although she credited her scientific parents, especially her mother, with her respect for 'empirically ascertainable fact'.[2] In December 1954 she triumphed in her university entrance exams, winning a Senior Scholarship in History at Lady Margaret Hall, Oxford, as well as an exhibition at Newnham College, Cambridge. But a glittering undergraduate career did not materialise. Margaret's disrupted childhood had left her socially and psychologically vulnerable, and she had a breakdown at Oxford, exacerbated, as she felt to the end of her life, by a lack of sympathy from her female tutors. Newnham, where her mother and elder sister had studied, was more to her taste, but ill-health again—and after a little more than a term in 1956–7—prompted her to withdraw from Cambridge to concentrate on caring for her disabled mother.

Somehow she persisted. Effective treatment improved her emotional stability, and she enrolled on a Cambridge adult education course on local history run by Esther Moir (de Waal). Work done for that class contributed to her first publication; an examination of the possible relationship between soil type and the width of selions (open strips of land) within two Cambridgeshire and seven Derbyshire parishes; characteristically, she concluded that there was none.[3] It was also through Esther Moir that she met her husband, the medieval economic historian Peter Spufford, at a party in the summer of 1959. Margaret and Peter were married on 7 July 1962, following Peter's appointment to an Assistant Lectureship at Keele. This passionate personal and intellectual partnership was crucial to the lives and careers of both scholars. As Margaret wrote of how she was 'so deeply fortunate in my marriage', so her son recalls his father's testimony that 'of course the biggest intellectual influence of my life was Margaret'.[4] Throughout their lives, Margaret and Peter Spufford were each other's staunchest supporters and fiercest critics, first readers of each other's work. Their mutual influence can be discerned in the systematic, quantitative elements that helped to structure Margaret's vivid accounts of the social and cultural lives of the common people, and in the social and human contexts discussed in Peter's analyses of money in Medieval Europe. There was no envy or rivalry; the scholarly work of both was facilitated through dogged juggling in the face of demanding, often traumatic family responsibilities. While Peter had the conventionally successful academic career, it was Margaret who first made a mark on her field with *Contrasting Communities*, and she had produced two monographs before Peter published a major book. In theory, they

---

[2] Spufford, *Celebration*, pp. 62, 65.
[3] H. M. Clark, 'Selion size and soil type', *Agricultural Historical Review*, 8 (1960), 91–8.
[4] Spufford, *Celebration*, p. 27; T. Dean, G. Parry and E. Vallance (eds.), *Faith, Place and People in Early Modern England, Essays in Honour of Margaret Spufford* (Woodbridge, 2018), dedication.

tried to take it in turns to work on major projects, but Margaret 'jumped the queue' on her second book, *Small Books and Pleasant Histories* (London, 1981) when she was immobilised by two accidents and could do nothing but write.[5]

The Spuffords were at Keele until 1979, living on campus as all academic staff were then obliged to do, but usually spending summers in Cambridge. The history department was an all-male, and rather misogynist, body; no woman was appointed to a substantive post there until 1991. Margaret's role at Keele was therefore somewhat anomalous, in formal terms 'merely' a 'staff wife', but also an increasingly distinguished scholar. In the early 1960s, encouraged by Esther Moir, she submitted an essay for the John Nichols Prize awarded by the Department of English Local History at Leicester University. She did not win but her work so impressed Professor Herbert Finberg, the head of the department, that he offered her a research studentship, overcoming the regulations that required holders to have a first degree, and thereby kick-starting her career as a scholar. Spufford began her 1995 inaugural lecture at Roehampton with praise for the 'Leicester school' of local historians, who had trained and nurtured her early work, and it was an ideal location for her study of Cambridgeshire.[6] W. G. Hoskins, Finberg and Joan Thirsk encouraged detailed, practical local research, trudging the fields as well as searching the archives. They were concerned with the landscape, with the varieties of human settlements, inheritance, housing and the everyday lives of the common people, alert to the character of specific places but also identifying broader regional patterns. Their themes and methods are evident in all Spufford's work, although she was also particularly interested in the culture and religious beliefs of the people. Her MA on Chippenham, later published as a Leicester Occasional Paper, was awarded in 1963, and her PhD, 'People, Land and Literacy in Cambridgeshire in the Sixteenth and Seventeenth Centuries', in 1970. By this time the Spuffords had two children, Francis born in 1964 and Bridget in 1967.[7]

Despite her odd position, Spufford made her mark on Keele, as she was to do wherever she went, and forged friendships that lasted for the rest of her life. It was during her time at Keele that she made her reputation as an historian. In the early 1960s she taught an adult education course with her husband at Eccleshall, laying the foundations for a significant publication some thirty years later. More immediately she worked on the book for which she is still best known, *Contrasting Communities*, published in 1974, and based partly on her thesis. Additional research was supported

[5] Spufford, *Celebration*, p. 67.
[6] M. Spufford, *Chippenham to the World: Microcosm to Macrocosm* (University of Roehampton, 1996), delivered 20 February 1995, pp. 2–5.
[7] M. Spufford, *A Cambridge Community: Chippenham from Settlement to Enclosure* (Leicester, 1966).

by an Eileen Power Research Studentship in Economic History and a Calouste Gulbenkian Research Fellowship, held at Lucy Cavendish College, Cambridge between 1969 and 1972. She was able to spend a full year at Cambridge when Peter Spufford had a sabbatical from Keele, but otherwise relied on regular visits to the archives from Keele. Following the publication of *Contrasting Communities*, Margaret was finally awarded an honorary lectureship at Keele, which came with a meagre stipend but more usefully provided support for grant applications. An award from the Social Science Research Council facilitated work on later seventeenth-century chapmen (completed at Cambridge); before the Spuffords left Keele she had published pioneering work on education and popular literacy and completed the manuscript of her book on the small 'merry books' and 'godly books' available to the common people of early modern England.[8]

All this was achieved despite the serious ill-health of herself and her daughter. Spufford was almost always in pain and frequently immobilised by broken bones, caused by early onset osteoporosis diagnosed, finally, after the birth of her children. Shortly afterwards came the crushing diagnosis of her daughter Bridget's incurable genetic disorder, cystinosis; in her son's words, this is 'a ridiculously rare disease, a disaster it was almost absurd to be afflicted by, like being struck by a meteorite'. Bridget's condition meant hourly feeds by tube, and regular, draining journeys to Great Ormond Street. The Spuffords were tireless and brave, but relied also on the help of au pairs, friends, colleagues and students. When Spufford was confined to bed, flat on her back, Keele University's workshop built an ingenious contraption, 'a special machine that went over the bed and adjusted to any angle', so that she could read her sources and write, and which was strong enough for the three-year old Francis to climb on it to play. In this way some of *Contrasting Communities* was written, and the book was completed while Spufford was spending months in Great Ormond Street hospital with her desperately ill small daughter. The manuscript was typed up by the department secretary, who also reproduced the medical charts essential to Bridget's survival.[9] Throughout all this, Spufford retained an enthusiasm for the research of others, and was a stimulating and ambitious presence on a sometimes introspective campus. She encouraged Marie Rowlands to begin research on early industrial development in the Black Country, and supported the work of Laura Weatherill on consumption and material culture.[10] These reciprocal relationships, which in many

[8] M. Spufford, 'First steps in literacy: the reading and writing experiences of the humblest seventeenth-century spiritual autobiographers', *Social History*, 4 (1979), 407–35; M. Spufford, *Small Books and Pleasant Histories: Popular Fiction and its Readership in Seventeenth-century England* (London, 1981), p. xxi.

[9] F. Spufford, *The Child That Books Built* (London, 2002), pp. 13–15; Spufford, *Celebration*, pp. 40–1.

[10] M. B. Rowlands, *Masters and Men in the West Midland Metalware Trades before the Industrial Revolution*

ways mirrored her understanding of early modern English social relations, took many forms. Shared interests in the reading habits of the labouring poor made her an effective mentor to the young historian David Vincent, and without his knowledge she arranged for a paperback edition of his first book. In turn he conducted on her behalf a successful appeal to the local benefits office for disability support.

It is misleading then to assess Spufford's career only through her individually authored works; it is also through her capacity to encourage others and to build research communities, not unconnected to her own need for practical support, that she had a major influence within and beyond early modern English history. When Peter moved from Keele to Cambridge, Margaret Spufford took up a fellowship at Newnham, converted in 1985 to a bye-fellowship (resigned in 1992). Her poor health prevented her teaching undergraduates and her relationships in the College were not always easy, but at Cambridge she was able to attract a remarkable group of postgraduate students, commonly known as the 'Spuffordians'. They came because of her books, rather than her formal status, and mostly shared her interests in social relationships, inheritance, popular religion, reading, cheap print and the circulation of ideas and goods. The Japanese scholar Motoyasu Takahashi had read *Contrasting Communities* and he came to Cambridge to build on Spufford's studies of Willingham and Chippenham. An article in both their names was published in 1996, and he later solicited her help in developing community studies in Japan. Michael Frearson was inspired by reading *Small Books and Pleasant Histories* at university in New South Wales to do research at Cambridge with Spufford. His 1993 thesis, 'The English Corantos of the 1620s', was a valuable contribution to the 'historical geography of the book trade'; like Spufford he explained the networks through which material circulated throughout the country as well as analysing the content of his texts.[11] Many achievements of the Spuffordians could be highlighted, but it is worth mentioning in particular Tessa Watt's *Cheap Print and Popular Piety, 1560–1640* (Cambridge, 1991) and Christopher Marsh's *The Family of Love in English Society, 1530–1630* (Cambridge, 1994). These books, based on their doctoral theses, remain standard works that build in creative fashion on Spufford's own concerns with piety and reading matter, and with religious dissent in communal contexts. In an influential, if controversial, collective work on patterns of religious dissent in England, Spufford presented work by Frearson, Marsh and Watt alongside studies by other students on the later Lollards and post-Restoration religious belief, and a substantial section of her own work. As

---

(Manchester, 1975); L. Weatherill, *Consumer Behaviour and Material Culture in Britain 1660–1760* (London, 1986).
[11] The phrase is from Patrick Collinson's 'Critical conclusion', in M. Spufford (ed.), *The World of Rural Dissenters, 1520–1725* (Cambridge, 1995), p. 389.

she wrote in the Preface, it demonstrated her conviction that 'to watch research students soar away, each into a different empyrean, is the ultimate academic pleasure', although she did acknowledge also 'the specific pleasure, for the historian, of finding a new and exciting document'.[12]

Spufford's students were invited into her family, as much as into an academic network. They met her, and each other, more often in her living room, kitchen or garden rather than in some austere study and, as they testified at her funeral, they were bowled over by her 'profound sense of fun and her irrepressible enthusiasm'.[13] They were expected to rally round in a crisis (and crises were frequent), filling the fridge and helping with dinner. During most of the time she had graduate students, Spufford's daughter was very sick and her own health precarious. Some students were overwhelmed by the situation, but most benefitted immeasurably from an atmosphere of mutual affection and perceptive support. When Michael Frearson was finishing his thesis the Spuffords held visiting fellowships at the Netherlands Institute of Advanced Study, and they paid for him to join them so that Margaret could go through his final draft.

Spufford's networks were not confined to her own students. Despite her own somewhat tense relationship with Keith Wrightson, the other early modern social historian at Cambridge, she is remembered with gratitude by several Wrightson students, and Henry French was jointly supervised.[14] As at Keele, the Spuffords' houses, at Girton, Haddenham, Bateman Street, Cambridge and finally the Guildhall at Whittlesford, offered generous hospitality and lively debate for historians and literary scholars. You did not have to agree with her; she enjoyed decades of 'stimulating and friendly disagreement' with Professor David Cressy over the penetration of cheap print in the English countryside and over standards of literacy.[15] To Professor Cressy, as to her own students and other protégés, Spufford was a passionate and persistent patron, although not always a very effective one. Her advocacy was particularly fierce on behalf of those whose careers, like hers, did not always run smoothly.

Spufford's work is beautifully written, often very personal and superficially artless. Her own reflections on her scholarship were ambiguous. She often presented her intellectual development as a process with a purely internal logic, prompted by the sources and her own preoccupations, denying any role to external methodological and/or theoretical positions: illness and family responsibilities had limited her reading of

---

[12] Spufford, *The World of the Rural Dissenters*, p. xvii.
[13] I am grateful for a copy of the address Michael Frearson gave at Spufford's funeral, written by himself and Christopher Marsh.
[14] Henry French and Steve Hindle contributed to *Faith, Place and People*, the volume in Spufford's honour.
[15] Margaret Spufford to David Cressy, 2 February 1977 (courtesy of Professor David Cressy).

other historians. 'Serendipity is not a methodology, but is nonetheless extremely useful', she wrote in 1995, but in her inaugural lecture the same year she repudiated the view that her research was wholly serendipitous, insisting on 'a quantitative skeleton to my work, to which I attach my qualitative work securely'. Indeed, throughout her career she turned to fiscal records, especially of the Hearth Tax, to establish basic patterns of population and wealth that she could connect to agricultural regions, and contrasting landscapes and cultures.[16] Hence, perhaps, her enduring admiration for the statistically minded herald and Staffordshire man, Gregory King, who like her was also a field worker who did not mind getting mud on his boots.[17]

Spufford always described herself as a local historian, with mud on her boots and often in her hair, but hers was a more sophisticated local history than she is sometimes given credit for. As we shall see, she came to regret that she had not been more methodologically self-conscious, feeling that it meant her work did not have the impact it deserved. She was always alert to the idiosyncrasies of particular places but did not accept that meant that 'everywhere is different' or that no generalisations could be drawn.[18] For local history, as for micro-history, the relationship between the particular and the general was crucial: 'this issue of typicality or a-typicality for an agricultural type seems to me the central problem with which micro-historians have to wrestle'. You could not claim typicality without some systematic work, and hence the attraction of the Hearth Tax.[19]

Spufford's first book, *Contrasting Communities*, remains her most influential. The first and most substantial section, 'People, families and land', based on her doctoral work, sought to address a long-standing concern in early modern English economic history, 'the disappearance of the small landowner'. Influenced by the work of the 'Leicester school', in particular the 'ecological' approach to farming regions associated with Joan Thirsk and Alan Everitt, she analysed developments in three different Cambridge communities, Willingham in the fens, Chippenham in the chalk lands and Orwell on the heavier clay soil. Her conclusions were founded on systematic analysis of population, landholding, inheritance practices and the treatment of widows, using taxation, manorial and probate records. In Chippenham and Orwell economic change, vulnerability to bad harvests and the vagaries of the market made smaller landholdings increasingly less viable in the late sixteenth and early seventeenth centuries—a

[16] Spufford, *The World of the Rural Dissenters*, p. xvii; Spufford, *Chippenham to the World*, pp. 7–9, 12.
[17] M. Spufford, *Poverty Portrayed: Gregory King and Eccleshall in Staffordshire in the 1690s* (Keele, 1995); see also A. Ailes, 'The Heralds and the Hearth Tax', in Dean, Parry and Vallance, *Faith, Place and People*, pp. 95–110.
[18] Spufford, *Chippenham to the World*, pp. 17–18.
[19] M. Spufford, 'The scope of local history, and the potential of the Hearth Tax returns', *The Local Historian*, 30 (2000), 203.

process exacerbated by over-generous inheritance arrangements in Orwell. In Willingham, however, the grazing and other rights afforded by the fens enabled a more egalitarian society to survive. Subsequent sections dealt with 'The schooling of the peasantry' and 'Parishioners and their religion'—perhaps not the most appropriate title as Spufford focused on religious dissent at least as much as on people's relationships with the established parish church. Both these sections built on earlier articles and covered themes that she returned to frequently during the rest of her career.[20] *Contrasting Communities* wears its ambition lightly, but it was an ambitious book, intended to have an impact on European social history. Spufford explained in her preface that she had not been able to read Emmanuel Le Roy Ladurie on *The Peasants of Languedoc* before publication, but she made several references to the work of Pierre Goubert on the Beauvais, and she used extensive comparisons with Le Roy Ladurie in recasting her work on Cambridgeshire in a comparative volume on family and inheritance in Western Europe.[21]

Spufford's next book, *Small Books and Pleasant Histories: Popular Fiction and its Readership*, was prompted initially by a desire to consider, in more depth than was possible in *Contrasting Communities*, what religious influences, besides their local vicar, were available to the common people, but the book presents vivid accounts of the 'small merry books' and romances with their tales of courtship, heroism and chivalry as well as discussing the godly books and prints that could be purchased for a penny. Spufford again offered comparisons with continental Europe in a chapter comparing her analysis of Pepys's cheap print collections with Robert Mandrou's account of 'le bibliothèque bleu'. At a time when most discussions of popular culture were based on the content of the cheap literature ordinary people were assumed to have read, Spufford's was a pioneering study that combined analysis of content with research on the distribution of cheap print and on the reading skills of the common people. She could thus demonstrate that 'small books' reached English villages through elaborate networks of 'pedlars, hawkers and petty chapmen', and she could show that it was likely that significant elements amongst the rural population could read this material. Her sensitive account of the ways in which reading pious handbooks or merry tales of courtship and adventure related to the everyday lives of the

---

[20] Amongst other examples are: M. Spufford, 'The schooling of the peasantry in Cambridgeshire, 1575–1700', in J. Thirsk (ed.), *Land, Church and People: Essays Presented to Professor H. P. R. Finberg*, Supplement to the *Agricultural History Review*, 18 (1970), pp. 112–47; M. Spufford, 'The dissenting churches in Cambridgeshire from 1660 to 1700', *Proceedings of the Cambridge Antiquarian Society*, 61 (1968), 67–95.

[21] M. Spufford, 'Peasant inheritance customs and land distribution in Cambridgeshire from the sixteenth to the eighteenth centuries', in J. Goody, J. Thirsk and E. P. Thompson (eds.), *Family and Inheritance. Rural Society in Western Europe, 1200–1800* (Cambridge, 1976), pp. 156–76.

peasantry was developed from substantial research on real pedlars, school mistresses and readers. Spufford's original synthesis of supply and demand, distribution and reception was developed by her own students, notably Tessa Watt and Michael Freason, and has had a productive influence on scholars of popular literacy in more recent times. Around the same time, she published 'First steps in literacy: the reading and writing experiences of the humblest seventeenth-century spiritual autobiographers'.[22] Where previous work on literacy had used statistical methods, using large data sets to discover what proportions of the population could sign their own names, Spufford built on her extensive research on education to uncouple reading and writing as distinct skills. Reading was taught before writing and with the widespread availability of semi-formal schools in the countryside she argued that many poor families could spare a few pence so their children could acquire rudimentary reading skills before they were required to work, even if they could not stay in school long enough to gain the more advanced capacity to write. She then turned to qualitative evidence, using spiritual autobiographies to demonstrate the strenuous and poignant efforts poor dissenters might take to preserve and improve their ability to read. She was more optimistic about the reading skills of the rural poor than many scholars, and she later acknowledged the importance of economic as well as religious influences on literacy, but her account of what reading might mean for the common people remains one of the most influential articles on the cultural history of early modern England ever written.[23]

Spufford's third book can also be seen as a natural outcome of questions raised earlier in *Contrasting Communities* and *Small Books*. Aided by a Senior Research Fellowship from the Social Science Research Council in 1978–80, she embarked on a study of the chapmen and women who brought reading matter to the people, more systematic than had been possible in the chapter in *Small Books*. Pedlars' packs held ribbons, buttons, textiles and ready-made clothes along with ballads, story books and religious tracts; the book's title, *The Great Reclothing of Rural England*, echoed a key achievement of the 'Leicester school'—W. G. Hoskins' article 'The rebuilding of rural England'.[24] This was another original contribution, establishing pedlars as

[22] M. Spufford, 'First steps in literacy', first published in *Social History*, 12 (1979), 407–35, was reprinted in H. J. Graff (ed.), *Literacy and Social Development in the West* (Cambridge, 1981) and in the collection of her essays: M. Spufford, *Figures in the Landscape* (Aldershot, 2000).
[23] In a comparative study, M. Spufford, 'Literacy, trade and religion in the commercial centres of Europe', in K. Davids and J. Lucassen (eds.), *A Miracle Mirrored: The Dutch Republic in European Perspective* (Cambridge, 1995), pp. 229–83, Spufford denied that she had ever questioned the basic human need to earn a living, and accepted that literacy was higher in towns than in the countryside.
[24] M. Spufford, *The Great Reclothing of Rural England. Petty Chapmen and their Wares in the Seventeenth Century* (London, 1984); W. G. Hoskins, 'The rebuilding of rural England, 1570–1640', *Past and Present*, 4 (1953), 44–59. For an astute discussion on the potential of this book, see 'Introduction', in Dean, Parry and Vallance, *Faith, Place and People*, p. 10.

cultural intermediaries, although her own treatment was rather under-theorised. Spufford's initial aim, to provide a systematic analysis of the chapmen licensed under national legislation of 1697–8, proved unworkable, and she provided instead a host of suggestive examples, based particularly on the creative use of wills and inventories, discovered through her own research and references from her extensive scholarly networks. Her final, posthumous, book, published more than thirty years later, built on this study. Chapmen are crucial to *The Clothing of the Common Sort*, produced with Susan Mee, one of her Roehampton PhD students, and seen through the press by Peter Spufford. This ground-clearing work explores what can be learnt of the largely uncharted territory of the clothing available to everyone from 'the poorest' to the 'chief inhabitants' of early modern communities. It covers both production and consumption; creative and painstaking research in poor relief and probate archives reveals the most common fabrics used, their transformation by 'women with a needle', and the widespread availability of ready-made clothing.[25]

Spufford's religious faith was fundamental to her life and, in paradoxical fashion, to her scholarship. She was a devout Anglican, with participation in the Eucharist at the heart of her faith. Yet most of her research and writing on early modern religion focused not on the orthodox, but on Quakers, Baptists and other dissenters from the established church. She cautioned against assumptions that the piety of the 'conformable' was consequently less powerfully felt, but she believed ('a shade too pessimistically' as Patrick Collinson noted) that: 'Very little can ever be said of the way that the beliefs of the orthodox amongst the laity affected them. Orthodoxy, like happiness has no history.'[26] If her specific religious beliefs were not reflected in her research and writing, her faith reinforced her opposition to accounts of historical change that explain belief, especially religious belief, solely in economic terms, or assume that ideas inevitably flow from the more prosperous to the poorer groups in society. In a later article she explored the possibilities of statistical analysis of religious belief, concluding with a pointed question: 'Can we weigh souls or count them?' In the process she attacked those who accepted Puritan judgements on the religious failings of the 'conformable': 'with a naivete that seems quite extraordinary, contemporary social historians swallow at their face value the judgements made by the "godly" on those they themselves considered "unreformed".'[27] This was a barely disguised dig at Keith

---

[25] M. Spufford and S. Mee, *The Clothing of the Common Sort 1570–1700* (Oxford, 2017).

[26] Spufford, *Contrasting Communities*, p. 319; Collinson, 'Critical conclusion', *The World of Rural Dissenters*, p. 395. This assumption has indeed been challenged by much recent scholarship on the history of religion and the history of emotions, and indeed by work done by Spufford's own students and associates, such as Christopher Marsh and Judith Maltby.

[27] M. Spufford, 'Can we count the "godly" and the "conformable" in the seventeenth century', *Journal of Ecclesiastical History*, 36 (1985), 438 and 434.

Wrightson in particular, and in this spirit she also challenged the links discerned by Christopher Hill and Wrightson between Puritanism and attempts to discipline or control unruliness amongst the lower classes.[28] Drives to close alehouses or particularly harsh punishment of illegitimacy occurred in periods of economic distress or population pressure, and were not a product of particular religious affiliations.[29] For the whole of her career she insisted, 'I do not myself believe in any economic determinism, for religious conviction or dissent, although there may be conditions that foster it.'[30]

Spufford's views on religion and society, with their implications for her broader understanding of early modern England, are demonstrated particularly clearly in the collective volume she edited, *The World of Rural Dissenters*. This began with some hundred pages of her own on 'the importance of religion in the sixteenth and seventeenth centuries', in part made up of revisions of recent articles, but the rest comprised a showcase for the work of her students and associates.[31] This is in some ways an odd book. It contained its own first review in the form of a 'Critical conclusion' by Patrick Collinson, in turn subject to some pointed responses in footnotes added by Spufford herself. As Collinson noted, there were important chapters by Eric Carlson, Tessa Watt and Michael Frearson that nonetheless did not quite fit the overall theme, and he also raised the question of whether there was anything distinctive about *rural* dissenters.[32] The chapters most relevant to Spufford's overall vision were those by Derek Plumb on the Lollards, Bill Stevenson on post-Restoration Dissenters, and Nesta Evans on 'The comparative mobility and immobility of Lollard descendants in early modern England'. Plumb and Stevenson both demonstrated that religious heterodoxy could not be connected to specific social groups but was found across all social groups, and in further support of Spufford's assumptions about English society they found (as Christopher Marsh did for the 'Family of love') that religious dissenters were mostly well integrated in their communities. Spufford connected their conclusions with the research of Nesta Evans on the survival of Lollard surnames amongst the seventeenth-century Quakers of the Buckinghamshire Chilterns. She noted the relative geographical immobility of people who lived in a

[28] C. Hill, *Society and Puritanism in Pre-Revolutionary England* (London, 1964); K. Wrightson and D. Levine, *Poverty and Piety in an English Village: Terling, 1525–1700* (New York, 1979).

[29] M. Spufford, 'Puritanism and social control?', in A. Fletcher and J. Stevenson (eds.), *Order and Disorder in Early Modern England* (Cambridge, 1985), pp. 41–57.

[30] Spufford, *Chippenham to the World*, p. 16.

[31] Sections were based on Spufford, 'Can we count the "godly"', and M. Spufford, 'The importance of the Lord's Supper to seventeenth-century dissenters', *Journal of the United Reformed Church History Society*, 5 (1993), 62–80.

[32] Collinson, 'Critical conclusion'; see also the thoughtful review by P. Griffiths, *Continuity and Change*, 11 (1996), 145–7.

region with excellent communication links (as Frearson showed), insisting that 'this relative immobility over time was the result of social acceptance in their own localities. They did not want to move because their neighbours, on the whole, tolerated them.'[33]

Spufford's account of religion and society is influential but not universally accepted. She had almost no interest in the 'Puritanism' which has attracted so much attention from historians, or in how the sixteenth-century Reformation transformed the status of Lollardy and complicated notions of orthodoxy and dissent. As Collinson pointed out, after 1662 many godly Puritans who had worked to reform the established church had themselves become dissenters but these Presbyterians and Congregationalists are missing from analyses that focus on Quakers and Baptists. Where she emphasised social integration and continuity, Christopher Hill used the same characteristics of familial patterns of dissent over time as an underground tradition of resistance in his article, 'From Lollards to Levellers', first published in 1978. While drawing on the work of Marsh, Plumb and Stevenson, later scholars have nonetheless seen a more fluid and complex interweaving of 'toleration' and confessional conflict in post-Reformation England and Europe.[34]

Spufford's ultimate ambition, in her own words, was to recreate, 'with love, and respect for these preceding human beings, all that I can currently grasp that needs to be known, and can be known, of their lives'.[35] In practice she devoted herself to the lives of 'ordinary people' in 'ordinary villages', and despite her broad interests in economic life, inheritance, piety and reading matter, there were significant omissions. Some of these she recognised herself. She speculated briefly in *Contrasting Communities* on the impact of Parliament's radical army during the English Civil War—'It is impossible to believe that Leveller ideas did not spread into Cambridgeshire.'[36] Here, she wrote, 'courage and time have failed me', but this simple explanation obscures the degree to which her own assumptions affected the choices she made and the time she allocated to particular themes. She could not work on a fen community like Willingham without paying some attention to struggles between landlords and tenants over collective resources threatened by fen drainage projects, but her account is comparatively low key, even humorous; the tenants have the best of a contest that appears relatively

[33] Spufford, *World of Rural Dissenters*, pp. 63–4.
[34] C. Hill, 'From Lollards to Levellers', first published in M. Cornforth (ed.), *Rebels and their Causes: Essays in Honour of A. L. Morton* (London, 1978) and in revised form in *The Collected Essays of Christopher Hill* vol. 2 (Brighton, 1985), pp. 89–116. Evans's chapter in *World of Rural Dissenters* echoes Hill's. On the complexities of toleration see, for example, A. Walsham, *Charitable Hatred: Tolerance and Intolerance in England, 1500–1700* (Manchester, 2006).
[35] Spufford, *Celebration*, pp. 63–4.
[36] Spufford, *Contrasting Communities*, p. xxi.

good natured.[37] In the Preface to *Contrasting Communities* (again) she explained: 'I have, purposely, avoided any consideration of the gentry and parochial clergy whose influence on their tenants and parishioners could obviously be an overriding one.' Although she added 'I think myself the docility of tenants to both their lords and their priests can be overstated', most of her work, as we have seen in discussion of religion, has stressed social cohesion rather than conflict.[38] Looking at crime or popular protest, for example, would have required more attention to matters that divided people rather than united them. And, for a scholar so passionately concerned with the lives and interests of the poor, there is surprisingly little on the workings of poor relief, although she used records of the poor law for material on the clothing of the poor. In an 'original, vivid and thought-provoking' account of the Staffordshire parish of Eccleshall, she used an extraordinarily detailed survey to illuminate the occupations and family relationships of the poor in 1690s. She used visual sources, and the nature of the survey itself, to explore how ways of understanding poverty changed over time, but there is little sense of whether or how the character of social relationships was transformed.[39]

We have suggested already that Spufford regretted the 'massive error' not to take up invitations to discuss her methodology, following the publication of *Contrasting Communities*: 'I thought it would be boring for my audiences.' This mattered because she believed this failure had limited her influence on English social history.[40] Her general comments were often an implicit and sometimes an explicit dialogue with or challenge to the interpretation of social change in early modern England associated with Keith Wrightson and his students. To put it at its simplest, she felt that the account of Terling by Wrightson and Levine had triumphed as a model for English social history over her Cambridgeshire villages.[41] In attempting a summing up of Spufford's work, the comparison with Wrightson cannot be avoided. In his detailed research on Terling, his perceptive articles and very influential general books, and through his talented students, Wrightson has established the dominant framework for early modern English social history. This is a more pessimistic model than Spufford's, and a more integrated account where growing economic inequality developed alongside social and cultural polarisation. Puritanism in this context is, in part, a means of

[37] Ibid., pp. 122–30.
[38] Ibid., p. xx.
[39] Spufford, *Poverty Portrayed*; the judgement is from Dr Jane Whittle, review of *Figures in the Landscape: Rural Society in England 1500–1700*, (review no. 237) https://reviews.history.ac.uk/review/237 (accessed 16 September 2019). This is an extremely perceptive account of Spufford's work.
[40] Spufford, *Chippenham to the World*, p. 7.
[41] Wrightson and Levine, *Poverty and Piety in an English Village*. The description of the 1995 Oxford University Press edition correctly has it: 'This classic study of a single community in early modern England has had a major influence on the interpretation of the social dynamics of the period.'

social differentiation and social control; social relationships are more marked by bitterness and aggression. As we have seen, Spufford sought in *Contrasting Communities* to provide a systematic and comparative account of economic change, which did demonstrate greater economic inequality. But she did not agree that growing economic differentiation necessarily implied cultural differences or social conflict. Through her study of inheritance practices in Cambridgeshire villages, she established that members of the same kinship networks might experience widely different economic fortunes, and with her student Motoyasu Takahashi she published an article that demonstrated 'poorer relations' witnessing the wills and attending the death beds of their richer kin (and vice versa). This occurred not only in the relatively egalitarian fen village of Willingham but even in later seventeenth-century Chippenham after the 'great economic gulf had developed between yeomen and their agricultural labourer relations'. This she argued was typical of a community in the 'chalk uplands' and, consequently, 'translating the economic gulf into a rigid social cleavage is purely a historians' construct'.[42] Spufford's work has thus been influential in resisting a deterministic account of culture, particularly in reference to forms of religious association and popular piety. Her stress on social cohesion also finds supporters, although for others her views of the fortunes of the 'common sort' and of social relations are over-optimistic. We must look elsewhere for accounts of the ways in which more discriminatory social relationships were embodied in the operation of the poor law and other forms of social regulation; of bitter quarrels over resources between landlords and tenants; or of collective popular agency in religious and political protest.[43]

Her scholarship remains a model in its imaginative rigour and in its humanity. In all her writings, Spufford used often unpromising sources to bring to life men and women within their communities: 'Until one has more adequately translated the statistics into human terms, it seems that despite all the care one takes, the human beings have slipped between the meshes of the net, and that one has not yet begun to

[42] M. Spufford and M. Takahashi, 'Families, will witnesses, and economic structure in the fens and on the chalk: sixteenth- and seventeenth-century Willingham and Chippenham', *Albion*, 28 (1996), 399 and 395. Her target in the last quotation is again Terling. Compare, for example, C. Marsh, *The Family of Love in English Society, 1530–1630* (Cambridge, 1994), pp. 183–7, where the bequests of Familists are used as evidence for the social integration of a group with radically distinctive religious beliefs.

[43] For different approaches, amongst a vast literature, see Wrightson and Levine, *Poverty and Piety*; S. Hindle, *On the Parish? The Micro-Politics of Poor Relief in Rural England, c. 1550–1750* (Oxford, 2004); J. Walter and K. Wrightson, 'Dearth and the social order in Early Modern England', *Past and Present*, 71 (1976), 22–42; J. Walter, 'Abolishing superstition with sedition? The politics of popular iconoclasm in England, 1640–1642', *Past and Present*, 183 (2004), 79–123; A. Wood, *The Politics of Social Conflict: The Peak Country 1520–1770* (Cambridge, 1999); P. Griffiths, *Lost Londons: Change, Crime and Control in the Capital City 1550–1660* (Cambridge, 2008); and for the latest summing up: K. Wrightson (ed.), *A Social History of England. 1500–1750* (Cambridge, 2017).

understand the real situation, which must have been so immediately apparent to the most illiterate peasant in every one of the alehouses of the villages concerned.'[44] She has introduced or popularised new sources, such as the probate accounts used as the foundation for her last book on clothing; and transformed approaches to familiar ones, as when she demonstrated the influence local scribes had on the religious clauses of early modern wills.[45] She offers unforgettable portraits of individual men and women, whose circumstances gently lead us to ponder important historical questions. There is Sister Sneesby, an elderly deaf Cambridgeshire widow, working as a casual labourer whose Baptist faith had been shaken by her reading Quaker books. Sister Sneesby, the records tell us, had been reduced to 'a sad, deplorable condition'. Her condition, Spufford wrote later, 'has haunted me ever since I first made her acquaintance', and she returned to Sneesby's troubles in many essays.[46] Sneesby embodies Spufford's insistence on the capacity of humble men and women for independent thought and action. In 'First steps in literacy', which completely transformed our assessment of literacy levels in early modern England, she described the young Oxfordshire shepherd (who could read but not write) who gave a lame young man one of his two sheep (**one of two**) 'to teach me to make the letters and joyn them together'.[47] And the sad case of a shipwrecked sailor, accused of vagrancy in Northumberland, while selling 'pictures, ballads, and other paper wares' bought on credit, sheds light on the complex family relationships and precarious existence of poorer chapmen in the eighteenth century.[48]

Spufford was sympathetic to women's history. She supervised Amy Erickson's important work on women and property, and offered sympathetic support to many other women scholars.[49] There are vivid accounts of women's experience in her studies of religious dissent, education and literacy, and chapwomen find a place alongside men in selling ballads, pins and clothes across England. Typically, she disclaimed any acquaintance with the feminist history emerging from the 1960s and 1970s: 'There was never any time for secondary reading of other historians, of theology as it interested me more, or feminism as it blossomed. My work developed in a vacuum.'[50] Nonetheless, Spufford's published work demonstrated a form of inspirational,

---

[44] Spufford, *Contrasting Communities*, p. 167.

[45] M. Spufford, 'The limitations of the Probate Inventory', in J. Chartres and D. Hey (eds.), *English Rural Society 1500–1800: Essays in Honour of Joan Thirsk* (Cambridge, 1990), pp. 139–74; Spufford and Mee, *Clothing of the Common Sort*. Peter Spufford and Amy Erickson had earlier highlighted the value of probate accounts.

[46] Spufford, *Contrasting Communities*, pp. 216–17; Spufford, *World of the Rural Dissenters*, p. 64.

[47] Spufford, 'First steps in literacy', 415–16.

[48] Spufford, *The Great Reclothing*, pp. 24–5.

[49] A. Erickson, *Women and Property in Early Modern England* (London, 1991).

[50] Spufford, *Celebration*, p. 68.

practical feminist scholarship in that it never hid the ways in which research and writing took place amongst personal difficulties and family responsibilities. In her inaugural lecture she explained that the idea for *Contrasting Communities*, 'the book of which I am most proud', came to her while she was driving to an adult evening class in Staffordshire, with her baby (Francis) 'stuffed under the seat in a carrycot'.[51] In the acknowledgements to that book, and in subsequent publications, she thanked those who had given her domestic support as well as more conventional intellectual influences, and grant-givers. She was frank about her own ill-health and about the difficulties in finding replacement care for her sick daughter. Such openness has become more common, but in the 1970s it was heartening to read a historian that admitted the hard work, the support from family and friends, the 'planning, organising, telephoning' necessary to clear a space to start, still more to complete, serious academic work.

While most of us engage in juggling acts to be parents, scholars, partners and friends, Spufford's dilemmas were of another order. She believed her sufferings and her faith enriched her work as a social historian by helping her understand better the people of the seventeenth century who were often in pain, usually devout and only too familiar with infant mortality. In *Celebration* she acknowledged the danger of 'over-identification' while insisting that 'Empathy is probably the historical virtue I most value'.[52] In this unflinching, deeply moving, surprisingly yet aptly titled book, Spufford wrote for new audiences as a committed Christian and a mother, as well as a dedicated historian, accepting but never facilely coming to terms with suffering. She explored her experience of three generations of 'physical evil': her mother's catastrophic stroke, her own ill-health and, especially, her daughter's chronic and incurable suffering through a genetic disorder, a particular example of the 'failures of God's creation'. As a convinced believer in an omnipotent and a loving God, Spufford pondered how he 'permitted such hurt'. Readers do not need to share her faith to be moved by the clear-sighted discussion of the dilemmas of families living on the frontiers of medical knowledge, where the search for a cure may be as troubling as the disease: as 'genuinely humane, high technology, modern medicine' brings nightmares as well as triumphs, and as, in the end, parents, 'utterly powerless and almost completely responsible', have to accept decisions made by sick, adult children. A kidney transplant from her father when she was eight bought Bridget precious time before her health deteriorated in young adulthood and she died in May 1989 aged twenty-two. *Celebration* is a notable contribution to medical ethics, posing the fundamental question of whether life

---

[51] Spufford, *Chippenham to the World*, p. 2; P. Spufford, 'Margaret', in Dean, Parry and Vallance, *Faith, Place and People*, p. 17.
[52] Spufford, *Celebration*, p. 70.

should always be sustained through 'massive and repeated medical intervention'. Spufford became an oblate of the Benedictine Community of St Mary's Abbey, West Malling in 1973, and it is clear that her strenuous Christian faith was fundamental to her life and work. At the end of *Celebration* she wrote, 'I loathe and detest my bone disease … But oddly, after twenty years, I can no longer wish that things were quite otherwise, except for my husband's sake. Learning to live with the disorder as creatively as possible has in the end formed the person I am … as historian, or mother, or oblate … the disease has indeed been a creative medium.'[53]

After Bridget Spufford died, a trust was established which between 1991 and 2003 supported a hostel for profoundly disabled students in Cambridge, enabling young people to live independently as Bridget had not. An 'Indian summer' for Margaret (and Peter) Spufford, of productive work, travel and new appointments was a paradoxical and unlooked for result of Bridget's death. They lectured in New Zealand and North America in 1991; held visiting fellowships in the Netherlands in 1992–3; and visited Japan for the first time in 1994, when Margaret was Visiting Professor at Rikkyo University, Tokyo. Spufford's former student, Motoyasu Takahashi, adopted her methods to develop local history in Japan, heading a team to study the village of Kami Shiojiri in Nagano Province, that specialised in breeding the eggs of silk moths, and in 2003 she visited Japan again, as a guest of the Japan Academy, to see for herself a place that had been much discussed in Cambridge and Whittlesford.

Meanwhile in 1994 Spufford was appointed as Research Professor in Social and Local History at Roehampton Institutute of Higher Education, a post she held until her retirement in 2001.[54] The appointment was the initiative of Roehampton's Professor Peter Edwards; he and Spufford were friends with a shared interest in the history of horses, whether they were carrying chapmen or going to war. Bridget Spufford would have studied at Roehampton had her health not collapsed. As Edwards wrote in an obituary for Spufford, the appointment came at 'the height of the RAE poaching frenzy' and aroused 'admiration and jealousy in equal measure'. Spufford raised the research profile and encouraged the ambitions of Roehampton's historians; the department duly achieved a high '5' rating in the 2001 Research Assessment Exercise. In 1995 Spufford established the Centre for Hearth Tax Research; she acted as Director until 2006 and it continues at Roehampton to this day.[55] As early as 1962 she had written an article on 'The significance of the Cambridgeshire Hearth Tax',

[53] Spufford, *Celebration*, pp. 49, 19, 99–114.
[54] The Institute was formed in 1975 through a federation of higher education colleges; it became the University of Roehampton in 2004.
[55] Peter Edwards, 'Obituary: Margaret Spufford, 1935–2014' that appeared on the Economic History Society website, https://web.archive.org/web/20140407092218/http://www.ehs.org.uk/news/obituary-margaret-spufford-1935–2014 (accessed 29 September 2019).

and almost forty years later in a lecture on the 'potential' of the Hearth Tax returns she repeated her conviction that 'each of our beloved village studies needs to be set in context for its significance to be fully known'.[56] The Hearth Tax, levied between 1662 and 1689, is the most remarkable source for the population of England between the Doomsday Book and the 1801 National Census, and illuminating also for research on wealth and housing. It is a vital resource for family and local historians as well as for academic historians and demographers. The Hearth Tax project is a remarkable collaboration between academic historians, local societies and dedicated volunteers across the country; appropriately it has been funded by both the British Academy and the Heritage Lottery Fund. By 2018, eleven volumes had been published (eight by the time of Spufford's death) by the British Record Society, often in cooperation with county record societies. It is a very fitting legacy.

Spufford was elected to the British Academy in 1995, and was awarded the OBE in 1996, 'for services to Social History and to Higher Education for People with Disabilities'. She was awarded a LittD by Cambridge University in 1986, and had honorary doctorates from the Open University (2002) and Keele University (2005). After her death on 6 March 2014 there were obituaries in the *Daily Telegraph*, *The Guardian* and *The Times*; a conference in her memory, 'After Margaret Spufford: English Local History Now', was held at the University of Roehampton in June 2015. The consequent volume in her honour was published in 2018.[57] She had planned a fund to support an undergraduate dissertation prize for a Newnham student, but so much money was raised that prizes in her name have been established for MA performance at all the institutions she was associated with: at Lucy Cavendish College Cambridge as well as Newnham, and Leicester, Roehampton and Keele Universities.

In an interview Francis Spufford explained that 'the qualities that made my mother extraordinary also made her difficult sometimes'; a lifelong friend stresses that she was always a fighter—for herself and her vocation as a historian, for her daughter and for her students and protégés.[58] Margaret filled any room she entered; the force of her personality, her convictions and her faith made her always inspiring if sometimes intimidating. Her family life and her remarkable scholarly achievements were only possible with the support of friends and students, but she repaid this help a thousand-fold. If Spufford had written only *Contrasting Communities* and her 'First

---

[56] H. M. Spufford, 'The significance of the Cambridgeshire Hearth Tax', *Proceedings of the Cambridge Antiquarian Society*, 55 (1962), 53–64; Spufford, 'The scope of local history', 213.

[57] Dean, Parry and Vallance, *Faith, Place and People in Early Modern England, Essays in Honour of Margaret Spufford*.

[58] Francis Spufford, interview with Terence Handley MacMath, 26 August 2016, www.churchtimes.co.uk/articles/2016/26-august/features/interviews/interview-francis-spufford-writer-and-lecturer (accessed 16 October 2019). I am relying also on discussions with Michael Frearson and David Vincent.

steps in popular literacy', her reputation as a social and cultural historian would be secure, but she leaves behind a broader corpus of pioneering studies of cheap print, consumption, communications, material culture, religious change and medical ethics, besides the research she inspired in her students, and the energy that established the team producing the Hearth Tax editions, sources of fundamental importance to early modern English economic and social history. She would never have wanted to be fashionable, and her scholarship worked to its own internal logic, but nonetheless, in her work on the history of the book and of reading, on consumption and material culture, on landscape and culture, she pioneered themes and methods that became decades later the focus of self-conscious, modish 'turns'.

Spufford's scholarship—personal, thoughtful and provocative—is of fundamental and enduring importance; the achievements of a remarkable historian and a remarkable woman in almost unimaginably difficult circumstances.

Acknowledgements
I did not know Margaret Spufford well at all, although I had the honour of giving the address when she was awarded an Honorary Degree at Keele in 2005. Consequently, I have been more than usually in need of help and advice with this obituary. I owe a great deal to the kindness of Michael Frearson, Amy Erickson and Judith Maltby amongst Margaret's students, while David Vincent and David Cressy have been particularly generous with personal testimony. Most of all I am indebted to Peter Spufford who provided me with warm hospitality at Whittlesford, copies of Margaret's books and offprints of her articles and a revised version of Margaret's own memoir prepared for the British Academy. I am more sorry than I can express that I was not able to complete this account before his death on 18 November 2017. For Peter Spufford's published account of Margaret Spufford's career, see his essay in the volume of essays in her honour.[59]

Note on the author: Ann Hughes is Professor of Early Modern History, Emerita, at Keele University.

[59] P. Spufford, 'Margaret', in Dean, Parry and Vallance, *Faith, Place and People in Early Modern England, Essays in Honour of Margaret Spufford*, pp. 15–26.

DAVID MARTIN

David Alfred Martin

30 June 1929 – 8 March 2019

elected Fellow of the British Academy 2007

by

JAMES A. BECKFORD
Fellow of the Academy

GRACE DAVIE

David Martin was Professor of Sociology at the London School of Economics and Political Science from 1971 until his early retirement in 1989, and the Elizabeth Scurlock Professor of Human Values at Southern Methodist University from 1986 to 1990. His numerous publications made distinguished and globally recognised contributions to the critical understanding of secularisation, the global spread of Pentecostalism, the interweaving of religion, music and poetry, and debates about religion and violence. His major works include *A Sociology of English Religion* (1967), *A General Theory of Secularization* (1978), *Tongues of Fire: the Explosion of Protestantism in Latin America* (1990), *Religion and Power: No Logos without Mythos* (2014) and *Ruin and Restoration: on Violence, Liturgy and Reconciliation* (2016). David Martin is also remembered for his leading role in the campaign to defend the Book of Common Prayer and the King James Bible.

Biographical Memoirs of Fellows of the British Academy, XVIII, 387–410
Posted 29 October 2019. © British Academy 2019.

DAVID MARTIN

Childhood and early years

David Martin was born on 30 June 1929 in Mortlake, in south-west London. The first chapter of his intellectual autobiography—*The Education of David Martin* (Martin 2013a)—contextualises this event by telling us more about his parents and grandparents and thus the influences on his early life. His maternal grandparents lived in Dorset, a part of the world that resonates at several points in David's life; his father's family came from rural Hertfordshire. Both father and mother worked 'in service' in London—the latter in a private house in Kensington and the former as a chauffeur then taxi driver, including a spell at Lambeth Palace during the time of Archbishop Davidson.

David's parents met at the Central Hall in Westminster, where he was baptised in 1929. This was an imposing building erected in the early years of the twentieth century, which 'announced' the presence of Wesleyan Methodists in central London (Martin 2013a, 26). It was Methodism, moreover, that infused David's upbringing and early life both directly and indirectly.

In terms of direct influences, his father is a key figure—a revivalist preacher who hoped, and no doubt prayed, that his son would follow in his footsteps. That didn't happen, at least not in the way envisaged, but Martin senior remains an active presence in the narrative—the more so in the sections that deal with David's later attention to Pentecostalism. The parallels with Methodism are nicely captured in the following: 'The moment I saw the Encyclopaedia and the Dictionary next to the Bible in the homes of Latin American Pentecostals I knew where I was. This was my childhood, my father's house and my mother's father's house, but far, far away and much later' (Martin 2013a, 6). The point is made in the initial pages of David's autobiography—the dénouement comes on pp. 209–16 in an account of a single day in Chile in November 1991.

The indirect influences are legion: the commitment to education, wide reading, singing, piano playing and—without exaggeration—the setting of a lifetime's agenda. The crucial questions were already forming: the need to make sense of the role of religion in society, the nature of power and politics, and especially sincerity and violence (Martin 2013a, 4).

More than a third of David's intellectual autobiography is taken up with the period prior to his eventual PhD at the London School of Economics (LSE). He arrived at the age of thirty by a roundabout route. This included regular church-going; primary and secondary (grammar school) education in south-west London, with short periods of evacuation in the early years of the war; a growing—though not always straightforward—passion for music; conscription in the Non-Combatant Corps from 1948 to 1950; teacher training at Westminster College in Oxford; a period of primary school teaching in Dorset; and an external University of London degree in sociology through a correspondence course.

Parts of this chronology require elaboration. First are the constant references to expanding knowledge—encyclopaedic reading in several disciplines (notably English literature and theology) with much gratitude to those (particular teachers) who pointed the way or opened new vistas. Much of this reading, however, was off-piste, well beyond any prescribed syllabus and at times a distraction from it. Importantly, the acquisition of knowledge included the history as well as the practice of music and, intuitively, its links to the transcendent. The chapter on military—or rather non-military—service jars in comparison, but becomes a crucial building block in David's later work on pacifism, war and violence. The sections on teaching, both training and practice, are set against the break-up of a brief and unhappy marriage but also the discovery of a 'way out' located both in sociology itself (a way of thinking that made sense of the world) and in the correspondence course devised by Wolsey Hall and delivered via the external University of London degree programme. The plan worked: in 1959 David was awarded a first-class degree for a set of papers that caught the attention of the examiners and permitted entry to LSE for a doctorate in sociology. The detail of his doctoral studies will be covered in a later section.

Family life

There was one more loop in the road before David finally settled at LSE as a member of the Sociology Department. This was a brief period of teaching in Sheffield at the beginning of the 1960s, which took place before the completion of his PhD. It was here that he met Bernice (née Thompson) who became not only David's wife but also his 'lifetime's critic and interlocutor' (Martin 2013a, 126) in a partnership of more than fifty years. They moved to London in the summer of 1962—she to teach at Bedford College and he to LSE. Appointed there as a lecturer he was promoted to Reader in 1967 and to Professor in 1971, retiring in 1989. At the time of moving, David already had one son (Jonathan); three further children followed—a daughter (Jessica) and two more boys (Izaak and Magnus).

Anyone one who knew David would be aware of the significance of Bernice's contribution both to his person and to his many and varied activities. Bernice is an accomplished musician and a distinguished scholar in her own right—the author of *A Sociology of Contemporary Cultural Change* (B. Martin 1981) and of important contributions to the understanding of Pentecostalism in Latin America, not least the place of women in this hugely significant movement (B. Martin 2013).

But quite apart from publication, Bernice and David, both singly and together, supported innumerable ventures and even more individuals in the sociology of religion and indeed beyond. Significant among these were 'non-standard' students to whom David showed both great sensitivity and much kindness. Such support took place in the largest of conferences and the smallest of workshops over many decades. More personally, many of their colleagues and students (both past and present) enjoyed not only welcome encouragement but warm hospitality in the Martins' home in Woking.

PhD and other early writings

David Martin's transition to full-time doctoral research at LSE had some elements of farce (Martin 2013a, 111–21). By his own account, he 'shuffled towards the sociology of religion sideways like a crab with uncertain intent' (Martin 2017, 59). Nevertheless, he took full advantage of the opportunity to mould his earlier experiences and extensive reading into a view of the world which was to remain largely unchanged throughout his adult life. His eccentric but erudite supervisor, Donald MacRae, excelled in mislaying students' papers and failing to keep appointments. But he approved of David's decision to study pacifism in Britain between the two World Wars; and he eventually helped him to see the benefits of adopting a sociology of knowledge approach to understanding the dialectics at work in ideological, religious and cultural movements. The PhD was completed in 1964.

A modified version was published a year later under the title *Pacifism: an Historical and Sociological Study* (Martin 1965a). In some ways it was a conventional treatment of the subject in so far as it interpreted pacifism in the light of a conceptual framework derived mainly from Ernst Troeltsch and Max Weber and with an emphasis on examples from modern British history. The central argument established the contrasting logics of 'sectarian absolutism and ecclesiastical compromise' (Martin 1965a, viii) not only in religion but also in politics—and particularly in religiously inflected politics. The sectarian impulse to reject or to withdraw from the world is contrasted to the church-like tendency to make compromises with vested interests and powers. This general idea was not entirely original: Milton Yinger, for instance, had expressed it in 1946 as the dilemma of purity and power. But David amplified and enriched it immeasurably by tracing its reverberations through examples taken from many different times, places, spheres of life and religious traditions. His analysis also explored in unprecedented detail the sometimes contradictory paths taken by different types of sect.[1] More importantly, he made the thoroughly original contribution of identifying

[1] At more or less the same time, another of Donald MacRae's former doctoral students, Bryan Wilson,

the sociological type that he labelled 'the denomination' and its characteristic stances in relation to political dissidence, voluntarism and pacifism.

The sociological distinctiveness of Christian denominations had long been assumed to lie in their emergence from sectarian origins, but in a seminar paper at LSE David offered a different interpretation. His paper, which first appeared in *The British Journal of Sociology* (Martin 1962), was included as an Appendix in *Pacifism*; it argued that groups of Christians such as Methodists, Congregationalists or Baptists had rarely displayed a sectarian spirit. They were not advanced sects. Instead, they were characterised for sociological purposes by a bundle of characteristics including their rejection of the principle of *extra ecclesiam nulla salus*, their pragmatic attitude to organisation, their subjective approach to sacraments, their traditional eschatology of heaven and hell, and their individualistic approach to morality. The article concluded that '[t]he sociological idea of the denomination is the idea of Her Majesty's Opposition, of disagreement within consensus, except that the opposition is permanently out of office' (Martin 1962, 224). Moreover, David pointed out that denominations tended to flourish in conditions of moderate social change rather than in conditions of turmoil when the contrasting attractions of sectarian rigour and ecclesiastical stability might prove more alluring. Strong echoes of these arguments about the sociological-cum-theological specificity of the denominational form and its underlying principle of voluntarism can be discerned in his explorations of global Pentecostalism some three decades later (Martin 2013b).

Indeed, David Martin's early writings about pacifism and denominations provide an essential key for unlocking many of the intellectual and broadly political preoccupations of his adult life. And, although some strands wore out, new strands of his thinking were added to the thread as fresh topics of interest were woven in. One of the original strands, which was expressed most forcefully and unequivocally in the Preface of *Pacifism*, proclaimed that he was 'entirely convinced that war and militarism are utterly repugnant to reason and religion' (Martin 1965a, x). But this stark affirmation eventually morphed into what he came to consider a more 'realist' version in many later writings, notably the view that 'pacifism brought about what it was most concerned to prevent, especially given the reluctance of its influential proponents to use pre-emptive force in the late 1930s' (Martin 2018, 164). Indeed, Bernice Martin records that '[h]is pacifism had finally died at Easter 1961' (B. Martin 2001, 208).

An additional strand of David's early writings reflected the inspiration that he had gained from reading Max Weber's essay 'Religious rejections of the world and their direction' (Weber, 1948a). It was Weber's insistence on the need to trace religious

---

had already elaborated his own, but different, typologies of religious sects and the tendency for some of them to develop into denominations: see, for example, Wilson (1959) and Barker (2009).

motives for rejecting the world through domains as different as the economy, politics, aesthetics, erotic life and the intellectual sphere that recommended itself to David as a methodological precept. Here was an early expression not only of his capacious intellectual curiosity but also of the kind of interdisciplinarity that he regarded as essential for capturing the patterned interconnections between so many disparate phenomena. In his view, '[o]ther disciplines may try to live in sealed off compartments but it is the task of sociology and of the sociology of religion in particular to think in terms of dialectic and of synthesis' (Martin 1966, 359). The interweaving of religion with music, poetry, architecture and politics was to be particularly close to his heart as well as to his intellectual project.

Nevertheless, David Martin never felt that his early enthusiasm for an interdisciplinary, comparative study of religion in all its subtlety and complexity was widely shared. On the contrary, he was acutely aware of the tendency for British social scientists to regard religion as a marginal epiphenomenon worthy of no more than a footnote. Indeed: 'Of all the different enclaves of contemporary specialization, the sociology of religion most resembles the republic of Venice just before Napoleon snuffed it out for ever' (Martin 1966, 355). Furthermore, the effect of this marginalisation was, he argued, to turn the sociology of religion in on itself to the point where the accumulation of knowledge about religious activities in isolation from the rest of the social and cultural world had become an end in itself. The result was that, as he captured it in one of his ironic *bons mots*, '[w]e now know the Standard Deviation of the time spent on shaving by Members of the Society of Jesus' (Martin 1966, 359). And, in anticipation of the sociological concern with 'lived religion', which was not to take root among sociologists of religion for a further three decades, he recommended that research should focus less on congruence between beliefs and the Athanasian Creed and more on 'the kind of religious and superstitious frameworks by which men live' (Martin 1966, 359)—or the 'subterranean theology' of everyday religion (Martin 2013a, 131).

This not to say, however, that David neglected the empirical investigation of religion. Indeed, he was among the pioneers who collected and analysed basic information about religious beliefs, practices and demographic variations in the UK; and he admired the work of Gabriel Le Bras—the doyen of methodical mapping of religion in France. Some of this material featured in the first course that he helped to teach at LSE on the social structure of modern Britain; and much of it underpinned his first book-length analysis of religion, which not only explored the social and cultural factors associated with religious belief, practice and organisation but also expressed his suspicions about the secularisation thesis (Martin 1967). In addition, he identified and defended intellectual spaces in which it was legitimate for sociologists to do research on religion and in which it made sense for religious leaders to take seriously the findings of such research. As the founding editor of *A Sociological Yearbook of Religion in Britain*, he introduced the idea of 'socio-religious studies' which were intended to be mutually beneficial to sociologists and 'churchmen' (Martin 1968, 9). He also pioneered studies of folk religiosity, 'the unknown gods of the English' (Martin 1969a, 103–13), the social class basis of different expressions of Christianity, religion in Central Europe and organisations ancillary to religious institutions. What he called 'the politico-religious nexus' (Martin 2014, 9) was at the heart of all these studies.

Although many of David's colleagues and students at LSE regarded the sociology of religion as irrelevant to their overriding concerns with social class and mobility, he relished the paradox of using 'the sceptical tools of sociology against its dogmatic assumptions' about the disappearance of religion as a chimera (Martin 2013a, 128). And his tongue-in-cheek self-description as 'an academic deviant living by a non-existent subject' (Martin 2013a, 127) should not be allowed to conceal his fervent determination to turn the tables on his critics for their adherence to what he regarded as historicist conceits and utopian delusions. This was to become a central theme of his intellectual project, especially his extensive work on secularisation (see below) and of his energetic engagement in contentious debates about higher education and culture. Nor did his self-ascribed status as an academic outsider prevent him from accomplishing the routine tasks that accompany increasing seniority as a scholar: for example as Dean of Students at LSE, as Chairman of the British Sociological Association's Study Group for the Sociology of Religion, or as President (for eight years) of the Société Internationale de Sociologie des Religions.

Politics, activism and violence

Witnessing at first hand the various waves of student rebelliousness that broke over LSE in the late 1960s David interpreted them as evidence of a new 'dissolution of the monasteries' (Martin 1969b). He regarded the then-fashionable forms of 'radical subjectivity', spontaneity and the advocacy for a 'free university' as ideological forces threatening to undermine the discipline, patience and objectivity required for effective teaching and learning. In his view: 'The disintegrations of the sixties … undermined the essential elements of rote and memory that provide the foundation of vision, flexibility, and creativity' (Martin 1983a, 172). In turn, these elements, which depended on the support of 'hierarchy and habit', were said to be 'preconditions of freedom' (Martin 2013a, 134). For David, 'order, discipline, and authority' are not only integral to politics but are 'necessary for human flourishing' (Martin 2012, 312).

Not surprisingly, then, he described himself as being 'on a direct collision course with the student revolutionaries who believed liberation followed from the disruption of habit and the destruction of hierarchy' (Martin 2013a, 134). His inaugural lecture at LSE in 1972 bravely took the theme of 'Order and rule', insisting that chaos could not lead to freedom. His aim was to defend 'masters and mastery, disciplines and discipleship, habit and continuity, the located and the familiar, the bounded and the particularized, rules, roles and relations' (Martin 1973, 142). Authority, he argued, must precede spontaneity—just as actors require a part before they can act.

If David's concern in the 1960s had been that 'antinomian students and seditious dons' (Martin 1983a, 183) were trying to undermine the intellectual case for disciplined and creative work in higher educational institutions, he was equally disturbed by what he saw as the British government's erosion of the autonomy of universities in the 1980s. The irony was not lost on him that the reasons for opposing student anarchy had been co-opted and traduced within two decades by the policies of Mrs Thatcher's governments which effectively forced the university sector to conform to what he regarded as narrowly utilitarian criteria for assessing the value of teaching and learning.

Taking the leading role in editing the volume on *Anarchy and Culture* was but the first of several high-profile forays that David Martin made into controversial issues in British public life. His love of music and English poetry was matched by a strong impulse to take a public stance in the defence of the institutions that he regarded as under threat from destructive forces: 'school, university, family, church and what I call ordinary politics' (Martin 2018, 178).

David's second foray into public life was sparked by responses to a Church of England working party's report of 1982 entitled 'The church and the bomb'. In particular, he quickly co-edited *Unholy Warfare: the Church and the Bomb* (Martin and Mullen 1983), a book that brought together contributors as diverse and as eminent as Enoch Powell, Tony Benn, Lord Soper and E. P. Thompson. The fact that so many of the contributors had a high public profile and that the book was published hard on the heels of the 1982 conflict with Argentina over the Falkland Islands—not to mention the bitterly contentious service of reconciliation that followed the war—served to evoke strong sentiments not only in the British establishment but also in wider movements for peace and against the use of nuclear weapons.

The chapter that David (1983b) contributed to *Unholy Warfare* was entirely consistent with the reasons that he had previously given for abandoning the pacifism of his early adult years. It was also a reflection of his theological conviction that 'God does not underwrite his Kingdom in political terms' (p. 106) and that 'Christianity cannot offer an unequivocal translation of the gospel of peace, love and universal fraternity into political terms and actions' (p. 93): it is redemptive rather than ethical.

His argument was for a form of political realism which precluded any policy of unilateral nuclear disarmament and which acknowledged that self-interest was the dominant force in international relations—an intriguing combination of Augustinian theology and *Realpolitik*.

In turn, these arguments against unilateral nuclear disarmament are part of David's broader understanding of religion, politics and violence. In his words, perhaps echoing Max Weber: 'Political life is a form of restricted warfare, and the state embodies an irreducible residue of violence' (Martin 1983b, 91). Rejecting the idea that religions are merely about salvation, he also regarded them as being necessarily engaged in conflicts over power and therefore essentially political. At the centre of these conflicts we find, once again, an oscillation between attempts, on the one hand, to link religion to dominant political powers and, on the other hand, to withdraw into sectarian enclaves. He was in no doubt, moreover, that both of these attempts at power-seeking could take a violent turn and that there was a potential for violence in all forms of human solidarity (Martin 2012, 300). He was equally sure that a 'holistic analysis of power, including the uses, occasions and triggers of violence' (Martin 2014, 9) was necessary for a sociological understanding of both religion and secularisation.

Nevertheless, the popular claim that religion is a primary cause of violence in the modern world was not credible in David Martin's eyes. On the contrary, he agreed with William Cavanaugh (2009) that the purported nexus between religion, irrationality and violence was not much more than an ideological product of the Enlightenment myth about 'an innocent secular liberal state' which legitimated itself as the only agency capable of managing violent and irrational others—as in the so-called, but misnamed, wars of religion. In short, his conclusion was that, while there is nothing specifically or uniquely violent about religion, good research should raise questions about the precise circumstances in which religions (or secular ideologies) have undoubtedly turned malignant and violent.

The reasons for the third of David's forays into public controversies are so deeply embedded in his views on relations between theology and sociology that they deserve separate treatment in the relevant section below (pp. 401–7). As before, the main point will be that activism and serious intellectual inquiry were two sides of the same coin—or, as he put it, '[t]hinking with your life' (Martin 2018, 405–6).

Secularisation

David Martin's writings about secularisation are arguably his best known and most influential contributions to the sociology of religion, but it is important to bear in mind that his core ideas in this field weave intricate patterns through his much broader interests in music, poetry, politics, violence and Pentecostalism. Furthermore, his persistent concern with the secular and with processes of secularisation showcase his insistence on the need to combine a search for patterns in historical change and continuity with a sensitivity to paradox, irony, contingency and reversibility. This clearly sets his work apart from that of scholars who frame secularisation as an inevitable, irreversible consequence of single causes such as modernisation, differentiation or rationalisation.

The radical character of David's approach to secularisation was evident in his early discussions of the concept's roots in counter-religious, utopian ideologies such as rationalism, Marxism and existentialism, which appealed to death-of-God theologians as well as to social scientists. Convinced that uses of the term secularisation were 'a barrier to progress in the sociology of religion' (Martin 1969a, 9) he argued, on the one hand, that the term needed to be explicated in detail and, on the other, that it should be 'erased from the sociological dictionary'. The fact that he saw no contradiction between these two positions both enhanced the distinctiveness of his work *and* attracted criticism from partisans on all sides of the secularisation debate.

Perhaps the most distinctive aspect of David Martin's analysis of both religion and secularisation is the centrality of struggles for power. He argued that religion's dual capacity both to exercise power and to validate the power of temporal authority places it in a dynamic tension with 'the world'.[2] Religion can lend legitimacy to temporal affairs; and it can challenge them. The outcomes of this continuous dialectic between religion and power vary across time and space. At one extreme lie countries such as France where a revolutionary conflict in the eighteenth century paved the way for a sharp dichotomy between religion and political power. By contrast, countries such as the USA and England experienced a relatively unproblematic transition to forms of democratic accommodation. But in both cases, as well as in the ones in between, David described the dynamic at work as one of thrust and recoil. In the history of Christianity, therefore, '[e]ach Christianization is a salient of faith driven into the secular from a different angle, each pays a characteristic cost which affects the character of the recoil, and each undergoes a partial collapse into some version of "nature"' (Martin 2005, 3). The main focus is on configurations of power and their varied inflections in different contexts, with particular emphasis on relations between religions and states. It is no exaggeration to say that this framework, which draws on sociology, history and theology, amounts to much more than a theory of secularisation.

[2] '[D]ifferent religious visions are in conflict with the world of power to varied degrees, ranging from Buddhism at the extreme position of tension, followed by Christianity, with Islam in the position of minimal conflict' (Martin 2018, 180).

It can work equally well for cross-national analyses of the political economy of religion and the secular.

This is the fundamental starting point for the cogent arguments that David subsequently elaborated not only in a full-fledged theory of secularisation but also in various self-critical revisions (Martin 2005). Secularisation in this perspective is definitely not about anything as simple as the decline of religion. It is about patterns of long-term, slow, partial, geographically specific and, above all, reversible shifts in the balance of power between religious and political forces—and the entanglement of these shifts with changes in elite and popular expressions of culture at the centre, and on the peripheries, of societies.

Charting an intellectual course at odds with most of his contemporaries in sociology, David recognised that modernisation had partially separated religion from other areas of society but he rejected any implication that modernity had *necessarily* relegated religion to the private sphere of life—or segregated it from the public sphere. On the grounds that religion and politics were necessarily interrelated, he argued that there was no inevitable progression towards the decline of religion—merely a balance between the religious and the secular which was continually shifting in response to historical contingencies and social forces. In short: 'The supposed association of modernity with secularity ... is contingent not necessary' (Martin 2014, 23). He never denied that secularisation *could* take place: but he rejected all unidirectional models which mechanically tied secularisation to modernity (Martin 2017, 37).

The most influential statement of David's theoretical ideas about high-level patterns of contention and accommodation between the religious and the secular was his book *A General Theory of Secularization*. The central idea had been heralded as early as 1965 (Martin 1965b) and further elaborated in Martin (1969c). The *General Theory* itself appeared in 1978 and is still an indispensable point of reference for discussions of secularisation. Its 'intellectual architecture' sought to explain how particular historical and cultural contexts refracted universal social processes to produce distinctive—albeit flexible—patterns of secularisation and de-secularisation in different countries and regions of the world. The six basic patterns, which were identified principally in terms of degrees and types of pluralism, included: total religious monopoly; religious duopoly; state church counterbalanced by free denominations; American religious pluralism; symbiosis of church and state (as in Nordic Lutheran and Eastern European Orthodox countries); and countries where 'Catholicism (or Orthodoxy) stood in for the state under conditions of external domination or external threat' (Martin 1978, 55).

The book drew on impressive amounts of detail from historical and social scientific studies to explore the historical origins, trajectory and outcomes of each of these basic patterns—and of their many variants around the world. Complex relations of power are shown to structure each pattern and variant, lending them 'particular character and colouring' (Martin 2014, 22). In subsequent publications David reflected self-critically on his general theory and offered further refinements of the basic framework and of its applicability to more and more cases. It was particularly gratifying for him to see that by the turn of the century 'an extraordinary reversal' (Martin 2005, 22) had occurred in the fortunes of conventional ways of thinking about secularisation. He welcomed the growing acceptance of ideas that included: the notion that religion persisted as a response to feelings of deprivation; the argument that western Europe was an exception to the continuing vitality of religion elsewhere in the world; the fact that religion had played a prominent role in the transition of states in Central and Eastern Europe from Soviet domination to self-determination; and the claim that tendencies towards cultural individualism had not necessarily excluded religion from all spheres of civil society. Other refinements emerged from extended exchanges with his critics (Martin 2018).

It is a mark of the imaginative originality, logical rigour and erudition of David's work on secularisation that other scholars still regard it as a classic in the sense of continuing to raise important questions, challenges and doubts (Carroll 2018; Koenig 2018). Indeed, it continues to generate a rich variety of hypotheses and hunches for other researchers to examine, especially as his publications after 1990 accorded more prominence to studies of religion in Latin America and to other regions of the world where the growing vitality of forms of evangelical Christianity has confirmed his theoretical expectations.

Pentecostalism

At Peter Berger's invitation, David Martin became an International Research Associate of the Institute for the Study of Economic Culture at Boston University in 1986. The following year he accepted the position of the Elizabeth Scurlock Professor of Human Values at Southern Methodist University in Dallas. These appointments gave David the opportunity to take his intellectual project in new directions while retaining a central focus on questions about secularisation and the renewal of religion in new contexts.

Given that religious developments in North America had avoided the 'spirals of antagonism' triggered by the clashes in Europe between Catholic monopolies, French secularism and the English pattern of a national church combined with denominations, David was drawn to the case of Latin America where a different pattern of development could be discerned. It seemed to him that emerging forms of popular Protestant evangelicalism—with loud echoes of eighteenth-century Methodism—

were replacing time-worn Catholic monopolies with more voluntaristic and entrepreneurial forms of Christianity.[3] Indeed, his reading of existing sources and his own fieldwork among Pentecostal groups in various countries of Latin America indicated that the latest twist in the struggle for power between religious and political forces had created a productive 'crossing of the "Anglo" and Hispanic patterns'—not as a replay of the old European dynamics but as 'a new moment with new possibilities' (Martin 1990, 295). In other words, he adapted and extended the framework forged in his *General Theory of Secularization* to take account of the rapid and large-scale growth of Pentecostal churches in Latin America. His first comprehensive assessment of this new twist in the *chassé-croisé* between secularising and de-secularising forces was *Tongues of Fire: the Explosion of Protestantism in Latin America* (Martin 1990). It was yet another reinforcement of his argument that the paths towards modernity could take different forms and that secularisation was not an inevitable location on, or destination of, any of them.

The unpredicted foundering of state socialist regimes in Central and Eastern Europe and their eventual replacement after 1990 by a variety of states with more liberal and democratic constitutions provided further support for David's view that modernity could follow widely differing trajectories. He seized the opportunity to examine these upheavals and their consequences for Christian churches while comparing events in Central and Eastern Europe with the rising strength of Pentecostalism in Latin America and elsewhere. His arguments, first aired in the 1991 F. D. Maurice lecture series at King's College London, were later published in *Forbidden Revolutions: Pentecostalism in Latin America, Catholicism in Eastern Europe* (Martin 1996). The central themes in both cases had robust roots in his earlier work on the revolutionary potential of the voluntary principle to overcome marginalisation at the hands of dominant systems (ideological or religious) and to replace them with democratic institutions. In his view, Pentecostals in Latin America and the Christian churches in Central and Eastern Europe had, in their different ways, contributed to 'the break-up of the hegemony of ideological power and the creation of autonomous space for the egalitarian exercise of personal and spiritual gifts' (Martin 1996, 6). Interest groups and voluntary associations were key to his reading of this transformation in which groups at the margins of a society were nevertheless able to transmit powerful messages to the centre, in some cases re-energising subcultures that had long been submerged. At the same time, David Martin was aware of the risks that Pentecostalism might favour machismo among its pastors and that political developments in post-communist Europe might aggravate deep-seated religio-ethnic tensions. But he remained confident

[3] For example: 'Pentecostalism in Latin America represented the appearance there of idiosyncratic versions of "the denomination" as the dominant form in North America' (Martin 2018, 165).

that, turning Karl Marx on his head, 'the beginning of criticism ... was undertaken by religion' (Martin 1996, 93) in both Latin America and Central and Eastern Europe.

David's pioneering work on Latin America was complemented twelve years later by an assessment of Pentecostalism's diffusion through other regions of the world—notably Africa and Asia. Indeed, his *Pentecostalism: the World their Parish* (Martin 2002a) raised the question of the extent to which Pentecostalism was becoming 'a global option'. In particular, he emphasised Pentecostalism's consonance not only with competitive pluralism, religious entrepreneurialism and voluntaristic forms of organisation but also with liberal capitalism on a global scale—albeit with national variations. The constant features of his analysis included the flexibility and trans-national portability of Pentecostal commitments among large masses of people in marginal or subdominant positions; the enhancement of women's status in families where the risk of machismo was challenged; ambivalence towards worldly politics; growth through contact with friends and family; and a positive attitude to material betterment. In short, David characterised Pentecostalism as a diffuse and ambiguous cultural revolution aimed at personal transformation principally among 'people on the move', most of whose 'movers and shakers' were women (Martin 2002a, 168).

At the same time, David was acutely aware that other commentators on the growth of Pentecostalism both in Latin America and elsewhere regarded it differently and were variously critical of his interpretation (Casanova 2018). Some found Pentecostal theologies and practices distasteful or anti-modern; others were sceptical about the motivations of Pentecostal leaders; yet others dismissed the spread of Pentecostalism as an export of American culture and entrepreneurialism; and a final group were not persuaded that Pentecostalism overcame tendencies towards machismo. None of these criticisms deflected David from his view that Pentecostalism was 'a dramatic instalment of "modernity" within the distinctive trajectory of Anglo-German Evangelicalism and Pietism' and at 'the confluence of black and white revivalism' (Martin 2017, 171).

Socio-theology, liturgy, poetry and music

It is already clear that David Martin's work straddled several disciplines. The significance of history in his understanding of the process—or rather processes—of secularisation is self-evident, as are the interactions of religion and state (and thus of sociology and political science) in his work on religion and violence. David's skilling in theology as well as social science demands, however, particular attention in that it manifested itself in multiple ways: in his academic thinking; in his role as a priest in the Church of England; and in his spirited defence of the Book of Common Prayer and the King James Bible. This last reflects, in turn, an unusual sensitivity to liturgy, language and poetry—thus extending interdisciplinarity yet further. The paragraphs that follow look first at the intersections of sociology and theology before turning to the Prayer Book controversy as such. A brief reference to David's final (posthumous) book: *Christianity and the World: Secularisation Narratives through the Lens of English Poetry 800AD to the Present* gathers a number of these ideas together, before a short note on music brings the section to an end.

The interweaving with David's biography is straightforward enough. The significance of his upbringing as a Methodist has already been noted, including protracted nurture in traditional forms of worship and scripture. Bit by bit, however, he moved towards Anglicanism and was confirmed into the Church of England in 1979. A relatively short time later, David was accepted for ordination, spending a term at Westcott House in Cambridge along the way; he was ordained deacon in 1983, priested a year later and became an honorary assistant priest at Guildford Cathedral for the rest of his life. His confirmation pretty much coincided with the publication of the collection 'Crisis for Cranmer and King James' in *Poetry Nation Review*, the key document of the Prayer Book controversy (Martin 1980a).

David held firmly to the idea that sociology and theology are commensurate disciplines. That view is not universal. On the one hand positivist readings of social science reflect on the emergence of sociology as an autonomous discipline, seeing this as a way of thinking that is antithetical not only to theology but to religion itself. Put bluntly, religion is seen as the intellectual and dying 'other', inimical to social progress and for this reason to be left on one side. On the other hand, theologians can be equally disparaging about the social sciences. David's own position regarding the latter stance was given book-length treatment first in *The Breaking of the Image* (Martin 1980b), then in *Reflections on Sociology and Theology* (Martin 1997) and more recently in *Ruin and Restoration: on Violence, Liturgy and Reconciliation* (Martin 2016).[4] Each of these will be considered in turn.

The Breaking of the Image was a published version of the 1977 Gore lectures, delivered in Westminster Abbey. It contains an innovative blend of theological and sociological insight which draws on a long-standing fascination with sign and symbol and the profound ambiguities that they express. The constant dialectic between cross and sword is a case in point: 'The cross will be carried into the realm of temporal power and will turn into a sword which defends the established order. It will execute the criminals and heretics in the name of God and the King' (Martin 1980b, 28). That, however, is not the whole story: temporal kingship is equally likely to be defended by reversed arms, that is by 'a sign of reversal and inversion' (p. 28). Empirical examples

---

[4] Also important in this context is the edited volume by Martin, Orme Mills and Pickering (2004).

of these complex dialectics follow, including a memorable description of the cross which dominates the US Airforce Chapel at Colorado Springs, itself a very striking building:

> At the centre of the huge arsenal is a chapel built of stained glass spurs like planes at the point of take-off. The cross is also like a sword. Looked at from another angle the combined cross and sword is a plane and a dove. The plane is poised to deliver death rather than to deliver *from* death and the dove signifies the spirit of peace and concord. (Martin 1980b, 28)

The extended discussion found in *Reflections on Sociology and Theology* had a different and very specific prompt: John Milbank's acclaimed but highly polemical *Theology and Social Theory: Beyond Secular Reason* (Milbank 1990). In this Milbank maintained that theology must not allow itself to be contaminated by social scientific thinking. The rationale is clear: social science is by definition secular (a profoundly negative term in Milbank's lexicon). For it to engage with theology is, therefore, for it to encroach unacceptably on the sublime. There is no room for compromise on these issues. David argued otherwise: that sociology, appropriately understood and carefully deployed, can (and indeed should) contribute to theological understanding without either discipline being compromised. The problem lies not in the disciplines as such, but in the fact that sociology is not always appropriately understood by theologians; nor is theology sufficiently valued by sociologists—a state of affairs that is regrettable.

For David, theological insights and the contexts from which they emerge are necessarily linked. In theological language, the Christian calling, both individual and collective, is to be 'in the world but not of it'. In David's more specific socio-theological discourse, there exists between the specificities of each situation (the context) and the exigencies of the Christian gospel 'an angle of eschatological tension'. Documenting and explaining the sharpness of this angle are, essentially, sociological tasks. So are suggestions of possible resolution if the tension becomes unbearable. Theologies of baptism in different parts of Europe offer a revealing illustration. Modes of initiation that 'fitted' the state churches of Northern Europe are no longer 'fitting', either socially or theologically, as these churches gradually mutate from ascription to voluntarism as the basis of membership (Martin 1997, 81; see also Davie, 2006). New understandings of baptism are required as new forms of ecclesiology emerge; they are more likely to succeed if the sociological shifts are not only taken into account but are properly understood.

In Chapter 10 of *Reflections on Theology and Sociology*, David explored the underlying tension further with reference to particular roles, one of which is the military chaplain—a position built into the structures of secular power (in this case the armed forces) but held by individuals commissioned by the Christian churches. In other words, the military chaplain is doubly commissioned. The tension moreover is unavoidable: chaplains receive 'the indelible stigmata of a social role' (Martin 1997, 149), yet are subjected to criticism to the extent that they cease to be distinctively Christian. Interestingly David observes that the criticism comes as much from those on the margins of the churches as it does from those within. The charges, moreover, are levelled both at Christian ministers who become chaplains, and at ministers who claim exemption from the obligations (military service) placed on ordinary citizens. This is a classic no-win situation.

The inevitability of the dilemma is once again worked out in terms of the 'angle of eschatological tension', itself set up by the impossible demands of the New Testament. It is plain, for example, that the teaching laid down in the Sermon on the Mount cannot be realised in practice either by a believing individual or by the institutional church. The former is asked to be in the world but not of it; the second to reconcile partnership with the state with its transformation. The role of the military chaplain displays this dilemma with particular clarity: he or she either joins up and takes the consequences in the form of persistent unease or opts out. In institutional terms, this mirrors very precisely the difference between a church and a sect—a persistent theme in David's writing.

In parenthesis, the role of the Christian politician is similar. Here David's discussion drew directly on Max Weber—specifically his iconic essay on 'Politics as a vocation' published in 1919. The core of Weber's argument lies in his conviction that politics is indeed a vocation which requires passion, so long as this is tempered by a sense of responsibility and proportion (Weber 1948b, 116). Crucially, the politician has to accept responsibility for the consequences of his or her actions, which implies in turn a right understanding not only of the relationship between ethics and politics, but also of the delicate connections between means and ends—a theme developed at some length. Towards the end of this discussion, Weber too returns to the Sermon on the Mount, recognising once again that this deals in absolutes. Politics, on the other hand, operates with a different set of assumptions: 'For if it is said, in line with the acosmic ethic of love, "Resist not him that is evil with force", for the politician the reverse proposition holds, "thou shalt resist evil by force", or else you are responsible for the evil winning out' (Weber 1948b, 119–20). The crucial point is to recognise the difference between the two realms. Arguments or actions that confuse them will almost certainly end badly.

David's most recent exploration of socio-theology can be found in *Ruin and Restoration: on Violence, Liturgy and Reconciliation* (2016), which includes an introductory essay by Charles Taylor. In this, David offers a particularly stark juxtaposition of the world which is governed by a dynamic of violence against which

Christianity and Buddhism offer non-violent alternatives. They are, he argues, the axial religions that lie most obviously against the 'grain of the world'. The book begins with a governing essay that develops this theme with reference to Christianity: specifically, it traces the tensions between 'the kingdom' and 'the world' and thus 'the tension between the social sciences as accounts of how "the world" works in practice and Christianity as a hope concerning a better world' (Martin 2016, 4). Six commentaries on the atonement follow in a volume which develops some of the ideas initiated— but not always followed through—in *The Breaking of the Image* (Martin 1980). The continuities are clear, but it is *Ruin and Restoration* that contains the fullest and most deliberate attempt to *integrate* sociology and theology.

The earlier section of this memoir entitled 'Politics, activism and violence' included two instances when David himself engaged a more public role—with reference to university life and to a Church of England working party on nuclear disarmament. Such prominence was equally true in relation to the Church's attempts to 'modernise' both its language and liturgy. Indeed, the section devoted to this question in David's autobiography is entitled 'Another culture war', for thus he saw it. It is quite clear, in fact, that it engaged him totally—body, mind and spirit. The reasons are clear: the Prayer Book, the King James Bible and classic hymnody were not only redolent of family and childhood but brought together the things that he valued most: 'poetry, music, poetry set to music, the poetics of place, the Church in a place, and articulate speech' (Martin 2013a, 161). Clearly, these sentiments predate by many decades his eventual embrace of Anglicanism.

The focus was an issue of *Poetry Nation Review*, entitled 'Crisis for Cranmer and King James', guest-edited by David (Martin 1980a). The issue was in effect a manifesto —a vigorous defence of the place of the Book of Common Prayer and the Authorised Version of the Bible in both the spiritual and more general culture of England. It took the form of forty-four essays and testimonials written by what can only be described as the cultural elite (political, literary and musical), and included a series of petitions addressed to the Church of England's General Synod. The list of signatories to the petitions is even more impressive than the contributors to the *Review* itself. The combination did its work, provoking a major and animated debate (both inside and outside the Church). Leaders appeared in the major dailies, alongside dozens of articles and letters. Sacks full of mail arrived at LSE. The Church however was resistant, with the effect that the debate moved to Parliament in the form of a bill which reached a second reading before it was withdrawn. The outcome was partial success: no *volte face* on the part of the Church but '[t]he Prayer Book was not to be consigned to the museum, and its services would remain available to worshippers' (Martin 2013a, 174). This is hardly the place to argue the rights and wrongs of the Church of England's policy regarding liturgical documents. More importantly, it is the place to note that, in addition to a distinguished academic career, David provoked on this occasion a major public debate.

David Martin's ordination followed, and offered—amongst many other things—a new way to combine priesthood and poetry. This was in the sermon, a mode of address that became deeply satisfying. Three collections have been published (Martin 1989, 2002, 2008) all of which demonstrate a very particular skill: sermons are crafted rather than written and (in David's words) constitute 'an art form that juxtaposes quotations and releases the charged-up energies stored in minute atoms of text and the multiple meanings of single words' (Martin 2013a, 175). In his hands, they did indeed.

It is important finally to note David's most recent book (in press), published after his death: *Christianity and the World: Secularisation Narratives through the Lens of English Poetry 800 AD to the Present.* This remarkable volume brings together many of the themes already addressed in this memoir, all of which find their focus in the relationship of Christianity to the dynamics of social order or what theologians might call 'the world'. The social order in this case is England and the medium of expression a thousand years of English poetry, through which it is possible to discern the thrusts and recoils of secularisation over the long term. Thus, in a single volume, David incorporates a lifetime's work on secularisation, a profound knowledge of English poetry and deep theological insight. A chronological (chapter by chapter) sequence of reflections relates each of these strands to the others. Those who are drawn to this collection will arrive by different routes, but all of them will be enriched by what they find.

Given its close connections to poetry, music constitutes a powerful sub-theme in this narrative. Indeed, any account of David Martin that did not consider the significance of music in both his life and his work would be seriously incomplete. Its centrality provides, therefore, a fitting 'note' on which to conclude this memoir.

Music was central to David's experience from the very beginning, unsurprisingly in that Methodism was—indeed still is—a singing religion. Hymns were poems set to music, and an early musical training (piano lessons) ensured that David was an asset to both choirs and congregations in local Methodist churches. His predilection for Handel showed at an early stage—see, for example, his reaction to hearing the *Hallelujah Chorus* for the first time ('I... rushed out of the room to hide my tears': Martin 2013a, 59). Playing the piano to an exacting standard gave him lifelong pleasure, most especially perhaps as an accompanist for his wife, herself an accomplished singer—a role established in the 1970s. In his own words, this was the (relatively late) moment when music finally 'came right' (p. 62).

Although David described his experience of taking diploma examinations for the Royal Schools of Music as 'humiliating' (Martin 2013a, 57), he continued to develop a profound understanding of music—a body of knowledge that became inextricably linked with his wider thinking. For example, in *A Sociology of English Religion* (Martin 1967, 85–6), different religious cultures are captured by the terms: 'carol', 'hymn' and 'chorus'. Clearly these labels have social as well as musical overtones. Singers of hymns and carols, moreover, demonstrate identifiable affinities with more complicated music: hymns are aligned with Handel and Mendelssohn; carols with Bach, Byrd and Britten. Choruses pull in a different direction, reflecting revivalist currents both in England and beyond.

More than fifty years later, David returned to the question of music in the retrospect that he contributed to *David Martin and the Sociology of Religion* (Martin 2018). In this he responded to the essay by Pål Repstad (2018) by taking time to clarify his own sociology of music, demonstrating at each stage how this related to his understanding of secularisation. Of particular note is the distinction between a high tradition of devotion found in forms of Catholic and Orthodox ceremonialism and a demotic tradition associated with 'participation, expressivity and sincerity' (Martin 2018, 173–4). Even more striking, however, is the comparative perspective that underpins this analysis. Identifiable patterns can be found in different parts of Europe and the USA, which relate closely to those associated with secularisation.

Indeed, the discussion turns full circle as David reminds us that France offers a dramatic contrast to England, 'based not on an evolutionary politics associated with Evangelicalism but on politics oscillating violently between revolution and restoration' (Martin 2018, 175). Thus, in France, in contrast to Britain—or indeed Germany—the linear development of choral singing was necessarily disturbed, as was the case in anticlerical Italy. Developments in architecture can be approached along similar lines. In London, for instance, Westminster Abbey is adjacent to the Houses of Parliament, whereas in France, the *mairie* almost always 'confronts' the Catholic church—a juxtaposition discovered in both the largest conurbation and the smallest commune; and in Rome, the huge Vittorio Emanuele II Monument obliterates the view of St Peter's.[5] Thus, for David Martin, these buildings and their spatial relationships mediate the shifting dispositions of religious and secular power no less powerfully than the developments of poetry, liturgy and music.

Conclusion

It is no easy task to capture the life and work of a scholar such as David Martin, who not only contributed with such distinction to an impressively wide array of intellectual

---

[5] This application of secularisation theory to European city architecture was explained at length in Martin (2010) and extended in Martin (2014) to North America, Moscow and Eurasia.

subjects but who also brought passion and reason to bear on debates about matters of public contention. One thing is crystal clear, however: his impact on the sociology of religion and socio-theology continues to be profound. His writings about pacifism, secularisation, religion and politics, Pentecostalism, liturgy and music have become standard references.[6] And his practice of reflecting critically on his own ideas has helped to make them more widely accessible. Not surprisingly, then, numerous students and researchers remain heavily indebted to him for providing a model of engaged scholarship—or, in his own words, 'thinking with your life'.

The impact of David Martin's life and work owes much to the sophistication of his writing style, which calls for special mention. His writings were not only artfully crafted and rooted in layers of erudition and artistic sensibility but were filled with striking metaphors and rhythms. Indeed, his writing combined Pascal's 'spirit of finesse' with his 'spirit of geometry': that is, poetry and musicality in the service of lucidity and logic. At the same time, humour, paradox and irony enlivened even his technical analyses of social structure and religious symbolism. The talks that he prepared for BBC radio programmes were models of wit as well as insight; and his book reviews sparkled with humour, notwithstanding the occasional poisoned barb.

David Martin was a complex individual. At times diffident and ill at ease, he was entirely sure of an argument once it was worked out and was ready to defend it with tenacity. This 'unlikely sociologist', had an evident taste for public controversy. Most of all, however, David Martin will be fondly remembered as an inspiring scholar, exacting teacher, supervisor, examiner, mentor and friend by the generations who follow in the sociology of religion—the sub-discipline that he did so much to promote.

Acknowledgements

In preparing this memoir, we have benefited from the assistance kindly offered by Bernice Martin, Jessica Martin and Robin Gill. We are deeply indebted to all of them for their willingness to answer questions at short notice, to provide invaluable guidance and to share our commitment to a memoir that does justice to both David Martin's personal qualities and his intellectual achievements.

Note on the authors: James A. Beckford is Professor Emeritus of Sociology at the University of Warwick; he was elected a Fellow of the British Academy in 2004. Grace Davie is Professor Emeritus of Sociology at the University of Exeter.

---

[6] A *David Martin Reader* was edited by Wei Dedong and Zhong Zhifeng (2015) and published in both English and Chinese, marking not only David's global reputation as a scholar but also a particular moment in the evolution of Chinese thinking about religion.

References

Barker, E. (2009). 'Bryan Ronald Wilson 1926–2004', *Proceedings of the British Academy*, 161, pp. 381–401.

Carroll, A. (2018). 'David Martin's theory of secularisation', in H. Joas (ed.), *David Martin and the Sociology of Religion* (London), pp. 16–31.

Casanova, J. (2018). 'Parallel reformations in Latin America. A critical review of David Martin's interpretation of the Pentecostal revolution', in H. Joas (ed.), *David Martin and the Sociology of Religion* (London), pp. 85–106.

Cavanaugh, W. T. (2009). *The Myth of Religious Violence* (New York).

Davie, G. (2006). 'Religion in Europe in the 21st century: the factors to take into account', *European Journal of Sociology*, 47, 271–96.

Davie, G. (2018). 'Understanding religion in modern Britain. Taking the long view', in H. Joas (ed.), *David Martin and the Sociology of Religion* (London), pp. 68–84.

Koenig, M. (2018). 'Revising secularization theory's paradigmatic core—David Martin on general processes, basic patterns and causal mechanisms of differentiation between religion and politics', in H. Joas (ed.), *David Martin and the Sociology of Religion* (London), pp. 32–49.

Luczewski, M. (2018). 'Converting: a general theory of David Martin', in H. Joas (ed.), *David Martin and the Sociology of Religion* (London), pp. 147–61.

Martin, B. (1991). *A Sociology of Contemporary Cultural Change* (Oxford).

Martin, B. (2001). '"Restoring intellectual day": theology and sociology in the work of David Martin', in A. Walker and M. Percy (eds.), *Restoring the Image. Essays on Religion and Society in Honour of David Martin* (Sheffield), pp. 203–26.

Martin, B. (2013). 'Tensions and trends in Pentecostal gender and family relations', in R. W. Hefner and P. L. Berger (eds.), *Global Pentecostalism in the 21st Century* (Bloomington, IN), pp. 115–48.

Martin, D. (1962). 'The denomination', *British Journal of Sociology*, 13, 1–14.

Martin, D. (1965a). *Pacifism: an Historical and Sociological Study* (London).

Martin, D. (1965b). 'Towards eliminating the concept of secularisation', in J. Gould (ed.), *Penguin Survey of the Social Sciences* (Harmondsworth), pp. 169–82.

Martin, D. (1966). 'The sociology of religion: a case of status deprivation?', *British Journal of Sociology*, 17, 353–9.

Martin, D. (1967). *A Sociology of English Religion* (London).

Martin, D. (1968). 'Introduction', *A Sociological Yearbook of Religion in Britain* (London), pp. 9–10.

Martin, D. (1969a). *The Religious and the Secular. Studies in Secularization* (London).

Martin, D. (ed.) (1969b). *Anarchy and Culture. The Problem of the Contemporary University* (London).

Martin, D. (1969c). 'Notes for a general theory of secularisation', *European Journal of Sociology*, 10, 192–201.

Martin, D. (1973). *Tracts against the Times* (Guildford).

Martin, D. (1975). 'Mutations: religio-political crisis and the collapse of Puritanism and humanism', in P. Seabury (ed.), *Universities in the Western World* (New York), pp. 85–97.

Martin, D. (1978). *A General Theory of Secularization* (Oxford).

Martin, D. (guest editor) (1980a). 'Crisis for Cranmer and King James', *Poetry Nation Review*, 13.

Martin D. (1980b). *The Breaking of the Image: a Sociology of Christian Theory and Practice* (Oxford).

Martin, D. (1983a). 'Trends and standards in British higher education', in J. W. Chapman (ed.), *The Western University on Trial* (Berkeley, CA), pp. 167–83.

Martin, D. (1983b). 'The Christian ethic and the spirit of security and deterrence', in D. Martin & P. Mullen (eds.), *Unholy Warfare: the Church and the Bomb* (Oxford), pp. 85–107.

Martin, D. (1989). *Divinity in a Grain of Bread* (Cambridge).

Martin, D. (1990). *Tongues of Fire. The Explosion of Protestantism in Latin America* (Oxford).

Martin, D. (1996). *Forbidden Revolutions: Pentecostalism in Latin America, Catholicism in Eastern Europe* (London).

Martin, D. (1997). *Reflections on Sociology and Theology* (Oxford).

Martin, D. (2001). 'Personal reflections in the mirror of Halévy and Weber', in R. K. Fenn (ed.), *The Blackwell Companion to Sociology of Religion* (Oxford), pp. 23–38.

Martin, D. (2002a). *Pentecostalism: the World Their Parish* (Oxford).

Martin, D. (2002b). *Christian Language in the Secular City* (Farnham).

Martin, D. (2005). *On Secularization: Towards a Revised General Theory* (Aldershot).

Martin, D. (2008). *Sacred History and Sacred Geography: Spiritual Journeys in Time and Space* (Vancouver).

Martin, D. (2010). 'Inscribing the general theory of secularization and its basic patterns in the architectural space/time of the city: from presecular to postsecular?', in A. Molendijk, J. Beaumont and C. Jedan (eds.), *Exploring the Postsecular: the Religious, the Political and the Urban* (Leiden), pp. 183–206.

Martin, D. (2012). 'Axial religions and the problem of violence', in H. Joas and R. N. Bellah (eds.), *The Axial Age and its Consequences* (Cambridge, MA), pp. 294–316.

Martin, D. (2013a). *The Education of David Martin: the Making of an Unlikely Sociologist* (London).

Martin, D. (2013b). 'Voluntarism. Niche markets created by a fissile transnational faith', in R. W. Hefner, J. Hutchinson, S. Mels and C. Timmerman (eds.), *Religions in Movement: the Local and the Global in Contemporary Faith Traditions* (New York), pp. 180–95.

Martin, D. (2013c). 'Pentecostalism: an alternative form of modernity and modernization?', in R. W. Hefner and P. L. Berger (eds.), *Global Pentecostalism in the 21ˢᵗ Century* (Bloomington, IN), pp. 37–62.

Martin, D. (2014). *Religion and Power: No Logos Without Mythos* (Farnham).

Martin, D. (2016). *Ruin and Restoration: On Violence, Liturgy and Reconciliation* (London).

Martin, D. (2017). *Secularisation, Pentecostalism and Violence: Receptions, Rediscoveries and Rebuttals in the Sociology of Religion* (London).

Martin, D. (2018). 'Thinking with your life', in H. Joas (ed.), *David Martin and the Sociology of Religion* (London), pp. 162–90.

Martin, D. (in press). *Christianity and the World. Secularisation Narratives through the Lens of English Poetry 800 AD to the Present* (Eugene, OR).

Martin, D. and Mullen, P. (eds.) (1981). *No Alternative: the Prayer Book Controversy* (Oxford).

Martin, D. and Mullen, P. (eds.) (1983). *Unholy Warfare: the Church and the Bomb* (Oxford).

Martin, D., Orme Mills OP, J. and Pickering, W. (eds.) (2004). *Sociology and Theology: Alliance and Conflict* (Hemel Hempstead).

Milbank, J. (1990). *Theology and Social Theory: Beyond Secular Reason* (Oxford—second edition, 2005).

Repstad, P. (2018). 'David Martin on Scandinavia and music', in H. Joas (ed.), *David Martin and the Sociology of Religion* (London), pp. 107–122.

Weber, M. (1948a). 'Religious rejections of the world and their direction', in H. H. Gerth and C. W. Mills (eds.), *From Max Weber. Essays in Sociology* (London), pp. 323–59.

Weber, M. (1948b). 'Politics as a vocation', in H. H. Gerth and C. W. Mills (eds.), *From Max Weber. Essays in Sociology* (London), pp. 77–128.

Wei, D. and Zhong, Z. (2015). *Sociology of Religion: a David Martin Reader* (Waco, TX).

Wilson, B. R. (1959). 'An analysis of sect development', *American Sociological Review*, 24, 3–15.

Yinger, J. M. (1946). *Religion in the Struggle for Power* (Durham, NC).

ALFRED STEPAN

Alfred Charles Stepan

22 July 1936 – 27 September 2017

elected Fellow of the British Academy 1997

by

ARCHIE BROWN

Fellow of the Academy

A fine boxer in his youth; an active duty officer in the US Marine Corps who spent the 1962 missile crisis at sea, twenty miles off the Cuban coast, in readiness to invade the island; a Marine officer in Vietnam; a special correspondent of *The Economist* who predicted the Brazilian military coup of March 1964; a Chicago native urged by the city's machine politicians to take over the seat of a retiring Democratic Congressman (with hints of a Senate opening to come); a professor who had a six-hour meeting with Fidel Castro in Havana (and a box of Cuban cigars from the revolutionary leader); the holder of prestigious Chairs and Deanships at Yale, Columbia and Oxford; the first President and Rector of the Central European University in Budapest; Chairman of the Board of the Richard Tucker Music Foundation—this would sound like an implausible combination for a character in a novel. Alfred Stepan, best known for his contributions to the comparative study of politics, did all these things and more.

Biographical Memoirs of Fellows of the British Academy, XVIII, 411–447
Posted 30 October 2019. © British Academy 2019.

ALFRED STEPAN

One of the most influential political scientists of his generation, Alfred Charles Stepan was born into 'a very Catholic family' of seven in Chicago on 22 July 1936.[1] He died of cancer, aged 81, on 27 September 2017. 'Al', as he was known to his family and friends, was the eldest of the sons. The five boys and two girls all went to university, but Al was the only one to choose an academic career. Although more bookish than his siblings, he was also an all-rounder. Extremely fit, he was good at sport, including American football—until his lack of height and weight made it impossible to compete with beefier late teenagers—and he excelled as a featherweight boxer. His grandparents, Czech-German on his father's side and Irish on his mother's, were immigrants or first-generation Americans. With an initial investment of just 500 dollars, Al's father, who was also Alfred C. Stepan, founded a chemical business in Chicago during the Depression. It became successful and in due course made the family comfortably off, but it was still developing during Al's childhood. Hard work was encouraged by his father as well as by his mother Mary Louise (Quinn before her marriage), and though Al went to one of Chicago's top Catholic schools, Loyola Academy, he did a paper round as a boy. Before Loyola, he had spent a year at a tough Chicago public school (in the traditional Scottish and hence American meaning of public school) at which he got into fights, and this provided an incentive to take up boxing.

His interest in the real world of politics began in the family and long preceded his academic studies in that field. His father and his brothers were Republicans, but Al's maternal grandfather, to whom he was close, was not only a committed Democrat but one on very friendly terms with Chicago's Irish-American machine politicians. He had a printing press which produced many of the publications of the city's Democratic Party organisations. From grandfather Quinn, Al learned a lot about how machine politics worked. He also shared his political leanings, supported Adlai Stevenson in the 1952 presidential election, and was puzzled by the extent to which Senator McCarthy's activities were found acceptable by so many Americans. From quite an early age, Al's political convictions were essentially social democratic. He was a staunch Democrat in the United States and sympathetic to the Labour Party in Britain. His partisanship as a citizen, though, did not get in the way of his political analysis. He could understand why others came to hold different views from his own, and when, for example, he studied the military in politics he was able to establish

[1] A. Stepan, 'Democratic governance and the craft of case-based research', in G. L. Munck and R. Snyder, *Passion, Craft, and Method in Comparative Politics* (Baltimore, MD, 2007), p. 395. This extended interview with Stepan was conducted over two days—on 15–16 October 2003. Many, though far from all, of the stories which Alfred Stepan relates in the interview I heard from him directly in the course of many conversations during our long friendship which began in the late 1970s and continued to his death. However, since Richard Snyder's interview with Stepan was recorded, I draw on it liberally in the certainty that I am being faithful to Stepan's own words.

relations of trust with many of his interlocutors, helped by the fact that he himself had been a military officer.

From his youth, Stepan developed broad academic and cultural interests alongside politics and sport. A lifelong lover of opera, he spent fifteen years as a member of the Board of Directors of the Richard Tucker Music Foundation, from 1985 to 1990 as its Chairman. His father was a personal friend of Tucker, the leading tenor over several decades in New York's Metropolitan Opera Company. Alfred Stepan senior, some of whose Central European forebears had been opera singers, was one of the most prominent early supporters and funders of the Lyric Opera of Chicago. A graduate of the University of Notre Dame, and later a trustee of that university, Al's father discovered that no Jew had ever been awarded an honorary degree at Notre Dame. He used his influence to make sure that Richard Tucker became the first. One evening not long after that occurred, the phone rang in the Stepan household at the unusually late hour of eleven o'clock. The father, whose early-to-bed, early-to-rise preferences were well known, answered with the intention of giving the disturber a piece of his mind. The caller, however, was Richard Tucker 'singing beautifully the Notre Dame fighting anthem, because Notre Dame had just won the national football championship'.[2]

As a teenager, Al Stepan read a lot, mainly novels, was fond of the theatre and won acting prizes. When he considered universities, he thought of Yale, but he was urged by his parents 'to set an example and go to a good Catholic university'.[3] He acquiesced and followed in his father's footsteps to Notre Dame (still at that time an all-male university), majoring in English and graduating in 1958. He discovered how much pleasure he derived from prolonged thinking during solitary walks around the campus lake—and on it during the coldest months of the Indiana winter—though, he recalled, his friends 'dreaded me walking into their rooms at midnight, because, after my period of solitude I would talk until three o'clock in the morning'.[4]

Notre Dame wanted Stepan to be one of their candidates for a Rhodes Scholarship at Oxford. He did not pursue that option because the American draft board said he could not leave the country until he had done his military service. Nor did they like the fact that, just a few days after his twenty-first birthday, he had gone to the 1957 World Youth Festival in Moscow.[5] Stepan discovered, however, that he would subsequently

[2] Ibid., p. 394.
[3] Ibid., p. 395.
[4] Ibid.
[5] Stepan was one of 34,000 young people, mainly Westerners, who arrived in Moscow for that event. Although Western security agencies viewed attendance there with deep suspicion, the outcome, as Rachel Polonsky puts it, was that for two weeks 'the Soviet Union felt like an open society'. She quotes the Russian dissident writer and art historian Igor Golomstock (who emigrated to Britain in 1972) saying 'It

be allowed out of the United States to study for two years if he somehow acquired a commission as a military officer. The let-out was to be conditional on serving for three years of active duty on return. Stepan rose to the challenge. He took the Marine Corps Platoon Leaders' Course which he described as 'a very brutal, Darwinian experience' and a course which many candidates started, but few finished. 'I finished', he noted. 'If I had been a more sensitive type, I guess I would have had a nervous breakdown.'[6]

In those days it was common for American students coming to Oxford after a first degree in the United States to take another first degree (in two years instead of the normal three) rather than a postgraduate course. In Stepan's case, this made the more sense because he was switching from English Literature to Politics, Philosophy and Economics (PPE). He entered Balliol in 1958 and graduated in 1960. He thought that the degree title was a misnomer because 'politics was barely covered', with that part of the degree in the 1950s (and 1960s) being mainly history and political philosophy. The teachers who made the biggest impact on Stepan were the economists Paul Streeten and Thomas Balogh. The latter, he said, 'loved to shock American students. The first essay I had to write for him was: "Why do Americans have such big tits on their cars?".'[7]

Al thoroughly enjoyed his time at Oxford and some of his fellow-students remained friends for life, among them Steven Lukes, later a Fellow of Balliol (and later still a professor at New York University at a time when Al was teaching at Columbia). In the university vacations he travelled a lot—unsurprisingly, for he had great curiosity about other countries and was an insatiable traveller throughout his life.[8] His most important

---

is hard to overestimate the part [the festival] played in the subsequent history of Russia', for the foreigners brought with them 'the fresh air of freedom': R. Polonsky, 'When the Soviets shimmied', *New York Review of Books*, 66 (13), 2019, 36; I. Golomstock, *A Ransomed Dissident: a Life in Art under the Soviets* (London, 2019), pp. 50–4, esp. p. 50. As a general rule, large-scale social and cultural contact between people from democratic and authoritarian states does more to open the minds and broaden the horizons of citizens of the latter than it does to serve the propaganda aims of their dictatorial rulers.

[6] Stepan, 'Democratic governance and the craft of case-based research', p. 396.

[7] Ibid.

[8] The travel included a skiing holiday in the Alps in early 1960, during which Stepan found himself at odds with Winston Churchill, grandson of the prime minister, later himself a Conservative MP. In Churchill's version of the story, 'I made the mistake', after too much alcohol, 'of playfully pushing away a diminutive American, called Al Stepan, who I judged was definitely smaller than me. Nobody had bothered to warn me that he was in fact the Light-Weight Boxing Champion of the US Marine Corps. The next thing I knew I was sailing backwards through a very large and very expensive plate glass window…' (W. S. Churchill, *Memories and Adventures* (London, 1990), p. 146). Though Churchill had been, Al Stepan told me, extremely annoying and 'I may have pushed him', the future junior minister's story was wrong in almost every particular. Far from being a champion boxer in the American Marines, Stepan had given up boxing before he arrived at Oxford. One day, after sparring with an Olympic boxer at a leading boxing club in Chicago, he finished up so dazed that he travelled for an hour in the wrong

meeting at Oxford, however, was with Nancy Leys, the sister of Colin Leys who taught at Balliol at that time. Nancy Leys Stepan, as she became after marrying Al in 1964, was a PPP (Psychology, Philosophy and Physiology) student who went on to become a historian of science and to hold a series of academic appointments, including a full professorship at Columbia. Nancy was born in Inverness but at the age of eight moved south when her father, a doctor who had studied at Oxford (her mother a Cambridge graduate), switched his place of work to London. Both her parents were staunch socialists and firmly irreligious, which made her introduction to the Stepan family somewhat delicate.

Military and journalistic interlude

After Oxford, Stepan had six months before he had to report for duty in the Marines. He used the time to travel to Iran, Pakistan, India, Indonesia, Japan and Vietnam, reading as much as he could about each country before going there. His intellectual and cultural curiosity led to many interesting meetings with people in each of these countries. It was somehow characteristic that on his first visit to Indonesia he found himself meeting President Sukarno in the presidential palace. His last stop was Vietnam because he believed that the defeat of the French and 'America's sense that it was going to control the world' would lead to the US 'getting involved there'.[9]

During his military service, he found himself playing what could have been an active role in an American invasion of Cuba. By October 1962 he was well into his second year as a Marine officer. His commanding officer told him that, since he knew Spanish and 'you've been to Oxford', he wanted him to 'read and interpret all the communications and intelligence reports and become the combat intelligence officer for our landing brigade'. If, he added, 'we get the order to invade, we're going in first, and you'll help to select the landing site'.[10] Although he didn't know it at the time, Stepan would have been part of what was designed to be a diversionary attack on the city of Santiago de Cuba, for the main attack was to take place further north, close to Havana. 'Everybody', Stepan recalled, 'was sure we were going into combat, and the amount of testosterone in the air was stunning and dangerous.' There was total radio

---

direction on the subway. When he got home, he announced that this was the last time he would box, and he stuck with that wise decision. Moreover, no one could have 'bothered to warn' Churchill in the academic year 1959–60 about the fighting qualities of a former US Marine, since the Alpine dispute occurred while Stepan was still an Oxford student and *before* he began his three-year service in the Marines.

[9] Stepan, 'Democratic governance and the craft of case-based research', p. 398.
[10] Ibid., pp. 398–9.

silence and he had to be 'ferried by helicopter among the boats in the invasion fleet to brief all our units about any changes in our plans'. The helicopter would drop him into a boat that sometimes pitched and drove his knees into his face. But that was the least of his worries. Even during the crisis, he managed to read about 'American perceptions and misperceptions of Cuba and realized, to my horror, that we had in fact mobilized our nuclear weapons for a war that I felt should never have reached that point'. In graduate school at Columbia, later in the 1960s, his first paper was on 'the role of mutually self-fulfilling prophecies in generating this near nuclear war'.[11]

About a year after the Cuban crisis Stepan's unit received what appeared to be contradictory instructions. One was to prepare the execution of a contingency plan to evacuate Americans from Vietnam which he assumed meant that President Kennedy was considering ending US involvement in Vietnam. But they were also given orders to prepare a contingency plan for landing the first US combat unit. It was about eighteen months later that the first American combat troops did land on the instructions of President Johnson. As with the Cuban operation, Stepan's unit spent over a month offshore from Vietnam. He spent time also in Vietnam and was already convinced that American active participation in the war would be 'a terrible mistake'. He had been involved in helping to train South Vietnamese officers in Okinawa, and they would ask him, 'How is your war going?'. He would reply, 'It's your war', to which they would respond, 'No, it's *your* war.' It was clear to him that if the officers of the country concerned regarded the war not as theirs but as that of the United States, no good would come from it.[12]

Stepan did not return to academia immediately after completing his military service, but spent almost a year in journalism, working for *The Economist*. He came to London and persuaded the journal to take him on as a special correspondent. He first went to Ghana and Nigeria, but he told his employers that his particular interest was in Latin America. He had visited Cuba two years before the Cuban revolution, and his personal experience of the Cuban missile crisis greatly increased his interest in the region. He had taken Spanish at high school and at Notre Dame, although he did not yet know Portuguese in which he later became fluent. Lucky breaks come to those with the acumen and resourcefulness to take advantage of them. On his flight to Rio de Janeiro, an airline steward saw him reading something by the Brazilian economist Celso Furtado, and they got into conversation. Al told him that he would be reporting from Brazil for *The Economist*. The steward asked him if he would like to meet some left-wing oppositionists. Stepan immediately said yes, 'and virtually the day we arrived, Nancy and I met some of them under very secret conditions'. He continued to have

[11] Ibid., p. 399.
[12] Ibid.

useful contacts in different quarters and was a fast learner. Six days before the military coup of 31 March 1964, he filed a story to *The Economist* saying that a coup was highly likely, explaining why it would happen, and why this would be to the detriment of the US-supported 'Alliance for Progress' which Kennedy had launched to counter the appeal of Cuban-style revolutionary politics. His London editors held the story up, believing that their 27-year-old stringer did not know enough about Brazil to be making such a bold prediction. Immediately after the coup took place, they published the piece, noting that their special correspondent had filed it ahead of the military takeover.

In his work for *The Economist*, which took him to Argentina, Chile, Paraguay, Bolivia, Peru and Venezuela as well as Brazil, he learned a lot about the art of in-depth interviewing. As Stepan put it: 'Even politicians get tired of talking only to other politicians and want to hear about the world. A successful interview is a transaction; it has to be interesting for both people. Someone like Salvador Allende would not wave you over several times in three days for a one-hour conversation unless he was learning something every time.'[13] Allende (who became Chilean president in 1970 and was killed in the 1973 military coup which overthrew his socialist government) was interested in talking about the coup in Brazil and he also wanted to talk about Argentina, both topics on which Stepan had something to offer in return. Politicians, Stepan observed, also believed that talking with a journalist would make that person and his publication more understanding of their perspective. One interview or conversation often led to another. When other leaders learned that he was about to write an article about the politics of their country in an influential international weekly, they would let him know that, since he had spoken to their rival, he should hear their viewpoint, too, before submitting his article.[14]

Return to academia

Stepan returned to academia in the autumn of 1964, beginning graduate studies at Columbia, which led to his PhD in 1969. His choice of university was influenced partly by the probable employment opportunities New York offered for his wife, Nancy, who was a science journalist at that time (later she, too, did a doctorate) and also by the availability of world-class opera. Among his political science teachers, he found Dankwart Rustow both knowledgeable and interesting. But the scholar who made by far the biggest impact on him, and with whom he was to go on to form one

---

[13] Ibid., pp. 401–2.
[14] Ibid., p. 402.

of the great partnerships in the academic study of politics, was Juan Linz. His first encounter with Linz was when he saw some students running across campus, and he asked them where they were going. 'To Linz', they said. 'Who's Linz?', Stepan asked. They told him that he was a young Spaniard. When he asked what Linz taught, 'Everything' was the answer. Al joined them in running to Linz's lecture. Juan Linz liked to teach for two hours just before lunch, so that he could continue the discussion with students who wished to join him over the meal. Sometimes the conversation continued until 4 p.m. Linz was interested in Stepan's up-to-date knowledge of Latin America and soon they were talking for three hours a week.[15]

While he was in graduate school, Stepan did a lot of writing in addition to course work and his doctoral thesis. He published review articles in academic journals and argumentative political pieces for *The Nation*, *New Politics* and *The New Republic*. He responded to requests to write policy briefs that came from time to time from Senators Frank Church and Robert Kennedy. Between 1966 and 1969 he was a Policy Analyst for the Rand Corporation. Rand supported his research in Latin America on the military in politics, awarding him a three-year grant to write the book based on his thesis. Among his Rand colleagues, he benefited especially from conversations with Alexander George, a major figure in the study of international relations. When Stepan presented his PhD research proposal—a study of the political role of the military in Brazil—to his Columbia research supervisors, he was told it was a non-starter because he would not have access to key sources. Instead he was steered into working on national integration in Brazil. After three months of work on that topic, he decided that he was far better prepared to say something new and distinctive about his original subject and quietly returned to it, without submitting a research plan. He simply got on with studying the Brazilian military and 'did a prospectus ex post facto'.[16]

Stepan studied all five Brazilian constitutions from 1891 and the debates surrounding them. He was astonished to find in all of them a clause which said that the military was responsible for maintaining the correct balance among the executive, legislative and judicial branches of government, something that would normally be a matter for the judiciary or politicians. More intriguingly, he found that this clause was never inserted by the subcommittee containing military men but by a second subcommittee containing no active-duty officers. He even found 'congressional testimony by the military *against* the clause which they feared was dangerous for the military as an institution because it would divide them'. Remarkably, over sixty years civilians had been inserting into the country's basic law a highly inappropriate judicial role for the armed forces. Stepan's hypothesis was that 'civilian politicians were embedding this

[15] Ibid., pp. 403–4.
[16] Ibid., p. 406.

role for the military in the constitution so they would have a basis for making public appeals to the military to carry out a coup d'état if, and when, the political elites wanted a coup'.[17] Content analysis of the editorials in the major Brazilian newspapers during sixty days before each coup attempt showed him that, in the case of every successful coup (but not prior to the unsuccessful coup attempts), the editorials were expressing overwhelming support for military intervention, citing the relevant article of the constitution and arguing that, as the president had upset the correct balance among the branches of government, it would be unconstitutional for the military to obey him.[18]

Stepan scrutinised the promotion book of the Brazilian military which contained basic biographical data on every officer. He found what the generals who led the most recent coup had in common in their army experience and education, with almost all having attended the same military college. Only after he had done a great deal of research did he begin his interviews with them. He told them he had been a Marine officer and a special correspondent with *The Economist* and that he was writing a book about a history in which they had played a part, a book he would be writing whether they spoke to him or not. As with his earlier journalistic experience, one interview led to another. A senior officer, often with Stepan still sitting in his office, would telephone a colleague and tell him that the young American knew what he was talking about and they should speak to him. Stepan's technique was to ask five questions, the answers to four of which he already knew. If his interlocutor said something that wasn't accurate, he would say, 'Yes, but come to think of it, General, it was actually 1939' or remind them that what they had been talking about did not happen in that particular battle but in another. He had learned a good deal about their military history, understood their hierarchy, and 'could recognize important medals from twenty-five yards'. He did a lot of his research at the elite military college which had educated the key figures in the military coup. Although he was prepared to be challenged and thrown out, Stepan managed to walk into and work regularly in the library of that college (the Escola Superior de Guerra, or ESG) in the company of numerous retired generals and colonels who went there to read the newspapers and reminisce. That he was never ejected owed something to having been, as he put it, always 'incredibly polite to librarians' and always wearing a suit.[19]

The book of Stepan's doctoral thesis, *The Military in Politics: Changing Patterns in Brazil* (Princeton, NJ, 1971) became a bestseller in Brazil in its Portuguese

[17] Ibid., p. 407.
[18] Ibid.
[19] Ibid., pp. 409–11.

translation. The book was banned, then uncensored, after which its sales soared, and then it was banned again. This, Stepan observed, was 'absolutely the best thing that could have happened for promoting the book'. The big impact it made was, as he said, 'not bad for the start of a career'.[20]

A distinguished former Brazilian president, Fernando Henrique Cardoso (who, during his two presidential terms, 1995–2003, did much to win the military's acceptance of democratic norms and institutions) has written of the 'groundbreaking role' that Stepan played in enhancing understanding of the part the military had played in Latin American societies and politics.[21] Notwithstanding their major impact, the military was an institution which had been largely neglected by social scientists. Stepan asked questions which in retrospect, noted Cardoso, might seem obvious but that had hitherto been overlooked, such as 'What are the inner dynamics of the military? How cohesive or fragmented are they? How can these differences favor or hinder processes of regime liberalization?'[22] More generally, at a time when political parties and Congress in Brazil were seen as 'hopelessly subservient to the repressive system', wrote Cardoso, 'Stepan called our attention to the role that political society might play in the transition to democracy', for even ritual elections for a relatively powerless legislature could, at certain moments, acquire real substance. This occurred in 1974 when, to the surprise of many, the Brazilian population seized the opportunity of national elections for Congress 'to vote en masse for opposition candidates'. This unexpected manifestation of political discontent led to the first 'faint intimations of a relaxation in authoritarian rule'.[23]

Stepan's concern with developments in the real political world went alongside a critical interest in what was happening in political science. The 1960s saw the 'behavioural revolution' in the discipline, in which the quantitative study of political behaviour (to the extent it could be measured by survey research) gained ground, while students of political pluralism focused on competition among various types of organised groups. In Stepan's view neither the 'behaviouralists' nor the 'pluralists' paid sufficient attention to political institutions and the state. Those who studied authoritarian regimes, whether in the Communist world or in many Latin American countries at that time, were, of course, less likely to overlook the continuing importance of state power. Stepan complained that in the books he was directed to read as a graduate student 'there was almost no state' and 'it was all interest groups'. While he

[20] Ibid., p. 412.
[21] F. H. Cardoso, 'Reconciling the Brazilian military with democracy: the power of Alfred Stepan's ideas', in D. Chalmers and S. Mainwaring (eds.), *Problems Confronting Contemporary Democracies: Essays in Honor of Alfred Stepan* (Notre Dame, IN, 2012), p. 67.
[22] Ibid., pp. 67–8.
[23] Ibid., p. 69.

was reading that literature, many of his friends in Brazil were 'being censored and even arrested by the authoritarian regime'.[24]

With the book of his doctorate already in the press, Stepan became an assistant professor of political science at Yale in 1970. While such posts are difficult to come by, securing tenure at an Ivy League university is harder still. Stepan's spectacularly speedy ascent saw him progress from assistant to associate to full professor within six years. Yale was at that time widely regarded as having the best political science department in the United States.[25] Stepan's years in New Haven were fruitful for him in many ways, but perhaps, above all, for his developing academic relationship, and great friendship, with Juan Linz who had moved from Columbia to Yale in 1968. Their work together was described by Richard Snyder as 'one of the most sustained and successful collaborations in modern social science'.[26] Stepan and Linz continued to publish separately, but their joint publications constituted some of their most important work. Each project involved hundreds of hours of conversation. Much of it took place in the library of Linz's New Haven home where, Stepan recalled, some of their best ideas came between midnight and three in the morning, following a lengthy day of discussion and reading. When Stepan was working as far away from Connecticut as Budapest and Oxford, they would arrange to be at the same conferences in many different countries. Their first book together was the massive and influential edited volume *The Breakdown of Democratic Regimes* (Baltimore, MD, 1978), for which Linz wrote a 124-page introduction as a prelude to studies of democratic breakdown in twelve different countries, with Stepan the author of the chapter on Brazil and Linz on Spain.

One of the main conclusions was that in every case they studied, 'democratic incumbents, the very people who should have been protecting democracy' facilitated and aided the breakdown of democratic norms and institutions by their ambivalence about violations of the law and their 'hesitation in using legitimate coercive force against antidemocratic groups' by, for example, allowing members of such groups to walk the streets wearing uniforms.[27] Having as a graduate student already documented civilian initiation of military rule in Brazil, Stepan was not surprised to find that civilian complicity in the degradation and destruction of democracy turned out to be a

---

[24] Stepan, 'Democratic governance and the craft of case-based research', pp. 415–16.
[25] Stepan's senior colleagues there included Robert A. Dahl, Robert E. Lane, Juan Linz (whose primary affiliation was, however, with the Department of Sociology), C. E. (Ed.) Lindblom, David Apter and Joseph LaPalombara. (Dahl, Lane and Linz were all elected to Corresponding Fellowships of the British Academy.) The collegial tone of the department was set by Dahl whom Stepan described as 'the nicest, easiest person in the world' (Stepan, 'Democratic governance and the craft of case-based research', p. 442).
[26] Ibid., p. 433.
[27] Ibid., p. 419.

much more widespread phenomenon, even when the civilians were supposedly committed democrats. Stepan and Linz were alert to the threat to democracy from both left and right, with Linz warning of the dangers posed by self-appointed spokesmen for a class or for 'the people' and noting that the 'vain hope of making democracies more democratic by undemocratic means has all too often contributed to regime crises and ultimately paved the way to autocratic rule'.[28]

Stepan became one of the authors who brought 'the state back in' to American political science (in Britain it was never really out[29]) with, for example, his book *The State and Society: Peru in Comparative Perspective* (Princeton, NJ, 1978). Later he reflected that this work would have had a still wider impact if he had published as a separate volume the first theoretical part on the state, rather than applying his framework of analysis to Peru within the same covers. He had, however, not separated the two parts because he believed it 'is terribly important to embed general theoretical arguments in an empirical context'.[30] In the first part of the book, Stepan noted that in 'most societies throughout most of history', people had not been able freely to combine in organised groups and, where such groups *were* to be found, it was important to study 'the institutional, class and ideological context' in which they operated.[31]

His analysis drew on the work of Philippe Schmitter and formed part of a revival of interest in the concept of state corporatism, though Stepan placed much more weight on the independent power of the state than did Schmitter.[32] He also broke down further Schmitter's distinction between state corporatism and societal corporatism—associational groups in the former dependent upon and penetrated by the state, and in the latter independent of the state. Stepan argued that the dynamics of state corporatism could not be adequately understood unless one distinguished an 'inclusionary pole' in which the state elite attempts 'to forge a new state-society equilibrium by policies aimed at incorporating salient working-class groups into the new economic and political model' from an 'exclusionary pole' where state power relies heavily on 'coercive policies to deactivate and then restructure salient working-class groups'. He went on to analyse the conditions influencing the adoption of one or other of these modes of state corporatism, taking the concrete examples of a variety of Latin American countries.[33]

Stepan was a strong believer in joint supervision of doctoral theses, partly because he believed the student benefited from the different perspectives of their advisers and,

---

[28] J. J. Linz and A. Stepan (eds.), *The Breakdown of Democratic Regimes* (Baltimore, MD, 1978), p. 97.

[29] As Stepan later noted in his book *Arguing Comparative Politics* (Oxford, 2001), p. 7.

[30] Stepan, 'Democratic governance and the craft of case-based research', p. 418.

[31] A. Stepan, *The State and Society: Peru in Comparative Perspective* (Princeton, NJ, 1978), pp. 14–15.

[32] P. C. Schmitter, 'Still the century of corporatism?', *Review of Politics*, 36 (1974), 85–139.

[33] Stepan, *The State and Society*, pp. 73–89, esp. p. 74.

in the field of comparative politics, expertise on different countries, but also in order that the student would not suffer when one of his advisers was on leave. Stepan himself liked to get away for uninterrupted research and writing every few years. He received many offers of visiting fellowships and was highly successful in obtaining research grants from such organisations as the Ford Foundation, the Carnegie Corporation of New York, the Guggenheim Foundation and the Social Science Research Council. During the period of his Yale professorship, he spent the 1978–9 academic year as Ford Visiting Scholar at St Antony's College, Oxford (which was when my own friendship with him began).

Chicago politics

It was while he was at Oxford that Stepan received a phone call from Chicago and, with it, the possibility of his career taking a radically different turn. He was offered the Democratic candidacy for an eminently winnable seat in Congress.[34] The caller from an influential group of Chicago Democrats informed him that Abner Mikva, who had won his last four elections for the 10th district of Chicago, was stepping down to become a federal judge. An imminent special election was being held to replace him and, having failed to agree on any local candidate, the group of kingmakers decided that Al would give them their best chance of holding on to the seat. They asked him to come and talk to them. Without commitment, he flew to Chicago for talks. He began by telling his political backers that he hadn't lived in the city for years and would be regarded as the ultimate carpetbagger. The response was that being away 'at college' didn't count. Asked how many relatives he had in the district, he answered, 'At least thirty'. His sponsors wanted to know how many would hold fundraising parties for him. Stepan said, if asked, all of them would, even the Republicans among them, for family ties would outweigh other affiliations. This was, naturally, music to the ears of his interlocutors whose response was that 'anyone who can organize thirty fundraising parties in a week with their relatives is no carpet bagger'.

Still not satisfied that he knew why the local Democrats were so keen for him to run, Stepan asked, 'What the hell is really going on?' The reply was, 'Well, Al, we're about the most perfect one-third, one-third, one-third constituency in America'. He

---

[34] More than once over the years I heard Al Stepan's account of this, for it was a story he loved to tell (probably because it threw light on American—or, at any rate, Chicago—politics, as well as on his own biography). Fortunately, my memory of how it went is echoed in Stepan's detailed answer to the question, 'Is it true that you nearly ran for Congress?' from his interviewer Richard Snyder (Stepan, 'Democratic governance and the craft of case-based Research', pp. 440–1).

asked what that meant, and was told, 'We're one-third Catholic.' He replied, 'I'm not the most orthodox or participatory Catholic.' That didn't matter, he was informed. He had gone to Loyola and Notre Dame—he would get the Catholic vote. What, he asked, was the next one-third. 'WASP',[35] he was told. But 'I'm not a WASP', he reminded them. 'You teach at Yale', they said—that was enough. To the question, 'What's the last one-third?', the answer was the Jewish vote. But 'I'm not Jewish', said Stepan. 'Yes, but you're an intellectual'—so that base was covered. Stepan was tempted. The campaign would have to start immediately, but if he won in the special election of 1979 and again in 1980, a Senate seat appeared to be opening up.

One of the Illinois Senators, Charles Percy, a liberal Republican, had told Stepan that he would not be standing again when his current term in the Senate ended. In fact, Percy contested his seat in 1984—and lost to the Democrat. But that Democrat was not Al Stepan. After a lot of thought, he decided not to make the career switch. He enjoyed the intellectual life that was, supposedly, going to commend him to a third of Chicago 10th District voters and worried about the extent to which he might be constrained in saying what he thought. A big factor for Stepan was his wife, Nancy, who had married a young academic and with no notion that she might be 'marrying Chicago politics'. To move into that world, he concluded, was 'too big a jump'. Nevertheless, he sometimes felt guilty about not having accepted the opportunity, for, as he put it, 'Aristotle said only gods or beasts do not have to live in a polis. We are not living in a well-run polis.'[36]

Stepan, however, never abandoned 'the polis' or his concern for the well-being and improvement of a great many polities. As will become still clearer, when further attention is paid to Stepan's writings, he continued to concern himself with problems of fundamental political importance and in a variety of countries. He was the main author of a much-cited joint article with Linz, published late in his career, in which he applied some of the lessons derived from comparative research to an analysis of the defects of American democracy. Al had no time for the kind of political science which was more preoccupied with the intellectual game of examining a falsifiable hypothesis than with bothering to ask whether solving the puzzle was of any earthly use. Throughout his career, as the editors of a Festschrift for him, Douglas Chalmers and Scott Mainwaring, observed, Stepan 'focused on issues of great importance in the real world and in scholarship', and did not 'seek to make minor incremental contributions to arcane debates'.[37]

[35] White Anglo-Saxon Protestant.
[36] Stepan, 'Democratic governance and the craft of case-based research', p. 441.
[37] Chalmers and Mainwaring, *Problems Confronting Contemporary Democracies*, p. 15.

From New Haven to New York

During the thirteen years he spent at Yale, Stepan published five books.[38] As early as six months into his Yale assistant professorship, he accepted the directorship of Yale's Council on Latin American Studies, although he was warned against taking on such administrative duties before he had tenure. He thought, however, that this body had been underperforming when one considered Yale's intellectual resources and library. It had only a $16,000 budget when he became director but a $600,000 budget by the time he left.[39] In his final year at Yale, 1982–3, he took on—in addition to his other administrative responsibilities, research, writing and teaching—the Directorship of the Yale Concilium on International and Area Studies. This was to be just the beginning, for it was a feature of Stepan's career that he went on to hold a series of major administrative posts while continuing to be an inspiring teacher and a prolifically productive scholar. When he returned to Columbia in 1983, it was as Dean of the School of International and Public Affairs (SIPA), along with a professorial appointment which became from 1987 a named chair—the Burgess Professorship of Political Science. To his administrative posts, Stepan brought intellectual leadership, vision and boundless energy. He also had a talent for fund-raising. The main reason, he once told me, why he found it easy to ask individual potential donors for money was that he knew how much pleasure his father had derived from his philanthropy. It had been a source of great satisfaction to him that he had helped to save the Chicago Opera when it fell on hard times, and his support for the University of Notre Dame was such that there is both a building and a road on the campus named after him.

Stepan's return to Columbia as Dean of SIPA was influenced by the greater career opportunities New York (as distinct from New Haven) offered his wife. Nancy had just published a second, and well-received, book on the history of science and medicine. On his own insistence, Stepan himself taught courses every year even while he was serving as a dean, and he continued to publish. He was extremely effective at wining large research grants, in attracting big names to Columbia, and in organising conferences. With the help of George Soros, he brought a number of significant Central European academics (who were also political dissidents) to New York. Jay Pritzker, the billionaire philanthropist from Chicago who founded the Hyatt hotel chain, was a longstanding personal friend of Stepan, and Al persuaded him to become

---

[38] Besides *The Military in Politics: Changing Patterns in Brazil* (Princeton, NJ, 1971), *The Breakdown of Democratic Regimes* (Baltimore, MD, 1978) and *The State and Society: Peru in Comparative Perspective* (Princeton, NJ, 1978), he had been co-editor (with Bruce Russett) and co-author of *Military Force in American Society* (New York, 1973) and editor of, and contributor to, *Authoritarian Brazil: Origins, Policies, and Future* (New Haven, CT, 1973).

[39] Stepan, 'Democratic governance and the craft of case-based research', p. 442.

chairman of the SIPA board. Pritzker agreed on condition that Stepan took him on one interesting trip a year. Their travels together included a meeting in Hanoi with General Giap who had commanded the North Vietnamese forces against the United States during the Vietnam War, what Stepan called 'a wild meeting with Lech Walesa in Gdansk', and the six-hour session with Fidel Castro in Havana, referred to in the introduction to this memoir.[40] That meeting ended with a present from Castro of the finest Cuban cigars. Stepan was an occasional cigar smoker but, keeping in mind the American prohibition on bringing Cuban cigars into the country, he gave them away. Asked at the US customs if he had any cigars, he said that he knew they were illegal, so had disposed of those he had before leaving Cuba. 'Too bad', he was told, 'the rules have just changed, and you could have brought them in'.

Central Europe

Stepan stepped down from his Deanship at Columbia in 1991 to have more time for his research which always involved a lot of travel. He was the reverse of a desk-bound scholar. The large theme that was his primary interest at any given time varied over the years, but whether it was the military in politics, the breakdown of authoritarian regimes, democratisation, federalism, or religion and politics, he was a frequent visitor to the countries which seemed to him to be most relevant to that particular subject of his comparative studies. When there, he would ask probing questions of politicians and scholars who, before long, were asking Al for guidance, having become eager to draw on his knowledge of how particular institutional arrangements had worked elsewhere.

Having been a successful dean at Columbia, and having reverted simply to his Burgess professorship, Stepan was being sounded out by leading American universities interested in his becoming their president. Al had, however, no interest in any of those positions, for he knew that they would mean 'the absolute end of my life as a field-based comparativist'.[41] Each move in his career he saw as an opportunity for learning as well as for teaching. Thus, his reaction was altogether more positive when, in Paraguay at the time, he took a telephone call from Budapest, asking him to consider becoming the first rector of the new university that was being created there. The invitation was on the initiative of the Hungarian political philosopher, János Kis, who had played a prominent part in the democratisation process in his country and was briefly a party leader before he returned to academia. The possibility of creating an

[40] Ibid., p. 443.
[41] Ibid.

independent university in central Europe had been mulled over by scholars from both sides of the East-West divide in the late 1980s, and with increasing optimism from 1989, the year in which the citizens of one central and east European country after another cast aside their Communist rulers while Soviet troops remained in their barracks.

The Central European University (CEU) became a reality thanks to major funding by George Soros. The intention was that it would have a presence in at least three countries—Czechoslovakia (as it then still was), Poland and Hungary—but in practice it was based mainly in Prague and Budapest. Petr Pithart, a Czech political scientist who had been an influential advocate of democratisation during the 1968 'Prague Spring' (and, in the wilderness years which followed, the author of important samizdat work) was, for two and a half years following the 'Velvet Revolution', Czech prime minister. He went out of his way to welcome the idea of the CEU being in Prague and earmarked a building to house it. When, however, he was succeeded in the premiership in July 1992 by Václav Klaus, whose suspicion of Soros presaged that of his Hungarian counterpart in the following decade, the attitude to the CEU changed to one of hostility. [42] Budapest became the university's principal institutional base and it was to be Stepan's main home during the three years, 1993–6, he spent as head of the CEU. Given that the university would not have got off the ground without the enormous moral and financial commitment to it of Soros, the appointment was very much in the hands of the philanthropist as well as resting on the support of central European intellectuals who were keen to attract Stepan. Soros and Stepan spoke for many hours and were, initially, not in full agreement. In providing financial support for opponents of authoritarianism and for intellectual freedom more generally, Soros (who had been a student of Karl Popper at the London School of Economics) was averse to making long-term commitments to particular institutions. Stepan believed that he had helped to persuade Soros that, if he were founding a university, endowment and long-term institutional commitment were absolutely necessary.[43]

The Soviet, post-Soviet, and Central and East European context was one of growing importance for democratisation studies. Being involved in the early years of a new central European institution, and charged with ensuring it reached high educational standards, suited Stepan admirably. The Central European University got off the ground remarkably quickly. It opened its doors to students in 1991. The chair of

---

[42] Long after Stepan's tenure, the CEU has been under fire from the Hungarian prime minister Viktor Orbán, whose studies at Oxford were funded by George Soros. The university, as a result, has now made Vienna its main institutional home. Their earlier anti-communist activism has not prevented some post-communist political leaders from succumbing, in their turn, to suspicion of truly independent institutions.

[43] Stepan, 'Democratic governance and the craft of case-based research', p. 444.

its Senate was Bill Newton-Smith who was concurrently Philosophy Tutor at Balliol and so could not be the formal administrative head of the new university, although he came as close as anyone did to being in charge prior to the appointment of Stepan. There was a lot of argument among the CEU's department heads about whether they should have an American-style university president or, as was more common in Europe, a rector. It was resolved by Newton-Smith's proposal that they should have both, but with the same person fulfilling both roles. Thus, Al Stepan became the first Rector and President of the Central European University.

Notwithstanding the extreme brevity of its existence prior to Stepan's arrival, the CEU already had a range of geographically dispersed departments which operated as separate fiefdoms. Although attending to mundane administrative detail was not his forte, Stepan was the right person in the right place at the right time, for he never lost sight of the big picture. One of his major tasks was to try to turn a collection of departments into a coherent university whose intellectual excellence and academic standards would be widely recognised internationally. This meant taking on the fiefdoms and, in the words of Jonathan Becker, who was Assistant Vice President of the CEU, at times that made for 'pretty fierce battles'.[44] Some of the freshly-appointed CEU staff were quite unaccustomed to the need to produce any kind of syllabus for their courses. Prominent among the teachers were those who had taught in dissident circles without syllabi, and whose previous experience had made them suspicious of all authority. Enraged by being asked for a syllabus, one faculty member wrote to Stepan (with colourful hyperbole) that 'even under high Stalinism, no one had interfered with his intellectual freedom as much as I had as rector'.[45] By the time Stepan left, the CEU had a more unified governmental structure and, in further alleviation of narrow departmentalism, a number of innovative inter-disciplinary programmes, including Environmental Studies, Gender Studies and a Centre for the Study of Nationalism.

One of the CEU colleagues whom Stepan esteemed most highly was Ernest Gellner, for whom the issue of nationalism had become his prime intellectual pre-occupation. It was Gellner who, with Stepan's strong support, set up the nationalism studies centre, to which prominent scholars in the field, such as Benedict Anderson and Rogers Brubaker, came as visiting professors. That centre remained in Prague so long as Gellner was alive, but after his untimely death in 1995 it moved to Budapest where the rest of the CEU's teaching and research was being concentrated. Among the new friendships Stepan formed during his CEU years were those with the

---

[44] Personal communication from Dr Jonathan Becker (now Executive Vice President and Vice President for Academic Affairs at Bard College in New York State).
[45] Stepan, 'Democratic governance and the craft of case-based research', p. 445.

Hungarian political sociologist Lázló Bruszt, who became the CEU's Academic Pro-Rector (and later acting director); the Polish historian Bronisław Geremek, who had been a leading figure in the socio-political movement, Solidarity; and Ralf Dahrendorf, Warden of St Antony's College at that time. Geremek and Dahrendorf became founding trustees of the CEU.

The benefits of Central Europe for Stepan's own research and understanding of post-Communism greatly exceeded the headaches. Discussing democracy with Václav Havel in Prague Castle 'was certainly a highlight', said Stepan, and 'George Soros attended many of our meetings and was a great part of that whole experience'.[46] In Stepan's view,

> CEU was the best base of all. The intellectual payoffs were immense. Many of my colleagues in Budapest and Prague had participated in the resistance movement against the old communist regimes, and I was able to talk to them at great length. Because I was traveling constantly across post-communist Europe to explore the possibility of opening branches of CEU in other countries, such as Russia, I also met all sorts of people who had been involved at various levels in the democratization process. I became attuned to a whole set of issues that the democratization literature had failed to address, especially the question of nationalism.[47]

As he pointed out, a very substantial study edited by Guillermo O'Donnell, Philippe Schmitter and Laurence Whitehead,[48] to which Stepan himself had been a contributor (and thus, 'I am as culpable as anyone'), had contained not a single chapter on nationalism.

In the preface to their 1978 book *The Breakdown of Democratic Regimes*, Linz and Stepan had written that 'high priority should now be given to the analysis of the conditions that lead to the breakdown of authoritarian regimes, to the process of transition from authoritarian to democratic regimes, and especially to the political dynamics of the consolidation of postauthoritarian democracies'.[49] That broad theme came high on their research agenda over the next two decades. By the first half of the 1990s, they were working on what became a major contribution to democratisation studies. In contrast with the 1978 volume on democratic breakdown, it was not a multi-author volume, but a tour de force of the duo. Stepan's three years presiding over the fledgling Central European University could not have been more timely, for it coincided with the writing of the justly acclaimed Linz and Stepan volume, *Problems of Democratic Transition and Consolidation: Southern Europe, South America, and*

[46] Ibid., p. 447.

[47] Ibid.

[48] G. O'Donnell, P. C. Schmitter and L. Whitehead (eds.), *Transitions from Authoritarian Rule: Prospects for Democracy*, 4 vols (Baltimore, MD, 1986).

[49] Linz and Stepan, *The Breakdown of Democratic Regimes*, p. x.

Post-Communist Europe.[50] That book was published in 1996, the year in which Stepan moved from Budapest to Oxford. When they were co-authors, Stepan did the actual writing, but he and Linz always argued each point through and neither of them was the sole author of chapters on any particular country or region. Of the two, Linz's knowledge of Southern Europe was especially profound and Stepan had the greater knowledge of South America. Strikingly, specialists on Communist and post-Communist Europe found their chapters on Central and Eastern Europe (Russia included), and their chapter on '"Stateness", nationalism, and democratization', no less rich and insightful.

Oxford

Stepan had agreed with Soros that he would serve as Rector and President of the Central European University for a limited time to get the CEU properly launched. Encouraged to apply for the Gladstone Chair of Government at Oxford, which came with a Fellowship of All Souls, he agreed and was duly appointed. He and Nancy had met in Oxford and had been coming back over the years. Al had many friends in the university, although more at St Antony's College than in All Souls. In the former there were people he knew well, specialists on different parts of the world and in almost every one of the college's regional studies centres—most obviously, the Latin American Centre. Stepan was elected to an Honorary Fellowship of St Antony's in 2006. His election to a Fellowship of the British Academy in 1997 came at the earliest possible date, for he was nominated during the very first academic year (1996–7) in which the appointment he held was at a British university.

Among the Oxford colleagues with whom he enjoyed many fruitful discussions were two leading figures in legal and political philosophy, Ronald Dworkin of University College and Joseph Raz at Balliol, and a specialist on Islamic political thought, James Piscatori (Wadham) who shared the new Gladstone Professor's interest in Islam and democracy. Stepan ran a democratisation workshop on approaches to democracy with Laurence Whitehead at Nuffield College and a seminar with me at his new academic home, All Souls, on problems of democracy in post-Communist Europe.[51] Nancy had obtained a senior fellowship at the Wellcome Unit for the History of Medicine at Oxford, which had been another factor influencing Al's acceptance of the Gladstone Chair.

[50] J. J. Linz and A. Stepan, *Problems of Democratic Transition and Consolidation: Southern Europe, South America, and Post-Communist Europe* (Baltimore, MD, 1996).
[51] Ibid., pp. 448–9.

For many who taught Politics at Oxford, as well as for graduate students in particular, Stepan was a wonderfully stimulating addition to the senior faculty. But the three years, 1996–9, he spent as a professor at the university where he had studied PPE forty years earlier were not entirely plain sailing. Although Oxford had the largest collection of people teaching Politics as an academic subject of any British university, thanks to the PPE degree which meant there were tutors in that field in every college, and the presence of a large cohort of graduate students, its organisation was somewhat amorphous.[52] It is as recently as 2000, a year after Stepan's departure, that the Sub-Faculty of Politics (as part of the Social Sciences Faculty) became the Department of Politics and International Relations. Stepan gave lectures for the core course in Comparative Politics but was unhappy with Oxford's separation of teaching from examining, whereby the setting and marking of examination questions at the end of the two-year MPhil in Politics might have only a tenuous link to the themes of his lectures, for examining was in the hands of 'a different group of colleagues'. He also strongly disliked the pressures from UK funding authorities (and the University's willingness to go along with them) for graduate students to complete their doctorates within four years. He held that this was particularly unhelpful for graduate students of comparative politics who might have to learn a new language and who certainly should spend a lengthy period in the country that was the primary focus of their research. It 'did not', he said, 'make intellectual sense to rush home from a great fieldwork experience'. Many of his outstanding earlier students— among them Nancy Bermeo, Evelyne Huber, Margaret Keck, Scott Mainwaring, Guillermo O'Donnell and Kathryn Sikkink—had, he pointed out, taken six years or longer to complete their doctoral degrees.[53]

There were other more personal reasons for the Stepans to return to the United States after only three years. Their two children, Adam and Tanya, lived in America, and grandchildren, whom they wished to see more often, were a further incentive to return to the US.[54] Moreover, not all of Stepan's new colleagues appreciated him as much as the majority of Oxford Politics specialists did and as his graduate students enthusiastically did. There were grumblings about papers getting stuck on his desk and about his not answering emails. His academic lifestyle—combining extensive research-related travel, a steady flow of innovative scholarship, inspirational teaching, and organisational tasks—meant he needed the support of a dedicated PA if mundane, but necessary, administrative matters were to be attended to promptly. The carping of a

---

[52] See C. Hood, D. King and G. Peele (eds.), *Forging a Discipline: a Critical Assessment of Oxford's Development of the Study of Politics and International Relations in Comparative Perspective* (Oxford, 2014).

[53] Ibid., p. 448.

[54] Ibid. In due course there were to be seven grandchildren: Isabel, Colin, Helena, Esther, Heloisa, Fiona and Erica.

minority of colleagues notwithstanding, Stepan's Oxford friends and advocates thought he was such a breath of fresh air and intellectual stimulus that the University should have accommodated itself to his way of working rather than risk losing him within a few short years. Had the transition from Sub-Faculty of Politics to Department of Politics and International Relations occurred a few years earlier, this might have happened.

Back to Columbia

It was in his interactions with both colleagues and graduate students in one-to-one discussion, small groups and in seminars that Stepan made his greatest contribution at Oxford. That was true also at Columbia to which Stepan returned as Wallace S. Sayre Professor of Government in 1999. He was also, however, an institutional innovator. He became the founder and first Director of Columbia's Center for the Study of Democracy, Tolerance and Religion which, funded by the Luce Foundation, began its life in 2006 and Co-Director of the Institute for Religion, Culture, and Public Life from 2007 to 2012. As those posts suggest, and as will be elaborated below, Stepan had become particularly interested, during the last two decades of his life, in the relationship between religion and democracy. He accepted that all the world's great religions had very different strands and tendencies within them—'multivocal' was his term—and he was interested in establishing what was required if they were to be compatible with democracy.

Although Columbia had good specialists on different parts of the world, Stepan felt that when he was there earlier the Political Science Department was relatively weak 'in terms of scholars doing systematic comparative analysis'. Things had improved in the intervening period. There had also been some progress in overcoming the artificial divide between comparative politics and the study of international relations (IR), although Stepan's friend and immediate successor as Dean of SIPA John Ruggie, a leading representative of the 'constructivist' tendency in IR, had left Columbia. Stepan's links with American studies had also improved, thanks to the arrival of Ira Katznelson. Specialists in the United States on American politics are often disparaging of 'area studies', although their ranks include many of the world's narrowest area specialists, with little knowledge of countries other than their own. Katznelson, an outstanding scholar with historical depth and a comparative dimension to his work, was the antithesis of that kind of specialist. Other significant new arrivals included Jon Elster and Brian Barry. With the latter, Stepan 'sparred over such issues as group rights'.[55]

---

[55] Stepan, 'Democratic governance and craft of case-based research', p. 449.

Committed though he was to comparative studies, Stepan deplored the tendency in modern political science whereby a young scholar—unless studying some aspect of politics in the United States (not, apparently, an 'area')—was expected, at the very outset of his or her academic career, to be working on several countries. He had come across doctoral theses in which the student had compared as many as six or eight countries, but relying entirely on secondary literature, and without 'having lived in a single foreign country'. He was a firm believer in young scholars acquiring in-depth knowledge of one country, substantiated by research *in* that country and supplemented by reading relevant secondary source materials on several other countries. The appropriate scope of research of the comparativist varied, he held, from one stage of a political scientist's career to another. It made sense for the broader comparative studies to be carried out when the scholars had established their credentials with work on the country of their primary speciality, and, having become better known, belonged to 'two or three invisible colleges'. Then they could tackle a big topic comparatively across a number of countries.[56] That had been Stepan's own approach. As a young scholar, his speciality was Brazil. As a mature scholar, he took up large themes, such as federalism and the part federations could play in holding together multinational states, or the compatibility of Islam and democracy, involving comparison of a variety of countries in which Islam was the dominant religion and including also the special case of India where Islam was the religion of a very substantial minority.

During his second, and final, period as a Columbia professor, Stepan received several honours and awards to add to his Fellowships of the American Academy of Arts and Sciences since 1991 and of the British Academy. In 2002 he was presented with the Ordem do Rio Branco, Commendador, of the Brazilian government by President Cardoso; in Rio de Janiero in 2009 he was given the Kalman Silvert Award for lifetime contributions to the study of Latin America by the Latin American Studies Association; and still more impressively (and deservedly), he received in 2012 the Karl Deutsch Award of the International Political Science Association, which is bestowed only once every three years, for especially distinguished cross-disciplinary research.[57] Stepan was unattracted by the idea of belonging to a fixed inter-disciplinary group as distinct from getting together with people interested in the same problem who happened to be from a variety of disciplines. He had 'lots of friends who are philosophers, economists, historians, sociologists, and anthropologists'. He read their work and they exchanged papers and argued. But, ultimately, he agreed with Albert Hirschman who said, 'The best inter-disciplinary work is done under one skull'.[58]

---

[56] Ibid., pp. 451–2.

[57] The last three recipients of the Karl Deutsch Award before Stepan were Juan Linz in 2003, Charles Tilly in 2006 and Giovanni Sartori in 2009.

[58] Stepan, 'Democratic governance and the craft of case-based research', p. 432.

Stepan as teacher

Working with graduate students was a component of academic life Stepan relished as much as he did research and writing. In the four institutions in which he taught—Yale, Columbia, the Central European University (even while he was Rector of the CEU) and Oxford—he left an indelible impression on those whose work attracted his scrutiny. Following his death, the *Journal of Democracy*, after describing Stepan as one of the 'most brilliant, prolific, and seminal scholars of the last half-century' in their field, noted that he was such 'a devoted teacher, generous mentor, and inspiring colleague' that the 'warmth, openness, and humanity' he brought to his personal interactions 'surpassed even his towering professional accomplishments'.[59] Vivienne Shue (now Emeritus Leverhulme Professor of Contemporary China Studies at Oxford) wrote: 'For me, as an assistant professor just starting out at Yale, Al was an immensely inspiring figure.' And he was one who always offered junior colleagues 'straight, no-nonsense counsel', distinguished by its integrity, directness and astuteness.[60]

Graduate students who were, in due course, to become good friends of Stepan could, nevertheless, recall their feelings of nervousness before submitting any work to him. Katherine Hite (now a Professor of Political Science at Vassar) said, 'I don't think I am entirely alone in my memory of how terrifying Al could be when we were graduate students—terrifying in the sense that it was impossible to wing an argument or fudge a concept with Al'. You 'had to come to graduate seminars absolutely over-prepared', and a meeting with him on dissertation chapters meant 'losing some sleep the night before with anxiety and then steeling oneself for questions relating to your work [that] you just would not know the answers to'. But the 'anxiety was inevitably worth it', for Al would come up with insights that led to a rethinking of the organisation of the thesis or of its arguments.[61] The editors of the 2012 Festschrift for Stepan described him as a 'vortex of energy' who 'challenges colleagues and students alike', confronting conventional wisdom and persuading people 'to reconceptualize problems in researchable ways', making 'an art form of collaboration' in the way he worked with scholars worldwide, and drawing 'many students into his projects, often giving them an indispensable start on their own careers'.[62]

Graduate students did not need to be among Stepan's official supervisees for him to spend a remarkable amount of time helping them to improve their work if it was in a field which interested him and he believed that they were capable of making a serious contribution. Thus, Jeffrey Kahn, now a Professor of Law at Southern Methodist

[59] 'Alfred C. Stepan (1936-2017)', *Journal of Democracy*, 29 (2018), 188–9.
[60] Vivienne Shue, email to the author of this memoir, 29 September 2017.
[61] 'Alfred C. Stepan (1936-2017)', 190.
[62] Chalmers and Mainwaring, *Problems Confronting Contemporary Democracies*, p. ix.

University, Dallas, remembered a day in Oxford when he was invited to the back garden of Stepan's house in Norham Road to work through the comments the Gladstone Professor had 'inked all over one of my dissertation chapters'. This took an entire afternoon as Stepan thrust page after page 'into my hands with his many suggestions (these were not phrased, I have to admit, as *suggestions* per se; I usually did what I was told, to my ultimate advantage)'. Describing Al Stepan as 'a force of nature', Kahn wrote: 'To be in his company, even for a short time, was an exhilarating experience. When his attention focused on you, the feeling was of being at the center of things with a trusted guide.'[63] Tomila Lankina, currently Professor of International Relations at the London School of Economics but studying at Oxford when Stepan held the Gladstone Chair, recalled seminars and meetings with him as among her 'most memorable and lasting intellectual experiences' as a doctoral student. Meeting him for the last time early in 2017 (the year of his death), receiving his wise advice on the book she had in progress, and learning about his own recent research visits to Tunisia and lectures in various Asian countries, she was impressed (as were so many) by his 'boundless intellectual curiosity and energy'.[64]

Al Stepan was a self-confident scholar, but never self-satisfied. He was as eager to draw on the expertise of others, not least graduate students and other younger scholars, as he was generous in sharing, with infectious enthusiasm, his own wide-ranging knowledge. Madhulika Banerjee and Yogendra Yadov, the latter of whom was subsequently to become a collaborator with Stepan in research, recalled their first meeting with him in Oxford in 1997. Describing themselves as 'academic nobodies from India', they were overwhelmed by the 'warm and unaffected Al Stepan', an 'internationally acclaimed scholar' who was prepared to spend hours with them. When they later became friends of Stepan, they learned that their experience had been no exception, and that he was 'willing to learn from anyone and everyone, irrespective of their rank or fame'. Writing that Stepan's 'curiosity knew no bounds' and that 'he was willing to go to any length to satisfy it', they added: 'Quite literally. He travelled all the way to Mizoram, a tiny state on the northeastern border of India, just because we were planning to write a few paragraphs on how the insurgency came to an end there.'[65]

---

[63] https://www.sant.ox.ac.uk/about/news/obituary-alfred-stepan (accessed 7 October 2019). In the Acknowledgements to the book of his thesis, Kahn wrote, 'Professor Alfred Stepan, in the capacity of an unofficial supervisor, was extraordinarily giving of his knowledge and guidance. An hour spent in his company was the equivalent of a full academic conference, but much more enjoyable': J. Kahn, *Federalism, Democratization, and the Rule of Law in Russia* (Oxford, 2002), p. vii.

[64] https://www.sant.ox.ac.uk/about/news/obituary-alfred-stepan.

[65] 'Alfred C. Stepan (1936–2017)', 191.

Reflecting on his relationship with his graduate students, Stepan described it as 'a lifelong commitment and mutual learning experience'. He continued to talk with his former students 'to get their feedback on my work and for pure pleasure'. The 'intensity may taper off', he said, 'but it remains a profound relationship. Students are a huge part of one's personal and professional life. We are in a very special profession that offers a continuous learning experience and many human rewards.' In what might fittingly serve as his last word on the adviser-graduate student relationship (though it was uttered in October 2003), Al said, 'It's not over until it's over, which means until one of you is dead.'[66]

Stepan's contribution to scholarship

During well over half a century Stepan was one of the world's most innovative and influential scholars in the field of comparative politics. The subjects to which he devoted himself were diverse, but they were united by being matters of profound consequence in the real world. They fell into six broad areas: (1) the military in politics; (2) the breakdown of democracy and advent of authoritarianism; (3) pathways from authoritarian rule and transition to and consolidation of democracy; (4) federalism, nationalism, and 'stateness'; (5) the role of the state and the quality of democracy; and (6) religion and politics (with particular reference to the relationship between religion and democracy).

Stepan's contribution to the first two of these broad subjects has already been discussed and his work on the third of them has been touched upon. Even as Stepan and his colleague Linz completed their large book on *The Breakdown of Democratic Regimes* in the late 1970s they were, as has already been noted, turning their attention to transitions from authoritarian rule. Stepan's contribution to the 1986 collective volume on *Transitions from Authoritarian Rule* was concerned with 'Paths to redemocratization'.[67] By the time his 1996 book with Linz on democratic transition and consolidation was published, they had also to take account of democratisation processes in countries which had never been democracies in the first place. What happened in the last years of the Soviet Union, and in the early post-Soviet era, in Russia and several other of the successor states was not 'redemocratization' but the advent of more democracy and greater freedom than those states had hitherto known.

---

[66] Stepan, 'Democratic governance and the craft of case-based research', pp. 452–3.
[67] A. Stepan, 'Paths toward redemocratization: theoretical and comparative considerations', in O'Donnell, Schmitter and Whitehead, *Transitions from Authoritarian Rule: Comparative Perspectives*, vol. 3, pp. 64–84.

This made the question whether it could be sustained and consolidated all the more salient.

In his 1986 chapter, written before the geopolitical map of Europe was transformed, Stepan outlined the varied paths as he then saw them which could theoretically lead towards redemocratisation (from which I pick out and italicise three). *Warfare and conquest* had historically been one of them, with Germany and Italy after the Second World War cases in point. As, however, was noted by a former student at Yale of both Linz and Stepan, Robert M. Fishman (now Professor of Sociology at the Carlos III University in Madrid), Stepan 'appreciated that the successful imposition of democracy by the Allies at the close of World War II was a historically bounded episode, not likely to prove replicable in the future'. Stepan and Linz explicitly warned, prior to the 2003 invasion of Iraq, that 'the plan to impose "regime change" on that country by military conquest was likely to lead not to successful democratic consolidation but instead to a far less felicitous outcome'.[68]

The key initiatives in moving away from dictatorial rule could in other instances come *from within the authoritarian regime itself*, as had occurred in post-Franco Spain. Alternatively, *oppositional forces* could play the major role in the transition to democracy. 'On theoretical grounds', Stepan wrote apropos the latter point, 'one is tempted to argue that society-led upheavals *by themselves* are virtually incapable of leading to redemocratization but are, nevertheless, often a crucial, or in some cases an indispensable, component to the redemocratization.'[69] There remains some force in that argument. It was too early for Stepan to cite it, but Poland was soon to illustrate his point. 'Solidarity' had been a mass movement which challenged the very existence of Communist rule in 1980–1, but the regime (with the might of the Soviet Union still standing behind it) had enough strength to impose martial law in December 1981. Solidarity's leaders were imprisoned, and the movement was confined to a subdued and underground existence. It remained a shadow of its former self until the late 1980s, by which time transformative change in Soviet domestic and foreign policy had dramatically altered the entire political context in East-Central Europe, making possible negotiations between Solidarity and the Polish party-state which facilitated rapid and peaceful transition to democracy.

Stepan was aware that democratic transition and the consolidation of democracy depended not only on institutions but on the values and political skill of leaders. He attached great weight to the collegial and inclusionary style of Adolfo Suárez, the Spanish prime minister who played a key role in Spain's democratic transition, and

---

[68] R. M. Fishman, 'Revisiting "Paths toward redemocratization"', in Chalmers and Mainwaring (eds.), *Contemporary Democracies*, p. 146.
[69] Stepan, 'Paths toward redemocratization', p. 79.

whom he interviewed at length. Examining the Spanish and Russian breaks with authoritarianism, Linz and Stepan in 1996 contrasted Boris Yeltsin's 'winners take all' approach and lack of interest in democratic institution-building with Suárez's consensus-building style and willingness to prioritise what was good for Spanish democracy over clinging to power.[70] But institutions, as well as people, mattered a great deal, for they could reframe the democratic process. Stepan and Linz dismissed the view that when former Communists formed governments in Central Europe, this signified a 'return to Communism'. As they put it, 'Even if some of the reformed Communists might not actually have undergone profound changes in their mentality (and many, of course, have not) the external reality to which [they] must respond has changed profoundly. As long as democracy is the only game in town, the incentive structure of those who seek governmental power is derived from the democratic context.'[71]

For Linz and Stepan the necessary conditions for the completion of transition from authoritarianism to democracy, and for the consolidation of democratic norms and institutions, were: the rule of law and freedom for civil society; the autonomy of political society, meaning, especially, free electoral competition among autonomous political parties; constitutional rules to allocate power democratically; a state bureaucracy that has not been politicised but is professional and capable of serving democratic governments; and sufficient autonomy for economic society to prevent fusion or excessive concentration of political and economic power (a criterion wholly compatible with a mixed ownership economy and regulation of the market).[72] Working on their magnum opus on democratic transition and consolidation was an illuminating experience for Stepan and Linz. Only after they had completed it, wrote Stepan in 2001, were some things still clearer to them. In particular, 'No state, no democracy. Free and fair elections are a necessary, but not sufficient, condition of democracy. A complete "free market" has never existed in a democracy and never can.' Moreover, in the many countries where there was more than one nation, 'nation-state building' and democracy building were conflicting logics. As human beings are capable of sustaining 'multiple and complementary identities', it was up to politicians to 'help create structures of inclusive citizenship' and to deliver a framework of rights, making loyalty towards what Stepan called a 'state-nation' possible.[73]

That last point leads into consideration of the fourth of the six broad areas of Stepan's work noted earlier—on federalism, nationalism and 'stateness'. Al became

---

[70] Linz and Stepan, *Problems of Democratic Transition and Consolidation*, esp. pp. 88–96 and 301–7.
[71] Ibid., p. 455.
[72] Ibid., pp. 3–15, esp. p. 7.
[73] Stepan, *Arguing Comparative Politics*, p. 18.

increasingly impatient with what he regarded as the French conception of the nation-state and the constant talk, even in the twenty-first century, of the need for 'nation-building' in states where this was liable to lead to disaster. His argument was that in countries with a variety of different languages and ethnic groups, state-building was entirely appropriate, but that the attempt to create a single nation in countries with profound cultural diversity, some of it territorially based and politically articulated by significant groups, was a recipe for oppression or civil war.[74] Contesting 'the old wisdom' that 'the territorial boundaries of a state must coincide with the perceived cultural boundaries of a nation' meant that his argument could be used against a homogenising state *and* against the insistence of different nations within a state that their sense of national identity necessitated their separate statehood. Stepan applied his analysis to many different countries and paid particular attention to India. As he and his co-authors wrote in 2011, 'The anti-Muslim pogrom of 2002 in Gujarat reminds us that the success of a state-nation is contingent on continuous political practices. Creating a state-nation is not a one-shot affair but a continual effort. It also reminds us that what is made can also be unmade. As in the case of nation-states, a state-nation is also a politically imagined community that needs to be sustained through continuous contestation and re-creation in the realm of ideas, institutions, and political practices.'[75]

Stepan recognised that 'nation-state and state-nation at one level are analytic ideal-type distinctions', but they could, nevertheless, be 'operationalized using a range of indicators'.[76] He challenged the idea that '*only* a nation-state can generate the necessary degree of strong identity and pride in membership of the state that is necessary for a democracy'. Drawing on the findings of the World Values Survey, which included scores for 'strong pride' in belonging to one's country, Stepan noted that the results were 'virtually indistinguishable between nation-states and state-nations, with the latter actually having marginally more pride'.[77] He devoted a lot of attention to different modes of federalism and the part they could play in sustaining democracy within multinational states. The academic literatures on democracy, federalism, and nationalism had, he noted, developed 'in relatively mutual isolation' from each other, and he did much to bring them together.[78] 'Asymmetrical federalism', he concluded, on the basis of wide-ranging comparison, could make a huge contribution to the preservation of democracy within a multinational state. Indeed, he went so far as to argue

---

[74] Ibid., pp. 315–61.

[75] A. Stepan, J. J. Linz and Y. Yadov, *Crafting State-Nations: India and Other Multinational Democracies* (Baltimore, MD, 2011), p. 88.

[76] Ibid., p. 7.

[77] Ibid., p. 38.

[78] Stepan, *Arguing Comparative Politics*, pp. 313–61, esp. p. 316.

that 'it may be true that all democracies that are strongly multinational are federal and asymmetrical', although that did not mean that they were immune from encouraging polarising identities or from threatening civic peace. Avoiding such calamities required a continuous focus on the political practices and incentives conducive to acceptance of multiple and complementary identities and of democracy.[79]

Stepan and Linz paid attention to the 'stateness' question in their analysis of problems of democratisation in the countries emerging from Communist rule. They note that an essential starting point was well expressed by Robert Dahl: '*The criteria of the democratic process presuppose the rightfulness of the unit itself.* If the unit itself is not [considered] proper or rightful—if its scope or domain is not justifiable—then it cannot be made rightful simply by democratic procedures.'[80] A bald insistence on majoritarianism does not resolve the problem if the appropriateness of the unit is not accorded legitimacy.[81] 'Because political identities are not fixed and permanent', Linz and Stepan observe, 'the quality of democratic leadership is particularly important. Multiple and complementary identities can be nurtured by political leadership. So can polar and conflictual political identities.' Conscious use of ethnic-cleansing as a strategy to construct nation-states in the former Yugoslavia produced civil war and destroyed harmonious inter-communal relations in places where they had previously existed, such as Sarajevo, 'a multinational urban area, whose citizens had multiple identities and one of the highest rates of interfaith marriages of any city in the world.'[82]

The fifth broad area identified earlier to which Stepan made an important contribution was on the state and the quality of democracy. He observed that in the democratisation literature, 'most of the theoretical reflection was on civil society, not enough on political society, and very little about what to do with the coercive apparatus of the state if and when democrats came to power'.[83] Yet, 'if there is no usable state with a democratically controlled coercive apparatus, citizens' rights cannot be effectively defended in a new democracy'.[84] Stepan concerned himself also, especially in the last decade of his life, with the quality of democracy in his own country, though the United States counted not only as a thoroughly consolidated democracy but one widely assumed (especially in America) to be an exemplar for the world. In an influential article co-authored with Linz (this time with the names not in alphabetical

[79] Ibid., p. 360.
[80] R. A. Dahl, *Democracy and its Critics* (New Haven, CT, 1989), p. 207.
[81] Linz and Stepan, *Problems of Democratic Transition and Consolidation*, p. 27.
[82] Ibid., p. 35.
[83] A. Stepan, 'Introduction', in A. Stepan (ed.), *Democracies in Danger* (Baltimore, MD, 2009), p. 6.
[84] Ibid.

order, for it was predominantly Stepan) in a journal of the American Political Science Association, he brought a comparative perspective to the study of the USA.[85]

Stepan and Linz made important points about American political science as well as about the defects of American democracy. Criticising the 'splendid isolation' in which the United States is so often studied in American universities, they noted that their country had become 'the world's most unequal longstanding democracy in the developed world', and that the preoccupation of many Americanists with Congress, the presidency and the Supreme Court obscured this important fact and its implications for the US political system.[86] They pointed to the fading of a tradition whereby some of the most important contributions to an understanding of American politics had been made by scholars who combined comparative research with work on the US—from Robert Dahl and Seymour Martin Lipset to Ira Katznelson. The failure to see the American political system in comparative context was being reinforced by trends in political science teaching. Writing in 2011, they remarked that two generations ago 'all of the best PhD programs in political science required the demonstration of at least a reading ability in one (or two) foreign languages', whereas now most of the programmes allowed doctoral candidates to substitute quantitative or formal modelling skills, with academic career incentives perversely promoting monolingualism. Of the twenty-five top PhD programmes in political science, by 2011 only New York University retained an explicit language requirement for all its doctoral candidates.[87]

In their substantive observations on American politics and society, Stepan and Linz focused on two issues in particular—the degree of inequality and the system's 'majority-constraining features'. In significant part a product of Franklin Roosevelt's New Deal, the Civil Rights movement and, not least, Lyndon Johnson's 'Great Society' reforms, the United States achieved in 1968 its best-ever Gini index of inequality (that is, its least unequal). Even then, the authors pointed out, 'during the heyday of income *equality* in the United States' no other democracy for which comparable data were available was as *unequal* as the US. They noted that inequality subsequently became substantially greater—from the 1970s onwards—and that 'by 2009 the US Census Bureau had put the US Gini at .469, America's worst Gini index in many decades'.[88]

Stepan and Linz saw a link between the 'inequality inducing' and 'majority constraining' aspects of American politics. The US Constitution, they observed, was by far the most difficult constitution to amend of any democracy, with minorities

---

[85] A. Stepan and J. J. Linz, 'Comparative perspectives on inequality and the quality of democracy in the United States', *Perspectives on Politics*, 9 (2011), 841–56.
[86] Ibid., pp. 841 and 853.
[87] Ibid., p. 842.
[88] Ibid., pp. 843–4.

possessing exceptional powers to block the wishes of majorities. That was nowhere more clearly manifested than in the equal representation of every state in a political institution as powerful as the Senate which, at the time they wrote their article, meant that a vote for a Senator in California had sixty-six times less weight than a vote in Wyoming. When there was an 83 per cent vote in the House of Representatives to abolish the Electoral College, the proposal for such a constitutional amendment was, entirely predictably, blocked by the Senate.[89] The authors were writing before, for the second time in a presidential election this century, the candidate who got fewer votes than his Democratic opponent (almost three million fewer in the case of Donald J. Trump) entered the White House. 'The time is long past', Stepan and Linz concluded in 2011, 'for unthinking acceptance of America's founding political institutions not only by citizens but also by academics.'[90] Six years later, in his valedictory piece as editor of the journal which published that article, Jeffrey C. Isaac wrote that the Stepan and Linz contribution had enhanced a much-needed understanding that the United States was a problematic polity among many, rather than being 'some exceptional "city on a hill"'.[91]

Finally, we come to Stepan's major interest in religion and politics, the subject which most preoccupied him during his last two decades. The very name of the 'Center for the Study of Democracy, Tolerance and Religion' he founded at Columbia indicated the scope of his concern with a major real-world problem—a world in which inter-communal and intra-communal conflict on religious lines and pretexts is pervasive. In several publications, Stepan elaborated his argument about the 'twin tolerations' that are needed if religion and democracy are to co-exist harmoniously within a given society.[92] This meant establishing, on the one side, acceptable boundaries of freedom of action for political institutions vis-à-vis religious authorities and, on the other side, for religious individuals and groups vis-à-vis political institutions. Since democracy, wrote Stepan, is, among other things, 'a system of conflict regulation that allows open competition over the values and goals that citizens want to advance', this meant that 'as long as groups do not use violence, do not violate the rights of other citizens, and stay within the rules of the democratic game, *all* groups are granted the right to advance their interests, both in civil society and in political society'.[93]

---

[89] Ibid., pp. 844–6.

[90] Ibid., p. 853.

[91] J. C. Isaac, 'Making America great again?', *Perspectives on Politics*, 15 (2017), 626.

[92] Most notably in A. Stepan, 'Religion, democracy, and the "twin tolerations"', *Journal of Democracy*, 11 (2000), 37–57; and, in a fuller version, A. Stepan, 'The world's religious systems and democracy: crafting the "twin tolerations"', in Stepan, *Arguing Comparative Politics*, pp. 213–53.

[93] 'Religion, democracy, and the "twin tolerations"', 37; and 'The world's religious systems and democracy', p. 216.

Having set out (in greater detail, of course) what he meant by the 'twin tolerations', Stepan was able to show that these have been respected at various times, including those we are living through, and in various places by each of the world's major religions. It was, he readily acknowledged, no less true that every one of those religions had on other occasions and in other places been brutally intolerant. He was sharply critical of Samuel Huntington's 'civilizational' approach, summarised as: in Islam God is Caesar, in Confucianism Caesar is God, and in Orthodoxy God is Caesar's junior partner. Stepan observed that all the world's major religions harbour diversity of belief and practices. He was a vigorous contributor to the debate on whether or not Islam is compatible with democracy, noting that while some strands of that religion are at odds with democracy, there are other strands which are compatible with democratic norms. His more empirical answer to the question was to point to the fact that several hundred million people have experienced democracy in countries in which the main religion has been Islam.[94]

Stepan noted that at one time there was a widespread belief, certainly by many Protestants, that if Catholicism was the main religion within a state, the chances of that country becoming a democracy were negligible. Yet, while the Catholic Church had, indeed, often been closely allied with authoritarian right-wing regimes, there were by now so many examples of predominantly Catholic, yet democratic, countries that the notion of such incompatibility was clearly untenable. Countries of 'Confucian civilization' (in Huntington's terms) were regarded as ill-equipped to make a transition from authoritarian rule, with China cited as the prime example. Yet democracy was vibrant enough in South Korea, Japan and Taiwan.

On the question of Islam and democracy, Stepan took a particularly keen interest in Tunisia, the one country where the high hopes of democracy raised by the 'Arab Spring' had not been extinguished at the time of his death.[95] Between March 2011 and January 2017, he made seven research visits to Tunisia (the last of them less than nine months before he died) and spoke with the main political and religious leaders. Especially notable among them was Rached Ghannouchi, the leader and founder of Tunisia's main Islamist movement and political party who was at the same time an influential proponent of the compatibility of Islam and western-style democracy. Stepan's first interviews with him took place in London and Oxford in 1997 when

[94] A. Stepan, 'The multiple secularisms of modern democratic and non-democratic regimes', in C. Calhoun, M. Juergensmeyer and J. Van Antwerpen (eds.), *Rethinking Secularism* (New York, 2011), pp. 114–44, esp. 136–7. Writing in early 2013, Stepan and Linz observed that 'close to 300 million Muslims have been living under democracy for each of the past ten years in the Muslim-majority countries of Albania, Indonesia, Senegal, and Turkey': A. Stepan and J. J. Linz, 'Democratization theory and the "Arab Spring"', *Journal of Democracy*, 24 (2013), 17.
[95] A. Stepan, 'Tunisia's transition and the twin tolerations', *Journal of Democracy*, 23 (2012), 89–103.

Ghannouchi was in exile. Following imprisonment in Tunisia, Ghannouchi left his native country in 1989 and successfully claimed political asylum in Britain in the early 1990s. After more than two decades in exile, he returned to Tunis at the end of January 2011. Less than two months later Stepan was there to see him, and they met on each of his subsequent visits to Tunisia. It was a two-way process. Ghannouchi was interested in Stepan's ideas on, and knowledge of, democratic transitions and on religion and democracy, while Stepan was greatly impressed by Ghannouchi and the part he was playing in promoting religious and political tolerance in an Islamic country emerging from authoritarian rule.[96] In Stepan's view, 'the more political actors do', in such circumstances, 'to reach consensual agreement on the rules of democratic contestation by negotiating among themselves, the better'. Tunisia in 2011 was following that course, while Egypt was doing the reverse.[97]

It was during one of Stepan's research trips to Tunisia that in 2013 he met the young scholar Monica Marks who was based there, conducting, as she put it, 'riveting interviews' but completely unsure about the direction of her doctoral research. As she discovered, 'Instead of sloughing off young scholars, Professor Stepan sought their expertise in the field.' She proceeded to sit in on most of his Tunisian interviews, including those in January 2017 when he was conducting up to six of them a day. Dr Marks (as she now is) wrote: 'The tenacious energy with which he approached his sharply insightful, question-driven research and the genuine concern he had for Tunisia, its people, and the survival of its fragile young democracy were unparalleled.'[98]

Stepan also interviewed major Islamic political figures in Indonesia, Turkey and Iran, but the country, in addition to Tunisia, to which he devoted special attention was the West African state of Senegal. He spent time there and conducted extensive interviews with Senegalese religious and political leaders. Some of his writing on Senegal, especially on 'rituals of respect', could have come from the hand of an anthropologist, had it not been for the fact that he used quantitative data (as he did whenever relevant survey research existed, often commissioning such research himself) as well as qualitative.[99]

---

[96] See A. Stepan, 'Multiple but complementary, not conflictual, leaderships: the Tunisian democratic transition in comparative perspective', *Daedalus*, 145 (3) (2016), esp. 101 and 105–6.

[97] Stepan, 'Tunisia's transition and the twin tolerations', 95.

[98] M. Marks, 'Foreword', in A. Stepan (ed.), *Democratic Transition in the Muslim World: a Global Perspective* (New York, 2018), p. x. This was Stepan's final book. It was just going to press at the time of his death in September 2017. His own chapter in it is called 'Mutual accommodation: Islamic and secular parties and Tunisia's democratic transition', pp. 43–71. He accorded pride of place as author of the opening chapter to an important contribution by Rached Ghannouchi.

[99] A. Stepan, 'Rituals of respect: sufis and secularists in Senegal in comparative perspective', *Comparative Politics*, 4 (2012), 379–401: 'Institutions matter', wrote Stepan, 'and I have devoted much of my scholarly life to studying them.' But 'Respect matters, too, and it is more difficult for institutionalists to study', he noted (p. 380), before going on to examine rituals in relation to inter-religious and intra-religious

While his many friends, colleagues and readers of his academic work greatly miss Al Stepan—as, still more, do his devoted family—one loss which should not go unnoticed is the book he had embarked on when cancer overtook him in the summer of 2017 and developed very fast. The divisiveness and aggressive rhetoric of such a president as Donald Trump made it the more essential, Stepan felt, to get his ideas on Islam and democracy across to a broader public. He had been thinking of doing this for some years, but his more specialised writing took precedence. However, he had produced a substantial outline and had made a start on a book aimed at a general readership which was to be called *The Minaret and the Ballot Box*. Whether it will be published in its outline form or filled out by another scholar, drawing on the substantial body of more specialised work Stepan produced on this subject, remains at the time of writing uncertain. That he did not live long enough to bring the book to completion himself is a matter of huge regret. With his journalistic experience in his earlier years, together with the vast knowledge he had accumulated over a lifetime, Al was more than capable of putting into plain and expressive language a narrative that would have challenged much of the conventional wisdom on Islam and democracy, while not glossing over the problems.

Stepan was realistic enough to caution social scientists and policymakers not to 'deceive themselves that all problems are solvable'. But, he added, 'we should also be aware that more appropriate, more timely actions might prevent some solvable problems from *becoming* insolvable'.[100] At heart, he remained an optimist, and one always on the lookout for ways to turn his deep academic knowledge to practical use. It may be fitting to give the last word to one of the many younger scholars who, regardless of whether or not they were one of Al Stepan's official supervisees, gained so much from having him as a mentor. Monica Marks concluded her Foreword to Al's posthumously published edited volume, *Democratic Transition in the Muslim World*, by writing: 'To have known Professor Stepan was to have received a rare education and to have encountered an extraordinary role model in research and in life. We are all in his debt.'[101]

Acknowledgements

I am particularly grateful to Nancy Leys Stepan for answering a number of my questions, for our conversations about her late husband, for reading (with a critical eye) what I have written, and for our long friendship. To Adam Stepan I owe thanks for sending a number of photographs of his father, from which we have chosen to accompany this memoir the official Columbia University portrait of Alfred Stepan

---

toleration in Senegal. See also A. Stepan, 'Stateness, democracy, and respect: Senegal in comparative perspective', in M. Diouf (ed.), *Tolerance, Democracy, and Sufis in Senegal* (New York, 2013), pp. 205–38.

[100] Stepan et al., *Crafting State-Nations*, p. 275.

[101] Marks, 'Foreword', p. x.

when he was Dean of its School of International and Public Affairs in the 1980s. I am much indebted also to a number of scholars who knew Al Stepan and his work—former doctoral students and friends of even longer standing—who read and commented on my draft of this memoir. In revising it, I have taken account of their valuable comments to make some additions and amendments. In alphabetical order, they are: Alan Angell (St Antony's College, Oxford); Dr Jonathan Becker (Bard College); Professor Jeffrey Kahn (Southern Methodist University); Professor Katherine Hite (Vassar College); Professor Tomila Lankina (London School of Economics); Professor Steven Lukes (New York University); Professor Scott Mainwaring (Kennedy School of Government, Harvard University); Professor Stephen Whitefield (Pembroke College, Oxford); and Dr Michael Willis (St Antony's College). I am grateful also to Professor Vivenne Shue (St Antony's College) for sharing her memories of Al Stepan at Yale.

My own four decades of friendship with Al Stepan included periods when we were colleagues not only in Oxford but also in the United States when I was a Visiting Professor of Political Science at Yale in 1980 and at Columbia in 1985. I have, accordingly, been able to draw on many conversations with Al in different places (Budapest and Moscow, among them) over the years. In some passages of this memoir, I have drawn lightly on a review article I published in *Government and Opposition*, 49 (2014), 313–30—'Alfred Stepan and the study of comparative politics'—and I am grateful to the journal's editors, Professors Laura Cram and Erik Jones, for granting permission to do so. The fullest appreciation of Alfred Stepan's work is to be found in the Festschrift edited by Douglas Chalmers and Scott Mainwaring, *Problems Confronting Contemporary Democracies: Essays in Honor of Alfred Stepan* (Notre Dame, IN, 2012), in which the editors and contributors engage with many of the issues of central concern to Stepan. The single most useful source on Stepan's life is the long interview he gave to Richard Snyder in Gerardo L. Munck and Richard Snyder, *Passion, Craft, and Method in Comparative Politics* (Baltimore, MD, 2007), pp. 392–455. Further illuminating reading in the same Munck and Snyder volume for anyone interested not only in Alfred Stepan but also in the big questions with which he engaged is the interview by Snyder with Juan J. Linz, 'Political regimes and the quest for knowledge', pp. 150–209.

Note on the author: Archie Brown is Emeritus Professor of Politics at the University of Oxford, and Emeritus Fellow of St Antony's College. He was elected a Fellow of the British Academy in 1991.

CHARLES BAWDEN

Charles Roskelly Bawden

22 April 1924 – 11 August 2016

elected Fellow of the British Academy 1971; resigned 1980; re-elected 1985

by

VERONIKA VEIT

Charles Bawden, Emeritus Professor of Mongolian Studies at the School of Oriental and African Studies (in the University of London), was born in Weymouth on the south coast of England (Dorset), on 22 April 1924. Scholar—Poet—Man of His Word: in such terms may be characterised the three vocations which were to guide and form the life celebrated in this memoir.

Biographical Memoirs of Fellows of the British Academy, XVIII, 449–469
Posted 21 November 2019. © British Academy 2019.

CHARLES BAWDEN

The scholar

Born of parents who were both school-teachers—the father at the local elementary school for boys—Charles himself describes his home as a modest one. 'There were few books at home,' he recalls, 'but important among them were the pre-first world war edition of Arthur Mee's *Children's Encyclopaedia*, and the *Harmsworth Encyclopedia*, which between them served as my childhood library.' In the late 1930s, however, Charles' father bought a wireless set, which the young boy calls 'his lifeline': from that set he was first able to listen to spoken French and German, which later were to prove his main academic interests, and even to hear music—another of his future lifelong interests—for Weymouth itself was, in those days, 'a cultural waste', without even a public library available, as Charles remembers. A further step in what he describes as his, in some ways, 'contradictory upbringing', and which directed his interests more definitely towards what was to become his future career, might best be described in his own words:

> On the one hand my father, especially, was a real pioneer in some things. He saw that I was academically able, and did all he could to help me. He it was who found out how one went about winning a State Scholarship—my school seems to have been quite uninformed about the mechanics of such things. He found out how to go about applying for admittance to Cambridge University. He saw the advantages of visits abroad—something unheard of in those days for children of our social milieu—and saw that we both went abroad in individual exchanges. My brother (Harry, older by two years) went twice to France, while I went to France for five weeks in 1938, and to Germany the following year, just before the war. These visits were of untold advantage to me, not only in building my self-confidence, but in the resulting improvement to my knowledge of the two languages.

The other side of what Charles calls his 'contradictory upbringing' was the fact that his parents were both very religious, devoted low church people. 'So, although my father wanted me to enlarge my outlook through foreign travel and university, I was expected to conform to strict low church ideals and mental limitations,' Charles recalls. Religious principles demanded church twice on Sundays, as well as scripture learning before the service; they further forbade the use of the family's boat on that day. Certainly this kind of attitude not only accounted for Charles' gradual defection from the Church of England, but later also led him to look with disillusion on all forms of organised religion.

Nevertheless, Charles' youth, altogether, was not without pleasure—pre-war days were spent with the family's boat, with fishing, sailing and swimming. No summer holiday away was taken—as there was nowhere better to go! Charles' formal education first began at the local church schools—Holy Trinity Infants' and Holy Trinity

Boys'. From there, Charles went to Weymouth Grammar School where, too, the education was sound, though neither broad nor deep. Again, Charles was lucky in finding there a teacher of learning and ability, Miss Marjorie Mitchell, later Mrs Brand, who became a lifelong friend. She taught biology, but was also a skilled musician and had a first-class knowledge of German. The school did not teach German, which Charles needed to fulfil his ambition of going up to Cambridge to read modern languages. So Miss Mitchell took him on in her spare time for German. Although he did not start the language until the autumn of 1938, and had only about two years to get to Higher School Certificate standard and then to Cambridge scholarship standard, he still managed it—thanks to his holiday in Germany and Marjorie's help and encouragement. There was one good thing about his school: it at least drilled its students well for examinations. Charles was exceptionally successful in the School Certificate exams of 1938 and the Higher exams in 1940 and 1941. On the strength of his performance in the latter, and his father's earlier prudent reconnaissance, Charles was awarded both County and State Scholarships.

The next step—Cambridge—also required money and, once again, he was lucky, as he calls it, to be awarded a minor scholarship at Peterhouse at the end of 1940. Charles had his own special view of what he calls 'being lucky', which he describes as follows:

> Luck, I would say, has played a large part in my life, and I believe that luck counts more than merit. I was lucky in my educational career, lucky not to have been killed in air raids when other people in the same town were, lucky to have kept my health, and lucky to have had a good marriage and four children of whom I can be proud.

Cambridge was a new experience, for which the young Charles, at first, must have felt completely unprepared. He stuck to it, however, and got a first in Part 1 of the Modern and Mediaeval Languages tripos in 1942.

As it was war time, call-up intervened, and in early February 1943 Charles joined the Royal Navy at HMS *Excalibur* as an Ordinary Seaman. Even before being called up, luck (in the above Charlesian sense of the word) or, one is tempted to say in this instance, 'fate', had once more intervened: Charles had been selected to learn Japanese. He was transferred to Bedford to join No. 4 Military Intelligence School and settled down to six months of Japanese under Captain Tuck RN and his assistant, Eric Ceadel, then a lieutenant in the Royal Corps of Signals and, until his early death, Librarian of Cambridge University. The group of eight young people—three girls among them—acquired a knowledge of written Japanese within the six months. Charles was then commissioned and underwent a two weeks' OLQ (Officer-Like Qualities) course at Portsmouth. Later he joined the staff at Bletchley Park, working on decoded Japanese messages. After a few months, together with two young colleagues (George Hunter, future Corresponding FBA, and Wilfred Taylor), Charles was appointed to HMS *Lanka* in Colombo, where they arrived in the summer of 1944. The stay only lasted until December 1945. Charles recalls this as perhaps the most formative period of his life, giving it words in a moving testimony, both professional and personal:

> It was not for us a violent period, but the experience of working on current enemy messages, always incomplete and requiring emendation, the experience, that is, of applying text-critical techniques, learned on the spot, to practical warfare, was something never to be forgotten. It was, too, a period when lifelong friendships were formed. We were a compact and harmonious group of civilians, naval officers and Wrens, and the unique association we formed then has lasted, for some of us, ever since.[1]

With the end of the war in August 1945, the group's services were no longer needed, and in December 1945 George, Wilfred and Charles were sent to Hong Kong via Australia. They reported to an intelligence officer, but there was no real work to do, apart from some days at the Supreme Court supervising Japanese internees who were translating depositions for a war crimes trial which was in progress. Charles writes with great sympathy of Hong Kong in those days:

> Hong Kong was in those days a ravaged city. Most of the houses above harbour level had been looted, right down to the doors and window frames, apparently in the interlude between Japanese collapse and the British resumption of authority. The population was small, about half a million, and the Hong Kong and Shanghai Bank occupied the tallest building in the city. As well as the British occupation forces there were US Navy vessels in the harbor, thousands of Japanese prisoners of war in camps, and a somewhat ragged and uninspiring Chinese army lounging around and waiting to be sent against the communists. But even then it was a bustling business and entertainment centre, and I have always been glad to have seen Hong Kong as a Chinese city before its development into an international market-place. Wilfred and I took lessons in Cantonese from an old gentleman called Sung Hok-pang who had been teaching since the beginning of the century. As it turned out, most of the teaching was done by his daughter Katherine, while he listened to us from behind a partition.

'I tell you two times,' Charles was fond of recalling Mr Sung, 'then you go and practice with my daughter!'

> Katherine Sung, many years later, who also worked as a civil servant and a dressmaker, came to this country and stayed two weeks with us. Before the fortnight was over she had taken a shop in Pont Street, where she became a well-known London dressmaker.

In October 1946 Charles resumed his life in Cambridge, reading for the preliminary exam to Part 2 of the tripos. Another first got him a wartime degree, after which he

---

[1] Wrens was the colloquial term for members of the Women's Royal Naval Service.

turned to study Chinese under Professor Gustav Haloun[2]—another lucky decision in the right direction towards his future career. A brief excursion, first, into the world of the Administrative Civil Service came to nothing—Foreign Service was missed, and Home Civil Service (being assigned to the German Section of the Foreign Office) did not last long. Nevertheless, while still in London one thing of great importance to Charles' personal life occurred—he met his future wife, Jean, younger sister of Margaret, Charles' Wren colleague in Ceylon. A group of the old Ceylon hands used to meet once a week in London for a meal, and on one occasion Margaret was joined by her younger sister Jean. It must have been love at first sight, for, as Charles says, 'we were married on 3 August 1949, less than a year after meeting, in the chapel at Shrewsbury School, where Jean's father, John Barham Johnson, was Director of Music'.

Still in 1949, Charles returned to Cambridge where, in the summer of 1950, he took his diploma in Chinese. In a subsequent curious interval, he was that year sent to Hong Kong again, en route to Peking, initiated by the Treasury committee. Nothing came of it—there was no academic programme, no introductions in Peking, in fact, Peking was never reached, but several rather frustrating months were spent in Hong Kong. Charles put them to good use, nevertheless, by learning as much Chinese as possible. Cambridge, as it was, had been entirely classical, and the adjustment to modern Chinese, accordingly, was not without problems.

Back home again, Charles started to work on his PhD. The theme, chosen by Haloun, was soon discarded, apart from the fact that Haloun suddenly died in 1951. By that time, Charles' interests had turned to Mongolian, a language he had started to learn earlier with Denis Sinor,[3] then teaching at Cambridge. No doubt as a result of the war experiences, Oriental Studies had seen a considerable promotion in some countries, Great Britain among them. At the proposal of Gustav Haloun, a post in Altaistic Studies had been established at Cambridge—the first holder of which was said Denis Sinor. Even while he was still in Hong Kong, Charles' interest in things Mongolian had started—not least through meeting some Mongols who were engaged in translating the New Testament. By yet another lucky occurrence, after he left Cheung Chau island off Hong Kong, Charles' room there was taken by one Magadbürin Haltod (1917–1977), a Chahar Mongol, who subsequently became lector at Bonn University and a good family friend. Back in 1954, having presented his thesis on the Mongolian chronicle *Altan Tobci* (a copy of the text having been in the University Library), Charles found himself at a loose end, with nothing to look forward to—but, as he puts it, once again luck played its part. In that year, the

---

[2] Gustav Haloun (1898–1951): see Franke (1952), 1–9.
[3] Denis Sinor (1916–2011): see Walravens (2011), 537–40.

International Congress of Orientalists met in Cambridge. Charles made the acquaintance of Walther Heissig,[4] whose work he already knew and had used. Heissig later was to become a close and lifelong friend of Charles; he was to be elected a Fellow of the School of Oriental and African Studies (SOAS), University of London (1983), and a Corresponding Fellow of the British Academy (1988). At the time, Heissig was much taken with Charles' thesis and agreed to publish it in the series *Göttinger Asiatische Forschungen* (founded by Heissig—and continuing today as *Asiatische Forschungen*). At the same time in 1954, Professor Kaare Gronbech,[5] the eminent Danish Orientalist, also interested himself in Charles' work, and from these meetings his academic career truly began.

In 1955, Bawden's first edition and translation of the said 17th-century Mongolian chronicle was published (Bawden, 1955). The work on the *Altan Tobci* proved significant in several respects. It marked the beginning of a long and fruitful scholarly co-operation with Walther Heissig, then Privatdozent in Göttingen (later appointed Professor and Head of the Seminar für Sprach- und Kulturwissenschaft Zentralasiens an der Rheinischen Friedrich-Wilhelms-Universität zu Bonn). It further led towards what was to become one of Bawden's main fields of research—traditional Mongolian historiography. Since Hartmut Walravens (2017), in his excellent essay in memory of Charles Bawden, also published a complete bibliography of Charles' scholarly work— monographs, brief studies, articles, reviews—the present memoir will forgo a repetition. Nevertheless, explicit mention will be made of major works representing Bawden's main fields of research. The *Altan Tobci* was followed by another pioneer edition, the biographies of the Khalkha Mongolian incarnation, *Jebtsundamba Khutukhtu* (Bawden, 1961).

This, furthermore, led to a follow-up step in Bawden's career. He was offered a lectureship in Mongolian at SOAS, a position he took up on 1 October 1955. SOAS was to remain 'his congenial academic home', as he called it, until his retirement in 1984. His further career at the School developed as follows: in 1959, he was accepted as a Recognized Teacher by the University of London, followed by the appointment as Reader in Mongolian, in October 1962; he became Professor and Head of the Department of the Languages and Cultures of the Far East, in October 1970; and Pro-Director of the School, in October 1982. To begin with, however, Charles felt rather isolated at SOAS. As he recalls:

> I was a member of the Department of the Far East under the headship of Professor Walter Simon, and though he received me most kindly I felt something of an outsider faced with the overwhelming preponderance of Chinese and Japanese research and

---

[4] Walther Heissig (1913–2005): see Walravens (2012); Veit (2018), 285–96.
[5] Kaare Gronbech (1901–1957): see Krueger (1957), 1–5, 13–18.

teaching in the Department. To begin with I had no students, a fact which, however, was soon to be remedied.[6] Also Mongolian itself was a very marginal subject. We had no relations with Mongolia and I did not even know the names of more than one or two academics there, let alone have any contact with them. There were no books to be bought until the end of the 1950s. Fortunately, Mongolian began to profit from the new interest in Altaic studies as a whole which was generated and promoted by some influential scholars at the 1957 International Congress of Orientalists at Munich, and with the founding of the PIAC (Permanent International Altaistic Conference) and its early meetings in Mainz one began to feel a member of a genuine group. Also, I had (continued to have) the sympathy of Walther Heissig, which meant a great deal in those early years.

The appointment to London had also led the Bawden family to move—at the end of 1955 they bought a house in Iver, where they lived until shortly before Charles died. Another fruitful scholarly co-operation Charles established was with Kaare Gronbech. Not only had he allowed Charles to make use of the *Jebtsundamba* manuscript, which he had brought back from Inner Mongolia, it also led to the Bawden family being invited to Copenhagen in 1956. Before, in 1953, the committee for a new catalogue of the Oriental collection in Demark had agreed upon entrusting Walther Heissig with describing the works of the Mongolian collection in the Royal Library, Copenhagen. Charles was called in to describe the sixty-seven divinatory and medical works. Professor Gronbech, adviser to the Royal Library on matters concerning the newly established Mongol collection, praised Bawden's 'extensive knowledge of literary Mongolian, sound acumen and untiring energy'. He attested to him never falling prey to arbitrary hypotheses or convenient shortcuts. The catalogue was finally published in 1971 (*Catalogue of Mongol Books, Manuscripts and Xylographs*, by Walther Heissig, assisted by Charles Bawden: Heissig, 1971).

Apart from the continued cataloguing of further Mongol collections (Walravens, 2017, 181–201), Charles' work in the Royal Library in Copenhagen opened an additional field in his truly pioneering scholarly activity: research on the linguistically as well as substantially difficult—albeit important—subject of Mongolian folk religion. Reports claim that Charles' scholarly enthusiasm, indeed Sherlock Holmesian meticulousness, led him to experiment himself with burning sheep shoulder-blades in the home fireplace—to the somewhat limited pleasure of the family—yet essential, when dealing with the Mongol tradition of divination by scapulimancy and the interpretation of the bones. The result was a number of outstanding studies in the form of articles, the likes of which have not been published since (Walravens, 2017, 181–210).

[6]To name but some: Veronika Veit (born 1944), at SOAS 1966/67, at present Professor Emeritus of Mongolian Studies at the University of Bonn; also Craig Clunas FBA (born 1954), at present Professor Emeritus of the History of Art (Ming China) at the University of Oxford.

What obviously served Charles well once more was what he had learned from decoding Japanese messages—that is, applying text-critical techniques. Charles was sometimes criticised as being 'finicky'. But a true scholar cannot be finicky enough: the number of errors that have been transmitted in footnotes (sometimes over a century), originating in negligent scholarship, are not few!

A new era began for Charles in 1958 with his first visit to Mongolia. The invitation seems to have been promoted by Ivor Montagu—a man of many interests, who had been to Mongolia a few years before and had published a book about his journey, *Land of Blue Sky* (Montagu, 1956). The chosen visitors were Group Captain H. St Clair Smallwood of the then Royal Central Asian Society, and Charles himself. There being no direct flights between London and Moscow at the time, they travelled via Copenhagen. The journey was written about in the *Journal of the Royal Central Asian Society* (Smallwood, 1959). Two things of note which came out of the visit may be worth mentioning: Charles and his colleague met one or two survivors of the group of Mongol children who had been sent to school in Germany in the 1920s (see Wolff, 1971). As a result of that encounter, Charles succeeded in making contact with the late Serge Wolff, who had been the European advisor for that group as well as for a trade delegation which came to Germany at the same time.

In 1959 Charles went to Mongolia again, this time travelling by ship to Leningrad, and then by train to Moscow and across Siberia (Bawden, 1960). The occasion was the holding of the First International Congress of Mongolists, a small but highly significant gathering, Charles recalls. Most of those attending were from Mongolia itself and other communist countries, but there were also scholars from the USA, Canada, Finland, Japan and Britain. The holding of this congress marked a turning point, not only in international scholarly relations but also, almost more important, in the slow recovery of scholarship in Mongolia itself after some very bad years previously. On the occasion, the Mongolian colleagues had even succeeded in founding a number of academic series.

Although Mongolian Studies in the UK were still a one-man-band, as Charles calls it, albeit somewhat improved with the appointment of Owen Lattimore as Professor of Chinese Studies (and a strong interest in Mongolian Studies) at the University of Leeds, Charles himself succeeded in doing much to establish the field on the academic map of Britain, not least by spreading his research interests over as wide an area as he could. Two books, highlights of his fine scholarship and his talent as a writer, appealing to scholars as well as an interested public, may serve as evidence in the said context. Encouraged by Bernard Lewis FBA, Charles contributed his book *The Modern History of Mongolia* to the series he was editing (Bawden, 1968). Although this book dealt with, amongst other topics, the dreadful story of the 1930s in Mongolia—albeit in a moderate, though critical, and always impeccably scholarly fashion—it was quite bitterly attacked both in Mongolia itself and by Ivor Montagu. Twenty years later, Charles had the satisfaction to see his book 'vindicated': where the political course in Mongolia had changed, Charles' book had not, and his Mongolian colleagues were praising it and longing for a reprint! This, indeed, came to pass in 1989 (Bawden, 1989). It still remains the standard treatment of the subject, surpassed by no other publication to date.

The second book to be mentioned is what Charles himself considers his most rewarding topic—the history of the London Missionary Society's mission to the Buryat Mongols in the early part of the 19th century (Bawden, 1985a). It seems worthwhile to relate Charles' own little background story to the enterprise:

> I had known something of this mission through reading James Gilmour's classic book 'Among the Mongols' many years before, but it was really quite by chance that I discovered, while reviewing another book, that the archives of the mission were not only preserved in the library of the Council for World Mission, but that this library was actually in the custody of our own library at SOAS.

The task of reconstructing the story of the mission was not only fascinating in itself, but brought new friendships, among them that of Professor Michael Stallybrass, a descendant of one of the members of the mission and an enthusiast for his family history. Charles' interest in the missionary activities among the Mongols continued, long after his retirement. Thus he came across the correspondence of the orthodox theologian (and Mongol scholar) W. A. Unkrig with the British and Foreign Bible Society[7] —to be transcribed in extenso in the three-volume Unkrig-edition. In connection with a documentation on the pioneer of Mongolian Studies, Isaak Jakob Schmidt,[8] a gap was discovered: two 'christliche Tractätgen' were mentioned in the literature, but they could not be identified. It took several years to discover them, and once again it was Charles who could be persuaded to deal with them. He took on this task with enthusiasm and carried it out in his precise and masterful way.[9]

In the autumn and winter of 1967–8, Charles had a long period of study leave in Mongolia, including a fortnight in western Mongolia, at that time almost unvisited by any foreigners. Political conditions limited the usefulness of the whole enterprise, as Charles relates, but nevertheless he thought it instructive—both academically and otherwise. Hence he not only gave his attention to traditional Mongolian historiography, but also saw the necessity to deal with documentary material concerning the social conditions in Mongolia during the Ch'ing period (1644–1911) and the period

---

[7] Wilhelm Alexander Unkrig (1883–1956): see Walravens (2003).
[8] Isaak Jakob Schmidt (1779–1847): see Walravens (2005).
[9] See Walravens (2017), 180, 197.

of the Mongol Autonomy (1912–1919), resulting in a number of fundamental articles.[10]

Charles' interest in all aspects of Mongolian culture also turned to literature and the specialised field of Mongol epics, which Walther Heissig, in his later years, had made his special concern. In a series of international conferences in Bonn, he promoted the study, individually as well as comparatively, of this almost exclusively oral field of literature. Amongst other endeavours, the recorded Mongolian texts were to be made available through translations, towards which Charles also contributed one volume (Bawden, 1985b), apart from a number of articles dealing with other aspects relevant to the subject of epics.[11] Written though it was after Charles' retirement, mention here should also be made of a book, again appealing to scholars as well as an interested public, that was an anthology of Mongolian traditional literature (Bawden, 2003). The translations are selected from history, legends, didactic literature, epics, prayers and rituals, folk-tales, Sino-Mongolian prose literature, tales of Indian origin, lyrics and other verse, reminiscences, a modern short story—presented here for the very first time in an English translation. Charles' gift for language and his love of words make the anthology readable, giving pleasure in every line.

Charles' retirement from official obligations did not mean a withdrawal from his scholarly activities, as has been seen. Apart from the above-mentioned anthology, he also completed a true treasure of his heart—in fact he called it 'his pet project': an extensive dictionary, Modern (Khalkha) Mongolian–English (Bawden, 1997). He had worked on this project almost his entire professional life (and beyond)—reading, collecting, correcting, improving—meticulously, indefatigably, once more always searching for what is meant and not only said, an echo, perhaps, of the decoding of Japanese messages in his youth? The result is considered to be outstanding and has (yet) to be bested.

Charles Bawden retired from his post at the School of Oriental and African Studies in September 1984, having been made Honorary Member of the School in June of that year, in recognition of his services, and Emeritus Professor of Mongolian in July 1984 'in recognition and appreciation of services to the University and his subject', as it says in the laudatio. He was elected to the British Academy in 1971; resigned 1980; and re-elected 1985. For a while he was Acting Head of the Percival David Foundation, sitting also on a number of other SOAS bodies at various times, including the Library Committee, Editorial Board of the *Bulletin*, and the Governing Body. He was co-editor of *Asiatische Forschungen*, sat on the editorial board of *Central Asiatic Journal*, and was vice-president of the International Association for Mongol Studies. The

[10] Ibid., 181–210.
[11] Ibid.

'Deutsche Forschungsgemeinschaft' took his expert opinion on numerous occasions. Charles was a recipient of the (Mongolian) Friendship Medal (1997) and the order of the Pole Star (Altan Ghadasun) of the Mongolian Republic (2007). In 2013 he was awarded the Indiana University Prize for Altaic Studies. On behalf of the British Academy he gave an excellent account of the life and work of the eminent German-born scholar Ernst Julius Walter Simon, Professor Emeritus of Chinese in the University of London, on the occasion of his death (Bawden, 1981).

A final field in connection with Charles' scholarly activities ought not to be forgotten, although it only indirectly bears a relation to his chosen field—his interest in collecting porcelain, Staffordshire Chinoiserie, to be precise. For his private use, Charles wrote a beautifully illustrated essay on his 'Collector's Enthusiasm', as well as a few articles on ceramic themes (included in Walraven's, 2017, bibliography). The interest was initiated by two events—one a book review he had been commissioned, the other a persistent 'feeling of dissatisfaction', as he describes it, in the early 1970s:

> I had been feeling dissatisfied with the way my life had become dominated by rather abstruse academic pursuits. I was feeling out of touch with reality, and felt there was something missing in the way life was going. Ceramics and their history now suddenly promised to fill this intellectual and aesthetic gap, and they have done so ever since. The review was Oliver Impey's book 'Chinoiserie', and in doing this, I had drawn attention to the wealth of early 19th century china decorated in a pseudo-Chinese style to be found in antique shops and fairs. … Our (active) interest was really aroused when in 1971 Joe and Lucy Felstead opened a little antique shop in Thorney Lane, Iver, just round the corner from our home in Richings Way. Lucy had some bowls and saucers on display which she was offering us at 25p each. They reminded us of what we once had, and I bought the lot, also a blue and white tea-bowl with a pattern of a tall pagoda on it. This looked different from the Chinese ware, and I was unsure of what it was. But in the end I did buy it, and I am glad I did, for unless I am mistaken, this was our first piece of Caughley, though we did not know it at the time. That was how we embarked on a hobby which has now lasted for thirty years [written in 2001—in fact, it lasted throughout Charles' lifetime].

The poet

Charles Bawden's gift for languages, his love of words and love for poetry led him to try his own hand at writing verse. The inclination towards such a fine pastime should surely not least be seen against the background of the first years in his academic career, when studying German and French at Cambridge. Poems he also saw in close connection with music, so it is not surprising that he particularly enjoyed Hugo von Hofmannsthal's lyrics written for the operas *Rosenkavalier* (Charles' favourite) and

Arabella. Another German poet he greatly admired was Heinrich Heine, some of whose poems he translated into English. The writer of the present memoir still has in her possession some letters written to her by Charles, in which the subject of poems was touched on. It seems worthwhile to quote a passage from one of them the better to illustrate what was important to Charles' mind, of literature in general and to Hofmannsthal/Strauss in particular:

> The Marschallin's great aria is one of the high points of literature, let alone the manner in which Strauss's music enhances it. What a chance it was that two men of genius in different fields should have been able to work together so productively. It is a pity that the stage performance hides so much of the intricacy of Hofmannsthal's words—one needs to see it.

Charles' wife Jean shared his enthusiasm, and since they were a couple of the most moving closeness they enjoyed a little game of words, taken from *Arabella*, for their private amusement. To quote from the same letter:

> When Mandryka comes on the scene with Waldner's hint to his now dead uncle to interest himself in Arabella, he says, (more or less)—'Wenn aber das der Fall gewesen wäre, dass mein Herr Onkel, der ein ganzer Mann gewesen ist, und in den besten Jahren? Gesetzt der Fall, es wäre so geschehen, dann hätten wir uns in einer unerwarteten Situation befunden'.[12] Jean and I used to use these words when we were faced with a dilemma—we might find ourselves in an unexpected situation.

When Charles had to move from his house in Iver in 2014, he became a resident at Cliveden Manor. He settled in very well, joining a poetry group and taking part in weekly quizzes. He took to writing more poetry and translating works that he enjoyed, particularly by Heinrich Heine and Betty Paoli—even Danish and Hungarian poetry he saw as a pleasant challenge to render into English. Unfortunately the writer of the present memoir has not kept examples of these enterprises, and it is only her memory which serves here as evidence.

Charles also rekindled an interest in 18th-century society, building up a small library of second-hand books that his son Richard was commissioned to purchase for him from AbeBooks. His own library he had donated, as early as 2001, to the Ancient India and Iran Trust, University of Cambridge. Although he used the common computer at Cliveden to scour the websites of his interest, Charles steadfastly refused to reinstate his own personal computer. He was particularly fond of the letters of Lieselotte von der Pfalz which he had a copy of in the German original. They appealed to his sense of humour, the true historian's curiosity in the small things in life, which

---

[12] But if that had been the case that my revered uncle—and a proper man he was—that that having been the case that it had all happened (in said manner), then we would have found ourselves in an unexpected situation.

tend to mirror much more accurately the conditions which form a society set in its time. When the writer of this memoir was about to leave for Mongolia, Charles sent her the following advice found in his copy of 'Lieselotte'—'always falling open at the same page', as he emphasised: 'Von einer Eiderdunen-Decke habe ich mein Leben nichts gehört; was mich recht warm im Bett haelt, seind sechs kleine Huendcher, so um mich herum liegen; keine Decke haelt so warm als die guten Huendcher.'[13] Similarly, Charles considered a word, ascribed to Heinrich Heine's uncle Salomon, as characteristic of the spirits of the contemporary times: when asked, on his deathbed, would he not convert and ask God for the forgiveness of his sins, Salomon was said to have replied—'No; HE will forgive, c'est son métier!'

Of the considerable number of poems left by Charles, a choice of only a few, in the following, may serve as examples of Charles' 'art of the word', his wit, his erudition, and last, though by no means least, his great love for his wife Jean.[14]

> *Beim Schlafengehen (Hermann Hesse)*
> *Going to Sleep*
> Now that day has tired me,
> my spirits long for
> starry night kindly
> to enfold them, like a tired child.
> Hands, leave all your doing;
> brow, forget all your thought!
> Now all my senses
> want to think themselves in slumber.
> And the soul unwatched,
> would soar in free flight,
> till in the magic circle of night
> it lives deeply and a thousandfold.

> *Fish at Cliveden*
> Carp in the safety of their shallow pond
> Have no conception of the Great Beyond.
> Contentedly and languidly they swim
> Unconscious products of a creator's whim?
> Lazily they glide along.
> Not knowing they might have it wrong.
> No wooden idol of a fishy god
> Protects them from the angler's line and rod.

---

[13] Of covers made of eiderdown I have never heard in all my life; yet what keeps me warm in bed be six small doggies thus lying around me—no cover keeps me as warm as those dear doggies.

[14] The poems are taken from the obituary for Jean Barham Bawden, 1 February 2010, and from the service for Charles Roskelly Bawden himself, 23 August 2016.

The heron, stiff upon his rocky perch
Alert, with beady eye appears to search
For piscine prey, but knows he must
Observe the bye-laws of the National Trust.
They don't know the superficial line
Which separates their world from the divine.
They dimly apprehend there may be sky
For ghostly images confront their eye.
Protective gods have left them in the lurch
The green pagoda is no shrine or church.
The wooden fish, erect upon his tail,
Looms out of sight, a mystery, of no avail.
No violence disturbs their peaceful lake,
No churchy dogma from priests upon the make,
No class distinction and no discrimination,
 No self regard, just aimless contemplation.

Jean and Charles never called each other by their Christian names—they had many changing ones, but the dearest to them were connected with cats:

The Cat
Observe my little concrete cat,
He cost ten pounds, including VAT.
Erect, on neat positioned paw
He guards the plot She never saw.
Tread circumspectly round my cat
Lest careless foot should knock him flat.
I would not like to see him fall
From his precarious pedestal.
May no intrusive dog or rat
Mar the composure of my cat.
Serene, his tail precisely curled,
Girl's Garden his allotted world.
Oblivious to sun and rain,
Exempt from illness and from pain,
Aloof, a feline autocrat,
Exemplar of a Stoic Cat.

Two Cats
I have a fire, I have a mat.
I wish I had a little cat.
So I could sit and stroke her fur
And hear the little creature purr.
I have a house and everything

That life and love and marriage bring.
And there I live in disarray
Without my Cat. She went away.

A Poem Too Late
You are so tired, my love, your weary eyes
Gaze steadfast into mine, demanding answer.
Your poor clenched hand seeks mine but cannot keep it.
You clasp my head and lay it on your cheek.
What answer can I give, except "I love you"?
Pale words, how can they bring you peace and comfort?
Yet they have magic power. They embrace
That world, unknown before, that we created.
Think kindly of me in your narrow room
As in our empty house I long for you.
Against my will I had to let you go,
And disregard your last despairing plea.

It was not only poetry—be it German, French, Italian, Danish, Hungarian (or, to refer to his professional interests, Mongolian and Chinese)—that caught Charles' interest, fired his imagination and afforded him great pleasure. So too did the world of the declining Austro-Hungarian empire of the Habsburgs, so admirably, if not incomparably, depicted in the books of Joseph Roth, Charles' favourite among the authors who dealt with that subject. This world, now lost forever, is equally preserved and most sensitively kept alive in Salcia Landmann's (1962) superb treasury of Jewish anecdotes and jokes. Charles was so fond of this book (as the writer of the present memoir always has been herself), that a cue alone would put both of us immediately 'on the scene', so to speak. We had, however, not (quite) reached the stage portrayed in the original anecdote, in which a group of salesmen habitually travelling together had numbered their favourite jokes, so that, when one just called out the right number, everyone laughed. A newcomer, fascinated, soon grasped the system and joined in, full of enthusiasm—but no one laughed. Deeply disappointed, the newcomer wanted to know the reason, was it not an excellent joke?—'You can't tell it properly, was the answer.' Such spice enlivened our many regular and long telephone conversations, on God and His world, on the follies of politics, on books and music, on Mongolia and China and things professional, which continued until shortly before Charles died.

Man of his word

Inspired by the title chosen for his much praised film on the present Pope, *Francis, a Man of His Word*, made by the well-known German film-director Wim Wenders in

2018, the author of this memoir believes this appellation also to be an apt depiction of Charles Bawden's character. 'A man of his word', as defined by the *Cambridge Academic Content Dictionary*, is a man of integrity, denoting people who do what they say they will do. Fine scholar, upright, truthful, modest, loyal to his academic calling and to his friends—all of this made up the man who was Charles Bawden, verily to be called a 'Man of his word'. Numerous instances, found in all matters that touched his life—official and private, in words or in actions—bear testimony to this quality.

The best known of these instances, perhaps, is the affair of the 'fourth man'. In 1979, the then Prime Minister, Margaret Thatcher, named Sir Anthony Blunt, a former security service officer and personal adviser on art to the Queen as 'the fourth man' in the Cambridge spy ring. The announcement—given in a written answer in the House of Commons—ended a fifteen-year cover-up. Mrs Thatcher revealed he had confessed to the authorities in 1964, but under a secret deal was granted immunity from prosecution. Minutes after the Prime Minister's statement, Buckingham Palace said he was being stripped of his knighthood. Blunt had been part of a Cambridge spy ring made up of Guy Burgess, Donald Maclean and Harold 'Kim' Philby—who was in charge of British intelligence's anti-communist counter-espionage in 1944–6. Burgess and Maclean defected in 1951 following a tip-off from Philby; he defected himself in 1963. Professor Blunt became a Marxist under the influence of his Cambridge friend Guy Burgess. After the Prime Minister's announcement, Professor Blunt made his own statement to the media on 20 November, in which he claimed the decision to grant him immunity from prosecution was taken by the then Prime Minister, Sir Alec Douglas-Home. He said he had come to 'bitterly regret' his spying activities, but, at the time, he had done so out of idealism. Anthony Blunt died in disgrace three years later. Charles' own reaction to the affair is best described—in extenso—in his own words:

> In 1971 I was elected a Fellow of the British Academy. This could have been passed over in a single sentence, were it not for the fact that a decade later I resigned from the Academy as a result of my disagreement with the non-action of the Fellows of the Academy over the matter of Anthony Blunt, who had been exposed as a Soviet agent. I do not want to re-open here a question which is now closed, but I do wish to say a little in explanation of my action. At the time I myself did not publicise it, and it never received any publicity. What then was the good of it? The answer is that I did not intend it to have any public result. I resigned because I felt that I could not share an honour with a man who had behaved as Blunt had apparently done. The question most discussed was whether the Academy, a non-political body, should concern itself with Blunt's alleged treason. I knew little of happenings in the USSR, but I did know something of what had happened in the dreadful years of the 1930s in her satellite Mongolia. There, too, the truth and decency had been suppressed, individuals and

families destroyed, and, worst of all from an academic point of view, honest scholars killed or imprisoned. Men whom I later knew and counted as colleagues and friends had been persecuted. Others, whose work I knew and respected, had been murdered. I did not feel justified in maintaining fellowship with one who had, however indirectly, connived at this, especially when he was under no compulsion to do so. So I left the Academy, to my great regret, though my section retained enough confidence in me to propose me once again some years later, and I was re-elected in 1985.

Need more be said?

Similarly, in his career as a professor, Charles Bawden stood out not only through his scholarly competence, but also through his unwavering objectivity, his strictly pertinent criticism and painstaking accuracy and honesty, as witnessed by his voluminous oeuvre. In his private life, as a husband, as a father, and finally as a friend, Charles Bawden was—and always will be—remembered for his kindness and hospitality, his open mind and reliability, his sense of humour and his great gift for lasting friendship. A few examples should suffice to bear witness. In the years 1963 and 1963–4, Charles hosted two Mongolian colleagues, who lived with the family in Iver. The first was Magadbürin Haltod, a Chahar Mongol mentioned earlier, who worked with Charles for three months; the second guest was Mr Sechin Jagchid (1916–2009), a Kharchin Mongol, later to become professor in the United States, at Brigham Young University, Provo, Utah, who then served as a temporary member of the staff at SOAS. Charles was able to work with him almost daily. Similarly, the author of this memoir had the good fortune to enjoy the Bawden family's hospitality on many occasions over the years.

His greatest piece of luck, however (always in the Charlesian sense of the word, as defined earlier), was undoubtedly to have met Jean, his much-loved wife, his congenial companion and partner. It was most unfortunate that she should fall ill with Parkinson's Disease in the 1980s, by which illness she became increasingly incapacitated. In the initial stage Charles himself took care of her in an exemplary fashion, until it was no longer physically possible for him, and Jean had to be admitted to a nursing home. She died there on 11 January 2010. Some of the poems Charles had dedicated to his wife have been quoted earlier in this memoir. Perhaps also his last tribute to her should be added to them: 'Let Man be noble, helpful and good, for that alone distinguishes him from all creatures that we know'. 'That was Jean' (J. W. von Goethe, translated by Charles Bawden).

Richard, the oldest of the four Bawden children, has put together some 'Reflections from the Next Generation'. Charles, as a father, clearly emerges from them fully consistent with the image of his personality as depicted in his other walks of life:

> My childhood memories of my father are of him being a somewhat remote person— often shut away in his study hard at work. It was my mother who really provided family cohesion and supervised the day-to-day running of the home. Dad's attitude to

life was a strange mixture of conservatism (born from his parents' low church adherence?), and academically inspired liberalism. He could be a strict disciplinarian and had a dim view of what he regarded as frivolities (television, sport, pop culture and riotous living), but equally was very relaxed with his offspring's love lives and could happily swap the most risqué of jokes and limericks. I don't remember his presence at childhood birthday parties and I think he was a reluctant attendee at school functions and the like. In his social life he related better to females rather than males. Although he was not one to push himself forward I think he was quietly proud of his achievements.

As has clearly emerged from many instances mentioned throughout this memoir, Charles also had a great gift for lasting friendships—witness his never losing touch with his old colleagues from his wartime activities, not to forget Katherine Sung from Hong Kong. Others are colleagues like the German scholar Walther Heissig, mentioned previously. In a brief memoir, Charles paid his friend a touching tribute (Bawden, 2012, 161–3):

> Walther Heissig was a man of extraordinary abilities. I assert this, not as a flattering eulogy of a departed friend, but as a fact. He was both scholar and an academic entrepreneur, two qualities which do not always coincide. He had a great capacity for friendship and was effective in promoting the interests of his students and younger colleagues. … Walther's life and mine were spent in different countries so that we only saw each other at irregular intervals. But it did not take long for an association to develop into a lasting friendship and indeed an intimate relationship between our two families. A group of friends grew up around the Heissigs, whose central point was Bonn, where we met on such occasions as the Epic seminars which Walther organized.

Veronika Veit, Charles' former student and later close friend, also belonged to that circle.

A final touching Charlesian piece of luck ought to be mentioned. Charles himself wrote:

> Some time after Jean's death in early 2010 my life was enriched by the re-entry into it of a dear friend, Patricia Adamson, after the passage of some 60 years. Pat and I had served in the same naval establishment, HMS Anderson, in Colombo, in the last stages of the Second World War. Her death, after only a few months of 'reunion' at a distance put an end to my emotional life.

***

An apt farewell to the scholar who was—and will remain—Charles Bawden may be found in the following hexameter:

> Grammata sola carent fato, mortemque repellunt
> (Hrabanus Maurus, Archbishop of Mainz, AD 776–865)

Another apt farewell to the man who was Charles Bawden may be found in the follow-ing verse—it was chosen by himself, much cherished by both Jean and Charles, and recited at the Services held to celebrate their lives:[15]

> Remember me when I am gone away,
> Gone far away into the silent land;
> When you can no more hold me by the hand,
> Nor I half turn to go, yet turning stay.
> Remember me when no more day by day
> You tell me of our future that you planned:
> Only remember me; you understand
> It will be late to counsel then or pray.
> Yet if you should forget me for a while
> And afterwards remember, do not grieve:
> For if the darkness and corruption leave
> A vestige of the thoughts that once I had,
> Better by far you should forget and smile
> Than that you should remember and be sad.
> (Christina Rossetti)

In an equally apt conclusion to the celebration of the life of the fine scholar and dear friend, the Service ended with Strauss' 'Waltzsequence' from Der Rosenkavalier Suite.

Acknowledgements
The author of the present biographical memoir wishes to express her gratitude to Mr Richard J. Bawden, who generously and most kindly allowed her to make use of his own notes—'Reflections From The Next Generation' (2016)—as well as several of his father's own personal notes from which the quotations here are taken: 'Some Notes For My Life' (1993); 'Collecting Porcelain—The Story of an Enthusiast' (2001); 'Some Notes For My Life'—addendum 2014. Charles Bawden himself gave the author a copy from the BBC—*On This Day*—16 November 1979, with reference to the Blunt affair.

Note on the author: Professor Dr Veronika Veit, University of Bonn.

References

Bawden, C. R. (1955) *The Mongol Chronicle Altan Tobci* (text, translation and critical notes, *Göttinger Asiatische Forschungen* 5) (Wiesbaden).

---

[15] Jean Barham Johnson, 1 February 2010; Charles Roskelly Bawden, 23 August 2016.

Bawden, C. R. (1960) 'Mongolia re-visited', *Journal of the Royal Central Asian Society*, 47, 127–40.

Bawden, C. R. (1961) *The Jebtsundamba Khutukhtus of Urga* (text, translation and notes, *Asiatische Forschungen* 9) (Wiesbaden).

Bawden, C. R. (1968) *The Modern History of Mongolia* (London).

Bawden, C. R. (1981) 'Ernst Julius Walter Simon, 1893–1981', *Proceedings of the British Academy*, 67, pp. 459–77.

Bawden, C. R. (1985a) *Shamans, Lamas and Evangelicals: the English Missionaries in Siberia* (London)

Bawden, C. R. (1985b) *Mongolische Epen X. Eight North Mongolian Epic Poems* (translated by C. R. Bawden, *Asiatische Forschungen* 75) (Wiesbaden).

Bawden, C. R. (1989) *The Modern History of Mongolia*, with afterword by Alan Sanders (London and New York)

Bawden, C. R. (1997) *Mongolian-English Dictionary* (London and New York)

Bawden, C. R. (2003) *Mongolian Traditional Literature: an Anthology* (London)

Bawden, C. R. (2012), 'Walther Heissig, a memoir', in H. Walravens (ed.), *Walther Heissig (1913–2005), Mongolist, Zentralasienwissenschaftler und Folklorist: Leben und Werk. Würdigungen, Dokumente, Forschungsberichte, Rundfunkprogramme* (Wiesbaden), pp. 161–4.

Franke, H. (1952), 'Gustav Haloun (1898–1951) in memoriam', *Zeitschrift der Deutschen Morgenländischen Gesellschaft*, 102, 1–9.

Heissig, W., assisted by Bawden, C. R. (1971) *Catalogue of Mongol Books, Manuscripts and Xylographs* (Copenhagen).

Krueger, J. R. (1957) 'In memoriam Kaare Gronbech 1901-1957', *Central Asiatic Journal*, 1, 1–5 and 13–18.

Landmann, S. (1962), *Der Jüdische Witz. Soziologie und Sammlung* (mit einem Geleiwort von Professor Carlo Schmid) (Freiburg).

Montagu, I. (1956) *Land of Blue Sky: a Portrait of Modern Mongolia* (London).

Smallwood, H. St. C. (1959) 'Visit to Mongolia', *Journal of the Royal Central Asian Society*, 46, 18–26.

Veit, V. (1994), 'Charles Bawden on the occasion of his 70th birthday', *Central Asiatic Journal*, 38:2, 149–54

Veit, V. (2018), 'Der Mongolist Walther Heissig (1913–2005), Spurensucher, Entdecker, Brückenbauer, Autor', *Die Bonner Orient- und Asienwissenschaftler* (*Orientierungen*, Themenband 18, Ostasien Verlag), 287–96

Walravens, H. (2003) *W. A. Ungkrig (1883–1956): Leben und Werk* (Wiesbaden).

Walravens, H. (2005), *Issak Jakob Schmidt (1779–1847): Leben und Werk des Pioniers der mongolischen und tibetischen Studien. Eine Dokumentation* (Wiesbaden).

Walravens, H. (2011), 'Denis Sinor (1916–2011) in memoriam', *Monumenta Serica*, 59, 537–40.

Walravens, H. (2012) (ed.), *Walther Heissig (1913-2005), Mongolist, Zentralasienwissenschaftler und Folklorist: Leben und Werk. Würdigungen, Dokumente, Forschungsberichte, Rundfunkprogramme* (Wiesbaden)

Walravens, H. (2017) 'Charles R. Bawden (1924-2016) zum Gedenken', *Monumenta Serica*, 65, 175–210.

Wolff, S. (1971), 'Mongolian educational venture in Western Europe (1926–1929)', *Zentralasiatische Studien*, 5, 247–320.

DONALD WINCH

Donald Norman Winch

15 April 1935 – 12 June 2017

elected Fellow of the British Academy 1986

by

STEFAN COLLINI
Fellow of the Academy

Although the history of economic thought had traditionally been regarded as an integral part of the discipline of Economics, in recent decades it has come more and more to be seen by economists as marginal or even antiquarian. At the same time, it has been increasingly cultivated within the field of Intellectual History, which encourages a more thoroughly historical and thick-textured treatment of past ideas. No single figure has been more central to this transition than Donald Winch. Trained as an economist, he developed an interest in the history of economic thought early on. Over time, encouraged especially by the innovative structure of the University of Sussex, where he taught for almost forty years, and by a group of congenial colleagues there, Winch became the leading intellectual historian of British economic thought of the eighteenth and nineteenth centuries, notably in *Riches and Poverty* (1996) and *Wealth and Life* (2009).

Biographical Memoirs of Fellows of the British Academy, XVIII, 471–496
Posted 21 November 2019. © British Academy 2019.

DONALD WINCH

The process we refer to as the 'professionalisation' of academic disciplines is never uniform or constant, but it does display a familiar tendency to move from encompassing, catholic, or baggy conceptions of a field to more purist senses of identity. Concerns that were once considered integral to a form of intellectual enquiry can come to be shunted to the sidelines, even expelled altogether. Yet in time this marginalised matter may find a home within a different specialism, perhaps one that is governed by other conceptions of rigour and relevance, or even one that is, for the time being, more hospitable to apparent untidiness. In recent decades, Economics has been a striking example of such disciplinary purification, as more technical, theoretical, and in many cases mathematical, approaches have come to dominate the field's understanding of its own nature and scope. One of the casualties of this narrowing focus has been the history of economic thought, once seen as an established part of the discipline and a required element in the education of economists, now increasingly regarded by many within the profession as a form of antiquarianism, best left to the retired or the also-rans. At the same time, the remarkable growth of Intellectual History in the past two generations has begun to re-insert past economic thinking into a much more thickly-textured understanding of the intellectual life of earlier periods. Instead of a triumphalist narrative that tended to tell a story of past error giving way to present truth, the intellectual history of economic thought attempts to recover the complexity of that thought, to appreciate its often various inspirations and purposes as well as its deep involvement with styles of enquiry that subsequently became the property of neighbouring scholarly disciplines. Few individuals experienced this transition in their own careers as intensely and fruitfully as Donald Winch; none made a more significant contribution to the present flourishing of the intellectual history of economic thought.

Donald studied Economics as an undergraduate at the London School of Economics (LSE) in the mid-1950s, a time and place confident in its understanding of that subject as a broad and fairly traditional discipline, one that was of central relevance to a wide range of policies. He did his PhD at Princeton in the late 1950s in an Economics department that was uneasily making the transition from a long-standing, heterogeneous conception of the field to one more dominated by a mathematised form of microeconomics. But already his own interests were coming to focus on the history of political economy, and although he was appointed to lectureships in Economics at, first, Edinburgh and, then, Sussex, the trajectory of his research and writing started to take him away from the hardening identity of his parent discipline. He found a more congenial home in the then still somewhat derogated or under-developed field of Intellectual History, and began to make major contributions to our understanding of social, political, and economic thinking in Britain from the middle of the eighteenth century to the middle of the twentieth. He ended his career as Emeritus Professor of Intellectual History, feted across the world for his learned, analytical, sometimes combative contributions to this broadened history. Yet he never altogether severed ties with the discipline of Economics in its contemporary form, remaining, for example, Publications Secretary of the Royal Economic Society until 2016 and an active member of the Economics section of the British Academy for over thirty years. His forthright championing of the claims of a genuinely historical approach to past economic thinking did not always make for amicable relations with those who understood their discipline as a more abstract and systematic enterprise, but his distinctive manner of combining mastery of theoretical issues and deep familiarity with historical context gave him a special standing and an unusual authority.

I

Donald Norman Winch was born on 15 April 1935, the only child of Iris (née Button) and Sidney Winch. Iris came from a family of agricultural workers in Suffolk, her widowed mother moving to London with her three young children and supporting them by working as a cleaner. Sidney belonged to a longer-established London working-class family: his father was a stone-mason, and Sidney was apprenticed to him in the 1920s. After they were married, the young couple managed to buy a small modern house on a new housing estate in North Cheam in south-west London, where Donald lived with his parents until he was 21 (apart from the period during the Second World War when he and his mother were evacuated to the Lake District). Sidney served in the Royal Navy during the war, contracting a kidney ailment that involved a long stay in hospital and meant he was not strong enough to resume work as a stone-mason once he was finally discharged. After the war he had a succession of jobs, including working as a cashier for a wholesale greengrocer's at Covent Garden. Only after Donald had left home to go as a postgraduate to the USA did Sidney and Iris sell the family home in North Cheam and buy a small greengrocer's shop in Sussex. Following their retirement in the mid-1970s, they and Donald jointly bought a large house in Cooksbridge, about four miles outside Lewes in East Sussex, which they divided into two separate establishments. Donald experienced the estrangement from many of his parents' tastes and ideas common to the highly educated child of relatively poorly educated parents, but the emotional bond was close and enduring, never more in evidence than in the tender care for his mother's welfare that Donald displayed in the years between Sidney's death in 1993 and her own, at age 100, in 2015.

In an unpublished autobiographical account, Donald paints a subtly nuanced picture of his family's class position and of the education that moved him away from it (as well as a wry sketch of the vantage-point from which he now surveyed this history, as 'a reasonably successful member of one of the shabbier branches of the professional middle-classes').[1] Already a clever boy at primary school, he was a beneficiary of the 11-plus system which won him a place at the nearby Sutton Grammar School. Writing half a century later, he could smile at the pretensions that survived from the school's more socially exclusive pre-1944 incarnation as well as at his own early antagonism to some of its more alien middle-class mores and snobberies. But, encouraged particularly by a sympathetic History teacher, he came in time to show more conscientiousness than belligerence (a dynamic or tension that remained visible throughout his career), and entered the sixth-form, a progression that was by no means to be taken for granted among children from his background at the time. He flourished in the intellectually stimulating and culturally rich environment of a 1950s grammar-school sixth-form, studying for A-levels in History, English, and Economics, while taking leading parts in debating, dramatic, and other school societies. His high marks qualified him for a State Studentship, which he chose to take up at LSE, attracted by its London location and its aura of engagement with the contemporary world. In October 1953 he embarked on the undergraduate course in Economics at 'the School' (as others, though rarely Donald, referred to it).

In later years, Donald retained a genuine respect for LSE, especially for the range and rigour of the syllabus he had to study, but he never quite seemed to have felt the affection and nostalgia that many others do for their *alma mater*. This may partly have been an expression of his cultivated briskness, even brusqueness, when talking about feelings and emotions, but it also owed something to the fact that he did not have the residential experience enjoyed by many students at other universities at the time. He commuted from the family home to the LSE on the Northern Line from Morden, or latterly on the back of a Vespa scooter owned by one of his fellow-students, and he retained his involvement with various local organisations and activities.

As an undergraduate, Donald responded to the intellectual stimulus of the diverse courses required in those days for the BSc(Econ) degree, especially classes in history and philosophy. Although it was not compulsory, he attended Michael Oakeshott's not-yet-famous lecture course on the history of political thought for two years in succession, seduced by its stylishness, intrigued by the subtlety of its textual and

[1] At some point in the mid-1990s, partly stimulated by reading Ralf Dahrendorf's history of the LSE, partly by having recently read John Burrow's autobiographical sketch of his early life, Donald wrote a two-part memoir entitled 'The London School of Economics and all that: I Getting there; II Being there'. In 2015–16 he wrote a further extended reflection on the making of his career entitled 'Intellectual history and the history of political economy'. He then attached the two LSE pieces as Appendixes to this account, subtitling the combined document 'Some autobiographical notes'. I quote from the continuously paginated version of this combined document: 'Some autobiographical notes', p. 85. An electronic copy forms part of the extensive collection of Donald's papers deposited at the University of Sussex archives in the East Sussex Record Office.

contextual analysis. But his focus was on economics, and within this field he discovered by his third year a special interest in international trade theory. The subject was taught by James Meade, later a Nobel-prize winner, and although their direct contact was limited and somewhat distant, Donald came to feel considerable estimation for Meade as one kind of model academic:

> The only time I met him outside the lecture hall at LSE was at a social event where he was pouring tea, rather bashfully, for members of his department. In later years I got to know a little more about him as a person – modest in manner, gentle, inventive, self-sufficient, almost saint-like in my estimation, if saints are allowed to be puckish. In retrospect, making use of my later trade as intellectual historian, I would say he was an archetypal representative of the best liberal socialist ideas of his day, with the emphasis falling on 'liberal' in one of its many senses. He was an admirable product of interwar, Second World War, and postwar economics, the period in which many of the intellectual foundations were laid for a world that his generation hoped would no longer be marred by heavy unemployment and large inequalities at home and economic autarky in international affairs.[2]

The hope of helping to make the world a better place had been a large part of the reason Donald had chosen to study Economics, but he also discovered in himself a more autonomous appetite for intellectual enquiry. It is true that he was (as he remained) on the left in the sense that he felt antagonistic to, even some disdain for, the old Tory establishment and the associated attitudes of snobbery and deference that it perpetuated, and he was, or at least longed to be, international in his outlook, irked by the parochialism of 1950s England. He had imbibed the secular progressive outlook that owed as much to, say, George Bernard Shaw or Aldous Huxley as to any more narrowly doctrinaire sources, and he had more than his share of the impatience common among clever young men. But as an undergraduate his development also started to take a more scholarly turn, experiencing a pleasure in ideas and their expression, even a taste for the hushed studiousness and sense of inheritance associated with great libraries.

In his final year he vaguely toyed with the idea of a career in one of the emerging international economic organisations, but when he was awarded a First he took up the opportunity provided by a Royal Insurance Company Fellowship to spend a year as a graduate student in the Economics Department at Princeton, where Meade's friend Jacob Viner taught international economics.[3] Donald distinguished himself in the first year graduate courses, thereby qualifying for funding that enabled him to stay and do

[2] Winch, 'LSE II: Being there', p. 133.
[3] Viner had published *Studies in the Theory of International Trade* in 1937 (London) before going on to the work in the history of economic thought for which he became better known, notably *The Long View and the Short: Studies in Economic Theory and Policy* (London, 1958).

a PhD, eventually submitted in 1960. Apart from international economics, the other graduate course that Viner taught was on the history of economic thought, and this encounter was to be decisive for the future direction of Donald's interests: 'Viner's course made some demanding assumptions about familiarity with the primary texts for an audience more accustomed to reading modern economic sources; but it also opened a window on the intricacies of textual interpretation that I was later to find enticing.'[4] For his dissertation, Donald tried to combine his interests in international economics with this new enthusiasm, following the thread of the export of capital and labour to the colonies in the nineteenth century, writing a dissertation somewhat cumbrously entitled 'The political economy of colonisation: a study in the development of the attitude of the English classical school to empire'. He later reflected that he must have been one of the last students at Princeton who had been permitted to do a dissertation on a subject in the history of economic thought, so rapidly was that ceasing to be regarded as a constituent element of the discipline as practiced in the leading US graduate schools (Viner retired in the year in which Donald submitted his dissertation). Donald subsequently wrote a sympathetic and moving memoir of Viner and, with Jacques Melitz, co-edited Viner's posthumous book *Religious Thought and Economic Society* (1978).[5] Curiously, Princeton was to be the scene of two of the major turning-points in Donald's intellectual life, the second coming some sixteen or seventeen years after the first.

Before he had submitted his dissertation, Donald obtained a one-year teaching post in the Economics department of the University of California at Berkeley (1959–60), and it must have seemed likely that he would make his career in the United States. American openness and energy spoke to him, especially at this stage of his life, and gave him a sense of freedom harder to come by in class-racked England. (The novels of David Lodge, Donald's exact contemporary, were memorably to capture this contrast, as Donald later recognised.) In 1957 he had married his long-standing English girlfriend, Marion Steed, who worked as a secretary in London, but even before the young couple moved to the West Coast it was clear that the marriage was in trouble. They separated during the year in Berkeley, something that may have encouraged Donald to think of returning to Britain. In 1960 he was appointed to a Lectureship in the Department of Political Economy at Edinburgh University.

---

[4] Winch, 'Some autobiographical notes', p. 13.
[5] D. Winch, 'Jacob Viner', *The American Scholar*, 50 (Autumn, 1981), 519–25; see also his 'Jacob Viner as intellectual historian', in W. J. Samuels (ed.), *The Craft of the Historian of Economic Thought* (Greenwich, CT, 1983), pp. 1–17.

Donald responded to the beauty and historical associations of Edinburgh without ever quite feeling at home in the still rather strait-laced academic society there. His first head of department, Alan Peacock, recognised the new recruit's talents and encouraged him in his interests, but some longer-established figures may have seemed less welcoming to the occasionally brash American-educated Englishman. Nonetheless, Donald's time at Edinburgh fostered his nascent interest in the Scottish traditions of political economy, an interest that had begun with his work on Adam Smith for his Princeton dissertation. In the early 1960s he was enlarging and extensively revising that work for publication, a project that led him to delve more deeply into the political and economic thinking of the early decades of the nineteenth century. The book was finally published in 1965 (under the auspices of the LSE), now more austerely titled *Classical Political Economy and Colonies*. Its Introduction quietly announced that it was a contribution to 'the history of ideas': it was not a study of policy-making, while 'at the same time it has been necessary to steer clear of the history of economic analysis for its own sake in order to remain close to the issues as seen by the participants. This study ... if it is to be classified, must be entered as a hybrid... .'[6] In his first academic publication, a polemical article entitled 'What price the history of economic thought?' in the *Scottish Journal of Political Economy* in 1962, Donald had already argued that the history of economic thought was becoming detached from the mainstream of the discipline, a development he resisted at the time, and his first monograph confirmed the historical turn in his own interests.[7] When the Scottish Economic Society inaugurated a short-lived series of editions of Scottish economic classics, Donald undertook the volume on James Mill's economic writings, and produced a substantial and learned edition that restored the elder Mill to his proper place among the classical economists; the book has lasted, being re-issued in 2006 and again in 2017.[8]

Having come to feel less comfortable in the Edinburgh department after the departure of Peacock to the founding chair at York, Donald took up a Lectureship in Economics at the University of Sussex in 1963. It was a fateful move: thereafter he spent his entire academic life at Sussex, becoming one of its most influential members and finding that, sometimes despite himself, much of his intellectual identity was bound up with the distinctiveness of the institution. The university, the earliest of the 'new' or 'plate-glass' universities founded in the 1960s, had taken its first fifty students

[6] D. Winch, *Classical Political Economy and Colonies* (London, 1965), p. 3. A Japanese translation was published in 1975.
[7] D. Winch, 'What price the history of economic thought?', *Scottish Journal of Political Economy*, 9 (1962), 193–204.
[8] D. Winch (ed.), *James Mill: Selected Economic Writings* (Edinburgh, 1966; reprinted in 2006 by Transaction Publishers, New Brunswick, NJ, and in 2017 by Routledge, London).

in the autumn of 1961, and it was still tiny and unformed when Donald arrived. Part of the defining aspiration of the university was to break down the over-specialised character of English (though not Scottish) higher education: from the outset, it set its face against orthodox departments and single-subject degrees.[9] The principal organising units were the Schools: the humanities and social sciences were initially divided among the School of English and American Studies, the School of European Studies, and the School of Social Studies (soon re-named the School of Social Sciences). Cutting across these units were 'Subject-groups', which essentially reflected traditional disciplinary identities. So, for example, the History Subject-group could have members in more than one School, as could the Philosophy Subject-group, the Politics Subject-group, and so on. Undergraduates were admitted to a School, and approximately half their courses were 'contextuals', common courses provided for all students in that School whatever their 'major'; the rest of their courses were in their chosen major. This structure made for flexible but complex teaching loads for the academic staff. One might teach courses provided by one's Subject-group to students from more than one School, while at the same time one might teach a range of Contextual courses to students in one's home School who were taking a variety of different majors (and, in some cases, one might teach Contextual courses in other Schools). Both the ethos and the structure of the university favoured innovation. The Contextual courses, in particular, had to be designed to provide a common intellectual framework for students taking widely different majors, a form of provision for which there was no real precedent in English universities, though the University of Keele (founded in 1949 and obtaining full university status in 1962) had begun to break away from the single-subject template. The structure also encouraged 'team teaching', either in the form of a group of staff sharing responsibility for designing and teaching a Contextual course taken by large numbers, or in the form of two members of staff from different Subject-groups coming together to provide a course that was intended to meld the approaches and insights of two complementary disciplines (imaginative courses of this type in History and Literature were a notable local specialty).

A grasp of this educational structure is essential to understanding Donald's institutional role and, to some extent, his intellectual development.[10] His post was in the School of Social Studies and he quickly became involved in designing one of its most distinctive pedagogic innovations. The course, called 'Concepts, Methods, and Values in the Social Sciences' (or, more familiarly, 'CMV'), taken by all students in the School in their final year, was intended to provide a unifying understanding of both

[9] See D. Daiches (ed.), *The Idea of a New University: an Experiment in Sussex* (London, 1964).
[10] For further details see S. Collini, 'General introduction', in S. Collini, R. Whatmore, and B. Young (eds.), *Economy, Polity, and Society: British Intellectual History 1750–1950* (Cambridge, 2000), pp. 1–21.

the philosophy and the history of the social sciences. In its earliest years, in the 1960s, Donald contributed to both parts of the course, throwing himself into teaching, say, Popper as well as Weber, but before long the two halves of the course acquired a semi-independent status, and Donald became the mainspring of the historical option.

The University of Sussex expanded very quickly in the 1960s: fifty undergraduates in 1961 became 400 in 1962 growing to 3,000 by 1968. Like any new university, it not only provided opportunities for curricular experiment but also for precocious career development. In 1968, at the early age of 33, Donald, already marked out by his energy, acumen and professional commitment, became Dean of the School of Social Sciences. It was not an auspicious year in which to occupy a senior administrative position at one of the universities in the forefront of student protests, and Donald's firm commitment to what he saw as core academic values did not always win him admirers from among the leaders of the insurgents. This was only the first of many occasions on which he engaged spiritedly on behalf of his conception of what a university was for, against attacks from both the right and the left, engagements that displayed his fearlessness, tactical adroitness, and natural pugnacity.

One of the more agreeable aspects of being a dean in an expanding new university was the influence it gave over creating and making new appointments. Having read with admiration John Burrow's first book, *Evolution and Society: a Study in Victorian Social Theory* (Cambridge, 1966), Donald invited John, then a lecturer in the School of European Studies at the University of East Anglia, to give a visiting lecture for CMV. That visit went well; both men held similar views about the need for a more historical understanding of the development of the social sciences; further correspondence ensued; finally, Donald engineered John's appointment to a post at Sussex in 1969. Although his title was to be 'Reader in History', his was not an appointment within the History Subject-group, which would have been the usual arrangement: it was a School appointment, specifically intended to support the teaching of the historical option of CMV. Thus began an association and a friendship that were to remain central to the lives of both men until John's death forty years later.

At much the same time, another piece of creative institutional entrepreneurship was taking place within the School of European Studies. Michael Moran, who had been appointed as a Lecturer in Philosophy in the School in its early years, found his interests in the history of ideas increasingly straying from, and at odds with, the style of analytic philosophy dominant at the time, and so he, together with a small group of colleagues similarly chafing at aspects of their disciplines' limits, such as Peter Burke in History and James Shiel in Classical and Medieval Studies, set up an MA in 'The History of Ideas'. The times were favourable to curricular experiment, enabling an undergraduate major in 'Intellectual History' to be established in 1969, based initially in the School of European Studies, and subsequently offered also in English and American Studies. This was the first, and for a long time the only, degree-course to be so designated in a British university. John Burrow quickly became a member of the new Intellectual History subject-group. Donald was at this point still a member of the Economics subject-group, but he soon became a secondary member of Intellectual History and later offered courses within the major. More consequentially, the fortunes of the Intellectual History major and the historical option of CMV were henceforth to be closely entwined. In a period of expansion, it was possible to obtain funding for a further post, and in 1972 Larry Siedentop was appointed to the first Lectureship in Intellectual History, the post carrying explicit responsibilities for also teaching CMV. When Larry returned to Oxford after one year, the post was re-advertised with the same remit, and I took up the appointment from October 1974. Thus, by a series of historical accidents, and certainly not as a result of any governing design, the elements were now in place for the development of what was often referred to thereafter as 'the Sussex School' of intellectual history.

II

Donald's research and writing in the second half of the 1960s continued to be focused on the history of economic thought, particularly its influence on policy. Boldly, he switched his attention to the twentieth century and set about exploring aspects of very recent history. *Economics and Policy: a Historical Study* appeared in 1969, almost indecently soon after the events it analysed. It examined the influence of economic thinking, and more particularly of economists themselves as advisers, on public policy in Britain and United States. Though it ranged from the Edwardian age to the 1960s, the book largely concentrated on the period from the mid-1920s to the mid-1940s, constituting an oblique account of the 'Keynesian revolution' in both economic theory and policy. It charted the profound shift involved in coming to see macro-economic management as perhaps the prime task of governments, although it might be thought that the book, written before the counter-attack of neo-liberalism in the 1980s, expressed an unwarranted confidence that the Keynesian techniques of demand management were permanent political acquisitions. *Economics and Policy* did not attempt to uncover the inner history of policy formation and implementation (the fifty-year rule, as it then was, on the disclosure of official archives made that impossible), nor was it an internal history of the development of economic theory in the period. Its focus, and the sources upon which it drew most heavily, were forms of public debate, that hard-to-delimit terrain on which convictions about questions of policy are shaped only partly as a result of expert opinion.

Economics and Policy was a strikingly accomplished and confident performance by a scholar still in his thirties who had not been trained as a historian. Although Donald declared in the introduction that 'I have approached my subject very much as a historian rather than as one concerned with contemporary issues',[11] the book reflected the confidence of the 1960s that the nurturing of economic growth was now largely a matter of fine-tuning. In the preface to the paperback edition published two years later, he expressed some misgivings about the potentially whiggish implications of his concentration on the success of 'the Keynesian revolution', and in subsequent years he took a still greater distance from the book. The relaxation in 1967 of the embargo period for official archives to thirty years enabled Donald to re-visit aspects of the story in the light of newly released government documents, leading to the study, co-written with Susan Howson, of the role of the Economic Advisory Council during the years of financial crisis and depression around 1931.[12] This was a more formidably technical work than its predecessor, lacking some of the brio, chastened by the demands of detailed narrative reconstruction, yet still displaying a trademark mastery of economic ideas in their historical setting.

Two other roles from this period signalled Donald's continuing engagement with the wider community of economists. In 1968, he, together with the Belfast-based historian of economic thought, R. D. C. (Bob) Black, organised the first meeting (at Sussex) of colleagues in the UK with interests in the history of economics.[13] These informal gatherings flourished and grew, coming eventually to be formalised as the History of Economics Society. One of the group's most valuable and enduring enterprises, in the curating of which Donald took a leading part, was *Economists' Papers 1750-1950*, a guide to archival collections, now continued and updated on its own website.[14] The other role was more purely institutional yet at the same time became more deeply personal. In 1971, Austin Robinson asked Donald to become Publications Secretary of the Royal Economic Society, a post he went on to occupy for, remarkably, forty-five years. This was a role Donald took extremely seriously (but then he took all his roles seriously), investing large amounts of administrative time and scholarly labour in it. (Along the way he also served as reviews editor of the *Economic Journal* between 1976 and 1983.) He was principally responsible for the Society's

---

[11] D. Winch, *Economics and Policy: a Historical Study* (London, 1969 [pbk ed. London, 1972]), p. 29.

[12] D. Winch and S. Howson, *The Economic Advisory Council, 1930–1939: a Study in Economic Advice during Depression and Recovery* (Cambridge, 1976).

[13] Donald later wrote an appreciative memoir of Black, with whom he maintained a close professional friendship: D. Winch, 'R. D. Collison Black, 1922–2008: a personal tribute', *History of Political Economy*, 42 (2010), 1–17.

[14] See P. Sturges, *Economists' Papers 1750-1950: a Guide to Archive and other Manuscript Sources for the History of British and Irish Economic Thought* (London, 1975); http://www.economistspapers.org.uk/ (accessed 13 November 2019).

support of major editions of leading economists, including Malthus, Jevons, Marshall and Edgeworth, as well as for the stewardship and further development of the mammoth edition of the works of Keynes. He co-edited (with John Hey) *A Century of Economics: One Hundred Years of the Royal Economic Society and the Economic Journal*, which appeared in 1990 (Oxford) to mark the Royal Economic Society's centenary, and later he was to write the Introduction to a reissue of the Society's edition of John Maynard Keynes's *Essays in Biography*, published in 2010 (Basingstoke). Not all of Donald's colleagues on the Society's council in later years were sympathetic to these ventures ('philistines' was the most printable of his descriptions of them), opposition that mobilised his formidable reserves of determination, loyalty and belligerence.

Having completed his eventful tenure as Dean, Donald (who had been promoted to Reader in 1966 and Professor three years later) took a sabbatical year in 1974–5 at the Institute for Advanced Study in Princeton, the scene for the second of those intellectual turning-points mentioned earlier. Although the first months of his fellowship were devoted to completing the book on the Economic Advisory Council, Donald's thinking was developing in new ways, spurred by conversation with others in Princeton, including Albert Hirschman among the permanent faculty and, especially, Quentin Skinner among the other visiting members that year. These conversations gave a sharper edge to his growing anti-whiggism and acquainted him with the recent work that had been undertaken in the history of political thought on the role of civic humanism and natural law in the seventeenth and eighteenth centuries. Bringing the fruits of this new reading to his understanding of Adam Smith, itself enriched by advance access to the then forthcoming Glasgow edition of Smith's unpublished lectures on jurisprudence, Donald realised that Smith's purposes needed to be understood in much broader terms than those in which he was celebrated as 'the founder of Economics'. The impending approach in 1976 of the bicentenary of the publication of *The Wealth of Nations* gave these insights an added topicality, and Donald embarked on an intellectually daring and provocative enterprise: what if one took Adam Smith out of the teleological story that saw him as the founder of modern Economics, complete with its premises about the self-correcting operation of free markets, and returned him to an eighteenth-century, and specifically Scottish, context, seeing him as addressing concerns about 'the history of civil society', the contrasts between 'rude' and 'polished' nations, the dangers associated with the decline of 'the martial spirit', and so on? Donald had rightly perceived that both Smith's capitalist champions and his Marxist detractors shared an understanding of the character of Smith's most famous work: both groups saw it as essentially an analytical enquiry into how the operation of markets contributed to prosperity, the one group lauding this analysis, the other group condemning it. 'Admirers and critics of what Smith was held to stand for ... were united in an unholy alliance not to disturb a stereotype that had become a necessary one for articulating both liberal and anti-liberal positions.'[15] In place of the stereotype, Donald recovered a Smith for whom 'the science of the legislator' was the over-arching intellectual enterprise, an author needing to be viewed alongside such Scottish peers as Francis Hutcheson and David Hume, and an active participant in topical disputes over such questions as the role of a citizen militia or the rights and wrongs of the rebellion in the American colonies.

Adam Smith's Politics: an Essay in Historiographic Revision was published in 1978 (Cambridge). The sub-title was exact: the short book was, in one sense of the term, an 'essay', not aspiring to comprehensiveness or a continuous narrative. It was, in effect, a sustained piece of argument, directed principally against those who had understood Smith through the lens of a later, market-based understanding of economics. The book made an immediate impact and was widely discussed: economists, in particular, did not always smile on it, but its central claims were irrefutable, and it has come to be seen as a foundational contribution to the enlarged and historically more sophisticated understanding of Smith that has developed in recent decades. Subsequent reprintings and translations of the book testify to its continuing influence.[16]

Upon his return from leave in 1975, Donald, now freed from major administrative duties and fired up by his recent engagement with eighteenth-century intellectual history, threw himself not just into the teaching of CMV but also into ideas for forms of publication that might express and vindicate the historical approach to the past of the social sciences embodied in that course. Over the years, he and John Burrow had fitfully tried to talk each other into some joint writing project, but without ever getting beyond the stage of sketching ambitious ideas over drinks. In the mid- and late 1970s I started to contribute to both the ideas and the drinks, and slowly we began to persuade ourselves that, improbably, we really could write a book together. A lot of ideas were aired and discarded (and a lot of drinks consumed) before we settled on the eventual shape of the book that was published in 1983 as *That Noble Science of Politics: a Study in Nineteenth-Century Intellectual History*.

Although the chapters of the book grew out of collective discussion and were subject to collective revision, the majority of them were in the first instance drafted by a single author. In this way, Donald was responsible for the first three chapters (or 'essays' as we more fastidiously liked to term them) covering the very late eighteenth and early nineteenth centuries, especially debates centring around the work of figures such as Dugald Stewart, Robert Malthus and James Mill. Donald and I co-wrote the

---

[15] Winch, 'Some autobiographical notes', p. 68.
[16] The book was last re-issued, with corrections, in 2008; it was translated into Japanese, with new introduction, 1989; Italian 1992; Chinese 2008.

chapter on Alfred Marshall, a singularly happy and conflict-free experience of collaboration in which it genuinely would be difficult to distinguish our separate contributions. All three authors had a hand in the occasionally polemical 'Prologue', which came to be cited as something of an anti-whiggish manifesto for its incitement to attend to what gets lost when the intellectual life of the past is divided up as the property of later academic disciplines. The briefest way to indicate the character of the book is to quote the following passage from the Preface, written in 1996, for the Japanese translation:

> As the Prologue to the book was intended to make clear, some of the intellectual energy that fuelled its writing came from our shared negative reaction to certain prevailing disciplinary dispensations. Most obviously, we repudiated those forms of 'the history of the social sciences' which consisted in finding 'precursors' and 'founding fathers' for contemporary social scientific specialisms from among past writers the specificity and integrity of whose concerns had thereby come in for some very rough treatment indeed. Our shared experience over several years of teaching 'The Historical Development of the Social Sciences' course at Sussex had left us dissatisfied with, in particular, the way eighteenth- and nineteenth-century concerns were treated in literature of this kind. Not only was there a tendency to bypass the political dimension of past thinking, but when that dimension was recognised it was treated reductively, either as mere party politics or as an aspect of a set of ideological allegiances, many of which would either have been rejected or unrecognisable to our chosen cast of authors. We also repudiated the coerciveness of the priorities encouraged by 'the history of political theory', an enterprise which has enjoyed such a strong institutional position in the Anglo-American scholarly world that political, economic, and social historians all too easily take it to *be* intellectual history. And, more obviously, we took our distance from those kinds of approaches which are united in little else than in assuming that intellectual activity is best understood as a reflection or by-product of some allegedly more fundamental social or economic process.[17]

The book explored a series of attempts by nineteenth-century authors to develop systematic knowledge of 'things political', that encompassing ancient category which covered enquiries later sub-divided among Political Science, Sociology, Economics and so on. The selection of figures for discussion paid little heed to subsequent forms of canonisation as 'founding fathers'—Dugald Stewart and Walter Bagehot received their due; E. A. Freeman was in his proper place alongside Sir Henry Maine; Henry Sidgwick was accorded no less attention than Alfred Marshall; and the treatment was deliberately episodic and discontinuous, tactics intended to disrupt residual teleological

[17] S. Collini, D. Winch and J. Burrow, *That Noble Science of Politics: a Study in Nineteenth-Century Intellectual History* (Cambridge, 1983); the Japanese translation was eventually published by Minerva, Tokyo, in 2005. The Preface to that translation was never published in English, though the above passage was also quoted in Collini, Whatmore and Young, *Economy, Polity, and Society*, p. 10.

expectations. Although the book was widely reviewed—far more widely than would be the case for a comparable publication today—and on the whole very favourably, it was hardly surprising that some reviewers expressed bafflement or irritation with these features. As one reviewer sympathetically put it: 'This is going to be a perplexing book for many. Librarians will wonder how to classify it. Specialists in politics and economics will be embarrassed at its demonstration of how what they thought sewn up can be unstitched. Tutors will wonder what passages their pupils can be trusted not to misunderstand.'[18]

Camping up the submission of our separate identities to the collective enterprise, we christened ourselves 'Burrinchini' and decided not to take the royalties (such as they were) individually, but to put them in a fund that was to be used to finance an annual reunion dinner of considerable extravagance. These dinners, which usually took place at Donald's house in Cooksbridge, were not for the faint-hearted, or at least not for the weak-livered, and after a couple of decades we had ruefully to recognise that the health of the fund was now considerably better than that of the authors. Thereafter, the residual monies were, at Donald's suggestion, used to subsidise activities associated with Intellectual History at Sussex.

Donald's contribution to *That Noble Science* signalled what were to be his principal preoccupations during the ensuing decade: on the one hand the question of the fate of Smith's ambitious programme in the hands of various putative successors, and, on the other, what was to prove a long engagement with the work and reputation of Robert Malthus. The former issued in several essays in the 1980s and early 1990s, studies that were never merely re-statements of a now-familiar case but always attempts to explore fresh ramifications of the re-orientation of the interpretation of Smith that Donald had done so much to stimulate.[19] The latter was a less predictable direction for his interests to have taken and requires a little more explanation.

[18] W. Thomas, 'Review of *That Noble Science of Politics*', *English Historical Review*, 101 (1986), 702–4.
[19] D. Winch, 'Adam Smith's enduring particular result; a political and cosmopolitan perspective', in I. Hont and M. Ignatieff (eds.), *Wealth and Virtue: the Shaping of Political Economy in the Scottish Enlightenment* (Cambridge, 1983), pp. 253–69; D. Winch, 'Adam Smith als politischer Theoretiker', in F. X. Kaufmann (ed.), *Markt, Staat und Solidarität bei Adam Smith* (Frankfurt, 1984), pp. 95–113; D. Winch, 'Science and the legislator: Adam Smith and after', *Economic Journal*, 93 (1983), 501–20 (reprinted in P. Roggi (ed.), *Gli economisti e la politica economia*, Edizione Scientifiche Italiane, 1985, pp. 81–107); D. Winch, 'The Burke-Smith problem in late eighteenth-century political and economic thought', *Historical Journal*, 28 (1985), 231–47; D. Winch, 'Adam Smith and the liberal tradition', in K. Haakonssen (ed.), *Traditions of Liberalism; Essays on John Locke, Adam Smith and John Stuart Mill* (Sydney, 1988), pp. 83–101, reprinted in K. Haakonssen (ed.), *Adam Smith* (International Library of Critical Essays in the History of Philosophy) (Aldershot, and Brookfield, VT, 1998); D. Winch, 'Adam Smith's politics revisited', *Quaderni di Storia dell'Economia Politica*, 9 (1991), 3–27; and D. Winch, 'Adam Smith: Scottish moral philosopher as political economist', *Historical Journal*, 35 (1992), 91–113, reprinted in Haakonssen, *Adam Smith*.

The second chapter of *That Noble Science*, 'Higher Maxims', had taken its title from a passage by Francis Horner, a pupil of Dugald Stewart and one of the first 'Edinburgh reviewers', who wrote: 'The truths of political economy form but a class among the principles of administration, and in their practical application must often be limited by higher maxims of state, to which in theory too they are held subordinate, as being less general.'[20] In his friendly exchanges and theoretical disputes with Ricardo, Malthus had in effect attempted to develop a form of political economy that could do justice to the truth of Horner's observation and provide the basis for those 'higher maxims'. This enterprise appealed to Donald at several levels, not least because it opened up a way of attending to the political and economic debates of the first three decades of the nineteenth century in ways that did not give centre-stage to ideas that later economists identified as precursors of their own. Although Donald certainly did not share Malthus's Anglican moralism, he warmed to his dogged, unfashionable attacks on unbridled optimism about human progress, and he wanted to do justice to a body of work that was too often pilloried as a simplistic misunderstanding of the consequences of population growth. His exemplary short study of Malthus for the Oxford University Press 'Past Masters' series, published in 1987, was the chief expression of this engagement, followed by his edition of Malthus's *An Essay on the Principle of Population* for the Cambridge University Press 'Texts in the History of Political Thought' series in 1992.[21] In addition, he published several important essays on aspects of Malthus's work and legacy, and was to return to him in greater detail in his 1996 book *Riches and Poverty*.[22] In his capacity as Publications Secretary of the Royal Economics Society he also sponsored and helped to see into print the major scholarly editions of Malthus's *Essay* and of his *Principles of Political Economy*, edited respectively by Patricia James and J. M. Pullen, two scholars whose close and detailed work he admired.

[20] Francis Horner, quoted in 'Higher maxims: happiness versus wealth in Malthus and Ricardo', in Collini, Winch and Burrow, *That Noble Science*, p. 63.

[21] The 'Past Masters' volume was reprinted in *Great Economists* (Oxford, 1997), with a foreword by Keith Thomas; an updated version appeared as part of Oxford University Press's 'Very Short Introduction' series in 2013. It was published in Japanese translation in 1992.

[22] D. Winch 'Robert Malthus: Christian moral scientist, arch-demoralizer, or implicit secular utilitarian?', *Utilitas*, 5 (1993), 239–53; D. Winch, 'Malthus versus Condorcet revisited', *European Journal of the History of Economic Thought*, 3 (1996), 45–62; D. Winch, 'The reappraisal of Malthus', *History of Political Economy*, 30 (1998), 60–72.

III

Donald had a highly developed sense of academic duty, one that put more selfish or more casual colleagues to shame. In 1986 he yielded, without enthusiasm, to the entreaties of others at Sussex who wanted him to take on the role of Pro-Vice-Chancellor (Arts and Social Sciences), in which capacity he served for three years. Being effectively the most senior figure on the non-scientific side of the university during the belt-tightening years of the later 1980s was never going to be a comfortable position, one that was not made easier by the appointment of Sir Leslie Fielding, a former diplomat, as Vice-Chancellor in 1987. Donald found Fielding's managerial style simultaneously high-handed and inattentive, more concerned with appearances than with reality, and the two clashed on several occasions. Donald always had a strong attachment to a traditional conception of a university as an institution committed to unfettered, open-ended enquiry, underpinned by the most rigorous standards of scholarship and science. But the times were requiring universities to be more immediately instrumental in their purposes and less demanding in their standards, pressures that Donald did his best to resist, a lonely and oftentimes thankless task. He was an extremely capable administrator, and no one could ever doubt his commitment to the welfare of the university or the demands he made upon himself, but he could on occasion be growly and impatient, characteristics that did not always endear him to colleagues who found themselves on the other side of an argument. His dismay at the direction taken by Sussex in particular and universities in general from the 1980s onwards was partially offset by Fellowship of the British Academy, an institution whose scholarly rationale he could endorse without reservation. He was an active Fellow following his election in 1986, serving with distinction as Vice-President in 1993–4, and as a valued and long-serving member of the Academy's Publications Committee (1990–9); he also co-edited (with Patrick O'Brien) *The Political Economy of British Historical Experience, 1688–1914*, which appeared in 2002, part of the Academy's centenary celebrations.[23] As a mark of his attachment, he left the Academy a substantial bequest to finance a Senior Research Fellowship in Intellectual History.

Donald was himself a beneficiary of one of these enlightened schemes for providing established academics with a little space in which to think and write when he was awarded a two-year British Academy Readership in 1993. This enabled him to extend

---

[23] Personal and institutional loyalties came together in Donald's last published piece of research, an exploration of Keynes's initial exclusion from, and subsequent role within, the Academy: D. Winch, 'Keynes and the British Academy', *Historical Journal,* 57 (2014), 751–71. A shorter version of this was published in *British Academy Review*, 22 (Summer 2013), 70–4.

his enquiries about Smith and Malthus into a much more ambitious undertaking. It can be unwise to dignify as a 'magnum opus' one work (or pair of works) by an author who continued to develop intellectually in the way that Donald did, but there can be no doubt that *Riches and Poverty: an Intellectual History of Political Economy in Britain, 1750-1834*, which appeared in 1996, and its sequel *Wealth and Life: Essays on the Intellectual History of Political Economy in Britain, 1848-1914*, published in 2009, constitute his most weighty as well as, it seems safe to say, enduring contributions to scholarship.

Building on his earlier re-situating of *The Wealth of Nations* within Smith's larger project of 'the science of the legislator', *Riches and Poverty* now asked what became of this project, both in the later years of Smith's career and in the hands of the next couple of generations of successors and critics. 'After Adam Smith' was one rejected title for the book (it was used for the Prologue instead), as was 'The Secret Concatenation', taken from Dr Johnson's observation about the links between luxury and poverty (this was the title Donald gave to his Carlyle lectures at Oxford), and each of these signals something about the eventual character of the book. But it is as much a history of political thought in the period as of anything later understood as 'economics'. Burke is scarcely a less central figure than Smith, while Ricardo's theorising is more than offset by the polemical contributions of the likes of Paine, Priestley and Price.[24] Malthus, the third central figure, is treated as a 'political moralist' for whom strictly economic questions were always subordinate to Christian imperatives, while Coleridge and Southey receive more detailed treatment than do some of the 'projectors' and 'calculators' whom they attacked.

One of the book's quiet achievements is the demonstration of how inseparable his protagonists' main ideas were from the more quotidian forms of political debate. This is most strikingly true of his account of the friendly controversies and exchanges between Ricardo and Malthus, where theoretical differences over large questions about value, land, currency and so on are shown to have grown piecemeal from other, more local differences over policy during the Napoleonic Wars or proposals for poor relief (he always had a high regard for, and duly acknowledged, the work of Boyd Hilton in this area). More generally, the book proceeds through the exploration of relations of 'affinity and discord' among figures normally categorised in other terms, with only occasional explicit condemnation of those later scholars who might have allowed some anachronistic category, whether capitalist or Marxist in inspiration, to

---

[24] Donald later extended his discussion of James Mackintosh, who had only received passing treatment in D. Winch, *Riches and Poverty: an Intellectual History of Political Economy in Britain, 1750-1834* (Cambridge, 1996), in the introduction to his edition of James Mackintosh, *Vindiciae Gallicae and Other Writings on the French Revolution* (Indianapolis, IN, 2006).

cloud their vision.[25] As Keith Tribe summarised the book's impact, it 'reorients our understanding of the origins of classical economics in a quite decisive manner'.[26]

Ideally, one should be able to exhibit Donald's prose at work rather than attempting to describe its characteristics, but it is not easy to excerpt briefly since his writing produced its effects by means of a kind of sustained command.[27] The following passage is simply one of dozens which display the book's incisive grasp of the choreography of intellectual alliance and antagonism as it introduces a discussion of the relations between the ideas of Smith, Burke, Paine, and Price at the end of the eighteenth century. Having remarked that Burke 'suggested the possibility of an inversion of the more familiar sequence expounded by Hume, Smith, and other Scottish historians of civil society, whereby commerce brings an improvement in manners and the arts and sciences in its train', Donald proceeds in characteristic fashion to allow historical complexity to erode the simplicities of later stereotypes:

> Paine's extrapolation of the more widely accepted sequence into the future, however, and the welcome given to Smith's system of natural liberty by other contemporary opponents of Burke, has proved as useful to students of turn-of-the-century radicalism as it has to students of what later was seen as Burke's conservatism. In Paine's case, it has allowed him to be characterised as a spokesman for an upwardly mobile society of self-interested economic individualists, as the radical embodiment of all those 'bourgeois' qualities that Smith, alongside and in harmony with Locke, is supposed to represent [a footnote hauls a selection of eminent miscreants into the dock at this point]. As in the case of Burke, some of the resulting characterisations have had an homogenising effect on the diverse qualities of radicalism in this period. Including Price alongside Paine in this comparative exercise acts as a reminder that supporters of revolution did not always speak with the same voice when diagnosing the economic conditions most likely to consort with republican institutions. Price did not fully share Paine's 'Smithian' confidence in the progressive potential contained in the spread of commerce and manufacturing. Nor, as we shall see, did Smith share Paine's belief in the capacity or necessity for commerce to civilise by revolutionising government.[28]

The passage is in some ways a promissory note, one made good by the rest of the chapter from the opening paragraphs of which it is taken. It is, typically, argumentative, and it is revisionist in the way complex, freshly-seen history is always revisionist, in refusing the mind any easy resting-place in familiar modern categories. The chapter

[25] Winch, *Riches and Poverty*, p. 10.
[26] K. Tribe, 'Donald Winch 1935–2017', *The European Journal of the History of Economic Thought*, 25 (2018), 200.
[27] This paragraph is adapted from S. Collini, 'General Introduction' to *Economy, Polity, and Society*, pp. 17–18.
[28] Winch, *Riches and Poverty*, p. 131.

is entitled 'Contested Affinities', a phrase emblematic of Donald's address to intellectual history, with its constant attempt to do justice both to family resemblances and to family quarrels. As in the book as a whole, the very structure of the prose vetoes any slack assimilation of what were subtly different positions, yet a clarity of outline survives through all attention to idiosyncrasy.

A variety of other tasks and distractions slowed the completion of the work that Donald always intended as a sequel to *Riches and Poverty*, with the result that *Wealth and Life* did not appear until thirteen years later. By modestly describing the book as 'essays', Donald may have contributed to a tendency to undervalue it as an original work of scholarship: without fanfare, it excavates a variety of overlooked or misunderstood debates from the period and is based on an exceptionally wide range of sources, including no fewer than sixteen archival collections, some previously little known or little used. Alongside such usual suspects as Mill, Jevons and Marshall, a large cast of characters come in for quite detailed discussion, including Bagehot, Cairnes, Cliffe Leslie, Cunningham, Fawcett, Foxwell, Hobson, J. N. Keynes, Mallet, Sidgwick and Toynbee among those with some claim to have contributed as economists, together with a still larger cast of critics and commentators including Carlyle, Cobden, Dickens, Henry George, Maine, Ruskin and the Webbs. The book deliberately refuses several of the familiar organising binaries. Referring to Toynbee's phrase about the 'bitter argument between economists and human beings', it exposes the fallacy involved in assigning concern with 'life' as opposed to 'wealth' exclusively to the side of the 'human beings': such broader issues were at the heart of economic thinking in this period, so that 'in the continuing debates over wealth and life no one group had an exclusive monopoly of either category'.[29] Nor does it tell a story of 'classical political economy' giving way to 'neo-classical economics' as a result of the so-called marginalist revolution: struggles with the legacy of Mill's *Principles*, attempts to clarify the notion of 'value', and insistence on the practical applicability of their science united figures whom the conventional story would assign to opposing schools. It should also be said that practically none of the figures whom Donald discusses in *Wealth and Life* exhibited that dogmatic adherence to the principle of *laissez-faire* which critics of the dismal science alleged to be characteristic of its exponents. The most telling chapter in this respect is the wonderfully intricate unravelling of Sidgwick's careful depositions in favour of 'economic socialism' in cases where his fundamental individualist principle could not operate successfully, a chapter which pays generous

---

[29] D. Winch, *Wealth and Life: Essays on the Intellectual History of Political Economy in Britain, 1848–1914* (Cambridge, 2009), p. 366. He administered a particularly sharp reproach to E. P. Thompson on this score, but then Thompson was a figure to whom Donald, provoked by some of Thompson's more high-handed ideological classifications, never quite did justice. See, in particular, the Appendix on 'Mr Gradgrind and Jerusalem', pp. 367–98.

tribute to Sidgwick's perspicuity at the same time as it indulges a wry smile at his laborious caution. And, finally, the book does not allow an easy distinction between 'academic' and 'non-academic' writers to structure the story: several figures straddled or crossed this supposed divide which was anyway less clear-cut in a period before fully self-sustaining academic careers became the norm. Although the book never makes this connection, one can even see its final chapters coming full circle to Donald's much earlier book, *Economics and Policy*, in that they explore some of the tensions involved in the earliest attempts by academic economists to deploy their scholarly authority on the contested terrain of policy-formation. But the connection also under-lines just how far Donald had travelled intellectually in the intervening forty years. *Wealth and Life* is a more nuanced, thickly textured, piece of scholarship, one that is alive to the religious, philosophical, and cultural dimensions of his cast's thinking in ways that the earlier study, focused on the interplay of economic theory and economic policy, had not been.

Structurally, Mill's *Principles of Political Economy*, published in 1848, occupies something of the position in this book that Smith's *Wealth of Nations* did in its prede-cessor, the *summa* which subsequent generations imbibed, refined, and criticised. But even while taking this much-studied figure as his starting-point, Donald managed to offer an original perspective. The chapter entitled 'Wild natural beauty, the religion of humanity, and unearned increments' explored what might now be termed Mill's 'envir-onmental' thinking, ingeniously weaving together 'the stationary state', the moral influence of natural beauty, commons preservation, 'peasant proprietorship', and Land Tenure Reform—a selection of Mill's enthusiasms that were united in their insistence on the centrality of nature and human rootedness in the land, commitments that were far removed from the stereotype of the 'desiccated calculating machine' and apologist for *laissez-faire*. This excavation of the deeper cultural and even sometimes temperamental sources of perspectives on supposedly 'economic' questions is a hall-mark of the book. As it says of one of the most familiar and hackneyed transitions in economic theorising: 'While there can be no doubt about the nature of Jevons's disagreement with Mill's political economy on this issue [sc. the theory of value], what the essay on him here tries to show is that Jevons's antipathy to Mill had deeper philosophical and religious roots.'[30] Donald elaborated this case in more program-matic terms in one of the most important of his later articles, teasingly entitled (adapting Marshall) 'The Old Generation of Economists and the New; an intellectual historian's approach to a significant transition'.[31]

---

[30] Winch, *Wealth and Life*, p. 21.
[31] D. Winch, 'The old generation of economists and the new; an intellectual historian's approach to a significant transition', *Journal of the History of Economic Thought*, 32 (2010), 23–37.

That article was the text of an invited lecture to the annual gathering of the History of Economics Society, of which he had been elected a Distinguished Fellow in 2007. Other tributes to his standing included being made an Honorary Member of the European Society for the History of Economic Thought in 2012 and being the subject of a chapter in Medema and Samuels, *Historians of Economics and Economic Thought*, while even the lengthy but bizarrely wrong-headed critique by Gregory C. G. Moore was back-handed testament to the eminence he had now achieved.[32] Since his death, there have been several admiring and heartfelt assessments of the figure described as 'one of the most inspirational intellectual historians of our time'.[33]

IV

In 1983 Donald married Doreen ('Dolly') Lidster, who taught the history of art, and over the remaining thirty-four years of his life he found a settled domestic happiness that had hitherto eluded him. Dolly's sociability and adaptability softened Donald's occasional tendency to irascible withdrawal, leading the Old Brewery, their house in Cooksbridge, to become the scene of countless high-spirited gatherings. She also did more than her share in helping and later caring for Donald's parents, as well as contributing hours of labour to the maintenance of the garden— though 'grounds' seems a more appropriate term for the four and a half acre plot at the foot of the Downs that Donald turned into a lush, bosky, many-roomed English garden in the Romantic tradition (charming nooks, seductive vistas, little regularity). His responsiveness to the natural world expressed itself in sometimes surprising ways, ranging from his discriminating judgements about several of the famous country-house gardens to, perhaps, that sympathetic responsiveness to the importance of environmental concerns in John Stuart Mill's social thought. Dolly also accompanied him on many of his academic travels, beginning their married life with a rather daunting year spent largely in Canberra, New Orleans and Calgary where Donald had visiting appointments. These were followed in later years by an extended visit to Japan (where he was particularly celebrated for his work on Malthus), numerous lecturing trips in Europe, and a

[32] G. Gilbert, 'Donald Winch as intellectual historian', in S. G. Medema and W. J. Samuels (eds.), *Historians of Economics and Economic Thought* (London, 2001); G. C .G. Moore, 'Placing Donald Winch in context: an essay on *Wealth and Life*', *History of Economics Review*, 52 (2010), 77–108.
[33] M. Albertone and E. Pasini, 'Editorial: homage to Donald Winch', *Journal of Interdisciplinary History of Ideas*, 6 (2017). See also Tribe, 'Donald Winch 1935–2017', 196–201; J. Stapleton and D. P. O'Brien, 'Professor Donald Norman Winch 1935–2017', *History of Political Economy*, 50 (2018), 421–4; S. Howson, 'Donald Winch (15 April 1935–12 June 2017)', *The Economic and Labour Relations Review*, 28 (2017), 565–8.

Visiting Fellowship at All Souls in Oxford in 1994. Much of the substance of the Carlyle Lectures in the History of Political Thought he gave at Oxford in 1995 was taken from *Riches and Poverty*, to be published the following year, but the six-lecture format led him to adopt a rather different perspective. The full text of the lectures is now available on the Intellectual History website at the University of St Andrews.[34]

Donald officially retired from Sussex in 2000. As he observed in a farewell speech: 'It has to be said that Sussex is not the kind of institution in which it is easy to grow old gracefully, to fade away from, as old soldiers are said to do. One reason for going now is to avoid growing old disgracefully, of becoming a gargoyle in buildings that were never designed for such things.'[35] But he cared too deeply about the fate of Intellectual History in the university to absent himself entirely, and having played an active part in the appointment of Knud Haakonssen to the Chair in Intellectual History in 2005 (in succession to Martin van Gelderen, who had succeeded John Burrow), he then gave Knud and Richard Whatmore much practical and moral support in their resourceful attempts to make the Sussex Centre for Intellectual History a flourishing hive of research activity—attempts which were impressively successful before being undermined by official obtuseness and indifference. Sussex had meant so much to Donald for so long; his understandable resentments about the behaviour of the university's 'senior management team' in his final years should not be allowed altogether to efface the loyalty and commitment to his conception of that institution's best self that had animated him over the decades. This and his scholarly eminence were recognised in an unusual way when he was awarded an honorary degree by his own university in 2006. In a moving speech of acceptance he recalled having deprived his parents of an important pleasure by heedlessly skipping his graduation ceremony at the LSE half-a-century earlier, emphasising the corresponding satisfaction it gave him to be able to make partial amends by having his 92-year-old mother present on this occasion.

For someone who was involved in so many collaborative enterprises, institutional and intellectual, and who had such a gift for close friendship, Donald lived a strikingly solitary academic existence for much of his life, largely spent in his small, smoke-suffused study at home in Cooksbridge rather than in any more sociable setting. But, a little like a member of the republic of letters from an earlier century, he stayed in touch with an extensive network of other scholars by means of a genre at which he excelled and which he cultivated with deliberate, unfashionable punctiliousness: the

---

[34] https://arts.st-andrews.ac.uk/intellectualhistory/islandora/object/intellectual-history%3A27 (accessed 12 November 2019).

[35] D. Winch, 'End', a typescript written in the late 1990s, p. 7; a copy is included in the Winch Papers, Sussex Archives.

extended exchange of letters on serious intellectual and scholarly matters. As he wrote in his autobiographical reflections: 'While it is reassuring to have sympathetic colleagues living in the same corridor or building, I have always found my real and ideal university through correspondence with like-minded people living elsewhere, usually abroad.'[36] His exchanges with other scholars of the eighteenth century such as Duncan Forbes and J. G. A. Pocock are models of intellectual engagement. The boxes of letters now deposited with his papers only include an occasional sample of his side of such exchanges, but anyone whose intellectual path crossed Donald's will testify to his striking attentiveness and generosity in this medium. As a reader of draft typescripts, he was thorough, sympathetic and meticulous; he was notably helpful to a number of younger scholars in this way, giving them the kind of informed, detailed, critical reading of their work which in some cases they had never encountered before. In addition, his files of letters on various contested matters of business would send a shiver down the spine of anyone in a position of administrative or bureaucratic responsibility—forensic, commanding, with a terrier-like determination not to let go till his correspondent ('adversary' seems more apt in some cases) dropped the bone or ran up the white flag. One of his favoured terms of disapprobation was 'slack': correspondents who did not reply as fully or promptly as Donald felt the situation demanded were prone to be classified as 'slack', an exasperated judgement to which he could impart an almost Old Testament damningness.

Though his published writing is measured and precise, Donald was a man of strong attachments and deep feelings, emotions sometimes masked from public view by a cultivated gruffness. As a friend—and he sustained numerous close friendships over many decades—he was wonderfully steadfast and unabashedly partisan, but also enormous fun. To sit up late over the whisky with him was a sure route to ever-greater affection and admiration as well as to a terrible hangover. In public settings he could sometimes appear rather formidable, but in the company of close friends he could be an engagingly expressive contributor to any gathering, responsive and appreciative rather than merely performative. He could also be a quite hilarious, pitch-perfect mimic. To hear him, for example, 'doing' a Glasgow taxi-driver on the theoretical defects of monetarism was to believe that Billy Connolly had a rival. And I remember thinking, after one rendition of the mechanic who failed to mend his car in Canberra, that Donald had been lucky to get out of Australia alive.

He was counter-suggestibly proud of the fact that he had never succumbed to any fashionable concern for his health or for 'staying in shape'. His eating, drinking, and, for many years, smoking habits ensured he could never be accused of 'looking after himself', yet until late in his life he retained remarkable physical strength, engaging

---

[36] Winch, 'Some autobiographical notes', p. 33.

with Gladstonian vigour in the felling and removing of surplus trees from his garden. But eventually his way of life caught up with him, involving unpleasant procedures to deal with growths on his bladder, operations to insert stents in his heart and medication for diabetes and for gout. Finally, he was diagnosed with lung cancer, which in his last months then spread to his brain. Donald had long admired the philosophic calm with which one of his heroes, David Hume, faced his own impending death. In everyday life, Donald didn't exactly *do* philosophic calm: his own dealings with circumstance always had a rather more combative edge to them. But as I think anyone would testify who saw him during those last dreadful eighteen months when even *his* ox-like constitution began to fail him, he displayed a quite remarkable dignity and stoicism in the face of the humiliations of dissolution.

The last time I saw Donald at the Old Brewery, not long before he was moved into the hospice where he was so well cared for in his final days, he was already much weakened and sleeping quite a lot. But he would make an effort to rouse himself for the rare visitor and, after the usual convivial dinner, he and I found ourselves sitting alone over the whisky at the evening's end, as we had done so often during the previous four decades. With the importunity permitted to an old friend, I asked him about his state of mind. 'Well', he said, reflectively but without either resentment or anguish, 'one can't, of course, imagine not being here, but, as the moment approaches, one just hopes to make a more or less orderly exit.' There was much of the man in that undemonstrative English idiom, and it requires no further commentary. But it does still seem unbearably difficult to adjust to his 'not being here', so large and central and loved a presence was he in so many lives.

Acknowledgements

Except where indicated, this memoir draws on personal knowledge and on the substantial cache of Donald's papers and digital archives in my possession. A much larger deposit of his papers, fully catalogued, is now available in the University of Sussex archives at the East Sussex Record Office. Further information, and the texts of some of his unpublished lectures, are available from the Intellectual History website at the University of St Andrews. For comments on earlier drafts of this memoir, I am grateful to Roger Backhouse, Peter Clarke, Knud Haakonssen, Boyd Hilton, Helen Small and John Thompson; special thanks are due to Dolly Winch.

Note on the author: Stefan Collini is Emeritus Professor of Intellectual History and English Literature, University of Cambridge. He was elected a Fellow of the British Academy in 2000.